EVERYMAN'S LIBRARY

REFERENCE

THESAURUS OF ENGLISH WORDS AND PHRASES

BY PETER ROGET · REVISED BY ANDREW BOYLE AND CHARLES LEE

IN 2 VOLS. VOL. 2

THESAURUS OF ENGLISH WORDS AND PHRASES

VOLUME TWO

PETER ROGET

LONDON: J. M. DENT & SONS LTD.
NEW YORK: E. P. DUTTON & CO. INC.

Made in Great Britain
by
The Temple Press Letchworth
for
J. M. Dent & Sons Ltd.
Aldine House Bedford St. London
First published in this edition 1912
Revised and reset 1925
Further revised 1930
Last reprinted 1950

X 144/33 m

CLASS VI—*continued*

WORDS RELATING TO THE SENTIENT AND MORAL POWERS—*continued*

SECTION II.—PERSONAL AFFECTIONS[1]

1°. Passive Affections

827. Pleasure (*Substantives*), gratification, enjoyment, fruition, relish, zest, gusto.

Well-being, satisfaction, content (831), comfort, *sans souci*, bed of roses, bed of down, velvet.

Joy, gladness, delight, glee, cheer, sunshine.

Physical pleasure, *see* 377.

Treat, regale, feast, *délice*, luxury, voluptuousness, clover.

Happiness, felicity, bliss, beatitude, beatification, enchantment, transport, rapture, ravishment, ecstasy, heaven, *summum bonum*, paradise, Eden, Arcadia, nirvana, elysium, empyrean (981).

Honeymoon, palmy days, halcyon days, golden age, *Saturnia regna*.

(*Verbs*). To be pleased, etc., to feel, receive, or derive pleasure, etc.; to take pleasure or delight in; to delight in, rejoice in, relish, like, enjoy, take in good part.

To indulge in, treat oneself, solace oneself, revel, riot, luxuriate in, gloat over; to be on velvet, in clover, in heaven, etc.; to enjoy oneself; to congratulate oneself, hug oneself.

(*Phrases*). To slake the appe-

828. Pain (*Substantives*), suffering; physical pain, *see* 378.

Displeasure, dissatisfaction, discontent, discomfort, malaise.

Uneasiness, disquiet, inquietude, weariness, dejection, *see* 837.

Annoyance, irritation, plague, bore, bother, botheration, worry, stew.

Care, anxiety, mortification, vexation, chagrin, trouble, trial, solicitude, cark, dole, dule, fret.

Grief, sorrow, distress, affliction, woe, bitterness, heartache, a heavy heart, a bleeding heart, a broken heart, heavy affliction, etc.

Unhappiness, infelicity, misery, wretchedness, desolation.

Dolour, sufferance, ache, aching, hurt, smart, cut, twitch, twinge, stitch, shoot, cramp, spasm, nightmare, convulsion, throe, *angina*.

Pang, anguish, agony, torture, torment, rack, crucifixion, martyrdom, purgatory, hell (982).

(*Phrases*). The cankerworm of care; a peck of troubles; a sea of troubles; the ills that flesh is heir to; the iron entering the soul.

[1] Or those which concern one's own state of feeling.

tite; to bask in the sunshine; to tread on enchanted ground; to have a good time.

(*Adjectives*). Pleased, enjoying, relishing, liking, gratified, glad, gladdened, rejoiced, delighted, charmed.

Cheered, enlivened, flattered, tickled, indulged, regaled, treated, etc.

Comfortable, at ease, easy, cosy, satisfied, content (831), luxurious, on velvet, in clover, on a bed of roses, *sans souci*, unalloyed, without alloy.

Happy, blest, blessed, blissful, overjoyed, enchanted, captivated, fascinated, transported, raptured, rapt, enraptured, in raptures, in ecstasies, in a transport, beatified, in heaven, in the seventh heaven, in paradise, etc.

(*Phrases*). With a joyful face; with sparkling eyes; happy as a king; pleased as Punch; in the lap of luxury; happy as the day is long; *ter quaterque beatus*.

(*Adverb*). Happily, etc.

A sufferer, victim, prey, martyr.

(*Verbs*). To feel, suffer, or experience pain, etc.; to suffer, ache, smart, ail, bleed, shoot, twinge, tingle, gripe, wince, writhe.

To grieve, fret, pine, mourn, bleed, worry oneself, chafe, yearn, droop, sink, give way, despair (859).

(*Phrases*). To sit on thorns; to be on pins and needles; to take to heart; to labour under afflictions; to have a thin time; to drain the cup of misery to the dregs; "*hæret lateri lethalis arundo.*"

(*Adjectives*). In pain; feeling, suffering, enduring, etc., pain; in a state of pain, of suffering, etc., sore, aching, suffering, ailing, etc., pained, hurt, stung, etc., *see* 830.

Displeased, annoyed, dissatisfied, discontented, weary, etc. (832), uneasy, ungratified, uncomfortable, ill at ease.

Concerned, afflicted, in affliction, sorry, sorrowful, in sorrow, *au désespoir*, bathed in tears (839).

Unhappy, unfortunate, hapless, unblest, luckless, unlucky, ill-fated, ill-starred, fretting, wretched, miserable, careworn, carking, disconsolate, inconsolable, woebegone, forlorn, comfortless, a prey to grief, etc., despairing, in despair (859), heart-broken, broken-hearted, the heart bleeding, doomed, devoted, accursed, undone.

829. Capability of giving pleasure.

PLEASURABLENESS (*Substantives*), pleasantness, gratefulness, welcomeness, acceptableness, acceptability, agreeableness, delectability, deliciousness, daintiness, sweetness, luxuriousness, lusciousness, voluptuousness.

Charm, attraction, attractiveness, attractability, fascination,

830. Capability of giving pain.

PAINFULNESS (*Substantives*), disagreeableness, unpleasantness, irksomeness, displeasingness, unacceptableness, bitterness, vexatiousness, troublesomeness.

Trouble, care, cross, annoyance, burden, load, nuisance, plague, bore, bother, botheration, pin-pricks.

Scourge, bitter pill, worm,

prestige, loveliness, takingness, likableness, invitingness, glamour.

A treat, dainty, tit-bit, bonbon, *bonne-bouche*, sweet, sweetmeat, sugar-plum, nuts, *sauce piquante.*

(*Verbs*). To cause, produce, create, give, afford, procure, offer, present, yield, etc., pleasure, gratification, etc.

To please, take, gratify, satisfy, indulge, flatter, tickle, humour, regale, refresh, interest.

To charm, rejoice, cheer, gladden, delight, enliven (836), to transport, captivate, fascinate, enchant, entrance, bewitch, ravish, enrapture, enravish, beatify, enthral, imparadise.

(*Phrase*). To do one's heart good; to take one's fancy.

(*Adjectives*). Causing or giving pleasure, etc., pleasing, agreeable, grateful, gratifying, pleasant, pleasurable, acceptable, welcome, glad, gladsome, comfortable.

Sweet, delectable, nice, palatable, dainty, delicate, delicious, dulcet, savoury, toothsome, luscious, luxurious, voluptuous, genial, cordial, refreshing, comfortable, scrumptious.

Fair, lovely, favourite, attractive, engaging, winning, taking, prepossessing, inviting, captivating, bewitching, fascinating, magnetic, seductive, killing, stunning, ripping, likable.

Charming, delightful, exquisite, enchanting, enthralling, ravishing, rapturous, heart-felt, thrilling, heavenly, celestial, elysian, empyrean, seraphic, ideal.

Palmy, halcyon, Saturnian, Arcadian.

(*Phrases*). To one's heart's content; doing one's heart good.

canker, cancer, ulcer, curse, gall and wormwood, sting, pricks, scorpion, thorn, brier, bramble, hornet, whip, lash, rack, wheel.

(*Phrases*). A thorn in one's side; a bitter pill; a crumpled rose-leaf; *amari aliquid.*

A mishap, misadventure, mischance, pressure, infestation, grievance, trial, crosses, hardship, blow, stroke, affliction, misfortune, reverse, infliction, dispensation, visitation, disaster, undoing, tragedy, calamity, catastrophe, adversity (735).

Provocation, infestation, affront, aggravation, indignity, outrage, *see* 900, 929.

(*Verbs*). To cause, produce, give, etc., pain, uneasiness, suffering, etc., to disquiet, etc.

To pain, hurt, wound, sting, pinch, grate upon, irk, gall, chafe, gnaw, prick, lacerate, pierce, cut, cut up, stick, gravel, hurt one's feelings, mortify, horrify, shock, twinge, gripe.

To wring, harrow, torment, torture, rack, scarify, cruciate, crucify, convulse, agonise.

To displease, annoy, incommode, discompose, trouble, disquiet, grieve, cross, tease, rag, tire, vex, worry, try, plague, fret, haunt, obsess, bother, pester, bore, gravel, flummox, harass, importune, tantalise, aggravate.

To irritate, provoke, nettle, aggrieve, enchafe, enrage.

To maltreat, bite, assail, badger, infest, harry, persecute, haze, rag.

To sicken, disgust, revolt, turn the stomach, nauseate, disenchant, repel, offend.

To horrify, prostrate.

(*Phrases*). To barb the dart; to set the teeth on edge; to stink in the nostrils; to tweak the nose; to break the heart; to add a nail to one's coffin; to plant a dagger in the breast; to put to the question; to break on the wheel, etc. (972); wring the heart; *surgit amari aliquid.*

(*Adjectives*). Causing, occasioning, giving, producing, creating, inflicting, etc., pain, etc., hurting, etc.

Painful, dolorific, dolorous, unpleasant, unpleasing, displeasing, unprepossessing, disagreeable, distasteful, uncomfortable, unwelcome, unsatisfactory, unpalatable, unacceptable, thankless, undesirable, untoward, unlucky, undesired, obnoxious.

Distressing, bitter, afflicting, afflictive, cheerless, joyless, depressing, depressive, mournful, dreary, dismal, bleak, melancholy, grievous, pathetic, woeful, disastrous, calamitous, tragical, deplorable, dreadful, lamentable, ill-omened.

Irritating, provoking, provocative, stinging, biting, vexatious, annoying, unaccommodating, troublesome, tiresome, irksome, plaguing, plaguy, teasing, pestering, bothering, bothersome, harassing, worrying, tormenting, aggravating, racking, importunate, insistent.

Intolerable, insufferable, insupportable, unbearable, unendurable, shocking, frightful, terrific, grim, appalling, dire, heart-breaking, heart-rending, heart-wounding, heart-corroding, dreadful, horrid, harrowing, horrifying, horrific, execrable, accursed, damnable.

Odious, hateful, unpopular, repulsive, repellent, uninviting, offensive, nauseous, disgusting, sickening, nasty, revolting, shocking, vile, abominable, loathsome, rotten.

Sharp, acute, sore, severe, grave, hard, harsh, bitter, cruel, biting, corroding, consuming, racking, excruciating, etc.

(*Phrase*). What flesh and blood cannot bear.

(*Adverb*). Painfully, etc.

831. CONTENT (*Substantives*), contentment, contentedness, satisfaction, entire satisfaction, serenity, sereneness, ease.

Comfort, snugness, well-being.

Moderation, patience, endurance, resignation, reconciliation.

(*Phrases*). "Patience sitting on a monument"; "patience, sovereign o'er transmuted ill."

(*Verbs*). To be content, etc.; to rest satisfied, to put up with; to take up with; to be reconciled to.

(*Phrases*). To make the best of; to let well alone.

832. DISCONTENT (*Substantives*), discontentment, dissatisfaction, disappointment, mortification.

Repining, taking on, inquietude, heart-burning, *see* Regret (833).

Nostalgia, home-sickness, *maladie du pays.*

(*Phrase*). *Laudator temporis acti.*

(*Verbs*). To be discontented, etc., dissatisfied; to repine, regret (833), grumble (839).

To cause discontent, etc., to disappoint, dissatisfy, mortify.

To render content, etc., to set at ease, to conciliate, reconcile, satisfy, indulge, slake, gratify, etc.

(*Phrases*). To set one's heart at ease, or at rest; to speak peace.

(*Adjectives*). Content, contented, satisfied, at ease, easy, snug, comfortable, cosy.

Patient, resigned to, reconciled to, unrepining.

Unafflicted, unvexed, unmolested, unplagued, etc., serene, at rest, *sine cura, sans souci.*

(*Adverb*). To one's heart's content.

(*Adjectives*). Discontented, dissatisfied, unsatisfied, malcontent, mortified, disappointed, cut up.

Repining, glum, grumbling, exigent, *exigeant*, exacting; nostalgic, home-sick; disgruntled.

(*Phrases*). Out of sorts; in the dumps; down in the mouth.

Disappointing, unsatisfactory.

---

833. Regret (*Substantives*), bitterness, repining; lamentation (839); *see* Penitence (950).

(*Verbs*). To regret, deplore, lament, rue, repent (950).

(*Adjectives*). Regretting, etc., regretful.

(*Phrases*). 'Tis pity; what a pity!

835. Aggravation (*Substantives*), heightening, exacerbation, exasperation.

(*Verbs*). To aggravate, to render worse, heighten, embitter, sour, acerbate, envenom, exacerbate, exasperate.

(*Adjectives*). Aggravating, etc., aggravated, etc., unrelieved; aggravable.

(*Phrase*). Out of the frying-pan into the fire.

834. Relief (*Substantives*), easement, alleviation, mitigation, palliation, solace, consolation, comfort, encouragement, refreshment (689), lullaby.

Delivery from evil, etc.

Lenitive, balm, oil, restorative, cataplasm, etc. (662), cushion, pillow, bolster, bed, etc. (215).

(*Phrases*). A crumb of comfort; balm in Gilead.

(*Verbs*). To relieve, ease, alleviate, mitigate, palliate, soften, soothe, assuage, allay, cheer, comfort, encourage, bear up, refresh, restore, remedy, cure.

(*Phrases*). To dry the tears; to wipe the tears; to pour balm into; to lay the flattering unction to one's soul; to breathe again; to breathe freely.

(*Adjectives*). Relieving, etc., consolatory; balmy, balsamic, lenitive, anodyne, etc. (662), remedial, curative; easeful.

---

836. Cheerfulness (*Substantives*), gaiety, cheer, spirits, high spirits, high glee, joyfulness, joyousness, *gaieté de cœur*, hilarity, exhilaration, liveliness, sprightliness, briskness, vivacity, *allégresse*, jocundity, levity, sportiveness, playfulness, jocularity.

837. Dejection (*Substantives*), depression, low spirits; lowness or depression of spirits, dejectedness; weight of oppression on the spirits, damp on the spirits, sadness.

Heaviness, dullness, infestivity, joylessness, gloom, dolefulness,

(*Phrases*). A flow of spirits; the sunshine of the mind.

Mirth, merriment, merry-making, laughter (*see* 838), amusement (*see* 840), nepenthe, Euphrosyne.

Gratulation, rejoicing, exultation, jubilation, jubilee, triumph, pæan, *Te Deum*, heyday, joy-bells.

(*Verbs*). To be cheerful, etc.; to be of good cheer, to cheer up, brighten up, light up; take heart, bear up.

To rejoice, make merry, exult, congratulate oneself, triumph, clap the hands, crow, sing, carol, lilt, frisk, prance, galumph, rollick, frivol.

(*Phrases*). To drive dull care away; to give a loose to mirth; to keep up one's spirits; care killed the cat; *ride si sapis*; laugh and grow fat.

To cheer, enliven, elate, exhilarate, entrance, etc., buck up, liven up.

(*Adjectives*). Cheerful, gay, blithe, cheery, cheerly, of good cheer, in spirits, in good or high spirits, *allegro*, light, lightsome, buoyant, debonair, bright, light-hearted, hearty, free and easy, airy, jaunty, canty, sprightly, lively, vivacious, sunny, breezy, chirpy, hopeful (858).

Merry, joyous, joyful, jocund, bonny, buxom, playful, *folâtre*, frisky, frolicsome, sportive, gamesome, jokesome, joky, jocose, jocular, jolly, frivolous.

Rejoicing, elated, exulting, jubilant, hilarious, flushed, rollicking, cock-a-hoop.

(*Phrases*). In high feather; gay as a lark; playful as a kitten; merry as a grig; full of beans.

dolesomeness, weariness (841), heaviness of heart, failure of heart, heart-sickness.

Melancholy, melancholia, dismals, mumps, dumps, doldrums, blues, mulligrubs, blue devils, megrims, spleen, hypochondria; *tædium vitæ*; *maladie du pays*.

Despondency, despair, pessimism, disconsolateness, prostration; the cave of despair, *see* 859.

Demureness, seriousness, gravity, solemnity, solemnness, sullenness, etc.

A hypochondriac, self-tormentor, *malade imaginaire*; a damper, a wet blanket; a pessimist.

(*Verbs*). To be dejected, sad, etc.; to grieve, to take on, to take to heart, to give way, droop, sink, lour, look downcast, mope, mump, pout, brood over, fret, pine, yearn, frown, *see* Despair (859).

(*Phrases*). To look blue; to hang down the head; to wear the willow; to laugh on the wrong side of the mouth.

To refrain from laughter; to keep one's countenance; to keep a straight face.

To depress, discourage, dishearten, dispirit, dull, deject, lower, sink, dash, unman, prostrate, overcloud.

(*Phrase*). To prey on the mind or spirits.

(*Adjectives*). Cheerless, unmirthful, mirthless, joyless, dull, flat, dispirited, out of spirits, out of sorts, out of heart, in low spirits, spiritless, lowering, frowning, sulky.

Discouraged, disheartened, down-hearted, downcast, cast down, depressed, chap-fallen, crest-fallen, dashed, drooping, sunk, heart-sick, dumpish,

(*Adverbs*). Cheerfully, cheerily, etc.

(*Interjections*). *Tant mieux!* hurrah! huzza! cheerio!

---

mumpish, desponding, pessimistic.

Dismal, melancholy, sombre, tristful, pensive, *penseroso*, mournful, doleful, moping, splenetic, gloomy, lugubrious, funereal, forlorn, care-worn, care-laden.

Melancholic, hipped, hypochondriacal, bilious, jaundiced, atrabilious, atrabiliar, saturnine, adust.

Disconsolate, despairing, in despair (859).

Grave, serious, sedate, staid, sober, solemn, demure, grim, grim-faced, grim-visaged (846), rueful, sullen.

(*Phrases*). Down in the mouth; sick at heart; with a long face; a prey to melancholy; dull as a beetle; dull as ditch-water; as melancholy as a gib-cat; grave as a judge.

Depressing, preying upon the mind, etc.

838. Expression of pleasure.

Rejoicing (*Substantives*), exultation, triumph, jubilation, jubilee (884), pæan (990).

Smile, simper, smirk, grin, broad grin.

Laughter, giggle, titter, snigger, crow, cheer, chuckle, guffaw, shout, hearty laugh, horse-laugh, a shout, burst, or peal of laughter.

Derision, risibility (856).

Momus, Democritus the Abderite.

(*Verbs*). To rejoice, exult, triumph (884).

To smile, simper, smirk, grin, mock; to laugh, giggle, titter, snigger, chuckle, chortle, burble, crow, cackle; to burst out, split, shout, guffaw.

(*Phrases*). To laugh in one's sleeve; to shake one's sides; to hold both one's sides; to split one's sides; to die with laughter.

To cause, create, occasion, raise, excite, or produce laughter, etc.; to tickle, titillate.

(*Phrases*). To tickle one's fancy; to set the table in a roar; to convulse with laughter; to be the death of one.

839. Expression of pain.

Lamentation (*Substantives*), complaint, murmur, mutter, plaint, lament, wail, sigh, suspiration, heaving.

Cry, whine, whimper, sob, tear, moan, snivel, grumble, groan.

Outcry, scream, screech, howl, whoop, yell, roar (414).

Weeping, crying, etc.; lachrymation, complaining, frown, scowl, sardonic grin or laugh.

Dirge (363), elegy, monody, threnody, jeremiad; coronach, keen, keening.

Plaintiveness, querimoniousness, languishment, querulousness.

Mourning, weeds, willow, cypress.

A grumbler, grouser, croaker, brawler; Heraclitus, Niobe.

(*Phrases*). The melting mood; wringing of hands and gnashing of teeth; *laudator temporis acti*.

(*Verbs*). To lament, complain, murmur, mutter, grumble, grouse, sigh; give, fetch, or heave a sigh.

To cry, weep, sob, greet, blubber, blub; snivel, whimper;

(*Adjectives*). Laughing, etc.; jubilant (836), triumphant.

Laughable, risible, ludicrous, side-splitting.

(*Phrases*). Ready to burst or split; *risum teneatis, amici?* "Laughter holding both his sides."

---

to shed tears; maunder, pule, take on, pine.

To grumble, groan, grunt, croak, whine, moan, bemoan, wail, bewail, frown, scowl.

To cry out, growl, mew, mewl, squeak, squeal, sing out, scream, cry out lustily, screech, bawl, howl, holloa, bellow, yell, roar, yammer.

(*Phrases*). To melt or burst into tears; to cry oneself blind; to cry one's eyes out; to beat one's breast; to wring one's hands; to gnash one's teeth; to tear one's hair; to roll on the ground; to roar like a bull; to bellow like an ox; to cry before one is hurt; to laugh on the wrong side of one's mouth; *infandum renovare dolorem.*

(*Adjectives*). Lamenting, complaining, etc.; tearful, lachrymose, plaintive, plaintful, querulous, querimonious.

(*Phrases*). Being in the melting mood; with tears in one's eyes; bathed or dissolved in tears; the eyes suffused, swimming, brimful, or overflowing with tears; with moistened or watery eyes; the tears standing in the eyes, or starting from the eyes; *les larmes aux yeux.*

(*Interjections*). Heigh-ho! alas! alack! O dear! ah me! well-a-day! well-a-way! alas the day! woe worth the day! *O tempora, O mores!*

840. AMUSEMENT (*Substantives*), diversion, entertainment, sport, divertisement, recreation, holiday, relaxation, distraction, avocation, pastime, *passe-temps*, red-letter day.

Fun, frolic, pleasantry, drollery, jocoseness, laughter (838).

Play, game, gambol, romp, prank, quip, quirk, rig, lark, fling, spree, burst, razzle-dazzle, escapade, *échappée,* jamboree.

Dance (309), ball, ballet (599), hop, jig, fling, reel, cotillion, quadrille, lancers, rigadoon, saraband, lavolta, pavane, galliard, hornpipe, cancan, tarantella, cachucha, fandango, bolero, minuet, gavotte, polka, mazurka, waltz (or valse), fox-trot, tango, one-step, etc.; folk-dance, morris-dance, square dance, round dance,

841. WEARINESS (*Substantives*), tedium, *ennui*, boredom, lassitude, fatigue (688), dejection, *see* 837.

Disgust, nausea, loathing, sickness, disgust of life, *tædium vitæ, Weltschmerz.*

Wearisomeness, irksomeness, tiresomeness, monotony, treadmill, grind.

A bore, a buttonholer, proser.

(*Phrases*). A twice-told tale; time hanging heavily on one's hands; a thin time.

(*Verbs*). To tire, weary, fatigue, bore; set to sleep, send to sleep.

To sicken, disgust, nauseate.

(*Phrase*). To harp on the same string.

(*Adjectives*). Wearying, etc., wearisome, tiresome, irksome, country dance, step-dance, clog-dance, sword-dance, egg-dance, break-down.

Festivity, festival, jubilee, merry-making, rejoicing, fête, gala, ridotto, revelry, revels, carnival, corroboree, saturnalia, night out.

Feast, banquet, entertainment, carousal, bean-feast, beano, jollification, regale, junket, wake, *kermis*, *fête champêtre*, symposium, wassail; jollity, joviality, jovialness.

Buffoonery, mummery, tomfoolery, raree-show, puppet-show, masquerade.

Bonfire, fireworks, *feu de joie*.

Toy, plaything, bauble, etc., *see* **643**.

A master of ceremonies or revels.

(*Phrases*). *Deus nobis hæc otia fecit*; "Quips and cranks and wanton wiles; Nods and becks and wreathèd smiles."

(*Verbs*). To amuse, divert, entertain, rejoice, cheer, re-create, enliven, solace; to beguile or while away the time; to drown care.

To play, sport, disport, make merry, take one's pleasure, make holiday, keep holiday; to game, gambol, revel, frisk, frolic, romp, jollify, skylark, dally; to dance, hop, foot it, jump, caper, cut capers, skip.

To treat, feast, regale, carouse, banquet.

(*Phrases*). To play the fool; to jump over the moon; to make a night of it; to have one's fling; *desipere in loco*; *ridentem dicere verum, quid vetat?*

(*Adjectives*). Amusing, amusive, diverting, etc., amused, etc.

Sportive, jovial, festive, jocose, tricksy, rompish, etc.

(*Phrases*). Playful as a kitten; "On the light fantastic toe"; *vive la bagatelle!*

uninteresting, devoid of interest, monotonous, humdrum, mortal, flat, tedious, prosy, prosing, slow, soporific, somniferous.

Disgusting, sickening, nauseating.

Weary, tired, etc.; unenjoyed, uninterested, flagging, used up, *blasé*, bored, stale, fed up, life-weary, weary of life; drowsy, somnolent, sleepy, etc.

(*Adverb*). Wearily, etc.

(*Phrase*). *Usque ad nauseam.*

---

842. WIT (*Substantives*), humour, imagination (515), fancy, fun, pleasantry, drollery, whim, jocularity, facetiousness, waggery, waggishness, wittiness, salt, Atticism, Attic wit, Attic salt, *esprit*, smartness, banter, badinage, farce, *espièglerie*.

Jest, joke, jape, conceit, quip, quirk, crank, wheeze, side-splitter, *concetto*, witticism, re-

843. DULLNESS (*Substantives*), heaviness, stolidness, stolidity, stupidity (499), flatness, prosiness, gravity (837), solemnity; prose, matter of fact; a wet blanket.

(*Verbs*). To be dull, etc.

To render dull, etc., damp, depress.

(*Phrase*). To throw cold water on.

partee, retort, *mot*, *bon-mot*, pleasantry, funniment, flash of wit, sally, point, dry joke, idle conceit, epigram, quibble, play upon words, pun (563), conundrum, anagram (533), quodlibet, *eu d'esprit*, *facetiæ*; a chestnut, a Joe Miller; an absurdity, *see* 497.

A practical joke, a rag.

(*Phrases*). The cream of the jest; the joke of it; *merum sal*; *le mot pour rire*.

(*Adjectives*). Dull (837), prosaic, prosing, prosy, unentertaining, flat, pointless, stolid, stupid, plodding, humdrum (841), pedestrian, literal, unimaginative, matter-of-fact, uninventive, slow; Bœotian.

(*Phrases*). *Davus sum, non Œdipus*; *aliquando bonus dormitat Homerus*; dull as ditch-water.

(*Verbs*). To joke, jest, jape, retort; to cut jokes, crack a joke, perpetrate a joke or pun.

To laugh at, banter, jeer (856), rag, to make fun of, make merry with.

(*Phrase*). To set the table in a roar.

(*Adjectives*). Witty, facetious, humorous, fanciful, quick-witted, ready-witted, nimble-witted, imaginative (515), *spirituel*, smart, jocose, jocular, waggish, comic, comical, laughable, droll, ludicrous, side-splitting, killing, funny, risible, farcical, roguish, sportive, pleasant, playful, sparkling, entertaining, arch.

(*Adverbs*). In joke, in jest, in sport, for fun.

844. A HUMORIST (*Substantives*), wag, wit, funny man, epigrammatist, *bel esprit*, jester, joker, Joe Miller, *drôle de corps*, *gaillard*.

A buffoon (599), *farceur*, merry-andrew, jack-pudding, tumbler, mountebank, charlatan, posture-master, harlequin, punch, punchinello, scaramouch, clown, pickle-herring, pantaloon, gipsy.

(*Phrase*). The life of the party.

2°. DISCRIMINATIVE AFFECTIONS

845. BEAUTY (*Substantives*), handsomeness, beauteousness, beautifulness, pulchritude, τὸ καλὸν, Æsthetics.

Form, elegance, grace, symmetry, *belle tournure*; good looks.

Comeliness, seemliness, shapeliness, fairness, prettiness, neatness, spruceness, attractiveness, loveliness, quaintness, speciousness, polish, gloss, nattiness; a good effect.

Bloom, brilliancy, radiance,

846. UGLINESS (*Substantives*), deformity, inelegance, plainness, homeliness, uncomeliness, ungainliness, uncouthness, clumsiness, stiffness, disfigurement, distortion, contortion, malformation, monstrosity, misproportion, want of symmetry, roughness, repulsiveness, squalor, hideousness, unsightliness, odiousness.

(*Phrases*). A forbidding countenance; a hanging look; a wry face; "*spretæ injuria formæ*."

splendour, magnificence, sublimity.

Concinnity, delicacy, refinement.

Venus, Hebe, the Graces, Peri, Houri, Cupid, Apollo, Hyperion, Adonis, Antinous, Narcissus.

Peacock, butterfly; the flower of, the pink of, etc.; a garden, a picture.

(*Phrases*). *Je ne sais quoi*; *le beau idéal*; a sight for sore eyes.

(*Verbs*). To be beautiful; to shine, beam, bloom.

To render beautiful, etc., to beautify, embellish, adorn, deck, bedeck, decorate, set out, set off, ornament (*see* 847), dight, bedight, array, garnish, furbish, smarten, trick out, rig out, fig out, dandify, dress up, prank, prink, perk, preen, trim, embroider, emblazon, adonise.

To polish, burnish, gild, varnish, japan, enamel, lacquer, etc.

To powder, rouge, make up, etc.

(*Adjectives*). Beautiful, handsome, fine, pretty, lovely, graceful, elegant, delicate, refined, fair, personable, comely, seemly, bonny, buxom, well-favoured, proper, shapely, well-made, well-formed, well-proportioned, symmetrical, becoming, goodly, neat, dapper, tight, spruce, smart, dashing, swagger, dandified, natty, sleek, quaint, jaunty, bright-eyed, attractive, seductive, curious.

Blooming, brilliant, shining, beaming, splendid, resplendent, dazzling, gorgeous, superb, magnificent, sublime, grand.

Picturesque, statuesque, artistic, æsthetic.

Passable, not amiss, undefaced, spotless, unspotted.

An eyesore, an object, a figure, a sight, fright, guy, spectre, scarecrow, hag, harridan, satyr, sibyl, toad, baboon, monster, Caliban, Hecate.

(*Phrase*). "*Monstrum horrendum, informe, ingens, cui lumen ademptum.*"

(*Verbs*). To be ugly, etc.

To render ugly, etc., to deform, deface, distort, disfigure, disfeature, misshape, blemish, spot, stain, distain, soil, tarnish, discolour, sully, blot, daub, bedaub, begrime, blur, smear, besmear (653), bespatter, maculate, denigrate, uglify.

(*Phrase*). To make faces.

(*Adjectives*). Ugly, plain, homely, unsightly, unornamental, unseductive, ill-looking, ordinary, unseemly, ill-favoured, hard-favoured, evil-favoured, hard-featured, hard-visaged, ungainly, uncouth, slouching, ungraceful, clumsy, graceless, rude, rough, rugged, homespun, gaunt, raw-boned, haggard, scraggy.

Misshapen, shapeless, misproportioned, ill-proportioned, deformed, ill-made, ill-shaped, disfigured, distorted, unshapen, unshapely, humpbacked, crooked, bandy, stumpy, dumpy, squat, stubby, bald, rickety.

Squalid, grim, grisly, gruesome, macabre, grim-faced, grim-visaged, ghastly, ghost-like, death-like, cadaverous, repulsive, forbidding, grotesque.

Frightful, odious, hideous, horrid, shocking, monstrous.

(*Phrase*). Ugly as sin.

Foul, soiled, tarnished, stained, distained, sullied, blurred, blotted, spotted, maculated, spotty, splashed, smeared, begrimed, spattered, bedaubed, besmeared; ungarnished.

847. Ornament (*Substantives*), adornment, decoration, embellishment, illustration, illumination, ornature, ornateness, gaud, pride.

Garnish, polish, varnish, gilding, japanning, enamel, lacquer, etc.

Cosmetic, rouge, powder, lip-salve, etc.

Jewel, gem, brilliant, etc. (650), *bijouterie*, spangle, trinket, carcanet.

Embroidery, broidery, brocade, galloon, lace, fringe, trapping, trimming, chiffon, hanging.

Wreath, festoon, garland, chaplet, tassel, knot, epaulette, frog, ermine.

Feather, plume, panache, aigrette.

Nosegay, bouquet, posy, buttonhole.

Tracery, moulding, arabesque.

Frippery, finery, bravery, gewgaw, fal-lal, tinsel, spangle, *clinquant*, tawdriness, etc.

Trope, flourish, flowers of rhetoric (577).

Excess of ornament, *see* 851.

(*Verbs*). To ornament, embellish, illustrate, illuminate, decorate, adorn, beautify, garnish, polish, gild, etc., bespangle, dizen, bedizen; embroider, etc., *see* 845.

(*Adjectives*). Ornamented, etc., beautified, rigged out, figged out, ornate, showy, dressy, gaudy (851), garish, gorgeous, *endimanché*.

(*Phrases*). Fine as a May-day queen; in full fig; in one's Sunday best; dressed up to the nines.

848. Blemish (*Substantives*), disfigurement, eyesore, defect, flaw, fleck.

Stain, blot, spot, speck, blur, *macula*, blotch, speckle, spottiness; soil, tarnish, smudge, smut, dirt, soot, etc. (653); freckle.

Excrescence, pimple, etc., *see* 250.

(*Verbs*). To disfigure, deface, etc., *see* 846.

849. Simplicity (*Substantives*), plainness, undress, chastity; freedom from ornament or affectation, homeliness.

(*Phrase*). *Simplex munditiis.*

(*Verbs*). To be simple, etc., to render simple, etc., to simplify.

(*Adjectives*). Simple, plain, homely, chaste, homespun, unaffected, severe, primitive.

Unadorned, unornamented, undecked, ungarnished, unarrayed, untrimmed, in dishabille.

---

850. Good taste.

Taste (*Substantives*), delicacy, refinement, gust, gusto, goût, virtuosity, virtuosoship, nicety, finesse, grace, virtu, τὸ πρέπον, polish, elegance.

Science of taste, Æsthetics.

A man of taste, connoisseur, judge, critic, *cognoscente*, virtuoso, amateur, æsthete, an Aristarchus, purist, *arbiter elegantiarum*.

851. Bad taste.

Vulgarity (*Substantives*), vulgarism, barbarism, Vandalism, Gothicism, *mauvais goût*, sensationalism, flamboyance.

Coarseness, grossness, indecorum, lowness, low life, *mauvais ton*, bad form, clownishness, rusticity, boorishness, brutishness, brutality, awkwardness, want of tact, tactlessness.

(*Verbs*). To appreciate, judge, discriminate, criticise (465).

(*Adjectives*). In good taste, tasteful, unaffected, pure, chaste, classical, attic, refined, æsthetic, elegant.

(*Adverb*). Elegantly, etc.

(*Phrases*). To one's taste or mind; after one's fancy; *tiré à quatre épingles*; *comme il faut*.

852. Fashion (*Substantives*), *ton*, tonishness, style, *bon ton*, mode, vogue.

Manners, breeding, politeness, gentility, decorum, *bienséance*, *savoir vivre*, punctilio, form, formality, etiquette, custom, demeanour, air, port, carriage, presence.

Show, equipage, turn-out, etc., *see* 882.

The world, the fashionable world, the *beau monde*, high life, society, town, court, gentility, civilisation, civilised life, *see* Nobility (875), the élite.

(*Phrase*). The height of fashion.

(*Verb*). To be fashionable, etc.

(*Adjectives*). Fashionable, in fashion, in vogue, *à la mode*, modish, tony, tonish, stylish, smart, courtly, *recherché*, genteel, *comme il faut*, well-bred, well-mannered, polished, gentleman-like, ladylike, well-spoken, civil, presentable, refined, thorough-bred, *dégagé*, jaunty, swell, swagger, unembarrassed.

(*Phrase.*) Having a run.

(*Adverbs*). Fashionably, in fashion, etc.

A bad joke; *une mauvaise plaisanterie*.

A rough diamond, a hoyden, tomboy, slattern, sloven, dowdy, frump, cub, clown, cad, etc. (876); an old fogy.

Excess of ornament, false ornament, tawdriness, finery, frippery, trickery, tinsel, gewgaw, *clinquant*.

(*Verb*). To be vulgar, etc.

(*Phrase*). To smell of the shop.

(*Adjectives*). In bad taste, vulgar, coarse, unrefined, gross, heavy, rude, unpolished, homely, homespun, homebred, uncouth, awkward, *gauche*, ungraceful, slovenly, slatternly, dowdy, frumpish, unlicked, ungenteel, impolite, ill-mannered, uncivil, tactless, underbred, ungentlemanly, unladylike, unfeminine, unmaidenly, unseemly, unpresentable, unkempt, uncombed.

Rustic, countrified, boorish, clownish, barbarous, barbaric, gothic, unclassical, heathenish, outlandish, untamed (876).

Obsolete, out of fashion, *démodé*, out of date, unfashionable, antiquated, fossil, old-fashioned, old-world, gone by.

(*Phrase*). A back number.

New-fangled, odd, fantastic, grotesque, *see* Ridiculous (853), affected, meretricious, extravagant, sensational, monstrous, shocking, horrid, revolting.

Gaudy, tawdry, bedizened, flamboyant, baroque, tricked out, gingerbread, loud, flashy.

(*Adverb*). Out of fashion, etc.

853. Ridiculousness (*Substantives*), ludicrousness, risibility.

Oddness, oddity, whimsicality, comicality, grotesqueness, fancifulness, quaintness, frippery, gawkiness, preposterousness, extravagance, monstrosity, *see* Absurdity (497).

Bombast, bathos, fustian, amphigouri, extravaganza.

(*Adjectives*). Ridiculous, absurd, extravagant, *outré*, monstrous, preposterous.

Odd, whimsical, quaint, queer, rum, droll, grotesque, fanciful, eccentric, bizarre, strange, out-of-the-way, fantastic, baroque, rococo.

Laughable, risible, ludicrous, comic, serio-comic, comical, funny, derisive, farcical, burlesque, *pour rire*, quizzical, bombastic, inflated, stilted.

Awkward, gawky, lumbering, lumpish, hulking, uncouth, etc.

(*Phrase*). As whimsical as a dancing bear.

854. Fop (*Substantives*), dandy, exquisite, coxcomb, beau, macaroni, blade, blood, jemmy, buck, spark, swell, toff, masher, dude, nut, dog, popinjay, puppy, *petit-maître*, jackanapes, jack-a-dandy, man-milliner, man about town, chappie.

855. Affectation (*Substantives*), mannerism, pretension, airs, frills, side, conceit, foppery, affectedness, preciosity, charlatanism, quackery, foppishness, pedantry, teratology, acting a part, pose, gush.

Prudery, Grundyism, demureness, coquetry, *minauderie*, sentimentality, lackadaisicalness, stiffness, formality, buckram.

Pedant, precisian, formalist, *poseur*, mannerist, *précieuse ridicule*; prude, Mrs. Grundy.

(*Phrases*). A lump of affectation; prunes and prism.

(*Verbs*). To affect, to give oneself airs, put on side or frills, to simper, mince, to act a part, overact, attitudinise, gush, pose.

(*Adjectives*). Affected, conceited, precious, pedantic, pragmatical, priggish, smug, puritanical, prim, prudish, starchy, stiff, formal, demure, goody-goody.

Foppish, namby-pamby, slip-slop, coxcombical, slipshod, simpering, mincing, niminy-piminy, la-di-da, sentimental, lackadaisical.

Exaggerated, etc. (549), overacted, overdone, gushing.

856. Ridicule (*Substantives*), derision, mockery, quiz, banter, irony, persiflage, raillery.

Jeer, gibe, quip, taunt, satire, scurrility, scoffing.

A parody, burlesque, travesty, skit, farce, comedy, tragi-comedy, doggerel, blunder, bull, *lapsus linguæ*, slip of the tongue, anticlimax.

Buffoonery, vagary, antic, mummery, tomfoolery, grimace, *simagrée*, monkey-trick, escapade, prank, gambade, extravaganza, practical joke, booby-trap.

(*Verbs*). To ridicule, deride, laugh at (929), laugh down, scoff, mock, jeer, banter, quiz, rally, fleer, flout, rag, rot, guy, roast, taunt, point at, grin at.

To parody, caricature, burlesque, travesty, take off.

(*Phrases*). To raise a smile; to set the table in a roar; "*risum teneatis, amici?*"

To turn into ridicule; to play upon; to make merry with; to make a fool of; to make an ass of; to make fun of; to make game of; to make faces at; to make mouths at; to lead one a dance; to run a rig upon; to make an April fool of; to laugh out of court; to pillory.

To laugh in one's sleeve.

(*Adjectives*). Derisory, scurrilous, burlesque, Hudibrastic.

857. Object and cause of ridicule.

LAUGHING-STOCK (*Substantives*), jesting-stock, gazing-stock, butt, target, quiz, square-toes, queer fish; an original, oddity, card, crank, eccentric, monkey, buffoon, jester (844), mime, mimer, etc. (599), scaramouch, punch, punchinello, mountebank, golliwog.

(*Phrase*). A figure of fun.

3°. PROSPECTIVE AFFECTIONS

858. HOPE (*Substantives*), trust, confidence, reliance, faith, assurance, credit, security, expectation, affiance, promise, assumption, presumption.

Hopefulness, reassurance, millennium, optimism, enthusiasm, etc.; Utopia.

(*Phrases*). Castles in the air, in Spain; *châteaux en Espagne*.

Anchor, mainstay, sheet-anchor, staff, etc., *see* Support (215).

(*Phrases*). A ray, gleam, or flash of hope.

(*Verbs*). To hope; to feel, entertain, harbour, cherish, feed, nourish, encourage, foster, etc., hope or confidence; to promise oneself.

To trust, confide, rely on, build upon, feel or rest assured, confident, secure, etc.; to flatter oneself, expect, presume, be reassured.

(*Phrases*). To see land; to live in hopes; to look on the bright side of; *voir en couleur de rose*; to pin one's hope or faith upon; to lay the flattering unction to one's soul; to catch at a straw; to hope against hope.

To give, or inspire hope; to augur well, shape well, bid fair, encourage, assure, promise, flat-

859. Absence, want, or loss of hope.

HOPELESSNESS (*Substantives*), despair, desperation, despondency, pessimism (837); forlornness, a forlorn hope, the Slough of Despond.

(*Verbs*). To despair, despond, give over; to lose, give up, abandon, relinquish, etc., all hope; to yield to despair.

To inspire or drive to despair; to dash, crush, or destroy one's hopes.

(*Phrases*). To trust to a broken reed; "*lasciate ogni speranza voi ch' entrate.*"

(*Adjectives*). Hopeless, having lost or given up hope, losing, etc., hope, past hope, despondent, pessimistic, forlorn, desperate, incurable.

Inauspicious, unpropitious, unpromising, threatening, etc.

860. FEAR (*Substantives*), timidity, diffidence, nervousness, restlessness, inquietude, disquietude, solicitude, anxiety, distrust, mistrust, hesitation, misgiving, suspicion, qualm, want of confidence, nerves.

Apprehension, flutter, trepidation, tremor, shaking, trembling, palpitation, quivering, the jumps, ter, buoy up, reassure, embolden, raise expectations, etc.

(*Adjectives*). Hoping, etc., in hopes, etc., hopeful, confident, secure, buoyant, buoyed up, sanguine, optimistic, enthusiastic, utopian.

Fearless, unsuspecting, unsuspicious; free or exempt from fear, suspicion, distrust, etc., undespairing.

Auspicious, promising, propitious, bright, rose-coloured, rosy, of good omen, *de bon augure*.

(*Phrases*). *Nil desperandum*; never say die; all for the best.

---

the creeps, ague-fit, fearfulness, despondency; stage-fright.

Fright, affright, alarm, dread, awe, terror, horror, dismay, obsession, panic, funk, stampede, scare, consternation, despair (859).

Intimidation, terrorism, reign of terror; an alarmist, scaremonger.

Object of fear: bugbear, bugaboo, bogy, scarecrow, goblin, etc. (980), *bête noire*, nightmare, Gorgon, ogre.

(*Phrases*). Raw head and bloody bones; fee-faw-fum.

(*Verbs*). To fear, be afraid, etc., to distrust, hesitate, have qualms, misgivings, suspicions, etc.

To apprehend, take alarm, start, wince, boggle, skulk, cower, crouch, tremble, shake, quake, shudder, quail, boggle, turn pale, blench, flutter, flinch, funk.

(*Phrases*). To smell a rat; to shake all over; to shake like an aspen-leaf; to stand aghast; to eye askance.

To excite fear, raise apprehensions, to give, raise, or sound an alarm, to intimidate, put in fear, frighten, fright, affright, alarm, scare, haunt, obsess, strike terror, daunt, terrify, awe, horrify, dismay, petrify, appal.

To overawe, abash, cow, browbeat, bully.

(*Phrases*). To fright from one's propriety; to strike all of a heap; to make the flesh creep; to give one the creeps.

(*Adjectives*). Fearing, timid, fearful, nervous, jumpy, funky, diffident, apprehensive, restless, haunted with the fear, apprehension, dread, etc., of, nervy.

Frightened, cowed, pale, alarmed, scared, terrified, petrified, aghast, awe-struck, dismayed, horror-struck, horrified, appalled, panic-struck, panic-stricken.

Inspiring fear, fearsome, alarming, formidable, redoubtable, portentous, perilous (665), ugly, fearful, dreadful, dire, shocking, terrible, tremendous, horrid, horrible, horrific, ghastly, awful, awesome, horripilant, creepy, crawly.

(*Phrases*). White as a sheet; *horresco referens*; the hair standing on end; not daring to say one's soul's one's own; more frightened than hurt; frightened out of one's senses or wits; in a blue funk.

(*Interjection*). *Absit omen!*

861. Absence of fear.

COURAGE (*Substantives*), bravery, valour, boldness, spirit, spiritedness, daring, gallantry,

862. Excess of fear.

COWARDICE (*Substantives*), pusillanimity, cowardliness, timidity, fearfulness, spiritless-intrepidity, contempt of danger, self-reliance, confidence, fearlessness, audacity.

Manhood, nerve, pluck, mettle, game, bottom, heart, spunk, face, virtue, hardihood, fortitude, firmness, resolution, sportsmanship.

Prowess, heroism, chivalry.

A hero, *preux chevalier*, Hector, Hotspur, Amazon, *beau sabreur*, fire-eater, etc. (863).

A lion, tiger, bulldog, gamecock, fighting-cock, sportsman.

(*Verbs*). To be courageous, etc., to face, front, affront, confront, despise, brave, defy, etc., danger; to take courage; to summon up, muster up, or pluck up courage; to rally.

To venture, make bold, face, defy, brave, beard, hold out, bear up against, stand up to.

(*Phrases*). To look in the face; to come up to the scratch; to "screw one's courage to the sticking-place"; to die game.

To give, infuse, or inspire courage; to encourage, embolden, inspirit.

(*Phrases*). To pat on the back; to make a man of.

(*Adjectives*). Courageous, brave, valiant, valorous, gallant, intrepid.

Spirited, high-spirited, high-mettled, mettlesome, self-reliant, manly, manful, resolute, stout, stout-hearted, lion-hearted, heart of oak, firm, indomitable, sportsmanlike.

Bold, daring, audacious, fearless, unfearing, dreadless, undaunted, aweless, unappalled, undismayed, unawed, unabashed, unalarmed, unflinching, unshrinking, unblenching, unblenched, unapprehensive, confident.

Enterprising, venturous, adventurous, venturesome, dashing, chivalrous, heroic, fierce, savage.

Unfeared, undreaded, etc.

(*Phrases*). Up to the scratch; brave as a lion; bold as brass; brave to the backbone; full of beans.

ness, faint-heartedness, softness, effeminacy, funk.

Poltroonery, baseness, dastardliness, Dutch courage, the white feather, a faint heart.

A coward, poltroon, dastard, recreant, funk, dunghill-cock, milksop, cry-baby.

A runaway, fugitive.

(*Verbs*). To quail, etc. (860), to flinch, fight shy, shy, turn tail, run away, cut and run, fly for one's life, stampede.

(*Phrases*). To show the white feather; to be in a sweat.

(*Adjectives*). Coward, cowardly, pusillanimous, shy, timid, skittish, timorous, poor-spirited, spiritless, weak-hearted, faint-hearted, chicken-hearted, lily-hearted, pigeon-hearted, white-livered, lily-livered, milk-livered, milksop.

Dastard, dastardly, base, craven, dunghill, recreant, unwarlike, unheroic.

(*Phrase*). "In face a lion, but in heart a deer."

(*Interjections*). *Sauve qui peut!* "The devil take the hindmost!"

---

863. RASHNESS (*Substantives*), temerity, audacity, presumption,

864. CAUTION (*Substantives*), cautiousness, discretion, prud-

precipitancy, precipitation, recklessness, overboldness, foolhardiness, desperation, Quixotism; carelessness, want of caution (460, 823), over-confidence.

Imprudence, indiscretion.

(*Phrases*). A blind bargain; a wild-cat scheme.

A desperado, rashling, bravo, dare-devil, *enfant perdu*, Hotspur, Don Quixote, knight-errant, Icarus.

(*Verbs*). To be rash, incautious, etc.

(*Phrases*). To buy a pig in a poke; to go on a forlorn hope; to go at it bald-headed; to rush on destruction.

(*Adjectives*). Rash, temerarious, headstrong, insane, foolhardy, slapdash, dare-devil, overbold, reckless, desperate, hot-headed, hare-brained, headlong, hot-brained, over-confident, precipitate, Quixotic.

Imprudent, indiscreet, uncalculating, incautious, improvident.

ence, reserve, wariness, cautel, heed, circumspection, calculation, deliberation, *see* 459.

Coolness, self-possession, presence of mind, sang-froid, self-command, steadiness, the Fabian policy.

(*Phrases*). "The better part of valour"; a safe man.

(*Verbs*). To be cautious, etc., to take care, to have a care, take heed, to be on one's guard, to look about one, to take no chances.

(*Phrases*). To look before one leaps; let sleeping dogs lie; to see which way the wind blows; to have one's wits about one.

(*Adjectives*). Cautious, wary, careful, heedful, cautelous, chary, circumspect, prudent, prudential, reserved, discreet, non-committal.

Unenterprising, unadventurous, cool, steady, self-possessed.

(*Phrases*). Without ballast; *tête baissée*; post-haste; neck or nothing; head-foremost; head-first; *à corps perdu*.

(*Interjections*). *Vogue la galère!* come what may!

865. Desire (*Substantives*), wish, mind.

Inclination, leaning, bent, fancy, partiality, penchant, predilection, liking, love, fondness, relish, keenness.

Want, need, exigency.

Longing, hankering, solicitude, anxiety, yearning, coveting, aspiration, ambition, over-anxiety.

Appetite, appetence, appetency, the edge of appetite, keenness, hunger, stomach, thirst, thirstiness, mouth-watering, itch, prurience, lickerishness, *cacoethes*, cupidity, lust, concupiscence, greed.

Avidity, greediness, covetous-

866. Indifference (*Substantives*), coldness, coolness, unconcern, insouciance, inappetency, listlessness, lukewarmness, *see* Disdain (930).

(*Verbs*). To be indifferent, etc.; to have no desire, wish, taste, or relish for; not to care for; to disdain, spurn (930).

(*Adjectives*). Indifferent, undesirous, cool, cold, unconcerned, insouciant, unsolicitous, unattracted, etc., lukewarm, half-hearted, listless, unambitious, unaspiring, phlegmatic.

Unattractive, unalluring, uninviting, undesired, undesirable, etc., uncared for, unwished, uncoveted, unvalued.

ness, craving, voracity, canine appetite, bulimia, rapacity.

Passion, rage, furore, mania, inextinguishable desire, vaulting ambition, impetuosity.

A gourmand, gourmet, glutton, cormorant, *see* 957.

An amateur, votary, devotee, aspirant, solicitant, candidate.

Object of desire: desideratum, attraction, allurement, fancy, temptation, magnet, whim, whimsy (608), maggot, hobby, hobby-horse, prestige.

(*Phrases*). The height of one's ambition; *hoc erat in votis*; the wish being father to the thought; *sua cuique voluptas*.

(*Verbs*). To desire, wish, long for, fancy, have a mind to, be glad of, want, miss, need, feel the want of, would fain have, to care for.

To hunger, thirst, crave, lust after, hanker after, itch for.

To desiderate, sigh, cry, gape, gasp, pine, pant, languish, yearn for, aspire after, catch at, jump at.

To woo, court, solicit, etc.

(*Phrases*). To have at heart; to find in one's heart; to set one's heart upon; to cast a sheep's eye upon; to set one's cap at; to run mad after.

To cause, create, raise, excite, or provoke desire; to allure, attract, solicit, tempt, hold out temptation or allurement, to tantalise, appetise.

(*Phrases*). To whet the appetite; to make one's mouth water.

To gratify desire, slake, satiate (827).

(*Adjectives*). Desirous, inclined, fain, keen, wishful, wishing, desiring, wanting, needing, hankering after, dying for, partial to.

Craving, hungry, esurient, Vapid, tasteless, insipid, unappètising, mawkish, namby-pamby, flat, stale, vain.

867. DISLIKE (*Substantives*), distaste, disrelish, disinclination, reluctance, backwardness, demur.

Repugnance, disgust, queasiness, turn, nausea, loathing, averseness, aversion, abomination, antipathy, abhorrence, horror, hatred, detestation (*see* 898), hydrophobia.

(*Verbs*). To dislike, mislike, disrelish.

To shun, avoid, eschew, withdraw from, shrink from, shrug the shoulders at, recoil from, shudder at.

To loathe, nauseate, abominate, detest, abhor, *see* Hate (898).

(*Phrase*). Not to be able to bear or endure or stand.

To cause or excite dislike; to disincline, repel, sicken, render sick, nauseate, disgust, shock.

(*Phrases*). To go against the grain; to turn one's stomach; to go against the stomach; to make one's blood run cold.

(*Adjectives*). Disliking, disrelishing, etc., averse from, adverse, shy of, disinclined.

Loathing, nauseating, sick of, dog-sick, queasy, sea-sick, abominating, abhorrent.

Disliked, disagreeable, unpalatable, unpopular, offensive, loathsome, loathly, sickening, nauseous, nauseating, repulsive, disgusting, detestable, execrable, abhorred (830), disgustful.

(*Adverb*). Disagreeably, etc.

(*Phrase*). *Usque ad nauseam.*

(*Interjections*). Faugh! ugh!

868. FASTIDIOUSNESS (*Substantives*), nicety, daintiness,

sharp-set, keen-set, peckish, thirsty, athirst, dry.

Greedy, voracious, lickerish, open-mouthed, agog, covetous, ravenous, rapacious, unsated, unslaked, insatiable, insatiate.

(*Phrases*). Pinched, or perished, with hunger; greedy as a dog; hungry as a horse; hungry as a hunter; having a sweet tooth; devoured by desire; nothing loth; *alieni appetens.*

Eager, bent on, intent on, aspiring, ambitious, vaulting, vehement, etc., *see* 825, would-be.

Desirable, desired, desiderated, etc., *see* Pleasing (829).

(*Interjections*). O for! would that!

squeamishness, niceness, particularity, difficulty in being pleased, *friandise*, epicurism.

Epicure, gourmet.

Excess of delicacy, prudery.

(*Verbs*). To be fastidious, etc., to disdain.

(*Phrase*). To turn up one's nose at.

(*Adjectives*). Fastidious, nice, difficult, dainty, lickerish, pernickety, squeamish, queasy, difficult to please, particular; prudish, strait-laced.

869. Satiety (*Substantives*), repletion, glut, saturation, surfeit.

A spoilt child; *enfant gâté.*

(*Verbs*). To sate, satiate, satisfy, saturate, quench, slake, pall, glut, gorge, surfeit, tire, spoil, sicken.

(*Adjectives*). Satiated, sated, *blasé*, used up, fed up, sick of.

(*Phrase*). *Toujours perdrix.*

(*Interjections*). Enough! *Eheu jam satis!*

4°. Contemplative Affections

870. Wonder (*Substantives*), surprise, marvel, astonishment, amazement, wonderment, admiration, awe, bewilderment, stupefaction, fascination, prestige, thaumaturgy (992), amazedness, etc.

(*Verbs*). To wonder, marvel, be surprised, admire, etc.; to stare, gape, start.

(*Phrases*). To open one's mouth or eyes; *tomber des nues*; to look blank; to stand aghast; not to believe one's eyes; not to account for; not to know whether one stands on one's head or one's heels.

To surprise, astonish, amaze, astound, dumbfound, strike, dazzle, startle, take by surprise, take aback, strike with

871. Absence of wonder.

Expectance (*Substantives*), expectation (507).

(*Verbs*). To expect, not to be surprised, not to wonder, etc., *nil admirari.*

(*Phrase*). To think nothing of.

(*Adjectives*). Expecting, etc., foreseen, unamazed, astonished at nothing, blasé (841).

Common, ordinary, *see* 82.

wonder, etc., electrify, stun, petrify, flabbergast, confound, stagger belief, stupefy, bewilder, fascinate.

(*Phrase*). To make one sit up.

To be wonderful, etc.

(*Phrases*). To beggar description; to stagger belief.

(*Adjectives*). Surprised, astonished, amazed, astounded, struck, startled, taken by surprise, taken aback, struck dumb, awe-struck, aghast, agape, dumbfounded, flabbergasted, thunderstruck, planet-struck, stupefied, open-mouthed, petrified.

(*Phrases*). Struck all of a heap; lost in wonder.

Wonderful, wondrous, surprising, astonishing, amazing, astounding, startling, stunning, unexpected, unforeseen, strange, uncommon, unheard of, unaccountable, incredible, inexplicable, indescribable, inexpressible, ineffable, unutterable, monstrous, prodigious, stupendous, beggaring description, miraculous, passing strange, uncanny, weird, phenomenal.

(*Adverbs*). Wonderingly, etc., with gaping mouth, all agog.

(*Interjections*). Lo! heyday! hallo! what! indeed! really! surely! humph! you don't say so! lack-a-daisy! my stars! my goodness! good gracious! gracious goodness! bless us! bless my heart! upon my word! O gemini! gad! dear me! only think! hoity-toity! *mirabile dictu!* who'd have thought it!

872. PRODIGY (*Substantives*), phenomenon, wonder, cynosure, marvel, miracle, monster (83), unicorn, phœnix, gazing-stock, curiosity, *rara avis*, lion, sight, spectacle, wonderment, sign, portent (512), eye-opener; wonderland, fairyland.

Thunderclap, thunderbolt, bursting of a shell or bomb, volcanic eruption.

(*Phrase*). A nine days' wonder.

5°. EXTRINSIC AFFECTIONS [1]

873. REPUTE (*Substantives*), Distinction, note, name, repute, reputation, figure, réclame, éclat, celebrity, fame, famousness, popularity, renown, memory, immortality.

Glory, honour, credit, kudos, account, regard, respect, reputableness, respectability, respectableness, illustriousness, gloriousness.

Dignity, stateliness, solemnity,

874. DISREPUTE (*Substantives*), discredit, ingloriousness, derogation, abasement, degradation, odium, notoriety.

Dishonour, shame, disgrace, slur, scandal, obloquy, opprobrium, ignominy, baseness, turpitude, vileness, infamy.

Tarnish, taint, defilement, pollution.

Stain, blot, spot, blur, stigma, brand, reproach, slur, black mark.

[1] Or personal affections derived from the opinions or feelings of others.

grandeur, splendour, nobleness, lordliness, majesty, sublimity.

Greatness, highness, eminence, supereminence.

Elevation, ascent (305), exaltation, superexaltation, aggrandisement.

Rank, standing, *pas*, station, place, status, order, degree, *locus standi*.

Dedication, consecration, enshrinement, glorification, deification, posthumous fame.

Chief, leader, etc. (745), hero, cock of the roost, cock of the walk, man of mark, *prima donna*.

A star, sun, constellation, galaxy, lion, paragon (650); honour, ornament, aureole, mirror.

(*Phrases*). A halo of glory; a fair name; blushing honours; *aura popularis*; *spolia opima*.

(*Verbs*). To be conscious of glory, to glory in, to be proud of (*see* 878), to exult, etc. (884), to be vain of (880).

To be glorious, distinguished, etc., to shine, to figure, to make or cut a figure, dash, or splash; to rival, outrival, emulate, outvie, eclipse, outshine; to throw into the shade.

To live, flourish, glitter, flaunt.

(*Phrases*). To acquire or gain honour, etc.; to bear the palm; to bear the bell; to take the cake; to win laurels; to make a noise in the world; to go far; to make a sensation; to be all the rage; to have a run; to catch on.

To confer or reflect honour, etc., on; to honour; to do honour to; to redound to one's honour; *fama volat*.

To pay or render honour, etc., to; to honour, lionise, dignify, glorify, ennoble, nobilitate, exalt,

(*Phrases*). A burning shame; *scandalum magnatum*; a badge of infamy; a blot on the scutcheon; a byword of reproach; a bad reputation.

(*Verbs*). To be conscious of shame, to feel shame, to blush, to be ashamed, humiliated, humbled, abashed, etc., *see* 879 and 881.

(*Phrases*). To feel disgrace; to take shame to oneself; to hide one's face; to look foolish; to hang one's head; to laugh on the wrong side of the mouth; to go away with a flea in one's ear; not to dare to show one's face; to hide its diminished head.

To be inglorious, abased, dishonoured, etc., to incur disgrace, etc.

(*Phrases*). To lose caste; to be in one's black books.

To cause shame, etc.; to shame, disgrace, put to shame, dishonour, throw, cast, fling, or reflect shame, etc., upon, to derogate from.

To tarnish, stain, blot, sully, taint, discredit, degrade, debase, defile.

To impute shame to, to brand, post, stigmatise, vilify, defame, slur, run down.

(*Phrase*). To hold up to shame.

To abash, humiliate, humble, dishonour, discompose, disconcert, shame, put down, confuse, mortify; to obscure, eclipse, outshine.

(*Phrases*). To put to the blush; to put out of countenance; to cast into the shade; to take the shine out of; to tread or trample under foot; to drag through the mud.

(*Adjectives*). Feeling shame, disgrace, etc., ashamed, abashed, enthrone, signalise, immortalise, deify.

To consecrate, dedicate to, devote to, to enshrine.

(*Phrases*). To exalt one's horn; to exalt to the skies.

(*Adjectives*). Distinguished, *distingué*, noted, notable, respectable, reputable, celebrated, famous, famed, far-famed, honoured, renowned, popular; imperishable, immortal, *ære perennius*, *see* 112.

Illustrious, glorious, splendid, bright, brilliant, radiant, full-blown, heroic.

Eminent, prominent, high, pre-eminent, peerless, signalised, exalted, dedicated, consecrated, enshrined.

Great, dignified, proud, noble, worshipful, lordly, grand, stately, august, imposing, transcendent, majestic, kingly, queenly, princely, sacred, sublime, commanding.

(*Phrases*). Redounding to one's honour; one's name living for ever.

(*Interjections*). Hail! all hail! *ave!* glory be to! honour be to!

etc., disgraced, etc., blown upon, branded, tarnished, etc.

Inglorious, mean, base, etc. (940), shabby, nameless, unnoticed, unnoted, unhonoured.

Shameful, disgraceful, despicable, discreditable, unbecoming, unworthy, disreputable, derogatory, vile, ribald, dishonourable, abject, scandalous, infamous, notorious.

(*Phrases*). *Infra dignitatem*, or *infra dig.*; shorn of its beams; unknown to fame; in bad odour; loaded with shame, infamy, etc.; under a cloud.

(*Interjections*). Fie! shame! for shame! *proh pudor!*

---

875. Nobility (*Substantives*), *noblesse*, aristocracy, peerage, gentry, gentility, quality, rank, blood, birth, donship, fashionable world, etc. (852), the *beau monde*, the upper ten, distinction, etc.

A personage, notability, man of distinction, rank, etc.; a nobleman, noble, lord, peer, grandee, magnate, magnifico, hidalgo, don, daimio, gentleman, squire, patrician, lordling, nob.

House of Lords, Lords Spiritual and Temporal.

Gentlefolk, squirearchy, *primates, optimates*.

Prince, duke, marquis, earl, viscount, baron, thane, banneret, baronet, knight, count, armiger,

876. Commonalty (*Substantives*), the lower or humbler classes or orders, the vulgar herd, the crowd, the people, the commons, the proletariat, the multitude, Demos, οἱ πολλοί, the populace, the million, the peasantry.

The middle classes, *see* 736.

The mob, rabble, rabble-rout, *canaille*; the scum or dregs of the people, or of society; the underworld; *profanum vulgus*; low company, vermin, nobody.

A commoner, one of the people, a proletary, proletaire, *roturier*; a peasant, boor, carle, churl, serf, kern, tyke (or tike), chuff, ryot, fellah, cottar, cottier.

A swain, clown, hind, clodhopper, bog-trotter, chaw-bacon,

esquire, etc.; nizam, begum, rajah, nawab, etc.

(*Verb*). To be noble, etc.

(*Adjectives*). Noble, exalted, of rank, titled, patrician, aristocratic, high-born, well-born, genteel, *comme il faut*, gentlemanlike, princely, etc., fashionable, etc. (852).

(*Phrases*). *Noblesse oblige*; born in the purple.

877. Title (*Substantives*), honour, knighthood, etc.

Highness, excellency, grace, lordship, worship, reverence, esquire, sir, master, sahib, etc.

Decoration, laurel, palm, wreath, medal, ribbon, cross, star, garter, feather, crest, epaulette, colours, cockade, livery; order, arms, shield, scutcheon.

(*Phrases*). A feather in one's cap; a handle to one's name.

hodge, joskin, yokel, bumpkin, ploughman, plough-boy, gaffer, loon, looby, lout, *gamin*, street-arab, guttersnipe, mudlark.

An upstart, *parvenu*, skipjack, *novus homo*, *nouveau riche*, outsider, vulgarian, snob, mushroom.

A beggar, pariah, muckworm, sansculotte, raff, tatterdemalion, ragtag and bobtail, ragamuffin, riffraff, caitiff.

(*Phrases*). A man of straw; nobody one knows; the great unwashed.

A Goth, Vandal, Hottentot, savage, barbarian, yahoo, an unlicked cub.

Barbarousness, barbarism.

(*Verbs*). To be ignoble, etc.

(*Adjectives*). Ignoble, mean, low, plebeian, proletarian, vulgar, untitled, homespun, homely, subaltern.

Base, base-born, beggarly, earth-born, rustic, agrestic, cockney, menial, sorry, scrubby, mushroom, dunghill, sordid, vile, uncivilised, loutish, boorish, churlish, rude, brutish, raffish, unlicked, barbarous, barbarian, barbaric.

878. Pride (*Substantives*), haughtiness, loftiness, hauteur, stateliness, pomposity, vainglory, superciliousness, assumption, lordliness, stiffness, primness, arrogance, *morgue*, starch, starchiness, side uppishness.

A proud man, etc., a highflier.

(*Verbs*). To be proud, etc., to presume, assume, swagger, strut, bridle.

(*Phrases*). To look big; toss the head; give oneself airs; ride the high horse; put on side; hold up one's head; to take the wall.

To pride oneself on, glory in, pique oneself, plume oneself, preen oneself, to stand upon.

879. Humility (*Substantives*), humbleness, meekness, lowness, lowliness, affability, condescension, abasement, self-abasement, self-contempt, humiliation, submission, resignation, verecundity, *see* Modesty (881), abasing.

(*Verbs*). To be humble, etc.; to deign, condescend; to humble or demean oneself; stoop, submit, knuckle to.

(*Phrases*). To lower one's flag; fall on one's knees, etc.; to knuckle down or under; to sing small; to eat humble-pie; to eat dirt; to kiss the rod; to pocket an affront; to stoop to conquer.

To render humble; to humble,

(*Phrases*). To put a good face upon; *odi profanum vulgus.*

(*Adjectives*). Proud, haughty, lofty, high, mighty, high-flown, high-minded, puffed up, flushed, supercilious, patronising, condescending, disdainful, overweening, consequential, on stilts, swollen, arrogant, pompous.

Stately, stiff, starchy, prim, perked up, in buckram, straitlaced, vainglorious, lordly, magisterial, purse-proud, stand-offish.

Unabashed, etc. (880).

(*Phrases*). High and mighty; proud as a peacock; proud as Lucifer.

humiliate, set down, abash, abase, take down, snub.

(*Phrases*). To throw into the shade; to put out of countenance; to teach one's distance; to take down a peg; to send away with a flea in one's ear.

(*Adjectives*). Humble, lowly, meek, sober-minded, submissive, resigned, self-contemptuous, under correction.

Humbled, humiliated, etc.

(*Phrases*). Out of countenance; shorn of one's glory; down on one's knees; humbled in the dust; not having a word to say for oneself.

880. VANITY (*Substantives*), conceit, conceitedness, self-conceit, self-confidence, self-sufficiency, self-esteem, self-approbation, self-importance, self-praise, self-laudation, self-admiration, complacency, self-complacency, megalomania, *amour-propre.*

Pretensions, mannerism, egotism, coxcombry, gaudery, vainglory (943), elation.

(*Phrases*). *Vox, et præterea nihil ; ne sutor ultra crepidam.*

A coxcomb, etc., *see* 854.

(*Verbs*). To be vain, etc., to egotise.

(*Phrases*). To have a high or overweening opinion of oneself, one's talents, etc.; to blind oneself as to one's own merit; to think no small beer of oneself; to put oneself forward; to show off; to fish for compliments.

To render vain, etc., to puff up, to inspire with vanity, etc.

(*Adjectives*). Vain, conceited, overweening, forward, vainglorious, puffed up, high-flown, inflated, flushed, stuck-up.

Self - satisfied, self - confident, self-sufficient, self-flattering, self-

881. MODESTY (*Substantives*), humility (879), diffidence, timidity, bashfulness, shyness, coyness, sheepishness, *mauvaise honte*, shamefacedness, blushing, verecundity, self-consciousness.

Reserve, constraint, demureness, *retenue.*

(*Verbs*). To be modest, humble, etc.; to retire, keep in the background, keep private, reserve oneself.

(*Phrases*). To draw in one's horns; to take a back seat.

(*Adjectives*). Modest, diffident, humble (879), timid, bashful, timorous, shy, skittish, coy, sheepish, shamefaced, blushing, self-conscious.

Unpretending, unobtrusive, unassuming, unostentatious, unboastful, unaspiring.

Abashed, ashamed, dashed, out of countenance, down in the mouth, chapfallen, crestfallen, dumbfounded.

Reserved, constrained, demure, undemonstrative.

(*Adverbs*). Humbly, etc., quietly, privately, unostentatiously.

admiring, self-applauding, self-opinionated, self-centred, complacent, self-complacent, *soi-disant*, *entêté*.

(*Phrases*). Without beat of drum; *sans façon*; *sans cérémonie*.

Unabashed, unblushing, unconstrained, unceremonious, free and easy.

(*Phrases*). Vain as a peacock; eaten up with pride.

(*Adverbs*). Vainly, etc., ostentatiously, etc. (882), with beat of drum, etc.

882. OSTENTATION (*Substantives*), display, show, flourish, parade, *étalage*, pomp, state, solemnity, pageantry, dash, splash, glitter, strut, magnificence, pomposity, showing off, swank, swagger, panache, *coup de théâtre*, stage-effect.

Flourish of trumpets, fanfare, salvo of artillery, salute, *feu de joie*.

Pageant, spectacle, procession, turn-out, set-out, fête, gala, regatta, field-day.

Ceremony, ceremonial, mummery; formality, form, etiquette, punctilio, punctiliousness, frippery, court-dress, etc.

(*Verbs*). To be ostentatious, etc.; to display, *prôner*, exhibit, show off, swank, come forward, put oneself forward, flaunt, emblazon, prink, glitter; make or cut a figure, dash, or splash.

To observe or stand on ceremony, etiquette, etc.

(*Adjectives*). Ostentatious, showy, gaudy, garish, flashy, dashing, flaunting, jaunty, glittering, sumptuous, theatrical, histrionic.

Pompous, solemn, stately, high-sounding, formal, stiff, ceremonious, punctilious.

(*Phrase*). *Ad captandum vulgus*.

(*Adverbs*). With flourish of trumpets, with beat of drum.

883. CELEBRATION (*Substantives*), jubilee, commemoration, solemnisation, ovation, pæan, triumph.

Triumphal arch, bonfire, salute, salvo, *feu de joie*, flourish of trumpets, fanfare.

Inauguration, installation.

(*Verbs*). To celebrate, keep, signalise, do honour to, pledge, drink to, toast, commemorate, solemnise.

To inaugurate, install.

(*Adjectives*). Celebrating, etc., in honour of, in commemoration of, etc.

(*Interjections*). Hail! all hail!

884. BOASTING (*Substantives*), boast, vaunt, vaunting, brag, swank, bluff, puff, puffing, puffery, flourish, fanfaronade, gasconade, braggadocio, bravado, vapouring, rodomontade, bombast, teratology, *see* Exaggeration (549), self-advertisement, *réclame*.

Exultation, triumph, flourish of trumpets, fanfare, jubilation.

A boaster, braggart, braggadocio, Gascon, fanfaron, puppy, peacock; a pretender, *soi-disant*.

(*Verbs*). To boast, make a boast of, brag, vaunt, puff, flourish, crake, crack, strut, swagger, swank, gas.

To exult, croak, crow, chuckle, triumph, glory.

(*Phrases*). To talk big; *se faire valoir*; *faire claquer son fouet*; to blow one's own trumpet.

(*Adjectives*). Boasting, vaunting, etc., vainglorious, braggart.

Elate, elated, flushed, jubilant.

(*Phrases*). On stilts; cock-a-hoop.

885. Undue assumption of superiority.

INSOLENCE (*Substantives*), haughtiness, arrogance, imperiousness, contumeliousness, superciliousness, bumptiousness, swagger, swank.

Impertinence, sauciness, pertness, flippancy, dicacity, petulance, malapertness.

Assumption, presumption, presumptuousness, forwardness, impudence, assurance, front, face, cheek, lip, side, brass, shamelessness, a hardened front, effrontery, audacity, procacity, self-assertion, nerve.

(*Phrases*). The Great Panjandrum himself; a cool hand.

(*Verbs*). To be insolent, etc.; to bluster, vapour, swagger, swank, swell, roister, arrogate, assume, bluff.

To domineer, bully, beard, snub, huff, outface, outlook, outstare, outbrazen, bear down, beat down, trample on, tread under foot, outbrave, hector.

To presume, take liberties or freedoms.

(*Phrases*). To give oneself airs; to lay down the law; to put on side; to ride the high horse; to lord it over; *traiter, ou regarder de haut en bas*; to ride rough-shod over; to carry with a high hand; to put on side; to carry it off; to brave it out.

(*Adjectives*). Insolent, etc.; haughty, arrogant, imperious, dictatorial, high-handed, contumelious, supercilious, uppish, self-assertive, bumptious, overbearing, intolerant, assumptive.

Flippant, pert, perky, cavalier, saucy, cheeky, forward, impertinent, malapert.

886. SERVILITY (*Substantives*), obsequiousness, suppleness, fawning, slavishness, abjectness, prostration, prosternation, genuflexion, etc. (990), abasement.

Fawning, mealy-mouthedness, sycophancy, *see* Flattery (833) and Humility (879).

A sycophant, parasite, toad-eater, toady, spaniel, lickspittle, hanger-on, tuft-hunter, time-server, reptile, cur (941).

(*Verbs*). To cringe, bow, stoop, kneel, fall on one's knees, etc.

To sneak, crawl, crouch, truckle to, grovel, fawn.

(*Phrases*). To pay court to; to dance attendance on; to pin oneself upon; to hang on the sleeve of; to lick the shoes of.

To go with the stream; to worship the rising sun; to hold with the hare and run with the hounds.

(*Adjectives*). Servile, subservient, obsequious, sequacious, supple, mean, crouching, cringing, fawning, slavish, grovelling, snivelling, beggarly, sycophantic, parasitical, abject.

(*Adverb*). Cap in hand.

Blustering, swaggering, swanky, vapouring, bluff, roistering, rollicking, high-flown, assuming, presuming, presumptuous, self-assertive, impudent, free, brazen, brazen-faced, shameless, unblushing, unabashed.

(*Adverbs*). *Ex cathedra*; cock-a-hoop.

887. BLUSTERER (*Substantives*), bully, swaggerer, fire-eater, roisterer, puppy, sauce-box, hussy, minx, malapert, jackanapes, jack-in-office, Drawcansir, Captain Bobadil, Sir Lucius O'Trigger, Bombastes Furioso, Hector, Thraso, Bumble.

SECTION III.—SYMPATHETIC AFFECTIONS

1°. SOCIAL AFFECTIONS

888. FRIENDSHIP (*Substantives*), amity, amicableness, amicability, friendliness, friendly regard, favour, brotherhood, fraternity, sodality, comradeship, *camaraderie*, confraternity, fraternisation, harmony, good understanding, concord (714), *entente cordiale*.

Acquaintance, introduction, intimacy, familiarity, fellowship, welcomeness, favouritism.

(*Verbs*). To be friends, to be friendly, etc., to fraternise, sympathise with (897), to be well with, to be thick with, to befriend (707), *tutoyer*, to be in with, to keep in with.

To become friendly, to make friends with, to chum up to.

(*Phrases*). To take in good part; to hold out the right hand of fellowship.

(*Adjectives*). Friendly, amical, amicable, brotherly, fraternal, harmonious, cordial, social, chummy, neighbourly, on good terms, on a friendly, a familiar, or an intimate footing, on friendly, etc., terms, well-affected, well-disposed, favourable.

Acquainted, familiar, intimate, thick, hand and glove, welcome.

Firm, staunch, intimate, familiar, bosom, cordial, tried, devoted, lasting, fast, warm, ardent.

(*Adverbs*). Friendlily, amicably, etc., *sans cérémonie*.

889. ENMITY (*Substantives*), *see* Hate (898) and Discord (713).

Unfriendliness, alienation, estrangement.

Animosity, umbrage, pique, hostility, bad blood, ill feeling.

(*Verbs*). To be inimical, etc., to estrange, to fall out, alienate.

(*Adjectives*). Inimical, unfriendly, at variance, at loggerheads, at daggers drawn, hostile, on bad terms, cold-hearted.

890. FRIEND (*Substantives*), well-wisher, *amicus curiæ*, *alter ego*, bosom friend, *fidus Achates*, favourer, *see* 711.

891. ENEMY (*Substantives*), foe, opponent (*see* 710), backfriend.

Persona grata.

Neighbour, acquaintance, associate, compeer, comrade, companion, confrère, *camarade*, mate, messmate, shopmate, shipmate, crony, confidant, chum, pal, boon companion, copesmate, pot-companion, schoolfellow, playfellow, playmate, bed-fellow, bed-mate.

Arcades ambo, Pylades and Orestes, Castor and Pollux, Nisus and Euryalus, Damon and Pythias, David and Jonathan, *par nobile fratrum.*

Host, Amphitryon, guest, visitor, *protégé.*

892. SOCIALITY (*Substantives*), sociability, sociableness, companionship, companionableness, consortship, intercommunication, intercommunion, consociation.

Conviviality, good fellowship, hospitality, heartiness, welcome, *savoir vivre*, festivity, merry-making.

Society, association, union, copartnership, fraternity, sodality, coterie, clan, club (72), circle, clique, party, welcomeness.

Assembly-room, casino, club-house, common-room.

Esprit de corps, nepotism (11).

An entertainment, party, levee, soirée, conversazione, rout, *ridotto*, at-home, house-warming, festival (840), interview, assignation, appointment, call, visit, visiting, reception (588).

(*Verbs*). To be sociable, etc., to associate with, keep company with, to club together, sort with, hob-nob with, consort; make, pick, or scrape acquaintance with, take up with.

To visit, pay a visit, interchange visits or cards, call upon, leave a card, make advances.

(*Phrases*). To beat up one's quarters; to make oneself at home.

To entertain, give a party, dance, etc.; to keep open house; to receive, to welcome.

(*Phrases*). To be at home to; to

893. SECLUSION (*Substantives*), privacy, retirement, recess, retiredness, rustication.

Solitude, singleness, estrangement from the world, loneliness, lonesomeness, retiredness, isolation; cloister, nunnery, etc. (1000).

Wilderness, depopulation.

Agoraphobia.

EXCLUSION (*Substantives*), excommunication, banishment, exile, ostracism, cut, cut direct, dead cut, inhospitality, inhospitableness, unsociability.

A recluse, hermit, cenobite, anchoret (or anchorite), stylite, santon, troglodyte, solitary, ruralist; outcast, pariah; foundling, waif, wastrel, etc.

(*Verbs*). To be secluded, etc., to retire, to live retired, secluded, etc.; to keep aloof; to keep snug; to shut oneself up, deny oneself.

(*Phrases*). *Aller planter ses choux*; to retire from the world.

To cut, refuse to associate with or acknowledge; repel, cold-shoulder, blackball, excommunicate, boycott, exclude, banish, exile, ostracise, rusticate, send down, abandon, maroon.

(*Phrases*). To send to Coventry; to turn one's back upon; to look cool upon.

To depopulate, dispeople.

(*Adjectives*). Secluded, sequesreceive with open arms; to give a warm reception to; to kill the fatted calf.

(*Adjectives*). Sociable, social, companionable, neighbourly, gregarious, clannish, clubbable, conversable, etc., on visiting terms, welcome, hospitable, convivial, festive.

(*Phrases*). Free and easy; hail fellow well met.

(*Adverbs*). *En famille*; in the family circle; *sans façon*; *sans cérémonie*; *sans gêne*.

tered, retired, private, bye, snug, domestic, claustral.

Unsociable, unsocial, offish, stand-offish, isolated, inhospitable, cynical, inconversible, retiring, unneighbourly, exclusive.

Solitary, lonesome, isolated, single, estranged, unfrequented.

Unvisited, cut, blackballed, uninvited, unwelcome, friendless, deserted, abandoned, lorn, forlorn, homeless, out of it.

(*Phrase*). Left to shift for oneself.

894. COURTESY (*Substantives*), good manners, good breeding, mannerliness, *bienséance*, urbanity, civilisation, polish, politeness, civility, amenity, suavity, good temper, easy temper, gentleness, mansuetude, graciousness, affability, obligingness, *prévenance*, amiability, good humour.

Compliment, fair words, soft words, sweet words, attentions, *petits soins*, salutation, reception, presentation, introduction, *accueil*, greeting, welcome, *abord*, respect, devoir.

Obeisance, reverence, bow, curtsy, scrape, salaam, kotow, capping, shaking hands, embrace, hug, squeeze, accolade, salute, kiss, buss, kissing hands, presenting arms, kneeling, genuflexion, prostration, obsequiousness.

Mark of recognition, nod.

Valediction, *see* 293.

(*Verbs*). To be courteous, civil, etc., to show courtesy, civility, etc., to speak fair; to make oneself agreeable; to unbend, thaw.

To visit, wait upon, present oneself, pay one's respects, kiss hands.

To receive, do the honours, greet, welcome, bid welcome, bid

895. DISCOURTESY (*Substantives*), ill-breeding; ill, bad, or ungainly manners; rusticity, inurbanity, impoliteness, ungraciousness, uncourtliness, insuavity, rudeness, incivility, barbarism, misbehaviour, *grossièreté*, roughness, ruggedness, brusqueness, brusquerie, bad form.

Bad or ill temper, churlishness, crabbedness, tartness, crossness, peevishness, moroseness, sullenness, sulkiness, grumpiness, acrimony, sternness, austerity, moodiness, asperity, captiousness, sharpness, snappishness, perversity, cussedness, sauciness, irascibility, *see* 901.

Sulks, dudgeon, mumps, black looks.

A bear, brute, blackguard, beast, cross-patch.

(*Verbs*). To be rude, etc., frown, scowl, glower, lour, pout; to cut, insult, etc.

(*Phrases*). To turn one's back upon; to turn on one's heel; to look black upon; turn a cold shoulder on.

To render rude, etc., to brutalise, decivilise, dehumanise.

(*Adjectives*). Discourteous, uncourteous, uncourtly, ill-bred, ill-mannered, ill-behaved, un-

God speed; hold or stretch out the hand; shake, press, or squeeze the hand.

To salute, kiss, smack, embrace, hug, drink to, pledge, hobnob; to move to, nod to, smile upon, bow, curtsy, scrape, uncover, cap, present arms, take off the hat, etc.

(*Phrases*). To make a leg; to steal a kiss.

To pay homage or obeisance, kneel, bend the knee, prostrate oneself, etc.

To render polite, etc., to polish, civilise, humanise.

(*Adjectives*). Courteous, courtly, civil, civilised, polite, well-bred, well-mannered, mannerly, urbane, gentlemanly, ladylike, refined (850), polished, genial.

Gracious, affable, familiar, well-spoken, fair-spoken, soft-spoken, fine-spoken, oily, bland, mild, obsequious, obliging, open-armed.

(*Phrases*). With open or outstretched arms; *suaviter in modo*; *à bras ouverts*; with a good grace.

(*Interjections*). Hail! welcome! well met! *ave!* all hail! *pax vobiscum!*

mannerly, mannerless, impolite, unpolished, ungenteel, ungentlemanly, unladylike, uncivilised.

Uncivil, rude, ungracious, cool, chilly, distant, stand-offish, offish, icy, repulsive, uncomplaisant, unaccommodating, ungainly, unceremonious, ungentle, rough, rugged, bluff, blunt, gruff, churlish, bearish, brutal, brusque, stern, harsh, austere, angular.

Ill-tempered, out of temper or humour, cross, crusty, tart, sour, crabbed, sharp, short, snappish, testy, peevish, waspish, captious, grumpy, snarling, caustic, acrimonious, ungenial, petulant, pettish, pert.

Perverse, cross-grained, ill-conditioned, wayward, humoursome, naughty, cantankerous, intractable, curst, froward, sulky, glum, grim, morose, scowling, glowering, surly, sullen, growling, splenetic, spleenful, spleeny, spleenish, moody, dogged, ugly.

(*Phrases*). Cross as a cat; cross as two sticks; cross as a dog; sour as a crab; surly as a bear.

(*Adverbs*). With a bad grace, grudgingly.

896. Congratulation (*Substantives*), felicitation, wishing joy.

(*Verbs*). To congratulate, felicitate, give or wish joy, tender or offer one's congratulations, etc.

(*Adjective*). Congratulatory, etc.

897. Love (*Substantives*), fondness, liking, inclination, regard, good graces, partiality, leaning, penchant, predilection; amativeness, amorousness.

Affection, sympathy, fellow-feeling, heart, affectionateness.

Attachment, yearning, amour, love-affair, *affaire de cœur*, passion, tender passion, *grande passion*, flame, devotion, enthusiasm,

898. Hate (*Substantives*), hatred, disaffection, disfavour, alienation, estrangement, odium, *see* Dislike (867) and Animosity (900).

Umbrage, pique, grudge, dudgeon, spleen, bitterness, acrimony, acerbity, malice (907), implacability.

Disgust, repugnance, aversion, averseness, loathing, abomination, enchantment, infatuation, adoration, idolatry, idolisation.

Eros, Cupid, Venus; *hiraeth*; the myrtle.

Maternal love, *στοργή*.

Attractiveness, etc., popularity.

Abode of love; agapemone.

A lover, suitor, follower, admirer, adorer, wooer, beau, sweetheart, flame, love, true-love, leman, paramour, amorist, *amoroso*, *cavaliere servente*, *cicisbeo*; turtle-doves.

Inamorata, idol, doxy, dona, Dulcinea, goddess.

Betrothed, affianced, *fiancée*.

(*Verbs*). To love, like, affect, abide, fancy, care for, regard, revere, cherish, admire, dote on, adore, idolise.

To bear love to; to take to; to be in love with; to be taken, smitten, etc., with; to have, entertain, harbour, cherish, etc., a liking, love, etc., for; to be fond of, be gone on; *aimer éperdument*.

(*Phrases*). To take a fancy to; to make much of; to look sweet upon; to cast sheep's eyes at; to fall in love with; to set one's affections on; to lose one's heart; become enamoured, etc.

To excite love; to win, gain, secure, etc., the love, affections, heart, etc.; to take the fancy of, to attract, attach, seduce, charm, fascinate, captivate, enamour, enrapture.

To get into favour; to ingratiate oneself, insinuate oneself, curry favour with, pay one's court to, *faire l'aimable*.

(*Adjectives*). Loving, liking, etc., attached to, fond of, taken with, struck with, gone on, sympathetic, sympathising with, charmed, captivated, fascinated, smitten, enamoured, lovesick, love-lorn.

Affectionate, tender, sweet upon, loving, lover-like, loverly, amorous, amatory, amative, spoony, erotic, uxorious, ardent, passionate, devoted, over-fond; amatorial.

(*Phrase*). Over head and ears in love.

tion, horror, detestation, antipathy, abhorrence.

Object of hatred: an abomination, aversion, antipathy, *bête noir*.

(*Verbs*). To hate, dislike, disrelish, etc. (867), loathe, nauseate, detest, abominate, shudder at, recoil at, abhor, shrink from.

To excite hatred, estrange, alienate, disaffect, set against, to be hateful, etc.

(*Phrases*). To make one's blood run cold; to have a down on.

(*Adjectives*). Hating, etc., averse from or to, set against.

Unloved, disliked, unwept, unlamented, undeplored, unmourned, unbeloved, uncared for, unvalued.

Crossed in love, forsaken, rejected, lovelorn.

Obnoxious, hateful, abhorrent, odious, repulsive, offensive, shocking, loathsome, sickening, nauseous, disgusting, abominable, horrid (649).

Invidious, spiteful, malicious, spleenful, disgustful.

Insulting, irritating, provoking.

(*Phrases*). Mutual hate: there being no love lost between them; being at daggers drawn.

Loved, beloved, etc., dear, precious, darling, favourite (899), pet, popular.

(*Phrases*). To one's mind, taste, or fancy; in one's good graces; dear as the apple of one's eye; nearest to one's heart; the idol of the people.

Lovely, sweet, dear, charming, engaging, amiable, winning, attractive, adorable, enchanting, captivating, fascinating, bewitching, taking, seductive (829).

899. FAVOURITE (*Substantives*), pet, cosset, dear, darling, jewel, idol, minion, spoilt child, *enfant gâté, persona grata.*

(*Phrases*). The apple of one's eye; a man after one's own heart.

900. RESENTMENT (*Substantives*), displeasure, animosity, anger, wrath, indignation.

Pique, umbrage, huff, miff, soreness, dudgeon, moodiness, acerbity, bitterness, asperity, spleen, gall, heart-burning, heart-swelling, rankling; temper (901), bad blood, ill blood.

Excitement, irritation, warmth, bile, choler, ire, fume, pucker, dander, passion, fit, tantrum, burst, explosion, paroxysm, storm, rage, fury, desperation.

Black looks.

(*Phrases*). The blood being up; the blood rising; the blood boiling; a towering passion; the vials of wrath; fire and fury.

Temper, petulance, procacity, angry mood, taking, snappishness.

Cause of umbrage: affront, provocation, offence, indignity, insult (929).

(*Phrases*). A sore subject; *casus belli.*

The Furies; the Eumenides.

(*Verbs*). To resent, take amiss, take offence, take umbrage, take huff, bridle up, bristle up, frown, scowl, lour, snarl, growl, gnash, snap.

To chafe, mantle, redden, colour, fume, froth up, kindle; get, fall, or fly into a passion, rage, etc.; fly out, take fire, fire up, flare up, boil, boil over, rage, storm, foam.

(*Phrases*). To take in bad part; to take it ill; to take exception; to stick in one's gizzard; to take in dudgeon; *ne pas entendre raillerie*; to stand on one's hind legs; to show one's teeth; to stamp the foot; to stamp, quiver, swell or foam with rage; to see red; to look as black as thunder; to breathe revenge; to cut up rough; to pour out the vials of one's wrath; to blaze up; to go on the war-path; "*Manet alta mente repostum.*"

To cause or raise anger; to affront, offend, give offence or umbrage; hurt the feelings; discompose, fret, ruffle, nettle, rile, excite, irritate, provoke, rile, chafe, wound, sting, incense, inflame, enrage, aggravate, embitter, exasperate, rankle, infuriate, to kindle wrath.

(*Phrases*). To put out of humour; to stir up one's bile; to raise one's dander or choler; to work up into a passion; to make one's blood boil; to lash into a fury; to drive one mad; to put one's monkey up.

(*Adjectives*). Angry, wroth, irate, warm, boiling, fuming, raging, etc., nettled, sore, bitter, riled, ruffled, chafed, exasperated, wrought up, worked up, snappish.

Fierce, wild, rageful, furious, infuriate, mad with rage, fiery, savage, boiling over, rankling, bitter, *acharné*, set against.

Relentless, ruthless, implacable, unpitying, pitiless (919), inexorable, remorseless, stony-hearted, immitigable.

(*Phrases*). One's back being up; up in arms; in a stew; the gorge rising; the eyes flashing; one's blood being up; "*Tantæne animis celestibus iræ ?*" in the height of passion.

901. Irascibility (*Substantives*), susceptibility, excitability, temper, procacity, petulance, irritability, fretfulness, testiness, tetchiness, touchiness, frowardness, peevishness, snappishness, hastiness, tartness, huffiness, resentfulness, vindictiveness, acerbity, protervity, aggressiveness, pugnacity, *see* 895.

Genus irritabile.

A shrew, vixen, termagant, virago; a tartar.

(*Verbs*). To be irascible, etc.; to take fire, fire up, flare up, etc., *see* 900.

(*Adjectives*). Irascible, susceptible, excitable, irritable, fretful, fretty, on the fret, fidgety, peevish, hasty, over-hasty, quick, warm, hot, huffish, huffy, touchy, testy, techy (or tetchy), pettish, waspish, snappish, petulant, peppery, fiery, passionate, choleric, short-tempered.

Ill-tempered, cross, churlish, sour, crabbed, out of sorts, fractious, splenetic, spleenful, froward, shrewish.

Quarrelsome, querulous, disputatious, cantankerous, sarcastic (932), resentful, vindictive, pugnacious, aggressive.

(*Phrases*). Like touchwood or tinder; a word and a blow; as cross as two sticks.

902. Expression of affection or love.

Endearment (*Substantives*), caress, blandishment, *épanchement*, fondling, billing and cooing, embrace, salute, kiss, buss, smack, osculation, deosculation.

Courtship, wooing, suit, addresses, attentions, *petits soins*, flirtation, philandering, gallivanting, serenading.

Honeymoon.

Love-tale, love-token, love-letter, *billet-doux*, valentine.

(*Verbs*). To caress, fondle, wheedle, dandle, dally, cuddle, cockle, cosset, nestle, nuzzle, snuggle, clasp, hug, embrace, kiss, salute, bill and coo.

To court, woo, flirt, philander, spoon, canoodle, mash, serenade.

(*Phrases*). To make much of; to smile upon; to make eyes at; to pat on the cheek; to make love; pay one's court or one's addresses to; set one's cap at; kill with kindness; pop the question.

To win the heart, affections, love, etc., of.

(*Adjectives*). Caressing, etc., caressed, etc., flirtatious, spoony.

903. MARRIAGE (*Substantives*), matrimony, wedlock, union, match, intermarriage, coverture, cohabitation, bed, the marriage-bond.

Wedding, nuptials, Hymen, spousals, espousals; leading to the altar; the torch of Hymen; nuptial benediction, epithalamium.

Bride, bridegroom, bridesmaid, bridesman, best man.

Honeymoon, honeymooner.

A married man, a husband, spouse, benedick, consort, goodman, hubby.

A married woman, a wife, mate, helpmate, helpmeet, rib, better half, *femme couverte* (or *feme coverte*), squaw.

A married couple, Darby and Joan, man and wife.

A monogamist, bigamist, polygamist, a much-married man, a Turk, a Bluebeard, a Mormon.

Monogamy, bigamy, digamy, deuterogamy, trigamy, polygamy, polyandry, endogamy, exogamy.

(*Verbs*). To marry, wed, espouse, wive.

(*Phrases*). To lead to the altar; to take to oneself a wife; to take for better for worse; to give one's hand to; to get spliced.

To marry, join, give away, handfast, splice.

(*Phrases*). To tie the nuptial knot; to give in marriage.

(*Adjectives*). Matrimonial, conjugal, connubial, nuptial, hymeneal, spousal, bridal, marital, epithalamic.

Monogamous, etc.

904. Unlawful marriage; a left-handed marriage; morganatic marriage; *mésalliance.*

CELIBACY (*Substantives*), singleness, misogamy.

(*Phrase*). Single blessedness.

An unmarried man, bachelor, old bachelor, celibate, misogamist.

An unmarried woman, a spinster, maid, maiden, old maid, virgin, *feme sole*, bachelor girl.

(*Verb*). To live single.

(*Adjectives*). Unwedded, celibate, wifeless, spouseless, lone.

(*Adverb*). *En garçon.*

905. DIVORCE (*Substantives*), separation, divorcement; widowhood, weeds.

A widow, relict, widower, dowager, a *divorcée*; a grass widow.

(*Verbs*). To live separate, divorce, put away.

(*Phrases*). *Separatio a mensa et thoro*; *a vinculo matrimonii*; a judicial separation.

2°. DIFFUSIVE SYMPATHETIC AFFECTIONS

906. BENEVOLENCE (*Substantives*), goodwill, good nature, kindness, kindliness, benignity, brotherly love, beneficence, charity, humanity, fellow-feeling, sympathy, good feeling, kind-

907. MALEVOLENCE (*Substantives*), ill will, unkindness, ill nature, malignity, malice, maliciousness, spite, spitefulness, despite, despitefulness.

Uncharitableness, venom, gall,

heartedness, amiability, complaisance, loving-kindness; toleration.

Charitableness, bounty, bounteousness, bountifulness, almsgiving, philanthropy (910).

Acts of kindness, a good turn, kind offices, attentions, good treatment.

(*Phrases*). The milk of human kindness; the good Samaritan.

(*Verbs*). To be benevolent, etc., to do good to, to benefit, confer a benefit, be of use, aid, assist (707), render a service, treat well, to sympathise with.

(*Phrases*). To have one's heart in the right place; to enter into the feelings of others; to do a good turn to.

(*Adjectives*). Benevolent, well-meaning, kind, obliging, accommodating, kind-hearted, tender-hearted, charitable, beneficent, humane, clement, benignant, benign, considerate.

Good-natured, *bon enfant*, *bon diable*, a good sort, spleenless, sympathising, sympathetic, responsive, complaisant, accommodating, amiable, gracious.

Kindly, well-meant, well-intentioned, brotherly, fraternal, friendly (888).

(*Adverbs*). With a good intention, with the best intentions.

(*Interjection*). God speed!

---

rancour, rankling, bitterness, acerbity, harshness, mordacity, acridity, virulence, *acharnement*, misanthropy (911).

Cruelty, hardness of heart, cruelness, brutality, brutishness, hooliganism, savageness, ferocity, barbarity, bloodthirstiness, immanity, pitilessness, truculence, devilry (or deviltry), devilment.

An ill turn, a bad turn; affront (900).

(*Phrases*). A heart of stone; the evil eye; the cloven hoof.

(*Verbs*). To injure, hurt, harm, molest, disoblige, do harm to, ill-treat, maltreat (649), do an ill office or turn to (830), to wrong.

To worry, harass, bait, oppress, grind, haze, persecute, hunt down, dragoon.

(*Phrases*). To wreak one's malice on; to bear or harbour malice against; to dip or imbrue one's hands in blood.

(*Adjectives*). Malevolent, malicious, ill-disposed, evil-minded, ill-intentioned, maleficent, malign, malignant.

Ill-natured, disobliging, inofficious, unfriendly, unsympathetic, unkind, uncandid, unaccommodating, uncharitable, ungracious, unamiable, unfriendly.

Surly, churlish (895), grim, spiteful, despiteful, ill-conditioned, foul-mouthed, acrid, mordacious, vitriolic, venomous.

Cold, cold-blooded, cold-hearted, hard-hearted, iron-hearted, flint-hearted, marble-hearted, stony-hearted.

Pitiless, unpitying, uncompassionate, without bowels, ruthless, merciless, unmerciful, inexorable, relentless, unrelenting, virulent, dispiteous.

Cruel, brutal, savage, ferocious, untamed, ferine, inhuman, barbarous, fell, Hunnish, bloody, blood-stained, bloodthirsty, bloody-minded, sanguinary, truculent (919), butcherly.

Fiendish, fiendlike, infernal, demoniacal, diabolical, devilish, hellish.

(*Phrases*). Betraying the cloven foot; having no bowels.

(*Adverbs*). Malevolently, etc., with bad intent or intention, despitefully.

908. MALEDICTION (*Substantives*), curse (641), malison, imprecation, denunciation, execration, anathema, ban, proscription, excommunication, commination (909), fulmination, *maranatha*.

Cursing, scolding, railing, Billingsgate, bad language, unparliamentary language.

(*Verbs*). To censure, curse, imprecate, beshrew, scold, swear at, rail at or against, execrate.

To denounce, proscribe, excommunicate, fulminate against, anathematise.

(*Phrases*). To devote to destruction; to invoke or call down curses on one's head; to swear like a trooper; to rap out an oath; curse with bell, book, and candle.

(*Adjectives*). Cursing, etc., accursed, cursed, etc.

(*Interjections*). Woe to! beshrew! *ruat cœlum!* ill betide! *Delenda est Carthago!*

909. THREAT (*Substantives*), menace, defiance (715), abuse, minacity, intimidation.

(*Verbs*). To threaten, threat, menace, fulminate, defy, snarl, growl, gnarl, mutter; to intimidate (860).

(*Phrases*). To hurl defiance; to throw down the gauntlet; to show one's teeth; to shake the fist at.

(*Adjectives*). Threatening, menacing, minatory, comminatory, minacious, abusive, *in terrorem*.

(*Interjection*). *Væ victis!*

910. PHILANTHROPY (*Substantives*), humanity, public spirit.

Patriotism, civicism, nationality, nationalism, love of country, *amor patriæ*, nostalgia; utilitarianism.

A philanthropist, humanitarian, utilitarian, cosmopolitan, cosmopolite, citizen of the world, patriot, nationalist, *amicus humani generis*.

911. MISANTHROPY (*Substantives*), egotism, incivism, moroseness, *see* Selfishness (943).

A misanthrope, egotist, cynic, man-hater, Timon, Diogenes.

Woman-hater, misogynist.

(*Adjectives*). Misanthropic, selfish, egotistical, morose, unpatriotic.

(*Adjectives*). Philanthropic, utilitarian, patriotic, etc., public-spirited.

(*Phrases*). "*Humani nihil a me alienum puto*"; *pro bono publico*; *pro aris et focis*; the greatest happiness of the greatest number.

912. BENEFACTOR (*Substantives*), saviour, good genius, tutelary saint, guardian angel, good Samaritan.

913. Maleficent being.

EVIL-DOER (*Substantives*), mischief-maker, marplot, firebrand, incendiary, evil genius (980).

(*Phrase*). *Deliciæ humani generis.*

———

Frankenstein's monster.

Savage, brute, ruffian, barbarian, caitiff, desperado, jail-bird, hooligan, apache (949).

Fiend, tiger, hyæna, bloodhound, butcher, blood-sucker, serpent, snake, adder, hell-hound, hag, hell-hag, beldam, Jezebel.

Monster, demon, imp, devil (980), anthropophagi, Attila, Hun.

(*Phrases*). A snake in the grass; a scourge of the human race; worker of iniquity; *fœnum habet in cornu.*

3°. Special Sympathetic Affections

914. Pity [1] (*Substantives*), compassion, commiseration, sympathy, fellow-feeling, tenderness, yearning.

Forbearance, mercy, humanity, clemency, leniency, ruth, long-suffering, quarter.

(*Phrases*). The melting mood; *coup de grâce*; bowels of compassion; *argumentum ad misericordiam.*

(*Verbs*). To pity, commiserate, compassionate, sympathise, feel for, yearn for, console, enter into the feelings of, have pity, etc.; show or have mercy; to forbear, relent, thaw, spare, relax, give quarter.

To excite pity, touch, soften, melt, propitiate.

To ask for pity, mercy, etc.; to supplicate, implore, deprecate, appeal to, cry for quarter, etc.; beg one's life, kneel, fall on one's knees, etc.

(*Adjectives*). Pitying, commiserating, etc.

Pitiful, compassionate, tender, clement, merciful, lenient, relenting, etc.; soft-hearted, sympathetic, tender, weak, soft, melting, unhardened (740).

(*Phrases*). Tender as a chicken; one's heart bleeding for.

(*Interjections*). For pity's sake! mercy! cry you mercy! God help you! poor thing! poor fellow!

915. Condolence (*Substantives*), lamentation, lament (*see* 839), sympathy, consolation.

(*Verbs*). To condole with, console, sympathise; express, testify, etc., pity; to afford or supply consolation, lament with, weep with, etc. (839).

4°. Retrospective Sympathetic Affections

916. Gratitude (*Substantives*), thankfulness, feeling of obligation.

Acknowledgment, recognition, thanksgiving, giving thanks.

917. Ingratitude (*Substantives*), thanklessness, oblivion of benefits.

(*Phrases*). "Benefits forgot"; "*Et tu, Brute!*"

[1] For Pitilessness *see* 907.

Thanks, praise, benediction, pæan, *Te Deum* (990).

Requital, thank-offering.

(*Verbs*). To be grateful, etc.; to thank, to give, render, return, offer, tender thanks, acknowledgments, etc.; to acknowledge, requite.

To lie under an obligation, to be obliged, beholden, etc., *savoir gré*.

(*Phrases*). To overflow with gratitude; to thank one's stars; never to forget.

(*Adjectives*). Grateful, thankful, obliged, beholden, indebted to, under obligation, etc.

(*Interjections*). Thanks! many thanks! gramercy! much obliged! thank heaven! heaven be praised!

(*Verbs*). To be ungrateful, etc.; to forget benefits.

(*Phrase*). To look a gift-horse in the mouth.

(*Adjectives*). Ungrateful, unmindful, unthankful, thankless.

Forgotten, unacknowledged, unthanked, unrequited, unrewarded.

(*Phrase*). Thank you for nothing.

---

918. FORGIVENESS (*Substantives*), pardon, condonation, grace, remission, absolution, amnesty, oblivion, indulgence, reprieve.

Reconcilement, reconciliation, shaking of hands, pacification (723).

Excuse, exoneration, quittance, acquittal, propitiation, exculpation.

Longanimity, placability.

(*Phrases*). *Amantium iræ; locus penitentiæ.*

(*Verbs*). To forgive, pardon, excuse, pass over, overlook, forgive and forget, absolve, pass, let off, remit, reprieve, exculpate, exonerate.

To allow for; to make allowance for.

To conciliate, propitiate, pacify, placate, reconcile.

(*Phrases*). To make it up; to shake hands; to heal the breach; to kiss and be friends; to let bygones be bygones.

(*Adjectives*). Forgiving, etc., unreproachful, placable.

Forgiven, etc., unresented.

919. REVENGE (*Substantives*), vengeance, revengement, avengement, vendetta, retaliation.

Rancour, vindictiveness, implacability, Nemesis.

Revenger, avenger, vindicator.

(*Verbs*). To revenge, take revenge, avenge.

(*Phrases*). To wreak one's vengeance; to visit the sins on; to breathe vengeance; to have a bone to pick with; to have accounts to settle; to have a rod in pickle; to get a knife into; to take one's change out of.

To harbour vindictive feelings; to rankle in the breast.

(*Adjectives*). Revengeful, vindictive, vengeful, rancorous, unforgiving, pitiless, unrelenting, relentless, implacable, rigorous.

(*Phrases*). "*Æternum servans sub pectore vulnus*"; *manet alta mente repostum.*

---

920. JEALOUSY (*Substantive*), jealousness.

(*Phrases*). A jaundiced eye; the green-eyed monster.

(*Verbs*). To be jealous, etc.; to view with jealousy.
(*Adjectives*). Jealous, jaundiced, yellow-eyed, unrevenged, horn-mad.

921. Envy (*Substantives*), rivalry, covetousness; a Zoilus.
(*Verbs*). To envy, covet.
(*Adjectives*). Envious, invidious.
(*Phrase*). *Alieni appetens.*

SECTION IV.—MORAL AFFECTIONS

1°. Moral Obligation

922. Right (*Substantives*), what ought to be, what should be, τὸ πρέπον.

Justice, equity, equitableness, fitness, fairness, fair play, impartiality, reasonableness, propriety.

Astræa, Nemesis, Aristides.

(*Phrases*). The scales of justice; even-handed justice; *suum cuique*; a clear stage and no favour; a fair field and no favour; *lex talionis*; "*Fiat justitia, ruat cœlum.*"

Morality, morals, ethics, etc., *see* Duty (926).

(*Verbs*). To be right, just, etc.

(*Phrases*). To do justice to; to see justice done; to hold the scales even; to see fair play; to see one righted; to serve one right; to put the saddle on the right horse; to give everyone his due; to give the devil his due; to give and take; *audire alteram partem*.

To deserve, merit; to be worthy of, to be entitled to, *see* 924.

(*Adjectives*). Right, just, equitable, fair, equal, even-handed, impartial, judicial, legitimate, justifiable, rightful, fit, proper, becoming, decorous, etc., *see* Duty (926).

Deserved, merited, condign, entitled to (924).

(*Adverbs*). Rightly, in justice, in equity, fairly, etc., in reason, without distinction.

(*Phrases*). *En règle ; selon les règles ; de jure.*

923. Wrong (*Substantives*), what ought not to be, what should not be.

Injustice, unfairness, inequity, foul play, partiality, favour, favouritism, party spirit, undueness (925), unreasonableness, unlawfulness (964), encroachment, imposition, etc.

(*Verbs*). To be wrong, unjust, etc.; to favour, lean towards; to encroach, impose upon, etc.

(*Adjectives*). Wrong, unjust, unfair, undue, inequitable, unequal, partial, invidious, one-sided, improper, unreasonable, unfit, immoral, *see* 945.

Unjustified, unjustifiable, unwarranted, unauthorised, unallowable, unwarrantable.

(*Phrases*). In the wrong; in the wrong box.

(*Adverbs*). Wrongly, unjustly, etc.

924. DUENESS (*Substantives*), due.

Right, privilege, prerogative, title, claim, qualification, pretension, birthright, prescription, immunity, licence, liberty, franchise, enfranchisement, vested interest.

Sanction, authority, warranty, tenure, bond, security, lien, constitution, charter, warrant (760), patent, letters patent, copyright, *imprimatur*.

A claimant, appellant, plaintiff.

Women's rights, feminism; feminist, suffragist, suffragette.

(*Verbs*). To be due, etc., to.

To have a right to, to be entitled to, to be qualified for, to have a claim upon, a title to, etc.; to deserve, merit, be worthy of, to deserve richly.

To demand, claim, call upon, exact, insist on, challenge, to come upon one for, to revendicate, make a point of, enforce, put in force, use a right.

To appertain to, belong to, etc. (777).

To lay claim to, assert, assume, arrogate, make good, vindicate a claim, etc., to make out a case.

To give or confer a right; to entitle, authorise, warrant, sanction, sanctify, privilege, enfranchise, license, legalise, ordain, prescribe.

(*Adjectives*). Having a right to, a claim to, etc.; due to, entitled to, deserving, meriting, worthy of, claiming, qualified.

Privileged, allowed, sanctioned, warranted, authorised, permitted, licit, ordained, prescribed, chartered, constitutional, official.

Prescriptive, presumptive, absolute, indefeasible, unalienable, inalienable, imprescriptible, inviolable, sacred, sacrosanct.

Condign, merited, deserved.

Allowable, permissible, lawful, legitimate, legal, legalised

925. Absence of right.

UNDUENESS (*Substantives*), unlawfulness, impropriety, unfitness, illegality (964).

Falseness, spuriousness, emptiness or invalidity of title, illegitimacy.

Loss of right, disfranchisement.

Usurpation, violation, breach, encroachment, stretch, relaxation.

(*Verbs*). Not to be due, etc., to; to be undue, etc.

To infringe, encroach, violate; to stretch or strain a point; to usurp.

To disfranchise, disentitle, disfrock, unfrock; to disqualify, invalidate, relax.

To misbecome, misbehave (945).

(*Adjectives*). Undue, unlawful, unmerited, undeserved, unearned, unconstitutional.

Unauthorised, unwarranted, unsanctioned, unjustified, unprivileged, illegitimate, spurious, supposititious, false, usurped, unchartered, unfulfilled, unofficial, unauthorised.

Unentitled, disentitled, unqualified.

Undeserved, unmerited, unearned.

Improper, unmeet, unbecoming, unfit, misbecoming, unseemly, preposterous.

(*Phrases*). Not being the thing; out of the question, out of court.

(963), proper, square, equitable, unexceptionable, reasonable (922).

(*Adverbs*). *Ex officio*, by divine right, *Dei gratia*, *jure divino*.

926. DUTY (*Substantives*), what ought to be done; moral obligation, accountableness, accountability, liability, *onus*, responsibility, bounden duty; dueness; the Decalogue.

Allegiance, fealty, tie, office, function, province, post, engagement (625).

Morality, morals, conscience, accountableness, conscientiousness.

(*Phrase*). "The still small voice within."

Dueness, *τὸ πρέπον*, propriety, fitness, decency, seemliness, decorum.

(*Phrases*). The thing; the proper thing; a case of conscience.

Science of morals: Ethics, Deontology; Moral or Ethical Philosophy, Casuistry, Ethology.

Observance, fulfilment, discharge, performance, acquittal, satisfaction, redemption, good behaviour.

(*Verbs*). To be the duty of, to be due to, to be up to; ought to be; to be incumbent on, to behove, befit, become, beseem, belong to, pertain to, devolve on, to lie on one's head, to owe to oneself.

(*Phrase*). To lie at one's door.

To be, or stand, or lie under the obligation, to be beholden or indebted to, to have to answer for, to be accountable for, to owe it to oneself, to be in duty bound, to be committed to, to be on one's good behaviour.

To impose a duty or obligation; to enjoin, require, exact, bind, pin down, saddle with, prescribe, assign, call upon, look to, oblige; must be.

To do one's duty, to enter upon a duty; to perform,

927. Dereliction of duty, guilt, etc., *see* 947.

EXEMPTION (*Substantives*), freedom, irresponsibility, immunity, liberty, licence, release, exoneration, excuse, dispensation, absolution, franchise, renunciation, discharge.

Non-observance, non-performance, neglect, relaxation, infraction, violation, transgression, failure, evasion.

(*Verbs*). To be exempt, free, at liberty, released, excused, exonerated, absolved, etc.

(*Phrase*). To wash one's hands of.

To exempt, release, excuse, exonerate, absolve, acquit, free, set at liberty, discharge, set aside, let off, license, dispense with; to give dispensation.

To violate, break through, break, infringe, set at naught, slight, neglect, trample on, evade, renounce, repudiate, escape, get off, beg off, transgress, fail.

(*Phrase*). To stretch a point.

(*Adjectives*). Exempt, free, released, at liberty, absolved, exonerated, excused, let off, discharged, licensed, acquitted, unencumbered, dispensed, scot free, immune.

Irresponsible, unaccountable, unanswerable, unbound.

---

observe, fulfil, discharge, adhere to; acquit oneself of, satisfy a duty, etc.

(*Phrases*). To be at one's post; to redeem one's pledge; to toe the mark or line; to do justice to.

(*Adjectives*). Obligatory, binding, behoving, incumbent on, chargeable on, meet, due to.

Being under obligation, obliged by, beholden to, bound by, tied by, saddled with, indebted to, in duty bound.

Amenable, liable, accountable, responsible, answerable, lying on one's head.

Right, proper, fit, due, seemly, fitting, befitting, decent.

(*Phrases*). Quite the thing; one's bounden duty.

Moral, ethical, casuistical, conscientious.

(*Adverbs*). Conscientiously, with a safe conscience; as in duty bound.

(*Phrases*). *In foro conscientiæ; quamdiu se bene gesserit.*

2°. Moral Sentiments

928. Respect (*Substantives*), deference, reverence, honour, esteem, distance, decorum, veneration, admiration.

Homage, fealty, obeisance, genuflexion, kneeling, salaam, kotow, presenting arms, etc. (*see* 896), prostration, *égards*, obsequiousness, devotion, worship (990).

(*Verbs*). To respect, honour, reverence, defer to, pay respect, deference, etc., to, render honour to, look up to, esteem, revere, to think much of, to think highly of, to venerate, hallow.

To pay homage to, bow to, take off one's hat to, kneel to, bend the knee to, present arms, fall down before, prostrate oneself.

(*Phrases*). To keep one's distance; to observe due decorum.

To inspire respect; to awe, dazzle.

(*Adjectives*). Respecting, etc., respectful, reverential, obsequious, ceremonious, bareheaded, cap in hand, etc.

929. Disrespect (*Substantives*), irreverence, dishonour, disparagement, slight, neglect, disesteem, superciliousness, contumely, indignity, insult.

Ridicule (856), derision, mockery, scoffing, sibilation.

A jeer, gibe, taunt, scoff, sneer, hiss, hoot, fling, flout, grin; *see* Contempt (930).

(*Verbs*). To treat with disrespect, etc., to disparage, dishonour, misprise, vilipend, slight, disregard, make light of, hold in no esteem, esteem of no account, set at naught, speak slightingly of, set down, pass by, overlook, look down upon, *see* 930.

To deride, scoff, sneer at, laugh at, ridicule (856), mock, jeer, taunt, hiss, hoot, boo.

(*Phrases*). Make game of; point the finger at; make a fool of; turn into ridicule; to laugh to scorn.

(*Adjectives*). Disrespectful, slighting, disparaging, dishonouring, etc., scornful (940), irreverent, supercilious, contumelious, deriding, derisive, derisory.

(*Phrase*). Saving one's presence.

Respected, honoured, hallowed, venerable, emeritus.

(*Interjections*). Hail! all hail! *esto perpetua!* may your shadow never be less!

Unrespected, unworshipped, unregarded, disregarded.

(*Adverbs*). Disrespectfully, cavalierly, etc.

---

930. CONTEMPT (*Substantives*), despisal, disdain, scorn, contumely, slight, sneer, spurn, sniff; a byword.

Scornfulness, disdainfulness, haughtiness, contemptuousness, superciliousness.

The state of being despised; despisedness.

(*Phrase*). "*Spretæ injuria formæ.*"

(*Verbs*). To despise, contemn, scorn, disdain, scout, spurn, look down upon, disregard, slight, make light of, hold cheap, hold in contempt, pooh-pooh, sneeze at, sniff at, whistle at, hoot, flout, kick, trample upon, abandon.

(*Phrases*). Not to care a straw, fig, button, etc., for (*see* 643); to turn up one's nose at; to shrug one's shoulders; to snap one's fingers at; to turn a cold shoulder upon; to laugh to scorn; to take the shine out of; to tread or trample under foot; *traiter de haut en bas*; to set at naught; to point the finger of scorn at.

(*Adjectives*). Contemptuous, disdainful, scornful, contumelious, derisive, supercilious, sniffy, sardonic.

Contemptible, despicable, poor, etc. (*see* 643), unenvied.

(*Interjections*). A fig for! hang it! pish! fudge! pooh-pooh! fiddlestick! fiddle-de-dee! tush! tut!

931. APPROBATION (*Substantives*), approval, approvement, endorsement, esteem, admiration, estimation, good opinion, appreciation, regard, account, popularity, kudos.

Commendation, praise, laud, good word; meed or tribute of praise, encomium, eulogium, eulogy, *éloge*, panegyric, homage.

Laudation, applause, plaudit, cheer, clap, clapping, clapping of hands, acclamation; pæan, benediction, blessing, benison, hosanna; *claque*.

(*Phrases*). A peal, shout, or chorus of applause; thunders of applause; *succès d'estime*.

(*Verbs*). To approve, think well of, think good or highly of,

932. DISAPPROBATION (*Substantives*), disapproval, blame, censure, obloquy, dispraise, contumely, odium, disesteem, depreciation, detraction, condemnation, ostracism.

Reprobation, exprobration, insinuation, animadversion, reflection, stricture, objection, exception, criticism, critique, correction, discommendation.

Satire, sneer, fling, wipe, gibe, skit, squib, quip, taunt, sarcasm, lampoon, cavil, pasquinade, invective, castigation.

Remonstrance, reprehension, reproof, admonition, expostulation, reproach, rebuke, reprimand, talking-to.

Evil speaking, hard words, foul

esteem, appreciate, value, admire, countenance, endorse.

To commend, speak well of, recommend, praise, laud, belaud, compliment, bepraise, clap, clap hands, applaud, cheer, panegyrise, celebrate, eulogise, cry up, crack up, write up, extol, glorify, magnify, puff, boom, exalt, swell, bless, give a blessing to.

(*Phrases*). To sing the praises of; to extol to the skies; to ring with the praises of; to say a good word for; to pat on the back.

To redound to the honour or praise of; to do credit to.

To deserve praise, etc., to be praised, etc.

(*Phrases*). To win golden opinions; *laudari a laudato viro*; to bring down the house.

(*Adjectives*). Approving, etc., commendatory, complimentary, benedictory, laudatory, panegyrical, eulogistic, encomiastic.

Approved, praised, uncensured, unimpeached, admired, popular, etc., deserving or worthy of praise, etc., praiseworthy, commendable, plausible, meritorious.

(*Phrases*). *Probatum est*; lavish of praise; lost in admiration.

(*Interjections*). Well done! *bravo! bravissimo! viva! euge! macte virtute!* hear, hear!

---

language, sauce, Billingsgate, unparliamentary language.

Upbraiding, abuse, vituperation, scolding, wigging, dressing, objurgation, jaw, railing, jobation, nagging, reviling, contumely, execration (908).

A set-down, trimming, slap, snub, frown, scowl, black look.

A lecture, curtain lecture, diatribe, jeremiad, tirade, philippic; clamour, outcry, hue and cry, hiss, hissing, sibilation.

A scold, shrew, vixen, Xanthippe; a lampooner.

(*Phrases*). A rap on the knuckles; a slap in the face.

(*Verbs*). To disapprove, dispraise, find fault with, criticise, glance at, insinuate, cut up, carp at, cavil, point at, peck at, nibble at, object to, take exception to, *fronder*, animadvert upon, protest against, frown upon, bar.

To disparage, depreciate, crab, speak ill of, decry, vilify, vilipend, defame, detract (*see* 934), revile, satirise, smoke, sneer, gibe, lampoon, inveigh against, write down, scalp.

(*Phrases*). "To hint a fault and hesitate dislike"; to cry "stinking fish."

To blame; lay or cast blame upon; to reflect upon; cast a slur upon; to censure; pass censure on; impugn, show up, censure, brand, stigmatise, reprobate, improbate.

To reprehend, reprimand, admonish, remonstrate, expostulate, reprove, pull up, take up, set down, snub, twit, taunt, reprimand, reproach, load with reproaches, rebuke, come down upon, sit on, pitch into.

To chide, scold, wig, rate, objurgate, upbraid, vituperate, abuse, call names, exclaim against, jaw, mob, trounce, trim, rail at, nag, nag at, bark at, blackguard, revile, ballyrag, rag, blow up, roast, lecture; castigate, chastise, correct, lash, flay, scalp; to fulminate against, fall foul of.

To cry out against, cry down, run down, clamour, hiss, hoot; to accuse (*see* 938), to find guilty, ostracise.

(*Phrases*). To set one's face against; to view with dark or jaundiced eyes; to bend or knit the brows; to pick holes in; to pluck a crow with; to have a fling at; to read a lecture; to take to task; to bring to book; to haul over the coals; to give a rap on the knuckles; to pull to pieces; to cut up; to cast in one's teeth; to abuse like a pickpocket; to speak or look daggers; to rail in good set terms; to give it one hot; to throw mud; to call names; not to mince matters.

To incur blame; to excite disapprobation; to scandalise, shock, revolt.

(*Phrases*). To forfeit the good opinion of; to catch it.

To take blame; to stand corrected.

(*Adjectives*). Disapproving, etc., disparaging, condemnatory, damnatory, reproachful, abusive, objurgatory, clamorous, vituperative, dyslogistic.

Censorious, critical, carping, satirical, sarcastic, cynical, dry, hypercritical, captious; sharp, cutting, mordant, biting, severe, scathing; squeamish, fastidious, strait-laced, etc. (868).

(*Phrases*). *Omnia suspendens naso*; sparing of praise; grudging praise.

Disapproved, etc., unapproved, blown upon, unblest, unlamented, unbewailed, etc.

Worthy of blame, uncommendable, exceptionable, *see* 649, 945.

(*Interjections*). Out upon it! *O tempora, O mores!* shame!

933. Flattery (*Substantives*), adulation, sycophancy, blandishment, cajolery, fawning, wheedling, coaxing, flunkeyism, toad-eating, toadyism, back-scratching, blandiloquence.

Incense, honeyed words, flummery, soft sawder, soft soap, blarney.

(*Verbs*). To flatter, wheedle, cajole, fawn upon, coax (615), humour, gloze, butter, toady, sugar, bespatter, beslaver, earwig, cog, truckle to, pander to, court, pay court to.

(*Phrases*). To curry favour with; to lay it on thick; to lay it on with a trowel; to lick the dust; to lay the flattering unction to the soul.

(*Adjectives*). Flattering, adula-

934. Detraction (*Substantives*), obloquy, scurrility, scandal, defamation, aspersion, traducement, slander, calumny, backbiting, criticism, slating, personality, evil-speaking.

Libel, lampoon, skit, sarcasm.

(*Verbs*). To detract, criticise, asperse, depreciate, cheapen, blow upon, bespatter, blacken, denigrate, defame, brand, malign, backbite, libel, slate, lampoon, traduce, slander, calumniate, run down, write down.

(*Phrases*). To speak ill of one behind one's back; to "damn with faint praise."

(*Adjectives*). Detracting, etc., disparaging, libellous, scurrilous, cynical (932), foul-tongued, foul-mouthed, slanderous, detory, mealy-mouthed, smooth, soapy, oily, unctuous, fair-spoken, plausible, servile, sycophantic, fulsome; courtier-like.

935. FLATTERER (*Substantives*), eulogist, encomiast, whitewasher, toady, sycophant, toad-eater, *prôneur*, touter, *claqueur*, spaniel, back-scratcher, flunkey, lickspittle, pick-thank, earwig, hanger-on, courtier, parasite, doer of dirty work, *âme damnée*, *Græculus esuriens*.

937. VINDICATION (*Substantives*), reply, justification, exoneration, exculpation, acquittal, whitewashing.

Extenuation, palliation, softening.

Plea, excuse, apology, defence, gloss, varnish, salvo (617).

(*Verbs*). To vindicate, justify, exculpate, acquit, clear, set right, exonerate, disculpate, whitewash.

To extenuate, palliate, excuse, soften, apologise, varnish, slur, gloze, gloss over, bolster up.

To plead, advocate, defend, stand up for, stick up for, speak for, make good, vindicate, bear out, say in defence, contend for.

(*Phrases*). To put in a good word for; to plead the cause of; to put a good face upon; to help a lame dog over a stile; to take the will for the deed; to make allowance for.

(*Adjectives*). Vindicatory, exculpatory; vindicating, etc.

Excusable, defensible, pardonable, venial, specious, plausible, justifiable, warrantable.

(*Phrases*). "*Honi soit qui mal y pense*"; *qui s'excuse s'accuse.*

famatory, calumnious, calumniatory.

936. DETRACTOR (*Substantives*), disapprover, critic, censor, caviller, carper, *frondeur*, defamer, backbiter, slanderer, traducer, libeller, calumniator, lampooner, Thersites.

938. ACCUSATION (*Substantives*), charge, imputation, inculpation, crimination, recrimination, invective, jeremiad, etc. (932).

Denunciation, denouncement, challenge, indictment, libel, delation, citation, arraignment, impeachment, appeachment, bill of indictment, *scandalum magnatum*, condemnation.

(*Phrases*). The gravamen of a charge; *argumentum ad hominem.*

(*Verbs*). To accuse, charge, tax, impute, twit, taunt with, slur, reproach, brand with, criminate, incriminate, inculpate, etc. (*see* 932), implicate, saddle with.

To inform against; to indict, denounce, arraign, impeach, challenge, show up, pull up, cite, summon.

(*Phrases*). To lay to one's door; to lay to one's charge; bring home to; to throw in one's teeth; to call to account; to bring to book; to take to task; to catch tripping; to put in the black book; to trump up a charge; to keep a rod in pickle for; to brand with reproach.

(*Adjectives*). Accusing, etc.,

accusatory, accusative, imputative, criminative, criminatory, incriminatory, accusable, imputable.

Indefensible, inexcusable, unpardonable, unjustifiable (945).

3°. Moral Conditions

939. Probity (*Substantives*), integrity, uprightness, honesty, faith, good faith, fairness, honour, fair play, justice, principle, constancy, fidelity, incorruptibility.

Trustworthiness, trustiness, reliability, dependableness, grace, uncorruptedness, impartiality, equity, candour, veracity (545), straightforwardness, truth, equitableness, singleness of heart.

Conscientiousness, punctiliousness, nicety, scrupulosity, delicacy, sense of decency, strictness, punctuality.

Dignity, reputableness, *see* 873.

A man of honour, a gentleman, a man of his word, a real sportsman, *preux chevalier*.

(*Phrases*). The court of honour; *argumentum ad verecundiam*.

(*Verbs*). To be honourable, etc.; to keep one's word; to give and take; to deal honourably, squarely, impartially, fairly, etc.

(*Phrases*). To give the devil his due; to put the saddle on the right horse; to play the game.

(*Adjectives*). Upright, honest, honourable, fair, right, just, equitable, impartial, evenhanded, square, constant, faithful, loyal, *see* 944, straight.

Trustworthy, trusty, reliable, dependable, tried, uncorrupt, straightforward, ingenuous (703), frank, open-hearted, candid.

Conscientious, tender-conscienced, high-principled, high-minded, high-toned, scrupulous, strict, nice, punctilious, overscrupulous, punctual, inviolable,

940. Improbity (*Substantives*), bad faith, unfairness, infidelity, faithlessness, want of faith, dishonesty, disloyalty, falseness, falsity, one-sidedness, disingenuousness, shabbiness, littleness, meanness, caddishness, baseness, vileness, abjectness, turpitude, unreliability, untrustworthiness, insidiousness, knavery, knavishness, fraud, etc. (545).

Disgrace, ignominy, infamy, tarnish, blot, stain, spot, slur, pollution, derogation, degradation, etc., *see* Dishonour (874).

Perfidy, perfidiousness, treason, high treason, perjury, apostasy, backsliding, breach of faith, defection, disloyalty, disaffection, foul play, double-dealing, treacherousness, treachery.

(*Phrases*). The kiss of Judas; Punic faith.

(*Verbs*). To be of bad faith, dishonest, etc.; to play false, break one's word, faith, etc., betray, forswear, shuffle (545).

To disgrace oneself, derogate, stoop, demean oneself, lose caste, dishonour oneself, sneak.

(*Phrases*). To seal one's infamy; to sell oneself; to go over to the enemy.

(*Adjectives*). Dishonest, unfair, one-sided, fraudulent, knavish, false, faithless, unfaithful, foul, disingenuous, trothless, trustless, untrustworthy, unreliable, slippery, double, crooked, tortuous, unscrupulous, insidious, treacherous, perfidious, false-hearted, perjured, rascally.

Base, vile, grovelling, dirty,

inviolate, unviolated, unbroken, unbetrayed.

Chivalrous, gentlemanlike, unbought, unbribed, unstained, stainless, untarnished, unsullied, untainted, unperjured (946), incorruptible.

(*Phrases*). Jealous of honour; as good as one's word; *sans peur et sans reproche*.

(*Adverbs*). Honourably, etc., *bona fide*; on the square.

---

scurvy, scabby, low, low-down, caddish, mean, paltry, pitiful, scrubby, beggarly, putid, unworthy, disgraceful, dishonourable, derogatory, low-thoughted, disreputable, unhandsome, unbecoming (925), unbefitting, ungentlemanly, unmanly, unwomanly, undignified, base-minded, recreant, low-minded, blackguard, pettifogging, underhand, underhanded, unsportsmanlike.

(*Phrases*). Double-tongued; lost to shame; dead to honour; *Parthis mendacior*; *contra bonos mores*.

(*Adverbs*). Dishonestly, etc., *mala fide*, on the crook.

941. KNAVE (*Substantives*) (*see* 949), blackleg, scab, trimmer, time-server, timist, turncoat, Vicar of Bray, Judas (607).

Apostate, renegade, pervert, black sheep, traitor, arch-traitor, betrayer, recreant, miscreant, cullion, outcast, mean wretch, *âme de boue*, slubberdegullion, a snake in the grass, *see* 949.

942. DISINTERESTEDNESS (*Substantives*), generosity, high-mindedness, nobleness, elevation, liberality, greatness, loftiness, exaltation, magnanimity, chivalry, chivalrous spirit, heroism, sublimity, unselfishness, altruism, self-forgetfulness, unworldliness.

Self-denial, self-abnegation, self-sacrifice, self-restraint, self-control, devotion, stoicism.

(*Phrases*). To put oneself in the background, in the place of others.

(*Adjectives*). Disinterested, generous, unselfish, self-forgetful, handsome, liberal, noble, princely, great, high, high-minded, elevated, lofty, exalted, spirited, stoical, self-devoted, magnanimous, chivalrous, heroic, sublime, unworldly.

Unbought, unbribed, pure, uncorrupted, incorruptible.

(*Adverb*). *En prince*.

---

943. SELFISHNESS (*Substantives*), egotism, egoism, self-regard, self-love, self-indulgence, worldliness, worldly-mindedness, earthly-mindedness, self-interest, opportunism.

Illiberality, meanness, baseness.

A time-server, tuft-hunter, fortune-hunter, jobber, worldling, self-seeker, opportunist.

(*Verbs*). To be selfish, etc., narrow-minded, to indulge oneself, to coddle oneself.

(*Phrases*). To look after one's own interest; to take care of number one; to have an eye for the main chance.

(*Adjectives*). Selfish, egotistical, egoistical, self-indulgent, apolaustic, self-regarding, illiberal, self-seeking, mercenary, mean, ungenerous, narrow-minded.

Worldly, earthly, mundane, time-serving, worldly-minded.

(*Phrases*). The dog in the manger; *après nous le déluge*; the charity that begins at home.

944. Virtue (*Substantives*), goodness, righteousness, morals, morality, rectitude, correctness, dutifulness, conscientiousness, integrity, probity (939), uprightness, nobleness, nobility.

Merit, worth, worthiness, desert, excellence, credit, self-control, self-conquest, self-government, self-respect.

Well-doing, good actions, good behaviour, the discharge, fulfilment, or performance of duty; a well-spent life.

Innocence, *see* 946.

(*Verbs*). To be virtuous, etc.; to act well; to do, fulfil, perform, or discharge one's duty, to acquit oneself, to practise virtue; to command or master one's passions, *see* 926.

(*Phrases*). To have one's heart in the right place; to keep in the right path; to set an example; to be on one's good behaviour.

(*Adjectives*). Virtuous, good, meritorious, deserving, worthy, correct, dutiful, duteous, moral, ethical, righteous, right-minded, etc. (*see* 939), laudable, well-intentioned, praiseworthy, excellent, admirable, sterling, pure, noble, well-conducted, well-behaved.

Exemplary, matchless, peerless, saintly, saint-like, heaven-born, angelic, seraphic, godlike.

(*Phrases*). Above or beyond all praise; *mens sibi conscia recti*.

(*Adverb*). Virtuously, etc.

---

945. Vice (*Substantives*), wickedness, sin, iniquity, unrighteousness, demerit, unworthiness, worthlessness, badness.

Immorality, incorrectness, impropriety, indecorum, laxity, looseness of morals, want of principle, obliquity, backsliding, gracelessness, infamy, demoralisation, pravity, depravity, depravation, obduracy, hardness of heart, brutality, corruption, pollution, dissoluteness, grossness, baseness, knavery, roguery, rascality, villainy, profligacy, abandonment, flagrancy, atrocity, devilry (or deviltry); cannibalism.

Criminality, etc., *see* Guilt (947).

Infirmity, weakness, feebleness, frailty, imperfection, error, weak side or point, blind side, foible, failing, failure, defect, deficiency, indiscretion, peccability.

(*Phrases*). The cloven hoof; the lowest dregs of vice; a sink of iniquity.

(*Verbs*). To be vicious, etc.; to sin, commit sin, do amiss, misdo, err, transgress, go astray, misdemean or misconduct oneself, misbehave; to fall, lapse, slip, trip, offend, trespass.

(*Phrases*). To deviate from the line of duty, or from the paths of virtue, rectitude, etc.; to hug a sin or fault; to sow one's wild oats.

(*Adjectives*[1]). Vicious, sinful, wicked, evil-minded, immoral, unprincipled, demoralised, unconscionable, worthless, unworthy, good for nothing, graceless, heartless, virtueless, undutiful, unrighteous, unmoral, amoral, bad.

Wrong, culpable, guilty, naughty, incorrect, indictable,

[1] Most of these adjectives are applicable both to the act and to the agent.

criminal, dissolute, disorderly, raffish, corrupt, profligate, depraved, abandoned, graceless, shameless, recreant, villainous, sunk, lost, obdurate, incorrigible, irreclaimable, ill-conditioned.

Weak, frail, lax, infirm, imperfect, indiscreet, erring, transgressing, sinning, etc., peccable, peccant.

Blamable, reprehensible, blameworthy, uncommendable, discreditable, disreputable, shady, exceptionable.

Indecorous, unseemly, improper, sinister, base, scurvy, foul, gross, vile, black, felonious, nefarious, scandalous, infamous, villainous, heinous, grave, flagrant, flagitious, atrocious, satanic, satanical, diabolic, diabolical, hellish, infernal, stygian, fiendlike, fiendish, devilish, miscreated, misbegotten, hell-born, demoniacal.

Unpardonable, unforgivable, indefensible, inexcusable, irremissible, inexpiable.

(*Phrases*). *Contra bonos mores*; of a deep dye; not having a word to say for oneself.

(*Adverbs*). Wrong, etc.; without excuse, too bad.

946. INNOCENCE (*Substantives*), guiltlessness, harmlessness, innocuousness, incorruption, impeccability, inerrability, blamelessness, sinlessness.

A lamb, a dove.

(*Verb*). To be innocent, etc.

(*Phrases*). *Nil conscire sibi, nulla pallescere culpa ; mens sibi conscia recti.*

(*Adjectives*). Innocent, guiltless, faultless, sinless, clear, spotless, stainless, immaculate, unspotted, innocuous, unblemished, untarnished, unsullied, undefiled.

Inculpable, unblamed, blameless, unblamable, clean-handed, irreproachable, unreproached, unimpeachable, unimpeached, unexceptionable, inerrable, unerring, salvable.

Harmless, inoffensive, unoffending, dovelike, lamblike, pure, uncorrupted, undefiled, undepraved, undebauched, unhardened, unsophisticated, unreproved.

(*Phrase*). Innocent as an unborn babe.

(*Adverbs*). Innocently, etc., with clean hands, with a clear conscience.

947. GUILT (*Substantives*), sin, guiltiness, culpability, criminality, criminousness, sinfulness.

Misconduct, misbehaviour, misdoing, malpractice, malefaction, malfeasance, misprision, deviation from rectitude, dereliction, *corpus delicti*.

Indiscretion, peccadillo, lapse, slip, trip, *faux pas*, fault, error, flaw, blot, omission, failure.

Misdeed, offence, trespass, transgression, misdemeanour, delinquency, felony, sin, crime, enormity, atrocity.

Science of crime: Criminology.

(*Phrase*). Besetting sin.

948. GOOD MAN (*Substantives*), trump, lamb, worthy, example,

949. BAD MAN (*Substantives*), evil-doer, culprit, delinquent,

pattern, mirror, model, paragon, phœnix, *rara avis*, *le cygne noir*, hero, *Uebermensch*, superman, demigod, seraph, angel, *see* Perfection (650), Saint (987).

A good fellow, a good sort, a trump.

---

criminal, recidivist, malefactor, wrongdoer, outlaw, felon, convict, lag, outcast, sinner (988).

Knave, rogue, rascal, scoundrel, scamp, scapegrace, scalawag, varlet, *vaurien*, blighter, rotter, good-for-nothing, son of a gun, blackguard, sweep, loose fish, bad egg, bad lot, vagabond, *mauvais sujet*, cur, sad dog, *drôle de corps*, raff, rip, rascallion, rapscallion, slubberdegullion, cullion, roisterer, Mohock, rowdy, hooligan, larrikin, apache, reprobate, *roué*, recreant, jail-bird, crook, *guet-apens*, villain, outlaw, outcast, ruffian, miscreant, caitiff, wretch, *âme damnée*, castaway, monster, Jonathan Wild, Jack Sheppard, Lazarillo de Tormes, Scapin, *see* 941.

Cur, dog, hound, skunk, viper, serpent, cockatrice, basilisk, reptile, urchin, tiger, imp, demon, devil, devil incarnate, cannibal, Mephistopheles (978), Jezebel, hell-hound, son of Belial, hell-cat, cut-throat, *particeps criminis*, incendiary.

(*Interjection*). Sirrah!

---

950. Penitence (*Substantives*), contrition, compunction, regret (833), repentance, remorse.

Self-reproach, self-reproof, qualms or prickings of conscience, self-condemnation.

Confession, acknowledgment, shrift, apology, *peccavi*, *locus pœnitentiæ*, *mea culpa*.

(*Phrases*). The stool of repentance; the cutty-stool; an awakened conscience.

(*Verbs*). To repent, regret, rue, repine, deplore, be sorry for.

(*Phrases*). To have a weight on one's mind; to plead guilty; to sing *miserere* or *de profundis*; to cry *peccavi*; to eat humble pie; to turn over a new leaf; to put on the new man.

To confess (529), acknowledge, apologise, to shrive oneself, humble oneself, to reclaim, to turn from sin, to stand in a white sheet.

(*Adjectives*). Penitent, repentant, contrite, repenting, self-reproachful, self-accusing, self-convicted, conscience-stricken or -smitten, etc.

(*Phrase*). "*Erubuit, salva res est.*"

Not hardened, unhardened, reclaimed.

951. Impenitence (*Substantives*), obduracy, recusance, hardness of heart, a seared conscience, induration.

(*Verbs*). To be impenitent, etc.; to steel or harden the heart.

(*Phrase*). To make no sign.

(*Adjectives*). Impenitent, uncontrite, obdurate, hard, hardened, seared, recusant, relentless, unrepentant, graceless, shriftless, lost, incorrigible, irreclaimable, irredeemable, unatoned, unreclaimed, unreformed, unrepented.

(*Adverbs*). In sackcloth and ashes, etc., down on one's marrow-bones.

952. ATONEMENT (*Substantives*), reparation, compromise, composition, compensation (30), quittance, quits; propitiation, expiation, redemption.

Amends, apology, *amende honorable*, satisfaction, peace-offering, sin-offering, scapegoat, sacrifice, burnt-offering.

Penance, fasting, maceration, sackcloth and ashes, white sheet, lustration, purgation, purgatory.

(*Verbs*). To atone, expiate, propitiate, make amends, redeem, make good, repair, ransom, absolve, do penance, apologise, purge, give satisfaction.

(*Phrases*). To wipe off old scores; set one's house in order; to pay the forfeit or penalty.

(*Adjectives*). Propitiatory, piacular, expiatory.

4°. MORAL PRACTICE

953. TEMPERANCE (*Substantives*), moderation, forbearance, abnegation, self-denial, self-conquest, self-control, self-command, self-discipline, sobriety, frugality, vegetarianism.

Abstinence, abstemiousness, system of Pythagoras.

A vegetarian, a teetotaller, a Pythagorean.

(*Phrase*). The simple life.

(*Verbs*). To be temperate, etc.; to abstain, forbear, refrain, deny oneself, spare.

(*Adjectives*). Temperate, moderate, sober, frugal, sparing, abstemious, abstinent, Pythagorean, vegetarian, teetotal.

---

954. INTEMPERANCE (*Substantives*), epicurism, epicureanism, hedonism, sensuality, luxury, excess, animalism, pleasure, effeminacy; the lap of pleasure or luxury; indulgence, self-indulgence, voluptuousness.

Dissipation, licentiousness, debauchery, dissoluteness, crapulence, brutishness, revels, debauch, orgy.

(*Phrases*). The Circean cup; system of Epicurus; the swine of Epicurus.

(*Verbs*). To be intemperate, sensual, etc.

To indulge, exceed, revel, dissipate; give a loose to indulgence, sensuality, etc.

(*Phrases*). To wallow in voluptuousness, luxury, etc.; to plunge into dissipation; to live on the fat of the land; sow one's wild oats.

To pamper, coddle, mollycoddle, wet-nurse, cocker, pander (or pandar), slake; to debauch, sensualise, animalise, brutalise.

(*Adjectives*). Intemperate, sensual, pampered, self-indulgent, fleshly, inabstinent, licentious, wild, dissolute, dissipated, fast, rakish, debauched, brutish, crapulous, hedonistic, epicurean, sybaritical, Sardanapalian, voluptuous, apolaustic, orgiastic, swinish, piggish.

Indulged, pampered.

A Sybarite, a mollycoddle, a debauchee, a man of pleasure, voluptuary, free liver, rake, rake-hell, rip, *roué*, a votary of Epicurus, pig, hog, swine, *see* 962.

955. ASCETICISM (*Substantives*), austerity, mortification, maceration, sackcloth and ashes, flagellation, etc., martyrdom, yoga.

An ascetic, anchorite, anchoret, yogi, martyr; a recluse, hermit, etc. (893).

(*Adjectives*). Ascetic, ascetical, puritanical.

956. FASTING (*Substantives*), fast, spare diet, meagre diet, Lent, *jour maigre*, a lenten entertainment, starvation, banyan-day, Ramadan.

(*Phrases*). A Barmecide feast; short commons.

(*Verbs*). To fast, starve.

(*Phrases*). To dine with Duke Humphrey; to make two bites of a cherry.

(*Adjectives*). Fasting, etc., unfed, famished.

957. GLUTTONY (*Substantives*), epicurism, greediness, good cheer, high living, edacity, voracity, gulosity, crapulence, hoggishness.

Gastronomy, *batterie de cuisine*.

A glutton, epicure, *bon vivant*, cormorant, gourmand, gourmet, hog, Apicius, gastronome, gastronomer, gastronomist.

(*Verbs*). To gormandise, gorge, stuff, guttle (296), pamper.

(*Phrases*). To eat out of house and home; to have the stomach of an ostrich.

(*Adjectives*). Gluttonous, greedy, gormandising, edacious, voracious, crapulent, swinish, hoggish, pampered, overfed; gastronomical.

958. SOBRIETY (*Substantives*), teetotalism, total abstinence; *see* Temperance (953).

Compulsory sobriety: Prohibition.

A water-drinker, teetotaller, abstainer, total abstainer, blue-ribbonite, Rechabite; prohibitionist.

(*Verbs*). To abstain, to take the pledge.

(*Adjectives*). Sober, teetotal.

(*Phrase*). Sober as a judge.

959. DRUNKENNESS (*Substantives*), insobriety, ebriety, inebriety, inebriation, intoxication, ebriosity, bibacity, drinking, topping, tippling, sottishness, tipsiness, bacchanals, compotation; dipsomania.

A drunkard, sot, toper, tippler, hard drinker, bibber, winebag, winebibber, dram-drinker, soaker, sponge, tun, toss-pot, reveller, carouser, Bacchanal, Bacchanalian, Bacchante, a devotee to Bacchus; a dipsomaniac.

(*Verbs*). To drink, tipple, tope, booze; to guzzle, swill, carouse, get drunk, etc.; to take to drinking, etc., to drink hard, to drink deep.

To inebriate, intoxicate, fuddle.

(*Phrases*). To get into the head; to take a drop too much; to drink like a fish; to splice the main-brace; to crook or lift the elbow.

(*Adjectives*). Drunk, drunken, tipsy, intoxicated, in liquor, inebriated, fuddled, mellow, boozy, fou, fresh, flush, flushed, flustered, groggy, top-heavy, pot-valiant, glorious, overcome, overtaken, elevated, whittled, screwed, corned, raddled, sewed up, lushy, squiffy, muddled, muzzy, maudlin, dead-drunk, disguised, tight, beery.

Bibacious, bibulous, sottish, bacchanal, bacchanalian.

(*Phrases*). In one's cups; *inter pocula*; the worse for liquor; having a drop too much; half-seas-over; three sheets in the wind; under the table; drunk as a piper; drunk as a fiddler; drunk as a lord; drunk as an owl; drunk as David's sow.

960. PURITY (*Substantives*), modesty, decency, decorum, delicacy, continence, chastity, honesty, pudency.

A vestal, a virgin, a Joseph, Hippolytus, Lucrece.

(*Adjectives*). Pure, modest, delicate, decent, decorous.

Chaste, continent, virtuous, Platonic, honest.

(*Phrase*). The white flower of a blameless life.

---

961. IMPURITY (*Substantives*), immodesty, grossness, coarseness, indelicacy, impropriety, impudicity, indecency, obscenity, ribaldry, smut, obsceneness, smuttiness, bawdiness, bawdry, *double entendre*, equivoque, pornography.

Concupiscence, lust, carnality, flesh, salacity, lewdness, prurience, lechery, lasciviousness, voluptuousness, lubricity.

Incontinence, intrigue, *faux pas*, gallantry, debauchery, libertinism, libertinage, fornication, liaison, wenching, concubinage, hetærism.

Seduction, defloration, violation, rape, adultery, *crim. con.*, incest, harlotry, stupration, procuration, white slave traffic.

A seraglio, harem, brothel, bagnio, stew, bawdy-house, *lupanar*.

(*Phrase*). The morals of the farmyard.

(*Verbs*). To intrigue, etc., to debauch, prostitute, procure.

(*Adjectives*). Impure, immodest, indecorous, indelicate, unclean, unmentionable, unseemly, improper, suggestive, indecent, loose, coarse, gross, broad, equivocal, risky, *risqué*, high-seasoned, nasty, smutty, scabrous, ribald, obscene, bawdy, lewd, pornographic, Rabelaisian, Aristophanic.

Concupiscent, prurient, lickerish, rampant, carnal, fleshly, sensual, lustful, lascivious, lecherous, libidinous, erotic, ruttish, salacious, Paphian.

Unchaste, light, wanton, debauched, dissolute, carnal-minded, riggish, incontinent, meretricious, rakish, gallant, dissipated, adulterous, incestuous, bestial.

(*Phrases*). On the town; on the streets; who is no better than she should be.

962. A LIBERTINE (*Substantives*), voluptuary, man of pleasure, rip, rake, debauchee, intrigant, gallant, seducer, fornicator, lecher, satyr, whoremonger, cuckold, *paillard*, adulterer, a gay Lothario, Don Juan, Bluebeard.

A courtesan, *hetæra*, strumpet, harlot, whore, prostitute, punk, *fille de joie*, *cocotte*, *lorette*, woman of the town, street-walker, Cyprian, miss, piece, the frail sisterhood, the *demi-monde*, loose fish, demirep, wench, trollop, trull, baggage, hussy, drab, quean, slut, harridan, an unfortunate, Jezebel, Messalina, Delilah, Thais, Aspasia, Phryne, Lais.

Concubine, odalisque, mistress, doxy, kept woman, hetæra.

Pimp, pander, *souteneur*, bawd, procuress.

(*Phrase*). A chartered libertine.

5°. INSTITUTIONS

963. LEGALITY (*Substantives*), legitimateness, legitimacy; legislature.

Law, code, constitution, pandect, enactment, edict, statute, rule, order, ordinance, injunction, precept, regulation, by-law, decree, firman, bull, ukase, decretal.

Legal process, form, formula, formality, rite.

The arm of the law.

Science of law: Jurisprudence, Legislation, Codification.

Equity, common law, *lex non scripta*, *lex scripta*, law of nations, international law, *jus gentium*, civil law, canon law, statute law, *lex mercatoria*, ecclesiastical law.

(*Verbs*). To enact, ordain, enjoin, prescribe, order; to pass a law, issue an edict or decree; to legislate, codify.

(*Adjectives*). Legal, according to law, legitimate, constitutional, chartered, vested.

Legislative, statutable, statutory.

(*Adverb*). Legally, etc.

(*Phrase*). In the eye of the law.

964. Absence or violation of law.

ILLEGALITY (*Substantives*), arbitrariness, antinomy, violence, brute force, despotism, outlawry.

Mob law, lynch law, club law.

Vehmgericht, Camorra, Ku Klux Klan, Judge Lynch.

(*Phrases*). *Le droit du plus fort*; *argumentum baculinum*; the unwritten law.

Informality, unlawfulness, illegitimacy, bastardy, the bar sinister.

Smuggling, poaching, simony.

(*Verbs*). To smuggle, run, poach.

(*Phrases*). To take the law into one's own hands; to set the law at defiance; to drive a coach and six through the law.

(*Adjectives*). Illegal, unlawful, illicit, illegitimate, injudicial, unofficial, lawless, unauthorised, unchartered, unconstitutional, informal, contraband.

Arbitrary, extrajudicial, despotic, irresponsible, unanswerable, unaccountable.

(*Phrase*). The law being a dead letter.

965. JURISDICTION (*Substantives*), judicature, soc, administration of justice.

Inquisition, inquest, coroner's inquest.

The executive: Municipality, corporation, magistracy, police, police force.

Sheriff, officer, constable, policeman, bailiff, tipstaff, bum-bailiff, catchpoll, beadle.

Sbirro, alguazil, gendarme, lictor, mace-bearer.

(*Adjectives*). Juridical, judicial, forensic, municipal, executive, administrative, inquisitorial, causidical.

(*Adverb*). *Coram judice.*

966. TRIBUNAL (*Substantives*), court, guild, board, bench, judicatory, senate-house, court of law, court of justice, Old Bailey, police-court, justice-seat, judgment-seat, mercy-seat, star-chamber, durbar, city hall, town hall, theatre, bar, dock, forum, hustings, drum-head, woolsack, jury-box, witness-box.

Assize, sessions, eyre, court-martial, wardmote, bailiwick.

967. JUDGE (*Substantives*), justice, chancellor, magistrate, stipendiary, coroner, arbiter, arbitrator, umpire, referee, jury, Justice of the Peace, J.P., Lord Chancellor, Lord Chief Justice.

Mullah, ulema, cadi (or kadi), kavass; police.

Prosecutor, plaintiff, accuser, appellant.

Defendant, panel, prisoner, the accused.

968. LAWYER (*Substantives*), the bar, advocate, counsellor, counsel, king's or queen's counsel, pleader, special pleader, conveyancer, bencher, proctor, civilian, barrister, jurist, jurisconsult, publicist, draughtsman, notary, notary-public, scrivener, attorney, solicitor, marshal, pundit; pettifogger.

(*Phrases*). The gentlemen of the long robe; the learned in the law; a limb of the law; a barrister-at-law.

(*Verbal Phrase*). To be called to the bar.

969. LAWSUIT (*Substantives*), suit, action, cause, trial, litigation.

Denunciation, citation, arraignment, prosecution, indictment, impeachment, apprehension, arrest, committal, imprisonment, *see* 751.

Pleadings, writ, summons, subpœna, plea, bill, affidavit, etc.

Verdict, sentence, judgment, finding, decree, arbitrament, adjudication, award, plebiscite.

(*Verbs*). To denounce, cite, apprehend, sue, prosecute, indict, impeach, attach, distrain; to commit.

(*Phrases*). To go to law; to take the law of; to appeal to the law; to join issue; file a bill; file a claim; to inform against; take an information; serve with a writ; bring an action against; bring to trial; bring to the bar; give in charge or custody; throw into prison.

To try, hear a cause, sit in judgment.

To pronounce, find, judge, adjudge, sentence, give judgment; bring in a verdict; doom, to arbitrate, adjudicate, award, report.

(*Phrases*). *Adhuc sub judice lis est; pendente lite.*

970. ACQUITTAL (*Substantives*), acquitment, absolution, quietus, *see* Pardon (918), clearance, discharge, release, reprieve, respite, compurgation.

Exemption from punishment: impunity.

(*Verbs*). To acquit, absolve, whitewash, clear, assoil, discharge, release, reprieve, respite.

(*Adjectives*). Acquitted, etc.

Uncondemned, unpunished, unchastised.

971. CONDEMNATION (*Substantives*), conviction, proscription, damnation, death-warrant.

Attainder, attainture, attaintment.

(*Verbs*). To condemn, convict, cast, find guilty, proscribe, attaint, damn, confiscate.

(*Adjective*). Condemnatory, etc.

972. PUNISHMENT (*Substantives*), punition, chastisement, castigation, correction, chastening, discipline, infliction.

Retribution, requital, reward (973), reckoning, Nemesis.

Imprisonment (751), transportation, exile (297), cucking- or ducking-stool, treadmill, crank, hulks, galleys, penal servitude, preventive detention.

A blow, slap, spank, swish, hit, knock, rap, thump, bang, stroke, cuff, kick, whack, thwack, box, punch, pummel.

Beating, lash, flagellation, flogging, etc., dressing, lacing, tanning, knock-out, fustigation, leathering, lathering, jacketing, gruelling, spiflication, bastinado, strappado, pillory, running the gauntlet, picketing, *coup de grâce*, *peine forte et dure*, strap-oil.

Execution, hanging, beheading, decollation, decapitation, electrocution, guillotine, garrotte, *auto da fé*, crucifixion, impalement, etc., martyrdom.

(*Verbs*). To punish, chastise, castigate, chasten, correct, inflict punishment, pay, do for, serve out, pay out, visit upon, give it to, strafe, spiflicate.

(*Phrases*). To make an example of; to serve one right.

To strike, hit, smite, knock, slap, flap, rap, bang, thwack, whack, thump, kick, punch, pelt, beat, buffet, thrash, swinge, pummel, clapperclaw, drub, trounce, baste, belabour, lace, strap, comb, lash, lick, whip, flog, scourge. knout, swish, spank, birch, tan, larrup, lay into, knock out, wallop, leather, flagellate, horsewhip, bastinado, lapidate, stone.

(*Phrases*). To give a dressing; to dust one's jacket; to tweak or pull the nose; to box the ears; to beat to a mummy, or jelly; to tar and feather; to give a black eye; to lay it on.

To execute, hang, behead, decapitate, decollate, electrocute, guillotine, garrotte, shoot, gibbet, picket, hang, draw and quarter; break on the wheel; crucify, impale, torture, etc.; lynch.

To be hanged, etc., to be spread-eagled.

(*Phrases*). To come to the gallows; to swing for it; to die in one's shoes.

(*Adjectives*). Punishing, etc., punitory, punitive, inflictive, castigatory.

Punished, etc.

973. REWARD (*Substantives*), recompense, remuneration, meed, guerdon, premium, indemnity, indemnification, compensation, reparation, requital, retribution, quittance, smart-money, hush-money, acknowledgment, amends, sop, atonement, redress, consideration, return, tribute, honorarium, prize; salvage.

Crown, laurel, bays, cross, medal, ribbon, decoration, etc.

(*Verbs*). To reward, recompense, requite, recoup, remunerate, compensate, make amends, indemnify, atone, satisfy, acknowledge, acquit oneself.

(*Phrase*). To get for one's pains.

(*Adjectives*). Remunerative, compensatory, retributive, reparatory.

974. PENALTY (*Substantives*), pain, penance.

Fine, mulct, amercement, forfeit, forfeiture, escheat, damages, deodand, sequestration, confiscation.

(*Verbs*). To fine, mulct, amerce, sconce, confiscate, sequester, sequestrate.

975. Instrument of punishment.

SCOURGE (*Substantives*), rod, cane, stick, rattan, switch, ferule, birch, cudgel.

Whip, lash, strap, thong, knout, cowhide, cat, cat-o'-nine-tails, sjambok, rope's end, boot.

Pillory, stocks, whipping-post, ducking-stool, triangle, wooden horse, treadmill.

Rack, wheel, stake, tree, block, scaffold, gallows, gibbet, axe, maiden, guillotine, electric chair, halter, bowstring.

Executioner, hangman, headsman, Jack Ketch.

SECTION V.—RELIGIOUS AFFECTIONS

1°. SUPERHUMAN BEINGS AND OBJECTS

976. DEITY (*Substantives*), Divinity, Godhead, Omnipotence, Providence.

Quality of being divine: Divineness, divinity.

GOD, Lord, Jehovah, The Almighty; The Supreme Being; The First Cause, *Ens Entium*; The Author, etc., of all things, The Infinite, The Eternal, The All-powerful, The All-wise, The All-merciful, The All-holy.

Attributes and Perfections: Infinite Power, Wisdom, Goodness, Justice, Mercy, Omnipotence, Omniscience, Omnipresence, Unity, Immutability, Holiness, Glory, Majesty, Sovereignty, Infinity, Eternity.

The Trinity, The Holy Trinity, The Trinity in Unity, The Triune God.

GOD THE FATHER, The Maker, The Creator.

Functions: Creation, Preservation, Divine Government, Theocracy, Thearchy, Providence, the ways, the dispensations, the visitations of Providence.

GOD THE SON, Christ, Jesus, The Messiah, The Anointed, The Saviour, The Redeemer, The Mediator, The Intercessor, The Advocate, The Judge, The Son of Man, The Lamb of God, The Word, The Logos, Emmanuel, The King of Kings and Lord of Lords, The King of Glory, The Prince of Peace, The Good Shepherd, The Way of Truth and Life, The Bread of Life, The Light of the World, The Sun of Righteousness.

The Incarnation, The Hypostatic Union.

Functions: Salvation, Redemption, Atonement, Propitiation, Mediation, Intercession, Judgment.

GOD THE HOLY GHOST, The Holy Spirit, Paraclete, The Comforter, The Spirit of Truth, The Dove.

Functions: Inspiration, Unction, Regeneration, Sanctification, Consolation.

(*Verbs*). To create, uphold, preserve, govern, etc.

To atone, redeem, save, propitiate, mediate, etc.

To predestinate, elect, call, ordain, bless, justify, sanctify, glorify, etc.

(*Adjectives*). Almighty, etc., holy, hallowed, sacred, divine, heavenly, celestial.

Superhuman, ghostly, spiritual, supernatural, theocratic.

977. Beneficent spirits.

ANGEL (*Substantives*), archangel.

The heavenly host; the host of heaven, the sons of God.

Madonna.

Seraphim, cherubim, ministering spirits, morning stars.

(*Adjectives*). Angelic, seraphic.

978. Maleficent spirits.

SATAN (*Substantives*), the Devil, Lucifer, Beelzebub, Belial, Sammael, Zamiel, the Prince of the Devils.[1]

The tempter, the evil one, the wicked one, the old Serpent, the Prince of darkness, the Prince of this world, the Prince of the power of the air; the foul fiend, the arch-fiend, the common enemy; the old malicious foe, Mephistopheles, Abaddon, Apollyon.

Diabolism, devilism, devilship; Satanism, Manichæism; the black mass.

Fallen Angels, unclean spirits; devils; the Rulers or Powers of darkness; inhabitants of Pandemonium.

(*Adjectives*). Satanic, diabolic, devilish.

[1] I have not inserted in the text the slang synonyms Old Nick, Old Scratch, Old Horny, Old Harry, the Deuce, the Old Gentleman, etc.

Mythological and other fabulous Deities and Powers

979. JUPITER (*Substantives*), Jove, etc., etc., Odin, etc., Brahma, Vishnu, Siva, Krishna, Buddha, Mithra, Ormuzd (or Ahura Mazda), Isis, Osiris, Moloch, Baal, Asteroth, etc.

Good genius, demiurge, familiar; fairy, fay, sylph, peri, kelpie, banshee, dryad, hamadryad, naiad, merman, mermaid (341), undine; Oberon, Mab, Titania, Puck, Robin Goodfellow, etc., etc.

(*Adjectives*). Fairy, fairy-like, sylph-like, sylphine.

---

980. DEMON (*Substantives*), evil genius, fiend, unclean spirit, cacodemon, incubus, succubus, succuba, flibbertigibbet; Belial, Mephistopheles, Asmodeus, Ahriman, Eblis, Abaddon, Demogorgon.

Fury, harpy, siren, satyr, etc.

Vampire, werewolf, ghoul, afreet (or afrite), ogre, gnome, imp, genie (or jinnee), lamia, bogy, bogle, nix, nixie, kobold, brownie, leprechaun, elf, pixy, troll, sprite.

Supernatural appearance, ghost, spectre, apparition, shade, vision, goblin, hobgoblin, spook, wraith, ***revenant***, ***doppelgänger***, ***poltergeist***.

(*Phrases*). The powers of darkness; the good people.

(*Adjectives*). Supernatural, ghostly, apparitional, elfin, elfish, unearthly, weird, spectral, spookish, spooky, ghostlike, fiendish, fiendlike, impish; demoniacal; haunted.

981. HEAVEN (*Substantives*), the kingdom of heaven; the kingdom of God, the heavenly kingdom; the throne of God, the presence of God.

(*Phrase*). The inheritance of the Saints in Light.

Paradise, Eden, the abode of the blessed; celestial bliss, glory, etc.

Mythological heaven, Olympus; mythological paradise: Elysium, the Elysian Fields; Valhalla (Scandinavian), Nirvana (Buddhist).

Translation, apotheosis, resurrection.

(*Adjectives*). Heavenly, celestial, supernal, unearthly, from on high, paradisaical, paradisical, paradisial, beatific.

982. HELL (*Substantives*), bottomless pit, place of torment; the habitation of fallen angels, Pandemonium, Abaddon.

Hell-fire, everlasting fire, the lake of fire and brimstone.

(*Phrases*). The fire that is never quenched; the worm that never dies.

Purgatory, limbo, Gehenna, abyss.

Mythological hell: Tartarus, Hades, Pluto, Avernus, Styx, the Stygian creek, the pit of Acheron, Erebus, Cocytus, Tophet.

(*Phrases*). The infernal regions; the shades below; the realms of Pluto.

(*Adjectives*). Hellish, infernal, stygian.

2°. RELIGIOUS DOCTRINES

983. Religious knowledge.

THEOLOGY (natural and revealed) (*Substantives*), divinity, religion, monotheism, hagiology, hagiography, hierography, theosophy; comparative religion, comparative mythology.

Creed, belief, faith, persuasion, tenet, dogma, articles of faith, declaration, profession or confession of faith.

983A. ORTHODOXY (*Substantives*), true faith, Christianity, Christianism, Christendom, Catholicism.

(*Phrase*). "The faith once delivered to the Saints."

A theologian, a divine, schoolman.

A Christian, a true believer.

The Church, the Catholic or Universal Church; the Church of Christ, the body of Christ, the Bride.

(*Phrases*). The members of Christ; the disciples or followers of Christ; the Christian community; the collective body of Christians; the temple of the Holy Ghost.

(*Adjectives*). Theological, divine, religious.

Orthodox, sound, faithful, true, scriptural, canonical, Christian, Catholic, schismless.

984. HETERODOXY (*Substantives*), heresy, schism, schismaticalness, dissent, latitudinarianism, recusancy, apostasy, backsliding, quietism, adiaphorism.

Antichrist.

Idolatry, superstition, bigotry, credulity, fanaticism.

Dissent, nonconformity, sectarianism, syncretism.

Unitarianism, Quakerism, theosophy.

Paganism, heathenism, ethnicism, mythology, polytheism, ditheism, tritheism, pantheism.

Judaism, Gentilism, Mahometanism (or Mohammedanism), Turcism, Buddhism, Hinduism, Taoism, Confucianism, Shintoism, etc., Sufism, Hylotheism, Mormonism.

A heretic, pagan, heathen, paynim, pantheist, idolator, sacrilegist, schismatic, recusant, bigot, fanatic, Ghazi.

Nonconformist, separatist, sectarian, sectarist, sectary; unitarian, theosophist, Quaker.

Jew, Mahometan (or Mohammedan), Mussulman, Moslem, Brahmin (or Brahman), Parsee, Sufi, Magus, Gymnosophist, Guebre, Fire-worshipper, etc.; Buddhist, Sabean, Gnostic, Rosicrucian.

(*Adjectives*). Heterodox, heretical, unorthodox, unscriptural, uncanonical, schismatic, sectarian, nonconformist, recusant, latitudinarian.

Credulous, bigoted, fanatical, idolatrous, superstitious, visionary.

Pagan, heathen, ethnic, gentile, pantheistic, polytheistic.

Judaical, Mohammedan, Brahminical, Buddhistic, etc.; Rosicrucian, etc.

985. REVELATION (*Substantives*), Word, Word of God, inspiration, Scripture, the Scriptures, Holy Writ, the Bible.

986. PSEUDO-REVELATION (*Substantives*), the Koran (or Alcoran), Shi King, Shaster, Veda, Zendavesta, Purana, etc.,

(*Phrases*). The sacred Scriptures; the inspired writing; the Holy Book, etc.

Old Testament: Septuagint, Vulgate, Pentateuch, Hagiographa, the Law, the Prophets, the Apocrypha, etc.; hierograph, hierogram.

New Testament: the Gospel, the Evangelists, the Epistles, the Apocalypse.

Talmud, Mishna, Masorah, Torah.

A Prophet, Seer, Evangelist, Apostle, Disciple, Saint, the Fathers.

Edda, Kalevala, Pitikas, Mahabharata.

Religious founders: Gotama (or Gautama), Zoroaster (or Zarathustra), Confucius, Lao-Tsze, Amida, Mahomet (or Mohammed), etc.

Idols: Golden calf, Baal, Moloch, Dagon, etc.

(*Adjectives*). Anti-scriptural, antichristian, profane, idolatrous, heathen, heathenish.

(*Phrases*). The Holy Men of old; the inspired penmen.

(*Adjectives*). Scriptural, biblical, sacred, prophetic, evangelical, apostolic, apostolical, inspired, theopneustic.

3°. Religious Sentiments

987. Piety (*Substantives*), religion, theism, faith, religiousness, godliness, reverence, humility, veneration, devoutness, devotion, theopathy, grace, unction, edification, unworldliness, other-worldliness; holiness, sanctity, sanctitude, sacredness, consecration.

(*Phrases*). The odour of sanctity; the beauty of holiness; spiritual existence.

Theopathy, beatification, adoption, regeneration, conversion, justification, salvation, inspiration.

A believer, theist, Christian, saint, one of the elect, a devotee.

The good, righteous, godly, elect, just.

(*Phrases*). The children of God, of light, etc.

(*Verbs*). To be pious, etc., to believe, have faith; to convert, edify, sanctify, beatify, re-

989. Impiety (*Substantives*), irreverence, profaneness, profanity, blasphemy, desecration, sacrilegiousness; scoffing, reviling.

Assumed piety: hypocrisy, pietism, lip-devotion, lip-service, lip-reverence, formalism, sanctimony, sanctimoniousness, pharisaism, precisianism, sabbatism, sabbatarianism, religiosity, *odium theologicum*.

Sinner, outcast, castaway, lost sheep, reprobate.

Hardening, backsliding, declension, reprobation.

A scoffer, hypocrite, pietist, religionist, precisian, formalist; sons of darkness, sons of men, sons of Belial, blasphemer, Pharisee.

A bigot, devotee, fanatic, sabbatarian.

The wicked, unjust, ungodly, unrighteous.

generate, inspire; to consecrate, enshrine.

(*Phrase*). To work out one's salvation.

(*Adjectives*). Pious, religious, devout, reverent, godly, humble, heavenly-minded, pure, holy, spiritual, saintly, saint-like, solemn, unworldly, other-worldly.

Believing, faithful, Christian, Catholic, etc.

Sanctified, regenerated, justified, adopted, elected, inspired, consecrated, converted, unearthly, sacred, solemn, not of the earth.

(*Verbs*). To be impious, etc., idolise.

To profane, desecrate, blaspheme, revile, scoff.

(*Adjectives*). Impious, profane, irreverent, sacrilegious, desecrating, blasphemous, unhallowed, unsanctified, hardened, perverted, reprobate.

Bigoted, priest-ridden, fanatical, churchy.

Hypocritical, pietistical, sanctimonious, over-righteous, righteous overmuch.

(*Phrases*). Under the mask, cloak, or pretence of religion.

988. Irreligion (*Substantives*), ungodliness, unholiness, gracelessness.

Scepticism, doubt, unbelief, disbelief, incredulity, incredulousness, faithlessness, want of faith or belief (485, 487).

Atheism, hylotheism.

Deism, infidelity, freethinking, rationalism, agnosticism, unchristianness, anti-christianity.

An atheist, sceptic, unbeliever, deist, freethinker, rationalist, agnostic, infidel, alien, giaour, heathen.

(*Verbs*). To be irreligious, disbelieve, lack faith, doubt, question, etc.

To dechristianise, rationalise.

(*Adjectives*). Irreligious, undevout, godless, atheistic, ungodly, unholy, unsanctified, graceless, without God, carnal-minded.

Sceptical, unbelieving, freethinking, agnostic, rationalistic, incredulous, unconverted, faithless, lacking faith, unhallowed.

Deistical, antichristian, unchristian, worldly-minded, mundane, carnal, earthly-minded.

(*Adverb*). Irreligiously, etc.

4°. Acts of Religion

990. Worship (*Substantives*), adoration, devotion, latria, cult, homage, service, humiliation, kneeling, genuflexion, prostration.

Prayer, invocation, supplication, rogation, petition, orison, holy breathing, asking, suffrage, etc. (765), litany, the Lord's prayer, paternoster, collect.

Thanksgiving, giving, or returning thanks, praise, glorification, benediction, doxology, hosanna, hallelujah, *Te Deum*, pæan (836); *non nobis, Domine*.

Psalmody, psalm, hymn, plainsong, chant, antiphon, response, anthem, *see* 415.

Oblation, sacrifice, incense, libation, burnt-offering, votive offering.

Discipline, self-discipline, self-examination, self-denial, fasting.

(*Verbs*). To worship, adore, do service, pay homage, humble oneself, kneel, bend the knee, prostrate oneself.

To pray, invoke, supplicate, petition, put up prayers or petitions; to ask, implore, beseech, etc. (765).

To return or give thanks; to say grace; to bless, praise, laud, glorify, magnify, sing praises, give benediction, lead the choir.

To propitiate, offer sacrifice, fast, deny oneself; vow, offer vows, give alms.

(*Phrase*). To work out one's salvation.

(*Adjectives*). Worshipping, etc., devout, solemn, devotional, reverent, pure, fervid, heartfelt, etc.

991. IDOLATRY (*Substantives*), idol-worship, idolism, demonism, demonolatry, fire-worship, devil-worship, fetishism.

Deification, apotheosis, canonisation.

Sacrifices, hecatomb, holocaust; human sacrifices, immolation, infanticide, self-immolation, suttee.

Idol, fetish, ju-ju, mumbo-jumbo, Juggernaut, etc.

(*Verbs*). To worship idols, pictures, relics, etc.; to deify.

(*Adjective*). Idolatrous.

992. OCCULT ARTS (*Substantives*), occultism, sorcery, magic, the black art, black magic, necromancy, theurgy, thaumaturgy, psychomancy, *diablerie*, bedevilment, witchcraft, witchery, glamour, fetishism, vampirism, Shamanism, voodooism, obeah (or obi), sortilege, conjuration, fascination, mesmerism, clairvoyance, mediumship, spiritualism, electro-biology, second-sight, spirit-rapping, psychometry, crystal-gazing, divination, enchantment, hocus-pocus (545), ordeal.

(*Verbs*). To practise sorcery, etc.; to conjure, exorcise, charm, enchant, bewitch, bedevil, entrance, mesmerise, hypnotise, fascinate; to taboo, wave a wand, cast a spell, call up spirits.

(*Adjectives*). Magic, magical, cabbalistic, talismanic, phylacteric, incantatory, occult, mediumistic, charmed, exorcised, etc.

993. SPELL (*Substantives*), charm, incantation, exorcism, weird, cabbala, exsufflation, cantrip, runes, abracadabra, open sesame, taboo, counter-charm, Ephesian letters; the evil eye.

Talisman, amulet, mascot, periapt, phylactery, philter.

Wand, caduceus, rod, divining-rod, the lamp of Aladdin.

994. SORCERER (*Substantives*), magician, conjurer, necromancer, thaumaturgist, occultist, adept, Mahatma, seer, wizard, witch, warlock, charmer, exorcist, mage, archimage, soothsayer (513), cunning-man, Shaman, medicine-man, witch-doctor, medium, spiritualist, clairvoyant; control.

(*Phrase*). *Deus ex machina.*

5°. Religious Institutions

995. Churchdom (*Substantives*), ministry, apostleship, sacerdotalism, priesthood, prelacy, hierarchy, church government, Christendom, church; (in a bad sense) priestcraft, theocracy, popery.

Monachism, monasticism; monkery.

Ecclesiastical offices and dignities: Pontificate, primacy, archbishopric, bishopric, bishopdom, episcopate, episcopacy, see, diocese; deanery, stall, canonry, canonicate, prebend, prebendaryship; benefice, incumbency, living, cure, rectorship, vicarship, vicariate, deaconry, deaconship, curacy, chaplaincy, chaplainship, abbacy.

Holy orders, ordination, institution, consecration, induction, preferment, translation.

Council, conclave, sanhedrim, synod, consistory, chapter, vestry (696).

(*Verbs*). To call, ordain, induct, prefer, translate, to take the veil.

(*Adjectives*). Ecclesiastical, clerical, sacerdotal, priestly, prelatical, pastoral, ministerial, capitular, theocratic.

Pontifical, papal, episcopal, archidiaconal, diaconal, canonical, clerical; monastic, monachal, monkish; levitical, rabbinical.

996. Clergy (*Substantives*), ministers, priesthood, presbytery.

A clergyman, divine, ecclesiastic, churchman, priest, presbyter, hierophant, pastor, father, shepherd, minister, father in Christ, patriarch, *padre*, clerk, cleric.

(*Phrases*). Black-coat; the cloth; sky-pilot; devil-dodger.

Dignitaries of the church: Primate, archbishop, bishop, prelate, diocesan, suffragan; dean, subdean, archdeacon, prebendary, canon, residentiary, beneficiary; rector, vicar, incumbent, parson, chaplain, curate, deacon, preacher, evangelist; capitular.

Churchwarden, sidesman; clerk, precentor, choir, almoner, verger, beadle, sexton (or sacristan), acolyte.

Roman Catholic priesthood: Pope, pontiff, cardinal, *abbé*, *curé*, confessor, spiritual director; (ancient) flamen.

Greek Church: Patriarch, metropolitan, archimandrite, pope.

Cenobite, conventual, abbot, prior, monk, oblate, friar, mendicant, Franciscan (or Grey Friars, Friars minor, Minorites), Observant, Capuchin, Dominican (or Black Friars), Carmelite, Augustin (or Austin Friars), Crossed or Crutched Friars, etc.

997. Laity (*Substantives*), flock, fold, congregation, assembly, brethren, people.

Temporality, secularisation.

A layman, parishioner.

(*Verb*). To secularise.

(*Adjectives*). Secular, lay, laical, civil, temporal, profane.

Abbess, prioress, canoness, *religieuse*, nun, beguine, novice.

Under the Jewish dispensation: Prophet, priest, high-priest, Levite, rabbi (or rabbin), scribe.

Mohammedan, etc.: Mullah, ulema, imam, sheik, muezzin, mufti, dervish, fakir, brahmin, guru, druid, bonze, santon, lama.

998. RITE (*Substantives*), ceremony, ordinance, observance, cult, formulary, ceremonial, solemnity, sacrament.

Baptism, christening, chrism, baptismal regeneration.

Confirmation, imposition or laying on of hands.

The Eucharist, the Lord's Supper, the communion, the sacrament, consubstantiation.

Matrimony (903), burial (363), visitation of the sick, etc., offertory, etc.

Roman Catholic rites and ceremonies: Mass, high mass, low mass, dry mass; matins, vespers; the seven sacraments, transubstantiation, impanation, extreme unction, viaticum, invocation of saints, canonisation, transfiguration, auricular confession, maceration, flagellation, sackcloth and ashes, telling of beads, etc.

Relics, rosary, beads, reliquary, pix (or pyx), host, crucifix, *Agnus Dei*, etc., censer, patera.

Liturgy, ritual, euchology, book of common prayer, litany, etc.; rubric, breviary, missal, processional, etc.

Service, duty, ministration, psalmody, etc. (*see* 990); preaching, predication; sermon, homily, lecture, discourse.

(*Verbs*). To perform service, do duty, minister, officiate; to baptise, dip, sprinkle, etc.; to confirm, lay hands on, etc.; to give or administer the sacrament; to take or receive the sacrament; to communicate.

To preach, sermonise, predicate, lecture.

(*Adjectives*). Ritual, ceremonial, baptismal, eucharistical, etc.

999. CANONICALS (*Substantives*), vestments, robe, gown, pallium, surplice, cassock, cope, soutane, scapulary, tonsure, cowl, hood, calotte, bands, etc.

Mitre, tiara, triple crown, crosier.

1000. Place of worship, house of God.

TEMPLE (*Substantives*), cathedral, pro-cathedral, minster, church, kirk, chapel, meeting-house, tabernacle, conventicle, bethesda, little Bethel, basilica, fane, holy place, chantry.

Synagogue, mosque, pantheon, pagoda, joss-house, etc., dagobah, tope.

Parsonage, rectory, vicarage, manse, presbytery, deanery, bishop's palace.

Altar, shrine, sanctuary, *sanctum sanctorum*, the Holy of Holies, sacristy, communion table, baptistery, font, holy table, table of the Lord.

Chancel, choir, nave, aisle, transept, vestry, crypt, stall, pew, pulpit, ambo, reading-desk, confessional, prothesis, credence.

Monastery, priory, abbey, convent, nunnery, cloister.

(*Adjectives*). Claustral, monastic, monasterial, conventual.

INDEX

N.B.—The numbers refer to the headings under which the words occur. The headings, too, are given in Italics, not to explain the meaning of the words, but to assist in the required reference. Words borrowed from another language have an asterisk prefixed to them.

Abbreviations.—Fr. French; L. Latin; It. Italian; Ger. German; Gr. Greek; Sp. Spanish; Port. Portuguese; R. Russian; Arab. Arabic; Ch. Chinese.

A

A1, *superiority*, 33.
Aback, *rear*, 235.
Abacus, *numeration*, 85.
Abaft, *rear*, 235.
Abalienate, *transfer*, 783.
Abandon, *a purpose*, 624.
property, 782.
*Abandon (Fr.), *artlessness*, 703.
Abandoned, *forsaken*, 893.
vicious, 945.
Abandonment, *purpose*, 624.
property, 782.
Abase, *depress*, 308, 874.
degrade, 879.
Abasement, *servility*, 886.
Abash, *daunt*, 860.
humiliate, 879.
shame, 874.
Abashed, *modesty*, 881.
Abate, *lessen*, 36.
a price, 813.
*A bâtons rompus (Fr.), *disorder*, 59.
irregularity, 139.
Abattis, *defence*, 717.
*Abattoir (Fr.), *killing*, 361.
Abbacy, *churchdom*, 995.
*Abbé (Fr.), *clergy*, 996.
Abbess, *clergy*, 996.
Abbey, *temple*, 1000.
Abbot, *clergy*, 996.
Abbreviate, *shorten*, 201, 596.
style, 572.
Abdicate, *resignation*, 757.
Abduct, *take*, 789.
steal, 791.
Abduction, *taking*, 789.
Abecedarian, *learner*, 541.
Abecedary, *letter*, 561.
Aberrant, *divergent*, 279, 291.
erroneous, 495.
exceptional, 83.
Aberration, *divergence*, 291.
deviation, 279.
mental, 503.
Abet, *aid*, 707.
*Ab extra (L.), *exterior*, 220.
Abeyance, *expectation*, 507.
extinction, 2
suspense, 141.
Abhor, *hate*, 898.
dislike, 867.
Abide, *continue*, 143.
permanence, 142.
diuturnity, 110.
endure, 821.
dwell, 186.
expect, 507.
Abide by, *resolution*, 604.
Abigail, *servant*, 746.
Ability, *power*, 157.
skill, 698.
*Ab imo pectore (L.), *affection*, 820.
*Ab incunabulis (L.), *beginning*, 66.
*Ab initio (L.), *beginning*, 66.
Abject, *servile*, 886.
vile, 874, 940.
Abjure, *renounce*, 607.
resign, 757.
deny, 536.
Ablation, *subduction*, 38.
taking, 789.
Ablaze, *heat*, 382.
light, 420.
Able, *skilful*, 157, 698.
Able-bodied, *strength*, 159.
Ablepsy, *blindness*, 442.
Ablution, *cleanness*, 652.

Abnegation, *denial*, 536, 764.
self-denial, 942.
forbearance, 953.
Abnormality, *unconformity*, 83.
Aboard, *ship*, 273.
present, 186.
Abode, *abode*, 189, 182.
Abodement, *prediction*, 511.
Abolish, *destroy*, 162.
abrogate, 756.
Abominable, *hateful*, 898.
bad, 649.
foul, 653.
painful, 830.
Abominate, *hate*, 898.
dislike, 867.
Abomination, *foulness*, 653.
*Abord (Fr.), *courtesy*, 894.
Aboriginal, *beginning*, 66.
Aborigines, *inhabitants*, 188.
Abortion, *failure*, 732.
Abound, *sufficiency*, 639.
About, *relative to*, 9.
near, 32, 197.
around, 227.
Above, *height*, 206.
Above all, *greatness*, 31.
Above-board, *visible*, 446.
plain, 518.
artless, 703.
true, 543.
Above ground, *alive*, 359.
Above par, *greatness*, 31.
*Ab ovo (L.), *beginning*, 66.
*Ab ovo usque ad mala (L.), *completeness*, 52.
duration, 106.
Abracadabra, *spell*, 993.
Abrade, *subduct*, 38.
Abrasion, *pulverulence*, 330.
friction, 331.
*A bras ouverts (Fr.), *courtesy*, 894.
Abreast, *lateral*, 236.
parallel, 216.
*Abrégé (Fr.), *compendium*, 596.
Abridge, *shorten*, 201.
lessen, 36.
deprive, 789.
in writing, 596.
Abroach, *dispersion*, 73.
Abroad, *extraneous*, 57.
distant, 196.
ignorant, 491.
perplexed, 704.
Abrogation, *abrogation*, 756, 764.
Abrupt, *sudden*, 132.
violent, 173.
transient, 111.
steep, 217.
Abrupt, *unexpected*, 508.
style, 579.
Abscess, *disease*, 655.
Abscission, *retrenchment*, 38.
division, 44.
Abscond, *escape*, 671.
fly from, 287.
Absence, *non-existence*, 2.
non-presence, 187.
inattention, 458.
thoughtlessness, 452.
Absentee, *absence*, 187.
Absent-minded, *inattentive*, 458.
*Absit omen (L.), *fear*, 860.
deprecation, 766.
Absolute, *not relative*, 1.
certain, 474, 31.
true, 494.
unconditional, 768A.
authoritative, 737.
severe, 739.
due, 924.
complete, 52.
Absolve, *forgive*, 918.
exempt, 927.
liberate, 750.
permit, 760.
acquit, 970.
Absonant, *unreasonable*, 495.
discordant, 414.
Absorb, *combination*, 48.
take in, 296.
think, 451.
attend to, 457.
feel, 821.
consume, 677.
Abstain, *refrain*, 603.
temperance, 953.
forbear, 623.
Abstemious, *temperance*, 953.
Absterge, *cleanness*, 652.
Abstersive, *remedy*, 662.
Abstinence, *disuse*, 678.
forbearance, 623, 953.
Abstinent, *temperance*, 953.
sobriety, 958.
Abstract, *separate*, 44.
idea, 451.
to abridge, 596, 572.
to take, 789.
to steal, 791.
Abstraction, *inattention*, 458.
unity, 87.
Abstruse, *recondite*, 519.
hidden, 528.
Absurd, *nonsensical*, 497, 499.
ridiculous, 853.
Abundant, *copious*, 639.
great, 31.

*Ab uno disce omnes (L.), *uniformity*, 16.
similarity, 17.
conformity, 82.
Abuse, *misuse*, 679.
ill-treat, 649.
threat, 909.
upbraid, 932.
deceive, 545.
of language, 523.
Abut, *rest on*, 215.
touch, 199.
Abyss, *depth*, 208.
space, 180.
hell, 982.
Academic, *teaching*, 537.
Academy, *school*, 542.
Accede, *consent*, 762.
Accelerate, *velocity*, 173, 274.
earliness, 132.
haste, 684.
Accension, *calefaction*, 384.
Accent, *tone of voice*, 580.
sound, 402.
Accept, *receive*, 785.
consent, 762.
assent, 488.
Acceptable, *agreeable*, 829.
expedient, 646.
Acceptance, *security*, 771.
Acceptation, *meaning*, 516.
Accepted, *conformity*, 82.
Access, *method*, 627.
Accessible, *facility*, 705.
Accession, *increase*, 35.
addition, 37.
to power, 737.
Accessory, *addition*, 37.
adjunct, 39.
auxiliary, 711.
aiding, 707.
accompanying, 88.
Accidence, *grammar*, 567.
Accident, *chance*, 156, 621.
event, 151.
Accidental, *external*, 6.
music, 413.
Acclamation, *approbation*, 931.
Acclimatise, *inure*, 613.
train, 673.
Acclivity, *obliquity*, 217.
*Accolade (Fr.), *courtesy*, 894.
Accommodate, *suit*, 23.
reconcile, 723.
lend, 787.
prepare, 673.
aid, 707.
give, 784.
Accommodating, *kind*, 906.
Accommodation, *lodging*, 189.
Accompaniment, *musical*, 415.
adjunct, 37, 39.
Accompanist, *musician*, 416.
Accompany, *coexist*, 88.
add, 37.
Accomplice, *auxiliary*, 711.
Accomplish, *execute*, 161.
finish, 729.
Accomplishment, *talent*, 698.
learning, 490.
Accord, *agree*, 23, 646.
assent, 488.
concord, 714.
give, 784.
grant, 760.
spontaneous, 600.
Accordingly, *reasoning*, 476.
According to, *relation*, 9.
conformably, 15.
evidence, 467.
Accordion, *musical instrument*, 417.
Accost, *allocation*, 586.
*Accoucheur (Fr.), *instrument*, 631.
Account, *money*, 811.
bill, 812.
computation, 85.
list, 86.
description, 594.
value, 644.
estimation, 484.
judgment, 480.
approbation, 931.
fame, 873.
sake, 615.
Account for, *attribution*, 155.
Accountable, *duty*, 926.
Accountant, *accounts*, 811.
Accoutre, *dress*, 225.
equip, 673.
Accredit, *money*, 805.
honour, 873.
Accretion, *coherence*, 46.
increase, 35.
Accrue, *result*, 154.
add, 37.
acquire, 775.
receive, 810.
benefit, 644.
*Accueil (Fr.), *courtesy*, 894.
Accumulate, *collect*, 72.
store, 636.
Accurate, *exact*, 494.
likeness, 17.
known, 490.
Accursed, *undone*, 828.
painful, 830.
disastrous, 649.
cursed, 908.

Accuse, *charge*, 938.
disapprove, 932.
Accuser, *judge*, 967.
Accustom, *habituate*, 613.
usual, 82.
Ace, *unit*, 87.
small in quantity, 32.
small in size, 193.
Ace, within an — of, *smallness*, 32.
Aceldama, *killing*, 361.
Acerbate, *embitter*, 659.
aggravate, 835.
Acerbity, *harshness*, 739.
spleen, 898, 900, 901.
malevolence, 907.
Acervate, *assemblage*, 72.
Acetous, *sourness*, 397.
*Acharné (Fr.), *resentment*, 900.
*Acharnement (Fr.), *malevolence*, 907.
Ache, *physical pain*, 378.
moral pain, 828.
Acheron, *hell*, 982.
Achievable, *possible*, 470.
easy, 705.
Achieve, *accomplish*, 729.
end, 67.
Achievement, *escutcheon*, 551.
Achromatism, *achromatic*, 429.
Acicular, *sharpness*, 253.
Acid, *sourness*, 397.
Acknowledge, *avow*, 535.
disclose, 529.
assent, 488.
consent, 762.
reward, 973.
repent, 950.
answer, 462.
observe, 772.
receive, 82.
Acme, *summit*, 210.
highest degree, 33.
perfection, 650.
Acolyte, *clergy*, 996.
Aconite, *bane*, 663.
*A corps perdu (Fr.), *rashness*, 863.
*A coup sûr (Fr.), *certainty*, 474.
Acoustics, *sound*, 402.
Acquaint, *information*, 527.
Acquaintance, *knowledge*, 490.
friendship, 888.
friend, 890.
Acquiesce, *assent*, 488.
consent, 762.
Acquire, *acquisition*, 775.
Acquirement, *knowledge*, 490.
learning, 539.
talent, 698.
Acquisition, *gain*, 775.
Acquisition, *knowledge*, 490.
Acquit, *absolve*, 970.
exempt, 927.
vindicate, 937.
liberate, 750.
Acquit oneself, *of a duty*, 926.
of an agreement, 772.
Acquittance, *payment*, 807.
Acres, *property*, 780.
Acrid, *unsavouriness*, 395.
Acrimony, *physical*, 171.
taste, 395.
hatred, 898.
discourtesy, 895.
Acrobat, *proficient*, 700.
Across, *transverse*, 219.
opposition, 708.
Acrostic, *neology*, 563.
puzzle, 533.
Act, *physical*, 170.
voluntary, 680.
to feign, 544.
to personate, 599.
to imitate, 19.
Action, *physical*, 170.
voluntary, 680.
battle, 720.
at law, 969.
*Actionnaire (Fr.), *participator*, 778.
Activity, *physical*, 171.
voluntary, 682.
Actor, *impostor*, 548.
player, 599.
Actual, *existing*, 1.
real, 494.
present, 118.
Actualise, *describe*, 594.
Actually, *truly*, 31.
Actuary, *accounts*, 811.
Actuate, *motive*, 615.
*Actum est (L.), *completion*, 729.
Acuity, *sharpness*, 253.
Aculeated, *sharpness*, 253.
Acumen, *wisdom*, 494.
Acuminated, *sharpness*, 253.
Acupuncture, *opening*, 260.
Acute, *pointed*, 253.
violent (*physically*), 173.
sensible (*physically*), 375.
painful (*morally*), 830.
strong feeling, 820.
musical tone, 410.
perspicacious, 498.
Acutely, *much*, 31.
Adage, *maxim*, 496.
*Adagio (It.), *slowness*, 275.
music, 415.
Adamant, *hard*, 323.
strong, 159.

Adapt, *fit*, 646.
adjust, 673.
agree, 23.
*Ad arbitrium (L.), *will*, 600.
*Ad captandum (L.), *plea*, 617.
deception, 545.
*Ad captandum vulgus (L.), *ostentation*, 882.
Add, *addition*, 37.
increase, 35.
numerically, 85.
Addendum, *adjunct*, 39.
Adder, *viper*, 663.
maleficent being, 913.
Addict, *habit*, 613.
Addition, *adjunction*, 37.
thing added, 39.
arithmetical, 85.
Additive, *addition*, 37.
Addle, *barren*, 169.
abortive, 732.
to spoil, 659.
Addle-headed, *imbecile*, 499.
Address, *speak to*, 586.
skill, 698.
request, 765.
residence, 189.
direction, 550.
lecture, 582.
Addresses, *courtship*, 902.
Adduce, *bring to*, 288.
evidence, 467.
Adept, *proficient*, 700.
sorcerer, 994.
Adequate, *sufficient*, 639.
power, 157.
strength, 159.
for a purpose, 644.
*Ad eundem (L.), *equality*, 27.
Adhere, *stick*, 46.
fidelity, 772.
resoluteness, 604.
Adherent, *follower*, 711.
Adhesive, *coherence*, 46.
Adhibit, *use*, 677.
*Ad hominem (L.), *speciality*, 79.
*Adieu (Fr.), *departure*, 293.
*Ad infinitum (L.), *infinity*, 105.
*Ad instar (L.), *conformity*, 82.
*Ad interim (L.), *duration*, 106.
Adipose, *unctuous*, 355.
Adiposity, *corpulence*, 192.
*A discrétion (Fr.), *choice*, 609.
Adit, *conduit*, 350.
orifice, 260.
Adjacent, *nearness*, 197.
Adjective, *adjunct*, 39.
Adjoin, *nearness*, 197.
Adjourn, *lateness*, 133.
Adjudge, *lawsuit*, 969.
Adjudication, *choice*, 609.
lawsuit, 969.
Adjunct, *thing added*, 39.
aid, 707.
Adjure, *request*, 765.
promise, 768.
Adjust, *fit*, 27.
preface, 673.
settle, 723.
Adjutage (or ajutage), *pipe*, 350.
opening, 260.
Adjutant, *auxiliary*, 711.
military, 745.
Adjuvant, *helper*, 707, 711.
*Ad libitum (L.), *will*, 600.
choice, 609.
sufficiency, 639.
Admeasurement, *measurement*, 466.
Administer, *give*, 784.
exercise authority, 737.
Administration, *of justice*, 965.
Admirable, *excellent*, 648.
virtuous, 944.
Admiral, *master*, 745.
Admire, *approve*, 931.
love, 897.
wonder, 870.
Admissible, *tolerable*, 651.
Admission, *ingress*, 294, 296.
inclusion, 76.
Admit, *let in*, 296.
accept, 785.
include, 76.
composition, 54.
concede in argument, 467.
allow, 760.
assent, 488.
Admit of, *possibility*, 470.
Admixture, *mixture*, 41.
Admonish, *advise*, 695.
warn, 668.
reprove, 932.
predict, 511.
Ado, *exertion*, 686.
activity, 682.
difficulty, 704.
Adolescence, *youth*, 131.
Adonis, *beauty*, 845.
Adopt, *choice*, 609.
Adore, *love*, 897.
worship, 990.
Adorn, *beauty*, 845.
Adown, *lowness*, 207.
*Ad rem (L.), *agreement*, 23.
reasoning, 473.
Adrift, *unrelated*, 10.
dispersed, 73.
at fault, 704.

Adroit, *skill*, 698.
Adscititious, *extrinsic*, 6.
added, 37.
supplementary, 52.
*Adscriptus glebæ (L.), *servant*, 746.
Adulation, *flattery*, 933.
Adult, *adolescence*, 131.
Adulterate, *mix*, 41.
deteriorate, 659.
falsify, 495.
Adulterer, *libertine*, 962.
Adultery, *impurity*, 961.
Adumbrate, *sketch*, 594.
painting, 556.
faint likeness, 21.
imitate, 19.
personify, 521.
*Ad unguem (L.), *perfection*, 650.
Adust, *burnt*, 384.
gloomy, 837.
*Ad valorem (L.), *price*, 812.
Advance, *progress*, 282, 731.
to promote, 658.
forward, 707.
increase, 35.
lend, 787.
assert, 535.
Advanced, *progressive*, 658.
Advances (to make), *sociality*, 892.
Advanced guard, *front*, 234.
Advantage, *good*, 618.
utility, 644.
goodness, 648.
superiority, 33.
inequality, 28.
success, 705, 731.
Advene, *addition*, 37.
Advent, *arrival*, 292.
event, 151.
futurity, 121.
Adventitious, *extrinsic*, 6.
casual, 156, 621.
Adventure, *event*, 151.
chance, 156, 621.
pursuit, 622.
trial, 675.
Adventurer, *deceiver*, 548.
Adventurous, *courageous*, 861.
dangerous, 665.
*Adversaria (L.), *register*, 551.
chronicle, 594.
Adversary, *opponent*, 710.
Adverse, *opposed*, 708.
disliking, 867.
unprosperous, 735.
Adversity, *adversity*, 735.
Advert, *attention*, 457.
Advertise, *publication*, 531.
Advertisement, *preface*, 64.
Advertisement, *information*, 527.
Advice, *counsel*, 695.
notice, 527.
news, 532.
Advisable, *expediency*, 646.
Advise, *inform*, 527.
counsel, 695.
predict, 511.
Advised, *voluntary*, 600.
Adviser, *counsellor*, 695.
teacher, 540.
Advocate, *counsellor*, 968.
to prompt, 615.
to vindicate, 937.
Saviour, 976.
*Advocatus diaboli (L.), *sophistry*, 477.
*Adytum (L.), *secret place*, 530.
room, 191.
prediction, 511.
Ædile, *authority*, 745.
Ægis, *defence*, 717.
Æolus, *wind*, 349.
Æon, *duration*, 106.
*Æquo animo (L.), *insensible*, 823.
Aerate, *air*, 338.
*Ære perennius (L.), *repute*, 873.
Aerial, *aeriform*, 334, 338.
elevated, 206.
Aerie, *abode*, 189.
Aeriform, *gaseity*, 334, 338.
Aerodrome, *arena*, 720.
Aeromancy, *prediction*, 511.
Aeronautics, *navigation*, 267.
Aeroplane, *ship*, 273.
Aerostatics, *gaseity*, 334.
navigation, 267.
Aerostation, *navigation*, 267.
Æsthetic, *taste*, 850.
beauty, 845.
sensibility, 375.
Æstivate, *sleep*, 68.
Ætiology, *knowledge*, 490.
attribution, 155.
disease, 655.
Afar, *distance*, 196.
Affable, *courteous*, 894.
humble, 879.
Affair, *business*, 625, 680.
event, 151.
topic, 454.
battle, 720.
*Affaire de cœur (Fr.), *love*, 897.
Affect, *desire*, 865.
love, 897
lend to, 176.
touch, 824.
Affectability, *sensibility*, 822.
Affectation, *pretension*, 855.

Affectation, *in style*, 577.
Affection, *state of soul*, 820.
love, 897.
Affiance, *trust*, 858.
promise, 768.
*Affiche (Fr.), *publication*, 531.
Affidavit, *evidence*, 467.
record, 551.
Affiliation, *relation*, 9.
kindred, 11.
Affinity, *relation*, 9.
similarity, 17.
Affirm, *assert*, 535.
confirm, 488.
Affirmatively, *assent*, 488.
Affix, *to join*, 43.
add, 37.
sequel, 39.
addition, 37.
Afflatus, *wind*, 349.
inspiration, 515.
Afflict, *painfulness*, 830.
Affliction, *calamity*, 619.
pain, 828.
Afflictive, *painfulness*, 830.
Affluent, *flowing*, 348.
wealthy, 803.
Afflux, *approach*, 286.
Afford, *supply*, 134, 784.
wealth, 803.
accrue, 810.
Affranchise, *liberation*, 750.
Affray, *contention*, 720.
Affright, *fear*, 880.
Affront, *insult*, 900.
courage, 861.
molest, 830.
Affuse, *water*, 337.
Afire, *heat*, 382.
Afloat, *at sea*, 273.
on shipboard, 273.
unstable, 149.
public, 531.
*A fond (Fr.), *completeness*, 52.
greatness, 31.
Afoot, *walking*, 266.
business, 625.
in preparation, 673.
*A force de (Fr.), *instrument*, 631.
Afore, *priority*, 116.
Aforesaid, *repetition*, 104.
priority, 116.
Aforethought, *intention*, 620.
*A fortiori (L.), *greatness*, 31.
superiority, 33.
evidence, 467.
reasoning, 476.
Afraid, *fear*, 860.
Afreet, *demon*, 980.
Afresh, *new*, 123.
repeated, 104.
frequent, 136.
Aft, *rear*, 235.
After, *in order*, 63.
in time, 117.
After all, *qualification*, 469.
After-clap, *disappointment*, 509.
After-course, *plan*, 626.
After-game, *plan*, 626.
After-life, *futurity*, 121.
Aftermath, *sequel*, 65.
effect, 154.
Afternoon, *evening*, 126.
After-part, *sequel*, 65.
After-piece, *drama*, 599.
After-taste, *taste*, 390.
Afterthought, *sequel*, 65.
thought, 451.
plan, 626.
After-time, *futurity*, 121.
Afterwards, *posteriority*, 117.
Aga, *master*, 745.
*Agacerie (Fr.), *motive*, 615.
Again, *repeated*, 104.
frequent, 136.
Against, *physical opposition*, 179.
voluntary opposition, 708.
anteposition, 237.
provision, 673.
Agape, *wonder*, 870.
curiosity, 455.
Age, *period*, 108.
present time, 118.
advanced life, 128.
Ageless, *perpetual*, 112.
Agency, *physical*, 170.
instrumentality, 157, 631, 755.
direction, 693.
*Agenda (L.), *business*, 625.
Agent, *physical*, 153.
voluntary, 690.
consignee, 758, 769.
Agentship, *commission*, 755.
Agglomerate, *assemblage*, 72.
Agglutinate, *coherence*, 46.
Aggrandise, *in degree*, 35.
in bulk, 194.
honour, 873.
Aggravate, *increase*, 35.
vehemence, 173.
distress, 835.
render worse, 659.
exasperate, 900.
exaggerate, 549.
provoke, 830.
Aggregate, *whole*, 50.
collection, 72.
Aggregation, *coherence*, 46.

Aggression, *attack*, 716.
Aggressive, *pugnacious*, 901.
Aggrieve, *distress*, 830.
injure, 649.
Aghast, *with wonder*, 870.
with fear, 860.
disappointed, 509.
Agile, *swift*, 274.
active, 682.
Agio, *discount*, 813.
Agiotage, *barter*, 794.
Agitate, *motion*, 315.
activity, 682.
to affect the mind, 821.
to excite, 824.
Agnation, *consanguinity*, 11.
Agnomen, *nomenclature*, 564.
Agnosticism, *unbelief*, 485, 988.
*Agnus Dei (L.), *canonicals*, 999.
Ago, *preterition*, 122.
Agog, *curiosity*, 455.
expectation, 507.
desire, 865.
Agonistic, *contention*, 720.
Agonise, *painfulness*, 830.
Agony, *physical*, 378.
mental, 828.
Agoraphobia, *seclusion*, 893.
Agrarian, *agriculture*, 371.
Agree, *accord*, 23.
concur, 178.
assent, 488.
consent, 762.
concord, 714.
Agreeable, *pleasant*, 829.
Agreeably, *conformably*, 82.
Agreement, *bargain*, 769.
Agrestic, *rural*, 371.
uncouth, 876.
Agriculture, *agriculture*, 371.
Agronomy, *agriculture*, 371.
Aground, *stranded*, 265, 704.
failure, 732.
Ague-fit, *fear*, 860.
Aguish, *cold*, 383.
Ahead, *in front*, 62, 234, 280.
Ahead (go), *progression*, 282.
to improve, 658.
Ahriman, *demon*, 980.
*A huis clos (Fr.), *concealment*, 528.
Aid, *to help*, 707, 712.
charity, 606.
Aide-de-camp, *auxiliary*, 711.
officer, 745.
Aigrette, *ornament*, 847.
*Aiguille (Fr.), *sharp*, 253.
Ail, *sick*, 655.
in pain, 828.
Ailment, *disease*, 655.
Aim, *direction*, 278.
purpose, 620.
Aimless, *chance*, 621.
Air, *gas*, 334.
atmospheric, 338.
wind, 349.
tune, 415.
appearance, 448.
unsubstantial, 4.
fashion, 852.
affectation, 855.
Air-balloon, *ship*, 273.
Air-built, *imagination*, 515.
Airiness, *levity*, 320.
Airing, *journey*, 266.
Air-man, *navigation*, 269.
Air-pipe, *air-pipe*, 351.
Air-pocket, *pitfall*, 667.
Air-tight, *closed*, 261.
Airy, *atmosphere*, 338.
gay, 836.
Aisle, *passage*, 260.
in a church, 1000.
Ajutage, *see* Adjutage.
Akimbo (to stand), 715.
angular, 244.
Akin, *consanguinity*, 11.
*A la (Fr.), *resemblance*, 17.
Alabaster, *whiteness*, 430.
*A la belle étoile (Fr.), *exterior*, 220.
air, 338.
*A la bonne heure (Fr.), *assent*, 488.
willingness, 602.
Alack! *lamentation*, 839.
Alacrity, *activity*, 682.
cheerfulness, 836.
*A la dérobée (Fr.), *concealment*, 528.
*A la mode (Fr.), *fashion*, 852.
Alarm, *fear*, 860.
notice of danger, 669.
signal, 550.
threatening, 665.
Alarum, *warning*, 669.
signal, 550.
loudness, 404.
Alas! *lamentation*, 839.
Alb, *dress*, 225.
Albeit, *counteraction*, 179.
Albescent, *white*, 430.
Albinism, *achromatism*, 429.
Albino, *dim-sightedness*, 443.
Album, *book*, 553.
compendium, 596.
Albuminous, *semiliquidity*, 352.
Alcade (or alcayde), *master*, 745.
Alchemy, *conversion*, 144.
Alcoran, *pseudo-revelation*, 986.
Alcove, *cave*, 252.
dwelling, 189.

Alderman, *master*, 745.
Alectryomancy, *prediction*, 511.
Alembic, *vessel*, 191.
laboratory, 691.
*Alentours (Fr.), *nearness*, 197.
Alert, *active*, 682.
watchful, 459.
Aleuromancy, *prediction*, 511.
Alexandrine, *length*, 200.
verse, 597.
Alexipharmic, *remedy*, 662.
Alfresco, *exterior*, 220.
air, 338.
Algebra, *numeration*, 85.
Algorism, *numeration*, 85.
*Alguazil (Sp.), *jurisprudence*, 965.
*Alias (L.), *misnomer*, 565.
*Alibi (L.), *absence*, 187.
Alien, *irrelevant*, 10.
foreign, 57.
Alienate, *transfer*, 783.
estrange, 889.
set against, 898.
Alienation (mental), *insanity*, 503.
*Alieni appetens (L.), *desire*, 865.
jealousy, 920.
Alight, *descend*, 306.
stop, 265.
arrive, 292.
light, 420.
Alike, *similarity*, 17.
Aliment, *food*, 298, 707.
materials, 635.
Alimentation, *aid*, 707.
Alimony, *dowry*, 810.
provision, 803.
*A l'improviste (Fr.), *inexpectation*, [508.
Aline, *arrange*, 60.
Aliquot, *part*, 51.
Alive, *living*, 359.
attentive, 457.
active, 682.
All, *whole*, 50.
complete, 52.
Allay, *moderate*, 174.
repress excitement, 826.
relieve, 834.
Allege, *evidence*, 467.
assert, 535.
plea, 617.
Allegiance, *duty*, 743, 926.
Allegory, *comparison*, 464, 521.
*Allegresse (Fr.), *cheerfulness*, 836.
*Allegretto (It.), *music*, 415.
*Allegro (It.), *cheerfulness*, 836.
music, 415.
Allemande, *dance*, 840.
Alleviate, *moderate*, 174.
allay, 826.
Alleviate, *relieve*, 834.
Alley, *passage*, 260.
way, 627.
court, 189.
All hands, *generality*, 78.
Alliance, *relation*, 9.
kindred, 11.
physical co-operation, 178.
voluntary co-operation, 709.
union, 714.
Alligation, *junction*, 43.
All-inclusive, *generality*, 78.
Alliteration, *similarity*, 17.
Allocation, *arrangement*, 60.
Allocution, *allocution*, 586.
Allodium, *property*, 780.
Allot, *arrange*, 60.
distribute, 786.
Allotropy, *variation*, 16.
multiformity, 81.
Allow, *permit*, 760.
assent, 488.
concede, 467.
give, 784.
discount, 813.
allot, 786.
pay, 809.
Allowable, *dueness*, 924.
Allowance, *qualification*, 469.
forgiveness, 918.
Alloy, *mixture*, 41.
debase, 65.
All-pervading, *generality*, 78.
Allude, *mean*, 516.
suggest, 514.
refer to, 521.
hint, 527.
Allure, *motive*, 615.
Allurement, *desire*, 865.
Allusion, *meaning*, 516.
reference, 521.
Allusive, *relation*, 9.
Alluvial, *plain*, 344.
Alluvium, *deposit*, 40.
soil, 653.
Ally, *auxiliary*, 711.
Alma Mater, *school*, 542.
Almanac, *chronometry*, 114.
record, 551.
Almighty (the), *deity*, 976.
Almoner, *clergy*, 996.
Almost, *nearly*, 32.
Alms, *giving*, 784.
Aloft, *height*, 206.
Alomancy, *prediction*, 511.
Alone, *unity*, 87.
Along, *length*, 200.
Along with, *together*, 88.
by means of, 631.

Alongside, *near*, 197.
parallel, 216.
side by side, 236.
Aloud, *loudness*, 404.
*A l'outrance (Fr.), *completeness*, 52.
*Alpha (Gr.), *beginning*, 66.
Alphabet, *letter*, 561.
Alps, *height*, 206.
Already, *antecedently*, 116.
even now, 118.
past time, 122.
Also, *addition*, 37.
accompaniment, 88.
Altar, *marriage*, 903.
church, 1000.
Alter, *vary*, 20.
change, 140.
Alterable, *mutability*, 149.
Altercation, *discord*, 713.
*Alter ego (L.), *identity*, 13.
similarity, 17.
friend, 890.
Alternate, *reciprocal*, 12.
periodic, 63, 138.
discontinuous, 70.
Alternative, *plan*, 626.
choice, 609.
Although, *counteraction*, 179.
opposition, 708.
counterevidence, 468.
Altitude, *height*, 206.
Altogether, *collectively*, 50.
entirely, 31.
*Alto rilievo (It.), *convexity*, 250.
sculpture, 557.
Altruism, *disinterestedness*, 942.
Alveolus, *concavity*, 252.
Always, *perpetuity*, 112.
uniformity, 16.
conformity, 82.
Amalgam, *mixture*, 41.
compound, 48.
Amanuensis, *writing*, 590.
Amaranthine, *perpetual*, 112.
Amass, *whole*, 50.
to collect, 72.
*Amateur (Fr.), *desire*, 865.
taste, 850.
Amateurish, *inferior*, 34.
Amatory, *love*, 897.
Amaurosis, *blindness*, 442.
Amaze, *wonder*, 870.
Amazingly, *greatness*, 31.
Amazon, *warrior*, 726.
courage, 861.
*Ambages (L.), *deviation*, 279.
Ambassador, *messenger*, 534.
Amber, *yellowness*, 436.
Ambidexter, *clever*, 678.
Ambidexter, *fickle*, 607.
right and left, 238.
Ambient, *circumscription*, 227.
Ambiguous, *uncertain*, 475, 520.
obscure, 571.
unintelligible, 519.
Ambit, *outline*, 229.
Ambition, *desire*, 865.
intention, 620.
Amble, *pace*, 266.
fleet, 274.
Ambo, *pulpit*, 542, 1000.
Ambrosial, *savouriness*, 394.
Ambulance, *remedy*, 662.
Ambulation, *journey*, 266.
Ambuscade, *ambush*, 530.
Ambush, *ambush*, 530.
*Ame damnée (Fr.), *servant*, 746.
flatterer, 935.
bad man, 949.
Ameer, *master*, 745.
Ameliorate, *improvement*, 658.
Amen, *assent*, 488.
Amenable, *duty*, 926.
Amend, *improvement*, 658.
*Amende honorable (Fr.), *atonement*, 952.
Amends, *compensation*, 30.
reward, 973.
atonement, 952.
Amenity, *courtesy*, 894.
Amerce, *penalty*, 974.
*A merveille (Fr.), *success*, 731.
Amethyst, *purple*, 437.
Amiable, *lovable*, 897.
benevolent, 906.
Amicable, *friendly*, 888.
assisting, 707.
*Amicus curiæ (L.), *friend*, 890.
Amida, *revelation*, 986.
Amidst, *interjacent*, 228.
middle, 68.
mixture, 41.
Amiss, *wrong*, 619.
inexpedient, 647.
Amity, *friendship*, 888.
concord, 714.
peace, 721.
Ammunition, *materials*, 635.
warlike, 727.
Amnesia, *oblivion*, 506.
Amnesty, *forgiveness*, 918.
pacification, 723.
Among, *interjacence*, 228.
mixture, 41.
Amorist, *love*, 897.
*Amoroso (It.), *love*, 897.
Amorous, *love*, 897.
Amorphous, *formless*, 241.

Amorphous, *irregular*, 83.
Amount, *quantity*, 25.
whole, 50.
numeration, 85.
sum of money, 800.
Amour, *love*, 897.
*Amour-propre (Fr.), *vanity*, 880.
Amphibious, *unconformity*, 83.
Amphibology, *equivocality*, 520.
Amphigouri, *ridiculous*, 853.
absurdity, 497.
Amphitheatre, *arena*, 728.
prospect, 441.
school, 542.
Amphitryon, *friend*, 890.
Ample, *much*, 31.
copious, 639.
large, 192.
broad, 202.
spacious, 181.
Amplify, *enlarge*, 35.
dilate, 194.
exaggerate, 549.
Amplitude, *degree*, 26.
size, 192.
breadth, 202.
Amputate, *subduction*, 38.
Amuck, run, *violence*, 173.
insanity, 503.
excitability, 825.
Amulet, *spell*, 993.
Amuse, *amusement*, 840.
Amylaceous, *semiliquidity*, 352.
An (*if*), 514.
Ana, *description*, 594.
Anachronism, *anachronism*, 115.
Anacoluthon, *discontinuity*, 70.
Anacreontic, *poetry*, 597.
Anæmia, *achromatism*, 429.
feebleness, 575.
Anæsthesia, *insensibility*, 376, 381, 823.
Anaglyph, *sculpture*, 557.
Anagogic, *concealment*, 528.
Anagram, *letter*, 561.
puzzle, 533, 842.
*Analecta (L.), *description*, 594.
Analeptic, *remedy*, 662.
Analogy, *relation*, 9.
similarity, 17.
comparison, 464.
Analysis, *decomposition*, 49.
arrangement, 60.
algebra, 85.
inquiry, 461.
Anamnesis, *memory*, 505.
Anamorphosis, *optical*, 443.
misrepresentation, 555.
Ananias, *deceiver*, 548.
Anarchy, *disorder*, 59.
social, 738.
Anastomosis, *junction*, 43.
crossing, 219.
Anastrophe, *inversion*, 218.
Anathema, *malediction*, 908.
Anatomy, *dissection*, 44.
skeleton, 329.
inquiry, 461.
Ancestor, *paternity*, 166.
Anchor, *safeguard*, 666.
hope, 858.
Anchorage, *roadstead*, 189, 265.
Anchorite, *asceticism*, 955.
Anchylosis, *immutability*, 150.
Ancient, *oldness*, 124.
Ancillary, *aid*, 707.
And, *addition*, 37.
*Andante (It.), *music*, 415.
*Andantino (It.), *music*, 415.
Androgynous, *unconformity*, 83.
Anecdotage, *loquacity*, 584.
Anecdote, *description*, 594.
Anent, *relation*, 9.
Anemometer, *wind*, 349.
Aneroid, *measurement*, 466.
Anew, *newness*, 123.
Anfractuosity, *angle*, 244.
convolution, 248.
Angel, *supernatural being*, 977.
object of love, 948.
Angelic, *virtue*, 944.
Anger, *resentment*, 900.
*Angina (L.), *pain*, 828.
Angle, *angularity*, 244.
Angle, to, *pursuit*, 622.
Anguilline, *narrow*, 203.
serpentine, 248.
Anguish, *physical*, 378.
moral, 828.
Angular, *angularity*, 244.
uncivil, 895.
Anhelation, *fatigue*, 688.
Anhydrous, *dryness*, 340.
Anility, *age*, 128.
Animadvert, *reprehend*, 932.
consider, 451.
Animal, *animal*, 366.
Animal cries, *ululation*, 412.
Animalcule, *minute*, 193.
Animalism, *sensuality*, 954.
Animality, *animality*, 364.
Animate, *excite*, 824.
stimulate, 615.
Animation, *life*, 359.
animality, 364.
excitation, 824.
Animosity, *enmity*, 889.
hatred, 898.

Animosity, *anger*, 900.
*Animus (L.), *will*, 600.
intention, 620.
Annalist, *recorder*, 114, 553.
Annals, *record*, 551.
history, 114.
account, 551.
Anneal, *harden*, 323.
Annex, *add*, 37.
join, 43.
Annihilate, *extinguish*, 2.
destroy, 162.
Anniversary, *periodicity*, 138.
Anno Domini, *period*, 108.
Annotation, *note*, 550.
glossary, 522.
Announce, *inform*, 527.
publish, 531.
predict, 511.
assert, 535.
Announcement, *programme*, 510.
Annoy, *pain*, 830.
Annoyance, *pain*, 828.
evil, 619.
badness, 649.
Annual, *year*, 108.
periodic, 138.
Annuity, *wealth*, 803, 810.
Annul, *abrogation*, 756.
Annular, *circularity*, 247.
Annulet, *circularity*, 247.
Annunciate, *inform*, 527.
publish, 531.
*Annus mirabilis (L.), *period*, 108.
Anodyne, *remedy*, 174, 662, 834.
Anoint, *coat*, 222.
oil, 355.
Anointed, *deity*, 976.
Anomalistic, *unconformity*, 83.
Anomaly, *irregularity*, 83.
disorder, 59.
Anon, *ere long*, 132.
shortly, 111.
Anonymous, *misnomer*, 565.
Another, *difference*, 15.
Answer, *to an inquiry*, 462.
reply, 468, 587.
to succeed, 731.
Answerable, *duty*, 926.
Answer for, *promise*, 768.
Answer to, *correspond*, 9.
Ant, *worker*, 690.
Antæus, *strength*, 159.
Antagonism, *difference*, 14.
voluntary, 708.
physical, 179.
Antagonist, *opponent*, 710.
Antecedence, *in order*, 62.
in time, 116.
Antecedent, *in order*, 64.
in time, 116.
Antechamber, *room*, 191.
Antedate, *anachronism*, 115.
Antediluvian, *oldness*, 124, 128.
priority, 116.
Antelope, *velocity*, 274.
Antemundane, *oldness*, 124.
Antenna, *touch*, 379.
Antepenultimate, *end*, 67.
Anterior, *in order*, 62.
in time, 116.
in place, 234.
Anteroom, *room*, 191.
Anthem, *worship*, 990.
Anthology, *poem*, 597.
collection, 596.
Anthropology, *mankind*, 372.
Anthropomorphic, *mankind*, 372.
Anthropophagi, *evil-doer*, 913.
Antic, *ridicule*, 856.
Antichristian, *irreligion*, 988.
Anticipate, *early*, 132.
future, 121.
anachronism, 115.
expect, 507.
foresee, 510.
prepare, 673.
priority, 116.
Anticlimax, *depth*, 208.
bathos, 856.
Anticyclone, *rotation*, 312.
Antidote, *remedy*, 662.
Antilogarithm, *number*, 84.
Antinomy, *illegality*, 964.
Antinous, *beauty*, 845.
Antiparallel, *obliquity*, 217.
Antiphon, *music*, 415.
answer, 462.
worship, 990.
Antiphrasis, *misnomer*, 565.
Antipodes, *distance*, 196.
antiposition, 237.
difference, 14.
depth, 208.
Antiposition, *antiposition*, 237.
Antiquated, *vulgarity*, 851.
Antique, *oldness*, 124.
Antiseptic, *remedy*, 662.
Antithesis, *contrast*, 14.
style, 574.
Antitoxin, *remedy*, 662.
Antitype, *prototype*, 22.
Antonomasia, *substitution*, 147.
Anvil, *support*, 215.
(on the), *plan*, 626.
preparing, 673.
Anxiety, *pain*, 828.
fear, 860.

Anxiety, *desire*, 865.
Aorist, *indefinite time*, 119.
*A outrance (Fr.), *violently*, 31.
contention, 720.
Apace, *swift*, 274.
short time, 111.
early, 132.
*Apache (Fr.), *ruffian*, 913, 949.
Apanage, *adjunct*, 39.
Apart, *distance*, 196.
singleness, 87.
difference, 15.
Apartment, *room*, 191.
Apartments, *abode*, 189.
Apathy, *physical*, 376.
moral, 823.
Ape, *imitation*, 19.
Apelles, *artist*, 559.
*Aperçu (Fr.), *compendium*, 596.
*A perte de vue (Fr.), *distance*, 196.
Aperture, *opening*, 260.
*A peu près (Fr.), *smallness*, 32.
nearness, 197.
Apex, *summit*, 210.
Aphasia, *aphony*, 581.
Aphelion, *distance*, 196.
Aphony, *aphony*, 581.
Aphorism, *maxim*, 496.
*A piacere (It.), *music*, 415.
Apicius, *gluttony*, 957.
Apiece, *disjunction*, 44.
particularity, 79.
Aplomb, *vertical*, 212.
intelligence, 498.
Apocalypse, *revelation*, 985.
Apocryphal, *uncertain*, 475.
false, 544.
Apodictic, *demonstration*, 478.
Apolaustic, *self-indulgent*, 943.
Apollo, *music*, 415.
beauty, 845.
Apologue, *description*, 521, 594.
Apology, *penitence*, 950.
vindication, 937.
atonement, 952.
Apophthegm, *maxim*, 496.
Apoplexy, *weakness*, 160.
Aposiopesis, *taciturnity*, 585.
Apostasy, *palinode*, 607.
dishonour, 940.
heterodoxy, 984.
Apostate, *knave*, 941.
Apostatise, *tergiversation*, 607.
Apostle, *teacher*, 540.
Apostolic, *revelation*, 985.
Apostrophe, *appeal*, 765.
address, 586, 589.
Apotheosis, *deification*, 981, 991.
Appal, *fear*, 860.
Appalling, *painfulness*, 830.
Appanage, *property*, 780.
Apparatus, *instrument*, 633.
Apparel, *vestment*, 225.
Apparent, *visible*, 446.
manifest, 525.
Apparition, *ghost*, 980.
appearance, 448.
Appeal, *request*, 765.
address, 586.
Appear, *come into being*, 1, 448.
come to light, 525.
come into view, 446.
Appearance, *sight*, 448
probability, 472.
Appear for, *deputy*, 759.
Appease, *physically*, 174.
morally, 826.
Appellant, *plaintiff*, 924, 967.
Appellation, *nomenclature*, 564.
Append, *addition*, 37.
sequence, 63.
Appendage, *adjunct*, 39.
Appendix, *sequel*, 65.
Apperception, *knowledge*, 490.
Appertain, *belong*, 777.
related to, 9.
right, 922.
inclusion, 76.
Appetence, *desire*, 865.
Appetiser, *whet*, 298, 615.
Appetite, *desire*, 865.
Applaud, *approbation*, 931.
Apple-green, *greenness*, 435.
Apple of discord, *discord*, 713.
Appliances, *means*, 632.
Applicable, *to use*, 644.
expedient, 646.
relative, 23.
Applicant, *petitioner*, 767.
Application, *use*, 677.
request, 765.
study, 457.
*Appoggiatura (It.), *music*, 415.
Appoint, *commission*, 755.
Appointment, *salary*, 809.
interview, 892.
Apportion, *allot*, 786.
arrange, 60.
portion, 51.
Apportionment, *dispersion*, 73.
Apposite, *agreeing*, 23.
relative, 9.
Apposition, *agreement*, 23.
closeness, 199.
Appraise, *value*, 812.
estimate, 466.
Appreciate, *measure*, 466.
taste, 850.

Appreciate, *judge*, 480.
approve, 931.
Apprehend, *know*, 490.
believe, 484.
fear, 860.
seize, 969.
Apprentice, *learner*, 541.
Apprenticeship, *learning*, 539.
training, 673.
Apprise, *information*, 527.
Approach, *move*, 286.
nearness, 197.
path, 627.
of time, 121.
Approbation, *approbation*, 931.
Appropinquation, *approach*, 197, 286,
Appropriate, *fit*, 23, 646.
to assign, 786.
to take, 789.
to steal, 791.
Appropriation, *stealing*, 791.
Approve, *commend*, 931.
corroborate, 467.
assent, 488.
Approximate, *approach*, 286.
nearness, 197.
in mathematics, 85.
resemble, 17.
related to, 9.
Appulse, *convergence*, 286, 290.
collision, 276.
Appurtenance, *part*, 51.
component, 56.
Apricot, *colour*, 439.
April-fool, *fool*, 501.
*A priori (L.), *reasoning*, 476.
Apron, *dress*, 225.
Apropos, *relation*, 9.
expedience, 646.
occasion, 134.
Apt, *consonant*, 23.
clever, 698.
docile, 539.
willing, 602.
expedient, 646.
tendency, 176.
Aptitude, *intelligence*, 498.
Aquarium, *cicuration*, 370.
collection, 636.
Aquatic, *water*, 337.
Aquatint, *engraving*, 558.
Aqueduct, *conduit*, 350.
Aqueous, *water*, 337.
Aquiline, *angularity*, 244.
Arabesque, *ornament*, 847.
Arable, *agriculture*, 371.
Aræometer, *density*, 321.
measure, 466.
Arbiter, *judge*, 480, 967.
Arbiter, *adviser*, 695.
*Arbiter elegantiarum (L.), *taste*, 850.
Arbitrament, *sentence*, 969.
judgment, 480.
choice, 609.
Arbitrary, *without law*, 964.
irregular, 83.
without relation, 10.
Arbitrate, *mediate*, 724, 969.
judge, 480.
Arbor, *support*, 215.
Arborescence, *branching*, 205, 242, 256.
Arboretum, *agriculture*, 371.
Arboriculture, *agriculture*, 371.
Arbour, *abode*, 189.
Arc, *curvature*, 245.
Arc lamp, *light*, 423.
Arcade, *arch*, 245.
passage, 189.
*Arcades ambo (L.), *similarity*, 17.
friend, 890.
Arcadian, *delightful*, 829.
Arcanum, *secret*, 533.
Arch, *curve*, 245.
great, 31.
cunning, 702.
roguish, 842.
greatness, 31.
Archaic, *oldness*, 124.
Archaism, *inelegance*, 579.
Archæology, *preterition*, 122.
Archangel, *angel*, 977.
Archbishop, *clergy*, 996.
Archdeacon, *clergy*, 996.
Archduke, *master*, 745.
Archetype, *prototype*, 22.
Arch-fiend, *Satan*, 978.
Archimage, *sorcerer*, 994.
Archimandrite, *clergy*, 996.
Archipelago, *sea*, 341.
Architect, *constructor*, 164.
agent, 690.
Architecture, *construction*, 161.
fabric, 329.
Architrave, *summit*, 210.
Archive, *record*, 551.
Archness, *cunning*, 702.
cleverness, 498.
intelligence, 450.
Arch-traitor, *knave*, 941.
Arctic, *polar*, 237.
cold, 383.
Arcuation, *curvature*, 245.
Ardent, *fiery*, 382.
feeling, 515, 821, 888.
expectant, 507.
Arduous, *difficulty*, 704.

Area, *region*, 181.
*A rebours (Fr.), *regression*, 283.
*A reculons (Fr.), *regression*, 283.
Arefaction, *dryness*, 340.
Arena, *field*, 181, 728.
workshop, 691.
Arenaceous, *pulverulence*, 330.
Areopagus, *council*, 696.
Areolar, *crossing*, 219.
*Arête (Fr.), *height*, 206.
sharpness, 253.
Argent, *whiteness*, 430.
Argillaceous, *softness*, 324.
Argosy, *ship*, 273.
Argot, *language*, 560.
Argue, *reason*, 476.
evidence, 467.
indicate, 550.
Argument, *evidence*, 467.
topic, 454.
meaning, 516.
compendium, 596.
*Argumentum ad hominem (L.), *speciality*, 79.
accusation, 938.
*Argumentum ad crumenam (L.), *money*, 800.
*Argumentum ad misericordiam (L.), *pity*, 914.
*Argumentum ad verecundiam (L.), *probity*, 939.
*Argumentum baculinum (L.), *compulsion*, 744.
Argus-eyed, *sight*, 441.
vigilant, 459.
Argute, *wisdom*, 498.
Aria, *music*, 415.
Arid, *dryness*, 340.
Ariel, *messenger*, 534.
swift, 274.
courier, 268.
spirit, 979.
Arietta, *music*, 415.
Aright, *goodness*, 618, 648.
Arise, *begin*, 66.
mount, 305.
appear, 446.
happen, 151.
proceed from, 154.
exist, 1.
Aristarchus, *taste*, 850.
Aristocracy, *power*, 737.
nobility, 875.
Arithmancy, *prediction*, 511.
Arithmetic, *numeration*, 85.
Ark, *asylum*, 666.
Arm, *instrument*, 266, 633.
part, 51.
power, 157.
Arm, *to provide*, 637.
to prepare, 673.
Armada, *ship*, 273.
Armageddon, *contention*, 720.
Armament, *arms*, 727.
Armature, *arms*, 727.
Armiger, *nobility*, 875.
Armistice, *pacification*, 723.
Armless, *impotence*, 158.
Armlet, *lake*, 343.
Armorial, *indication*, 550.
Armour, *arms*, 727.
Armoury, *store*, 636.
Arms, *blazon*, 550.
scutcheon, 877.
war, 722.
weapon, 727.
See Arm.
Arm's length, *distance*, 196.
Army, *troops*, 726.
multitude, 102.
collection, 72.
Aroma, *fragrance*, 400.
Around, *circumjacent*, 227.
Arouse, *motive*, 615.
Arpeggio, *music*, 415.
Arquebus, *arms*, 727.
Arraign, *accuse*, 938.
indict, 969.
Arrange, *order*, 60.
plan, 626.
to prepare, 673.
to settle, 723.
Arrangement, *order*, 58.
music, 415.
Arrant, *greatness*, 31.
Array, *order*, 58.
series, 69.
dress, 225.
prepare, 673.
beauty, 845.
multitude, 102.
assemblage, 72.
Arrears, *debt*, 806.
Arrest, *stop*, 265.
imprison, 751.
commit, 969.
*Arrière-pensée (Fr.), *plan*, 626.
Arrive, *reach*, 292.
happen, 151.
complete, 729.
Arrogant, *insolent*, 885.
severe, 739.
proud, 878.
Arrogate, *assume*, 885.
claim, 922.
*Arrondissement (Fr.), *region*, 181.
Arrow, *swift*, 274.
missile, 284.

Arrow, *arms*, 727.
Arrow-headed, *angular*, 244.
Arrowy, *sharp*, 253.
Arsenal, *store*, 636.
military, 727.
Arson, *calefaction*, 384.
Art, *skill*, 698.
cunning, 702.
deception, 545.
representation, 554.
Arterialise, *to aerate*, 338.
Artery, *conduit*, 350.
Artesian well, *conduit*, 348.
Artful, *cunning*, 702.
deceitful, 544.
Article, *thing*, 3.
goods, 798.
part, 51.
conditions, 770.
dissertation, 595.
Articles, *belief*, 484, 983.
Articulation, *speech*, 580.
junction, 43.
Artifice, *cunning*, 702.
plan, 626.
deception, 545.
Artificer, *agent*, 690.
Artificial, *cunning*, 702.
fictitious, 544.
style, 579.
Artillery, *arms*, 727.
corps of, 726.
explosion, 404.
Artisan, *agent*, 690.
Artist, *contriver*, 626.
painter, etc., 559.
agent, 690.
*Artiste (Fr.), *the drama*, 599.
Artistic, *skilful*, 698.
beautiful, 845.
Artless, *natural*, 703.
veracious, 543.
As, *motive*, 615.
Ascend, *ascent*, 305.
Ascendancy, *power*, 157, 175.
success, 731.
Ascent, *rise*, 305.
acclivity, 217.
glory, 873.
Ascertain, *judgment*, 480.
Asceticism, *asceticism*, 955.
Ascribe, *attribution*, 155.
Ashamed, *shame*, 874.
modest, 881.
Ash colour, *grey*, 432.
Ashes, *residue*, 40.
corpse, 362.
Ashore, *land*, 342.
Ashy, *colourless*, 429.
Aside, *laterally*, 236.
privately, 528.
soliloquy, 589.
Aside (to put), *relinquish*, 624.
disuse, 678.
Asinine, *imbecile*, 499.
Ask, *inquire*, 461.
request, 765.
as price, 812.
supplicate, 990.
Askance, *obliquity*, 217.
doubt, 485.
Askew, *oblique*, 217.
distorted, 243.
Aslant, *obliquity*, 217.
Asleep, *inactivity*, 683.
Aslope, *obliquity*, 217.
Aspect, *appearance*, 448.
state, 7.
feature, 5.
situation, 183.
relation, 9.
of thought, 453.
Asperge, *sprinkle*, 337.
Asperity, *roughness*, 256.
tartness, 895.
anger, 900.
Asperse, *detraction*, 934.
Asphyxiate, *killing*, 361.
Aspirate, *voice*, 580.
Aspire, *rise*, 305.
desire, 865.
project, 620.
Ass, *beast of burden*, 271.
fool, 501.
Assagai, *arms*, 727.
Assail, *attack*, 716.
plain, 830.
Assailant, *opponent*, 710.
attacker, 716, 726.
Assassinate, *killing*, 361.
Assault, *attack*, 716.
Assay, *experiment*, 463.
Assemble, *assemblage*, 72.
Assembly-room, *sociality*, 892.
Assent, *agree*, 488.
consent, 762.
Assert, *affirm*, 535.
claim as a right, 924.
Assess, *measure*, 466.
judge, 480.
price, 812.
Assessor, *adviser*, 695.
Assets, *property*, 780.
money, 800.
Asseverate, *affirm*, 535.
Assiduous, *activity*, 682.
Assign, *attribute*, 155.
give, 784.

Assign, *allot*, 786.
duty, 926.
*Assignat (Fr.), *money*, 800.
Assignation, *sociality*, 892.
Assignment, *allotment*, 786.
commission, 755.
Assimilate, *resemble*, 17, 144.
imitate, 19.
agree, 23.
Assist, *aid*, 707.
benefit, 906.
Assistant, *auxiliary*, 711.
Assize, *measure*, 466.
tribunal, 966.
Associate, *accompany*, 88.
unite, 43.
mixture, 41.
assemble, 72.
friend, 890.
society, 892.
Association, *relation*, 9.
Assoil, *free*, 750.
acquit, 970.
Assonance, *similarity*, 17.
poetry, 597.
Assort, *arrange*, 60.
Assortment, *class*, 75.
collection, 72.
Assuage, *physically*, 174.
morally, 826.
relieve, 834.
Assume, *suppose*, 514.
evidence, 467.
hope, 858.
right, 924.
insolence, 739, 885.
pride, 878.
falsehood, 544.
Assumption, *qualification*, 469.
severity, 739.
Assurance, *assertion*, 535.
promise, 768.
certainty, 474.
belief, 484.
hope, 858.
insolence, 885.
Assuredly, *positively*, 31.
safety, 664.
Asterisk, *indication*, 550.
Astern, *rear*, 235.
Asteroid, *world*, 318.
Asteroth, *deity*, 979.
Asthenia, *weakness*, 160.
Astigmatism, *dim-sightedness*, 443.
Astonish, *wonder*, 870.
Astonishing, *great*, 31.
Astound, *surprise*, 870.
excite, 824.
Astræa, *right*, 922.
Astral, *world*, 318.
immaterial, 317.
Astray, *deviation*, 279.
Astriction, *junction*, 43.
Astride, *support*, 215.
Astringent, *contraction*, 195.
Astrology, *prediction*, 511.
Astronomy, *world*, 318.
Astrophysics, *world*, 318.
Astute, *wisdom*, 498.
Asunder, *separate*, 44.
distant, 196.
disjunction, 44.
Asylum, *retreat*, 666.
hospital, 662.
defence, 717.
Asymmetry, *disorder*, 59, 243.
Asymptote, *convergence*, 290.
Ataraxia, *insensibility*, 823.
*A tâtons (Fr.), *experiment*, 463.
*Atelier (Fr.), *workshop*, 691.
Athanor, *furnace*, 386.
Atheism, *irreligion*, 988.
Athirst, *desire*, 865.
Athletic, *strength*, 159.
Athletics, *training*, 673.
At-home, *sociality*, 892.
Athwart, *oblique*, 217.
crossing, 219.
opposing, 708.
Atlantes, *support*, 215.
Atlantis, *visionary*, 515.
Atlas, *support*, 215.
strength, 159.
maps, 554.
Atmosphere, *air*, 338.
circumambience, 227.
Atoll, *island*, 346.
Atom, *small in degree*, 32.
in size, 193.
Atomiser, *spray*, 353, 337.
Atonality, *melody*, 413.
At once, *transientness*, 111.
Atone, *atonement*, 952.
Atonement, *religious*, 976.
reward, 973.
Atony, *weakness*, 160.
*A tort et à travers (Fr.), *obstinacy*, 606.
Atrabilious, *dejection*, 837.
Atrocious, *vice*, 945.
guilt, 947.
Atrophy, *shrinking*, 195.
disease, 655.
Attach, *join*, 43.
love, 897.
legal, 969.
*Attaché (Fr.), *servant*, 746.
consignee, 758.

Attachment, *see* Attach.
Attack, *attack*, 716.
Attain, *arrive*, 292.
succeed, 731.
Attainable, *possible*, 470.
easy, 705.
Attainder, *condemnation*, 971.
Attainment, *learning*, 539.
Attar, *fragrance*, 400.
Attemper, *mix*, 41.
moderate, 174.
Attempt, *undertaking*, 676.
Attend, *accompany*, 88.
follow, 281.
apply the mind, 457.
be present, 186.
Attendant, *servant*, 746.
Attention, *attention*, 451, 457.
Attentions, *courtesy*, 894.
courtship, 902.
kindness, 906.
Attenuate, *lessen*, 36.
contract, 195.
narrow, 203.
Attest, *bear testimony*, 467.
indicate, 550.
adjure, 768.
Attestation, *record*, 551.
Attic, *garret*, 191.
high, 206.
wit, 842.
taste, 850.
Atticism, *wit*, 842.
Attila, *bane*, 663.
evil-doer, 913.
Attire, *vestment*, 225.
Attitude, *posture*, 183, 240.
circumstance, 8.
Attitudinise, *affectation*, 855.
Attorney, *consignee*, 758, 769.
in law, 968.
Attract, *bring towards*, 289.
please, 829.
allure, 865.
Attractive, *beautiful*, 845.
pleasing, 829.
lovely, 897.
Attrahent, *attraction*, 288.
Attribute, *power*, 157.
Attribution, *attribution*, 155.
Attrition, *friction*, 331.
*Attroupement (Fr.), *assemblage*, 72.
Attune, *music*, 415.
prepare, 673.
Aubade, *music*, 415.
Auburn, *brown*, 433.
*Au courant, (Fr.), *knowledge*, 490.
Auction, *sale*, 796.
Auctorial, *book*, 593.
Audacity, *courage*, 861.
insolence, 863, 885.
*Au désespoir (Fr.), *pain*, 828.
*Audi alteram partem (L.), *evidence*, 468.
right, 922.
Audible, *sound*, 402.
Audience, *hearing*, 418.
conversation, 588.
Audiphone, *hearing*, 418.
Audit, *accounts*, 811.
numeration, 85.
Audition, *hearing*, 418.
Auditor, *hearer*, 418.
accounts, 811.
Auditory, *hearing*, 418.
*Au fait (Fr.), *knowledge*, 490.
*Au fond (Fr.), *truth*, 494.
Auger, *perforation*, 262.
Aught, *part*, 51.
whole, 50.
Augment, *to increase*, 35.
thing added, 39.
Augmentation, *expansion*, 194.
Augur, *predict*, 507, 511.
soothsayer, 513.
Augury, *prediction*, 511, 512.
August, *repute*, 873.
Augustine, *clergy*, 996.
*Au pied de la lettre (Fr.), *truth*, 494.
meaning, 516.
Aura, *touch*, 380.
emanation, 295.
Aureate, *yellowness*, 436.
Aureolin, *orange*, 439.
*Au revoir (Fr.), *departure*, 292.
Auricular, *hearing*, 418.
Aurora, *light*, 420.
dawn, 125.
Auroral, *rosy*, 434.
Auscultation, *hearing*, 418.
Auspices, *patronage*, 175, 707.
Auspicious, *hopeful*, 858.
prosperous, 734.
expedient, 646.
opportune, 134.
Auster, *wind*, 349.
Austere, *harsh taste*, 395.
severe, 739.
discourteous, 895.
ascetic, 955.
Austromancy, *prediction*, 511.
Authentic, *truth*, 494.
Authenticate, *record*, 551.
Author, *producer*, 164.
writer, 590.
Authoritative, *certain*, 474.
peremptory, 741.

Authority, *power*, 737.
command, 741.
right, 924.
permission, 760.
testimony, 467.
sign, 500.
Autobiography, *description*, 594.
Autocar, *vehicle*, 272.
Autochthonous, *inhabitant*, 188.
Autocracy, *severity*, 739.
Autocrat, *master*, 745.
*Auto da fé (Sp.), *burning*, 384.
execution, 972.
Autograph, *warranty*, 467.
signature, 550.
writing, 590.
Autolycus, *merchant*, 797.
Automatic, *mechanical*, 601.
insensible, 823.
Autonomy, *freedom*, 748.
Autopsy, *vision*, 441.
Autotype, *imitation*, 19.
engraving, 558.
Auxiliary, *aid*, 707.
helper, 711.
*Aux abois (Fr.), *death*, 360.
danger, 665.
*Aux aguets (Fr.), *care*, 459.
Avail, *use*, 677.
utility, 644.
Avalanche, *fall*, 306.
debâcle, 348.
Avant-courier, *pioneer*, 673.
precursor, 64.
*Avant-propos (Fr.), *precursor*, 64.
Avarice, *parsimony*, 819.
Avast, *quiescence*, 265.
Avaunt, *disappear*, 449.
depart, 293.
repulse, 289.
Avenge, *revenge*, 919.
Avenue, *method*, 627.
Aver, *affirmation*, 535.
Average, *mean*, 29.
ordinary, 82.
Avernus, *hell*, 982.
Averse, *unwilling*, 603.
repugnant, 616.
Aversion, *dislike*, 867.
hate, 898.
Avert, *hindrance*, 706.
Aviary, *collection*, 370, 636.
Aviation, *locomotion*, 267.
Avidity, *desire*, 865.
avarice, 819.
Avifauna, *animals*, 366.
Avocation, *business*, 625.
Avocation, *diversion*, 840.
Avoid, *shun*, 623, 867.
*A volonté (Fr.), *will*, 600.
Avouch, *affirmation*, 535.
Avow, *assert*, 535.
assent, 488.
disclose, 529.
Avulsion, *separation*, 44.
extraction, 301.
Await, *future*, 121.
impend, 152.
Awake, *excite*, 824.
incite, 615.
active, 682.
attentive, 457.
careful, 459.
Award, *lawsuit*, 969.
decision, 609.
Aware, *knowledge*, 490.
Away, *absence*, 187.
Awe, *wonder*, 870.
fear, 860.
Aweless, *courage*, 861.
Awe-struck, *fear*, 860.
Awful, *great*, 31.
fearful, 860.
Awhile, *transientness*, 111.
Awkward, *unskilful*, 699.
vulgar, 851.
ridiculous, 853.
difficult, 704.
Awl, *perforator*, 262.
Awn, *bristle*, 253.
Awning, *tent*, 222.
dwelling, 189.
height, 210.
Awry, *oblique*, 217.
distorted, 243.
Axe, *edge tool*, 253.
weapon, 727.
for beheading, 975.
Axinomancy, *prediction*, 511.
Axiom, *maxim*, 496.
Axiomatic, *truth*, 494.
demonstrable, 469, 478.
Axis, *rotation*, 312.
length, 200.
support, 215.
centre, 223.
Ay, *yes*, 488.
affirmation, 535.
Aye, *ever*, 112.
Azimuth, *direction*, 278.
obliquity, 217.
Azoic, *lifeless*, 360.
Azure, *blueness*, 438.
Azygous, *unity*, 87.

B

Baa, *animal sound*, 412.
Baal, *divinity*, 979.
idol, 986.
Babble, *talk*, 584.
faint sound, 405.
Babe, *infant*, 129.
novice, 701.
Babel, *confusion*, 59.
discord, 414.
Baboon, *ugliness*, 846.
Baby, *fool*, 501.
Babyhood, *youth*, 127.
Babyish, *folly*, 499.
Bacca, *tobacco*, 298A.
Bacchanals, *drunkenness*, 959.
Bacchus, *drunkenness*, 959.
Bachelor, *celibacy*, 904.
Bacillus, *bane*, 663.
Back, *rear*, 235.
convexity, 250.
to recede, 283.
to aid, 707.
Back down, *revoke*, 607.
Back out, *revoke*, 607.
relinquish, 624.
Backbite, *traduce*, 932.
detract, 934.
Backbiter, *detractor*, 936.
Backbone, *frame*, 215.
interior, 221.
strength, 159.
decision, 604.
intrinsic, 5.
Back-friend, *opponent*, 710.
enemy, 891.
Back-handed, *oblique*, 717.
unexpected, 508.
Backhander, *attack*, 716.
Back-scratcher, *flatterer*, 935.
Backsheesh, *gratuity*, 784.
Backsliding, *dishonour*, 940.
delinquency, 945.
(religious), 984.
Backstairs influence, *concealment*, 528.
Backward, *regression*, 283.
traction, 285.
tardy, 133.
unwilling, 603.
Backwardness, *unwillingness*, 603.
dislike, 867.
Backwoodsman, *inhabitant*, 188.
Bacon, to save one's, *escape*, 671.
Bad, *badness*, 649, 945.
putrid, 653.
Badge, *indication*, 550.
Badger, *to maltreat*, 830.
Badinage, *wit*, 842.
Baedeker, *guide*, 266.
Baffle, *thwart*, 706.
defeat, 731.
Baffled, *failure*, 731.
Baffling, *bewildering*, 528.
Bag, *receptacle*, 191.
to take, 789, 791.
to receive, 810.
to pocket, 184.
Bagatelle, *unimportance*, 643.
Baggage, *property*, 780.
materials, 634.
hussy, 962.
Bagman, *agent*, 758.
Bagnio, *impurity*, 961.
Bagpipe, *musical instrument*, 417.
Baggy, *loose*, 47.
bulging, 250.
Bail, *security*, 771.
Bailiff, *director*, 694.
servant, 746.
officer, 965.
factor, 758.
Bailiwick, *tribunal*, 966.
Bairn, *infant*, 129.
Bait, *allurement*, 615.
food, 299.
to harass, 907.
Bake, *heat*, 384.
Bakehouse, *furnace*, 386.
Baker's dozen, *thirteen*, 98.
Balance, *equality*, 27.
remainder, 40.
numeration, 85.
measure, 466.
money, 800.
accounts, 811.
mean, 29.
steadiness, 265.
Balcony, *convexity*, 250.
Bald, *bare*, 226.
ugly, 846.
in style, 575.
Baldachin, *canopy*, 222.
Balderdash, *absurdity*, 497.
Baldric, *girdle*, 247.
Bale, *bundle*, 72.
evil, 619.
Baleful, *badness*, 649.
Bale out, *ejection*, 297.
Balk, *hinder*, 706.
fail, 731.
disappoint, 509.
deceive, 545.
Ball, *globe*, 249.
missile, 284.
(cannon), 727.
dance, 840.

Ballad, *song*, 415.
poem, 597.
Ballade, *poem*, 597.
music, 415.
Ballad-opera, *drama*, 599.
catapult, 276.
Ballast, *weight*, 319.
steadiness, 150.
wisdom, 498.
*Ballet (Fr.), *amusement*, 840.
Ballista, *arms*, 727.
Ballistics, *propulsion*, 284.
Balloon, *ship*, 273.
Ballot, *choice*, 609.
Ballyrag, *abuse*, 932.
Balm, *fragrance*, 400.
relief, 834.
remedy, 662.
Balmy, *foolish*, 499.
*Balourdise (Fr.), *failure*, 732.
Balsam, *see* Balm.
Balsamic, *salubrious*, 656.
Baluster, *support*, 215.
Balustrade, *enclosure*, 232.
Bamboozle, *deception*, 545.
Ban, *prohibition*, 761.
denunciation, 908.
Banal, *commonplace*, 82, 643.
feeble, 575.
Band, *ligature*, 45.
assemblage, 72.
party, 712.
of music, 416.
shackle, 752.
Bandage, *ligature*, 45.
to lie, 43.
Bandbox, *receptacle*, 191.
Banderole, *flag*, 550.
Bandit, *thief*, 792.
Bandog, *warning*, 668.
Bands, *canonicals*, 999.
Bandy, *agitate*, 315.
contest, 476, 720.
exchange, 148.
crooked, 245.
deformed, 846.
Bane, *badness*, 663.
Baneful, *badness*, 649.
Bang, *sound*, 406.
to impel, 276.
to beat, 972.
Banish, *exclude*, 55, 297.
seclude, 893.
Banister, *support*, 215.
Banjo, *musical instrument*, 417.
Bank, *side of lake*, 342.
acclivity, 217.
store, 636.
money, 802.
Banker, *treasurer*, 801.
Bankruptcy, *failure*, 732.
non-payment, 808.
*Banlieue (Fr.), *nearness*, 197.
Banner, *indication*, 550.
Banneret, *nobility*, 875.
Banquet, *meal*, 298.
feast, 840.
Banshee, *fairy*, 979.
Bantam, *small*, 193.
Banter, *wit*, 842.
ridicule, 856.
Bantling, *child*, 129.
offspring, 167.
Banyan, *fast*, 956.
scanty, 640.
Baptise, *name*, 564.
Baptism, *rite*, 998.
Baptistry, *temple*, 1000.
Bar, *hindrance*, 706.
line, 200.
to exclude, 55.
enclosure, 232.
prison, 752.
prohibition, 761.
tribunal, 966.
legal profession, 968.
*Baragouin (Fr.), *absurdity*, 497.
Barb, *spike*, 253.
nag, 271.
Barbarian, *evil-doer*, 913.
Barbarism, *discourtesy*, 895.
solecism, 568.
Barbarous, *maleficent*, 907.
vulgar, 851.
rude, 876.
style, 579.
Barbican, *defence*, 717.
*Barbouillage (Fr.), *writing*, 590.
Bard, *poetry*, 597.
Bare, *mere*, 32.
nude, 226.
scanty, 640.
exposed to view, 446.
Barefaced, *visible*, 446.
shameless, 885.
Bareheaded, *respect*, 928.
Barely, *smallness*, 32.
Baresark, *violence*, 173.
combatant, 726.
Bargain, *compact*, 769.
barter, 794
promise, 768.
cheap, 813, 815.
Bargain, into the, *addition*, 37.
Barge, *ship*, 273.
Baritone, *deep-toned*, 408.
Bark, *rind*, 223.
ship, 273.

Bark, *to yelp*, 412.
to censure, 932.
Barm, *yeast*, 353.
Barn, *abode*, 189.
Barnacles, *optical instrument*, 445.
Barometer, *measurement*, 466.
Baron, *nobility*, 875.
Baronet, *nobility*, 875.
Baronetage, *list*, 86.
Baroque, *ridiculous*, 853.
Barrack, *abode*, 189.
Barracoon, *defence*, 717.
Barrage, *obstacle*, 706.
Barred, *crossed*, 219.
striped, 440.
Barrel, *vessel*, 191.
cylinder, 249.
Barren, *sterile*, 169.
useless, 645.
Barricade, *fence*, 232.
prison, 752.
obstacle, 706.
Barrier, *fence*, 232.
obstacle, 706.
Barring, *except*, 83.
save, 38.
Barrister, *lawyer*, 968.
Barrow, *vehicle*, 272.
grave, 363.
Barter, *exchange*, 794.
Bascule, *instrument*, 633.
Base, *lowest part*, 211.
support, 215.
bad, 649.
dishonourable, 940.
shameful, 874.
vicious, 945.
cowardly, 862.
plebeian, 876.
Baseless, *unreal*, 2.
erroneous, 495.
Basement, *base*, 211.
Base-minded, *improbity*, 940.
Bashaw, *ruler*, 745.
tyrant, 739.
Bashful, *modesty*, 881.
Basic, *support*, 215.
Basilica, *temple*, 1000.
Basilisk, *serpent*, 949.
cannon, 727.
Basin, *hollow*, 252.
vessel, 191.
plain, 344.
dock, 189.
Basis, *preparation*, 673.
foundation, 215.
Bask, *warmth*, 382.
physical enjoyment, 377.
moral enjoyment, 827.
Bask, *prosperity*, 734.
Basket, *receptacle*, 191.
Bas-relief, *convexity*, 250.
Bass, *deep-sounding*, 408, 413.
*Basso rilievo (It.), *convexity*, 250.
sculpture, 557.
Bassoon, *musical instrument*, 417.
Bass-viol, *musical instrument*, 417.
Bastard, *spurious*, 544.
erroneous, 495.
Bastardy, *illegitimacy*, 964.
Baste, *beat*, 276.
punish, 972.
Bastille, *prison*, 752.
Bastinado, *punishment*, 972.
Bastion, *defence*, 717.
Bat, *club*, 727.
mall, 633.
Batswing, *light*, 423.
Batch, *assemblage*, 72.
quantity, 25.
Bate, *diminish*, 36, 38.
reduce price, 813.
Bath, *immersion*, 300, 337.
Bathe, *immersion*, 300.
Bathos, *depth*, 208.
anticlimax, 497.
ridiculous, 853.
Bathymetric, *depth*, 208.
Baton, *sceptre*, 747.
Battalion, *troop*, 726.
assemblage, 72.
Batten, *feed*, 296.
Batter, *beat*, 276.
destroy, 162.
Battered, *imperfect*, 651.
Battering-ram, *weapon*, 276, 727.
Battery, *instrument*, 633.
Battle, *contention*, 720.
Battle array, *warfare*, 722.
arrangement, 60.
Battle-axe, *arms*, 727.
Battlefield, *arena*, 728.
Battlement, *bulwark*, 666.
defence, 717.
enclosure, 232.
embrasure, 257.
*Battre la générale (Fr.), *alarm*, 669.
Battue, *pursuit*, 622.
Baulk, *see* Balk.
Bauble, *trifle*, 643.
toy, 840.
*Bavardage (Fr.), *absurdity*, 497.
Bawd, *libertine*, 962.
Bawdy, *impurity*, 961.
Bawl, *cry*, 411, 839.
Bay, *gulf*, 343.
brown, 433.
to howl, 412.

Bay, at, *defence*, 717.
Bayadère, *dancer*, 599.
Bayard, *carrier*, 271.
perfection, 650.
Bayonet, *arms*, 727.
Bays, *trophy*, 733.
reward, 973.
Bazaar, *mart*, 799.
Be, to, *existence*, 1.
Be off, *departure*, 293.
Beach, *land*, 342.
Beacon, *sign*, 423, 550.
warning, 668.
Beadle, *janitor*, 263.
officer, 745.
law officer, 965.
church, 996.
Bead-roll, *list*, 86.
Beads, *rite*, 998.
Beak, *front*, 234.
nose, 250.
Beaker, *receptacle*, 191.
Beam, *support*, 215.
of a balance, 466.
of light, 420.
beauty, 845.
Beamless, *darkness*, 421.
Bean-feast, *pleasure*, 827, 840.
meal, 298.
Bear, *sustain*, 215.
produce, 161.
carry, 270.
suffer, 821.
admit, 470.
brute, 895.
Bear down upon, *attack*, 716.
Bear off, *taking*, 789.
Bear out, *confirm*, 467.
vindicate, 937.
Bear up, *cheerfulness*, 836.
Bear upon, *influence*, 175.
evidence, 467.
to relate to, 9.
Beard, *sharp*, 253.
rough, 256.
to defy, 715.
courage, 861.
insolence, 885.
Beardless, *youth*, 127.
Bearer, *carrier*, 271.
Bear-garden, *arena*, 728.
Bearing, *support*, 215.
direction, 278.
meaning, 516.
demeanour, 692.
situation, 183.
Bearish, *discourtesy*, 895.
Bear-leader, *teacher*, 540.
Beast, *animal*, 366.
Beast, *blackguard*, 895.
Beastly, *uncleanness*, 653.
Beat, *strike*, 716, 972.
be superior, 33.
periodic, 138.
oscillation, 314.
agitation 315.
crush, 330.
sound, 407.
succeed, 731.
line of pursuit, 625.
Beating, *impulse*, 276.
Beat down, *chaffer*, 794.
insolence, 885.
Beat hollow, *superiority*, 33.
Beat off, *defence*, 717.
Beat time, *chronometry*, 114.
Beatify, *enrapture*, 829.
sanctify, 987.
Beatitude, *pleasure*, 827.
Beat up for, *seek*, 461.
Beau, *fop*, 854.
man, 373.
admirer, 897.
*Beau-idéal, (Fr.), *beauty*, 845.
perfection, 650.
*Beau-monde (Fr.), *fashion*, 852.
nobility, 875.
*Beau sabreur (Fr.), *hero*, 861.
Beautify, *ornament*, 847.
Beauty, *beauty*, 845.
Beaver, *hat*, 225.
Becalm, *quiescence*, 265.
Because, *attribution*, 155.
reasoning, 476.
motive, 615.
Bechance, *eventuality*, 151.
Beck, *rill*, 348.
signal, 550.
mandate, 741.
Beckon, *signal*, 550.
Becloud, *darkness*, 421.
Become, *change to*, 144.
behove, 926.
Become of, *event*, 151.
Becoming, *proper*, 646.
beautiful, 845.
just, 922.
Bed, *layer*, 204.
support, 215.
lodgment, 191.
Bedabble, *splash*, 337.
Bedarken, *darkness*, 421.
Bedaub, *cover*, 222.
dirt, 653.
deface, 846.
Bedazzle, *light*, 420.
Bedeck, *beauty*, 845.
Bedevil, *derange*, 61.

Bedevil, *bewitch*, 992.
Bedew, *moisture*, 339.
Bed-fellow, *friend*, 890.
Bedight, *beauty*, 845.
Bedim, *darkness*, 421.
Bedizen, *beautify*, 845.
ornament, 851.
Bedlam, *insanity*, 503.
Bedlamite, *madman*, 504.
Bedraggle, *soil*, 653.
Bed-ridden, *disease*, 655.
Bedstead, *support*, 215.
Bee, *agent*, 690.
active, 682.
Bee-line, *direction*, 278.
Bee-witted, *folly*, 499.
Beefy, *corpulent*, 192.
Beelzebub, *Satan*, 978.
Beery, *drunken*, 959.
Beetle, *high*, 206.
projecting, 250.
Befall, *eventuality*, 151.
Befitting, *right*, 926.
expedient, 646.
Befool, *deceive*, 503, 545.
Before, *precedence*, 62.
Before Christ, *period*, 108.
Beforehand, *priority*, 116, 132.
Befoul, *uncleanness*, 653.
Beg, *request*, 765.
Beg the question, *evidence*, 467.
Beget, *produce*, 161.
Beggar, *petitioner*, 767.
poor, 804.
Beggarly, *mean*, 643.
vulgar, 876.
servile, 886.
vile, 940.
Begilt, *ornament*, 847.
Begin, *beginning*, 66.
Begin again, *repetition*, 104.
Beginner, *learner*, 541.
Beginning to end, from, *whole*, 50.
completeness, 52.
duration, 106.
Begird, *encircle*, 227, 231.
Begone, *depart*, 293.
disappear, 449.
repel, 289.
Begrime, *soil*, 653.
deface, 846.
Begrudge, *refusal*, 764.
Beguile, *deceive*, 545.
amuse, 840.
Beguine, *nun*, 996.
Begum, *nobility*, 875.
Behalf, *advantage*, 618.
aid, 707.
Behave, *conduct*, 692.
Behead, *punish*, 972.
Behest, *command*, 741.
Behind, *in order*, 63.
in space, 235.
Behindhand, *late*, 133.
adversity, 735
shortcoming, 304.
Behold, *vision*, 441.
Beholden, *grateful*, 916.
obligatory, 926.
Behoof, *good*, 618.
Behove, *duty*, 926.
Being, *abstract*, 1.
concrete, 3.
Belabour, *thump*, 972.
buffet, 276.
Belated, *late*, 133.
confused, 491.
Belaud, *approbation*, 931.
Belay, *junction*, 43.
*Bel canto (It.), *music*, 415.
Belch, *ejection*, 297.
Beldam, *old woman*, 130.
hag, 913.
Beleaguer, *attack*, 716.
*Bel esprit (Fr.), *humorist*, 844.
Belial, *demon*, 980.
Belie, *falsify*, 544.
misinterpret, 523.
deny, 536.
disagreement, 24.
Belief, *credence*, 484.
religious creed, 983.
Believer, *piety*, 987.
Belike, *probability*, 472.
Bell, *sound*, 417.
funeral, 363.
alarm, 669
Belle, *woman*, 374.
*Belles-lettres (Fr.), *language*, 560.
knowledge, 490.
Bellicose, *warlike*, 722.
Belligerent, *warfare*, 722.
Bellow, *cry*, 412.
complain, 839.
Bellows, *wind*, 349.
Bell-shaped, *globose*, 249.
concave, 252.
Bell-wether, *precursor*, 64.
Belly, *receptacle*, 191.
interior, 221.
to bulge, 250.
Bellyful, *sufficiency*, 639.
Belly-timber, *food*, 298.
Belomancy, *prediction*, 511.
Belong to, *related*, 9.
property, 717.
attribute, 157.
duty, 926.

Belong, *inclusion*, 76.
Beloved, *favourite*, 897, 899.
Below, *lowness*, 207.
Belt, *girdle*, 247.
outline, 229.
Belvedere, *vision*, 441.
Bemire, *soil*, 653.
Bemoan, *lament*, 839.
Bemuddle, *bewilder*, 458.
Bemuse, *bewilder*, 458.
Bench, *support*, 215.
council, 696.
tribunal, 966.
Bencher, *lawyer*, 968.
Bend, *curve*, 245.
angularity, 244.
circle, 247.
yield, 324, 725.
circuit, 311.
obliquity, 217.
descent, 806.
deviation, 279.
stoop, 879.
Bend to, *tend*, 176.
habit, 613.
Bending, *pliant*, 324.
Beneath, *under*, 207.
unbecoming, 940.
Benedick, *marriage*, 903.
Benediction, *approval*, 931.
gratitude, 916.
worship, 990.
Benefaction, *giving*, 784.
Benefactor, *benevolence*, 912.
Benefice, *churchdom*, 995.
Beneficent, *benevolence*, 906.
Beneficial, *useful*, 644.
good, 648.
Beneficiary, *clergy*, 996.
Benefit, *advantage*, 618.
acquisition, 775.
benevolence, 906.
Benevolence, *kindness*, 906.
tax, 812.
Benighted, *ignorance*, 491.
Benignant, *benevolence*, 906.
Benison, *approbation*, 931.
Bent, *direction*, 278.
inclination, 602.
desire, 865.
tendency, 176.
intentions, 629.
affections, 820.
Bent on, *willing*, 602.
resolved, 604, 620.
desirous, 865.
*Ben trovato (It.), *probable*, 472.
falsehood, 544.
deception, 545.
Benumb, *cold*, 383.
general insensibility, 376.
tactual insensibility, 381.
affective sensibility, 823.
Be of, *inclusion*, 76.
Beplaster, *cover*, 222.
Bepraise, *approbation*, 931.
Bequeath, *giving*, 784.
Bequest, *gift*, 784.
acquisition, 775.
Bereave, *take away*, 789.
Bereavement, *loss*, 789.
Bereft, *poor*, 804.
*Berceuse (Fr.), *music*, 415.
*Bergschrund (Ger.), *interval*, 198.
Berlin, *vehicle*, 272.
Berry, *brown*, 433.
*Bersagliere (It.), *combatant*, 726.
Berserker, *combatant*, 726.
violence, 173.
Berth, *lodging*, 189.
bed, 191.
repose, 215.
Beseech, *request*, 765.
pray, 990.
Beseem, *duty*, 926.
Beset, *surround*, 227.
difficulty, 704.
entreaty, 765.
beshrew, 908.
by the side of, 216.
Beshrew, *curse*, 908.
Beside, *except*, 83.
accompaniment, 216.
Beside oneself, *insanity*, 503.
Beside the mark, *irrelation*, 10.
Besides, *addition*, 37, 88.
Besiege, *attack*, 716.
solicit, 765.
Beslaver, *flattery*, 933.
Beslime, *uncleanness*, 653.
Beslobber, *uncleanness*, 653.
Besmear, *soil*, 653.
deface, 846.
Besmirch, *soil*, 653.
deface, 846.
Besom, *cleanness*, 652.
Besotted, *prejudiced*, 481.
foolish, 499.
Bespangle, *ornament*, 847.
Bespatter, *soil*, 653.
spoil, 659.
deface, 846.
revile, 932.
flatter, 933.
Bespeak, *indicate*, 516.
hire, 755.
earliness, 132.
request, 765.

Bespeckle, *variegation*, 440.
Bespotted, *variegation*, 440.
Besprinkle, *mix*, 41.
spirt, 296.
Best, *perfection*, 650.
to outwit, 545.
Bestial, *impurity*, 961.
Bestir, *activity*, 682, 686.
Bestow, *giving*, 784.
Bestraddle, *sit*, 215.
Bestrew, *disperse*, 73.
Bestride, *mount*, 206.
sit, 215.
Bestud, *emboss*, 250.
Bet, *chance*, 621.
Betake, *business*, 625.
*Bête noire (Fr.), *fear*, 860.
hate, 898.
Bethink, *memory*, 505.
Bethump, *beat*, 276.
Betide, *eventuality*, 151.
Betimes, *earliness*, 132.
Betoken, *indicate*, 550.
predict, 511.
Betray, *disclose*, 529.
deceive, 545.
dishonour, 940.
appear, 446.
Betroth, *promise*, 768.
Betrothed, *affianced*, 897.
Better (to), *improvement*, 658.
Between, *interjacence*, 228.
Betwixt, *interjacence*, 228.
Bevel, *obliquity*, 217.
Bever, *food*, 298.
*Bévue (Fr.), *failure*, 732.
Bevy, *assemblage*, 72, 102.
Bewail, *lamentation*, 839.
Beware, *warn*, 668.
afraid, 862.
Bewilder, *confuse*, 458.
mislead, 538.
perplex, 519, 528.
astonish, 870.
Bewildered, *ignorant*, 491.
Bewitch, *please*, 829.
exorcise, 992.
influence, 615.
Bewray, *disclose*, 529.
Bey, *master*, 745.
Beyond, *distance*, 196.
Bias, *slope*, 217.
prepossession, 481.
(mental), 602.
tendency, 176.
motive, 615.
disposition, 820.
Bibacious, *drunkenness*, 959.
Bibber, *toper*, 959.
*Bibelot, (Fr.), *trifle*, 643.
Bible, *revelation*, 985.
Bibliography, *list*, 86.
book, 593.
Bibliolatry, *heterodoxy*, 984.
Bibliology, *book*, 593.
Bibliomancy, *prediction*, 511.
Bibliomania, *erudition*, 490.
book, 593.
Bibliophil, *book*, 593.
Bibulous, *spongy*, 322.
drunken, 959.
Bicentenary, *period*, 138.
Bicentric, *duality*, 89.
Bicker, *flutter*, 315.
discord, 713.
quarrel, 720.
Biscuspid, *bisection*, 91.
Bid, *order*, 741.
offer, 763.
Bid for, *bargain*, 794.
Biddable, *obedient*, 743.
Bide, *tarry*, 133.
remain, 142.
Bide one's time, *futurity*, 121.
*Bienséance (Fr.), *polish*, 852.
manners, 894.
Bier, *interment*, 363.
Bifacial, *duplication*, 90.
Bifarious, *duality*, 89.
Bifocal, *duality*, 89.
Bifold, *duplication*, 90.
Biform, *duplication*, 90.
bisection, 91.
Biformity, *duality*, 89.
*Bifrons (L.), *duality*, 89.
Bifurcation, *bisection*, 91.
fork, 244.
Big, *in degree*, 31.
in size, 192.
Bigamy, *marriage*, 903.
Bight, *lake*, 343.
bend, 245.
Bigot, *impiety*, 989.
Bigoted, *imbecile*, 499.
Bigotry, *prejudice*, 481.
obstinacy, 606.
heterodoxy, 984.
Big-wig, *sage*, 500.
pedant, 492.
notability, 642.
*Bijou (Fr.), *gem*, 650.
Bilander, *ship*, 273.
Bilateral, *duality*, 89.
Bilbo, *arms*, 727.
Bilboes, *prison*, 752.
Bile, *resentment*, 900.
Bilge-water, *uncleanness*, 653.
Bilious, *dejection*, 837.

Bilk, *deception*, 545.
Bill, *money account*, 811.
charge, 812.
money-order, 800.
in law, 969.
placard, 531.
ticket, 550.
hatchet, 633.
weapon, 727.
Bill of fare, *food*, 298.
list, 86.
Billet, *epistle*, 592.
ticket, 500.
to apportion, 786.
to locate, 184.
*Billet-doux (Fr.), *correspondence*, 592.
endearment, 902.
Billingsgate, *scolding*, 932.
imprecatory, 908.
Billion, *numbers*, 98.
Billow, *wave*, 348.
Billycock, *hat*, 225.
Bimetallism, *money*, 800.
Bin, *receptacle*, 191.
Binary, *duality*, 89.
Bind, *connect*, 43.
compel, 744.
obligation, 926.
condition, 770.
Binomial, *duplication*, 90.
Biograph, *spectacle*, 448.
Biography, *description*, 594.
Biology, *organisation*, 357.
Bioscope, *spectacle*, 448.
Bipartition, *duplication*, 91.
Biplane, *air-vessel*, 273.
Birch, *scourge*, 975.
to punish, 972.
Bird, *animal*, 366.
Bird's eye view, *appearance*, 448.
Birds of a feather, *inclusion*, 76.
conformity, 82.
Bird-lime, *vinculum*, 45.
Bird's-eye, *tobacco*, 298A.
Bireme, *ship*, 273.
Biretta, *cap*, 225.
Birth, *beginning*, 66.
nobility, 875.
Birthplace, *origin*, 153.
Birthright, *dueness*, 924.
*Bis (Fr.), *duplication*, 89.
*Bise (Fr.), *wind*, 349.
Bisection, *duality*, 91.
Bishop, *clergy*, 996.
Bishopric, *churchdom*, 995.
Bissextile, *period*, 108.
Bisulcate, *fold*, 258, 259.
Bit, *part*, 51.
Bit, *mixture*, 41.
small quantity, 32.
curb, 747, 752.
Bit by bit, *part*, 51.
degree, 26.
Bite, *pain*, 378.
painful, 830.
cheat, 545.
Biting, *cold*, 383.
pungent, 392.
painful, 830.
Bitter, *taste*, 395.
cold, 383.
animosity, 898.
wrath, 900.
regret, 833.
painful, 830.
Bivouac, *repose*, 265.
to encamp, 186.
camp, 189.
watch, 664.
Bizarre, *ridiculous*, 853.
unconformity, 83.
Blab, *disclosure*, 529.
Black, *colour*, 431.
crime, 945.
Blackamoor, *blackness*, 431.
Black art, *sorcery*, 992.
Black-ball, *exclude*, 55.
reject, 610.
seclude, 893.
Blacken, *disapprobation*, 932.
Blackguard, *rude*, 895.
vagabond, 949.
to revile, 932.
Black-hole, *prison*, 752.
Black-leg, *sharper*, 548.
thief, 792.
traitor, 941.
Black-letter, *printing*, 591.
Black looks, *discourtesy*, 895.
Blackmail, *theft*, 791.
booty, 793.
Black out, *obliterate*, 552.
Bladder, *receptacle*, 191.
Blade, *instrument*, 633.
man, 372.
fop, 854.
*Blague, (Fr.), *humbug*, 545.
Blain, *swelling*, 250.
Blamable, *vice*, 945.
Blame, *disapprobation*, 932.
Blameless, *innocence*, 946.
Blameworthy, *vice*, 945.
Blanch, *whiteness*, 430.
Bland, *courteous*, 894.
mild, 174.
Blandiloquence, *flattery*, 933.
Blandishment, *flattery*, 902, 933.

Blank, *insubstantiality*, 2, 4.
simple, 42.
vacant, 187.
verse, 597.
Blare, *loudness*, 404.
Blarney, *flattery*, 933.
*Blasé (Fr.), *weariness*, 841
fastidious, 868.
Blasphemy, *impiety*, 989.
Blast, *wind*, 349.
sound, 404.
evil, 619.
explosion, 173.
destroy, 162.
Blast-furnace, *furnace*, 386.
Blatant, *cry*, 412.
loud, 404.
silly, 499.
Blaze, *light*, 420.
heat, 382.
Blaze abroad, *publication*, 531.
Blazon, *publication*, 531.
Blazonry, *colour*, 428.
Bleach, *discolour*, 429.
whiten, 430.
Bleak, *cold*, 383.
dreary, 830.
Blear-eyed, *dim-sighted*, 443.
Bleat, *animal cry*, 412.
Bleb, *swelling*, 250.
bubble, 353.
Bleed, *physical pain*, 378.
moral pain, 828.
despoil, 789.
Blemish, *ugly*, 846.
defect, 848.
Blench, *avoid*, 623.
fear, 860.
Blend, *mix*, 41.
combine, 48.
Bless, *approbation*, 931.
Blessed, *happy*, 827.
Blessing, *good*, 618.
Blether, *nonsense*, 497, 499.
loquacity, 584.
Blight, *evil*, 619.
decay, 659.
deterioration, 659.
Blighter, *knave*, 949.
Blind, *cecity*, 442.
ignorant, 491.
screen, 424.
falsehood, 546.
deception, 545.
concealment, 528.
necessity, 601.
heedless, 458.
pretext, 617
imperforate, 261.
Blind alley, *closure*, 261.
Blindfold, *sightless*, 442.
ignorant, 491.
Blind side, *obstinacy*, 606.
prejudice, 481.
Blink, *wink*, 442.
neglect, 460.
overlook, 458.
shirk, 623.
Bliss, *pleasure*, 827.
Blister, *swelling*, 250.
Blithe, *cheerfulness*, 836.
Blizzard, *wind*, 349.
Bloated, *size*, 192, 194.
Block, *mass*, 192.
dense, 321.
fool, 501.
execution, 975.
Block in, *sketch*, 556.
Block out, *form*, 240.
Block up, *plug*, 261.
impede, 706.
Blockade, *closure*, 261.
hindrance, 706.
Blockhead, *fool*, 501.
Blockhouse, *defence*, 716.
Blockish, *folly*, 499.
Bloke, *man*, 373.
Blonde, *whiteness*, 430.
Blood, *relation*, 11.
killing, 361.
affections, 820.
nobility, 875.
fop, 854.
Blood-guilty, *killing*, 361.
Bloodhound, *evil-doer*, 913.
detective, 461.
Blood-red, *redness*, 434.
Bloodshed, *killing*, 361.
Blood-stained, *murderous*, 361.
maleficent, 907.
Blood-sucker, *evil-doer*, 913.
Bloodthirsty, *malevolence*, 907.
Bloody, *malevolence*, 907.
Bloom, *youth*, 127.
prosperity, 734.
success, 731.
blueness, 438.
Bloomer, *error*, 495.
dress, 225.
Blooming, *beauty*, 845.
health, 654.
Blossom, *success*, 731.
prosperity, 734.
Blot, *obliterate*, 552.
darken, 431.
disappear, 449.
discoloration, 429.
forget, 506.

Blot, *ugly*, 846.
blemish, 848.
disgrace, 874.
dishonour, 940.
guilt, 947.
Blotch, *blackness*, 431.
blemish, 848.
Blouse, *dress*, 225.
Blow, *wind*, 349.
knock, 276.
action, 680.
evil, 619.
pain, 828.
disappointment, 732.
mishap, 830.
to prosper, 734.
Blow down, *destruction*, 162.
Blow-hole, *air-pipe*, 351.
Blow-out, *extinguish*, 385.
Blow over, *preterition*, 122.
Blowpipe, *wind*, 349.
Blow up, *fan*, 615.
wind, 349.
inflame, 194.
eruption, 173.
objurgation, 932.
Blow upon, *censure*, 934.
Blown, *fatigued*, 688.
Blowzy, *red*, 434.
sluttish, 653.
Blubber, *cry*, 839.
fat, 356.
Bludgeon, *club*, 276.
weapon, 727.
Blue, *colour*, 438.
learned, 490.
Blue book, *record*, 551.
Blue devils, *dejection*, 837.
Blue lights, *firework*, 423, 669.
Bluestocking, *scholar*, 492.
Bluff, *high*, 206.
blunt, 254.
insolent, 885.
discourteous, 895.
boasting, 884.
deception, 545.
Blunder, *error*, 495.
folly, 499.
awkwardness, 699.
mistake, 732.
ridiculous, 856.
Blunderbuss, *arms*, 727.
Blunderheaded, *folly*, 499.
Blunt, *inert*, 172.
obtuse, 254.
insensible, 376.
inexcitable, 826.
stupid, 499.
cash, 800.
Blunt, *discourteous*, 895.
frank, 543.
to moderate, 174.
to damp, 616.
Blunt-witted, *folly*, 499.
Blur, *deformity*, 846.
blemish, 848.
disrepute, 874.
Blurred, *invisibility*, 447.
Blurt out, *disclosure*, 529.
Blush, *redden*, 434.
feel, 821.
be ashamed, 874.
appearance, 448.
Bluster, *violence*, 173.
insolence, 885.
defiance, 715.
Blusterer, *swagger*, 887.
Blustering, *windy*, 349.
Board, *layer*, 204.
food, 298.
to attach, 716.
council, 696.
tribunal, 966.
theatre, 599.
Boast, *brag*, 884.
Boat, *ship*, 273.
Bob, *rise*, 305.
stoop, 306.
oscillate, 314.
agitate, 315.
Bobadil, *blusterer*, 887.
Bobbery, *disturbance*, 315.
Bode, *prediction*, 511.
Bodega, *drink*, 298.
Bodice, *dress*, 255.
Bodily, *substantiality*, 3.
Bodkin, *perforator*, 262.
go-between, 228.
Body, *substance*, 3.
matter, 316.
whole, 50.
person, 373.
assemblage, 72.
party, 712.
political, 737.
Bœotian, *dull*, 843.
foolish, 499.
Bog, *swamp*, 343.
dunghill, 653.
Boggle, *demur*, 603.
hesitate, 605.
difficulty, 704.
awkward, 699.
Bogle, *demon*, 980
Bogy, *demon*, 980.
alarm, 669.
Bohemian, *unconformity*, 83, 614.
Boil, *heat*, 382.

Boil, *wheat*, 384.
bubble, 353.
effervesce, 315.
be excited, 825.
be irate, 900.
Boil down, *shorten*, 201, 596.
Boiler, *furnace*, 386.
Boisterous, *violent*, 173.
hasty, 684.
excitable, 825.
Bold, *brave*, 861.
prominent, 250.
Bolero, *dance*, 840.
Bolshevism, *authority*, 737.
Bolster, *support*, 215.
aid, 707.
repair, 658.
relief, 834.
Bolt, *fastening*, 45.
to fasten, 43.
to propel, 284.
decamp, 287.
swallow, 296.
move rapidly, 274.
escape, 671, 750.
shackle, 752.
upright, 212.
Bolthead, *receptacle*, 191.
Bolus, *mouthful*, 298.
Bomb, *arms*, 727.
Bombard, *attack*, 716.
Bombardier, *combatant*, 726.
Bombast, *absurd*, 497.
ridiculous, 853.
boasting, 884.
style, 549, 573, 577, 853.
*Bona fide (L.), *veracity*, 543.
meaning, 516.
Bonanza, *good luck*, 618.
*Bon-bon (Fr.), *sweet*, 396.
pleasurable, 829.
Bond, *relation*, 9.
tie, 45.
compact, 769.
security, 771.
right, 924.
fetters, 752.
Bondage, *subjection*, 749.
Bondsman, *servant*, 746.
*Bon enfant (Fr.), *benevolence*, 906.
Bone of contention, *discord*, 713.
Bones, *corpse*, 362.
Bonfire, *rejoicing*, 838.
*Bon gré (Fr.), *willing*, 602.
*Bon gré, mal gré (Fr.), *unwilling*, 603.
*Bonhomie (Fr.), *credulity*, 486.
veracity, 543.
candour, 703.
*Bon-mot (Fr.), *wit*, 842.
*Bonne (Fr.), *servant*, 746.
*Bonne-bouche (Fr.), *dainty*, 829.
savoury, 394.
Bonnet, *hat*, 225.
to assault, 716.
Bonny, *pretty*, 845.
cheerful, 836.
*Bon ton, *fashion*, 852.
Bonus, *advantage*, 618.
gift, 784.
money, 810.
addition, 39.
*Bon vivant (Fr.), *glutton*, 957.
Bonze, *clergy*, 996.
Boo, *cry*, 412
deride, 927.
Booby, *fool*, 501.
ignoramus, 493.
Book, *volume*, 593.
enter account, 811.
to record, 551.
to register, 86.
to bespeak, 132.
Bookish, *erudite*, 490.
scholarly, 492.
Book-keeper, *recorder*, 553.
Book-keeping, *accounts*, 811.
Bookless, *ignorant*, 493.
Bookworm, *scholar*, 492.
Boom, *bar*, 633.
defence, 717.
obstacle, 706.
to sail, 267.
rush, 274.
sound, 404.
praise, 931.
Boomerang, *arms*, 727.
recoil, 277.
Booming, *impulse*, 276.
Boon, *giving*, 784.
good, 618.
Boor, *clown*, 876.
ridiculous, 851.
Boot (to), *addition*, 37.
dress, 225.
advantage, 618.
important, 642.
punishment, 975.
Booth, *abode*, 189.
Bootless, *useless*, 645.
failing, 732.
Booty, *plunder*, 793.
Booze, *drunkenness*, 959.
Bo-peep, *vision*, 441.
Border, *edge*, 230.
to be near, 197.
Bore, *hole*, 260.
diameter, 202.

Bore, *to trouble*, 828.
to plague, 830.
to weary, 841.
tide, 348.
Boreal, *polar*, 237.
cold, 383.
Boreas, *wind*, 349.
Borer, *perforator*, 262.
*Borné (Fr.), *folly*, 499.
Borough, *abode*, 189.
Borrow, *borrowing*, 788.
Boscage, *vegetation*, 367.
Bosom, *breast*, 221.
mind, 450.
will, 600.
affection, 820.
Bosom-friend, *friend*, 890.
Boss, *convexity*, 250.
to direct, 693, 737.
master, 745.
Botanic, *plant*, 367.
Botanomancy, *prediction*, 511.
Botany, *botany*, 369.
Botch, *to mend*, 658.
to fail, 732.
unskilful, 699.
imperfect, 651.
Both, *duality*, 89.
Bother, *trouble*, 828.
to trouble, 830.
Bottle, *receptacle*, 191.
Bottle-green, *green*, 435.
Bottle up, *preserve*, 670.
enclose, 231.
remember, 505.
Bottle-washer, *servant*, 746.
Bottom, *lowest part*, 211.
base, 215.
ship, 273.
pluck, 604.
courage, 861.
Bottom, at, *intrinsicality*, 5.
Bottomless, *depth*, 208.
*Boudoir (Fr.), *room*, 191.
Bough, *part*, 51.
curve, 245.
Boulder, *mass*, 192.
*Boulevards (Fr.), *circumjacence*, 227.
*Bouleversé (Fr.), *excitation*, 824.
*Bouleversement (Fr.), *change*, 140.
destruction, 162.
Bounce, *violence*, 173.
motion, 274.
exaggeration, 549.
Bounce upon, *arrival*, 292.
surprise, 508.
Bouncer, *untruth*, 546.
Bouncing, *large*, 192.
Bound, *limit*, 233.
Bound, *circumscribe*, 231.
spring, 274.
ascend, 305.
leap, 309.
Boundary, *limit*, 233.
Bounden duty, *duty*, 926.
Bounder, *upstart*, 876.
Boundless, *great*, 31.
infinite, 105.
space, 180.
Bounteous, *benevolent*, 906.
Bountiful, *liberal*, 816.
Bounty, *gift*, 784.
liberality, 816.
benevolence, 906.
Bouquet, *fragrance*, 400.
ornament, 847.
*Bourgeois (Fr.), *middle class*, 736.
Bourne, *limit*, 233.
Bout, *turn*, 138.
job, 680.
fight, 720.
*Boutade (Fr.), *absurdity*, 497.
caprice, 608.
Bovine, *inert*, 172, 823.
Bow, *curve*, 245.
fore-part, 234.
propeller, 284.
arms, 727.
to stoop, 306.
reverence, 894.
obeisance, 743.
servility, 886.
respect, 928.
prominence, 250.
Bowdlerise, *expurgate*, 652.
Bowels, *interior*, 221.
of compassion, 914.
Bower, *alcove*, 189.
chamber, 191.
Bowie-knife, *arms*, 727.
Bowl, *vessel*, 191.
hollow, 252.
to propel, 284.
Bow-legged, *curvature*, 245.
Bowler, *hat*, 225.
Bowling-green, *horizontality*, 213.
Bowshot, *nearness*, 197.
Bowstring, *scourge*, 975.
Box, *chest*, 191.
house, 189.
to strike, 972.
to fight, 720.
Boxer, *combatant*, 726.
Boxing, *contention*, 720.
Boy, *infant*, 129.
Boyhood, *youth*, 127.
Boycott, *exclude*, 893.
Brace, *to tie*, 43.

Brace, *fastening*, 45.
two, 89.
to refresh, 689.
to strengthen, 159.
Bracelet, *circularity*, 247.
Brachygraphy, *writing*, 590.
Bracing, *strengthening*, 159.
refreshing, 689.
Bracket, *tie*, 43.
support, 215.
vinculum, 45.
couple, 89.
Brackish, *pungent*, 392.
Brad, *vinculum*, 45.
Bradawl, *perforator*, 262.
Brag, *boasting*, 884.
Braggadocio, *boasting*, 884.
Braggart, *boasting*, 884.
Brahma, *deity*, 996.
Brahmin, *clergy*, 996.
Braid, *to tie*, 43.
ligature, 45.
intersection, 219.
Braille, *printing*, 591.
Brain, *intellect*, 450.
skill, 498.
Brainless, *imbecile*, 499.
Brain-sick, *giddy*, 460.
Brake, *copse*, 367.
curb, 752.
Bramble, *thorn*, 253.
painful, 830.
Bran, *pulverulence*, 330.
Bran-new, *newness*, 123.
Branch, *member*, 51.
duality, 91.
posterity, 167.
ramification, 256.
Branch off, *divergence*, 291.
Branch out, *style*, 573.
divide, 91.
Brand, *to burn*, 384.
fuel, 388.
to stigmatise, 932.
to accuse, 938.
reproach, 874.
Brandish, *oscillate*, 314.
flourish, 315.
Brangle, *discord*, 713.
*Bras croisés (Fr.), *inactivity*, 683.
Brasier, *furnace*, 386.
Brass, *insolence*, 885.
colour, 439.
Brat, *infant*, 129.
Bravado, *boasting*, 884.
Brave, *courage*, 861.
to defy, 715.
Bravery, *courage*, 861.
ornament, 847.
*Bravo (It.), *assassin*, 361.
applause, 931.
*Bravura (It.), *music*, 415.
Brawl, *cry*, 411.
discord, 713.
contention, 720.
Brawny, *strong*, 159.
stout, 192.
Bray, *cry*, 412.
to grind, 330.
Brazen-faced, *insolent*, 885.
Breach, *crack*, 44.
quarrel, 713.
violation, 925.
exception, 83.
Bread, *food*, 298.
Bread-stuffs, *food*, 298.
Breadth, *thickness*, 202.
of mind, 498.
Break, *fracture*, 44.
shatter, 162.
interval, 70, 198.
vehicle, 272.
crumble, 328.
violation, 773.
bankruptcy, 808.
to infringe, 927.
to disclose, 529.
to tame, 749.
to decline, 659.
to swerve, 311.
Break down, *fail*, 732.
Break ground, *undertaking*, 676.
Break in, *teach*, 537.
train, 673.
Break loose, *escape*, 671.
liberate, 750.
Break off, *a habit*, 614.
leave off, 141.
abrogate, 756.
Break out, *fly out*, 825.
Break the ranks, *derangement*, 61.
Break the record, *superiority*, 33.
Break up, *destroy*, 162.
decompose, 49.
Break with, *discord*, 713.
Breaker, *wave*, 348.
danger, 667.
Breakfast, *food*, 298.
Break-neck, *perilous*, 665.
precipitous, 217.
Breakwater, *refuge*, 666.
Breast, *interior*, 221.
mind, 450.
will, 600.
soul, 820.
to oppose, 708.
Breastplate, *defence*, 717.
Breastwork, *defence*, 717.

Breath, *air*, 349.
sound, 405.
life, 359, 364.
Breathe, *exist*, 1.
live, 359.
blow, 349.
mean, 516.
utter, 580.
repose, 687.
Breather, *preparation*, 673.
Breathing, *life-like*, 17.
Breathing-space, *interval*, 106.
pause, 265.
Breathless, *calm*, 265.
out of breath, 688.
feeling, 821.
Breech, *rear*, 235.
Breeches, *dress*, 225.
Breed, *kind*, 75.
to multiply, 161.
progeny, 167.
Breeding, *fashion*, 852.
Breeze, *wind*, 349.
Breezy, *lively*, 836.
Brevet, *warrant*, 741.
commission, 755.
permission, 760.
Breviary, *liturgy*, 998.
Brevity, *space*, 201.
Brew, *mix*, 41.
prepare, 673.
impend, 121.
Bribe, *buy*, 795.
offer, 763.
gift, 784.
fee, 809.
tempt, 615.
*Bric-à-brac, (Fr.), *trifle*, 643.
Brick, *materials*, 635.
Brickbat, *propulsion*, 284.
Bride, *marriage*, 903.
Bridegroom, *marriage*, 903.
Bridewell, *prison*, 752.
Bridge, *intermedium*, 45.
way, 627.
escape, 671.
Bridge over, *junction*, 43.
Bridle, *curb*, 752.
to restrain, 751.
to moderate, 174.
to swagger, 878.
Bridle up, *resentment*, 900.
Brief, *time*, 111.
space, 201.
style, 572.
compendium, 596.
Briefly, *transientness*, 111.
Brier, *sharp*, 253.
painful, 830.
Brier, *tobacco-pipe*, 351.
Brig, *ship*, 273.
Brigade, *combatant*, 726.
Brigand, *thief*, 792.
Brigantine, *ship*, 273.
Bright, *shining*, 420.
colour, 428.
cheerful, 836.
auspicious, 858.
glorious, 873.
Brilliant, *shining*, 420.
beautiful, 845.
glorious, 873.
perfect, 650.
gem, 847.
Brim, *edge*, 230.
Brim-full, *sufficient*, 639.
Brinded, *brown*, 433.
Brindled, *variegated*, 440.
Brine, *salt*, 392.
sea, 341.
Bring, *transfer*, 270.
induce, 615.
Bring about, *cause*, 153.
achieve, 729.
succeed, 731.
Bring forth, *produce*, 161.
Bring forward, *manifest*, 525.
Bring home to, *convince*, 537
adduce, 467.
Bring in, *price*, 812.
Bring into, *existence*, 1.
Bring off, *deliver*, 672.
accomplish, 161.
Bring out, *manifest*, 525.
publish, 531.
Bring over, *persuade*, 484, 615.
Bring to, *restore*, 658.
Bring under, *subdue*, 824.
Bring up, *educate*, 537.
Brink, *edge*, 230.
Brink, on the — of, *nearly*, 32.
*Brio (It.), *vivacity*, 682.
Brisk, *quick*, 274.
energetic, 171.
active, 682.
prompt, 111.
Bristle, *sharpness*, 253.
Bristle up, *resentment*, 900.
Brittle, *brittleness*, 328.
Broach, *begin*, 66.
put forth, 535.
Broad, *space*, 202.
indelicate, 961.
meaning, 516, 535.
Broadcast, *scattered*, 73.
shed, 291.
Broad-minded, *wisdom*, 498.
Broadside, *side*, 236.

Broadside, *cannonade*, 716.
Broadsword, *arms*, 727.
Brobdignagian, *size*, 192.
Brocade, *ornament*, 847.
*Brochure (Fr.), *book*, 593.
Brogue, *language*, 560.
  shoe, 225.
Broidery, *ornament*, 847.
Broil, *heat*, 382.
  to fry, 384.
  fray, 720.
Broken, *weakness*, 160.
Broken-hearted, *unhappy*, 828.
Broken-winded, *fatigue*, 688.
Broker, *agent*, 758, 769.
  merchant, 797.
Brokerage, *pay*, 812.
Bronze, *brown*, 433.
  sculpture, 557.
Brooch, *fastening*, 45.
Brood, *posterity*, 167.
Brood over, *think*, 451.
  mope, 837.
Brook, *stream*, 348.
  to bear, 821, 826.
Broom, *cleanness*, 652.
Broth, *food*, 298.
Brothel, *impurity*, 961.
Brother, *kin*, 11.
  similar, 17.
  equal, 27.
  friend, 888.
Brougham, *vehicle*, 272.
*Brouillerie (Fr.), *discord*, 713.
*Brouillon (Fr.), *rough copy*, 21.
Brow, *summit*, 210.
  edge, 230.
Browbeat, *intimidate*, 860.
  swagger, 885.
Brown, *colour*, 433.
Brownie, *imp*, 980.
Brown study, *reverie*, 458.
Browse, *feed*, 296.
Bruise, *hurt*, 619.
  to injure, 649.
Bruiser, *fighter*, 726.
Bruit, *publication*, 531.
  news, 532.
Brumal, *cold*, 383.
Brummagem, *spurious*, 544.
Brumous, *foggy*, 422.
Brunette, *brown*, 433.
Brunt, *impulse*, 276.
  attack, 716.
Brush, *rapid motion*, 274.
  to clean, 652.
  painting, 559.
  fight, 720.
  rough, 256.
Brush up, *memory*, 505.
Brushwood, *plant*, 367.
Brusque, *discourteous*, 895.
Brutal, *vicious*, 945.
  ill-bred, 895.
  savage, 907.
Brutalise, *harden*, 823, 895.
Brute, *animal*, 366.
  rude, 895.
  maleficent, 913.
Brute force, *illegality*, 964.
Brute matter, *materiality*, 316.
  inanimate matter, 358.
Brutish, *vulgar*, 876.
  intemperate, 954.
*Brutum fulmen (L.), *impotence*, 158.
  laxity, 738.
Bubble, *air*, 353.
  light, 320.
  trifle, 643.
  error, 495.
  vision, 515.
  deceit, 545.
  excitement, 824.
Buccaneer, *thief*, 792.
Buck, *to wash*, 652.
  fop, 854.
Buck up, *hasten*, 274.
  stimulate, 615.
  cheer, 836.
Bucket, *receptacle*, 191.
Buckle, *to tie*, 43.
  vinculum, 45.
  distort, 243.
Buckle to, *apply oneself*, 682.
Buckle with, *grapple*, 720.
Buckler, *defence*, 666, 717.
Buckram, *hardness*, 323.
  affectation, 855.
Bucolic, *pastoral*, 371.
  poem, 597.
Bud, *beginning*, 66.
  to expand, 194.
  effect, 154.
  graft, 300.
Buddha, *deity*, 979.
Buddhism, *heterodoxy*, 984.
Budge, *move*, 264.
Budget, *heap*, 72.
  store, 636.
  news, 532.
  finance, 881.
Buff, *yellow*, 436.
Buffer, *defence*, 717.
  fellow, 373.
Buffet, *cupboard*, 191.
  beat, 276, 972.
  attack, 716.

*Buffo (It.), *the drama*, 599.
Buffoon, *humorist*, 844.
butt, 857.
actor, 599.
Buffoonery, *amusement*, 840.
ridiculous, 856.
Bugaboo, *fear*, 860.
Bugbear, *fear*, 860.
alarm, 669.
imaginary, 515.
Buggy, *vehicle*, 272.
Bugle, *instrument*, 417.
war-cry, 722.
Buhl, *variegation*, 440.
Build, *construct*, 161.
compose, 54.
Build upon, *expect*, 507, 858.
Builder, *producer*, 164.
Building, *abode*, 189.
Bulb, *knob*, 249.
projection, 250.
Bulbous, *swollen*, 194.
Bulge, *convexity*, 250.
Bulk, *whole*, 50.
size, 192.
Bulkhead, *hindrance*, 706.
Bulky, *size*, 192.
Bull, *absurdity*, 497.
error, 495.
solecism, 568.
law, 963.
ordinance, 741.
Bull-calf, *fool*, 501.
Bulldog, *courage*, 861.
Bullet, *ball*, 249.
missile, 284.
arms, 727.
Bulletin, *message*, 532.
Bullion, *money*, 800.
Bully, *bluster*, 885.
blusterer, 887.
fight, 726.
frighten, 860.
Bulrush, *unimportance*, 643.
Bulwark, *defence*, 717.
refuge, 666.
Bumboat, *ship*, 273.
Bump, *projection*, 250.
thump, 276.
Bumper, *sufficiency*, 639.
Bumpkin, *commonalty*, 876.
Bumptious, *insolent*, 885.
Bunch, *protuberance*, 250.
collection, 72.
Bundle, *packet*, 72.
to move, 275.
Bung, *stopper*, 263.
Bungalow, *abode*, 189.
Bungle, *unskilfulness*, 699.
Bungle, *failure*, 732.
Bungler, *unskilful*, 701.
Bunk, *bed*, 191.
escape, 671.
Bunker, *obstruction*, 706.
Bunkum, *humbug*, 545.
Bunting, *flag*, 550.
Buoy, *float*, 320.
to raise, 307.
to hope, 858.
Buoyant, *floating*, 305.
levity, 320.
elastic, 325.
hopeful, 858.
cheerful, 836.
Bur, *rough*, 256.
clinging, 46.
Burden, *weight*, 319.
clog, 706.
chorus, 104.
frequency, 136.
lading, 190.
care, 830.
oppression, 828.
*Bureau (Fr.), *cabinet*, 691
office, 799.
Bureaucracy, *direction*, 693.
Burgee, *flag*, 550.
Burgeon, *expansion*, 194.
Burgess, *citizen*, 188, 373.
Burglar, *thief*, 792.
Burglary, *stealing*, 791.
Burgomaster, *master*, 745.
Burgrave, *master*, 745.
Burial, *corpse*, 362.
Buried, *depth*, 208.
Burin, *engraving*, 559.
Burke, *kill*, 361.
destroy, 162.
suppress, 528.
Burlesque, *imitation*, 19.
travesty, 21.
drama, 599.
ridicule, 856.
ridiculous, 853.
Burletta, *the drama*, 599.
Burly, *size*, 192.
Burn, *heat*, 382.
consume, 384.
passions, 821.
rivulet, 348.
Burnish, *polish*, 255.
beautify, 845.
shine, 420.
Burnous, *dress*, 225.
Burrow, *excavate*, 252.
lodge, 186.
Bursar, *treasurer*, 801.
Bursary, *treasury*, 802.

Burst, *explosion*, 173.
sound, 406.
of anger, 900.
paroxysm, 825.
spree, 840.
Burst forth, *appear*, 446.
sprout, 194.
Burst out, *ejaculate*, 580.
Burst upon, *inexpectation*, 508.
Bury, *inter*, 363.
conceal, 528.
Bus, *vehicle*, 272.
Busby, *hat*, 225.
Bush, *branch*, 51.
shrub, 367.
Bushel, *receptacle*, 191.
Bushy, *roughness*, 256.
Business, *occupation*, 625.
event, 151.
topic, 454.
action, 680.
barter, 794.
Business-like, *activity*, 682.
order, 58.
Buskin, *dress*, 225.
drama, 599.
Buss, *ship*, 272.
kiss, 902.
Bustle, *activity*, 682.
haste, 684.
energy, 171.
earliness, 132.
Busy, *activity*, 682.
Busybody, *activity*, 682.
But, *exception*, 83, 179.
counter-evidence, 468.
Butcher, *evil-doer*, 913.
Butchery, *killing*, 361.
Butler, *servant*, 746.
Butt, *aim*, 620.
laughing-stock, 857.
to push, 276.
to attack, 716.
Butt-end, *end*, 67.
Butter, *softness*, 324.
oiliness, 356.
to flatter, 933.
Butter-fingers, *bungler*, 701.
Butterfly, *beauty*, 845.
fickleness, 605.
Butt in, *intervene*, 228.
Button, *knob*, 250.
to fasten, 43.
fastening, 45.
hanging, 214.
trifle, 643.
Buttoned up, *reserved*, 528.
taciturn, 585.
Buttonhole, *ornament*, 847.
Buttonholer, *weariness*, 841.
Buttons, *servant*, 746.
Buttress, *defence*, 717.
Buxom, *plump*, 192.
comely, 845.
cheerful, 836.
Buy, *purchase*, 795.
Buyer, *merchant*, 797.
Buzz, *sound*, 409, 412.
to publish, 531.
news, 532.
Buzzard, *fool*, 501.
By and by, *transientness*, 111.
By the by, *opportunity*, 134.
Bye, *departure*, 293.
sequestered, 893.
By fits and starts, *disorder*, 59.
Bygone, *former*, 122.
forgotten, 506.
By-law, *legality*, 963.
By-name, *misnomer*, 565.
By-path, *road*, 627.
Byssus, *roughness*, 256.
Bystander, *spectator*, 444.
near, 197.
By-way, *road*, 627.
Byword, *maxim*, 496.
cant term, 563.
contempt, 930.

C

Cab, *vehicle*, 272.
Cabbage, *purloin*, 791.
Cabal, *confederacy*, 712.
plan, 626.
Cabbala, *spell*, 993.
Cabbalistic, *mysterious*, 528.
Cabin, *room*, 189.
receptacle, 191.
Cabinet, *receptacle*, 191.
workshop, 691.
council, 696.
Cable, *vinculum*, 45.
Cabriolet, *vehicle*, 272.
Cache, *hiding-place*, 530.
Cachexy, *disease*, 655.
Cachinnation, *rejoicing*, 838.
Cachuca, *dance*, 840.
Cacique, *master*, 745.
Cackle, *of geese*, 412.
talk, 588.
laughter, 838.
Cacodemon, *demon*, 980.
Cacodyl, *fetor*, 401.
*Cacoethes (L.), *habit*, 613.
itch, 865.
writing, 590.

*Cacoethes loquendi (L.), *loquacity*, 584.
*Cacoethes scribendi (L.), *writing*, 590.
Cacography, *writing*, 590.
Cacophony, *stridor*, 410.
discord, 414.
style, 579.
Cad, *vulgarity*, 851.
*Cadastre (Fr.), *list*, 86.
Cadaverous, *pale*, 429.
hideous, 846.
Caddish, *mean*, 940.
Caddy, *receptacle*, 191.
Cadence, *accent*, 580.
music, 415.
descent, 306.
Cadenza, *music*, 415.
Cadet, *junior*, 129.
officer, 745.
Cadge, *request*, 765.
Cadger, *merchant*, 797.
Cadi, *judge*, 967.
Cadre, *framework*, 215.
Caduceus, *spell*, 993.
Caducity, *transientness*, 111.
*Cæcum (L.), *closure*, 261.
Cæsar, *master*, 745.
Cæsura, *break*, 70.
disjunction, 44.
*Cætera desunt (L.), *incomplete*, 53.
*Cæteris paribus (L.), *circumstance*, 8.
equality, 27.
Café, *food*, 298.
Caftan, *dress*, 225.
Cage, *prison*, 231, 752.
to immure, 751.
abode, 189.
Caïque, *ship*, 273.
Cairn, *grave*, 363.
sign, 550.
*Caisson (Fr.), *receptacle*, 191.
Caitiff, *ruffian*, 913.
villain, 949.
churl, 876.
Cajole, *persuade*, 615.
flatter, 933.
Cake, *aggregate*, 46.
density, 321.
Calabash, *receptacle*, 191.
tobacco-pipe, 351.
Calamity, *evil*, 619.
adversity, 735.
suffering, 830.
Calash, *vehicle*, 272.
cap, 225.
Calcine, *calefaction*, 384.
Calculate, *reckon*, 85.
Calculate, *expect*, 507.
believe, 484.
investigate, 461.
Calculated, *tending to*, 176.
premeditated, 600.
Calculating, *prudent*, 498.
Calculation, *consideration*, 615.
caution, 864.
Calculus, *numeration*, 85.
Caldron, *mixture*, 41.
vessel, 191.
heating, 386.
laboratory, 691.
Calefaction, *heating*, 384.
*Calembour (Fr.), *pun*, 563.
Calendar, *of time*, 114.
list, 86.
record, 551.
Calender, *to glaze*, 255.
Calf, *fool*, 501.
Caliban, *ugliness*, 846.
Calibre, *size*, 192.
breadth, 202.
opening, 260.
intellectual capacity, 698.
Calidity, *heat*, 382.
Caliph, *master*, 745.
Caliphate, *authority*, 737.
Call, *to name*, 564.
motive, 615.
visit, 892.
inspiration, 985.
Call down, *malediction*, 908.
Call for, *order*, 741.
ask, 765.
require, 630.
Call forth, *resort to*, 677.
Call on, *ask*, 765.
Call over, *numeration*, 85.
Call up, *memory*, 505.
summon, 741.
Call upon, *behove*, 926.
visit, 892.
claim, 924.
Calligraphy, *writing*, 590.
Calling, *business*, 625.
Callipers, *measurement*, 466.
Callisthenics, *training*, 673.
Callosity, *hardness*, 323.
Callous, *obtuse*, 376.
insensible, 823.
Callow, *infant*, 129.
young, 127.
Calm, *physical*, 174.
moral, 826.
quiet, 265.
dissuade, 616.
Calorific, *heat*, 382.
Calorimeter, *thermometer*, 389.

*Calotte (Fr.), *vestment*, 225, 999
Calumet, *pacification*, 723.
Calumny, *detraction*, 934.
Calumniator, *detractor*, 936.
Calyx, *integument*, 222.
*Camarade (Fr.), *friend*, 890.
*Camaraderie (Fr.), *friendship*, 888.
*Camarilla (Sp.), *party*, 712.
Camber, *curvature*, 250.
Camel, *carrier*, 271.
Cameo, *sculpture*, 557.
Camera, *optical instrument*, 445.
*Camisade (Fr.), *attack*, 716.
Camouflage, *concealment*, 528.
deception, 545.
Camisole, *dress*, 225.
Camorra, *illegality*, 964.
Camp, *to locate*, 184.
abode, 186.
Campaign, *warfare*, 722.
plan, 626.
conduct, 692.
Campagna, *space*, 180.
*Campanile (It.), *tower*, 206.
Campaniliform, *bell-shaped*, 249.
cupped, 252.
Campanologist, *musician*, 416.
Can, *power*, 157.
mug, 191.
to preserve, 670.
*Canaille (Fr.), *commonalty* 876.
Canal, *opening*, 260.
Canard, *deception*, 545.
Cancan, *dance*, 840.
Cancel, *obliterate*, 552, 773.
abrogate, 756.
Cancellated, *crossing*, 219.
*Cancelli (L.), *lattice*, 219.
Cancer, *disease*, 655.
foulness, 653.
painful, 830.
Candelabra, *luminary*, 423.
Candescence, *heat*, 382.
Candid, *sincere*, 543.
ingenuous, 703.
honourable, 939.
Candidate, *petitioner*, 767, 865.
Candidature, *solicitation*, 765.
Candle, *luminary*, 423.
Candle-ends, *remainder*, 40.
Candle-holder, *auxiliary*, 711.
Candlestick, *luminary*, 423.
Candour, *veracity*, 543.
artlessness, 703.
honour, 939.
Candy, *sweetness*, 396.
Cane, *scourge*, 975.
to beat, 276.
punish, 972.
Cangue, *shackle*, 752.
Canicular, *heat*, 382.
Canister, *receptacle*, 191.
Canker, *disease*, 655.
bane, 663.
deterioration, 659.
pain, 830.
Cankering, *badness*, 649.
Cannibal, *sinner*, 949.
Cannon, *arms*, 727.
collision, 276.
Cannonade, *attack*, 716.
Cannoneer, *combatant*, 726.
Canny, *cunning*, 702.
intelligent, 498.
thrifty, 817.
Canoe, *ship*, 273.
Canon, *rule*, 80.
music, 415.
precept, 697.
priest, 996.
Canonical, *orthodox*, 983A.
Canonicals, *holy orders*, 999.
Canonise, *rites*, 998.
Canoodle, *endearment*, 902.
Canopy, *height*, 206.
roof, 210.
covering, 222.
Canorous, *resonant*, 402.
melodious, 415.
Cant, *neology*, 563.
oblique, 217.
hypocrisy, 544.
Cantankerous, *discourtesy*, 895.
Cantata, *music*, 415.
*Cantatrice, (It.), *musician*, 416.
Canted, *obliquity*, 217.
Canteen, *receptacle*, 191.
feeding, 298.
Canter, *move*, 266.
gallop, 274.
Canticle, *music*, 415.
Cantilever, *support*, 215.
Cantle, *part*, 51.
Canto, *poetry*, 597.
Canton, *region*, 181.
Cantonment, *location*, 184.
abode, 189.
Canty, *cheerfulness*, 836.
Canvas, *sail*, 267.
Canvass, *investigate*, 461.
solicit, 765.
Canyon, *ravine*, 198.
Canzonet, *song*, 415.
poem, 597.
Caoutchouc, *elasticity*, 325.
Cap, *hat*, 225.
height, 206.
to be superior, 33, 194.

Cap, *to salute*, 894.
Capability, *power*, 157.
strength, 159.
facility, 705.
endowment, 5.
Capacity, *space*, 180.
size, 192.
endowment, 5.
power, 157.
intellect, 450.
aptitude, 539.
talent, 698.
wisdom, 498.
utility, 644.
office, 625.
*Cap-à-pie (Fr.), *preparation*, 673.
Caparison, *vestment*, 225.
Cape, *land*, 342.
projection, 250.
height, 206.
cloak, 225.
Caper, *rise*, 305.
leap, 309.
dance, 840.
Capillary, *thinness*, 203, 205.
Capital, *excellent*, 648.
important, 642.
summit, 210.
money, 800.
wealth, 803.
Capitalist, *wealth*, 803.
Capitation, *numeration*, 85.
Capitol, *defence*, 717.
Capitular, *clergy*, 996.
Capitulate, *submission*, 725.
Capnomancy, *prediction*, 511.
Capote, *vestment*, 225.
*Capriccio (It.), *caprice*, 608.
Caprice, *chance*, 608.
music, 415.
Capricious, *irregular*, 139.
whimsical, 608.
Capriole, *leap*, 309.
Capsize, *inversion*, 218.
wreck, 731.
Capsized, *failure*, 732.
Capstan, *instrument*, 633.
Capsule, *vessel*, 191.
tunicle, 222.
Captain, *master*, 745.
Caption, *indication*, 550.
Captious, *capricious*, 608.
censorious, 932.
discourteous, 795.
Captivated, *fascinated*, 827, 897.
Captivating, *pleasing*, 829.
lovely, 897.
Captive, *prisoner*, 754.
Captivity, *restraint*, 751.
Capture, *taking*, 789.
Capuchin, *clergy*, 996.
*Caput mortuum (L.), *remainder*, 40.
unclean, 653.
Car, *vehicle*, 272.
Carabineer, *combatant*, 726.
*Caracole (Fr.), *rise*, 305.
leap, 309.
journey, 266.
Carafe, *receptacle*, 191.
*Carambole (Fr.), *impulse*, 276.
Carapace, *covering*, 222.
Caravan, *vehicle*, 272.
Caravansary, *abode*, 189.
Carbine, *arms*, 727.
Carbonise, *calefaction*, 384.
Carboy, *receptacle*, 191.
Carcass, *corpse*, 362.
Card, *ticket*, 550.
plan, 626.
oddity, 857.
to unravel, 60.
Cardiac, *remedy*, 662.
Cardigan, *dress*, 225.
Cardinal, *important*, 642.
excellent, 648.
red, 434.
dress, 225.
priest, 996.
Care, *attention*, 459.
pain, 828, 830.
custody, 751.
Care for, *desire*, 865.
love, 642, 897.
Careen, *slant*, 217, 306.
repair, 658.
Career, *business*, 625.
conduct, 692.
Careful, *caution*, 864.
Careless, *inattentive*, 458.
neglectful, 460.
insensible, 823.
Caress, *endearment*, 902.
*Caret (L.), *incomplete*, 53.
to want, 640.
Care-worn, *pain*, 828.
Cargo, *goods*, 798.
contents, 190.
property, 780.
materials, 635.
large quantity, 31.
Caricature, *likeness*, 19.
misrepresentation, 555.
ridicule, 856.
*Caries (L.), *disease*, 655.
Carillon, *musical instrument*, 417.
Carking, *pain*, 828.
Carle, *boor*, 876.
Carmelite, *clergy*, 996.

Carminative, *remedy*, 662.
Carmine, *redness*, 434.
Carnage, *killing*, 361.
Carnal, *impure*, 961.
irreligious, 988.
Carnation, *redness*, 434.
Carnival, *amusement*, 840.
Carny, *to coax*, 615.
Carol, *music*, 415.
cheerful, 836.
Carouse, *feast*, 296.
festivity, 840.
drink, 959.
Carp, *disapprobation*, 932.
*Carpe diem (L.), *occasion*, 134.
Carper, *detractor*, 936.
Carpet, on the, *preparation*, 673.
*Carrefour (Fr.), *road*, 627.
Carriage, *transference*, 270.
vehicle, 272.
gait, 264.
aspect, 448.
conduct, 692.
fashion, 852.
Carrier, *porter*, 271.
Carriole, *vehicle*, 272.
Carrion, *carcass*, 362.
foulness, 653.
Carronade, *arms*, 727.
Carroty, *redness*, 434.
Carry, *support*, 215.
transfer, 270.
tend, 176.
induce, 615.
Carry off, *take*, 789.
steal, 791.
Carry on, *conduct*, 692.
continue, 143.
pursue, 622.
Carry out, *complete*, 729.
conduct, 692.
Carry through, *complete*, 729.
conduct, 692.
Cart, *vehicle*, 272.
to transfer, 270.
Cartage, *transference*, 270.
*Carte blanche (Fr.), *permission*, 760.
liberality, 816.
*Carte de visite (Fr.), *indication*, 550.
*Carte du pays (Fr.), *plan*, 626.
Cartel, *defiance*, 715.
truce, 723.
security, 771.
Cart-load, *quantity*, 31.
abundance, 639.
Cartography, *representation*, 554.
Cartoon, *painting*, 556.
Cartouche, *scroll*, 248.
Cartridge, *arms*, 727.
Cartulary, *record*, 551.
Caruncle, *convexity*, 250.
Carve, *sculpture*, 557, 857.
to form, 240.
to produce, 161.
disjunction, 44.
Carver, *artist*, 559.
Caryatides, *support*, 215.
Cascade, *river*, 348.
Case, *state*, 7.
sheath, 222.
receptacle, 191, 232.
Case, in good, *stout*, 192.
Case-harden, *harden*, 823.
strengthen, 159.
train, 673.
Casemate, *defence*, 717.
Cash, *money*, 800.
Cash register, *numeration*, 85.
Cashier, *to dismiss*, 756.
treasurer, 801.
Casino, *sociality*, 892.
Cask, *receptacle*, 191.
Casket, *receptacle*, 191.
*Casserole (Fr.), *receptacle*, 191.
Cassock, *dress*, 225.
canonicals, 999.
Cast, *to throw*, 284.
state, 7.
bias, 820.
mould, 21.
form, 240.
to throw down, 308.
small quantity, 32.
tinge, 428.
aspect, 448.
to peel, 226.
to condemn, 971.
to allot, 786.
drama, 599.
Cast about, *inquiry*, 461.
Castilian, *poetry*, 597.
Cast anchor, *stop*, 265.
arrive, 293.
Castanet, *musical instrument*, 417.
Castaway, *lost*, 732.
to relinquish, 782.
reprobate, 949.
sinner, 949.
Cast down, *dejection*, 837.
Caste, *class*, 75.
Castellan, *keeper*, 753.
servant, 746.
Caster, *receptacle*, 191.
Cast forth, *dispersion*, 73.
Castigate, *punish*, 972.
reprove, 932.
Castle, *defence*, 717.

Castle, *edifice*, 189.
Castle-building, *imagination*, 515.
Cast of the eye, *squint*, 443.
Cast off, *remainder*, 40.
discard, 678.
Castor, *hat*, 225.
Cast out, *ejection*, 297.
Castrate, *mutilate*, 38, 44, 53.
Castrated, *weakened*, 160.
purified. 652.
Cast up, *add*, 85.
happen, 151.
eject, 297.
Casual, *by chance*, 156, 621.
irregular, 139.
mutable, 149.
uncertain, 475.
unmethodical, 59.
Casualty, *event*, 151.
chance, 156, 621.
Casuistry, *sophistry*, 477.
scruple, 485.
ethics, 926.
*Casus belli (L.), *discord*, 713.
resentment, 900.
*Casus fœderis (L.), *condition*, 770.
Cat, *scourge*, 975.
to vomit, 297.
Catachresis, *metaphor*, 521.
misinterpretation, 523.
Cataclysm, *deluge*, 348.
convulsion, 146.
redundance, 641.
Catacomb, *interment*, 363.
Catafalque, *interment*, 363.
Catalectic, *poetry*, 597.
Catalepsy, *quiescence*, 265.
Catalogue, *list*, 86, 551.
*Catalogue raisonné (Fr.), *list*, 86.
Catalysis, *decomposition*, 49.
Catamaran, *vessel*, 273.
Cataplasm, *remedy*, 662.
Catapult, *projection*, 276, 284.
arms, 727.
Cataract, *river*, 348.
Catastrophe, *end*, 67.
disaster, 619.
adversity, 735.
calamity, 830.
Catch, *take*, 134, 789.
receive, 785.
learn, 539.
gather meaning, 518.
cheat, 545.
vinculum, 45.
Catch at, *receiving*, 785.
Catching, *infectious*, 657.
Catch on, *success*, 731.
Catch-penny, *trumpery*, 643.
Catch-penny, *false*, 544.
Catchpoll, *jurisprudence*, 965.
Catch up, *overtake*, 292.
Catchword, *formula*, 80.
Catechetical, *inquiry*, 461.
Catechise, *inquiry*, 461.
Catechumen, *learner*, 541.
Categorical, *true*, 494.
positive, 474.
demonstrative, 478.
affirmative, 535.
Category, *class*, 75.
state, 7.
Catenation, *continuity*, 69.
Cater, *provision*, 637.
Caterwauling, *ululation*, 412.
Cates, *food*, 298.
Cathedral, *temple*, 1000.
Catholic, *universal*, 78.
religion, 987.
broad-minded, 448.
Catholicism, *theology*, 983.
Catholicity, *generality*, 78.
broad-mindedness, 498.
Catholicon, *remedy*, 662.
Cat-o'-nine-tails, *scourge*, 975.
Catoptromancy, *prediction*, 511.
Cat's-cradle, *crossing*, 219.
Cat's-paw, *instrument*, 631.
Caucus, *assemblage*, 72.
Caudal, *end*, 67.
Caudate, *pendency*, 214.
Cauldron, *see* Caldron.
Caulk, *repair*, 658.
Causality, *cause*, 153.
power, 157.
Causation, *cause*, 153.
agency, 170.
Cause, *source*, 153.
final, 620.
lawsuit, 969.
Causeless, *casual*, 156.
aimless, 621.
*Causeur (Fr.), *talker*, 588.
Causeway, *road*, 627.
Causidical, *jurisprudence*, 965.
Caustic, *energetic*, 171.
gruff, 895.
Cautelous, *caution*, 864.
Cauterise, *calefaction*, 384.
Caution, *care*, 459.
warning, 668.
prudence, 864.
advice, 695.
security, 771.
Cavalcade, *continuity*, 69.
Cavalier, *horseman*, 268.
insolent, 885.
*Cavaliere servente (It.), *lover*, 897.

Cavalierly, *inattention*, 458.
Cavalry, *combatant*, 726.
*Cavatina (It.), *music*, 415.
Cave, *cavity*, 252.
cell, 191.
dwelling, 189.
*Caveat (L.), *warning*, 668.
*Caveat emptor (L.), *purchase*, 795.
Cave in, *submit*, 729.
Cavendish, *tobacco*, 298A.
Cavern, *hollow*, 252.
cell, 191.
dwelling, 189.
Cavernous, *hollow*, 252.
porous, 322.
Caviar, *pungent*, 171, 392.
Cavil, *censure*, 932.
Caviller, *detractor*, 936.
Cavity, *concavity*, 252.
Caw, *animal cry*, 412.
Cayenne, *condiment*, 393.
pungent, 171.
Cease, *cessation*, 141.
Ceaseless, *perpetuity*, 112.
Cecity, *blindness*, 442.
Cede, *relinquish*, 782.
Ceiling, *height*, 206.
summit, 210.
*Cela va sans dire (Fr.), *conformity*, 82.
effect, 154.
Celebrate, *solemnise*, 883.
publish, 531.
praise, 931.
Celebration, *fête*, 883.
Celebrity, *repute*, 873.
Celerity, *velocity*, 274.
Celestial, *physical*, 318.
moral, 829.
religious, 976, 981.
Celibacy, *bachelor*, 904.
Cell, *cavity*, 252.
receptacle, 191.
abode, 189.
prison, 752.
Cellar, *receptacle*, 191.
Cellaret, *receptacle*, 191.
Cellule, *receptacle*, 191.
Cembalo, *musical instrument*, 417.
Cement, *uniting medium*, 45.
to unite, 46.
concord, 714.
Cemetery, *interment*, 363.
Cenobite, *recluse*, 893.
anchorite, 996.
Cenotaph, *interment*, 363.
Censer, *temple*, 1000.
Censor, *detractor*, 936.
Censorious, *disapprobation*, 932.
Censorship, *authority*, 737.
Censure, *disapprobation*, 932.
Census, *counting*, 85.
Centaur, *unconformity*, 83.
Centenary, *numbers*, 98.
Centennial, *numbers*, 98.
period, 108.
Centesimal, *number division*, 99.
*Cento (It.), *poetry*, 597.
Central, *centrality*, 223.
Centralise, *combine*, 48.
focus, 72.
concentrate, 223.
Centre, *in order*, 68.
in space, 223.
Centre in, *convergence*, 290.
Centrifugal, *divergence*, 291.
Centripetal, *convergence*, 290.
Centuple, *number*, 98.
Centurion, *master*, 745.
Century, *period*, 108.
duration, 106.
Cerberus, *janitor*, 263.
custodian, 664.
Cerebration, *thought*, 451.
Cerebrum, *intellect*, 450.
Cerement, *interment*, 363.
Ceremony, *parade*, 882.
religious, 998.
Ceremonious, *respect*, 928.
Cerise, *red*, 434.
Certain, *sure*, 474.
special, 79.
indefinite number, 100.
Certainly, *assent*, 488.
Certificate, *voucher*, 551.
evidence, 467.
Certify, *evince*, 467.
inform, 527.
Certitude, *certainty*, 474.
Cerulean, *blue*, 438.
Cess, *tax*, 812.
Cessation, *ceasing*, 141.
Cession, *surrender*, 725, 782.
gift, 784.
Cesspool, *uncleanness*, 633.
Cestus, *girdle*, 225.
ligature, 45.
ring, 247.
Chafe, *warm*, 384.
pain, 378.
irritate, 825, 828.
vex, 830.
incense, 900.
Chaff, *trash*, 643.
vulgar, 876.
Chaffer, *bargain*, 769.
sale, 794.
Chafing-dish, *furnace*, 386.

Chagrin, *pain*, 828.
Chain, *series*, 69.
to fasten, 43.
vinculum, 45.
to imprison, 752.
Chain-mail, *arms*, 727.
Chain-shot, *arms*, 727.
Chair, *support*, 215.
vehicle, 272.
professorship, 542.
throne, 747.
Chairman, *director*, 694, 745.
Chairmanship, *direction*, 693.
Chaise, *vehicle*, 272.
*Chalet (Fr.), *abode*, 189.
Chalice, *cup*, 191.
hollow, 252.
Chalk, *mark*, 550.
drawing, 556.
Chalk out, *plan*, 626.
Chalky, *white*, 430.
Challenge, *defy*, 715.
accuse, 938.
claim, 924.
Cham, *master*, 745.
Chamber, *room*, 191.
council, 696.
mart, 799.
Chamberlain, *servant*, 746.
Chamber-maid, *servant*, 746.
Chamber-music, *music*, 415.
Chameleon, *variegation*, 440.
inconstancy, 149, 605.
Chamfer, *furrow*, 259.
Champ, *eat*, 296.
Champaign, *plain*, 344.
Champion, *auxiliary*, 711.
proficient, 700.
defence, 717.
combatant, 726.
Championship, *aid*, 707.
superiority, 33.
Chance, *absence of cause*, 156.
absence of aim, 621.
opportunity, 134.
Chancel, *temple*, 1000.
Chancellor, *president*, 745.
judge, 967.
Chance-medley, *chance*, 156.
Chancy, *risky*, 665.
uncertain, 475.
Chandelier, *luminary*, 423.
Change, *alteration*, 140.
mart, 799.
small coin, 800.
Changeable, *mutable*, 149, 607.
irresolute, 605.
Changeful, *mutable*, 149.
volition, 607.
Changeling, *changed*, 147.
fool, 501.
Channel, *opening*, 260.
conduit, 350.
way, 627.
furrow, 259.
Chant, *sing*, 415.
worship, 990.
rites, 998.
*Chantage, (Fr.) *blackmail*, 791.
Chanty, *music*, 415.
Chaomancy, *prediction*, 511.
Chaos, *disorder*, 59.
secret, 533.
Chap, *man*, 373.
fissure, 198.
Chap-book, *book*, 593.
Chapel, *temple*, 1000.
*Chaperon (Fr.), *safety*, 664, 753.
accompaniment, 88.
Chap-fallen, *dejected*, 837.
abashed, 881.
Chaplain, *clergy*, 996.
Chaplet, *circle*, 247.
dress, 225.
ornament, 847.
trophy, 733.
Chapman, *merchant*, 797.
Chaps, *orifice*, 66.
Chapter, *part*, 51.
topic, 454.
book, 593.
church, 995.
Char, *calefaction*, 384.
*Char-à-banc (Fr.), *vehicle*, 272.
Character, *nature*, 5.
disposition, 820.
state, 7.
letter, 561.
type, 591.
drama, 599.
class, 75.
unconformity, 83.
Character, out of, *disagreement*, 24.
Characterise, *nomenclature*, 564.
Characteristic, *special*, 79.
intrinsic, 5.
Charade, *secret*, 533.
Charcoal, *fuel*, 388.
black, 431.
Charge, *business*, 625.
direction, 693.
advice, 695.
commission, 755.
load, 639.
order, 741.
accusation, 938.
attack, 716.
price, 812.

Charge, *custody*, 751.
*Chargé d'affaires (Fr.), *deputy*, 759.
Charger, *carrier*, 271.
Chariot, *vehicle*, 272.
Charioteer, *director*, 694.
Charitable, *giving*, 784.
  liberal, 816.
  benevolent, 906.
Charity, *giving*, 784.
  benevolence, 906.
  bounty, 816.
*Charivari (Fr.), *loudness*, 404.
  discordance, 413.
Charlatan, *impostor*, 548.
  mountebank, 844.
Charlatanism, *quackery*, 545, 855.
Charm, *to please*, 829.
  love, 897.
  motive, 615.
  to conjure, 992.
  spell, 993.
Charnel-house, *interment*, 363.
Chart, *representation*, 554.
Charter, *privilege*, 924.
  compact, 769.
  security, 771.
  commission, 755.
Chary, *economical*, 817.
  cautious, 864.
Chase, *pursue*, 622.
  follow, 281.
  wood, 367.
Chasm, *discontinuity*, 4, 70.
  interval, 198.
Chassis, *framework*, 215.
Chaste, *simple*, 849.
  good taste, 850.
  pure, 960.
  style, 576.
Chasten, *punish*, 972.
  refine, 658.
  moderate, 826.
Chastise, *punish*, 932, 972.
Chat, *interlocution*, 588.
*Château (Fr.), *abode*, 189.
*Chatoyant (Fr.), *variegation*, 440.
Chattels, *goods*, 635.
  property, 780.
Chatter, *talk*, 584.
  cold, 383.
Chatterbox, *loquacity*, 584.
Chauffeur, *driver*, 694.
Chauvinistic, *bellicose*, 722.
Chaw-bacon, *boor*, 876.
Cheap, *low price*, 815.
  worthless, 643.
Cheapen, *barter*, 794.
  depreciate, 483.
Cheat, *deceiver*, 548.
Cheat, *to deceive*, 545.
Check, *restrain*, 174.
  pacify, 826.
  slacken, 275.
  counteract, 179.
  hinder, 706.
  dissuade, 616.
  evidence, 467.
  ticket, 550.
  money order, 800.
  numerical, 85.
Checkmate, *success*, 731.
Cheek, *side*, 236.
  insolence, 885.
Cheer, *mirth*, 836.
  rejoicing, 838.
  amusement, 840.
  pleasure, 827.
  to give pleasure, 830.
  relief, 834.
  cry, 411.
  repast, 298.
  applaud, 931.
Cheered, *pleasure*, 827.
Cheerful, *pleasurable*, 836.
Cheerless, *dejection*, 830, 837.
Cheese-parings, *remainder*, 40.
  parsimony, 819.
*Chef (Fr.), *director*, 694.
*Chef-d'œuvre (Fr.), *masterpiece*, 650.
  capability, 648.
  master-stroke, 698.
Chela, *novice*, 541.
Chemise, *dress*, 225.
Chemistry, *conversion*, 144.
Cheque, *money*, 800.
Chequer, *variegation*, 440.
Cherish, *love*, 897.
  entertain, 820.
Cheroot, *tobacco*, 298A.
Cherub, *angel*, 977.
Chest, *box*, 191.
  coffer (*money*), 802.
Chesterfield, *seat*, 215.
Chest-note, *resonance*, 408.
Chestnut, *brown*, 433.
  joke, 842.
*Cheval de bataille (Fr.), *plea*, 617.
  instrument, 631.
Cheval-glass, *mirror*, 445.
*Chevalier d'industrie (Fr.), *thief*, 792.
*Chevaux de frise (Fr.), *defence*, 717.
  spikes, 253.
*Chevelure (Fr.), *hair*, 256.
Chevron, *indication*, 550.
Chew, *eat*, 296.
Chew the cud, *thought*, 451.

*Chez soi (Fr.), *at home*, 221.
*Chiaroscuro (It.), *shade*, 424.
Chibouque, *tobacco-pipe*, 351.
Chicane, *cunning*, 702.
Chicanery, *sophistry*, 477.
wrangling, 713.
Chicken, *youth*, 127.
weakness, 160.
Chicken-hearted, *cowardice*, 862.
Chide, *disapprobation*, 932.
Chief, *principal*, 642.
master, 745.
Chieftain, *master*, 745.
*Chiffon (Fr.), *ornament*, 847.
*Chignon (Fr.), *head-dress*, 225.
Child, *youth*, 129.
fool, 501.
offspring, 167.
Childish, *foolish*, 499.
trifling, 643.
Child's-play, *unimportance*, 643.
Chiliad, *numbers*, 98.
duration, 106.
Chill, *cold*, 383.
discouragement, 616, 706.
Chilly, *ungracious*, 895.
Chime, *resonance*, 408.
roll, 407.
repetition, 104.
to harmonise, 413.
Chime in with, *agree*, 23.
conformity, 82.
assent, 488.
Chimera, *monster*, 83.
error, 495.
imaginary, 515.
Chimney, *air-pipe*, 351.
fissure, 198.
opening, 260.
egress, 295.
Chink, *gap*, 198.
sound, 408.
Chip, *bit*, 51.
small part, 193.
to detach, 44.
to reduce, 195.
Chip in, *conversation*, 588.
Chip of the old block, *similarity*, 17.
Chirography, *writing*, 590.
Chiromancy, *prediction*, 511.
Chirp, *as a bird*, 412.
sing, 415.
Chirpy, *cheerful*, 836.
Chirrup, *see* Chirp.
Chisel, *sculpture*, 557.
form, 240.
fabricate, 161.
Chit, *infant*, 129.
small, 193.
Chit, *letter*, 592.
Chit-chat, *interlocution*, 588.
Chivalrous, *martial*, 722.
honourable, 939.
bold, 861.
generous, 942.
Chlorosis, *achromatism*, 429.
Chlorotic, *achromatism*, 429.
Chock-full, *sufficiency*, 639.
Chocolate, *brown*, 433.
Choice, *election*, 609.
excellent, 648.
Choir, *music*, 415.
orchestra, 416.
church, 1000.
Choke, *close*, 261.
hinder, 706.
suffocate, 361.
Choke off, *dissuade*, 616.
Choler, *resentment*, 900.
Choleric, *irascible*, 901.
Choose, *choice*, 609.
Chop, *disjoin*, 44.
change, 140.
Chop logic, *reasoning*, 476.
Chopping, *large*, 192.
Chops, *orifice*, 66.
Choral, *music*, 415.
Chord, *harmony*, 413.
Choreography, *dance*, 840.
Chorister, *musician*, 416.
sacerdotal, 997.
Chorography, *situation*, 183, 554.
Chortle, *to laugh*, 838.
Chorus, *sound*, 404.
voices, 411.
musicians, 416.
unanimity, 488.
*Chose jugée (Fr.), *judgment*, 480.
Chouse, *deception*, 545.
Chrism, *rite*, 998.
Christ, *deity*, 976.
Christen, *nomenclature*, 564.
Christian, *piety*, 987.
Christianity, *theology*, 983.
Chromatic, *colour*, 428.
musical scale, 413.
Chromatrope, *optical instrument*, 445.
Chromolithograph, *engraving*, 558.
Chronic, *diuturnity*, 110.
Chronicle, *annals*, 551.
measure of time, 114.
account, 594.
*Chronique scandaleuse (Fr.), *gossip*, 532, 588.
Chronology, *time measurement*, 114.
Chronometry, *time measurement*, 114.
Chrysalis, *youth*, 127, 129.

Chubby, *size*, 192.
Chuck, *throw*, 284.
cry, 412.
Chuck out, *expel*, 297.
Chuck up, *abandon*, 624.
Chuckle, *laugh*, 838.
exult, 884.
Chuckle-head, *fool*, 501.
Chum, *friend*, 890.
Chummy, *friendly*, 888.
Chunk, *size*, 192.
Church, *orthodoxy*, 983A.
temple, 1000.
Churchdom, *church*, 995.
Churchman, *clergy*, 996.
Churchwarden, *clergy*, 996.
tobacco-pipe, 351.
Churchy, *bigoted*, 989.
Churchyard, *interment*, 363.
Churl, *boor*, 876.
rude, 895.
irascible, 901.
niggard, 819.
Churn, *agitation*, 315, 352.
Chute, *obliquity*, 217.
Chutney, *condiment*, 393.
Cicatrix, *junction*, 43.
Cicatrise, *improvement*, 658.
*Cicerone (It.), *teacher*, 540.
director, 694.
*Cicisbeo (It.), *love*, 897.
Cicuration, *cicuration*, 370.
*Ci-devant (Fr.), *preterition*, 122.
Cigar, *tobacco*, 298A.
Cigarette, *tobacco*, 298A.
Ciliated, *roughness*, 256.
Cimmerian, *darkness*, 421.
Cinch, *grip*, 781.
Cincture, *circularity*, 247.
Cinders, *remainder*, 40.
Cinema, *theatre*, 599.
Cinematograph, *spectacle*, 448.
Cineration, *calefaction*, 384.
Cinerator, *furnace*, 386.
Cinereous, *grey*, 432.
Cingulum, *belt*, 229.
Cinque, *numbers*, 98.
Cipher, *zero*, 101.
number, 84.
to compute, 85.
secret, 533.
mark, 550.
monogram, 562.
writing, 590.
unimportant, 643.
Circe, *seductor*, 615.
sensuality, 954.
Circle, *form*, 247.
space, 181.
Circle, *social*, 892.
Circuit, *deviation*, 279.
indirect path, 629.
winding, 248.
turn, 311.
tour, 266.
space, 181.
Circuitous, *devious*, 279.
turning, 311.
indirect, 629.
Circular, *round*, 247.
advertisement, 531.
letter, 592.
Circulate, *rotate*, 312.
publish, 531.
Circumambient, *circumjacence*, 227.
Circumambulate, *move*, 266.
wind, 311.
Circumbendibus, *winding*, 248.
circuit, 629.
circuition, 311.
Circumference, *outline*, 229.
Circumfluent, *circuition*, 311.
Circumfuse, *dispersion*, 73.
Circumgyration, *rotation*, 312.
Circumjacence, *surrounding*, 227.
Circumlocution, *phrase*, 566, 573.
Circumnavigation, *navigation*, 267.
circuition, 311.
Circumrotation, *rotation*, 312.
Circumscribe, *surround*, 231.
limit, 761.
Circumspect, *attentive*, 457.
careful, 459.
cautious, 864.
Circumstance, *phrase*, 8.
event, 151.
Circumstantial, *diffuse*, 573.
evidence, 472.
Circumvallation, *enclosure*, 232.
defence, 717.
Circumvent, *cheat*, 545.
defeat, 731.
cunning, 702.
Circumvolution, *rotation*, 312.
Circus, *arena*, 728.
edifice, 189.
Cistern, *receptacle*, 191.
store, 636.
Citadel, *fort*, 666.
defence, 717.
Cite, *quote as example*, 82, 564.
as evidence, 467.
summon, 741.
accuse, 938.
arraign, 969.
Cithern, *musical instrument*, 417.
Citizen, *inhabitant*, 188.
man, 373.

Citrine, *yellow*, 436.
City, *abode*, 189.
Civet, *fragrance*, 400.
Civic, *urban*, 189.
public, 372.
Civicism, *patriotism*, 910.
Civies, *dress*, 225.
Civil, *courteous*, 894.
laity, 997.
Civilian, *lawyer*, 968.
non-combatant, 726A.
Civilisation, *courtesy*, 894.
mankind, 372.
Clack, *talk*, 588.
snap, 406.
animal cry, 412.
Clad, *dressed*, 225.
Claim, *demand*, 741, 765.
right, 924.
Claimant, *dueness*, 924.
Clairvoyance, *occult arts*, 992.
insight, 490.
foresight, 510.
Clamber, *ascent*, 305.
Clammy, *semiliquid*, 352.
Clamour, *loudness*, 404.
Clamp, *to fasten*, 43.
fastening, 45.
Clan, *class*, 75.
clique, 892.
Clandestine, *concealment*, 528.
Clang, *loudness*, 404.
resonance, 408.
Clank, *stridor*, 410.
Clap, *explosion*, 406.
to applaud, 931.
Clap on, *addition*, 37.
Clapperclaw, *beat*, 972.
Claptrap, *plea*, 617.
pretence, 546.
Clap up, *restraint*, 751.
*Claqueur (Fr.), *flatterer*, 935.
Clarence, *vehicle*, 272.
Clarify, *cleanness*, 652.
Clarinet, *musical instrument*, 417.
Clarion, *musical instrument*, 417.
Clarity, *transparency*, 425.
perspicuity, 570.
Clash, *oppose*, 708.
disagree, 24.
discord, 713.
contest, 720.
concussion, 276.
sound, 406.
Clasp, *to unite*, 43.
fastening, 45.
entrance, 903.
come close, 197.
Class, *category*, 75.
Class, *to arrange*, 60.
learner, 541.
Classic, *masterpiece*, 650.
Classical, *taste*, 578, 850.
Classify, *arrangement*, 60.
Clatter, *roll*, 407.
Clause, *part*, 51.
passage, 593.
condition, 770.
Claustral, *secluded*, 893.
Clavichord, *musical*, 417.
Claw, *hook*, 633.
to grasp, 789.
Clay, *earth*, 342.
corpse, 362.
tobacco-pipe, 351.
Clay-cold, *cold*, 383.
Claymore, *arms*, 727.
Clean, *unstained*, 652.
entirely, 31.
Clean-handed, *innocence*, 946.
Cleanse, *purge*, 652.
Clear, *transparent*, 425.
light, 420.
visible, 446.
intelligible, 518.
perspicuous style, 570.
to prepare, 673.
to free, 750.
to vindicate, 937.
to acquit, 970.
innocent, 946.
simple, 42.
easy, 705.
to pay, 807.
to pass, 302.
Clear decks, *preparation*, 673.
Clear of, *distant*, 196.
Clear out, *eject*, 297.
Clear up, *interpret*, 522.
Clearance, *payment*, 807.
Clear-sighted, *vision*, 441.
shrewd, 498.
Cleave, *adhere*, 46.
sunder, 44, 91.
Cleek, *club*, 276.
Clef, *music*, 413.
Cleft, *chink*, 198.
Clement, *lenient*, 740.
kind, 906.
pitiful, 914.
Clench, *see* Clinch.
Clepsydra, *chronometry*, 114.
Clergy, *clergy*, 996.
Clerical, *churchdom*, 995.
Clerk, *scholar*, 492.
recorder, 553.
writer, 590.
agent, 758.

Clerk, *church*, 996.
Clerkship, *commission*, 755.
Cleromancy, *prediction*, 511.
Clever, *skill*, 698.
*Cliché (Fr.), *stereotyped*, 82.
Click, *snap*, 406.
Client, *dependant*, 746.
Clientship, *subjection*, 749.
Cliff, *height*, 206.
verticality, 212, 217.
Climacteric, *age*, 128.
Climate, *region*, 181.
weather, 338.
Climax, *summit*, 210.
in degree, 33.
Climb, *ascent*, 305.
Clime, *region*, 181.
Clinch, *snatch*, 789.
fasten, 43.
an argument, 478.
Clincher, *confutation*, 479.
Cling, *cohere*, 46.
Clinic, *medicine*, 662.
Clink, *resonance*, 408.
prison, 752.
Clinker, *concretion*, 321.
*Clinquant (Fr.), *ornament*, 847, *vulgarity*, 851.
Clip, *prune*, 38.
contract, 195.
shorten, 201.
stammer, 583.
Clipper, *ship*, 273.
swift, 274.
Clipping, *part*, 51.
first-rate, 648.
*Clique (Fr.), *party*, 712.
sociality, 892.
Cloaca, *conduit*, 350.
foulness, 653.
Cloak, *dress*, 225.
conceal, 528.
disguise, 546.
Clock, *chronometry*, 114.
Clockwise, *rotation*, 312.
Clockwork, *instrument*, 633.
Clod, *earth*, 342.
fool, 591.
Clod-hopper, *boor*, 876.
Clod-pated, *folly*, 499.
Clod-poll, *fool*, 501.
Clog, *hindrance*, 706.
boot, 225.
Clog-dance, *dance*, 840.
Cloister, *temple*, 1000.
seclusion, 893.
Close, *near*, 197.
short, 201.
narrow, 203.
Close, *dense*, 321.
tight, 43.
similar, 17.
to shut, 261.
warm, 382.
end, 67.
to complete, 729.
thinking, 451.
taciturn, 585.
stingy, 819.
piece of land, 780.
house, 189.
Close-fisted, *parsimony*, 819.
Close in upon, *convergence*, 290.
Close with, *arrive*, 292.
combat, 720.
assent, 488.
compact, 769.
Closeness, *junction*, 43.
Close quarters, *nearness*, 197.
Closet, *room*, 191.
Closure, *closing*, 261.
Clot, *concretion*, 46.
density, 321.
earth, 342.
Clothes, *dress*, 225.
Cloud, *dimness*, 422.
shade, 424.
opacity, 426.
concealment, 528.
crowd, 72.
smoke, 334.
Cloud - capt, cloud - topt, cloud - touching, *height*, 206.
Clouded, *variegated*, 440.
Cloudless, *light*, 420.
Cloudy, *opaque*, 426.
dark, 421.
Clout, *blow*, 276.
to repair, 658.
Cloven, *bisection*, 91.
Cloven-footed, *malevolent*, 907.
Clover, *luxury*, 377.
comfort, 827.
Clown, *rustic*, 876.
buffoon, 844.
pantomimic, 599.
Clownish, *vulgar*, 851.
Cloy, *satiety*, 641, 869.
Club, *bludgeon*, 276.
instrument, 633.
weapon, 727.
party, 712.
to co-operate, 709.
social meeting, 892.
assemblage, 72.
focus, 74.
Club-law, *illegality*, 964.
Cluck, *animal cry*, 412.

Clue, *ball*, 249.
key, 462.
Clump, *projecting mass*, 250.
assemblage, 72.
trees, 367.
to tread, 266.
Clumsy, *unskilful*, 647, 699.
graceless, 846.
style, 579.
Cluster, *assemblage*, 72.
Clutch, *seize*, 134, 789.
retain, 781.
Clutches, *authority*, 737.
Clutter, *roll*, 407.
Coacervation, *assemblage*, 72.
Coach, *carriage*, 272.
to teach, 537.
tutor, 540.
Coachman, *director*, 694.
Coaction, *compulsion*, 744.
Coadjutor, *auxiliary*, 711.
Coagency, *co-operation*, 709.
Coagulate, *density*, 321.
Coagulum, *density*, 321.
Coal, *fuel*, 388.
Coal-black, *blackness*, 431.
Coalesce, *identity*, 13.
combine, 48.
Coalition, *co-operation*, 709.
Coaptation, *agreement*, 23.
Coarctation, *narrow*, 203.
decrease, 36.
Coarse, *texture*, 329.
vulgar, 851.
dirty, 653.
impure, 961.
Coast, *land*, 342.
to navigate, 267.
to skirt, 230.
to slide down, 306.
Coaster, *ship*, 273.
Coat, *layer*, 204.
exterior, 220.
habit, 225.
to paint, 222.
lining, 224.
Coating, *lining*, 224.
Coax, *flatter*, 933.
persuade, 615.
Cob, *horse*, 271.
Cobble, *to mend*, 658.
Coble, *ship*, 273.
Cobra, *bane*, 663.
Cobweb, *light*, 320.
flimsy, 643.
dirty, 653.
untruth, 546.
Cockade, *badge*, 550.
title, 877.
Cock-a-hoop, *exulting*, 731, 884.
gay, 836.
Cock-and-bull, *absurdity*, 497.
Cockatrice, *bane*, 663.
miscreant, 949.
Cock-boat, *ship*, 273.
Cock-crow, *morning*, 125.
Cocker, *caress*, 902.
pamper, 954.
Cockle up, *fold*, 258.
Cockney, *commonalty*, 876.
townsman, 188.
Cockpit, *arena*, 728.
of a ship, 191.
council, 696.
Cocktail, *stimulus*, 615.
Cock up, *stick up*, 212.
project, 250.
*Cocotte (Fr.), *prostitute*, 962.
Coction, *calefaction*, 384.
Cocytus, *hell*, 982.
*Coda (It.), *end*, 67.
Coddle, *pamper*, 954.
Code, *law*, 963.
precept, 697.
secret, 533.
signal, 550.
Codger, *parsimony*, 819.
Codicil, *adjunct*, 39.
sequel, 65.
Codify, *legality*, 963.
Coefficient, *co-operating*, 709.
accompanying, 88.
factor, 84.
Coemption, *purchase*, 795.
Cœnobite, *seclusion*, 893.
Coequal, *equality*, 27.
Coerce, *restrain*, 751.
compel, 744.
dissuade, 616.
Coessential, *identity*, 13.
Coetaneous, *synchronism*, 120.
Coeternal, *perpetuity*, 112.
Coeval, *synchronism*, 120.
Coexist, *synchronism*, 120.
accompany, 88.
contiguity, 199.
Coextension, *equality*, 27.
parallelism, 216.
Coffee-house, *food*, 298.
Coffer, *chest*, 191.
money-chest, 802.
store, 636.
Coffin, *interment*, 363.
Cog, *tooth*, 253.
ship, 273.
deceive, 545.
flatter, 933.
Cogent, *powerful*, 157.

Cogent, *argument*, 467, 476.
Cogitate, *thought*, 451.
Cognate, *rule*, 80.
relation, 9.
Cognation, *relation*, 9.
Cognisance, *knowledge*, 490.
Cognition, *knowledge*, 490.
Cognomen, *nomenclature*, 564.
Cognoscence, *knowledge*, 490.
*Cognoscente (It.), *taste*, 850.
Cognoscible, *knowledge*, 490.
Cohabitation, *marriage*, 903.
Cohere, *unite*, 46.
dense, 321.
Cohesive, *uniting*, 46.
dense, 321.
tenacious, 327.
Cohort, *combatant*, 726.
*Cohue (Fr.), *assemblage*, 72.
Coif, *dress*, 225.
*Coiffure (Fr.), *dress*, 225.
Coil, *convolution*, 248.
circuition, 311.
disorder, 59.
Coin, *money*, 800.
to fabricate, 161.
to imagine, 515.
Coincidence, *identity*, 13.
in time, 120.
in place, 199.
in opinion, 488.
Coke, *fuel*, 388.
Colander, *opening*, 260.
Cold, *frigidity*, 383.
style, 575.
insensible, 823.
indifferent, 866.
Cold-blooded, *malevolent*, 907.
dispassionate, 823, 826.
Cold-shoulder, *exclusion*, 893.
Coliseum, *arena*, 728.
Collaborate, 88, 709.
Collapse, *contraction*, 195.
prostration, 160.
fatigue, 688.
failure, 732.
Collar, *dress*, 225.
shackle, 749, 752.
seize, 789.
Collate, *compare*, 464.
Collateral, *relation*, 11.
lateral, 236.
consequential, 467.
Collation, *food*, 299.
comparison, 464.
Colleague, *auxiliary*, 711.
co-operating, 709.
Collect, *assemble*, 72.
take, 789.
Collect, *acquire*, 775.
learn, 539.
opine, 480.
understand, 518.
prayer, 990.
*Collectanea (L.), *assemblage*, 72.
compendium, 596.
Collected, *calm*, 826.
Collection, *store*, 636.
assemblage, 72.
Collectivism, *participation*, 780.
Collectiveness, *whole*, 50.
Collector, *assemblage*, 72.
Colleen, *woman*, 374.
College, *school*, 542.
Collide, *see* Collision.
Collier, *ship*, 273.
man, 373.
Colligate, *assemblage*, 72.
Colligation, *junction*, 43.
Collimation, *direction*, 278.
Collimator, *optical instrument*, 445.
Collision, *approach*, 286.
percussion, 276.
clashing, 179.
opposition, 708.
encounter, 720.
Collocate, *arrange*, 60.
assemble, 72.
Collocution, *interlocution*, 588.
Collogue, *confer*, 588.
Colloid, *semiliquid*, 352.
Collop, *part*, 51.
Colloquialism, *solecism*, 568.
Colloquy, *interlocution*, 588.
Collusion, *deceit*, 545.
conspiring, 709.
Colon, *stop*, 141.
Colonel, *master*, 745.
Colonise, *location*, 184, 188.
Colonnade, *continuity*, 69.
Colony, *settlement*, 184, 188.
Colophon, *end*, 67.
Coloration, *colour*, 428.
*Coloratura (It.), *music*, 415.
Colossal, *size*, 192.
height, 206.
Colour, *hue*, 428.
plea, 617.
disguise, 545.
to blush, 434.
Colourable, *deceptive*, 545.
ostensible, 472.
Colouring, *meaning*, 516.
exaggeration, 549.
Colourless, *achromatism*, 429.
Colours, *standard*, 550.
decoration, 877.

Colporteur, *agent*, 758.
Colt, *fool*, 501.
horse, 271.
Column, *series*, 69.
height, 206.
monument, 551.
cylinder, 249.
troop, 726.
Coma, *insensibility*, 823.
Combat, *contention*, 720, 722.
Combatant, *contention*, 726.
Combination, *union*, 48.
Combinations, *arithmetical*, 84.
dress, 225.
Combine, *join*, 48.
syndicate, 778.
Combustible, *heating*, 384.
fuel, 388.
Come, *arrive*, 292.
approach, 286.
happen, 151.
Come about, *eventuality*, 151.
Come after, *sequence*, 63.
Comeatable, *accessible*, 705.
Come away, *recession*, 287.
Come before, *precedence*, 62.
Come by, *acquisition*, 775.
Come down, *descend*, 306.
cheapness, 815.
pay, 809.
Come forth, *existence*, 1.
Come from, *effect*, 154.
Come in for, *obtain*, 775.
Come into existence, *existence*, 1.
Come near, *approach*, 286.
Come off, *disjunction*, 44.
take place, 151.
Come on, *follow*, 63.
defy, 715.
prosper, 731.
Come out, *egress*, 294.
Come over, *induce*, 615
Come to, *whole*, 50.
Come to the same thing, *equality*, 27.
Come up to, *equal*, 27.
Come up with, *arrival*, 292.
Come upon, *arrival*, 292.
Comedian, *the drama*, 599.
Comedy, *drama*, 599.
ridicule, 856.
Comely, *beauty*, 845.
Comestible, *food*, 298.
Comet, *wanderer*, 268.
Comfit, *sweetness*, 396.
Comfort, *pleasure*, 827.
content, 831.
relief, 834.
Comfortable, *pleased*, 827.
Comfortable, *pleasing*, 829.
Comforter, *deity*, 976.
Comfortless, *unhappy*, 828.
Comic, *witty*, 842.
ridiculous, 853.
*Comitia (L.), *council*, 696.
*Comitium (L.), *assemblage*, 72.
council, 696.
Comma, *stop*, 141.
Command, *order*, 741.
authority, 737.
Commandeer, *impress*, 744.
Commander, *master*, 745.
Commanding, *dignified*, 873.
*Commando (Port)., *armed force*, 726.
*Comme il faut (Fr.), *taste*, 850.
fashion, 852.
Commemorate, *celebration*, 883.
Commence, *beginning*, 66.
Commend, *approbation*, 931.
Commensurate, *accordant*, 23.
adequate, 639.
Comment, *reason*, 476.
interpret, 522.
Commerce, *interlocution*, 588.
barter, 794.
Commination, *threat*, 909.
Commingle, *mixture*, 41.
Comminute, *pulverulence*, 330.
disjunction, 44.
incoherence, 47.
Commiserate, *pity*, 914.
Commissariat, *provision*, 298, 637.
Commissary, *consignee*, 758.
deputy, 759.
Commission, *business*, 625.
consignee, 755.
fee, 809.
Commissionaire, *agent*, 690.
Commissioner, *consignee*, 758.
Commissure, *junction*, 43.
Commit, *act*, 680.
delegate, 755.
imprison, 751.
arrest, 969.
Committee, *director*, 693.
council, 696
assemblage, 72.
Commix, *mixture*, 41.
Commode, *receptacle*, 191.
Commodious, *expedience*, 646.
Commodity, *merchandise*, 798.
Commodore, *master*, 745.
Common, *ordinary*, 82.
general, 78.
frequent, 136.
plain, 344.
Commonalty, *common*, 876.

Commoner, *commonalty*, 876.
Commonplace, *unimportant*, 643.
hackneyed, 496.
Common-room, *sociality*, 892.
Common sense, *intellect*, 450.
wisdom, 498.
Commons, *commonalty*, 876.
food, 298.
Commonwealth, *man*, 373.
Commotion, *agitation*, 315.
Commune, *muse*, 451.
converse, 588.
territorial division, 181.
Communicate, *tell*, 527.
participate, 778.
join, 43.
Communication, *information*, 527, 532.
connection, 43.
Communion, *society*, 712.
participation, 778.
sacrament, 998.
Communism, *participation*, 778.
Community, *man*, 373.
fellowship, 712.
participation, 778.
Commute, *barter*, 794.
substitution, 147.
exchange, 148.
Compact, *close*, 43.
dense, 321.
compendious, 201, 572.
bargain, 769.
unity, 87.
*Compages (L.), *whole*, 50.
texture, 329.
Compagination, *junction*, 43.
Companion, *friend*, 890.
Companionable, *sociality*, 892.
Companionship, *accompaniment*, 88.
sociality, 892.
Company, *assembly*, 72.
accompaniment, 88.
partnership, 797.
Comparable, *relation*, 9.
Comparative, *degree*, 26.
magnitude, 31.
Compare, *comparison*, 464.
Compartment, *cell*, 191.
region, 181.
place, 182.
Compass, *degree*, 26.
space, 180.
surround, 227.
measure, 466.
to enclose, 231.
achieve, 729.
intend, 620.
Compassion, *pity*, 914.
Compatible, *consentaneous*, 23.
possible, 470.
Compatriot, *inhabitant*, 188.
Compeer, *equal*, 27.
friend, 890.
Compel, *compulsion*, 744.
Compendious, *compendium*, 596.
Compendium, *short*, 201.
writing, 596.
Compensate, *make up for*, 30.
requite, 973.
Compete, *oppose*, 708.
contend, 720.
Competence, *power*, 157.
sufficiency, 639.
wealth, 803.
skill, 698.
Competition, *opposition*, 708.
contention, 720.
Competitor, *opponent*, 710.
combatant, 726.
Compilation, *dissertation*, 595.
Complacent, *content*, 831.
self-satisfied, 880.
Complaint, *murmur*, 839.
illness, 655.
Complaisant, *benevolent*, 906.
Complement, *adjunct*, 39.
remainder, 40.
part, 52.
arithmetical, 84.
Complete, *entire*, 52.
great, 31.
end, 67.
to finish, 729.
Complex, *mixture*, 41.
disorder, 59.
Complexion, *state*, 7.
appearance, 448.
Compliance, *observance*, 772.
consent, 762.
obedience, 743.
Complicated, *disorder*, 59.
Complicity, *deceit*, 545.
conspiring, 709.
Compliment, *courtesy*, 894.
praise, 931.
Comply, *consent*, 762.
obey, 743.
observe, 772.
Component, *component*, 56
Comport, *conduct*, 692.
Comport with, *agree*, 23.
*Compos (L.), *sanity*, 502.
Compose, *make up*, 54.
produce, 161.
moderate, 174.
pacify, 723.
assuage, 826.

Compose, *music*, 415.
write, 590.
Composed, *self-possessed*, 826.
Composite, *mixture*, 41.
Composition, *constitution*, 54.
combination, 48.
music, 415.
writing, 590.
style, 569.
compromise, 774.
atonement, 952.
Compositor, *printer*, 591.
Compost, *manure*, 653.
Composure, *inexcitability*, 826.
Compotation, *drunkenness*, 959.
Compound, *mix*, 41.
combination, 48.
compromise, 774.
Compound for, *compact*, 769.
barter, 794.
Comprehend, *include*, 76.
compose, 54.
understand, 518.
know, 490.
Comprehensive, *general*, 78.
wide, 192.
Compress, *condense*, 321, 572.
narrow, 203.
curtail, 201.
contract, 195.
Comprise, *inclusion*, 76.
Compromise, *compound*, 774.
atone, 952.
endanger, 665.
mean, 29.
compensation, 30.
*Compte rendu (Fr.), *compendium* 596.
Comptroller, *director*, 694.
master, 745.
Compulsion, *force*, 744.
Compunction, *penitence*, 950.
Compurgation, *acquittal*, 970.
Compute, *numeration*, 85.
Comrade, *friend*, 890.
Con, *memory*, 505.
thought, 451.
to steer, 693.
*Con amore (It.), *willing*, 602.
Concatenation, *junction*, 43.
continuity, 69.
Concave, *concavity*, 252.
Conceal, *hide*, 528.
invisible, 447.
Concede, *consent*, 762.
admit, 467.
give, 784.
assent, 488.
permit, 760.
Conceit, *idea*, 453.
belief, 484.
supposition, 514.
imagination, 515.
affectation, 855.
vanity, 880.
wit, 842.
Conceited, *folly*, 499.
Conceive, *believe*, 484.
imagine, 515.
Concentrate, *assemble*, 72.
converge, 290.
Concentric, *centrality*, 223.
Concept, *idea*, 453.
Conception, *intellect*, 450.
idea, 453.
belief, 484.
knowledge, 490.
imagination, 515.
Conceptual, *thought*, 451.
Concern, *relation*, 9.
grief, 828.
importance, 642.
business, 625.
firm, 797.
Concerning, *relation*, 9.
Concert, *music*, 415.
co-operation, 709.
agreement, 23.
*Concerto (It.), *music*, 415.
Concertina, *musical*, 417.
Concession, *grant*, 762, 784.
assent, 488.
permit, 760.
*Concetto (It.), *wit*, 842.
Conchoid, *curvature*, 245.
*Concierge (Fr.), *keeper*, 263, 753.
Conciliate, *talk over*, 615.
satisfy, 831.
Concinnity, *style*, 578.
beauty, 845.
Concise, *conciseness*, 572.
Conclave, *assembly*, 72.
council, 696.
church, 995.
Conclude, *end*, 67.
infer, 476.
opine, 480.
complete, 729.
determine, 604.
Conclusions (to try), *contention*, 720.
Conclusive, *demonstration*, 478.
Concoct, *prepare*, 673.
plan, 626.
Concomitant, *synchronous*, 120.
accompanying, 88.
Concord, *agreement*, 23.
in music, 413.
assent, 488.

Concord, *harmony*, 714.
amity, 888.
Concordance, *see* Concord.
*Concordat (L.), *compact*, 769.
*Concours (Fr.), *contention*, 720.
Concourse, *assemblage*, 72.
convergence, 290.
Concrete, *mass*, 46.
density, 321.
Concubine, *libertine*, 962.
Concupiscence, *desire*, 865.
impurity, 961.
Concur, *co-operate*, 178.
in concert, 709.
converge, 290.
assent, 488.
Concurrence, *agreement*, 23.
coexistence, 120.
Concussion, *impulse*, 276.
Condemn, *censure*, 932.
convict, 971.
Condense, *contraction*, 195.
density, 321.
style, 572.
Condescend, *humility*, 879.
Condescending, *patronising*, 878.
Condign, *dueness*, 922, 924.
Condiment, *condiment*, 393.
Condition, *state*, 7.
term, 770.
modification, 469.
Conditionally, *circumstance*, 8.
Condole, *condolence*, 915.
Condonation, *forgiveness*, 918.
*Condottiere (It.), *master*, 745.
Conduce, *tend*, 176.
concur, 178.
avail, 644.
contribute, 153.
Conduct, *lead*, 693.
transfer, 270.
procedure, 692.
music, 415.
Conductor, *guard*, 666.
director, 694.
musician, 416.
conveyer, 271.
Conduit, *conduit*, 350.
Condyle, *convexity*, 250.
Cone, *round*, 249.
pointed, 253.
Confabulation, *interlocution*, 588.
Confection, *sweetness*, 396.
Confederacy, *party*, 712.
co-operation, 709.
Confederate, *auxiliary*, 711.
Confer, *give*, 784.
converse, 588.
advise, 695.
Confess, *avow*, 529, 535.
assert, 488.
penitence, 950.
rite, 998.
Confessedly, *affirmation*, 535.
admission, 467.
Confessional, *temple*, 1000.
Confidant, *auxiliary*, 711.
friend, 890.
Confide, *trust*, 484.
hope, 858.
Confidence, *courage*, 861.
Confidential, *concealment*, 528.
Configuration, *form*, 240.
Confine, *limit*, 233.
imprison, 751.
circumscribe, 231.
frontier, 199.
Confined, *ailing*, 655.
Confirm, *corroborate*, 467.
consent, 762.
rites, 998.
Confirmed, *fixed*, 150.
Confiscate, *condemn*, 971.
take, 789.
Conflagration, *calefaction*, 384.
Conflation, *combination*, 48.
Conflict, *contention*, 720.
disagreement, 24.
Conflicting, *opposing*, 179, 708.
Confluence, *convergence*, 290.
Conflux, *assemblage*, 72.
Conform, *assent*, 488.
accustom, 613.
agree, 646.
Conformation, *form*, 240.
frame, 7.
Conformity, *to rule*, 16, 82.
Confound, *disorder*, 61.
injure, 649.
perplex, 475.
confuse, 519.
astonish, 870.
Confoundedly, *greatness*, 31.
Confraternity, *friendship*, 888.
*Confrère (Fr.), *friend*, 890.
Confront, *face*, 234.
compare, 467.
resist, 719.
Confucius, *religious founder*, 986.
Confuse, *derange*, 61.
obscure, 519.
perplex, 458, 475.
abash, 874.
style, 571.
Confusion, *disorder*, 59.
shame, 874
Confutation, *disproof*, 479.
*Congé (Fr.), *dismissal*, 756.

Congeal, *cold*, 385.
Congealed, *dense*, 321.
Congener, *consanguinity*, 11.
similar, 17.
included, 76.
Congenial, *agreeing*, 23.
expedient, 646.
Congenital, *intrinsic*, 5.
habitual, 613.
Congeries, *assemblage*, 72.
Congestion, *collection*, 72.
redundance, 641.
Conglobation, *assemblage*, 72.
Conglomerate, *assemblage*, 72.
Conglutinate, *coherence*, 46.
Congratulate, *congratulation*, 896.
Congregate, *assemblage*, 72.
Congregation, *laity*, 997.
Congress, *assemblage*, 72, 290.
council, 696.
Congruous, *agreeing*, 23.
expedient, 646.
Conical, *round*, 249.
pointed, 253.
Conjecture, *supposition*, 514.
Conjoin, *junction*, 43.
Conjointly, *together*, 37, 43.
Conjugal, *marriage*, 903.
Conjugate words, *word*, 562.
Conjugation, *junction*, 43.
pair, 89.
phase, 144.
grammar, 567.
Conjunct, *junction*, 43.
Conjunction, *vinculum*, 45.
Conjuncture, *contingency*, 8.
occasion, 134.
Conjuration, *deception*, 545.
sorcery, 992.
Conjure, *entreat*, 765.
exorcise, 992.
Conjurer, *sorcerer*, 994.
adept, 700.
*Con moto (It.), *music*, 415.
Connate, *cause*, 153.
intrinsic, 5.
Connatural, *uniform*, 16.
similar, 17.
Connect, *relate*, 9.
link, 43.
Connection, *kindred*, 11.
Connective, *vinculum*, 45.
Connive, *overlook*, 460.
allow, 760.
*Connoisseur (Fr.), *taste*, 850.
proficient, 700.
Connotation, *indication*, 550.
Connubial, *marriage*, 903.
Conquer, *success*, 731.
Conquered, *failure*, 732.
Conqueror, *success*, 731.
Conquest, *success*, 731.
Consanguinity, *kindred*, 11.
Conscience, *moral sense*, 926.
knowledge, 490.
Conscientious, *virtuous*, 944.
scrupulous, 726A, 939.
true, 494.
Consciousness, *intuition*, 450.
knowledge, 490.
Conscript, *soldier*, 726.
Conscription, *compulsion*, 744.
Consecrate, *dedicate*, 873.
sanctify, 987.
Consectary, *corollary*, 480.
Consecution, *sequence*, 63.
Consecutive, *following*, 63.
continuous, 69.
Consecutively, *gradually*, 144.
Consensus, *agreement*, 23.
assent, 488.
Consent, *grant*, 762.
assent, 488.
Consentaneous, *agreeing*, 23.
expedient, 646.
Consequence, *effect*, 154.
event, 151.
importance, 642.
Consequent, *sequence*, 63.
Consequential, *arrogant*, 878.
deducible, 467.
Consequently, *reasoning*, 154, 476.
Conservation, *preservation*, 670.
Conservative, *permanence*, 142.
*Conservatoire (Fr.), *school*, 542.
Conservatory, *store*, 636.
hot-house, 386.
Conserve, *sweet*, 396.
Consider, *think*, 451.
attend to, 457.
inquire, 461.
Considerable, *in degree*, 31.
in size, 192.
important, 642.
Considerate, *judicious*, 498.
benevolent, 906.
Consideration, *motive*, 615.
qualification, 469.
importance, 642.
requital, 973.
Considering, *reasoning*, 476.
Consign, *transfer*, 783.
commission, 755.
give, 784.
Consignee, *delegate*, 758.
Consignment, *commission*, 755.
Consistence, *density*, 321.
Consistency, *uniformity*, 16.

Consistent, *agreement*, 23.
Consist in, *existence*, 1.
Consist of, *composition*, 54.
Consistory, *council*, 696.
church, 995.
Consociation, *sociality*, 892.
Console, *relieve*, 834.
pity, 914.
table, 215.
keyboard, 417.
Consolidate, *unite*, 46, 48.
condense, 321.
Consonance, *agreement*, 23.
expedience, 646.
music, 413.
Consonant, *letter*, 561.
Consort, *accompany*, 88.
associate, 892.
spouse, 903.
Consortship, *sociality*, 892.
Consort with, *fit*, 646.
Conspectus, *compendium*, 596.
Conspicuous, *visible*, 446.
Conspiracy, *plot*, 626.
Conspire, *concur*, 178.
Constable, *governor*, 745.
officer, 965.
Constant, *uniformity*, 16.
immutable, 150.
regular, 80, 82.
resolute, 604.
faithful, 939.
Constantly, *frequently*, 136.
Constellation, *stars*, 318, 423.
glory, 873.
Consternation, *fear*, 860.
Constipate, *density*, 321.
Constituent, *component*, 54, 56.
voter, 609.
Constitute, *compose*, 54, 56.
produce, 161.
Constitution, *nature*, 5.
state, 7.
texture, 329.
charter, 924.
law, 963.
Constrain, *power*, 157.
restrain, 751.
compel, 744.
abash, 881.
Constrict, *narrow*, 203.
Constringe, *narrow*, 203.
Construct, *production*, 161
Construction, *form*, 240.
meaning, 522.
Construe, *meaning*, 522.
Consubstantiation, *rite*, 998.
Consul, *deputy*, 759.
Consult, *advice*, 695.
Consume, *destroy*, 162.
waste, 638.
use, 677.
ravage, 649.
Consuming, *painful*, 830.
Consummate, *great*, 31.
complete, 729.
skill, 698.
Consummation, *end*, 67.
Consumption, *shrinking*, 195.
waste, 638.
use, 677.
Contact, *contiguity*, 199.
*Contadino (It.), *peasant*, 876.
Contagious, *insalubrious*, 657.
Contain, *include*, 76.
be composed of, 54.
Contaminate, *spoil*, 659.
soil, 653.
Contango, *discount*, 813.
Contemn, *contempt*, 930.
Contemper, *moderation*, 174.
Contemplate, *view*, 441.
think, 451.
purpose, 620.
expect, 507.
Contemporaneous, *synchronism*, 120
Contemporary, *synchronism*, 120.
Contempt, *despise*, 930.
Contemptible, *unimportant*, 643.
Contend, *fight*, 720.
assert, 535.
Content, *satisfied*, 827, 831.
calm, 826.
assentient, 488.
patience, 821.
will, 600.
Contention, *discord*, 713.
struggle, 720.
Contents, *ingredients*, 56.
components, 190.
list, 86.
compendium, 596.
end, 67.
Conterminal, *end*, 67.
limit, 233.
Conterminous, *adjoining*, 199.
Contest, *contention*, 720.
Context, *printing*, 591.
Contexture, *state*, 7.
texture, 329.
Contiguous, *touching*, 199.
Continence, *purity*, 960.
Continent, *land*, 342.
Contingent, *conditional*, 8.
eventual, 151.
chance, 156.
liable, 177.
possible, 470.

Contingent, *uncertain*, 475.
casual, 621.
allotment, 786.
part, 51.
duration, 108A.
Continually, *frequency*, 136.
Continuation, *sequence*, 63.
sequel, 65.
adjunct, 39.
Continue, *persist*, 143.
endure, 106.
Continued, to be, *sequel*, 65.
Continuity, *persistence*, 69.
Contortion, *distortion*, 243.
convolution, 246.
deformity, 846.
Contour, *outline*, 229, 448.
*Contra (L.), *opposition*, 708.
Contraband, *illicit*, 964.
false, 544.
Contract, *decrease*, 36.
shrivel, 195.
curtail, 201.
narrow, 203.
promise, 768.
bargain, 769.
Contractility, *corrugation*, 195.
elasticity, 325.
Contradict, *evidence*, 468.
deny, 536.
dissent, 489.
Contradiction, *contrariety*, 14.
Contradistinction, *difference*, 15.
Contralto, *melody*, 413.
Contraposition, *reversion*, 237.
inversion, 218.
Contrapuntal, *melody*, 413.
Contrary, *opposite*, 14, 179.
opposing, 708.
capricious, 608.
Contrast, *contrariety*, 14.
comparison, 464.
Contravallation, *defence*, 717.
Contravene, *counteract*, 179.
oppose, 14, 708.
hinder, 706.
counter-evidence, 468.
argue, 476.
deny, 536.
*Contrecoup (Fr.), *counteraction*, 179.
*Contretemps (Fr.), *difficulty*, 704.
intempestivity, 135.
Contribute, *tend*, 176.
concur, 178.
give, 784.
cause, 153.
Contribution, *giving*, 784.
expenses, 809.
Contrition, *abrasion*, 331.
Contrition, *penitence*, 950.
Contrive, *plan*, 626, 702.
Contriving, *artful*, 702.
Control, *power*, 157.
authority, 737.
to regulate, 693.
to check, 179, 708.
Controversy, *discussion*, 476.
dispute, 713.
Controvertible, *dubious*, 475.
Contumacy, *obstinacy*, 606.
disobedience, 742.
Contumely, *disrespect*, 929.
arrogance, 885.
rudeness, 895.
scorn, 930.
reproach, 932.
Contund, *pulverise*, 330.
Contuse, *pulverise*, 330.
Conundrum, *secret*, 533.
pun, 563.
wit, 842.
problem, 461.
Convalescence, *improvement*, 658.
Convection, *transference*, 270.
*Convenances (Fr.), *rule*, 80.
Convene, *assemblage*, 72.
Convenient, *expedient*, 646.
Convent, *temple*, 1000.
Conventicle, *church*, 1000.
assembly, 72.
Convention, *compact*, 769.
treaty of peace, 723.
assembly, 72.
rule, 80.
Conventional, *uniform*, 82.
Conventual, *clergy*, 996.
Converge, *convergence*, 290.
Conversable, *sociable*, 588, 892.
Conversant, *knowing*, 490.
skilful, 698.
Conversation, *interlocution*, 588.
*Conversazione (It.), *meeting*, 72.
sociality, 892.
Converse, *reverse*, 14.
talk, 588.
Conversion, *change*, 144.
religious, 987.
Convert, *opinion*, 484.
learner, 541.
to change to, 144.
to use, 677.
Convertible, *identical*, 13.
equal, 27.
Convex, *convexity*, 250.
Convey, *transfer*, 270.
Conveyance, *vehicle*, 272.
Conveyancer, *lawyer*, 968.
Convict, *condemn*, 971.

Convict, *to convince*, 537.
prisoner, 754.
condemned, 949.
Conviction, *belief*, 484.
Convince, *teaching*, 537.
Convincement, *belief*, 484.
Convivial, *social*, 892.
Convocation, *council*, 696, 995.
Convoke, *assemblage*, 72.
Convolution, *coil*, 248.
rotation, 312.
Convoy, *transfer*, 270.
guard, 664.
Convulse, *violent*, 173.
agitate, 315.
pain, 378.
torture, 830.
Coo, *animal cry*, 412.
Cook, *heat*, 384.
prepare, 673.
falsify, 544.
accounts, 811.
Cool, *cold*, 383.
to refrigerate, 385.
judicious, 498.
to moderate, 174.
to dissuade, 616.
to allay, 826.
indifferent, 866.
torpid, 826.
Cool one's heels, *futurity*, 121.
Cooler, *refrigerator*, 387.
Cool-headed, *torpid*, 826.
judicious, 498.
Coolie, *carrier*, 271.
Coombe, *valley*, 252.
Coop, *confine*, 752.
restrain, 751.
Co-operate, *physically*, 178.
voluntarily, 709.
Co-operation, *agreement*, 23.
Co-operator, *auxiliary*, 711.
Co-ordinate, *equality*, 27.
Copartner, *participator*, 778.
associate, 892.
accompanying, 88.
Cope, *contend*, 720.
equal, 27.
canonicals, 999.
*Copia verborum (L.), *diffuseness*, 573.
speech, 582.
Copious, *abundant*, 639.
style, 573.
Copper, *money*, 800.
colour, 439.
Copperplate, *engraving*, 558.
Coppice (or copse), *plant*, 367.
Coprology, *impurity*, 653, 961.
Copula, *junction*, 45.
Copy, *imitation*, 21.
prototype, 22.
to write, 590.
represent, 554.
Copying, *imitating*, 19.
Copyist, *writing*, 590.
Copyright, *privilege*, 924.
Coquetry, *affectation*, 855.
Coracle, *boat*, 273.
*Coram judice (L.), *jurisdiction*, 965.
*Cor anglais (Fr.), *musical*, 417.
*Corbeille (Fr.), *receptacle*, 191.
Cord, *tie*, 45.
filament, 205.
Cordage, *junction*, 45.
Cordial, *grateful*, 829.
warm, 821.
willing, 602.
friendly, 888.
remedy, 662.
Cordon, *outline*, 229, 232.
circular, 247.
badge, 550.
Corduroy, *furrow*, 259.
Core, *centrality*, 223.
Coriaceous, *tenacity*, 327.
Co-rival, *see* Corrival.
Cork, *lightness*, 320.
plug, 263.
Cork up, *closure*, 261.
Corkscrew, *perforator*, 262.
spiral, 248.
Cormorant, *gluttony*, 865, 957.
Corn, *projection*, 250.
Corn-cob, *tobacco-pipe*, 351.
Corned, *drunk*, 959.
Corner, *place*, 182.
receptacle, 191.
Corner-stone, *support*, 215.
to engross, 777.
syndicate, 778.
Cornet, *music*, 417.
officer, 745.
Cornice, *summit*, 210.
Cornucopia, *sufficiency*, 639.
Cornute, *sharp*, 253.
Corollary, *deduction*, 480.
addition, 37, 39.
Corona, *circularity*, 247.
light, 420.
Coronach, *lamentation*, 839.
Coronet, *sceptre*, 747.
Corporal, *officer*, 745.
Corporality, *materiality*, 316.
Corporate, *junction*, 43.
Corporation, *association*, 712.
bulk, 192.
Corporeal, *materiality*, 316.

Corps, *assemblage*, 72.
troops, 726.
*Corps de réserve (Fr.), *store*, 636.
*Corps diplomatique (Fr.), *consignee*, 758.
Corpse, *body*, 362.
Corpulent, *size*, 192.
Corpuscle, *atom*, 193.
jot, 32.
*Corpus delicti (L.), *guilt*, 947.
Corradiation, *focus*, 74.
Corral, *enclosure*, 232, 752.
Correct, *true*, 494.
reason, 476.
virtuous, 944.
style, 570.
to improve, 658.
to censure, 932.
to punish, 972.
Corrective, *remedy*, 662.
*Corregidor (Sp.), *master*, 745.
Correlation, *relation*, 9.
reciprocity, 12.
Correspond, *agree*, 23.
write, 592.
Corridor, *place*, 191.
passage, 627.
Corrie, *hollow*, 252.
Corrigible, *improvement*, 658.
Corrival, *combatant*, 726.
Corrivalry, *contention*, 720.
Corroborant, *remedy*, 662.
Corroborate, *evidence*, 467.
Corroboree, *festivity*, 840.
Corrode, *erode*, 162, 659.
consume, 649.
afflict, 830.
Corrosion, *evil*, 619.
Corrosive, *acrid*, 171.
destructive, 649.
Corrugate, *constrict*, 195.
narrow, 203.
rumple, 258.
derange, 61.
Corrupt, *foul*, 653.
noxious, 649.
evil, 619.
to spoil, 659.
vicious, 945.
*Corruptio optimi pessima (L.), *badness*, 649.
Corruption, *decomposition*, 49.
Corsage, *dress*, 225.
Corsair, *thief*, 792.
Corse, *corpse*, 362.
Corset, *dress*, 225.
*Corso (It.), *arena*, 728.
*Cortège (Fr.), *suite*, 746.
continuity, 39, 69.
Cortes, *council*, 696.
Cote, *hut*, 189.
Cortex, *covering*, 222.
Coruscate, *light*, 420.
*Corvée (Fr.), *compulsion*, 744.
Corvette, *ship*, 273.
Corybantic, *insanity*, 503.
Coryphæus, *leader*, 745.
Coscinomancy, *prediction*, 511.
Cosmetic, *remedy*, 662.
ornament, 847.
Cosmic, *world*, 318.
Cosmogony, *world*, 318.
Cosmography, *world*, 318.
Cosmopolitan, *world-wide*, 78.
Cosmopolite, *philanthropy*, 910.
Cosmorama, *painting*, 558.
view, 448.
Cossack, *combatant*, 726.
Cosset, *favourite*, 899.
Cost, *price*, 812.
Costermonger, *merchant*, 797.
Costive, *taciturn*, 585.
style, 576.
Costly, *dearness*, 814.
Costume, *dress*, 225.
Cosy, *comfortable*, 827, 829.
Cot, *abode*, 189.
Coterie, *party*, 712.
sociality, 892.
Cotillion, *amusement*, 840.
Cottage, *abode*, 189.
Cottar, *inhabitant*, 188.
peasant, 876.
Couch, *bed*, 215.
to lie, 213.
to stoop, 306.
lie in wait, 530.
express, 566.
Couchant, *horizontal*, 213.
*Couci-couci (Fr.), *imperfection*, 651.
*Couloir (Fr.), *gully*, 198.
Council, *senate*, 696.
ecclesiastical, 995.
Counsel, *advice*, 695.
Counsellor, *adviser*, 695.
lawyer, 968.
Count, *compute*, 85.
expect, 507.
believe, 484.
estimate, 480.
signify, 642.
lord, 875.
Countenance, *face*, 234.
favour, 707.
appearance, 448.
to approve, 931.
Counter, *contrary*, 14.
against, 179, 708.

Counter, *number*, 84.
token, 550.
table, 215.
shop-board, 799.
to retaliate, 718.
Counteract, *physically*, 179.
voluntarily, 708.
hinder, 706.
compensate, 30.
Counter-attraction, *dissuasion*, 616.
avoidance, 623.
Counterbalance, *compensation*, 30.
Counterblast, *counteraction*, 179.
retaliation, 718.
Counterchange, *reciprocality*, 12, 148.
Countercharm, *spell*, 993.
Countercheck, *hindrance*, 706.
Counter-evidence, *contrary*, 468.
Counterfeit, *simulate*, 544.
imitate, 19.
copy, 21.
Counter-irritant, *counteraction*, 179.
Countermand, *abrogation*, 756.
Countermarch, *regression*, 283.
Countermark, *indication*, 550.
Countermine, *opposition*, 708.
Counter-movement, *regression*, 283.
Counter-order, *abrogation*, 756.
Counterpane, *covering*, 222.
Counterpart, *reverse*, 14.
copy, 21.
match, 17.
Counterplot, *retaliation*, 718.
plan, 626.
Counterpoint, *harmony*, 413.
Counterpoise, *compensation*, 30.
Counterpoison, *remedy*, 662.
Counter-project, *retaliation*, 718.
plan, 626.
Counter-revolution, *revolution*, 146.
Countersign, *indication*, 550.
Counter-subject, *music*, 415.
Counter-stroke, *retaliation*, 718.
Counter-tenor, *melody*, 413.
Countervail, *compensate*, 28, 30.
oppose, 179, 708.
evidence, 468.
Counterwork, *opposition*, 708.
Counting-house, *mart*, 799.
Countless, *infinity*, 105.
Countrified, *rural*, 185.
Country, *definite region*, 181, 189.
Countryman, *inhabitant*, 185.
Counts, *particulars*, 79.
County, *definite region*, 181.
*Coup (Fr.), *action*, 680.
*Coup de grâce (Fr.), *death-blow*, 361.
destruction, 162.
Coup de grâce (Fr.), *completion*, 729.
end, 67.
pity, 914.
punishment, 972.
*Coup de main (Fr.), *violence*, 173.
action, 680.
*Coup de maître (Fr.), *skill*, 698.
success, 731.
*Coup d'essai (Fr.), *essay*, 675.
*Coup d'état (Fr.), *action*, 680.
plan, 626.
*Coup de théâtre (Fr.), *appearance*, 448.
ostentation, 882.
*Coup d'œil (Fr.), *vision*, 441.
appearance, 448.
*Coupé (Fr.), *vehicle*, 272.
Couple, *two*, 89.
to unite, 43.
Couplet, *poetry*, 597.
Coupon, *money*, 800.
ticket, 550.
Courage, *bravery*, 861.
Courier, *messenger*, 534.
Course, *order*, 58.
continuity, 69.
of time, 109.
direction, 278.
motion, 264.
locomotion, 266.
effect, 154.
rapidity, 274.
pursuit, 622.
teaching, 537.
plan, 626.
way, 627.
conduct, 692.
arena, 728.
dinner, 298.
Courser, *carrier*, 271.
swift, 274.
Court, *house*, 189.
hall, 191.
council, 696.
to invite, 615.
to pursue, 622.
to solicit, 765.
to wish, 865.
to woo, 902.
to flatter, 933.
gentility, 852.
tribunal, 966.
retinue, 746.
Courtesan, *libertine*, 962.
Courtesy, *politeness*, 894.
Courtier, *flatterer*, 935.
Courtier-like, *flattery*, 933.
Courtly, *fashion*, 852.
polite, 894.

Court-martial, *tribunal*, 966.
Courtship, *endearment*, 902.
Cousin, *consanguinity*, 11.
*Coûte que coûte (Fr.), *resolution*, 604.
obstinacy, 606.
Cove, *cell*, 191.
haunt, 189.
hollow, 252.
bay, 343.
man, 373.
Covenant, *compact*, 769, 770.
Cover, *dress*, 225.
superpose, 222.
conceal, 528.
retreat, 530.
safety, 664.
to compensate, 30.
stopper, 263.
Covert, *invisibility*, 447.
Coverture, *marriage*, 903.
Covetous, *miserly*, 819.
desirous, 865.
Covey, *assemblage*, 72, 102.
Cow, *intimidate*, 860.
Coward, *fearful*, 862.
Cow-catcher, *defence*, 717.
Cower, *fear*, 860.
stoop, 306.
Cowl, *dress*, 225.
sacerdotal, 999.
Co-worker, *worker*, 690.
Coxcomb, *fop*, 854.
Coxcombical, *vain*, 880.
affected, 855.
Coxswain, *steersman*, 694.
Coy, *modesty*, 881.
Cozen, *deception*, 545.
Crab, *sourness*, 397.
to depreciate, 932.
Crabbed, *sour*, 397.
difficult, 704.
uncivil, 895.
testy, 901.
Crab-like, *deviation*, 279, 283.
Crack, *split*, 44.
snap, 328.
fissure, 198.
furrow, 259.
to destroy, 162.
sound, 406.
to boast, 884.
excellent, 648.
proficient, 698, 700.
Crack, in a, *instantaneity*, 113.
Crack-brained, *imbecility*, 499.
Cracked, *mad*, 504.
faulty, 651.
Cracker, *snap*, 406.
Cracker, *untruth*, 546.
Crackle, *snap*, 406.
Cradle, *bed*, 215.
beginning, 66.
origin, 153.
infancy, 127.
to place, 184.
to train, 673.
Craft, *cunning*, 702.
skill, 698.
plan, 626
apparatus, 633.
business, 623.
shipping, 273.
Crag, *sharpness*, 253.
height, 206.
Cragged, *rough*, 256.
Cram, *stuff*, 194.
fill, 639.
gorge, 296.
teach, 537.
choke, 261.
*Crambe repetita (L.), *repetition*, 104.
Crammer, *teacher*, 540.
untruth, 546.
Cramp, *hinder*, 706.
restrain, 751.
narrow, 203.
fasten, 45.
paralyse, 158.
weaken, 160.
spasm, 378, 828.
Cramped, *style*, 572, 579.
Crane, *instrument*, 633.
Crane-neck, *curvature*, 245.
Cranium, *intellect*, 450.
Crank, *instrument*, 633.
wit, 842.
eccentric, 499.
punishment, 972.
Crankle, *to bend*, 244.
Cranky, *eccentric*, 499.
opinionated, 606.
insane, 503.
Cranny, *interval*, 198.
Crapulence, *intemperance*, 954.
Crash, *sound*, 406.
destruction, 162.
impulse, 276.
Crasis, *nature*, 5.
coherence, 46.
Crass, *great*, 31.
ignorance, 491.
Crassitude, *breadth*, 202.
thickness, 352.
Crate, *receptacle*, 191.
Crater, *hollow*, 252.
depth, 208.
receptacle, 191.

Cravat, *dress*, 225.
Crave, *ask*, 765.
desire, 865.
Craven, *cowardice*, 862.
Craw, *receptacle*, 191.
Crawl, *move*, 275.
servility, 886.
Crayon, *painting*, 556.
pencil, 559.
Craze, *caprice*, 608.
Crazy, *weak*, 160.
mad, 503.
Creak, *stridor*, 410.
Cream, *emulsion*, 354.
oil, 355.
perfection, 650.
Cream-coloured, *white*, 430.
Creamy, *semiliquid*, 352.
Crease, *fold*, 258.
Create, *produce*, 161.
cause, 153.
imagine, 515.
Creationism, *causation*, 153.
Creator, *deity*, 976.
Creature, *animal*, 366.
thing, 3.
effect, 154.
Creature comforts, *food*, 298.
*Crèche (Fr.), *nursery*, 542.
Credence, *belief*, 484.
Credential, *evidence*, 467.
Credible, *probability*, 472, 484.
Credit, *belief*, 484.
authority, 737.
pecuniary, 805.
account, 811.
influence, 737.
hope, 858.
repute, 873.
desert, 944.
Creditor, *credit*, 805.
Credulity, *belief*, 486,
superstition, 984.
Creed, *belief*, 484, 496.
tenet, 983.
Creek, *gulf*, 343.
Creep, *crawl*, 275.
Creeper, *plant*, 367.
Creeping, *sensation*, 380.
Creepy, *fearsome*, 860
Cremation, *burning*, 384.
of corpses, 363.
*Crême de la crême (Fr.), *goodness*, 648.
Cremona, *musical instrument*, 417.
Crenated, *notch*, 257.
Crepitate, *snap*, 406.
Crepuscule, *dawn*, 125.
dimness, 422.
*Crescendo (It.), *increase*, 35.
music, 415.
Crescent, *curve*, 245.
street, 189.
Cresset, *torch*, 423.
Crest, *summit*, 210.
tuft, 256.
armorial, 550, 877.
Crestfallen, *dejected*, 837.
humiliated, 881.
Cretin, *fool*, 501.
*Crevasse (Fr.), *interval*, 198.
Crevice, *interval*, 198.
Crew, *assemblage*, 72.
party, 712.
inhabitants, 188.
Crib, *bed*, 215.
to steal, 791.
interpretation, 522.
Crick, *pain*, 378.
Crier, *messenger*, 534.
Crime, *guilt*, 947.
Criminal, *culprit*, 949.
vicious, 945.
Criminality, *guilt*, 947.
Criminate, *accusation*, 938.
Criminology, *crime*, 947.
Crimp, *curl*, 248.
ridge, 247.
fold, 258.
to steal, 791.
Crimson, *red*, 434.
Cringe, *submit*, 743.
servility, 886.
Crinkle, *fold*, 258.
angle, 244.
Crinoline, *dress*, 225.
Cripple, *weaken*, 160.
disable, 158.
injure, 649.
disease, 655.
Crisis, *conjuncture*, 8.
event, 151.
difficulty, 704.
opportunity, 134.
Crisp, *brittle*, 328.
rough, 256.
rumpled, 248.
Criss-cross-row, *letter*, 561.
Criterion, *trial*, 463.
evidence, 467.
Crithomancy, *prediction*, 511.
Critic, *taste*, 850.
reviewer, 590.
detractor, 936.
Critical, *opportune*, 134.
important, 642.
Criticise, *taste*, 850.
Criticism, *disapprobation*, 932.

Criticism, *dissertation*, 595.
Critique, *discrimination*, 465.
dissertation, 595.
disapprobation, 932.
Croak, *cry*, 412.
stammer, 583.
complain, 839.
boast, 884.
predict, 511.
Croceate, *yellow*, 436.
Crochet, *knit*, 43.
Crocodile tears, *falsehood*, 544.
Crœsus, *wealth*, 803.
Croft, *hut*, 189.
Crock up, *failure*, 732.
Crock, *weakness*, 160.
Cromlech, *interment*, 363.
Crone, *veteran*, 130.
Crony, *friend*, 890.
Crooked, *angular*, 244.
distorted, 243, 846.
sloping, 217.
dishonourable, 940.
Croon, *to hum*, 405, 415.
Crop, *stomach*, 191.
to shorten, 201.
to gather, 775.
to take, 789.
to eat, 297.
harvest, 154.
Crop up, *inexpectation*, 508.
Crosier, *canonicals*, 999.
Cross, *intersection*, 219.
swindle, 545.
opposition, 708.
vexation, 828.
vexatiousness, 830.
ill-tempered, 895.
fretful, 901.
failure, 732.
mixture, 41.
decoration, 877.
reward, 973.
rites, 998.
Cross-bow, *arms*, 727.
Cross-breed, *unconformity*, 83.
Cross-cut, *method*, 627.
Cross-examine, *inquiry*, 461.
Cross-grained, *obstinate*, 606.
ill-tempered, 895.
Crossing, *crossing*, 219.
Cross-patch, *ill-tempered*, 895.
Cross-purposes, *error*, 495.
misinterpretation, 523.
Cross-question, *inquiry*, 461.
Cross-reading, *misinterpretation*, 523.
Cross-road, *way*, 627.
Cross-word, *puzzle*, 533.
Crotch, *angularity*, 244.
Crotchet, *music*, 413.
caprice, 608.
Crotchety, *folly*, 499.
Crouch, *stoop*, 306.
lower, 207.
servility, 886.
fear, 860.
Croup, *rear*, 235.
*Croûte (Fr.), *daub*, 555.
Crow, *cry*, 412.
laugh, 838.
boast, 884.
exult, 836.
lever, 633.
Crowbar, *instrument*, 633.
Crowd, *assemblage*, 72.
multitude, 102.
closeness, 197.
the vulgar, 876.
Crow flies, as the, *direction*, 278.
Crown, *top*, 210.
end, 67.
circle, 247.
trophy, 733.
sceptre, 747.
reward, 973.
to complete, 729.
Crucial, *crossing*, 219.
experimental, 463.
demonstrative, 478.
Crucible, *receptacle*, 191.
laboratory, 691.
Crucifix, *rite*, 998.
canonicals, 999.
Cruciform, *crossing*, 219.
Crucify, *torture* (*physical*), 378.
agony (*mental*), 828.
torturing, 830.
execution, 972.
Crude, *unprepared*, 674.
inelegant, 579.
Cruel, *painful*, 830.
inhuman, 907.
Cruet, *receptacle*, 191.
Cruise, *navigation*, 267.
Cruiser, *ship*, 273.
Crumb, *small part*, 51.
grain, 193.
powder, 330.
bit, 32.
Crumble, *pulverise*, 330.
destroy, 162.
spoil, 659.
brittleness, 328.
Crumple, *ruffle*, 256.
crease, 258.
Crunch, *bruise*, 44.
masticate, 297.
pulverise. 330.

Crupper, *rear*, 235.
Crusade, *warfare*, 722.
Cruse, *vessel*, 191.
Crush, *pulverise*, 330.
destroy, 162.
injure, 649.
Crust, *covering*, 222.
Crusty, *discourtesy*, 895.
Crutch, *support*, 215.
angle, 244.
instrument, 633.
Crux, *question*, 461.
Cry, *animal*, 412.
human, 411.
loudness, 404.
voice, 580.
publish, 531.
weep, 839.
Cry down, *disapprove*, 932.
Cry for, *desire*, 865.
Cry to, *beseech*, 765.
Cry up, *praise*, 931.
Crypt, *cell*, 191.
grave, 363.
altar, 1000.
Cryptic, *latent*, 526, 528.
Cryptogram, *cipher*, 533.
Cryptography, *writing*, 590.
Crystalline, *dense*, 321.
transparent, 425.
Cub, *young*, 129.
clown, 876.
Cube, *triality*, 92.
Cubist, *artist*, 559.
Cuckold, *libertine*, 962.
Cuckoo, *repetition*, 104.
imitation, 19.
cry, 412.
fool, 501.
Cuddle, *caress*, 902.
Cudgel, *beat*, 975.
bludgeon, 276, 727.
Cue, *hint*, 527.
watchword, 550.
plea, 617.
Cuff, *beat*, 276, 972.
*Cui bono (L.), *utility*, 644.
Cuirass, *defence*, 717.
Cuirassier, *combatant*, 726.
*Cuisine (Fr.), *food*, 298.
*Culbute (Fr.), *inversion*, 218.
descent, 306.
*Cul-de-lampe (Fr.), *tail-piece*, 67.
*Cul-de-sac (Fr.), *concavity*, 252.
closure, 261.
difficulty, 704.
Culinary, *food*, 298.
Cull, *choice*, 609.
Cullender, *sieve*, 260.
Cullion, *wretch*, 941, 949.
Cully, *dupe*, 547.
Culminate, *maximum*, 33.
height, 206, 210.
Culpability, *guilt*, 947.
Culpable, *vice*, 945.
Culprit, *sinner*, 949.
Cult, *worship*, 990.
rite, 998.
Cultivate, *improve*, 658.
till, 371.
Culture, *tillage*, 371.
teaching, 537.
knowledge, 490.
Culverin, *arms*, 727.
Culvert, *conduit*, 350.
*Cum grano salis (L.), *qualify*, 469.
unbelief, 485.
Cumber, *load*, 319.
to incommode, 647.
to obstruct, 706.
Cumulation, *assemblage*, 72.
Cummerbund, *girdle*, 247.
Cumulative, *increase*, 35.
addition, 37.
Cumulus, *cloud*, 353.
Cunctation, *delay*, 133.
inactivity, 683.
Cuneiform, *angular*, 244.
Cunning, *art*, 702.
sagacity, 698.
well-planned, 626.
Cup, *hollow*, 252.
vessel, 191.
Cupboard, *receptacle*, 191.
Cupid, *beauty*, 845.
love, 897.
Cupidity, *avarice*, 819.
desire, 865.
Cupola, *dome*, 250.
height, 206.
Cur, *knave*, 949.
Curable, *improvement*, 658.
Curacy, *churchdom*, 995.
Curate, *clergy*, 996.
Curative, *remedial*, 834.
Curator, *consignee*, 758.
Curb, *restrain*, 751.
hinder, 706.
shackle, 752.
moderate, 174.
check, 826.
dissuade, 616.
counteract, 179.
slacken, 275.
Curd, *mass*, 46.
density, 321.
pulp, 354.
Curdle, *condense*, 321.

Curdle, *coagulate*, 46.
Cure, *remedy*, 662, 834.
reinstate, 660.
religious, 995.
preserve, 670.
improve, 656.
*Curé (Fr.), *priest*, 996.
Cureless, *deterioration*, 659.
Curfew, *evening*, 126.
Curio, *toy*, 643.
*Curiosa felicitas (L.), *elegance*, 578.
Curiosity, *curiosity*, 455.
phenomenon, 872.
Curious, *true*, 494.
exceptional, 83.
beautiful, 845.
Curl, *bend*, 245, 248.
cockle up, 258.
Curlicue, *convolution*, 248.
Curmudgeon, *parsimony*, 819.
Currency, *publicity*, 531.
money, 800.
Current, *existing*, 1.
present, 118.
happening, 151.
stream, 347.
river, 348.
course, 109.
opinion, 484.
public, 531.
prevailing, 82.
*Currente calamo (L.), *diffuseness*, 573.
Curricle, *vehicle*, 272.
Curriculum, *teaching*, 537.
Curry, *condiment*, 393.
Curry favour, *flattery*, 933.
Curse, *malediction*, 908.
bane, 663.
evil, 619.
badness, 649.
painfulness, 830.
Cursory, *transient*, 111.
inattentive, 458.
neglecting, 460.
hasty, 684.
Curst, *perverse*, 895.
Curt, *short*, 201.
Curtail, *shorten*, 201, 572.
retrench, 38.
decrease, 36.
deprive, 789.
Curtain, *shade*, 424.
ambush, 530.
Curtain-raiser, *play*, 599.
Curtsy, *obeisance*, 743, 894.
stoop, 306.
Curve, *curvature*, 245.
Curvet, *rise*, 305.
Curvet, *leap*, 309.
oscillate, 314.
agitate, 315.
Cushion, *pillow*, 215.
softness, 324.
to frustrate, 706.
relief, 834.
Cusp, *point*, 253.
angle, 244.
Custodian, *keeper*, 753.
Custody, *captivity*, 664, 751, 781.
captive, 754.
Custom, *rule*, 80.
habit, 613.
fashion, 852.
sale, 796.
barter, 794.
tax, 812.
Custom-house, *mart*, 799.
Customer, *purchaser*, 795.
dealer, 797.
Cut, *divide*, 44.
bit, 51.
interval, 70, 198.
sculpture, 557.
curtail, 201.
layer, 204.
notch, 257.
form, 240.
road, 627.
print, 558.
pain, 828.
to give pain, 830.
affect, 824.
decline acquaintance, 893, 895.
state, 7.
cold, 385.
Cut across, *passage*, 302.
Cut along, *velocity*, 274.
Cut and dried, *ready*, 673.
trite, 82.
Cut and run, *escape*, 671.
Cutaneous, *covering*, 222.
Cut capers, *leap*, 309.
dance, 840.
Cut down, *diminish*, 36.
destroy, 162.
shorten, 201.
lower, 308.
kill, 361.
Cuticle, *covering*, 222.
Cutlass, *arms*, 727.
Cut off, *kill*, 361.
subduct, 38.
impede, 706.
disjunction, 44.
Cut out, *surpass*, 33.
retrench, 38.
plan, 626.

Cut-purse, *thief*, 792.
Cut short, *shorten*, 201, 572.
decrease, 36.
contract, 195.
Cutter, *ship*, 273.
Cut-throat, *killing*, 361.
sinner, 949.
Cutting, *cold*, 383.
affecting, 821.
censorious, 932.
Cut up, *divide*, 44.
destroy, 162.
censure, 932.
Cycle, *period*, 138.
circle, 247.
Cycloid, *circularity*, 247.
Cyclone, *violence*, 173.
rotation, 312.
Cyclopædia, *knowledge*, 490.
Cylinder, *rotundity*, 249.
Cymbal, *musical instrument*, 417.
Cynical, *censorious*, 932.
detracting, 483.
unsociable, 893.
cross, 895.
Cynosure, *indication*, 550.
prodigy, 872.
Cypher, *see* Cipher.
Cypress, *lamentation*, 839.
Cyst, *receptacle*, 191.
Czar, *master*, 745.

D

Dab, *clever*, 700.
to paint, 222.
to slap, 276.
Dabble, *meddle*, 680.
fribble, 683.
moisten, 337.
*Da capo (It.), *repetition*, 104.
duplication, 90.
frequency, 136.
Dacoit, *thief*, 792.
Dactyliomancy, *prediction*, 511.
Dactylology, *language*, 560.
Dad, *paternity*, 166.
Dado, *lining*, 224.
Dædal, *convoluted*, 248.
Dædalian, *skill*, 698.
Daft, *insane*, 503.
Dagger, *arms*, 727.
Daggers drawn, *discord*, 713.
enmity, 889.
Daggle, *pendency*, 214.
Daguerreotype, *painting*, 556.
copy, 21.
Dahabeeyah, *ship*, 273.
Dainty, *savoury*, 394.
pleasing, 829.
fastidious, 868.
Dais, *support*, 215.
Dale, *concavity*, 252.
Dally, *irresolute*, 605.
delay, 133.
inactive, 683.
amuse, 840.
fondle, 902.
Dam, *parent*, 166.
lock, 350.
close, 261.
obstruct, 348, 706.
Damage, *evil*, 619.
to injure, 649.
to spoil, 659.
payment, 812.
Damages, *penalty*, 974.
Damask, *redness*, 434.
Dame, *woman*, 374.
Damn, *condemn*, 971.
expletive, 641.
Damnify, *damage*, 649.
Damnable, *execrable*, 830.
spoil, 659.
*Damnosa hereditas (L.), *burden*, 706.
Damp, *moist*, 339.
cold, 386.
to moderate, 174.
to dissuade, 616.
depress, 837.
calm, 826.
Damper, *silencer*, 417.
Damsel, *youth*, 129.
lady, 374.
Dance, *oscillate*, 314.
agitate, 315.
rise, 305.
jump, 309.
sport, 840.
Dander, *resentment*, 900.
Dandify, *adorn*, 845.
Dandle, *endearment*, 902.
Dandruff, *uncleanness*, 653.
Dandy, *fop*, 854.
Danger, *danger*, 665.
Dangle, *hang*, 214.
swing, 314.
Dank, *moist*, 339.
Dapper, *thin*, 203.
elegant, 845.
Dapple, *brown*, 433.
Dappled, *variegation*, 440.
Darbies, *fetter*, 752.
Dare, *defy*, 715.
face danger, 861.
Dare-devil, *rashness*, 863.
Daring, *courage*, 861.

Dark, *obscure*, 421.
dim, 422.
invisible, 447.
unintelligible, 519.
ignorant, 491.
blind, 442.
latent, 526.
Darling, *favourite*, 899.
beloved, 897.
Darn, *improve*, 658.
Dart, *missile*, 727.
to propel, 284.
swift, 274.
Darwinism, *causation*, 153.
Dash, *sprinkling*, 32, 193.
to mix, 41.
throw down, 308.
display, 882.
depress, 837.
shine, 873.
mark, 550.
expletive, 641.
vivacity, 682.
Dashing, *brave*, 861.
smart, 845.
Dash off, *sketch*, 556.
Dash out, *rush*, 274.
haste, 684.
Dastard, *coward*, 862.
Data, *evidence*, 467.
reasoning, 476.
Date, *chronometry*, 114.
Daub, *cover*, 222.
dirt, 653.
bad painting, 555.
to deform, 846.
Daughter, *posterity*, 167.
Daunt, *frighten*, 860.
Dauntless, *courage*, 861.
Dawdle, *slow*, 275.
tardy, 133.
inactive, 683.
Dawn, *morning*, 125.
precursor, 116.
to begin, 66.
dim, 422.
glimpse, 490.
Day, *period*, 108.
light, 420.
Day-book, *list*, 86.
Day-break, *morning*, 125.
beginning, 66.
Day-dream, *imagination*, 515.
Day-labourer, *workman*, 690.
Daylight, *light*, 420.
publicity, 531.
Day-dream, *inattention*, 458.
Day of Judgment, *end*, 67.
Daze, *light*, 420.
Daze, *confuse*, 442.
stupefy, 823.
Dazzle, *light*, 420.
confuse, 442.
Deacon, *clergy*, 996.
Dead, *lifeless*, 360.
insensible, 823.
colourless, 429.
Dead-beat, *fatigue*, 688.
Deaden, *weaken*, 158, 160.
moderate, 174, 826.
benumb, 823.
Dead-drunk, *drunkenness*, 959.
Dead heat, *equality*, 27.
Deadlock, *stoppage*, 265.
hindrance, 706.
Deadly, *mortal*, 361, 657.
pernicious, 649.
Deadness, *numbness*, 381.
inertness, 172, 823.
Dead shot, *proficient*, 700.
Dead weight, *hindrance*, 706.
Deaf, *deafness*, 419.
Deafening, *loud*, 404.
Deal, *quantity*, 31.
mingle, 41.
give, 784.
allot, 786.
barter, 794.
Dealer, *merchant*, 797.
Deal out, *distribute*, 73, 784.
Dean, *clergy*, 996.
Deanery, *office*, 995.
house, 1000.
Dear, *loved*, 897, 899.
high-priced, 814.
Dear-bought, *worthless*, 645.
Dearth, *insufficiency*, 640.
Death, *death*, 360.
Death-blow, *end*, 67.
killing, 361.
failure, 732.
Deathless, *perpetuity*, 112.
Deathlike, *hideous*, 846.
silence, 403.
*Débâcle (Fr.), *river*, 348.
descent, 306.
destruction, 162.
Debar, *prohibit*, 761.
hinder, 751.
Debark, *arrive*, 292.
Debase, *depress*, 308.
deteriorate, 659.
foul, 653.
Debatable, *uncertain*, 475.
Debate, *reason*, 476.
dispute, 713, 720.
hesitate, 605.
talk, 588.

Debauch, *spoil*, 659.
intemperance, 954.
impurity, 961.
Debenture, *certificate*, 551.
security, 771.
Debility, *weakness*, 160.
Debit, *debt*, 806.
accounts, 811.
Debonair, *cheerfulness*, 836.
Debouch, *march out*, 292.
Débris, *part*, 51.
pulverulence, 330.
unimportance, 643.
Debt, *debt*, 806.
Debtor, *debt*, 806.
Début, *undertaking*, 676.
Decade, *number*, 98.
period, 108.
duration, 106.
Decadence, *deterioration*, 659.
Decadent, *feeble*, 575.
Decagon, *number*, 98.
Decamp, *move off*, 287, 293.
escape, 671.
Decant, *transfer*, 270.
Decanter, *receptacle*, 191.
Decapitate, *kill*, 361, 972.
Decay, *spoil*, 659.
disease, 655.
shrivel, 195.
decrease, 36.
Decayed, *imperfect*, 651.
old, 124.
adversity, 735.
Decease, *death*, 360.
Deceit, *deception*, 545.
Deceiver, *deceiver*, 548.
Decent, *modest*, 960.
tolerable, 651.
seemly, 926.
Decentralise, *disperse*, 73.
Deception, *deception*, 545.
sophistry, 477.
Decide, *judge*, 480.
choose, 609.
Decided, *resolved*, 604.
positive, 535.
certain, 475.
great, 31.
Deciduous, *transitory*, 111.
spoiled, 659.
Decimal, *number*, 84, 98.
Decimate, *subduct*, 38, 103.
Decipher, *interpret*, 522.
solve, 462.
Decision, *intention*, 620.
conclusion, 480.
resolution, 604.
Decisive, *final*, 67.
Decisive, *evidence*, 467.
resolution, 604.
demonstration, 478.
Decivilise, *brutalise*, 895.
Deck, *floor*, 211.
to beautify, 845.
Declaim, *speech*, 582.
Declare, *assert*, 535.
inform, 516, 527.
Declension, *descent*, 306.
deterioration, 659.
grammar, 567.
Declensions, *intrinsicality*, 5.
Decline, *decrease*, 36.
weaken, 160.
decay, 735.
disease, 655.
become worse, 659.
reject, 610.
refuse, 764.
be unwilling, 603.
grammar, 567.
Declivity, *obliquity*, 217.
Decoction, *calefaction*, 384.
Decode, *interpret*, 522.
Decollate, *punishment*, 972.
Decoloration, *achromatism*, 429.
Decompose, *decomposition*, 49, 653.
Decorate, *embellish*, 845, 847.
Decoration, *repute*, 873.
title, 877.
Decorous, *decent*, 960.
befitting, 922.
Decorticate, *divest*, 226.
Decorum, *politeness*, 852.
respect, 928.
purity, 960.
*Décousu (Fr.), *discontinuity*, 70.
failure, 732.
Decoy, *entice*, 615.
deceive, 545.
deceiver, 548.
Decrease, *in degree*, 36.
in size, 195.
Decree, *law*, 963.
judgment, 969.
order, 741.
Decrepit, *old*, 124, 128.
weak, 160.
frail, 651.
Decrepitude, *age*, 128.
feebleness, 160.
*Decrescendo (It.), *decrease*, 36, 415.
Decretal, *law*, 963.
order, 741.
Decry, *depreciate*, 483.
censure, 932.
Decumbent, *horizontality*, 213.
Decuple, *number*, 98.

Decurrent, *descent*, 306.
Decursive, *descent*, 306.
Decussation, *crossing*, 219.
Dedicate, *consecrate*, 873.
*De die in diem (L.), *period*, 108.
recurrence, 138.
Deduce, *infer*, 480.
retrench, 38.
Deducible, *evidence*, 467, 480.
Deduct, *retrench*, 38.
deprive, 789.
Deduction, *abatement*, 813.
Deed, *act*, 680.
record, 467, 551.
security, 771.
Deem, *belief*, 484.
Deep, *profound*, 208, 451.
the sea, 341.
cunning, 702.
feeling, 821.
sound, 404.
greatness, 31.
Deep-mouthed, *loud*, 404.
Deep-seated, *interior*, 221.
deep, 208.
Deep-toned, *resonant*, 408.
Deface, *render ugly*, 846.
destroy form, 241.
*De facto (L.), *existence*, 1.
truth, 494.
Defalcation, *shortcoming*, 304.
contraction, 195.
incompleteness, 53.
insufficiency, 640.
non-payment, 808.
Defame, *detract*, 934.
shame, 874.
censure, 932.
Defamer, *detractor*, 936.
Default, *insufficiency*, 640.
non-payment, 806, 808.
Defaulter, *debtor*, 806.
Defeat, *to confute*, 479.
failure, 732.
Defecate, *clean*, 652.
improve, 658.
Defect, *incomplete*, 53.
imperfect, 651.
failing, 945.
Defection, *disobedience*, 742.
disloyalty, 940.
Defective, *incomplete*, 53.
imperfect, 651.
insufficient 640.
Defence, *resistance*, 717.
vindication, 937.
safety, 664.
Defenceless, *weak*, 158, 160.
exposed, 665.
Defendant, *judge*, 967.
Defer, *put off*, 133.
Defer to, *respect*, 928.
assent, 488.
Deference, *subordination*, 743.
respect, 928.
Defiance, *daring*, 715.
threat, 909.
Deficiency, *inferiority*, 34.
frailty, 945.
Deficient, *incomplete*, 53.
imperfect, 651.
insufficient, 640.
inferior, 34.
insane, 502.
Deficit, *debt*, 806.
Defile, *ravine*, 198, 203.
march, 266.
dirt, 653.
spoil, 659.
shame, 874.
Define, *name*, 564.
explain, 522.
Definite, *exact*, 494.
clear, 516.
special, 79.
visible, 446.
limited, 233.
intelligible, 518.
Definitive, *decided*, 604.
final, 67.
Deflagration, *calefaction*, 384.
Deflate, *contract*, 195.
Deflection, *curvature*, 245.
Defloration, *impurity*, 961.
soil, 653.
Defluxion, *river*, 348.
Deform, *deface*, 241, 846.
Defraud, *cheat*, 545.
non-payment, 808.
Defray, *pay*, 807.
Deft, *clever*, 698.
suitable, 23.
Defunct, *dead*, 360.
Defy, *dare*, 715.
disobey, 742.
threaten, 909.
*Dégagé (Fr.), *freedom*, 748.
fashion, 825.
Degenerate, *deterioration*, 659.
Deglutition, *swallowing*, 296.
Degradation, *shame*, 874.
dishonour, 940.
deterioration, 659.
Degree, *quantity*, 26.
term, 71.
honour, 873.
Degustation, *taste*, 390.
*De haut en bas (Fr.), *contempt*, 930.

Dehortation, *dissuasion*, 616.
advice, 695.
warning, 668.
Dehumanise, *brutalise*, 895.
Deification, *idolatry*, 991.
honour, 873.
Deign, *condescend*, 879.
consent, 762.
*Dei gratiâ (L.), *dueness*, 924.
Deiseal, *rotation*, 312.
Deism, *irreligion*, 988.
Deity, *deity*, 976.
fabulous, 979.
Dejection, *sadness*, 828, 837, 841.
*Déjeuner (Fr.), *food*, 298.
*De jure (L.), *right*, 922.
*Délâbrement (Fr.), *deterioration*, 659.
destruction, 162.
Delation, *accusation*, 938.
Delay, *lateness*, 133.
*Dele (L.), *obliteration*, 552.
Delectable, *savoury*, 394.
agreeable, 829.
Delegate, *consignee*, 758, 759.
to commission, 755.
Deleterious, *pernicious*, 649.
unwholesome, 657.
Deletion, *obliteration*, 552.
Deliberate, *think*, 451.
cautious, 864.
leisurely, 685.
advised, 695.
Deliberately, *slowly*, 133.
designedly, 600.
Delicacy, *of texture*, 329.
slenderness, 203.
weak, 160.
tender, 655.
savoury, 394.
dainty, 298.
of taste, 850.
fastidiousness, 868.
exactness, 494.
pleasing, 829.
beauty, 845.
honour, 939.
purity, 960.
difficulty, 704.
scruple, 603, 616.
*Delicatessen (Ger.), *food*, 298.
Delicious, *taste*, 394.
pleasing, 829.
Delight, *pleasure*, 827.
Delightful, *pleasurableness*, 829.
Delilah, *temptress*, 615.
Delimit, *circumscribe*, 231.
Delineate, *describe*, 594.
represent, 554.
Delinquency, *guilt*, 947.
Delinquent, *sinner*, 949.
Deliquescent, *liquid*, 333.
*Deliquium (L.), *weakness*, 160.
fatigue, 688.
Delirium, *raving*, 503.
passion, 825.
Delitescence, *latency*, 526.
Deliver, *transfer*, 270.
give, 784.
liberate, 750.
relieve, 834.
utter, 582.
rescue, 672.
escape, 671.
Dell, *concavity*, 252.
Delta, *land*, 342.
Delude, *deceive*, 495, 545.
Deluge, *flow*, 337, 348.
redundance, 641.
Delusion, *error*, 495.
deceit, 545.
(self), *credulity*, 486.
Delve, *dig*, 252.
depth, 208.
Demagogue, *leader*, 745.
agitator, 742.
Demagogy, *authority*, 737.
Demand, *claim*, 924.
ask, 765.
inquire, 461.
order, 741.
price, 812.
Demarcation, *limit*, 199, 233.
*Démarche (Fr.), *procedure*, 680.
Dematerialise, *immateriality*, 317.
Demean, *humble*, 879.
dishonour, 940.
Demeanour, *conduct*, 692.
air, 448.
fashion, 852.
Dementation, *insanity*, 503.
*Démenti (Fr.), *contradiction*, 536.
Demerit, *vice*, 945.
inutility, 645.
Demesne, *property*, 780.
Demi, *bisection*, 91.
Demigod, *hero*, 948.
Demijohn, *receptacle*, 191.
Demi-rep, *libertine*, 962.
Demise, *death*, 360.
to transfer, 783.
to give, 784.
Demiurge, *deity*, 979.
Demobilise, *disperse*, 73.
Democracy, *authority*, 737.
*Démodé (Fr.), *obsolete*, 851.
*Demoiselle (Fr.), *woman*, 374.
Demolish, *destroy*, 162.

Demolish, *confute*, 479.
damage, 649.
Demon, *devil*, 980.
wretch, 913.
bane, 663.
violent, 173.
Demoniacal, *wicked*, 945.
furious, 825.
diabolic, 649, 980.
Demonism, *idolatry*, 991.
Demonolatry, *idolatry*, 991.
Demonstrate, *prove*, 85, 478.
manifest, 525.
Demonstrative, *evidential*, 467, 478.
excitable, 825.
Demoralise, *vice*, 945.
Demos, *commonalty*, 876.
Demotic, *writing*, 590.
Demulcent, *mild*, 174.
soothing, 662.
Demur, *unwillingness*, 603.
hesitation, 605.
to disbelieve, 485.
dissent, 489.
dislike, 867.
Demure, *grave*, 826.
sad, 837.
modest, 881.
affected, 855.
Den, *cell*, 189.
prison, 752.
sty, 653.
Denary, *number*, 98.
Denaturalised, *unconformity*, 83.
Dendriform, *rough*, 256.
Denegation, *negation*, 536.
Denial, *negation*, 536.
Denigrate, *blacken*, 431.
decry, 483, 934.
Denization, *liberation*, 750.
Denizen, *inhabitant*, 188.
man, 373.
Denominate, *nomenclature*, 564.
Denomination, *class*, 75.
Denominator, *number*, 84.
Denote, *indication*, 550.
*Dénouement (Fr.), *result*, 154.
end, 67.
elucidation, 522.
completion, 729.
Denounce, *accuse*, 908.
cite, 965.
*De novo (L.), *repetition*, 104.
frequency 136.
Dense, *close*, 321.
crowded, 72.
Density, *closeness*, 46, 321.
Dent, *notch*, 257.
hollow, 252.
Denticulated, *sharp*, 253.
Denude, *divest*, 226.
Denunciation, *see* Denounce.
Deny, *negative*, 536.
dissent, 489.
refuse, 764.
Deodand, *penalty*, 974.
Deodorise, *disinfect*, 652.
Deontology, *duty*, 926.
*Deo volente (L.), *conditions*, 770.
Depart, *set out*, 293.
die, 360.
Departed, *gone*, 2.
Department, *class*, 75.
region, 181.
business, 625.
Depauperate, *impoverish*, 804.
Depend, *hang*, 214.
be contingent, 475.
Depend upon, *trust*, 484.
be the effect of, 154.
affirm, 535.
Dependable, *belief*, 484.
probity, 939.
Dependent, *liable*, 177.
servant, 746.
Dependence, *subjection*, 749.
Depict, *paint*, 556.
describe, 594.
Depletion, *insufficiency*, 640.
Deplorable, *bad*, 649.
disastrous, 735.
painful, 830.
Deplore, *regret*, 833.
complain, 839.
remorse, 950.
Deploy, *expansion*, 194.
Deponent, *evidence*, 467.
Depopulate, *displace*, 185.
desert, 893.
Deportation, *displace*, 185.
transfer, 270.
emigration, 297.
Deportment, *conduct*, 692.
Depose, *evidence*, 467.
tell, 527.
record, 551.
dethrone, 756.
declare, 535.
Deposit, *place*, 184.
secure, 771.
store, 636.
expenditure, 809.
Depository, *store*, 636.
Depot, *store*, 636.
focus, 74.
mart, 799.
Deprave, *spoil*, 659.
Depraved, *bad*, 649.

Depraved, *vicious*, 945.
Deprecate, *deprecation*, 766.
pity, 914.
Depreciate, *detract*, 483.
censure, 932.
decrease, 36.
Depredation, *stealing*, 791.
Depredator, *thief*, 792.
Depression, *lowering*, 308.
lowness, 207.
depth, 208.
concavity, 252.
dejection, 837.
Deprive, *take*, 789.
subduct, 38.
lose, 776.
Depth, *physical*, 208.
mental, 450, 490.
Depurate, *clean*, 652.
improve, 658.
Depuratory, *remedy*, 662.
Depute, *commission*, 755.
Deputy, *substitute*, 147, 759.
Derangement, *mental*, 503.
physical, 61.
*De règle (Fr.), *rule*, 80.
Dereliction, *relinquishment*, 624.
guilt, 947.
Deride, *ridicule*, 856.
disrespect, 929.
trifle with, 643.
scoff, 483.
*De rigueur (Fr.), *rule*, 80.
Derisive, *ridiculous*, 853.
Derivation, *origin*, 153.
verbal, 562.
Derivative, *effect*, 154.
Derive, *attribute*, 155.
receive, 785.
acquire, 775.
Dermal, *covering*, 22.
income, 810.
*Dernier ressort (Fr.), *plan*, 626.
Derogate, *disparage*, 483.
demean, 940.
shame, 874.
Derringer, *arms*, 727.
Dervish, *clergy*, 996.
Descant, *dissert*, 595.
dwell upon, 584.
diffuseness, 573.
Descendant, *posterity*, 167.
Descent, *slope*, 217.
motion downwards, 306.
order, 58.
Describe, *set forth*, 594.
Description, *kind*, 75.
narration, 594.
Descry, *vision*, 441.
Desecrate, *misuse*, 679.
profane, 989.
Desert, *solitude*, 101, 893.
waste, 645.
empty, 4.
Desert, *merit*, 944.
to relinquish, 624.
to escape, 671.
Deserter, *apostate*, 607.
Desertless, *vice*, 945.
Deserve, *merit*, 944.
right, 922, 924.
Deshabille, *undress*, 225.
unprepared, 674.
simplicity, 849.
Desiccate, *dryness*, 340.
Desiderate, *desire*, 865.
require, 630.
Desideratum, *desire*, 865.
inquiry, 461.
requirement, 630.
Design, *intention*, 620.
cunning, 702.
plan, 626.
delineation, 554.
prototype, 22.
Designate, *specify*, 79, 564.
Designation, *kind*, 75.
Designed, *intended*, 600.
Designer, *artist*, 559, 626.
Designing, *false*, 544.
artful, 702.
Desirable, *expedient*, 646.
Desire, *longing*, 865.
Desist, *discontinue*, 141.
relinquish, 624.
inaction, 681.
Desk, *support*, 215.
receptacle, 191.
Desolate, *alone*, 87.
secluded, 893.
afflicted, 828.
to ravage, 162.
Desolation, *evil*, 619.
*Désorienté (Fr.), *ignorance*, 491.
Despair, *hopelessness*, 859
dejection, 837.
Despatch, *see* Dispatch.
Desperado, *rashness*, 863.
Desperate, *great*, 31.
violent, 173.
rash, 863.
difficult, 704.
impossible, 471.
Desperation, *hopelessness*, 859.
Despicable, *shameful*, 874.
contemptible, 930.
trifling, 643.
Despise, *contemn*, 930.

Despise, *deride*, 483.
Despite, *notwithstanding*, 179, 708.
malevolence, 907.
Despoil, *take*, 789.
rob, 791.
hurt, 649.
Despondency, *sadness*, 837.
fear, 860.
despair, 859.
Despot, *master*, 745.
Despotism, *arbitrariness*, 964.
authority, 737.
severity, 739.
Desquamation, *divestment*, 226.
Dessert, *food*, 298.
Destination, *fate*, 152, 601.
arrival, 292.
intention, 620.
Destiny, *fate*, 601.
chance, 152.
Destitute, *insufficient*, 640.
poor, 804.
Destroy, *demolish*, 162.
injure, 649.
deface, 241.
Destroyed, *inexistence*, 2.
Destroyer, *ship*, 272.
Destruction, *demolition*, 162, 732.
evil, 619.
Destructive, *hurtful*, 649.
Desuetude, *disuse*, 614, 678.
Desultory, *discontinuous*, 70.
irregular, in time, 139.
disordered, 59.
multiform, 81.
deviating, 149, 279.
agitated, 315.
Detach, *separate*, 10, 44, 47.
Detached, *irrelated*, 10, 47.
unity, 87.
Detachment, *part*, 51.
army, 726.
Detail, *to describe*, 594.
special portions, 79.
Detain, *retention*, 781.
Detect, *judgment*, 480.
Detective, *inquiry*, 461.
Detention, *retention*, 781.
imprisonment, 751.
*Détenu (Fr.), *prisoner*, 754.
Deter, *dissuasion*, 616.
Detergent, *remedy*, 662.
remedial, 656.
Deteriorate, *deterioration*, 659.
Determinate, *special*, 79.
exact, 474.
resolute, 604.
Determination, *resolution*, 604.
will, 600.
Determination, *purpose*, 604.
judgment, 480.
Determine, *judge*, 480.
intend, 620.
direction, 278.
resolve, 604.
designate, 79.
Determinism, *necessity*, 601.
Detersive, *cleanness*, 652.
Detest, *hate*, 867, 898.
Detestable, *bad*, 649, 867.
Dethrone, *abrogation*, 756.
Dethronement, *anarchy*, 738.
Detonate, *sound*, 406.
explode, 173.
Detour, *circuit*, 629.
curvature, 245.
deviation, 279.
Detract, *subduct*, 38.
depreciate, 483.
censure, 932.
slander, 934.
Detractor, *slanderer*, 936.
Detrain, *arrival*, 292.
Detriment, *evil*, 619.
Detrimental, *hurtful*, 649.
Detritus, *part*, 51.
pulverulence, 330.
*De trop (Fr.), *redundance*, 641.
Detrude, *cast out*, 297.
cast down, 308.
Detruncation, *subduction*, 38.
disjunction, 44.
Deuce, *duality*, 89.
demon, 980.
Deuced, *great*, 31.
*Deus ex machina (L.), *helper*, 711.
wonder-worker, 994.
Deuterogamy, *marriage*, 903.
Devastate, *destroy*, 162.
injure, 649.
Devastation, *havoc*, 659.
Develop, *cause*, 153.
produce, 161.
increase, 35.
expand, 194.
evolve, 313.
Development, *effect*, 154.
Deviate, *differ*, 15.
vary, 20.
change, 140.
turn, 279.
diverge, 291.
circuit, 629.
bend, 245.
Device, *expedient*, 626.
motto, 550.
Devices, *inclination*, 602.
Devil, *Satan*, 978.

Devil, *maleficent being*, 913.
culprit, 949.
seasoned food 392.
Devilish, *great*, 31.
bad, 649.
Devilry (or Deviltry), *evil*, 619.
cruelty, 907.
wickedness, 945.
sorcery, 992.
Devious, *deviating*, 245, 279.
different, 15.
Devise, *plan*, 620, 626.
imagine, 515.
bequeath, 784.
Devoid, *empty*, 640.
absent, 187.
not having, 776.
*Devoir (Fr.), *courtesy*, 894.
Devolution, *delegation*, 755.
Devolve, *transfer*, 783.
Devolve on, *duty*, 926.
Devote, *attention*, 457.
curse, 908.
employ, 677.
consecrate, 873.
Devoted, *loving*, 897.
friendly, 888.
doomed, 152, 735, 828.
Devotee, *pious*, 988.
resolute, 604.
Devotion, *piety*, 987.
worship, 990.
respect, 928.
love, 897.
disinterestedness, 942.
Devour, *eat*, 296.
destroy, 162.
Devout, *pious*, 897.
Dew, *moisture*, 339.
Dew-pond, *lake*, 343.
Dexter, *right*, 238.
Dexterous, *skill*, 698.
Dey, *master*, 745.
Dhow, *ship*, 273.
*Diablerie (Fr.), *sorcery*, 992.
Diabolic, *malevolent*, 907.
wicked, 945.
bad, 649.
satanic, 978.
Diacoustics, *sound*, 402.
Diadem, *ensign*, 747.
Diagnostic, *intrinsicality*, 5.
speciality, 79.
discrimination, 465.
Diagonal, *oblique*, 217.
Diagram, *representation*, 554.
Diagraph, *imitation*, 19.
Dial, *clock*, 114.
Dialect, *neology*, 563.
Dialectic, *argumentation*, 476.
language, 560.
Dialogue, *interlocution*, 588.
Diameter, *breadth*, 202.
Diamond, *lozenge*, 244.
gem, 650.
Diapason, *melody*, 413.
Diaper, *reticulation*, 219.
Diaphanous, *transparent*, 425.
Diaphoresis, *excretion*, 298.
Diaphragm, *partition*, 228.
middle, 68.
Diary, *record*, 551.
journal, 114.
Diastole, *expansion*, 194.
pulse, 314.
Diathermancy, *calefaction*, 384.
Diathesis, *state*, 7.
habit, 613.
Diatonic, *harmony*, 413.
Diatribe, *disapprobation*, 932.
Dibble, *perforator*, 262.
Dicacity, *insolence*, 885.
Dice, *chance*, 156.
Dichotomy, *bisection*, 91.
angularity, 244.
Dichroism, *variegation*, 440.
Dicker, *barter*, 794.
Dicky, *seat*, 215.
Dictate, *command*, 741.
authority, 737.
enjoin, 615.
write, 590.
Dictator, *master*, 745.
Dictatorial, *severe*, 739.
insolent, 885.
Dictatorship, *authority*, 737.
Diction, *style*, 569.
Dictionary, *word*, 562.
*Dictum (L.), *maxim*, 496.
affirmation, 535.
command, 741.
Didactic, *teaching*, 537.
Diddle, *deception*, 545.
Die, *chance*, 156.
to expire, 2, 360.
cease, 141.
Die for, *desire*, 865.
*Dies non (L.), *neverness*, 107.
Diet, *food*, 298.
remedy, 662.
council, 696.
Dietetics, *remedy*, 662.
Difference, *difference*, 15, 28.
discord, 713.
numerical, 84.
Differential, *number*, 84.
Differentiation, *numeration*, 85.
difference, 15.

Differentiation, *discrimination*, 465.
*Difficile (Fr.), *troublesome*, 704.
Difficult, *fastidious*, 868.
Difficulty, *hardness*, 704.
question, 461.
Diffident, *modest*, 881.
fearful, 860.
Diffraction, *curvature*, 245.
Diffluent, *liquefaction*, 335.
Diffuse, *style*, 573.
disperse, 73, 291.
publish, 531.
permeate, 186.
Dig, *excavate*, 252.
deepen, 208.
poke, 276.
Digamy, *marriage*, 903.
Digest, *arrange*, 60, 826.
think, 451.
plan, 626.
compendium, 596.
Diggings, *abode*, 189.
Dight, *dressed*, 225.
Digit, *number*, 84.
Digitated, *pointed*, 253.
Dignify, *honour*, 873.
Dignitary, *cleric*, 996.
Dignity, *glory*, 873.
honour, 939.
Digress, *deviate*, 279.
style, 573.
Dike, *ditch*, 198, 232.
defence, 666, 717.
Dilaceration, *disjunction*, 44.
Dilapidation, *destruction*, 162.
deterioration, 659.
Dilate, *increase*, 35.
swell, 194.
lengthen, 202.
rarefy, 322.
style, 573.
discourse, 584.
Dilatory, *slow*, 275.
inactive, 683.
Dilemma, *difficulty*, 704.
logic, 476.
doubt, 485.
*Dilettante (It.), *scholar*, 492.
taste, 850.
Diligence, *coach*, 272.
activity, 682.
Dilly-dally, *irresolution*, 605.
lateness, 133.
Dilution, *weakness*, 160.
water, 337.
Diluvian, *old*, 124, 128.
Dim, *dark*, 421.
obscure, 422.
invisible, 447.
Dimension, *size*, 192.
Dimidiation, *bisection*, 91.
Diminish, *lessen*, 32, 36.
contract, 195.
*Diminuendo (It.), *music*, 415.
Diminutive, *in degree*, 32.
in size, 193.
Dimness, *dimness*, 422.
Dimple, *concavity*, 252.
notch, 257.
Dimsighted, *dimsightedness*, 443.
foolish, 499.
Din, *noise*, 404.
repetition, 104.
loquacity, 584.
Dine, *to feed*, 297.
Ding-dong, *repeat*, 104.
noise, 407.
Dinghy, *boat*, 273.
Dingle, *hollow*, 252.
Dingy, *dark*, 421, 431.
dim, 422.
colourless, 429.
grey, 432.
Dinner, *food*, 298.
Dint, *power*, 157.
instrumentality, 631.
dent, 257.
Diocesan, *clergy*, 996.
Diocese, *churchdom*, 995.
Diorama, *view*, 448.
painting, 556.
Dip, *plunge*, 310.
direction, 278.
slope, 217.
dive, 208.
insert, 300.
immerse, 337.
Dip into, *examine*, 457.
investigate, 461.
Diphthong, *letter*, 561.
Diploma, *commission*, 755.
document, 551.
Diplomacy, *mediation*, 724.
artfulness, 702.
negotiation, 769.
Diplomatic, *artful*, 544, 702.
tactful, 498, 698.
Diplomatist, *messenger*, 534.
Dipsomania, *drunkenness*, 959.
craving, 865.
Dire, *fearful*, 860.
grievous, 830.
hateful, 649.
Direct, *straight*, 246, 628.
to order, 737.
to command, 741.
to teach, 537.
artless, 703.

Direction, *tendency*, 278.
course, 622.
place, 183.
management, 693.
precept, 697.
Directly, *soon*, 111.
towards, 278.
Director, *manager*, 694.
master, 745.
teacher, 540.
Directorship, *authority*, 737.
Directory, *council*, 696.
list, 86.
Dirge, *song*, 415.
lament, 839.
funeral, 363.
Dirigible, *air-ship*, 273.
Dirk, *arms*, 727.
Dirt, *uncleanness*, 653.
trifle, 643.
ugly, 846.
blemish, 848.
Dirty, *dishonourable*, 940.
Disability, *impotence*, 158.
Disable, *weaken*, 158, 160, 674.
Disabuse, *disclosure*, 529.
Disadvantage, *evil*, 649.
inexpedience, 647.
badness, 649.
Disaffection, *hate*, 898.
disloyalty, 940.
Disagreeable, *unpleasant*, 830.
disliked, 867.
Disagreement, *incongruity*, 24.
difference, 15.
discord, 713.
dissent, 489.
Disallow, *prohibit*, 761.
Disannul, *abrogate*, 756.
Disapparel, *divest*, 226.
Disappear, *vanish*, 2, 449.
Disappoint, *discontent*, 832.
fail, 732.
baulk, 509.
Disapprobation, *blame*, 932.
Disarm, *incapacitate*, 158.
weaken, 160.
Disarrange, *derange*, 61.
Disarray, *disorder*, 59.
undress, 226.
Disaster, *evil*, 619.
failure, 732.
adversity, 735.
calamity, 830.
Disavow, *negation*, 536.
Disband, *disperse*, 73.
separate, 44.
Disbelief, *doubt*, 485.
religious, 989.
Disbranch, *disjunction*, 44.
Disburden, *facilitate*, 705.
disclose, 529.
Disburse, *expend*, 809.
Disc, *see* Disk.
Discard, *dismiss*, 624, 756.
disuse, 678.
refuse, 764.
thought, 452.
repudiate, 773.
Discern, *behold*, 441.
Discernible, *visibility*, 446.
Discerning, *wisdom*, 498.
Discernment, *wisdom*, 498.
Discerption, *disjunction*, 44.
Discharge, *emit*, 297.
sound, 406.
violence, 173.
propel, 284.
excrete, 299.
flow, 348.
duty, 926.
acquit oneself, 692.
observe, 772.
pay, 807.
exempt, 927.
accomplish, 729.
liberate, 750.
forget, 506.
acquit, 970.
Disciple, *learner*, 541.
Disciplinarian, *master*, 540.
martinet, 739.
Discipline, *order*, 58.
teaching, 537.
training, 673.
restraint, 751.
punishment, 972.
religious, 990.
Disclaim, *deny*, 536.
refuse, 764.
repudiate, 756.
abjure, 757.
Disclose, *disclosure*, 529.
Discoid, *horizontality*, 213.
Discolour, *achromatism*, 429.
to stain, 846.
Discomfit, *success*, 731.
Discomfiture, *failure*, 732.
Discomfort, *pain*, 828.
Discommendation, *blame*, 932.
Discommodious, *inutility*, 645.
hindrance, 706.
Discommodity, *inexpedience*, 647.
Discompose, *derange*, 61.
hinder, 706.
put out, 458.
to vex, 830.
disconcert, 874.

Discompose, *provoke*, 900.
Disconcert, *hinder*, 706.
frustrate, 731.
distract, 458.
confuse, 874.
Disconcerted, *inattention*, 458.
Disconformity, *disagreement*, 24.
Discongruity, *disagreement*, 24.
Disconnect, *disjunction*, 44.
irrelation, 10.
Disconnected, *confused*, 519.
Disconsolate, *sad*, 837.
grief, 828.
Discontent, *dissatisfaction*, 832.
Discontented, *pain*, 828.
Discontinuance, *cessation*, 141.
Discontinue, *interrupt*, 70.
relinquish, 624.
Discord, *disagreement*, 24.
dissension, 713.
musical, 414.
Discordance, *incongruity*, 24.
sound, 410.
dissent, 489.
Discount, *abatement*, 813.
to anticipate, 673.
disregard, 460, 483.
qualify, 469.
Discountenance, *refuse*, 764.
disfavour, 706.
rudeness, 895.
Discourage, *dissuade*, 616.
sadden, 837.
disfavour, 706.
Discourse, *talk*, 588.
speech, 582.
dissert, 595.
Discourtesy, *rudeness*, 895.
Discover, *perceive*, 441.
find, 480.
solve, 462.
Discredit, *disbelief*, 485.
dishonour, 874.
Discreditable, *vice*, 945.
Discreet, *careful*, 459.
cautious, 864.
prudent, 498.
clever, 698.
Discrepancy, *disagreement*, 24.
Discrete, *separate*, 44.
single, 87.
Discretion, *wisdom*, 498.
caution, 864.
skill, 698.
will, 600.
care, 459.
choice, 609.
Discrimination, *distinction*, 465.
difference, 15.
Discrimination, *taste*, 850.
wisdom, 498.
Disculpate, *vindicate*, 937.
Discursive, *moving*, 264.
migratory, 266.
wandering, 279.
style, 573.
dissertation, 595.
Discuss, *reason*, 476.
inquire, 461.
reflect, 451.
treat of, 595.
eat, 296.
Disdain, *contempt*, 930.
indifference, 866.
fastidiousness, 868.
Disdainful, *proud*, 878.
Disease, *illness*, 655.
Disembark, *arrive*, 292.
Disembarrass, *facilitate*, 705.
Disembodied, *immaterial*, 317.
Disembody, *decompose*, 49.
Disembogue, *flow out*, 348.
emit, 295.
Disembowel, *extraction*, 300.
Disenable, *impotence*, 158.
Disenchant, *dissuade*, 616.
Disencumber, *facility*, 705.
Disendow, *taking*, 789.
Disengage, *detach*, 44.
facilitate, 705.
liberate, 750.
Disentangle, *separate*, 44.
arrange, 60.
facilitate, 705.
decipher, 522.
Disenthral, *liberate*, 750.
Disentitled, *undueness*, 925.
Disestablish, *displace*, 185.
Disesteem, *disrespect*, 929.
censure, 932.
Disfavour, *hate*, 898.
to oppose, 708.
Disfeature, *deface*, 241.
deform, 846.
Disfigure, *deface*, 241.
deform, 846.
blemish, 848.
Disfranchise, *disentitle*, 925.
Disgorge, *emit*, 297.
restore, 790.
flow out, 348.
Disgrace, *shame*, 874.
dishonour, 940.
Disguise, *conceal*, 528.
falsify, 544.
deceive, 545.
mask, 530.
untruth, 546.

Disguised, *in liquor*, 959.
Disgust, *dislike*, 867.
hatred, 898.
offensive, 830.
weary, 841.
taste, 395.
Dish, *plate*, 191.
food, 299.
to foil, 731.
Dishabille, *see* Deshabille.
Dishearten, *dissuade*, 616.
deject, 837.
Dished, *failure*, 732.
Dishevelled, *loose*, 47.
disordered, 61.
intermixed, 219.
twisted, 248.
Dishonest, *false*, 544.
faithless, 940.
Dishonour, *baseness*, 940.
to repudiate a bill, 808.
disrespect, 929.
Dishonourable, *disrepute*, 874.
Disillusion, *dissuasion*, 616.
Disincline, *dissuade*, 616.
Disinclined, *unwilling*, 603.
disliking, 867.
Disinfect, *purify*, 652.
improve, 658.
Disinfectant, *remedy*, 662.
Disingenuous, *false*, 544.
dishonourable, 940.
Disinherit, *transfer*, 783.
Disintegrate, *separate*, 44.
pulverise, 330.
Disinter, *exhume*, 363.
discover, 525.
Disinterested, *unselfish*, 942.
Disjoin, *loosen*, 44.
Disjointed, *loosened*, 44.
in disorder, 59.
Disjunction, *incoherence*, 47.
decomposition, 49.
Disk, *face*, 234.
exterior, 220.
Dislike, *distaste*, 867.
hate, 898.
reluctance, 603.
Dislocate, *loosen*, 44.
Dislodge, *displace*, 185.
Disloyal, *improbity*, 940.
Dismal, *dejection*, 837.
Dismantle, *destroy*, 162.
disuse, 678.
despoil, 649.
injure, 659.
Dismast, *disuse*, 678.
dismantle, 659, 674.
Dismay, *fear*, 860.
Dismember, *loosen*, 44.
Dismiss, *discard*, 678, 756.
liberate, 750.
Dismount, *descend*, 306.
arrive, 292.
disable, 674.
Disobey, *disobedience*, 742.
Disobliging, *malevolent*, 907.
Disorder, *confusion*, 59.
to derange, 61.
disease, 655.
Disorderly, *violent*, 173.
Disorganise, *derange*, 61.
destroy, 162.
spoil, 659.
Disown, *negation*, 536.
Disparage, *depreciate*, 483.
disrespect, 929.
censure, 932.
Disparate, *different*, 15.
dissimilar, 18.
single, 87.
disagreeing, 24.
unequal, 28.
Disparity, *dissimilarity*, 18.
Dispart, *disjoin*, 44.
Dispassionate, *calm*, 826.
Dispatch, *speed*, 274.
haste, 684.
earliness, 132.
to conduct, 692.
complete, 729.
kill, 162, 361.
epistle, 592.
intelligence, 532.
Dispel, *destroy*, 162.
scatter, 73.
Dispensable, *disuse*, 678.
Dispensation, *licence*, 760.
calamity, 830.
Dispense, *exempt*, 927.
permit, 760.
disuse, 678.
relinquish, 624.
give, 784.
disperse, 73.
retail, 796.
Dispeople, *seclusion*, 893.
Disperse, *scatter*, 73, 638.
separate, 44.
diverge, 291.
Dispersion, *removal*, 270.
Dispirit, *sadden*, 837.
discourage, 616.
Displace, *remove*, 185.
transfer, 270.
derange, 61.
Display, *show*, 525.
appear, 448.

Display, *parade*, 882.
Displease, *painfulness*, 830.
Displeased, *pain*, 828.
Displeasure, *pain*, 828.
anger, 900.
Displosion, *violence*, 173.
Disport, *amusement*, 840.
Dispose, *arrange*, 60.
prepare, 673.
tend, 176.
induce, 615.
Dispose of, *sell*, 796.
give, 784.
relinquish, 782.
use, 677.
Disposition, *order*, 58.
arrangement, 60.
inclination, 602.
mind, 820.
Dispossess, *take away*, 789.
transfer, 783.
Dispossessed, *deprived*, 776.
Dispraise, *disapprove*, 932.
Disprize, *depreciate*, 483.
Disproof, *counter-evidence*, 468.
confutation, 479.
Disproportion, *irrelation*, 10.
disagreement, 24.
Disprove, *confute*, 479.
Disputant, *debater*, 476.
combatant, 726.
Disputatious, *irritable*, 901.
Dispute, *discord*, 713.
denial, 485, 536.
discussion, 476.
Disqualified, *incapacitated*, 158.
incompetent, 699.
Disqualify, *incapacitate*, 158.
weaken, 160.
disentitle, 925.
unprepared, 674.
Disquiet, *excitement*, 825.
uneasiness, 149, 828.
to give pain, 830.
Disquietude, *apprehension*, 860.
Disquisition, *dissertation*, 595.
Disregard, *overlook*, 458.
neglect, 460.
indifferent, 823.
slight, 483.
Disrelish, *dislike*, 867.
hate, 898.
Disreputable, *vicious*, 945.
Disrepute, *disgrace*, 874.
Disrespect, *irreverence*, 929.
Disrobe, *divestment*, 226.
Disruption, *disjunction*, 44.
schism, 713.
Dissatisfaction, *discontent*, 832.
Dissatisfaction, *sorrow*, 828.
Dissect, *anatomise*, 44, 49.
investigate, 461.
Dissemble, *falsehood*, 544.
Dissembler, *liar*, 548.
Disseminate, *scatter*, 73.
diverge, 291.
publish, 531.
pervade, 186.
Dissension, *discord*, 713.
Dissent, *disagree*, 489.
refuse, 764.
heterodoxy, 984.
discord, 713.
Dissertation, *disquisition*, 595.
Disservice, *disadvantage*, 619.
inexpedience, 647.
Dissever, *disjoin*, 44.
Dissidence, *disagreement*, 24.
dissent, 489.
Dissilience, *violent*, 173.
Dissimilar, *unlike*, 18.
Dissimulate, *falsehood*, 544.
Dissipate, *scatter*, 73.
waste, 638.
prodigality, 818.
dissolute, 961.
licentiousness, 954.
Dissociation, *irrelation*, 10.
separation, 44.
Dissolute, *intemperate*, 954.
profligate, 945.
debauched, 961.
Dissolution, *decomposition*, 49.
liquefaction, 335.
death, 360.
Dissolve, *vanish*, 2.
disappear, 449.
abrogate, 756.
liquefy, 335.
Dissonance, *disagreement*, 24.
discord, 414.
Dissuade, *dissuasion*, 616.
Distain, *ugliness*, 846.
Distance, *longinquity*, 196.
to overtake, 282.
to leave behind, 303, 732.
respect, 928.
of time, 110.
Distant, *far*, 196.
discourteous, 895.
Distaste, *dislike*, 867.
Distasteful, *disagreeable*, 830.
Distemper, *disease*, 655.
painting, 556.
Distend, *expansion*, 194.
Distended, *size*, 192.
Distich, *poetry*, 597.
Distil, *evaporate*, 336.

Distil, *flow*, 348.
drop, 295.
Distinct, *visible*, 446.
intelligible, 516, 518, 535.
disjoined, 44.
Distinction, *difference*, 15.
discrimination, 465.
fame, 873.
style, 574.
*Distingué (Fr.), *repute*, 873.
Distinguish, *perceive*, 441.
Distortion, *obliquity*, 217.
twist, 243, 555.
of vision, 443.
perversion, 523.
ugliness, 846.
Distracted, *insane*, 503.
confused, 491.
Distraction, *inattention*, 458.
amusement, 840.
Distrain, *seize*, 789, 969.
*Distrait (Fr.), *incogitancy*, 452.
inattention, 458.
Distraught, *see* Distracted.
Distress, *affliction*, 828.
cause of pain, 830.
poor, 804.
Distribute, *disperse*, 73.
arrange, 60.
allot, 786.
diverge, 291.
District, *region*, 181.
Distrust, *disbelief*, 485.
fear, 860.
Disturb, *derange*, 61.
alter, 140.
agitate, 315.
Disunion, *separation*, 44.
discord, 713.
Disuse, *unemployment*, 678.
desuetude, 614.
Ditch, *conduit*, 350.
hollow, 252.
trench, 259, 343.
Dither, *shiver*, 315, 383.
Dithyrambic, *poetry*, 597.
Ditto, *repetition*, 104, 136.
Ditty, *music*, 415.
Diurnal, *period*, 108, 138.
Diuturnal, *diuturnity*, 110.
Divan, *sofa*, 215.
council, 696.
Divarication, *divergence*, 291.
deviation, 279.
difference, 15.
Dive, *plunge*, 310.
inquire, 461.
Divellicate, *disjoin*, 44.
Divergence, *variation*, 20.
Divergence, *difference*, 15.
dispersion, 73.
separation, 291.
disagreement, 24.
deviation, 279.
Divers, *many*, 102.
different, 15.
multiform, 81.
Diversified, *varied*, 15, 18, 20, 81.
Diversion, *amusement*, 840.
Diversity, *difference*, 15.
dissimilarity, 18.
multiform, 81.
Divert, *turn*, 279.
amuse, 840.
abstract, 452.
*Divertissement (Fr.), *drama*, 599.
Dives, *wealth*, 803.
Divest, *denude*, 226.
take, 789.
Divest oneself of, *leave*, 782.
Divide, *separate*, 44.
part, 51, 91.
apportion, 786.
Dividend, *part*, 51.
number, 84.
portion, 786.
Divination, *prediction*, 511.
occult arts, 992.
Divine, *Deity*, 976.
clergyman, 983A, 996.
to guess, 514.
perfect, 650.
Divining-rod, *spell*, 993.
Divinity, *Deity*, 976.
theology, 983.
Division, *separation*, 44.
part, 51.
class, 75.
arithmetical, 85.
discord, 713.
distribution, 786.
Divisor, *number*, 84.
Divorce, *matrimonial*, 905.
separation, 44.
Divulge, *disclose*, 529.
Divulsion, *disjoin*, 44.
Dizen, *beautify*, 845.
ornament, 847.
Dizzard, *fool*, 501.
Dizzy, *confused*, 458.
vertigo, 503.
Do, *act*, 680.
produce, 161.
suffice, 639.
complete, 729.
cheat, 545.
Do away with, *remove*, 185, 678.
destroy, 162, 681.

Do for, *injure*, 659.
defeat, 731.
kill, 361.
suit, 646.
punish, 972.
Do in, *kill*, 361.
Do into, *interpret*, 522.
Do like, *imitation*, 19.
Do over, *cover*, 222.
Do up, *repair*, 658.
pack, 72.
Docetic, *immateriality*, 317.
Docile, *teachable*, 539.
willing, 602.
Dock, *cut off*, 38.
diminish, 36.
shorten, 201.
port, 189.
yard, 636, 691.
tribunal, 966.
incompleteness, 53.
Docker, *workman*, 690.
Docket, *indication*, 467, 550.
Doctor, *sage*, 492.
physician, 695.
to restore, 660.
remedy, 658.
Doctrinaire, *ignoramus*, 493.
Doctrinal, *teaching*, 537.
Doctrine, *tenet*, 484.
knowledge, 490.
Document, *record*, 551.
Dodge, *oscillate*, 314.
pursue, 461.
deceive, 545.
avoid, 623.
shift, 264.
contrivance, 626.
cunning, 702.
Doer, *agent*, 690.
originator, 164.
Doff, *put off*, 226.
Dog, *to pursue*, 622.
Dog-cart, *vehicle*, 272.
Dog-cheap, *cheapness*, 815.
Dog-days, *heat*, 382.
Doge, *master*, 745.
Dogged, *obstinate*, 606.
discourteous, 895.
Dogger, *ship*, 273.
Doggerel, *verse*, 597.
Dogma, *tenet*, 484.
theological, 983.
Dogmatic, *obstinate*, 606.
assertion, 535.
intolerant, 481.
Dog's-ear, *fold*, 258.
Dog-tired, *fatigue*, 688.
Dog-trot, *slowness*, 275.
Doings, *actions*, 680.
events, 151.
Doit, *trifle*, 643.
coin, 800.
Doited, *insane*, 503.
*Dolce far niente (It.), *inactivity*, 638.
Doldrums, *dejection*, 837.
Dole, *small quantity*, 32.
to give, 784.
to allot, 786.
expenditure, 809.
grief, 828.
Doleful, *dejected*, 837.
Doll, *image*, 554.
small, 193.
Dollar, *money*, 800.
Dolman, *dress*, 225.
Dolmen, *grave*, 363.
Dolorous, *pain*, 830.
Dolour, *physical*, 378.
moral, 828.
Dolt, *fool*, 501.
Doltish, *folly*, 499.
Domain, *region*, 181.
property, 780.
Dome, *convexity*, 250.
Domestic, *interior*, 188, 221.
servant, 746.
secluded, 893.
Domesticate, *tame*, 537.
Domicile, *abode*, 189.
Dominance, *influence*, 175.
Dominant, *prevailing*, 737.
note in music, 413.
Domination, *authority*, 737.
Domineer, *tyrannise*, 739.
insolence, 885.
Dominican, *clergy*, 996.
Dominie, *teacher*, 540.
Domino, *dress*, 225.
mask, 530.
Don, *to put on*, 225.
noble, 875.
Dona, *woman*, 374.
sweetheart, 897.
Donation, *gift*, 784, 804.
Done, *finished*, 729.
cheated, 547.
Donjon, *defence*, 717.
Donkey, *ass*, 271.
fool, 591.
*Donna (It.), *woman*, 374.
Do-nothing, *inactivity*, 683.
Doodle, *fool*, 501.
Doom, *fate*, 152.
necessity, 601.
destruction, 162, 360.
to sentence, 969.
end, 67.

Doomed, *undone*, 828.
fated, 152, 601.
Doomsday, *futurity*, 121.
end, 67.
Door, *opening*, 260.
passage, 627.
brink, 230.
entrance, 66, 294.
barrier, 232.
Door-keeper, *janitor*, 263.
Doorway, *opening*, 260.
Dope, *semiliquid*, 352.
stupefy, 376.
*Doppelgänger (Ger.), *ghost*, 980.
Dormant, *latent*, 526.
inert, 172, 683.
Dormitory, *room*, 191.
Dormouse, *inactivity*, 683.
Dorsal, *rear*, 235.
*Dorsum (L.), *rear*, 235.
convexity, 250.
Dose, *part*, 51.
mixture, 41.
Doss-house, *inn*, 189.
Dossier, *record*, 551.
evidence, 461.
Dot, *speck*, 32, 193.
mark, 550.
*Dot (Fr.), *dowry*, 810.
Dotage, *age*, 128.
folly, 499.
Dotard, *fool*, 501.
Dote, *drivel*, 499, 503.
love, 897.
Dotted, *variegated*, 440.
Double, *duplex*, 90.
turn, 283.
fold, 258.
false, 544.
similarity, 17.
Double-dealing, *falsehood*, 544.
dishonour, 940.
Double-Dutch, *jargon*, 497.
Double-edged, *energy*, 171.
equivocal, 520.
*Double-entendre (Fr.), *equivocalness*, 520.
indecency, 961.
Double-faced, *deceitful*, 544.
trimming, 607.
Doublet, *dress*, 225.
Double-tongued, *false*, 544.
equivocal, 520.
Doubt, *disbelief*, 485.
scepticism, 988.
Doubtful, *uncertain*, 475.
incredulous, 485.
Doubtless, *certainty*, 474.
*Douceur (Fr.), *expenditure*, 809.
*Douceur (Fr.), *giving*, 784.
Douche, *water*, 337.
Dough, *pulp*, 354.
inelastic, 324.
Doughty, *courageous*, 861.
Dour, *severe*, 739.
Douse, *immerse*, 310.
splash, 337.
Dove, *deity*, 976.
Dovelike, *innocent*, 946.
Dovetail, *intervene*, 228.
intersect, 219.
insert, 300.
angular, 244.
join, 43.
agree, 23.
Dowager, *widow*, 905.
lady, 374.
Dowdy, *vulgar*, 851.
dirty, 653.
ugly, 846.
Dower, *wealth*, 803, 810.
Dowerless, *poverty*, 804.
Down, *levity*, 320.
smoothness, 255.
plumose, 256.
bed of, 377.
below, 207.
Downcast, *dejection*, 837.
Downfall, *ruin*, 162, 732.
calamity, 619.
Down-hearted, *dejection*, 837.
Downhill, *obliquity*, 217.
Downright, *absolute*, 31.
plain, 516.
sincere, 703.
Downs, *plains*, 344.
uplands, 206.
Downwards, *lowness*, 207.
Downy, *hairy*, 256.
soft, 324.
cunning, 702.
Dowry, *wealth*, 803, 810.
Doxology, *worship*, 990.
*Doyen (Fr.), *oldness*, 124.
Doze, *inactivity*, 683.
Dozen, *assemblage*, 72.
number, 98.
Drab, *colour*, 432.
hussy, 962.
Draconian, *severe*, 739.
Draff, *uncleanness*, 653.
Draft, *copy*, 21.
transfer, 270.
sketch, 554.
abstract, 596.
depth, 208.
plan, 626.
cheque, 800.

Drag, *traction*, 285.
attract, 288.
crawl, 275.
slowness, 275.
brake, 752.
Draggle, *hang*, 214.
Drag-net, *generality*, 78.
assemblage, 72.
Dragoman, *interpreter*, 524.
Dragon, *fury*, 173.
monster, 83.
Dragonnade, *evil*, 619, 791.
Dragoon, *combatant*, 726.
to persecute, 907.
Drag up, *elevation*, 307.
Drain, *conduit*, 350.
to dry, 340.
exhaust, 789.
waste, 638.
dissipate, 818.
flow out, 295.
empty itself, 297, 348.
drink up, 296.
Dram, *stimulus*, 615.
drink, 298.
Drama, *the drama*, 599.
Dramatic, *impressive*, 824.
*Dramatis personæ (L.), *the drama*, 599.
interlocution, 588.
agent, 690.
party, 712.
Drapery, *clothes*, 225.
Drastic, *energy*, 171.
Draught, *drink*, 296.
traction, 285.
stream of air, 349.
depth, 208.
abundance, 639.
remedy, 662.
cheque, 800.
Draughtsman, *artist*, 559.
Draw, *pull*, 285.
attract, 288.
extract, 301.
induce, 615.
delineate, 556.
equal, 27.
unfinished, 730.
money order, 800.
Draw back, *regress*, 283, 287.
avoid, 623.
Drawback, *hindrance*, 706.
imperfection, 651.
discount, 813.
evil, 619.
Drawbridge, *escape*, 671.
Drawcansir, *blusterer*, 887.
Drawee, *money*, 800.
Drawer, *receptacle*, 191.
money, 800.
Drawers, *dress*, 225.
Draw in, *contract*, 195.
Drawing, *sketch*, 556.
Drawing-room, *room*, 191.
Drawl, *creep*, 275.
prolong, 200.
in speech, 583.
sluggish, 683.
Drawn, *distorted*, 217.
Draw near, *approach*, 286.
time, 121.
Drawn game, *equality*, 27.
Draw on, *event*, 151.
entice, 615.
Draw out, *extract*, 301.
prolong, 200.
protract, 110.
exhibit, 525.
Draw together, *assemble*, 72.
Draw up, *writing*, 590.
Dray, *vehicle*, 272.
Dread, *fear*, 860.
Dreadful, *great*, 31.
fearful, 860.
calamitous, 830.
Dreadless, *courage*, 861.
Dreadnought, *ship*, 273.
Dream, *vision*, 515.
unsubstantial, 4.
error, 495.
inactivity, 683.
Dream of, *think*, 451.
intend, 620.
Dreamy, *inattentive*, 458.
Dreary, *solitary*, 87.
melancholy, 830.
Dredge, *raise*, 307.
extract, 301.
collect, 72.
Dregs, *refuse*, 643.
dirt, 653.
remainder, 40.
Drench, *drink*, 296.
affusion, 337.
redundance, 641.
Dress, *clothe*, 225.
prepare, 673.
fit, 23.
clip, 38.
trim, 27.
Dresser, *support*, 215.
Dressing, *punishment*, 972.
Dress up, *adorn*, 845.
scolding, 932.
Dressy, *smart*, 847.
Dribble, *flow out*, 295.
drop, 348.

Driblet, *part*, 51.
scanty, 193.
Drift, *direction*, 278.
meaning, 516.
intention, 620.
approach, 286.
to float, 267.
to accumulate, 72.
Driftless, *chance*, 621.
Drill, *auger*, 262.
to train, 673.
teach, 537.
pierce, 260.
Drink, *to swallow*, 296.
liquor, 298.
to tipple, 959.
Drink in, *learn*, 539.
imbibe, 296.
Drip, *ooze*, 295.
flow out, 348.
Dripping, *fat*, 356.
Drive, *impel*, 276.
propel, 284.
repel, 289.
urge, 615.
pursue, 622.
fatigue, 688.
compel, 744.
airing, 266.
Drive at, *intend*, 620.
mean, 516.
Drive in, *insert*, 300.
ingress, 294.
Drive out, *ejection*, 297.
Drivel, *folly*, 499.
fatuity, 503.
Driveller, *fool*, 501.
loquacious, 584.
Driver, *director*, 694.
Drizzle, *distil*, 295.
rain, 348.
Droll, *witty*, 842.
odd, 853.
Drollery, *amusement*, 840.
Dromedary, *carrier*, 271.
Drone, *inactive*, 683.
slow, 275.
sound, 412.
Droop, *sink*, 306.
flag, 688.
weakness, 160.
disease, 655.
sorrow, 828.
dejection, 837.
decline, 659.
Drop, *fall*, 306.
discontinue, 141.
expire, 360.
relinquish, 624.
Drop, *faint*, 160.
fatigue, 688.
flow out, 348.
spherule, 249.
small quantity, 32, 193.
Drop astern, *regression*, 283.
Drop in, *immerse*, 300.
arrive, 292.
Drop off, *die*, 360.
Dropsical, *swollen*, 192.
redundant, 641.
*Droshky (R.), *vehicle*, 272.
Dross, *dirt*, 653.
trash, 643.
remainder, 40.
Drought, *insufficiency*, 640.
Drove, *assemblage*, 72, 102.
Drown, *kill*, 361.
immerse, 300.
affusion, 337.
ruin, 731, 732.
Drowsy, *slow*, 275.
inactive, 683.
weary, 841.
Drub, *beat*, 276.
punish, 972.
Drudge, *agent*, 690.
to work, 680.
to plod, 682.
Drug, *remedy*, 662.
superfluity, 641.
trash, 643.
Druid, *priest*, 996.
Drum, *cylinder*, 249.
music, 417.
sound, 407.
to repeat, 104.
Drum-head, *tribunal*, 966.
Drunk, *ebriety*, 959.
Dry, *arid*, 340.
style, 576.
thirsty, 865.
scanty, 640.
wit, 844.
cynical, 932.
Dry up, *waste*, 638.
Dry-nurse, *aid*, 707.
teach, 537.
teacher, 540.
Dry-point, *engraving*, 558.
Dry-rot, *deterioration*, 653, 659.
Duality, *duality*, 89.
Dub, *name*, 564.
Dubious, *uncertain*, 475.
Dubitation, *doubt*, 485.
Duchy, *region*, 181.
Duck, *immerse*, 300.
plunge, 310.
affuse, 337.

Duck, *stoop*, 308.
Ducking-stool, *punishment*, 975.
Duct, *conduit*, 350.
Ductile, *flexible*, 324.
easy, 705.
useless, 645.
Dud, *defective*, 651.
Dude, *fop*, 854.
Dudeen, *tobacco-pipe*, 351.
Dudgeon, *anger*, 900.
discourteous, 895.
club, 727.
Duds, *clothes*, 225.
Due, *proper*, 924, 926.
owing, 806.
expedient, 646.
Duel, *contention*, 720.
Duellist, *combatant*, 726.
Dueness, *right*, 924.
Duenna, *teacher*, 540.
accompaniment, 88.
attendant, 281.
keeper, 753.
Dues, *price*, 812.
Duet, *music*, 815.
Duffer, *fool*, 501.
bungler, 700.
Dug-out, *refuge*, 666.
canoe, 273.
Duke, *noble*, 875.
ruler, 745.
Dulcet, *sound*, 405.
melodious, 413.
agreeable, 829.
Dulcify, *sweeten*, 396.
Dulcimer, *musical instrument*, 417.
Dulcinea, *favourite*, 899.
Dull, *inert*, 172.
insensible, 376.
tame, 575.
callous, 823.
blunt, 254.
weak, 160.
moderate, 174.
colourless, 429.
dejected, 837.
inexcitable, 826.
stolid, 699.
prosing, 843.
unapt, 499.
Dullard, *fool*, 501.
Dull-brained, *folly*, 499.
Dull-witted, *folly*, 499.
Duma, *council*, 696.
Dumb, *aphony*, 581.
Dumbfound, *astonish*, 870.
abash, 881.
disappoint, 509.
Dumb-show, *the drama*, 599.
Dumb-show, *language*, 560.
Dummy, *aphony*, 581.
effigy, 554.
Dump, *deposit*, 184.
Dumps, *sadness*, 837.
mortification, 832.
Dumpy, *broad*, 202.
ugly, 846.
Dun, *colour*, 432.
to importune, 765.
a creditor, 805.
Dunce, *ignoramus*, 493.
fool, 501.
Dunderhead, *fool*, 501.
Dundreary, *whisker*, 256.
Dune, *hillock*, 206.
Dung, *uncleanness*, 653.
Dungarees, *dress*, 225.
Dungeon, *prison*, 752.
Dunghill, *vulgar*, 876.
cowardly, 862.
Duodecimal, *numbers*, 99.
Duodecimo, *littleness*, 193.
printing, 591.
Duodenary, *numbers*, 98.
Duologue, *interlocution*, 588.
drama, 599.
Dupe, *to deceive*, 545.
deceived, 547.
credulous, 486.
Duplex, *double*, 89, 90.
Duplicate, *double*, 89, 90.
copy, 21.
pledge, 550, 805.
Duplication, *imitation*, 19.
Duplicity, *falsehood*, 544, 702.
Durable, *lasting*, 110.
stable, 150.
Durance, *restraint*, 751.
Duration, *period*, 106.
Durbar, *tribunal*, 966.
Duress, *restraint*, 751.
During, *lasting*, 106.
During good behaviour, *contingent duration*, 108A.
During pleasure, *contingent duration*, 108A.
Dusk, *evening*, 126.
obscurity, 422.
Dusky, *darkness*, 421.
Dust, *powder*, 330.
levity, 320.
dirt, 653.
trash, 643.
to clean, 652.
contest, 720.
money, 800.
Duteous, *virtue*, 944.
Dutiful, *virtue*, 944.

Duty, *obligation*, 926.
business, 625.
work, 686.
tax, 812.
rite, 998.
Dwarf, *small*, 193.
to lessen, 36.
Dwell, *tarry*, 265.
reside, 186.
Dwell on, *descant*, 573, 584.
Dweller, *inhabitant*, 188.
Dwelling, *abode*, 189.
residence, 184.
Dwindle, *diminish*, 32, 195.
lessen, 36.
Dyadic, *duality*, 89.
Dye, *colour*, 428.
Dying, *death*, 360.
Dynamics, *force*, 159, 276
Dynasty, *authority*, 737.
Dyslogistic, *disapproving*, 932.

E

Each, *speciality*, 79.
Eager, *ardent*, 507, 821.
desirous, 865.
active, 682.
Eagle, *swift*, 274.
sight, 441.
standard, 550.
Eagre, *tide*, 348.
Ear, *hearing*, 418.
Ear-deafening, *loudness*, 404.
Earl, *nobility*, 875.
Earless, *deaf*, 419.
Early, *earliness*, 132.
Earn, *acquire*, 775.
Earnest, *intention*, 620.
strenuous, 682.
emphatic, 642.
pledge, 771.
pay in advance, 809.
eager, 821.
Ear-phone, *hearing*, 418.
Ear-piercing, *loud*, 404.
Ear-shot, *nearness* 197.
Earth, *land*, 342.
ground, 211.
world, 318.
Earth-born, *commonalty*, 876.
Earthly-minded, *selfish*, 943.
worldly, 988.
Earthquake, *violence*, 146, 173.
Ear-trumpet, *hearing*, 418.
Earwig, *to flatter*, 933.
flatterer, 935.
Ear-witness, *evidence*, 467.
Ease, *facility*, 705.
relief, 834.
content, 831.
in style, 578.
Easel, *frame*, 215.
painter's, 559.
Easy, *slow*, 275.
Easy-going, *inactive*, 683.
Eat, *swallow*, 296.
Eatable, *food*, 298.
Eaves, *projection*, 250.
Eaves-dropping, *hearing*, 418.
*Ebauche (Fr.), *plan*, 626.
copy, 21.
Ebb, *regress*, 283.
decrease, 36.
contract, 195.
waste, 638.
spoil, 659.
Eblis, *demon*, 980.
Ebony, *blackness*, 431.
Ebriety, *drunkenness*, 959.
Ebullition, *heat*, 384.
energy, 171.
violence, 173.
excitation, 825.
*Ecce signum (L.), *evidence*, 467.
indication, 550.
Eccentric, *irregular*, 83.
exterior, 220.
wrong-headed, 499.
oddity, 857.
Ecclesiastic, *clergy*, 996.
*Ecervelé (Fr.), *insanity*, 503.
*Echappée (Fr.), *amusement*, 840.
*Echappée belle (Fr.), *escape*, 671.
Echelon, *series*, 69.
Echo, *repeat*, 104.
imitate, 19.
loudness, 404.
resonance, 408.
answer, 462.
*Eclaircissement (Fr.), *interpretation*, 522.
*Eclat (Fr.), *repute*, 873.
Eclectic, *choice*, 609.
Eclipse, *hide*, 528.
darkness, 421, 422.
outshine, 33, 874.
Eclogue, *poetry*, 597.
Economy, *order*, 58.
plan, 626.
conduct, 692.
frugality, 817.
Ecstasy, *fancy*, 515.
rapture, 821, 827.
Ectype, *copy*, 21.
Edacity, *gluttony*, 957.

Eddy, *current*, 348.
whirlpool, 312.
Eden, *heaven*, 981.
Edge, *brink*, 230.
energy, 171.
to move forward, 282.
to move sideways, 236.
to instigate, 615.
Edge-tool, *sharpness*, 253.
Edible, *food*, 298.
Edict, *legality*, 963.
Edifice, *abode*, 189.
Edify, *build*, 161.
teach, 537.
piety, 987.
Edit, *publish*, 531.
alter, 140.
Editorial, *dissertation*, 595.
Educate, *teach*, 537.
train, 673.
Education, *learning*, 490.
Educe, *elicit*, 525.
Educt, *remainder*, 40.
Edulcorate, *sweeten*, 396.
clean, 652.
Eel, *convolution*, 248.
Eerie, *unconformity*, 83.
Efface, *obliterate*, 552.
oblivion, 506.
disappear, 449.
Effect, *consequence*, 154.
to produce, 161.
to complete, 729.
Effects, *property*, 780.
goods, 798.
materials, 635.
Effective, *capable*, 157.
impressive, 821.
real, 1.
Effectual, *useful*, 644.
Effeminate, *weak*, 160.
sensual, 954.
timorous, 862.
Effendi, *master*, 745.
Effervesce, *bubble up*, 353.
agitate, 315.
energy, 171.
violence, 173.
excited, 825.
Effete, *old*, 124.
weak, 160.
useless, 645.
spoiled, 659.
Efficacy, *power*, 157.
Efficiency, *utility*, 644.
Effigy, *representation*, 554.
copy, 21.
*Effleurer (Fr.), *skim*, 267.
slur over, 458
Efflorescence, *pulverulence*, 330.
Effluence, *egress*, 295.
Effluvium, *odour*, 398.
vapour, 334.
Efflux, *flow*, 348.
Effort, *exertion*, 686.
Effrontery, *insolence*, 885.
Effulgence, *light*, 420.
Effusion, *outpouring*, 295.
ejection, 297, 299,
speech, 582.
Effusiveness, *feeling*, 821.
Eftsoons, *soon*, 111.
early, 132.
*Egards (Fr.), *respect*, 928.
Egg on, *urge*, 615.
Egg-shaped, *round*, 247, 249.
Ego, *self*, 13.
Egotism, *selfishness*, 911, 943.
vanity, 880.
Egregious, *exceptional*, 83.
extravagant, 499.
Egregiously, *greatness*, 31.
Egress, *emergence*, 295.
*Eidolon (Gr.), *idea*, 453.
Eirenicon, *mediation*, 724.
Eisteddfod, *assemblage*, 72.
Either, *choice*, 609.
Ejaculate, *propel*, 284.
utter, 580.
Eject, *displace*, 185.
emit, 297.
Eke, *addition*, 37.
to complete, 52.
spin out, 110.
Elaborate, *preparation*, 673.
detail, 594.
*Elan (Fr.), *ardour*, 821.
activity, 682.
Elapse, *pass*, 122.
flow, 109.
Elastic, *resilient*, 325.
strong, 159.
Elate, *to cheer*, 836.
boast, 884.
Elbow, *angle*, 244, 258.
projection, 250.
to push, 276.
Elbow-room, *freedom*, 748.
Elder, *oldness*, 124.
age, 128.
veteran, 130.
Elect, *choice*, 609.
Election, *necessity*, 601.
choice, 609
Elector, *master*, 745.
voter, 609.
Electric, *feeling*, 821.
Electricity, *velocity*, 274.

Electrify, *excite*, 824.
astonish, 870.
energise, 171.
Electrocute, *punish*, 972.
Electron, *atom*, 193.
Electroplate, *to cover*, 222.
Electrotype, *engraving*, 558.
imitation, 19.
Eleemosynary, *giving*, 784.
Elegance, *beauty*, 845.
in style, 578.
taste, 850.
Elegy, *dirge*, 415.
plaint, 839.
Element, *component*, 56.
matter, 316.
cause, 153.
rudimental knowledge, 490.
Elementary, *simple*, 42.
Elenchus, *sophistry*, 477.
Elephant, *large*, 192.
carrier, 271.
Elevation, *height*, 206.
raising, 307.
plan, 554.
improvement, 658.
of mind, 942.
style, 574.
glory, 873.
Elevator, *lift*, 627.
Eleventh hour, *occasion*, 134.
Elf, *infant*, 129.
little, 193.
demon, 980.
Elicit, *manifest*, 525.
discover, 480.
draw out, 301.
Elide, *strike out*, 552.
Eligible, *expedience*, 646.
Eliminate, *exclude*, 55.
extract, 301.
weed, 103.
Elimination, *subduction*, 38.
Elision, *separation*, 44.
shortening, 201.
*Elite (Fr.), *perfection*, 650.
Elixir, *remedy*, 662.
*Elixir vitæ (L.), *remedy*, 662.
Ellipse, *circularity*, 247.
Ellipsis, *curtailment*, 201.
style, 572.
Ellipsoid, *circularity*, 247.
rotundity, 249.
Elocution, *speech*, 582.
*Eloge (Fr.), *approval*, 931.
Elongation, *lengthening*, 200
distance, 196.
Elope, *escape*, 671.
Eloquence, *of style*, 574.
Eloquence. *speech*, 582.
Else, *addition*, 37.
Elsewhere, *absence*, 187.
Elucidate, *interpret*, 522.
Elude, *avoid*, 623.
escape, 671.
palter, 773.
sophistry, 477.
succeed, 731.
Elusory, *falsehood*, 544.
Elysium, *paradise*, 981.
bliss, 827.
Emaciation, *contraction*, 193.
smallness, 195.
slenderness, 203.
Emanate, *go out of*, 295.
excrete, 299.
proceed from, 154.
Emanation, *odour*, 398.
Emancipate, *free*, 750.
facilitate, 705.
Emasculate, *weakness*, 160.
style, 575.
Embalm, *preserve*, 670.
memory, 505.
to perfume, 400.
Embankment, *defence*, 717.
Embargo, *prohibition*, 706, 761.
stoppage, 265.
Embark, *depart*, 293.
engage, in 676.
Embarrass, *render difficult*, 704.
hinder, 706.
perplex, 475, 528.
hesitation, 485.
Embase, *deterioration*, 659.
Embassy, *errand*, 532, 755.
Embattled, *arranged*, 60.
warfare, 722.
Embed, *locate*, 184.
insert, 300.
Embellish, *beautify*, 845.
ornament, 847.
Embers, *fuel*, 388.
Embezzle, *steal*, 791.
Embitter, *aggravate*, 835.
deteriorate, 659.
acerbate, 900.
Emblazon, *colour*, 428.
beautify, 845.
display, 882.
Emblem, *indication*, 550.
Embody, *combine*, 48.
compose, 54.
join, 43.
form a whole, 50.
materialise, 316.
Embolden, *encourage*, 861.
hope, 858.

Embolism, *insertion*, 300.
*Embonpoint (Fr.), *size*, 192.
Embosomed, *middle*, 68.
lodged, 184.
begirt, 227.
Embossed, *convex*, 250.
*Embouchure (Fr.), *opening*, 260.
lipping, 415.
Embrace, *include*, 76.
compose, 54.
enclose, 227.
courtesy, 894.
endearment, 902.
Embrasure, *notch*, 257.
Embrocation, *remedy*, 662.
Embroider, *beauty*, 845.
ornament, 847.
exaggerate, 549.
Embroil, *discord*, 713.
derange, 61.
Embryo, *cause*, 153.
preparation, 673.
beginning, 66.
Emendation, *improvement*, 658.
Emerald, *green*, 435.
Emerge, *egress*, 295.
Emergency, *difficulty*, 704.
conjuncture, 8.
event, 151.
Emeritus, *retired*, 757.
respected, 928.
Emersion, *egress*, 295.
*Emeute (Fr.), *resistance*, 716.
Emigrant, *traveller*, 268.
Emigrate, *remove*, 266.
egress, 295.
Eminence, *height*, 206.
fame, 873.
Eminently, *superiority*, 33.
Emir, *master*, 745.
Emissary, *messenger*, 534.
consignee, 758.
Emission, *ejection*, 297.
Emmet, *little*, 193.
Emollient, *remedy*, 662.
softness, 324.
Emolument, *acquisition*, 775.
receipt, 810.
Emotion, *feeling*, 821.
Emotional, *sensibility*, 822.
Empale, *see* Impale.
Emperor, *master*, 745.
Emphasis, *accent*, 580.
Emphatic, *positive assertion*, 535.
style, 574.
important, 642.
Empire, *dominion*, 737.
domain, 780.
Empirical, *tentative*, 675.
Empiricism, *experiment*, 463.
quackery, 545.
Employ, *use*, 677.
commission, 755.
business, 625.
*Employé (Fr.), *servant*, 746.
agent, 758, 690.
Emporium, *mart*, 799.
Empower, *power*, 157.
commission, 755.
permit, 760.
*Empressement (Fr.), *activity*, 682.
feeling, 821.
Emprise, *undertaking*, 676.
Emption, *purchase*, 795.
Empty, *vacant*, 187.
transfer, 270.
insufficient, 640.
unimportant, 643.
drain, 297.
Empty-headed, *ignorant*, 491.
Empyrean, *sky*, 318.
blissful, 827, 829.
Emulate, *rival*, 708.
imitate, 19.
glory, 873.
Emulsion, *semiliquidity*, 352.
Emunctory, *conduit*, 350.
Enable, *power*, 157.
Enact, *order*, 741.
a law, 963.
Enamel, *painting*, 556.
smooth, 255.
adorn, 845, 847.
Enamour, *love*, 897.
*En bloc (Fr.), *assent*, 488.
Encage, *circumscribe*, 231.
restrain, 751.
Encamp, *locate*, 184, 265.
inhabit, 186.
Encase, *circumscribe*, 231.
Encaustic, *painting*, 556.
*Enceinte (Fr.), *region*, 181.
enclosure, 232.
pregnant, 168.
Enchain, *bind*, 43, 751.
Enchant, *please*, 829.
love, 897.
conjure, 992.
Enchiridion, *book*, 593.
Encircle, *begird*, 227.
Enclave, *enclosure*, 232.
Enclose, *circumscribe*, 231.
Enclosure, *fence*, 752.
space, 181.
Encomiast, *flatterer*, 935.
Encomium, *approval*, 931.
Encompass, *begird*, 227.
*Encore (Fr.), *repetition*, 104.

Encounter, *meet*, 292.
clash, 276.
contest, 720.
withstand, 708.
Encourage, *animate*, 615.
aid, 707.
embolden, 861.
hope, 858.
comfort, 834.
Encroach, *transgress*, 303.
infringe, 925.
Encrust, *line*, 224.
coat, 222.
Encumbrance, *hindrance*, 704, 706.
Encyclical, *publication*, 531.
Encyclopædia, *knowledge*, 490.
assembly, 72.
generality, 78.
End, *termination*, 67, 154.
object, 620.
Endamage, *injure*, 659.
harm, 649.
Endanger, *danger*, 665.
Endeavour, *attempt*, 676.
pursue, 622.
intend, 620.
Endemic, *special*, 79.
disease, 655, 657.
*Endimanché (Fr.), *ornament*, 847.
Endless, *infinite*, 105.
multitudinous, 102.
Endogamy, *marriage*, 903.
Endorsement, *evidence*, 467.
sign, 550, 590
voucher, 771.
ratification, 769.
approval, 931.
Endosmose, *passage*, 302.
Endow, *confer power*, 157.
Endowment, *gift*, 784.
capacity, 5.
power, 157.
talent, 698.
Endue, *empower*, 157.
Endure, *time*, 106.
to continue, 142.
to last, 110.
event, 151.
to bear, 821.
to submit, 826.
Endways, *length*, 200.
Enemy, *enemy*, 891.
Energumen, *madman*, 503.
fanatic, 515.
Energy, *physical*, 171.
strength, 159.
style, 574.
activity, 682.
resolution, 604.
Enervate, *weakness*, 160.
*En famille (Fr.), *sociality*, 892.
*Enfant gâté (Fr.), *prosperity*, 734.
favourite, 899.
*Enfant perdu (Fr.), *rashness*, 863.
*Enfant terrible (Fr.), *artlessness*, 703.
Enfeeble, *weaken*, 160.
Enfilade, *pierce*, 260.
pass through, 302.
Enfold, *circumscribe*, 231.
Enforce, *urge*, 615.
compel, 744.
require, 924.
Enfranchise, *liberate*, 750, 924.
Engage, *induce*, 615.
the attention, 457.
in a pursuit, 622.
promise, 768, 769.
undertake, 676.
Engagement, *business*, 625.
contest, 720.
promise, 768.
duty, 926.
Engaging, *pleasing*, 829.
amiable, 897.
*En garçon (Fr.), *celibacy*, 904.
Engender, *produce*, 161.
Engine, *instrument*, 633.
Engineering, *means*, 632.
Engirdle, *circumjacence*, 227.
Engorge, *reception*, 296.
Engorgement, *redundance*, 641.
Engraft, *insert*, 301.
join, 43.
add, 37.
teach, 537.
implant, 6.
Engrained, *imbued*, 5.
combined, 48.
Engrave, *mark*, 550.
on the memory, 505.
Engraver, *artist*, 559.
Engraving, *engraving*, 558.
Engross, *possess*, 777.
write, 590.
the thoughts, 451.
the attention, 457.
Engulf, *destroy*, 162.
plunge, 310.
swallow up, 296.
Enhance, *increase*, 35.
improve, 658.
Enharmonic, *harmony*, 413.
Enigma, *secret*, 533.
question, 461.
Enigmatic, *concealed*, 528.
obscure, 519.
uncertain, 475.

Enjambement, *transcursion*, 303.
Enjoin, *command*, 741.
induce, 615.
enact, 963.
Enjoy, *physically*, 377.
morally, 827.
possess, 777.
Enkindle, *induce*, 615.
Enlace, *surround*, 227.
entwine, 219, 248.
Enlarge, *increase*, 35.
swell, 194.
liberate, 750.
in writing, 573.
Enlighten, *illuminate*, 420.
inform, 527.
instruct, 537.
Enlightened, *wise*, 498.
Enlightenment, *knowledge*, 490.
Enlist, *commission*, 755.
engage, 615.
Enliven, *amuse*, 840.
cheer, 836.
delight, 829.
Enmesh, *entwine*, 219.
Enmity, *hate*, 889.
discord, 713.
Ennoble, *glorify*, 873.
*Ennui (Fr.), *weariness*, 841.
Enormity, *crime*, 947.
Enormous, *in degree*, 31.
in size, 192.
Enough, *much*, 31.
sufficient, 639.
satiety, 869.
Enough, well, *smallness*, 32.
*En passant (Fr.), *method*, 627.
irrelation, 10.
journey, 266.
*En prince (Fr.), *generosity*, 942.
Enrage, *incense*, 900.
provoke, 830.
*En rapport (Fr.), *agreement*, 23.
Enrapture, *excite*, 824.
beatify, 829.
love, 897.
Enravish, *beatify*, 829.
*En règle (Fr.), *conformity*, 82.
*En revanche (Fr.), *compensation*, 30.
Enrich, *wealth*, 803.
Enrobe, *invest*, 225.
Enrol, *record*, 551.
Enrolment, *list*, 86.
*En route, (Fr.), *journey*, 266.
*Ens (L.), *essence*, 1.
Ensample, *prototype*, 22.
Ensanguined, *red*, 434.
Ensconce, *safety*, 664.
Ensconce, *conceal*, 528.
*Ensemble (Fr.), *whole*, 50.
Enshrine, *memory*, 505, 873.
sanctify, 987.
Enshroud, *conceal*, 528.
Ensiform, *sharpness*, 253.
Ensign, *standard*, 550.
officer, 726.
master, 745.
Enslave, *subjection*, 749.
Ensnare, *cheat*, 545.
endanger, 665.
Ensue, *follow*, 63.
happen, 151.
Ensure, *certainty*, 474.
Entablature, *summit*, 210.
Entail, *cause*, 153.
involve, 467.
impose, 741.
Entangle, *derange*, 61.
entwine, 219.
disorder, 59.
embroil, 713.
perplex, 528.
mixture, 41.
*Entente cordiale (Fr.), *friendship*, 888.
concord, 714.
Enter, *go in*, 294.
note, 551.
accounts, 811.
Enter in, *converge*, 290.
Enter into, *component*, 56.
Enterprise, *pursuit*, 622.
attempt, 676.
Enterprising, *active*, 682.
courageous, 861.
Entertain, *amuse*, 840.
support, 707.
sociality, 892.
an idea, 451, 484.
Entertainment, *repast*, 298.
Enter upon, *begin*, 66.
*Entêté (Fr.), *obstinate*, 606.
prejudiced, 481.
Enthral, *subdue*, 749.
delight, 829.
Enthrone, *repute*, 873.
Enthusiasm, *feeling*, 821.
imagination, 515.
love, 897.
hope, 850, 858.
Enthusiastic, *sensibility*, 822.
excitability, 825.
Enthymeme, *reasoning*, 476.
Entice, *motive*, 615.
Enticing, *pleasure*, 829.
Entire, *whole*, 50.
complete, 52.

Entirely, *greatness*, 31.
Entitle, *name*, 564.
give a right, 924.
Entity, *existence*, 1.
Entomb, *inter*, 231, 363.
imprison, 751.
*Entourage (Fr.), *environment*, 227.
retinue, 746.
Entrails, *interior*, 221.
Entrain, *depart*, 293.
*Entr'acte (Fr.), *interval*, 106.
Entrance, *beginning*, 66.
ingress, 294.
fee, 809.
to enrapture, 824, 829.
to conjure, 992.
Entrap, *deceive*, 545.
ensnare, 665.
Entreat, *request*, 765.
*Entrechat (Fr.), *leap*, 309.
*Entremet (Fr.), *food*, 298.
Entrench, *defence*, 717.
*Entre nous (Fr.), *concealment*, 528.
*Entrepôt (Fr.), *store*, 636.
mart, 799.
*Entrepreneur (Fr.), *organiser*, 626.
Entresol, *interjacence*, 228.
Entrust, *consign*, 784.
charge with, 755.
Entry, *ingress*, 294.
beginning, 66.
record, 551.
evidence, 467.
Entwine, *join*, 43.
intersect, 219.
convolve, 248.
Enumerate, *number*, 85.
Enunciate, *publish*, 531.
inform, 527.
voice, 580.
Envelop, *invest*, 225.
conceal, 528.
Envelope, *covering*, 222.
enclosure, 232.
Envenom, *poison*, 649.
deprave, 659.
exasperate, 835.
*Environs (Fr.), *nearness*, 197.
circumjacence, 227.
Envisage, *view*, 441.
confront, 234.
intuition, 477.
Envoy, *messenger*, 534.
postscript, 39.
Envy, *jealousy*, 921.
Enwrap, *invest*, 225.
*Epanchement (Fr.), *sociality*, 902.
Epaulet, *badge*, 550.
decoration, 877.
Epaulet, *ornament*, 847.
*Éperdu (Fr.), *excited*, 824.
Ephemeral, *transient*, 111.
changeable, 149.
Ephemeris, *calendar*, 114.
record, 551.
Epic, *poem*, 597.
Epicedium, *interment*, 363.
Epicene, *exceptional*, 83.
multiform, 81.
Epicure, *sensual*, 954.
glutton, 957.
fastidious, 868.
Epicycle, *circularity*, 247.
Epicycloid, *circularity*, 247.
Epidemic, *disease*, 655.
Epidermis, *covering*, 222.
Epigram, *wit*, 842.
Epigrammatic, *pithy*, 516.
Epigrammatist, *humorist*, 844.
Epigraph, *indication*, 550.
Epilepsy, *convulsion*, 315.
Epilogue, *sequel*, 65.
Episcopal, *clergy*, 995.
Episode, *event*, 151.
Episodic, *unrelated*, 10.
style, 573.
Epistle, *letter*, 592.
Epitaph, *interment*, 363.
*Epithalamium (Gr.), *marriage*, 903.
Epithem, *remedy*, 662.
Epithet, *nomenclature*, 564.
Epitome, *compendium*, 596.
miniature, 193.
Epizootic, *insalubrity*, 657.
Epoch, *time*, 113.
period, 114.
Epopee, *poetry*, 597.
Equable, *right*, 922.
Equal, *equality*, 27.
equitable, 922.
Equanimity, *inexcitability*, 826.
Equate, *equality*, 27.
Equator, *middle*, 68.
Equerry, *servant*, 746.
Equestrian, *traveller*, 268.
Equidistant, *middle*, 68.
Equilibrium, *equality*, 27.
steadiness, 265.
Equip, *dress*, 225.
prepare, 673.
Equipage, *vehicle*, 272.
instrument, 633.
materials, 635.
Equipoise, *equal*, 27.
Equipollent, *equal*, 27.
identical, 13.
Equiponderant, *equal*, 27.

Equitable, *just*, 922.
fair, 480, 939.
due, 924.
Equitation, *journey*, 266.
Equity, *justice*, 922.
law, 963.
honour, 939.
Equivalence, *equal*, 27.
Equivalent, *identity*, 13.
compensation, 30.
synonymous, 516.
Equivocal, *dubious*, 475.
double meaning, 520, 961.
Equivocate, *pervert*, 477.
prevaricate, 520.
Equivoque, *equivocalness*, 520.
uncertainty, 475.
impurity, 961.
error, 495.
Era, *duration*, 106.
Eradicate, *destroy*, 162.
Erase, *efface*, 162, 499, 552.
Ere, *priority*, 116.
Erebus, *dark*, 421.
hell, 982.
Erect, *raise*, 307.
build, 161.
vertical, 212.
Erection, *house*, 189.
Ere long, *earliness*, 132.
Erewhile, *preterition*, 122.
priority, 116.
*Ergo (L.), *reasoning*, 476.
Eriometer, *optical*, 445.
Ermine, *ornament*, 847.
badge of authority, 747.
Erode, *destroy*, 162.
injure, 659.
Erotic, *amorous*, 897.
impure, 961.
Err, *in opinion*, 495.
morally, 945.
Errand, *commission*, 755.
business, 625.
message, 532.
Erratic, *capricious*, 149, 608.
wandering, 264, 279.
Erratum, *error*, 495.
misprint, 555.
Error, *false opinion*, 495.
failure, 732.
vice, 945.
guilt, 947.
Erst, *preterition*, 122.
Erubescence, *redness*, 434.
Eructate, *eject*, 297.
Erudition, *knowledge*, 490.
Eruption, *egress*, 295.
violence, 173.
Escalade, *mount*, 305.
attack, 716.
Escalator, *way*, 627.
Escapade, *freak*, 608.
prank, 840.
vagary, 856.
Escape, *flight*, 671.
liberate, 750.
evade, 927.
forget, 506.
Escarpment, *slope*, 217.
Eschatology, *intention*, 620.
Escheat, *penalty*, 974.
Eschew, *avoid*, 623.
dislike, 867.
Escort, *to accompany*, 88.
safeguard, 664.
keeper, 753.
Esculent, *food*, 298.
Escutcheon, *indication*, 550.
Esoteric, *private*, 79.
concealed, 528.
Especial, *private*, 79.
Esperanto, *language*, 560.
Espial, *vision*, 441.
*Espièglerie (Fr.), *wit*, 842.
Espionage, *inquiry*, 461.
Esplanade, *flat*, 213.
plain, 344.
Espousal, *marriage*, 903.
*Esprit (Fr.), *shrewdness*, 498.
wit, 842.
*Esprit de corps (Fr.), *party*, 712.
misjudgment, 481.
belief, 484.
sociality, 892.
*Esprit fort (Fr.), *sage*, 500.
Espy, *vision*, 441.
Esquire, *title*, 877.
Essay, *try*, 463.
endeavour, 675.
dissertation, 595.
Essayist, *writing*, 590.
Essence, *nature*, 5.
odour, 398.
pith, 642.
Essential, *great*, 31.
requisite, 630.
Establish, *fix*, 184.
demonstrate, 478.
create, 161.
substantiate, 494.
settle, 150.
Established, *received*, 82.
Establishment, *fixture*, 142.
location, 184.
*Estancia (Sp.), *property*, 780.
Estate, *condition*, 7.
property, 780.

Esteem, *judge*, 480.
believe, 484.
approve, 931.
Estimable, *good*, 648.
Estimate, *measure*, 466.
judge, 480.
count, 85.
Estimation, *opinion*, 484.
good, 648.
Estrade, *horizontal*, 213.
Estrange, *alienate*, 889.
hate, 898.
seclude, 893.
Estuary, *gulf*, 343.
Esurient, *hungry*, 865.
*Etat-major (Fr.), *combatant*, 726.
Etcetera, *addition*, 37.
inclusion, 76.
plurality, 100.
*Etalage (Fr.), *ostentation*, 882.
Etch, *engraving*, 558.
Eternal, *perpetuity*, 112.
Ether, *sky*, 313, 338.
vapour, 334.
levity, 320.
Ethical, *virtue*, 944.
Ethics, *duty*, 926.
Ethiopic, *blackness*, 431.
Ethnic, *heterodox*, 984.
racial, 372.
Ethnology, *mankind*, 372.
Etiolate, *bleach*, 429, 430.
Etiquette, *fashion*, 852.
custom, 613.
ceremony, 882.
*Etourderie (Fr.), *neglect*, 460.
*Etude (Fr.), *music*, 415.
Etymology, *word*, 562.
Etymon, *origin*, 153.
verbal, 562.
Eucharist, *rite*, 998.
Euchology, *rite*, 998.
Eugenics, *production*, 161.
Eulogy, *approval*, 931.
Euphemism, *misnomer*, 565.
Euphonious, *musical*, 413.
style, 578.
Euphony, *harmony*, 413.
Euphuism, *ornament*, 577.
Eurasian, *mixture*, 41.
*Eureka (Gr.), *judgment*, 480.
Eurhythmics, *training*, 673.
Euterpe, *music*, 415.
Euthanasia, *death*, 360.
Evacuate, *emit*, 297.
excrete, 299.
Evade, *avoid*, 623.
escape, 671.
sophistry, 477.
Evade, *exempt*, 927.
Evaluate, *appraise*, 466, 812.
Evanescent, *transient*, 111.
minute, 32, 193.
disappearing, 449.
Evangelise, *convert*, 484.
Evangelist, *revelation*, 985.
Evaporate, *vapour*, 336.
Evasion, *escape*, 623, 671.
sophistry, 477.
falsehood, 544.
untruth, 546.
dereliction, 927.
Eve, *evening*, 126.
priority, 116.
Even, *equal*, 27.
level, 213.
smooth, 265.
straight, 246.
although, 179, 469.
Even-handed, *equitable*, 922.
honourable, 939.
Evening, *evening*, 126.
Even so, *assent*, 488.
Event, *eventuality*, 151.
Eventful, *stirring*, 151.
remarkable, 642.
Eventide, *evening*, 126.
Eventual, *futurity*, 121.
Ever, *always*, 112.
seldom, 137.
Ever and anon, *repetition*, 104.
Ever-changing, *mutability*, 149.
Evergreen, *newness*, 123.
diuturnity, 110.
perpetuity, 112.
Everlasting, *perpetual*, 112, 136.
Evermore, *perpetual*, 112.
Ever-recurring, *repetition*, 104.
Every, *generality*, 78.
Everyday, *conformity*, 82.
perpetuity, 112.
Everyman, *mankind*, 372.
Everywhere, *space*, 180, 186.
Eviction, *displacement*, 185.
Evidence, *evidence*, 467.
Evident, *visible*, 446.
demonstrable, 478.
manifest, 525.
Evil, *harm*, 619.
producing evil, 649.
Evil-doer, *maleficent*, 913.
culprit, 949.
Evil eye, *malevolence*, 907.
Evil-minded, *malevolent*, 907.
vicious, 945.
Evil-speaking, *detraction*, 934.
Evince, *show*, 467.
prove, 478.

Eviscerate, *extract*, 301.
mutilate, 38.
Evoke, *call upon*, 765.
excite, 824.
Evolution, *numerical*, 85.
effect, 154.
development, 161.
turning out, 313.
circuition, 311.
Evulsion, *extraction*, 301.
Ewer, *receptacle*, 191.
Exacerbate, *increase*, 35.
aggravate, 835.
exasperate, 173.
Exact, *true*, 494.
similar, 17.
require, 741.
claim, 924.
tax, 812.
Exactly, *just so*, 488.
Exaggerate, *increase*, 35.
overestimate, 482.
misrepresent, 549.
Exalt, *increase*, 35.
elevate, 307.
extol, 931.
boast, 884.
Exalted, *heroic*, 942.
Examine, *inquiry*, 457, 461.
Example, *instance*, 82.
pattern, 22.
model, 948.
Exanimate, *listless*, 683.
lifeless, 360.
Exarch, *ruler*, 745.
deputy, 759.
Exasperate, *increase*, 35.
exacerbate, 173.
aggravate, 835.
inflame, 900.
*Ex cathedrâ (L.), *affirmation*, 535.
insolence, 885.
Excavate, *dig*, 252.
Exceed, *surpass*, 33.
expand, 194.
transgress, 303.
Exceeding, *remaining*, 40.
Exceedingly, *greatness*, 31.
Excel, *superiority*, 33.
goodness, 648, 650.
Excellent, *good*, 648.
virtuous, 944.
Excellency, *skill*, 698.
title, 877.
*Excelsior (L.), *ascent*, 305.
Except, *subduct*, 38.
exclude, 55.
Exception, *to a rule*, 83.
qualification, 469.

Exception, *censure*, 932.
Exceptionable, *vicious*, 945.
blameworthy, 932.
Exceptional, *special*, 79.
irregular, 83.
*Exceptis excipiendis (L.), *qualification*, 469.
Excerpt, *extract*, 596.
Excess, *superiority*, 33.
remainder, 40.
redundance, 641.
intemperance, 954.
Excessive, *greatness*, 31.
Exchange, *mutual change*, 148.
transfer, 783.
barter, 794.
mart, 799.
Exchequer, *treasury*, 802.
Excise, *price*, 812.
Excision, *subduction*, 38.
Excitability, *excitement*, 825.
irascibility, 901.
Excitation, *excitation*, 824.
Excite, *violent*, 173.
morally, 824.
anger, 900.
Exclaim, *voice*, 580.
Exclude, *leave out*, 55.
prohibit, 761.
ostracise, 893.
subduction, 38.
Exclusive, *omitting*, 55.
special, 79.
irregular, 83.
unsociable, 893.
Excogitation, *thought*, 451.
imagination, 515.
Excommunicate, *exclude*, 55, 893.
hate, 898.
curse, 908.
*Ex concesso (L.), *reasoning*, 476.
assent, 488.
Excoriate, *flay*, 226.
Excrement, *uncleanness*, 653.
Excrescence, *projection*, 250.
blemish, 848.
Excretion, *excretion*, 299.
Excruciating, *pain*, 378, 830.
Exculpate, *forgive*, 918.
vindicate, 937.
Excursion, *tour*, 266.
circuit, 311.
Excursive, *style*, 573.
Excursus, *appendix*, 65.
Excuse, *plea*, 617.
exempt, 927.
forgive, 918.
vindicate, 937.
*Exeat (L.), *leave*, 760.

Execrable, *bad*, 649.
offensive, 830.
nauseous, 867.
Execrate, *malediction*, 908.
Execute, *conduct*, 692.
perform, 739.
in law, 771.
music, 415.
Executioner, *killing*, 361.
Executive, *jurisprudence*, 965.
Executor, *agent*, 690.
Exegesis, *interpretation*, 522.
Exemplar, *prototype*, 22.
Exemplary, *virtue*, 944.
Exemplify, *quote*, 82.
illustrate, 522.
Exempt, *absolve*, 927.
free, 748.
permit, 760.
Exemption, *exception*, 83.
Exenterate, *extract*, 300.
mutilate, 38.
*Exequatur (L.), *commission*, 755.
Exequies, *interment*, 363.
Exercise, *employ*, 677.
act, 680.
exert, 686.
teach, 537.
train, 673.
task, 625.
Exercitation, *dissertation*, 595.
Exert, *exertion*, 686.
Exertion, *physical*, 171.
Exfoliation, *divestment*, 226.
Exhalation, *vapour*, 336.
odour, 398.
excretion, 299.
Exhaust, *drain*, 638, 789.
fatigue, 688.
weaken, 160.
misemploy, 679.
squander, 818.
complete, 52.
Exhaustless, *infinite*, 105.
plentiful, 639.
Exhibit, *show*, 525.
display, 882.
Exhilarate, *cheer*, 836.
Exhort, *advise*, 695.
induce, 615.
Exhume, *interment*, 363.
Exigency, *crisis*, 8.
difficulty, 704.
requirement, 630.
need, 865.
dearth, 640.
Exigent, *severe*, 739
exacting, 832.
Exiguous, *little*, 193.
Exile, *displace*, 185.
send out, 297.
seclude, 893.
Exility, *thinness*, 203.
Existence, *being*, 1.
thing, 3.
in time, 118.
in space, 186.
Exit, *departure*, 293.
egress, 295.
*Ex-libris (L.), *label*, 550.
*Ex mero motu (L.), *will*, 600.
*Ex necessitate rei (L.), *destiny*, 152.
Exodus, *departure*, 293.
*Ex officio (L.), *truth*, 494.
authority, 737.
dueness, 924.
Exogamy, *marriage*, 903.
Exonerate, *exempt*, 927.
vindicate, 937.
forgive, 918.
disburden, 705.
release, 756.
Exorbitant, *enormous*, 31.
redundant, 641.
dear, 814.
Exorcise, *conjure*, 992.
Exorcism, *theology*, 993.
Exorcist, *heterodoxy*, 994.
*Exordium (L.), *beginning*, 66.
Exosmose, *passage*, 302.
Exoteric, *disclosed*, 531.
public, 529.
Exotic, *alien*, 10.
exceptional, 83.
Expand, *swell*, 194.
increase, 35.
in breadth, 202.
rarefy, 322.
in writing, 573.
Expanse, *space*, 180, 202.
size, 192.
*Ex parte (L.), *evidence*, 467.
Expatiate, *in writing*, 573.
in discourse, 582, 584.
Expatriate, *deport*, 295.
exclude, 55.
Expect, *look for*, 121, 507.
not wonder, 871.
hope, 858.
Expectorant, *remedy*, 662.
Expectorate, *eject*, 296.
Expedience, *utility*, 646.
Expedient, *means*, 632.
plan, 626.
Expedite, *accelerate*, 274.
earliness, 132.
aid, 707.
Expedition, *speed*, 274.

Expedition, *march*, 266.
Expel, *displace*, 185.
drive from, 297.
Expend, *use*, 677.
waste, 638.
pay, 809.
Expense, *price*, 812.
Expensive, *dear*, 814.
Experience, *knowledge*, 490.
undergo, 821.
event, 151.
Experienced, *skilled*, 698.
Experiment, *trial*, 463.
endeavour, 675.
*Experimentum crucis (L.), *demonstration*, 478.
Expert, *skill*, 698.
adept, 700.
*Experto crede (L.), *knowledge*, 490.
Expiate, *atonement*, 952.
Expire, *death*, 360.
end, 67.
breathe out, 349.
Explain, *expound*, 522.
inform, 527.
teach, 537.
answer, 462.
Explain away, *misinterpret*, 523.
Expletive, *redundance*, 573, 641.
Explication, *interpret*, 522.
Explicit, *distinct*, 516, 518, 535.
Explode, *burst*, 173.
sound, 406.
refute, 479.
passion, 825.
anger, 900.
Exploit, *action*, 680.
to use, 677.
Explore, *investigate*, 461.
experiment, 463.
Explosion, *see* Explode.
Exponent, *index*, 550.
numerical, 84.
interpreter, 522.
Export, *transfer*, 270.
send out, 297.
thing sent, 295.
*Exposé (Fr.), *account*, 596.
disclosure, 529.
Expose, *show*, 525.
interpret, 522.
confute, 479.
denude, 226.
endanger, 665.
Exposition, *answer*, 462.
disclosure, 529.
Expositor, *interpreter*, 524.
teacher, 540.
Expository, *information*, 527, 595.
*Ex post facto (L.), *preterition*, 122.
Expostulate, *deprecate*, 766.
reprehend, 932.
dissuade, 616.
advise, 695.
Exposure to, *liability*, 177.
Expound, *interpret*, 522.
teach, 537.
answer, 462.
Express, *voluntary*, 600.
intentional, 620.
declare, 525.
mean, 516.
inform, 527.
phrase, 566.
intelligible, 518.
name, 564.
squeeze out, 301.
rapid, 274.
Expression, *aspect*, 448.
Expressive, *style*, 574.
Exprobation, *disapproval*, 932.
Expropriate, *take*, 789.
Expulsion, *see* Expel.
Expunge, *efface*, 552.
destroy, 162.
disappear, 449.
Expurgation, *cleanness*, 652.
Exquisite, *excellent*, 648.
pleasurable, 829.
savoury, 394.
fop, 854.
Exquisitely, *great*, 31.
Exsiccate, *dryness*, 340.
Exsufflation, *sorcery*, 992.
Extant, *being*, 1.
Extempore, *instantly*, 113.
early, 132.
off-hand, 612.
unprepared, 674.
Extend, *prolong*, 200.
expand, 194.
reach, 196.
increase, 35.
Extensile, *pliable*, 324.
Extensive, *spacious*, 180.
considerable, 31.
Extent, *degree*, 26.
space, 180.
Extenuate, *decrease*, 36.
diminish, 192.
excuse, 937.
Exterior, *exteriority*, 220.
Exterminate, *destruction*, 162.
Exterminator, *destroyer*, 165.
External, *exteriority*, 220.
Extinction, *destruction*, 162.
of life, 360.
Extinguish, *destroy*, 162.

Extinguish, *darken*, 421.
blow out, 385.
Extinguisher, *destroyer*, 165.
Extirpate, *destruction*, 162.
Extol, *praise*, 931.
over-estimate, 482.
Extort, *despoil*, 789.
compel, 744.
Extra, *additional*, 37, 39.
supernumerary, 641.
Extract, *take out*, 301.
quotation, 596.
Extradition, *deportation*, 270.
expulsion, 297.
Extrajudicial, *illegality*, 964.
Extramundane, *immateriality*, 317.
*Extra muros (L.), *exteriority*, 220.
Extraneous, *extrinsic*, 6.
Extraneous, *not related*, 10.
foreign, 57.
Extraordinary, *unconformity*, 83.
greatness, 31.
Extravagant, *exaggerated*, 549.
unwarranted, 514.
irrational, 477.
absurd, 497.
ridiculous, 853.
foolish, 499.
redundant, 641.
high-priced, 814.
prodigal, 818.
vulgar, 851.
inordinate, 31.
*Extravaganza (It.), *fanciful*, 515.
burlesque, 853.
the drama, 599.
Extravasate, *excretion*, 299.
Extreme, *greatness*, 31.
Extremist, *zealot*, 604.
Extremity, *end*, 67.
exterior, 220.
Extricate, *take out*, 301.
liberate, 750.
deliver, 672.
facilitate, 705.
Extrinsic, *extrinsicality*, 6.
Extrude, *eject*, 297.
Exuberant, *redundant*, 641.
style, 573.
feeling, 821.
Exude, *excretion*, 299.
egress, 295.
Exult, *crow*, 836.
rejoice, 838.
boast, 873, 884.
*Exuviæ (L), *remainder*, 40.
Eye, *organ of sight*, 441.
opening, 260.
circle, 247.
Eye-glass, *optical instrument*, 445.
Eyeless, *blind*, 442.
Eyelet, *opening*, 260.
Eye-opener, *enlightenment*, 527.
portent, 870.
Eyesight, *vision*, 441.
Eyesore, *ugliness*, 846.
Eyewitness, *evidence*, 467.
Eyre, *jurisprudence*, 965.
Eyrie, *abode*, 189.

F

Fabian policy, *inactivity*, 683.
delay, 133.
Fable, *fiction*, 546.
error, 495.
description, 594.
Fabric, *texture*, 329.
house, 189.
effect, 154.
state, 7.
Fabricate, *make*, 161.
invent, 515.
forge, 544.
falsify, 546.
Fabulous, *imagination*, 515.
greatness, 31.
Façade, *front*, 234.
Face, *exterior*, 220.
front, 234.
lining, 224.
impudence, 885.
confront, 861.
aspect, 448.
Face about, *deviation*, 279.
Face down, *withstand*, 719.
Face to face, *manifestation*, 525.
Facet, *exterior*, 220.
Facetious, *wit*, 842.
Facia, *indication*, 550.
Facile, *irresolute*, 605.
persuasible, 615.
easy, 705.
*Facile princeps (L.), *superiority*, 33.
goodness, 648.
Facility, *ease*, 705.
aid, 707.
Facing, *lining*, 224.
*Façon de parler (Fr.), *meaning*, 516.
metaphor, 521.
exaggeration, 549.
phrase, 566.
Facsimile, *copy*, 21.
representation, 554.
Fact, *event*, 151.
truth, 494.
existence, 1, 2.

Faction, *party*, 712.
Factious, *discord*, 713.
Factitious, *artificial*, 544.
Factor, *numerical*, 84.
director, 694.
consignee, 758.
merchant, 797.
Factory, *workshop*, 691.
Factotum, *manager*, 694.
employé, 758.
Faculty, *power*, 157.
skill, 698.
profession, 625.
Fad, *caprice*, 608.
Fade, *vanish*, 2.
disappear, 449.
lose colour, 429.
spoil, 659.
droop, 160.
change, 149.
become old, 124.
*Fade (Fr.), *insipid*, 391.
Fadge, *agreement*, 23.
Fæces, *excretion*, 298.
foulness, 653.
Fag, *labour*, 686.
activity, 682.
fatigue, 688.
drudge, 690.
Fag-end, *remainder*, 40.
end, 67.
Faggot, *bundle*, 72.
fuel, 388.
Fail, *incomplete*, 53, 651.
shortcoming, 304.
non-observance, 732.
non-payment, 808.
dereliction, 927.
droop, 160.
vice, 945.
Fain, *wish*, 865.
willing, 602.
compulsive, 744.
*Fainéant (Fr.), *idler*, 683.
Faint, *weak*, 160.
sound, 405.
colour, 429.
small in degree, 32.
swoon, 688.
Faint-hearted, *coward*, 862.
Fair, *in degree*, 31.
white, 430.
just, 922.
honourable, 939.
true, 543.
pleasing, 829.
beautiful, 845.
mart, 799.
Fairing, *gift*, 784.
Fair sex, *woman*, 374.
Fairly, *great*, 31.
Fair play, *justice*, 922.
honour, 939.
Fair-spoken, *courteous*, 894.
flattering, 933.
Fairy, *fabulous being*, 979.
*Fait accompli (Fr.), *completion*, 729.
Faith, *belief*, 484.
hope, 858.
honour, 939.
creed, 983.
piety, 987.
Faithful, *likeness*, 17.
true, 494.
observant, 772.
Faithless, *false*, 544.
dishonourable, 940.
sceptical, 988.
Fake, *imitation*, 19.
deception, 545.
to forge, 544.
Fakir, *clergy*, 996.
Falcated, *curved*, 245.
sharp, 244.
Falchion, *arms*, 727.
Falciform, *angularity*, 244.
curvature, 245.
Fall, *descend*, 306.
destruction, 162.
slope, 217.
fail, 732.
die, 360.
adversity, 735.
decline, 659.
happen, 151.
vice, 945.
autumn, 126.
Fall away, *decrease*, 36.
shrink, 195.
Fall back, *recede*, 283, 287.
relapse, 661.
Fall behind, *sequence*, 281.
Fall down, *descend*, 306.
worship, 990.
Fall foul of, *oppose*, 708.
encounter, 720.
reprimand, 932.
Fall in, *marshal*, 58, 60.
happen, 151.
Fall in with, *find*, 480.
uniformity, 16.
agree, 23.
Fall off, *deterioration*, 659.
decrease, 36.
disjunction, 44.
Fall out, *happen*, 151.
quarrel, 713.

Fall out, *drop*, 297.
Fall short, *shortcoming*, 304, 730.
fail, 53.
insufficiency, 640.
Fall to, *work*, 686.
devour, 296.
fight, 722.
Fall to pieces, *disjunction*, 44.
Fall through, *failure*, 732.
Fall under, *inclusion*, 76.
Fall upon, *attack*, 716.
discover, 480.
devise, 626.
Fallacy, *error*, 495.
uncertainty, 475.
sophistry, 477.
Fal-lal, *ornament*, 847.
Fallible, *uncertain*, 475, 477.
Fallow, *yellow*, 436.
unready, 674.
False, *untrue*, 544.
error, 495.
sophistry, 477.
spurious, 925.
dishonourable, 940.
False-hearted, *improbity*, 940.
Falsehood, *lie*, 546.
Falsetto, *music*, 413.
affected, 577.
Falsify, *misinterpret*, 523.
Falsify, *accounts*, 811.
deceive, 495.
lie, 544.
Falstaffian, *fat*, 192.
Falter, *stammer*, 583.
hesitate, 605.
demur, 603.
slowness, 275.
Fame, *renown*, 873.
rumour, 531.
news, 532.
Familiar, *common*, 82.
known, 490.
friendly, 888.
affable, 894.
spirit, 979.
Family, *class*, 75.
consanguinity, 11.
posterity, 167.
Famine, *insufficiency*, 640.
Famished, *fasting*, 956.
Famous, *repute*, 873.
greatness, 31.
Fan, *blow*, 349.
excite, 615.
Fanatic, *extravagant*, 515.
Fanaticism, *folly*, 499.
obstinacy, 606.
religious, 984.
Fanciful, *capricious*, 608.
imaginative, 515.
mistaken, 495.
unreal, 2.
Fancy, *think*, 451.
believe, 484.
wit, 842.
idea, 453.
suppose, 514.
imagine, 515.
caprice, 608.
choice, 609.
desire, 865.
love, 897.
pugilism, 726.
Fandango, *dance*, 840.
Fane, *temple*, 1000.
Fanfare, *loudness*, 404.
ostentation, 882.
Fanfaronade, *boasting*, 884.
Fantasia, *music*, 415.
imagination, 515.
Fantastic, *odd*, 83.
imaginary, 515.
capricious, 608.
ridiculous, 853.
Fantasy, *caprice*, 608.
imagination, 515.
idea, 453.
*Fantoccini (It.), *marionettes*, 554, 599.
Far, *distant*, 196.
Far from it, *dissimilarity*, 18.
Farce, *drama*, 599.
ridiculous, 856.
*Farceur (Fr.), *humorist*, 844.
Farcical, *ridiculous*, 856.
witty, 842.
trifling, 643.
Fardel, *assemblage*, 72.
Fare, *circumstance*, 8.
event, 151.
to eat, 296.
food, 298.
price, 812.
Farewell, *departure*, 293.
Far-fetched, *irrelation*, 10.
irrelevant, 24.
irrational, 477.
obscure, 519.
Farm, *house*, 189.
property, 780.
to rent, 795.
Farrago, *mixture*, 41.
confusion, 59.
Far-seeing, *foresight*, 510.
Farthing, *coin*, 800.
worthless, 643.
Farthingale, *dress*, 225.

*Fasces (L.), *sceptre*, 747.
Fascia, *band*, 205.
circle, 247.
Fascicle, *assemblage*, 72.
Fascinate, *please*, 829.
excite, 824, 825.
astonish, 870.
love, 897.
conjure, 992.
Fascination, *spell*, 993.
Fashion, *form*, 144, 240.
custom, 613.
mould, 140.
mode, 852.
nobility, 875.
Fashion, after a, *smallness*, 32.
Fast, *rapid*, 274.
steadfast, 150, 888.
stuck, 265.
joined, 43.
dissolute, 954.
not to eat, 956.
Fast and loose, *false*, 544.
changeful, 607.
Fasten, *join*, 45, 214.
fix, 150.
restrain, 751.
Fastening, *vinculum*, 45.
Fastidious, *dainty*, 868.
squeamish, 932.
Fasting, *abstinence*, 956.
atonement, 952.
Fastness, *asylum*, 666.
defence, 717.
Fat, *oleaginous*, 356.
unctuous, 355.
corpulent, 192.
Fatal, *lethal*, 361.
pernicious, 649.
Fatalism, *destiny*, 152.
necessity, 601.
*Fata Morgana (It.), *dim sight*, 443.
imagination, 515.
Fate, *necessity*, 601.
chance, 152, 621.
end, 67, 360.
Fat-head, *fool*, 501.
Father, *paternity*, 166.
priest, 996.
Fatherland, *home*, 189.
Father upon, *attribute*, 155.
Fatherless, *unsustained*, 160.
Fathom, *measure*, 466.
investigate, 461.
Fathomless, *depth*, 208.
Fatidical, *prediction*, 511.
Fatigue, *lassitude*, 688.
weariness, 841.
*Fatras (Fr.), *unimportance*, 643.
Fatten on, *feeding*, 296.
Fatuity, *folly*, 499.
Fat-witted, *folly*, 499.
*Faubourg (Fr.), *suburb*, 227.
*Fauces (L.), *beginning*, 66.
Faugh! *dislike*, 867.
Fault, *imperfection*, 651.
vice, 945.
guilt, 947.
error, 495.
failure, 732.
ignorance, 491.
Faultless, *perfect*, 650.
innocent, 946.
*Fauna (L.), *animal*, 366.
*Faute de mieux (Fr.), *shift*, 626.
*Fauteuil (Fr.), *support*, 215.
*Faux pas (Fr.), *failure*, 732.
vice, 945.
impurity, 961.
Favour, *aid*, 707.
permit, 760.
friendship, 888.
partiality, 923.
gift, 784.
letter, 592.
to resemble, 17.
Favourable, *advantageous*, 648.
friendly, 707, 888.
Favourite, *pleasing*, 829.
beloved, 897, 899.
Favouritism, *wrong*, 923.
Fawn, *colour*, 433.
cringe, 886.
flatter, 933.
Fay, *fairy*, 979.
Fealty, *duty*, 926.
respect, 928.
obedience, 743.
Fear, *fear*, 860.
Fearful, *great*, 31.
Fearless, *hopeful*, 858.
courageous, 861.
Feasible, *possible*, 470.
easy, 705.
Feast, *repast*, 298.
to devour, 296.
revel, 840.
enjoyment, 827.
Feat, *action*, 680.
Feather, *tuft*, 256.
lightness, 320.
trifle, 643.
class, 75.
ornament, 847.
decoration, 877.
Feather-bed, *softness*, 324.
Feathery, *roughness*, 256.
Feature, *character*, 5.

Feature, *form*, 240.
appearance, 448.
lineament, 550.
to resemble, 17.
Feckless, *feeble*, 160.
Feculence, *uncleanness*, 653.
Fecund, *productive*, 168.
Federation, *co-operation*, 709.
party, 712.
Fed up, *weariness*, 841.
satiety, 869.
Fee, *expenditure*, 795, 809.
Feeble, *weak*, 160.
scanty, 32.
silly, 477.
writing, 575.
Feeble-minded, *foolish*, 499.
irresolute, 605.
Feed, *eat*, 296.
supply, 637.
meal, 298.
Feel, *touch*, 379.
sensibility, 375.
moral, 821.
Feel for, *seek*, 461.
sympathise, 914.
Feet, *journey*, 266.
Feign, *falsehood*, 544.
Feint, *deception*, 545.
Felicitate, *congratulate*, 896.
Felicitous, *expedient*, 646.
favourable, 648.
skilful, 699.
successful, 731.
happy, 827.
Felicity, *happiness*, 827.
skill, 698.
Feline, *stealthy*, 528.
sly, 702.
Fell, *mountain*, 206.
to cut down, 308.
dire, 162.
wicked, 907.
Fellah, *commonalty*, 876.
Fellow, *similar*, 17.
equal, 27.
companion, 88.
man, 373.
dual, 89.
Fellow-creature, *man*, 373.
Fellow-feeling, *love*, 897.
sympathy, 906, 914.
Fellowship, *sociality*, 892.
partnership, 712.
friendship, 888.
*Felo-de-se (L.), *killing*, 361.
Felon, *sinner*, 949.
Felonious, *vice*, 945.
Felony, *guilt*, 947.
Felt, *matted*, 219.
Felucca, *ship*, 273.
Female, *woman*, 374.
Feminality, *feebleness*, 160.
Feminine, *woman*, 374.
Feminism, *rights*, 924.
*Femme couverte (Fr.), *marriage*, 903.
*Femme de chambre (Fr.), *servant*, 746.
Fen, *marsh*, 345.
Fence, *circumscribe*, 231.
enclose, 232.
defence, 717.
fight, 722.
safety, 664.
refuge, 666.
prison, 752.
to evade, 544.
Fencible, *combatant*, 726.
Fend, *defence*, 717.
provision, 637.
Fenestrated, *windowed*, 260.
Feoff, *property*, 780.
Ferine, *malevolence*, 907.
Ferment, *disorder*, 59.
energy, 171.
violence, 173.
agitation, 315.
effervesce, 353.
Ferocity, *brutality*, 907.
violence, 173.
Ferret, *tape*, 45.
Ferret out, *inquiry*, 480.
Ferry, *transference*, 270.
way, 627.
Fertile, *productive*, 168.
abundant, 639.
imaginative, 515.
Ferule, *scourge*, 975.
Fervour, *heat*, 382.
animation, 821.
Fester, *disease*, 655.
corruption, 653.
*Festina lente (L.), *haste*, 684.
Festive, *amusement*, 840.
sociality, 892.
Festoon, *ornament*, 847.
Fetch, *bring*, 270.
arrive, 292.
stratagem, 626.
evasion, 545.
price, 812.
*Fête (Fr.), *amusement*, 840.
ostentation, 882.
convivial, 892.
*Fête champêtre (Fr.), *amusement*, 840.
Fetid, *fetor*, 401.

Fetishism, *idolatry*, 991.
sorcery, 992.
Fetlock, *chain*, 45.
shackle, 752.
Fetter, *hinder*, 706.
restrain, 751.
shackle, 752.
Fettle, *preparation*, 673.
Feud, *discord*, 713.
Feudal, *authority*, 737.
Feudatory, *subjection*, 749.
*Feu de joie (Fr.), *firework*, 840.
salute, 882.
Feuilleton, *essay*, 595.
Fever, *heat*, 382.
excitement, 825.
Few, *fewness*, 103.
Fez, *cap*, 225.
*Fiasco (It.), *failure*, 732.
Fiat, *command*, 741.
*Fiancée (Fr.), *love*, 897.
Fib, *falsehood*, 544, 546.
Fibre, *link*, 45.
filament, 205.
Fibrous, *thin*, 203.
Fichu, *dress*, 225.
Fickle, *irresolute*, 605.
Fictile, *form*, 240.
Fiction, *untruth*, 546.
fancy, 515.
story, 594.
Fictitious, *false*, 544.
Fiddle, *to play*, 415.
violin, 417.
Fiddle-de-dee, *trifling*, 643.
contemptible, 930.
Fiddle-faddle, *trifle*, 643.
dawdle, 683.
Fiddler, *musician*, 416.
Fiddlestick, *contemptible*, 930.
absurd, 497.
trifling, 643.
Fiddling, *trifling*, 643.
Fidelity, *honour*, 939.
observance, 772.
Fidget, *excitability*, 825.
irascibility, 901.
activity, 682.
Fiducial, *belief*, 484.
*Fidus Achates (L.), *auxiliary*, 711.
Fie! *disrepute*, 874.
Fief, *property*, 780.
Field, *plain*, 344.
arena, 728.
scope, 180.
property, 780.
Field of view, *vista*, 441.
idea, 453.
Field-day, *pageant*, 882.
Field-marshal, *master*, 745.
Field-piece, *arms*, 727.
Fiend, *demon*, 980.
ruffian, 913.
Fiendish, *malevolent*, 907.
wicked, 945.
Fierce, *violent*, 173.
passion, 825.
daring, 861.
angry, 900.
Fiery, *violent*, 173.
excitable, 825.
hot, 382.
fervent, 821.
ardent, 515.
Fiery cross, *warfare*, 722.
Fife, *musical instrument*, 417.
Fig, *unimportant*, 643.
dress, 225.
adorn, 845, 847.
Fight, *contention*, 720, 722.
Fighter, *combatant*, 726.
Figment, *imagination*, 515.
*Figurante (It.), *the drama*, 599.
Figuration, *form*, 240.
Figurative, *metaphorical*, 521.
style, 577.
comparison, 464.
Figure, *state*, 7.
number, 84.
form, 240.
metaphor, 521, 566.
imagine, 515.
represent, 550, 554.
reputation, 873.
ugliness, 846.
parade, 882.
Figure-head, *effigy*, 554.
inaction, 683.
Figurine, *sculpture*, 557.
Filament, *slender*, 205.
ligature, 45.
Filamentous, *thin*, 203.
Filch, *steal*, 791.
File, *to smooth*, 255.
to pulverise, 330.
to string together, 60.
row, 69.
list, 86.
register, 551.
File off, *march*, 266.
diverge, 291.
Filiation, *consanguinity*, 11.
posterity, 167.
derivation, 155.
Filibeg, *dress*, 225.
Filibuster, *thief*, 792.
Filigree, *crossing*, 219.
Filings, *pulverulence*, 330.

Fill, *occupy*, 186.
Filling, *stopper*, 263.
Fill out, *expand*, 194.
Fill up, *complete*, 52.
close, 261.
satisfy, 639.
composition, 54.
compensate, 30.
*Fille de joie (Fr.), *libertine*, 962.
Fillet, *band*, 45.
circle, 247.
Fillip, *stimulus*, 615.
impulse, 276.
Filly, *horse*, 271.
young, 129.
Film, *layer*, 204.
dimness, 421, 426.
Filmy, *texture*, 329.
Filter, *clean*, 652.
percolate, 295.
amend, 658.
Filth, *uncleanness*, 653.
Fimbriated, *rough*, 256.
Fin, *instrument*, 267, 633.
Final, *end*, 67.
conclusive, 478.
resolved, 604.
*Finale (It.), *music*, 415.
Finance, *money*, 800.
Financier, *treasurer*, 801.
Find, *discover*, 480.
term, 71.
provide, 637.
sentence, 969.
acquisition, 775.
Fine, *rare*, 322.
textural, 329.
good, 648.
beautiful, 845.
thin, 203.
mulct, 974.
to clarify, 652.
Fine-draw, *improve*, 658.
Finery, *ornament*, 847, 851.
Fine-spoken, *courtesy*, 894.
Fine-spun, *thinness*, 203.
Finesse, *cunning*, 702.
manœuvre, 545.
tact, 698.
taste, 850.
Finger, *touch*, 379.
instrument, 633.
Finger-post, *indication*, 550.
Finger-print, *evidence*, 467.
Finical, *unimportant*, 643.
Finikin, *unimportant*, 643.
*Finis (L.), *end*, 67.
Finish, *complete*, 52.
achieve, 729.
Finish, *end*, 67.
symmetry, 242.
Finished, *perfect*, 242, 650.
accomplished, 698.
greatness, 31.
Finite, *smallness*, 32.
Fiord, *gulf*, 343.
Fire, *heat*, 382, 384.
to excite, 825.
to urge, 615.
to attack, 716.
Fire away, *begin*, 66.
Fire-brand, *brand*, 388.
incendiary, 913.
Fire-drake, *light*, 420.
Fire-eater, *blusterer*, 887.
Fire-fly, *luminary*, 423.
Firelock, *arms*, 727.
Fire off, *propulsion*, 284.
Fire-place, *furnace*, 386.
Fire-proof, *incombustible*, 383.
Fire-ship, *ship*, 273.
Fireside, *abode*, 189.
Fire up, *resentment*, 900.
Firework, *fire*, 382.
light, 423.
Fire-worshipper, *heterodoxy*, 984.
Firing, *fuel*, 388.
explosion, 406.
Firkin, *receptacle*, 191.
Firm, *hard*, 323.
junction, 43.
belief, 484.
stable, 150.
resolute, 604.
brave, 861.
party, 712.
partnership, 797.
friendship, 888.
Firmament, *world*, 318.
Firman, *order*, 741.
permit, 760.
decree, 963.
First, *beginning*, 66.
First-born, *age*, 124, 128.
First-rate, *ship*, 273.
excellent, 648.
superiority, 33.
First to last, from, *whole*, 50.
completeness, 52.
duration, 106.
Firth, *gulf*, 343.
Fisc, *treasury*, 802.
Fiscal, *money*, 800.
Fish, *animal*, 366.
Fish out of water, *disagreement*, 24.
Fish out, *judgment*, 480.
Fish up, *elevation*, 307.
Fishy, *dubious*, 475, 478.

Fissile, *brittle*, 328.
Fission, *disjunction*, 44.
Fissure, *chink*, 198.
Fistula, *opening*, 260.
Fit, *state*, 7.
paroxysm, 173.
caprice, 608.
to prepare, 673.
excitement, 825.
anger, 900.
duty, 926.
agreement, 23.
expedient, 646.
right, 922.
Fitful, *capricious*, 608.
irresolute, 605.
irregular, 139.
Fitness, *agreement*, 23.
Fit out, *preparation*, 673.
Fitting, *expedient*, 646.
right, 922, 926.
Fit up, *preparation*, 673.
Five, *number*, 98.
Fix, *place*, 150, 184.
solidify, 321.
arrangement, 60.
difficulty, 704.
Fixed, *determined*, 604.
permanent, 142, 150.
belief, 484.
quiescent, 265.
Fix together, *junction*, 43.
Fixture, *property*, 780.
Fix upon, *choose*, 609.
Fizgig, *firework*, 423.
Fizz, *sibilation*, 409.
Fizzle, *hiss*, 409.
Fizzle out, *failure*, 732.
Flabbergast, *astound*, 870.
Flabby, *soft*, 324.
Flaccid, *shrivelled*, 172, 193.
empty, 640.
Flag, *streamer*, 550.
flat stone, 204.
weakness, 160.
floor, 211.
droop, 688.
infirm, 655.
slowness, 275.
Flagellation, *flogging*, 972.
asceticism, 955.
Flageolet, *musical*, 417.
Flagitious, *vice*, 945.
Flagrant, *notorious*, 531.
atrocious, 945.
Flagship, *ship*, 273.
Flagstaff, *sign*, 550.
high, 206.
Flail, *impulse*, 276.
*Flair (Fr.), *intelligence*, 498.
Flake, *layer*, 204.
Flam, *untruth*, 546.
*Flambé (Fr.), *failure*, 732.
Flambeau, *luminary*, 423.
Flamboyant, *vulgar*, 851.
ornamented, 577.
Flame, *light*, 420.
fire, 382.
luminary, 423.
passion, 825.
love, 897.
favourite, 899.
Flame-colour, *orange*, 439.
Flamen, *clergy*, 996.
Flaming, *feeling*, 821.
excited, 825.
*Flâneur (Fr.), *idler*, 683.
Flange, *support*, 215.
Flank, *side*, 236.
safety, 664.
Flap, *adjunct*, 39.
hanging, 214.
move about, 315.
beat, 972.
Flapdoodle, *deception*, 545.
Flapper, *memory*, 505.
girl, 129, 374.
Flapping, *loose*, 47.
Flare, *glare*, 420.
violence, 173.
Flaring, *colour*, 428.
Flare up, *kindle*, 825.
anger, 900.
Flash, *instant*, 113.
fire, 382.
light, 420.
thought, 451.
sudden act, 612.
violence, 173.
Flash note, *money*, 800.
Flashy, *gaudy colour*, 428.
bad taste, 851.
ostentatious, 882.
Flask, *receptacle*, 191.
Flat, *level*, 251.
horizontal, 213.
novice, 701.
low, 207.
vapid, 391.
inert, 172, 823.
dull, 841, 843.
dejected, 837.
sound, 408.
indifferent, 866.
positive, 535.
apartment, 191.
Flatter, *please*, 829.
encourage, 858.

Flatter, *adulation*, 933.
Flatterer, *eulogist*, 935.
Flatulent, *windy*, 338.
style, 573.
*Flatus (L.), *wind*, 349.
Flaunt, *display*, 873, 882.
gaudy, 428.
ornament, 847.
Flautist, *musician*, 416.
Flavour, *taste*, 390.
Flaw, *crack*, 198.
error, 495.
imperfection, 651.
blemish, 848.
fault, 947.
Flay, *divest*, 226.
Flea-bite, *unimportance*, 643.
Fleckered, *variegation*, 440.
Fledged, *preparation*, 673.
Flee, *escape*, 671.
avoid, 623.
Fleece, *tegument*, 222.
to rob, 791.
to strip, 789.
impoverish, 804.
Fleer, *ridicule*, 856.
Fleet, *swift*, 274.
ships, 273.
Fleeting, *transient*, 111.
Flesh, *mankind*, 372.
carnality, 961.
Flesh-colour, *redness*, 434.
Fleshly, *sensual*, 954, 961.
Flesh-pots, *food*, 298.
Fleshy, *corpulent*, 192.
Flexible, *pliant*, 324.
tractable, 705.
Flexion, *bending*, 245.
fold, 258.
Flexuous, *convolution*, 248.
Flexure, *bending*, 245.
fold, 258.
Flick, *propel*, 284.
Flicker, *flutter*, 315.
waver, 149, 605.
Flickering, *irregular*, 139.
Flight, *departure*, 287, 293.
volitation, 267.
swiftness, 274.
multitude, 102.
Flight of fancy, *imagination*, 515.
idea, 453.
Flighty, *insane*, 503.
fickle, 605.
Flim-flam, *lie*, 546.
caprice, 608.
Flimsy, *texture*, 329.
soft, 324.
irrational, 477.
Flimsy, *trifling*, 643.
frail, 651.
manuscript, 590.
Flinch, *fear*, 860, 862.
avoid, 623.
swerve, 607.
Fling, *propel*, 284.
censure, 932.
attack, 716.
jeer, 929.
amusement, 840.
Fling away, *relinquish*, 782.
Flint, *hardness*, 323.
Flint-hearted, *malevolence*, 907.
Flip, *propel*, 284.
Flippant, *pert*, 885.
fluent, 584.
Flipper, *fin*, 267.
Flirt, *propel*, 284.
coquette, 902.
Flit, *move*, 264, 266.
depart, 293.
escape, 671.
swift, 274.
thought, 451.
Flitter, *scrap*, 51.
flutter, 315.
Flitting, *evanescent*, 111, 149.
roving, 266.
Float, *navigate*, 267.
buoy up, 305.
lightness, 320.
sound, 405.
Flocculent, *soft*, 324.
pulverulent, 330.
Flock, *herd*, 366.
assemblage, 72, 102.
laity, 997.
Flog, *punishment*, 972.
Flood, *water*, 348.
abundance, 639.
increase, 35.
of light, 420.
Flood-gate, *conduit*, 350.
Floor, *base*, 211.
level, 204.
horizontal, 213.
support, 215.
to puzzle, 485, 704.
to overthrow, 731.
Flop, *flutter*, 315.
Flora, *plant*, 367.
Florid, *colour*, 428.
red, 434.
health, 654.
style, 577.
Flotilla, *ship*, 273.
Flotsam, *fragments*, 51.
Flounce, *quick motion*, 274.

Flounce, *agitation*, 315.
trimming, 230.
fold, 258.
Flounder, *toss*, 315.
waver, 149, 314.
mistake, 495.
to blunder, 499, 732.
struggle, 704.
Floundering, *bungling*, 699.
Flourish, *brandish*, 314.
succeed, 731, 734.
display, 873, 882.
boast, 884.
exaggerate, 549.
of speech, 577, 582.
Flout, *mock*, 856.
sneer, 929.
Flow, *stream*, 347.
motion, 264.
course, 109.
result from, 154.
Flow out, *egress*, 295.
Flow over, *run over*, 348.
abound, 641.
Flower, *ornament*, 845.
perfection, 650.
prosper, 734.
of life, 127.
of speech, 577.
honour, 873.
Flowing, *style*, 573.
sound, 405.
abundant, 639.
Fluctuate, *oscillate*, 314.
wavering, 605.
Flue, *air-pipe*, 351.
egress, 295.
opening, 260.
down, 320.
dross, 643, 653.
Fluent, *speech*, 584.
style, 573.
flowing, 348.
Fluid, *liquidity*, 333.
Fluke, *angularity*, 244.
chance, 621.
Flummery, *vain*, 643.
flattery, 933.
absurd, 497.
Flummox, *bewilder*, 458.
Flunkey, *lackey*, 746.
flatterer, 935.
Fluorescence, *light*, 420.
Flurry, *hurry*, 684.
agitation, 821, 825.
Flush, *flat*, 251.
flood, 348.
heat, 382.
light, 420.
Flush, *redness*, 434.
abundance, 639.
feeling, 821.
passion, 825.
rich, 803.
in liquor, 959.
Flushed, *elated*, 836, 884.
vain, 880.
proud, 878.
Fluster, *excitement*, 824.
Flustered, *tipsy*, 959.
Flute, *musical*, 417.
Fluted, *furrow*, 259.
Flutter, *move*, 315.
fear, 860.
excitement, 821, 824, 825.
Fluviatile, *river*, 348.
Flux, *flow*, 109, 348.
motion, 264.
changes, 140.
Fluxions, *numeration*, 85.
Fly, *depart*, 293.
take wing, 267.
escape, 671.
recede, 287.
shun, 623.
run away, 862.
lose colour, 429.
minute, 193.
time, 109, 111.
burst, 173, 328.
Fly at, *attack*, 716.
Fly-boat, 273.
Fly back, *recoil*, 277.
elastic, 325.
Fly-blown, *unclean*, 653.
Fly-leaf, 228.
book, 593.
Fly out, *burst*, 173.
passion, 825.
anger, 900.
Fly-wheel, *instrument*, 633.
Flying, *swiftness*, 274.
volitation, 267.
Foal, *young*, 129.
Foam, *spray*, 353.
passion, 173, 900.
Fob, *pocket*, 191.
to cheat, 545.
evade, 773.
Focus, *reunion*, 74.
centre, 223.
Fodder, *materials*, 635.
food, 298.
Foe, *antagonist*, 710.
enemy, 891.
Fœtus, *infant*, 129.
Fog, *cloud*, 353.
dimness, 422.

Foggy, *obscure*, 447.
shaded, 426.
*Föhn (Ger.), *wind*, 349.
Foible, *vice*, 945.
Foil, *contrast*, 14.
success, 731.
Foiled, *failure*, 732.
Foist in, *insert*, 228, 300.
Foist upon, *deception*, 545.
*Folâtre (Fr.), *cheerful*, 836.
Fold, *plait*, 258.
pen, 752.
bisection, 91.
congregation, 996.
bisect, 91.
Foliaceous, *layer*, 204.
Foliage, *plant*, 367.
Foliated, *layer*, 204.
Folk, *man*, 373.
Folk-dance, *dance*, 840.
Folk-tale, *legend*, 594.
Follicle, *hollow*, 252.
opening, 260.
cyst, 191.
Follow, *in order*, 63.
in time, 117.
in motion, 281.
to imitate, 19.
pursue, 622.
result from, 154.
obey, 743.
Follow on, *continue*, 143.
Follow suit, *conformity*, 82.
Follow up, *inquiry*, 461.
Follower, *sequence*, 281.
partisan, 746.
Folly, *irrationality*, 499.
nonsense, 497.
building, 189.
Foment, *promote*, 707.
excite, 173.
Fond, *love*, 897.
Fondle, *endearment*, 902.
Fondling, *favourite*, 899.
Fondness, *love*, 897.
desire, 865.
Font, *altar*, 1000.
Food, *eatable*, 298.
materials, 635, 637.
Fool, *silly*, 501.
to deceive, 548.
Foolhardy, *rashness*, 863.
Foolish, *unwise*, 499.
trifling, 643.
irrational, 477, 497.
misguided, 699.
Foot, *stand*, 211.
metre, 597.
Foot it, *walk*, 266.
Foot it, *dance*, 840.
Footfall, *motion*, 264.
trace, 551.
Foothold, *influence*, 175.
support, 215.
Footing, *situation*, 8, 183.
foundation, 211.
place, 58.
rank, 71.
influence, 175.
Footing, to be on, *state*, 7.
Footlights, *drama*, 599.
Footman, *servant*, 746.
Footmark, *record*, 551.
Foot-pace, *slowness*, 275.
Footpad, *thief*, 792.
Foot-path, *way*, 627.
Footprint, *record*, 551.
Footstep, *record*, 551.
Footstool, *support*, 215.
Foozle, *bungle*, 699, 732.
Fop, *fop*, 854.
Foppery, *affectation*, 855.
Foppish, *affectation*, 855.
For, *reason*, 476.
motive, 615.
For all the world like, *similarity*, 17.
Forage, *provision*, 637.
materials, 635.
booty, 793.
to steal, 791.
food, 298.
Foraminous, *opening*, 260.
Forasmuch as, *reasoning*, 476.
Foray, *attack*, 716.
robbery, 791.
havoc, 619.
Forbear, *avoid*, 623.
spare, 678.
pity, 914.
abstain, 953.
sufferance, 826.
Forbears, *ancestors*, 130, 166.
Forbid, *prohibit*, 761.
Forbidding, *repulsive*, 846.
Force, *power*, 157.
validity, 476.
strength, 159.
agency, 170.
to compel, 744.
to induce, 615.
of style, 574.
Forced, *out of place*, 24.
Ford, *way*, 627.
Fore, *front*, 234.
Fore and aft, *whole*, 50.
Forearmed, *preparation*, 673.
Forebode, *prediction*, 511.

Forecast, *foresee*, 510.
plan, 626.
prepare, 673.
Foreclose, *hindrance*, 706.
Foredoom, *necessity*, 601.
Forefather, *old*, 130.
ancestor, 166.
Foregoing, *past*, 122.
preceding, 62.
Foreground, *front*, 234.
Forehead, *front*, 234.
Foreign, *alien*, 10.
extraneous, 57.
Forejudge, *misjudgment*, 481.
Foreknow, *foresight*, 510.
Foreland, *high*, 206.
projection, 250.
Foreman, *director*, 694.
Foremost, *front*, 234.
beginning, 66
Forename, *name*, 564.
Forenoon, *morning*, 125.
Forensic, *jurisprudence*, 965.
Foreordain, *predestine*, 152.
Fore-rank, *front*, 234.
Forerun, *priority*, 116.
Forerunner, *in order*, 64.
in time, 116.
omen, 512.
Foresee, *foreknow*, 510.
expect, 507.
Foreshadow, *prediction*, 511.
Foreshorten, *shortness*, 201.
Foresight, *foresight*, 510.
Forest, *plant*, 367.
Forestall, *early*, 132.
expect, 507.
Forestry, *agriculture*, 371.
Foretaste, *foresight*, 510.
Foretell, *prediction*, 511.
priority, 116.
Forethought, *care*, 459.
Foretoken, *prediction*, 511.
Forewarn, *warn*, 668.
advise, 695.
predict, 511.
Foreword, *preamble*, 64.
Forfeit, *lose*, 776.
fail, 773.
penalty, 974.
Forfend, *guard*, 717.
hinder, 706.
Forge, *produce*, 161.
workshop, 691.
trump up, 544.
Forgery, *untruth*, 546.
imitation, 19.
Forget, *oblivion*, 506.
Forgive, *forgiveness*, 918.
Forgo, *relinquish*, 782.
renounce, 757.
For good, *diuturnity*, 110.
Forgotten, *unremembered*, 506.
ingratitude, 917.
Fork, *angularity*, 244.
bisection, 91.
Forlorn, *abandoned*, 893.
dejected, 837.
woebegone, 828.
Forlorn hope, *hopeless*, 859.
danger, 665.
Form, *shape*, 240.
state, 7.
arrange, 60.
rule, 80.
to make up, 54.
produce, 161.
educate, 537.
habituate, 613.
bench, 215.
part, 569.
fashion, 852.
etiquette, 882.
law, 963.
fours, 58.
manner, 627.
beauty, 845.
likeness, 21.
pupils, 541.
Formal, *regular*, 82.
affected, 855.
positive, 516, 535.
Formalism, *hypocrisy*, 989.
Formality, *ceremony*, 852.
parade, 882.
law, 963.
Format, *style*, 7.
Formation, *production*, 161.
shape, 240.
Formed of, *composition*, 54.
Former, *in order*, 62.
in time, 122.
Formication, *itching*, 380.
Formidable, *fear*, 860.
Formless, *amorphism*, 241.
Formula, *rule*, 80.
precept, 697.
law, 963.
number, 84.
Fornication, *impurity*, 961.
Fornicator, *libertine*, 962.
Forsake, *relinquish*, 624.
Forsooth, *truth*, 494.
Forswear, *renounce*, 624.
refuse, 764.
perjure, 544, 940.
Fort, *defence*, 717.
refuge, 666.

Forte, *excellence*, 698.
*Forte (It.), *loudness*, 404.
Forth, *progression*, 282.
Forth, and so, *addition*, 37.
Forthcoming, *futurity*, 121, 673.
Forthwith, *transient*, 111.
Fortification, *defence*, 717.
refuge, 666.
Fortify, *strength*, 159.
Fortitude, *courage*, 861.
endurance, 826.
Fortress, *defence*, 716.
prison, 752.
Fortuitous, *chance*, 156, 621.
Fortunate, *opportune*, 134.
prosperous, 734.
Fortune, *chance*, 156.
accident, 621.
wealth, 803.
Fortune-teller, *oracle*, 513.
Fortune-telling, *prediction*, 511.
Forum, *tribunal*, 966.
school, 542
Forward, *early*, 132.
to advance, 282
to help, 707.
active, 682.
willing, 602.
vain, 880.
impertinent, 885.
Fosse, *furrow*, 259.
enclosure, 232.
Fossil, *antiquated*, 851.
Foster, *aid*, 707.
Fou, *drunken*, 959.
Foul, *bad*, 649.
corrupt, 653.
odour, 401.
ugly, 846.
vicious, 945.
Foul-mouthed, *malevolent*, 907.
Foul-tongued, *scurrilous*, 934.
Found, *cause*, 153.
prepare, 673.
Foundation, *base*, 211.
support, 215.
Founder, *originator*, 164.
sink, 732.
Foundling, *outcast*, 893.
Fount, *origin*, 153.
type, 591.
Fountain, *cause*, 153.
river, 348.
store, 636.
Fountain-pen, *writing*, 590.
Four, *number*, 95.
Fourfold, *number*, 96.
Four-square, *number*, 95.
Fourscore, *number*, 98.
Fours, on all, *disagreement*, 24.
Fourth, *number*, 97.
Fowl, *animal*, 366.
Fowling-piece, *arms*, 727.
Fox, *cunning*, 702.
Fox-trot, *dance*, 840.
*Fracas (Fr.), *contention*, 720.
Fraction, *part*, 51.
numerical, 84.
Fractious, *irascibility*, 901.
Fracture, *disjunction*, 44.
discontinuity, 70, 198.
to break, 328.
Fragile, *brittle*, 328.
frail, 149.
Fragment, *part*, 51.
Fragrant, *fragrant*, 400
Frail, *brittle*, 328.
mutable, 149.
irresolute, 605.
imperfect, 651.
failing, 945.
Frame, *condition*, 7.
support, 215.
texture, 329.
form, 240.
substance, 316.
to construct, 161.
border, 230.
Franchise, *right*, 924.
freedom, 748.
exemption, 927.
Franciscan, *clergy*, 996.
Frangible, *brittle*, 328.
Frank, *artless*, 703.
open, 525.
sincere, 543.
honourable, 939.
Frankincense, *fragrant*, 400.
Frantic, *delirious*, 503.
violent, 173.
excited, 825.
Fraternal, *brotherly*, 11.
friendly, 888, 906.
Fraternise, *co-operate*, 709.
harmonise, 714.
Fraternity, *assemblage*, 72.
company, 712, 892.
Fraud, *deception*, 545.
dishonour, 940.
Fraught, *having*, 777.
full of, 639.
Fray, *contention*, 720.
to abrade, 331.
Freak, *caprice*, 608.
unconformity, 83.
Freakish, *irresolution*, 605.
Freckle, *blemish*, 848.
Freckled, *variegation*, 440.

Free, *detached*, 44.
at liberty, 748.
spontaneous, 600, 602.
exempt, 927.
unobstructed, 705.
liberal, 816.
gratuitous, 815.
insolent, 885.
Freebooter, *thief*, 792.
Free-born, *freedom*, 748.
Freedom, *liberty*, 748.
looseness, 47.
full play, 705.
exemption, 927.
space, 180.
Free gift, *giving*, 784.
Freehold, *property*, 780.
Free-lance, *writer*, 590.
Freemasonry, *secrecy*, 528.
sign, 550.
fraternity, 712.
Free play, *freedom*, 748.
Free-spoken, *veracity*, 543.
Free-thinking, *religion*, 988.
Free-will, *will*, 600.
Freeze, *frigefaction*, 385.
Freight, *contents*, 190.
cargo, 798.
transfer, 270.
Frenzy, *insanity*, 503.
Frequent, *in time*, 136.
in number, 102.
in space, 186.
Frequency, *repetition*, 104.
Fresco, *painting*, 556.
Fresh, *new*, 123.
cold, 383.
colour, 428.
unforgotten, 505.
healthy, 654.
good, 648.
tipsy, 959.
Freshet, *flood*, 348.
Freshman, *learner*, 541.
Fret, *suffer*, 378.
grieve, 828.
to gall, 830.
sadness, 837.
to irritate, 900.
Fretful, *irascibility*, 901.
Fretwork, *crossing*, 219.
Friable, *pulverulence*, 330.
*Friandise (Fr.), *fastidious*, 868.
Friar, *clergy*, 996.
Fribble, *trifle*, 643.
dawdle, 683.
Friction, *rubbing*, 331.
obstacle, 179.
discord, 713.
Friend, *well-wisher*, 890.
auxiliary, 711.
Friendless, *seclusion*, 893.
Friendly, *amical*, 714, 888.
helping, 707.
Friendship, *amical*, 714, 888.
Frieze, *summit*, 210.
Frigate, *ship*, 273.
Fright, *alarm*, 860.
ugliness, 846.
Frightful, *great*, 31.
hideous, 846.
dreadful, 830.
Frigid, *cold*, 383.
callous, 823.
reluctant, 603.
Frigorific, *refrigeration*, 385.
Frill, *border*, 230.
Frills, *affectation*, 855.
Fringe, *lace*, 256.
ornament, 847.
Frippery, *dress*, 225.
trifle, 643.
ornament, 847, 851.
ostentation, 882.
ridiculous, 853.
Frisk, *brisk*, 682.
gay, 836.
amuse, 840.
Frisky, *nimble*, 274, 305.
in spirits, 836.
Frith, *strait*, 343.
chasm, 198.
Fritter, *small part*, 51.
waste, 135, 638, 683.
misuse, 679.
Frivolous, *unimportant*, 643.
silly, 499.
frisky, 836.
Frizzle, *curl*, 248.
fold, 258.
Frock, *dress*, 225.
Frog, *ornament*, 847.
Frolic, *amusement*, 840.
Frolicsome, *cheerful*, 836.
Front, *fore-part*, 234.
beginning, 66.
exterior, 220.
resistance, 719.
Frontal, *beginning*, 66.
exterior, 220.
Frontier, *limit*, 233.
vicinity, 199.
Fronting, *antiposition*, 237.
Frontispiece, *prefix*, 64.
front, 234.
Frost, *cold*, 383.
Froth, *bubble*, 353.
trifle, 643.

Froth, *style*, 577.
Froward, *irascible*, 901.
discourteous, 895.
Frown, *disapprove*, 932.
anger, 900.
scowl, 839, 895.
lower, 837.
Frowzy, *fetor*, 401.
Fructify, *productive*, 168.
prosper, 734
Frugal, *temperate*, 953.
economical, 817.
Fruit, *result*, 154.
acquisition, 775.
Fruitful, *productive*, 168.
Fruition, *pleasure*, 827.
fulfilment, 729.
Fruitless, *useless*, 645.
abortive, 732.
Frump, *dowdy*, 851.
Frustrate, *defeat*, 731.
prevent, 706.
Frustration, *failure*, 732.
Frustum, *part*, 51.
Fry, *young*, 129.
small, 193.
heat, 384.
Frying-pan, *furnace*, 386.
Fuddled, *drunk*, 959.
Fudge, *nonsense*, 497.
trivial, 643.
Fuel, *combustible*, 388.
materials, 635.
Fugacious, *transitory*, 111.
Fugitive, *escape*, 287, 671.
changeful, 149, 607.
transitory, 111.
evasive, 623.
emigrant, 268.
Fugleman, *prototype*, 22.
leader, 745.
Fugue, *music*, 415.
Fulcrum, *support*, 215.
Fulfil, *observe*, 772.
duty, 926.
complete, 729.
Fulgent, *light*, 420.
Fulguration, *light*, 420.
Fuliginous, *black*, 422, 431.
opaque, 426.
Full, *much*, 31.
complete, 52.
sound, 404.
abundant, 639.
Full-blown, *expansion*, 194.
Full-flavoured, *savoury*, 394.
Full-grown, *expansion*, 194.
Fullness of time, *occasion*, 124
Fully, *great*, 31.
Fulminate, *loud*, 404.
violent, 173.
malediction, 908.
threat, 909.
Fulsome, *nauseous*, 395.
adulatory, 933.
Fulvous, *yellow*, 436.
Fumble, *derange*, 61.
handle, 379.
awkward, 699.
Fumbler, *bungler*, 701.
Fume, *exhalation*, 334.
odour, 398.
violence, 173.
excitement, 825.
anger, 900.
Fumigate, *cleanness*, 652.
Fun, *amusement*, 840.
Funambulist, *proficient*, 700.
Function, *business*, 625.
duty, 926.
utility, 644.
number, 84.
Functionary, *consignee*, 758.
Fund, *capital*, 800.
store, 636, 639.
Fundamental, *basis*, 211, 215
note, 413.
Fundamentally, *greatness*, 31.
Funds, *money*, 800.
Funeral, *interment*, 363.
Fungus, *convexity*, 250.
Funk, *fear*, 860.
cowardice, 862.
Funk-hole, *refuge*, 666.
Funnel, *opening*, 260.
Funnel-shaped, *concave*, 252.
Funny, *witty*, 842.
ridiculous, 853.
Fur, *hair*, 256.
dirt, 653.
Furbish, *improve*, 658.
prepare, 673.
beautify, 845.
ornament, 847.
Furfur, *unclean*, 653.
Furfuraceous, *pulverulent*, 330.
Furious, *great*, 31.
violent, 173.
passion, 825.
enraged, 900.
velocity, 274.
Furl, *roll up*, 312.
Furlough, *permission*, 760.
Furnace, *furnace*, 386.
Furnish, *provide*, 637.
prepare, 673.
give, 215, 784.
Furniture, *materials*, 635.

Furniture, *goods*, 780.
*Furor (L.), *excitement*, 825.
excitement, 825.
Furore, *rage*, 865.
excitement, 825.
Furrow, *furrow*, 198, 259.
Further, *aid*, 707.
Furthermore, *addition*, 37.
Furtive, *clandestine*, 528.
false, 544.
stealing, 791.
Fury, *violence*, 173.
excitation, 825.
anger, 900.
demon, 980.
bane, 663.
Fuscous, *brown*, 433.
Fuse, *melt*, 335.
heat, 382, 384.
combine, 48.
Fusiform, *pointed*, 253.
angular, 244.
Fusilier, *combatant*, 726.
Fusillade, *killing*, 361.
Fusion, *liquefaction*, 335.
heat, 384.
union, 48.
Fuss, *haste*, 684.
activity, 682.
hurry, 825.
Fustian, *nonsense*, 497.
ridiculous, 853.
style, 477.
Fusty, *fetor*, 401.
Futile, *useless*, 645.
unavailing, 732.
Future, *futurity*, 121.
Futurist, *artist*, 559.
Fylfot, *cross*, 219.

G

Gab, *speech*, 582.
Gabble, *loquacity*, 584.
Gabelle, *tax*, 812.
Gaberdine, *dress*, 225.
Gad about, *journey*, 266.
Gadget, *contrivance*, 626.
tool, 633.
Gaffer, *man*, 373.
veteran, 130.
clown, 876.
Gag, *speechless*, 581, 585.
muzzle, 403, 751.
interpolation, 228.
Gage, *security*, 771.
Gaiety, *see* Gay.
*Gaillard (Fr.), *humorist*, 844.
Gain, *acquisition*, 775.
advantage, 618.
to learn, 539.
Gain ground, *improve*, 658.
Gain upon, *approach*, 286.
become a habit, 613.
Gainful, *utility*, 644, 810.
Gainless, *inutility*, 645.
Gainsay, *negation*, 536.
Gait, *walk*, 264.
speed, 274.
Gaiter, *dress*, 225.
Gala, *festival*, 840.
display, 882.
Galaxy, *stars*, 318.
assembly, 72.
luminary, 423.
multitude, 102.
glory, 873.
Gale, *wind*, 349.
*Galimatias (Fr.), *absurd*, 497.
Gall, *bitterness*, 395.
pain, 378.
to pain, 830.
malevolence, 907.
anger, 900.
Gallant, *brave*, 861.
licentious, 961, 962.
Galleon, *ship*, 273.
Gallery, *room*, 191.
passage, 260.
Galley, *ship*, 273.
Galliard, *dance*, 840.
Gallicism, *neology*, 563.
Galligaskins, *dress*, 225.
Gallimaufry, *mixture*, 41.
Gallipot, *receptacle*, 191.
Gallivant, *travel*, 266.
Gallop, *ride*, 266.
scamper, 274.
Galloway, *carrier*, 271.
Gallows, *scourge*, 975.
Galosh, *dress*, 225.
Galumph, *exult*, 836.
Galvanic, *violent*, 173.
Galvanise, *energise*, 171.
Galvanism, *excitation*, 824.
*Gambade (Fr.), *leap*, 309.
prank, 856.
*Gambado (Sp.), *dress*, 225.
Gamble, *chance*, 156, 621.
Gambol, *amusement*, 840.
Game, *chance*, 156.
pursuit, 622.
plan, 626.
intent, 620.
amusement, 840.
resolute, 604.
brave, 861.

Game-cock, *courage*, 861.
Gamesome, *cheerful*, 836.
*Gamin (Fr.), *commonalty*, 876.
Gammon, *untruth*, 546.
to hoax, 545.
Gamut, *harmony*, 413.
Gamy, *pungent*, 392.
Gang, *party*, 712.
knot, 72.
Gangrene, *disease*, 655.
Gangway, *way*, 627.
Gaol, *see* Jail.
Gap, *discontinuity*, 70.
chasm, 4, 198.
Gape, *open*, 260.
wonder, 870.
curiosity, 455.
desire, 865.
Gar, *to make*, 161.
Garage, *house*, 189.
Garb, *dress*, 225.
Garbage, *unclean*, 653.
Garble, *retrench*, 38.
exclude, 55.
misinterpret, 523.
falsify, 544.
Garbled, *incomplete*, 53.
*Garçon (Fr.), *servant*, 746.
Garden, *beauty*, 845.
Gardening, *agriculture*, 371.
Gargantuan, *size*, 192.
Gargoyle, *spout*, 350.
Garish, *colour*, 428.
light, 420.
ornament, 847.
display, 882.
Garland, *ornament*, 847.
Garment, *dress*, 225.
Garner, *collect*, 72.
store, 636.
Garnish, *adorn*, 845.
ornament, 847.
addition, 39.
Garret, *room*, 191.
high, 206.
Garrison, *combatant*, 726.
defend, 664.
Garrotte, *killing*, 361.
punishment, 972.
Garrulity, *loquacity*, 584.
Gas, *rarity*, 322.
gaseity, 334.
to chatter, 584.
to boast, 884.
Gas-bag, *loquacity*, 584.
Gasconade, *boasting*, 884.
Gash, *disjunction*, 44, 198.
Gasp, *pant*, 688.
desire, 865.
Gasp, *droop*, 655.
Gastronomy, *gluttony*, 957.
Gate, *beginning*, 66.
way, 627.
mouth, 260.
barrier, 232.
Gather, *collect*, 72, 789.
acquire, 775.
enlarge, 194.
learn, 539.
conclude, 480.
fold, 258.
unite in a focus, 74.
*Gauche (Fr.), *unskilful*, 699.
ill-mannered, 851.
Gaud, *ornament*, 847.
Gaudery, *vanity*, 880.
Gaudy, *colouring*, 428.
ornamental, 847, 851.
flaunting, 882.
Gauge, *measure*, 466.
Gaunt, *bulky*, 192.
spare, 203.
ugliness, 846.
Gauntlet, *defiance*, 715.
punishment, 972.
glove, 225.
anger, 909.
Gauze, *shade*, 424.
Gauzy, *filmy*, 329.
Gavotte, *dance*, 840.
music, 415.
Gawky, *awkward*, 699.
ridiculous, 853.
Gay, *cheerful*, 836.
colour, 428.
Gaze, *vision*, 441.
Gazebo, *look-out*, 441.
Gazelle, *velocity*, 274.
Gazette, *publication*, 531.
record, 551.
Gazetted, *bankrupt*, 808.
Gazetteer, *list*, 86.
Gazing-stock, *prodigy*, 872.
Gear, *clothes*, 225.
harness, 633.
Gehenna, *hell*, 982.
Geisha, *dancer*, 599.
Gelatine, *pulpiness*, 354.
Gelatinous, *semiliquid*, 352.
Gelding, *carrier*, 271.
Gelid, *cold*, 383.
Geloscopy, *prediction*, 511.
Gem, *jewel*, 650.
Gemination, *duplicate*, 90.
Gemini, *duality*, 89.
*Gendarme (Fr.), *police*, 965.
Gender, *class*, 75.
Genealogy, *continuity*, 69.

Genealogy, *filiation*, 155.
General, *generic*, 78.
officer, 745.
Generalisssimo, *master*, 745.
Generality, *generic*, 78.
Generalship, *conduct*, 692.
Generate, *production*, 161, 168.
Generation, *mankind*, 372.
period, 108.
Generic, *general*, 78.
Generous, *liberal*, 816.
disinterested, 942.
Genesis, *production*, 161.
Genial, *warm*, 382.
cordial, 602, 829.
courteous, 894.
Geniculated, *angular*, 244.
Genie, *demon*, 980.
Genius, *talent*, 498.
intellect, 450.
skill, 698.
spirit, 979.
proficient, 700.
*Genius loci (L.), *location*, 184.
*Genre (Fr.), *class*, 75.
style, 7.
painting, 556.
Genteel, *fashionable*, 852.
Gentile, *heathen*, 984.
Gentility, *rank*, 875.
politeness, 852.
Gentle, *moderate*, 174.
meek, 826.
lenient, 740.
courteous, 894.
sound, 405.
Gentleman, *person*, 373.
squire, 875.
man of honour, 939.
Gentlemanly, *polite*, 852.
noble, 875.
courteous, 894.
Gently, *slowly*, 174, 275.
Gentry, *nobility*, 875.
Genuflexion, *homage*, 743.
respect, 928.
servility, 886.
worship, 990.
Genuine, *true*, 494.
good, 648.
Genus, *class*, 75.
Geodesy, *measurement*, 466.
Geography, *place*, 183.
Geology, *mineral*, 358.
Geometry, *measurement*, 466.
Germ, *rudiment*, 153, 674.
bane, 663.
Germane, *relation*, 23.
Germinate, *sprout*, 194.
Germinate, *produce*, 153.
Gerrymander, *garble*, 544.
Gestation, *pregnancy*, 168.
preparation, 673.
Gesticulate, *sign*, 550.
Gesture, *hint*, 527.
indication, 550.
Get, *acquire*, 775.
Get about, *publication*, 531.
Get among, *mixture*, 41.
Get at, *tamper with*, 682.
Get-at-able, *attainable*, 705.
Get back, *arrival*, 292.
Get before, *precedency*, 62.
Get down, *descend*, 306.
Get home, *arrive*, 292.
Get off, *depart*, 293.
liberating, 750.
escape, 927.
Get on, *advance*, 282.
succeed, 731.
improve, 658.
Get round, *circumvent*, 702.
Get the start, *precede*, 62.
Get to, *arrive*, 292.
Get together, *assemble*, 72.
Get up, *rise*, 305.
prepare, 673.
style, 7.
Gewgaw, *trifle*, 643.
ornament, 847.
tinsel, 851.
Geyser, *heat*, 382.
furnace, 386.
Ghastly, *tedious*, 846.
frightful, 860.
Ghost, *soul*, 450.
apparition, 980.
shade, 362.
emaciated, 193.
(Holy), 976.
Ghoul, *demon*, 980.
Giant, *tall*, 206.
large, 192.
Gibber, *stammer*, 583.
Gibberish, *jargon*, 519.
nonsense, 517.
absurdity, 497.
Gibbet, *gallows*, 975.
to execute, 972.
Gibbous, *globose*, 249.
convex, 250.
distorted, 244.
Gibe, *jeer*, 856, 932.
taunt, 929.
Giddiness, *caprice*, 608.
inattention, 458.
bungling, 699.
Giddy, *careless*, 460.

Giddy, *irresolute*, 605.
bungling, 699.
light-headed, 503.
Gift, *given*, 784.
power, 157
talent, 698.
Gig, *vehicle*, 272.
ship, 273.
Gigantic, *large*, 192.
tall, 206.
Giggle, *laugh*, 838.
Gild, *adorn*, 845.
ornament, 847.
coat, 222.
Gilding, *covering*, 222.
Gill, *river*, 348.
Gimbals, *rotation*, 312.
Gimcrack, *brittle*, 328.
valueless, 645.
imperfect, 651.
ornament, 847.
whim, 865.
Gimlet, *perforator*, 262.
Gin, *trap*, 667.
Ginger, *pungency*, 392.
Gingerbread, *flimsy*, 651.
ornament, 847.
Gingerly, *carefully*, 459.
slowly, 275.
Ginger up, *excite*, 824.
Gipsy, *deceiver*, 548.
fortune-teller, 513.
Girandole, *luminary*, 423.
Gird, *bind*, 43.
surround, 227.
enclose, 231.
strengthen, 159.
Girder, *bond*, 45.
beam, 215.
Girdle, *circular*, 247.
outline, 229.
Girl, *young*, 129.
female, 374.
Girth, *band*, 45.
outline, 229.
Gist, *essence*, 5.
important, 642.
meaning, 516.
Gittern, *musical instrument*, 417.
Give, *giving*, 784.
regress, 283.
Give and take, *probity*, 939.
Give back, *restitute*, 790.
Give ear, *listen*, 418.
Give entrance to, *reception*, 296.
Give forth, *publish*, 531.
Give in, *submit*, 725.
obey, 743.
Give notice, *inform*, 527.
Give notice, *warn*, 668.
Give out, *emit*, 297.
bestow, 784.
publish, 531.
teach, 537.
end, 67.
Give over, *relinquish*, 624.
cease, 141.
lose hope, 859.
Give up, *relinquish*, 624.
resign, 757.
yield, 743.
reject, 610.
property, 782.
Give way, *yield*, 725.
obey, 743.
despond, 837.
Gizzard, *receptacle*, 191.
Glabrous, *smooth*, 255.
Glacial, *cold*, 383.
Glaciate, *frigefaction*, 385.
Glacier, *cold*, 383.
Glacis, *defence*, 717.
Glad, *pleasure*, 827.
Gladden, *pleasurableness*, 829.
Glade, *opening*, 260.
hollow, 252.
thicket, 367.
Gladiator, *combatant*, 726.
Gladiatorial, *warfare*, 722.
Gladsome, *pleasurable*, 829.
Glairy, *semiliquid*, 352.
Glamour, *sorcery*, 992.
Glance, *look*, 441.
rapid motion, 274.
attend to, 457.
hint, 527.
Glare, *light*, 420.
visible, 446.
colour, 428.
obvious, 518.
Glaring, *greatness*, 31.
Glass, *vessel*, 191.
brittle, 328.
spectacles, 445.
Glassy, *dim*, 422.
transparent, 425.
colourless, 429.
Glaucous, *green*, 435.
Glazed, *smooth*, 255.
Gleam, *ray*, 429.
Glean, *choose*, 609.
take, 789.
acquire, 775.
learn, 539.
Glebe, *smooth*, 342.
Glee, *satisfaction*, 827.
merriment, 836.
music, 415.

Gleeman, *musician*, 416.
Glen, *concavity*, 252.
Glib, *voluble*, 584.
facile, 705.
Glide, *move*, 266.
slowly, 275.
course, 109.
Glider, *airship*, 273.
Glimmer, *light*, 420.
dimness, 422.
Glimmering, *slight knowledge*, 490. 491.
Glimpse, *sight*, 441.
knowledge, 490.
Glint, *shine*, 420.
Glissade, *descent*, 306.
*Glissando (It.), *music*, 415.
Glisten, *shine*, 420.
Glitter, *shine*, 420, 873.
display, 882.
Gloaming, *evening*, 126.
dimness, 422.
Gloat, *look*, 441.
revel, 827.
Globe, *sphere*, 249.
world, 318.
Globe-trotter, *traveller*, 268.
Globule, *spherule*, 249.
minute, 193.
Glockenspiel, *musical*, 417.
Glomeration, *assembly*, 72.
Gloom, *darkness*, 421.
sadness, 837.
Glorify, *approve*, 931.
worship, 990.
Glory, *honour*, 873.
light, 420.
boast, 884.
pride, 878.
Gloss, *light*, 420.
smoothness, 255.
beauty, 845.
plea, 617.
falsehood, 546.
interpretation, 522.
Glossary, *interpretation*, 522.
verbal, 562.
Gloss over, *neglect*, 460.
inattention, 458.
sophistry, 477.
vindication, 937.
falsehood, 544.
Glossy, *smooth*, 255.
Glove, *cartel*, 715.
Glow, *shine*, 420.
colour, 428.
warmth, 382.
passion, 821.
style, 574.
Glower, *scowl*, 895.
Glow-worm, *luminary*, 423.
Gloze, *flatter*, 933.
palliate, 937.
Glucose, *sweetness*, 396.
Glue, *cement*, 45.
to cement, 46.
Glum, *discontented*, 832.
sulky, 895.
Glut, *redundance*, 641.
satiety, 869.
Glutinous, *coherence*, 46.
semiliquid, 352.
Gluttony, *excess*, 957.
desire, 865.
Glycerine, *semiliquid*, 352.
Glyphography, *engraving*, 558.
Gnarled, *rough*, 256.
Gnash, *anger*, 900.
Gnat, *littleness*, 193.
Gnaw, *eat*, 296.
corrode, 659.
pain, 378.
give pain, 830.
Gnome, *demon*, 980.
maxim, 496.
Gnomic, *sententious*, 572.
Gnosis, *knowledge*, 490.
Gnostic, *intellectual*, 450.
mystic, 528.
Go, *move*, 264.
depart, 293.
Go about, *undertake*, 676.
Go across, *passage*, 302.
Goad, *motive*, 615.
Go ahead, *advance*, 282.
improve, 658.
activity, 682.
Goal, *object*, 620.
reach, 292.
Go-between, *agent*, 758.
intermedium, 228, 631.
Gobble, *devour*, 296.
cry, 412.
*Gobemouche (Fr.), *credulous*, 486.
fool, 501.
dupe, 547.
Go beyond, *pass*, 303.
Goblin, *ghost*, 980.
bugbear, 860.
Go by, *pass*, 303.
Go-by, *evasion*, 623.
God, *Deity*, 976.
Goddess, *favourite*, 899.
Godless, *irreligion*, 988.
Godlike, *virtue*, 944.
Godliness, *piety*, 987.
Go down, *sink*, 306.
decline, 659.

Godsend, *luck*, 621.
advantage, 618.
success, 731.
Goer, *horse*, 271.
Go forth, *depart*, 293.
publish, 531.
Goggle, *optical instrument*, 445.
to stare, 441.
Goggle-eyed, *dimsighted*, 443.
Go halves, *divide*, 91.
Go hand in hand with, *accompany*, 88.
Go in for, *business*, 625.
Gold, *money*, 800.
Golden, *yellow*, 436.
Golden age, *pleasure*, 827.
Golden-mouthed, *ornament*, 577.
Gombeen-man, *usurer*, 805.
Goliath, *strength*, 159.
Gondola, *ship*, 273.
Gone, *non-extant*, 2.
absent, 187.
dead, 360.
Go near, *approach*, 286.
Gone by, *past*, 123.
Gone on, *loving*, 897.
Gonfalon, *flag*, 550.
Gong, *resonance*, 417.
Good, *advantage*, 618.
advantageous, 648.
virtuous, 944.
Good-bye, *departure*, 293.
Good day, *arrival*, 292.
Good-fellowship, 892.
Good, for, *end*, 67.
Good-for-nothing, *rascal*, 949.
Goodly, *large*, 192.
beautiful, 845.
Good manners, *courtesy*, 894.
Good nature, *benevolence*, 906.
Goods, *effects*, 780.
Goodwill, *benevolence*, 906.
merchandise, 798.
materials, 635.
Goody, *woman*, 374.
Go off, *cease*, 142.
die, 360.
fare, 151.
Go on, *continue*, 143.
Goose, *fool*, 501.
Goose-cap, *fool*, 501.
Goose-skin, *cold*, 383.
Goose-step, *quiescence*, 265.
Go over, *change sides*, 607.
Gordian knot, *problem*, 461.
difficulty, 704.
Gore, *opening*, 260.
angularity, 244.
Gorge, *ravine*, 198.
Gorge, *narrowness*, 203.
to devour, 296.
full, 641.
gluttony, 957.
satiety, 869.
Gorgeous, *colour*, 428.
splendid, 845.
ornamented, 847.
Gorgon, *fear*, 860.
Gormandise, *gluttony*, 957.
reception, 296.
Go round, *circuition*, 311.
Gospel, *scripture*, 985.
truth, 494.
certainty, 474.
Gossamer, *texture*, 329.
slender, 205.
light, 320.
Gossip, *conversation*, 588.
chatterer, 584.
news, 532.
Gossoon, *boy*, 129, 373.
Goth, *barbarian*, 876.
Gothic, *vulgarity*, 851.
Go through, *pass*, 302.
complete, 729.
endure, 821.
Go to, *direction*, 278.
remonstrance, 695.
*Gouache (Fr.), *painting*, 556
Go under, *name*, 564.
sink, 310.
ruin, 735.
Go up, *ascent*, 305.
*Goût (Fr.), *taste*, 850.
Go with, *assent*, 488.
suit, 646.
Gourmand, *gluttony*, 957.
Gourmet, *desire*, 865.
gluttony, 957.
Govern, *direct*, 693.
authority, 737.
Governess, *teacher*, 540.
Governess-cart, *vehicle*, 272.
Governor, *director*, 694.
tutor, 540.
Gown, *dress*, 225.
Grab, *snatch*, 789.
steal, 791.
booty, 793.
Grabble, *fumble*, 379.
Grace, *elegance*, 845.
polish, 850.
forgiveness, 918.
honour, 939.
title, 877.
piety, 987.
worship, 990.
beseech, 765.

Grace, *style*, 578.
Graceless, *ungraceful*, 846.
vicious, 945.
impenitent, 951.
Grace-note, *music*, 415.
Grace-stroke, *killing*, 361.
Gracile, *slender*, 203.
Gracious, *courteous*, 894.
good-natured, 906.
*Gradatim (L.), *degree*, 26.
order, 58.
conversion, 144.
Gradation, *degree*, 26.
order, 58.
arrangement, 60.
continuity, 69.
Grade, *degree*, 26.
term, 71.
Gradient, *obliquity*, 217.
Gradual, *degree*, 26.
continuity, 69.
Graduate, *to arrange*, 60.
to adapt, 23.
to measure, 466.
scholar, 492.
*Gradus (L.), *dictionary*, 562.
*Graffito (It.), *drawing*, 556.
Graft, *join*, 43.
insert, 300.
locate, 184.
teach, 537.
Grain, *essence*, 5.
minute, 32.
particle, 193.
texture, 329.
soul, 820.
Grammar, *grammar*, 567.
Grammercy, *gratitude*, 916.
Gramophone, *reproduction*, 19.
music, 417.
Granary, *store*, 636.
Grand, *important*, 642
beautiful, 845.
glorious, 873.
Grandam, *veteran*, 130.
Grandee, *master*, 875.
Grandeur, *repute*, 873.
Grandiloquence, *eloquence*, 582.
style, 577.
Grandiose, *style*, 577.
Grandsire, *old*, 130.
ancestor, 166.
Grange, *abode*, 189.
Grangerise, *addition*, 36.
Granite, *hardness*, 323.
Grant, *give*, 784.
allow, 760.
consent, 762.
assent, 488.
Granulate, *pulverulence*, 330.
Granule, *littleness*, 193.
Grape-shot, *arms*, 727.
Graphic, *painting*, 556.
description, 594.
intelligible, 518.
Grapnel, *anchor*, 666.
Grapple, *contend*, 720.
undertake, 676.
Grappling-iron, *fastening*, 45.
safety, 666.
Grasp, *seize*, 789.
retain, 781.
comprehend, 518.
power, 737.
Grass, *plant*, 367.
Grass-green, *green*, 435.
Grass widow, *divorce*, 905.
Grate, *rub*, 330.
friction, 331.
harsh, 410, 414.
furnace, 386.
pain, physical, 378.
moral, 830.
Grateful, *thankful*, 916.
agreeable, 829.
Gratification, *animal*, 377.
moral, 827.
Gratify, *pleasure*, 829.
Grating, *noise*, 410.
lattice, 219.
Gratis, *cheap*, 815.
Gratitude, *thanks*, 916.
Gratuitous, *spontaneous*, 600.
unwarranted, 514.
payless, 815.
Gratuity, *giving*, 784.
Gratulation, *rejoicing*, 836.
Gravamen, *importance*, 642.
grievance, 619.
Grave, *sad*, 836.
serious, 642.
distressing, 830.
heinous, 945.
to engrave, 559.
impress, 505.
tomb, 363.
sound, 408.
greatness, 31.
Gravel, *offend*, 830.
puzzle, 704.
Graveolent, *odour*, 398.
Graver, *artist*, 559.
Graveyard, *interment*, 363.
Gravid, *pregnant*, 168.
Gravity, *weight*, 319.
dullness, 843.
seriousness, 837.
importance, 642.

Gravity, *composure*, 826.
Gravy, *liquid*, 333.
Graze, *browse*, 296.
touch, 199.
Grease, *oil*, 356.
unctuous, 355.
Great, *much*, 31.
big, 192.
important, 642.
glorious, 873.
magnanimous, 942.
Great-coat, *garment*, 225.
Greaten, *enlarge*, 35.
Greaves, *garment*, 225.
Greedy, *voracious*, 957.
desirous, 865.
avaricious, 819.
Green, *colour*, 435.
new, 123.
unskilled, 699.
unprepared, 674.
credulous, 484.
ignorant, 491.
Greenback, *money*, 800.
Green-eyed, *jealousy*, 920.
Greenhorn, *fool*, 501.
novice, 493.
bungler, 701.
Green-room, *the drama*, 599.
Greet, *hail*, 894.
weep, 839.
Gregarious, *social*, 892.
Grenade, *arms*, 727.
Grenadier, *soldier*, 726.
tall, 206.
Grey, *colour*, 432.
age, 128.
Greybeard, *veteran*, 130.
Grey-headed, *age*, 128.
Greyhound, *swift*, 274.
Grid, *lattice*, 219.
Gridelin, *purple*, 437.
Gridiron, *lattice*, 219.
Grief, *dejection*, 837
Grievance, *injury*, 619.
pain, 830.
Grieve, *complain*, 828, 839.
afflict, 830.
injure, 649.
Griffin, *unconformity*, 83.
keeper, 753.
*Griffonage (Fr.), *writing*, 590.
Grig, *cheerful*, 836.
Grill, *calefaction*, 384.
Grille, *lattice*, 219.
Grim, *ugly*, 846.
frightful, 828.
discourteous, 846.
ferocious, 907.
Grimace, *ridicule*, 856.
Grime, *unclean*, 653.
Grim-visaged, *grave*, 837.
Grin, *laugh*, 838.
ridicule, 856.
scorn, 929.
Grind, *pulverise*, 330.
an organ, 415.
oppress, 907.
learn, 539.
sharpen, 253.
Grinder, *teacher*, 540.
Grip, *power*, 737.
Gripe, *seize*, 789.
retain, 781.
pain, 378, 828.
to give pain, 830.
power, 737.
Griping, *avaricious*, 819.
*Grisette (Fr.), *woman*, 374.
Grisly, *ugliness*, 846.
Grist, *provision*, 637.
materials, 635.
Grit, *pulverulence*, 330.
determination, 604.
Gritty, *hard*, 323.
Grizzled, *variegation*, 440.
Grizzly, *grey*, 432.
Groan, *cry*, 411.
lament, 839.
Groggy, *drunk*, 959.
Groin, *angular*, 244.
Groom, *servant*, 746.
Groove, *furrow*, 259.
habit, 613.
Grope, *feel*, 379.
experiment, 463.
inquire, 461.
try, 675.
Gross, *whole*, 51.
vulgar, 851.
vicious, 945.
impure, 961.
greatness, 31.
*Grossiéreté (Fr.), *discourtesy*, 895.
Grot, *see* Grotto.
Grotesque, *deformed*, 846.
ridiculous, 851, 853.
outlandish, 83.
Grotto, *alcove*, 189.
hollow, 252.
Ground, *land*, 342.
support, 215.
base, 211.
region, 181.
cause, 153.
motive, 615.
plea, 617.
property, 780.

Ground, *teach*, 537.
Grounded, *knowing*, 490.
wrecked, 732.
Groundless, *erroneous*, 495.
sophistical, 477.
Groundling, *commonalty*, 876.
Grounds, *lees*, 653.
Ground-swell, *surge*, 348.
agitation, 315.
Groundwork, *basis*, 211.
support, 215.
cause, 153.
precursor, 64.
preparation, 673
Group, *cluster*, 72.
to marshal, 58.
Grouse, *grumble*, 839.
Grout, *vinculum*, 45.
Grove, *wood*, 367.
house, 189.
Grovel, *move slowly*, 275.
be low, 207.
cringe, 886.
base, 940.
Grow, *increase*, 35.
expand, 194.
Grow from, *effect*, 154.
Growl, *cry*, 412.
complain, 839.
threaten, 909.
anger, 900.
Growth, *in degree*, 35.
in size, 194.
Groyne, *refuge*, 666.
Grub, *little*, 193.
food, 298.
Grub up, *extract*, 301.
destroy, 162.
discover, 480.
Grudge, *hate*, 898.
stingy, 640, 819.
unwilling, 603.
Gruelling, *punishment*, 972.
Gruesome, *ugly*, 846.
Gruff, *morose*, 895.
sound, 410.
Grumble, *sound*, 411.
complain, 832, 839.
Grumous, *dense*, 321.
Grumpy, *discourteous*, 895.
Grundyism, *prudery*, 855.
Grunt, *cry*, 412.
complain, 839.
Guano, *manure*, 653.
Guarantee, *security*, 771.
evidence, 467.
promise, 768.
Guard, *defend*, 717.
safety, 664.
Guarded, *circumspect*, 459.
conditional, 770.
Guardian, *safety*, 664, 717.
Guardless, *danger*, 665.
Guard-room, *prison*, 752.
Guardsman, *combatant*, 726.
Gudgeon, *dupe*, 547.
Guebre, *heterodoxy*, 984.
Guerdon, *reward*, 973.
Guerrilla, *combatant*, 726.
Guess, *suppose*, 514.
Guest, *friend*, 890.
*Guet-apens (Fr.), *untruth*, 546.
ambush, 530.
Guffaw, *laughter*, 834.
Guggle, *see* Gurgle.
Guide, *direct*, 693.
director, 694.
advice, 695.
teach, 537.
teacher, 540.
road-book, 266.
Guideless, *danger*, 665.
Guide-post, *indicator*, 550.
warning, 668.
Guild, *corporation*, 712.
tribunal, 966.
partnership, 797.
Guild-hall, *mart*, 799.
Guile, *cunning*, 702.
deceit, 545.
Guileless, *artless*, 703.
sincere, 543.
Guillotine, *engine*, 975.
to decapitate, 972.
Guilt, *crime*, 947.
vice, 945.
Guiltless, *innocence*, 946.
*Guindé (Fr.), *conciseness*, 572.
Guise, *state*, 7.
appearance, 448.
plea, 617.
Guiser, *the drama*, 599.
Guitar, *music*, 417.
Gules, *redness*, 434.
Gulf, *sea*, 343.
depth, 208.
Gull, *dupe*, 547.
credulous, 486.
Gullet, *throat*, 260.
rivulet, 348.
Gullible, *credulity*, 486.
Gully, *conduit*, 350.
opening, 260.
hollow, 252.
ravine, 198.
Gulosity, *gluttony*, 957.
Gulp, *swallow*, 297.
believe, 484.

Gum, *vinculum*, 45.
coherence, 46.
semiliquid, 352.
Gumption, *capacity*, 498.
Gun, *arms*, 727.
Gunboat, *ship*, 273.
Gunner, *combatant*, 726.
Gurgitation, *rotation*, 312.
Gurgle, *sound*, 405, 408.
bubble, 353.
Gurkha, *soldier*, 726.
Gush, *flow*, 295.
flood, 348.
feeling, 821.
affectation, 855.
Gusset, *angularity*, 244.
Gust, *wind*, 349.
physical taste, 390.
enjoyment, 826.
moral taste, 850.
Gustatory, *taste*, 390.
Gusto, *relish*, 827.
taste, 850.
Gut, *opening*, 260.
to sack, 789.
vitals, 221.
Gutter, *conduit*, 350.
groove, 259 .
Guttersnipe, *commonalty*, 876.
Guttle, *devour*, 296.
gorge, 957.
Guttural, *stammer*, 583.
Guy, *rope*, 45.
ugliness, 846.
to ridicule, 856.
Guzzle, *drink*, 296,
tipple, 959.
Gymkhana, *contention*, 720.
Gymnasium, *school*, 542.
training, 673.
Gymnast, *proficient*, 700.
Gymnastic, *exertion*, 686.
Gymnosophist, *heterodoxy*, 984.
Gynæcocracy, *authority*, 737.
Gyration, *rotation*, 312.
Gyre, *rotation*, 312
Gyromancy, *prediction*, 511.
Gyroscope, *rotation*, 312.
Gyve, *chain*, 45.
shackle, 752.

H

Haberdashery, *dress*, 225.
Habergeon, *defence*, 717.
Habiliment, *dress*, 225.
Habilitation, *skill*, 698.
Habit, *intrinsic*, 5.
Habit, *custom*, 613.
coat, 225.
Habitat, *abode*, 189.
Habitation, *abode*, 189.
location, 184.
Habitual, *regular*, 82, 613.
Habituate, *accustom*, 613.
train, 673.
Habitude, *state*, 7.
relation, 9.
habit, 613.
*Hacienda (Sp.), *property*, 780.
Hack, *cut*, 44.
shorten, 201.
horse, 271.
Hackneyed, *regular*, 82.
trite, 496.
habitual, 613.
experienced, 698.
Hackle, *cut*, 44.
Hades, *hell*, 982.
*Hadgi (Arab.), *pilgrim*, 268.
Haft, *instrument*, 633.
Hag, *ugly*, 846.
wretch, 913.
Haggard, *ugly*, 846.
wild, 824.
insane, 503.
intractable, 606.
Haggle, *bargain*, 769.
chaffer, 794.
Hagiography, *theology*, 983.
Ha-ha, *ditch*, 198.
defence, 717.
Haik, *dress*, 225.
Hail, *call*, 586.
salute, 928
ice, 383.
Hair, *thread*, 45.
filament, 205.
roughness, 256.
Hair's breadth, *thin*, 203.
Halberd, *arms*, 727.
Halberdier, *combatant*, 726.
Halcyon, *prosperous*, 734, 829.
joyful, 827.
calm, 174.
Hale, *health*, 654.
Half, *bisection*, 91.
Half and half, *mixture*, 41.
Half a dozen, *six*, 98.
Half-baked, *incomplete*, 53.
witless, 499.
Half-blood, *unconformity*, 83.
Half-breed, *unconformity*, 83.
Half-caste, *mixture*, 41.
unconformity, 83.
Half-hearted, *indifferent*, 866.
timorous, 862.

Half-moon, *curvature*, 245.
Half-seas-over, *drunk*, 959.
Half-way, *middle*, 68.
Half-wit, *fool*, 501.
Half-witted, *folly*, 499.
Hall, *chamber*, 189.
receptacle, 191.
mart, 799.
Hallelujah, *worship*, 990.
Hall-marked, *genuine*, 494.
Hallo! *call*, 586.
wonder, 870.
Halloo, *cry*, 411.
Hallowed, *venerated*, 928.
Deity, 976.
Hallucination, *error*, 495.
delusion, 503.
Halo, *light*, 420.
glory, 873.
Halt, *stop*, 265.
flag, 655.
rest, 687.
limp, 275.
Halter, *rope*, 45.
punishment, 975.
Halting, *lame*, 160.
Halve, *bisect*, 91.
Halyard, *rope*, 45.
Hamadryad, *nymph*, 979.
Hamlet, *abode*, 189.
*Hammal (Arab.), *carrier*, 271.
*Hammam (Arab.), *furnace*, 386.
Hammer, *to knock*, 276.
instrument, 633.
auction, 796.
repetition, 104.
Hammer at, *thought*, 583.
action, 682.
Hammock, *support*, 215.
Hamper, *basket*, 191.
obstruct, 706.
Hamstring, *injure*, 649.
weaken, 160.
incapacitate, 158.
Hand, *instrument*, 633.
indicator, 550.
agent, 690.
side, 236.
writing, 590.
to give, 784.
agency, 170.
Hand-barrow, *vehicle*, 272.
Handbook, *advice*, 695.
Handcuff, *tie together*, 43.
manacle, 752.
Handfast, *marriage*, 903.
Handful, *quantity*, 25, 103.
smallness, 32.
Hand-gallop, *velocity*, 274.
Handicap, *inequality*, 28.
disadvantage, 651.
Handicraft, *action*, 680.
Handicraftsman, *agent*, 690.
Hand (in), *possession*, 777.
business, 625.
Hand in hand, *accompaniment*, 88.
Handiwork, *action*, 680.
Handkerchief, *dress*, 225.
Handle, *instrument*, 633.
plea, 617.
feel (*touch*), 379.
describe, 594.
dissert, 595.
work, 680.
Handling, *treatment*, 692.
Handmaid, *servant*, 746.
Hand, on the other, *compensation*, 30.
Handsel, *security*, 771.
pay, 809.
Hands off! *resist*, 719.
prohibit, 761.
Handsome, *beautiful*, 845.
liberal, 816.
disinterested, 942.
Handspike, *instrument*, 633.
Handwriting, *omen*, 512.
signature, 550.
autograph, 590.
Handy, *near*, 197.
skilful, 698.
attainable, 705.
Hang, *pendency*, 214.
kill, 361.
execute, 972.
Hang about, *loiter*, 275.
Hangar, *building*, 189.
Hang back, *hesitate*, 603.
Hanger, *arms*, 727.
Hanger-on, *servant*, 746.
accompany, 88.
parasite, 886.
flatterer, 935.
Hang fire, *reluctance*, 603.
vacillation, 605.
refuse, 764.
slowness, 275.
Hangings, *ornaments*, 847.
Hangman, *executioner*, 975.
Hang out, *reside*, 188.
Hang over, *futurity*, 121.
destiny, 152.
height, 206.
Hang together, *junction*, 43.
Hang up, *defer*, 133.
Hank, *skein*, 219.
Hanker, *desire*, 865.
Hanky-panky, *deception*, 545.

Hansom, *vehicle*, 272.
Hap, *chance*, 156, 621.
Haphazard, *chance*, 156, 621.
Hapless, *hopeless*, 859.
miserable, 828.
Haply, *chance*, 156.
Happen, *event*, 151.
Happy, *glad*, 827.
expedient, 646
agreement, 23.
Happy-go-lucky, *careless*, 460.
Happy medium, *middle*, 68.
*Hari-kari (Japanese), *suicide*, 361.
Harangue, *speech*, 582.
Harass, *worry*, 907.
fatigue, 688.
vex, 830.
Harbinger, *omen*, 512.
precursor, 64, 116.
Harbour, *refuge*, 666.
haven, 292.
to cherish, 821.
Harbourless, *exposed*, 665.
Hard, *dense*, 323.
difficult, 704.
grievous, 830.
obdurate, 951.
sour, 397.
Hard-and-fast, *exact*, 494.
strict, 739.
Harden, *accustom*, 613.
train, 673.
render callous, 823.
impious, 989.
impenitent, 951.
Hard-favoured, *ugly*, 846.
Hard-headed, *skill*, 698.
Hard-hearted, *malevolence*, 907.
Hardihood, *courage*, 861.
Hardly, *scarcely*, 32.
infrequency, 137.
Hard-mouthed, *obstinacy*, 606.
Hardness of heart, *vice*, 945.
Hardship, *pain*, 830.
Hard-up, *poverty*, 804.
Hard-working, *exertion*, 682, 686.
Hardy, *strong*, 159.
healthy, 654.
Hare, *velocity*, 274.
Hare-brained, *rash*, 460, 863.
Harem, *apartment*, 191.
impurity, 961.
Hark, *hearing*, 418.
Harlequin, *motley*, 440.
pantomimic, 599.
humorist, 844.
Harlot, *libertine*, 962.
Harlotry, *impurity*, 961.
Harm, *evil*, 619.
Harm, *badness*, 649.
malevolence, 907.
Harmattan, *wind*, 349.
Harmless, *safe*, 664.
innocent, 946.
innocuous, 648.
Harmonic, *music*, 413.
Harmonica, *musical*, 417.
Harmonise, *uniformity*, 16.
Harmonium, *musical instrument*, 417.
Harmony, *agreement*, 23.
melody, 413.
concord, 714.
peace, 721.
conformity, 82.
friendship, 888.
Harness, *fasten*, 43.
fastening, 45.
accoutrement, 225.
instrument, 633.
subjection, 749.
Harp, *musical instrument*, 417.
to repeat, 104.
to weary, 841.
Harper, *musician*, 416.
Harpoon, *arms*, 727.
Harpsichord, *musical*, 417.
Harpy, *demon*, 980.
thief, 792.
miser, 819.
Harquebus, *arms*, 727.
Harridan, *hag*, 846.
trollop, 962.
Harrow, *pain*, 830.
Harry, *pain*, 830.
Harsh, *severe*, 739.
morose, 895.
disagreeable, 830.
malevolent, 907.
acrid, 171.
sound, 410.
Harum-scarum, *disorder*, 59
*Haruspex (L.), *oracle*, 513.
Haruspicy, *prediction*, 511.
Harvest, *acquisition*, 775, *effect*, 154.
Hash, *mixture*, 41.
to cut, 44.
Hasp, *lock*, 45.
to lock, 43.
Hassock, *support*, 215.
Haste, *in time*, 132.
in motion, 274.
in action, 684.
activity, 682.
Hasten, *to promote*, 707.
Hasty, *transient*, 111.
irritable, 901.
Hat, *dress*, 225.

Hatch, *produce*, 161.
plan, 626.
prepare, 673.
door, 66.
Hatchet, *instrument*, 633.
Hatchment, *record*, 551.
Hatchway, *way*, 627.
Hate, *hate*, 898.
Hateful, *noxious*, 649.
painful, 830.
Hauberk, *arms*, 717.
Haughty, *proud*, 878
severe, 739.
insolent, 885
Haul, *traction*, 285.
Haunch, *side*, 236.
Haunt, *presence*, 186
alarm, 860.
abode, 189.
trouble, 830.
Hautboy, *musical instrument*, 417.
*Haute politique (Fr.), *government*, 693.
Hauteur, *pride*, 878.
*Haut-goût (Fr.), *pungency*, 392.
Have, *possession*, 777.
Have it, *belief*, 484.
Haven, *refuge*, 292, 666.
Haversack, *receptacle*, 191.
Havoc, *evil*, 162, 619.
Haw, *stammering*, 583.
Hawk, *sell*, 796.
publish, 531.
Hawker, *merchant*, 797.
Hawk-eyed, *vision*, 441.
Hawser, *rope*, 45.
Hazard, *chance*, 156, 621.
danger, 665.
obstacle, 706.
Haze, *mist*, 353.
dimness, 422.
opacity, 426.
to harass, 830, 907.
Hazel, *brown*, 433.
Hazy, *indistinct*, 447.
Head, *beginning*, 66
class, 75.
summit, 210.
to lead, 280.
froth, 353.
intellect, 450.
wisdom, 498.
master, 745.
direction, 693.
director, 694.
topic, 454.
Headache, *pain*, 378.
Head and shoulders, *whole*, 50.
Header, *plunge*, 310.
Head-foremost, *rash*, 863.
obstinate, 606.
Head-gear, *dress*, 225.
Headiness, *obstinacy*, 606.
Heading, *title*, 550.
beginning, 66.
Headland, *projection*, 250.
cape 342.
height, 206.
Headlong, *rashly*, 460, 863.
hastily, 684.
obstinately, 606.
swiftly, 274.
Head-piece, *intellect*, 450.
skill, 698.
wisdom, 498.
Headquarters, *focus*, 74.
abode, 189.
Heads, *compendium*, 596.
Headstrong, *rash*, 863
obstinate, 606.
violent, 173.
Headway, *space*, 180.
progress, 282.
Head-work, *thought*, 451.
Heady, *obstinate*, 606.
Heal, *repair*, 658.
forgive, 918.
Health, *health*, 654.
Healthy, *salubrity*, 656.
Heap, *collection*, 72.
store, 636.
much, 31, 50.
Hear, *audition*, 418.
learn, 539.
Hearken, *audition*, 418.
Hearsay, *news*, 532.
Hearse, *interment*, 363.
Heart, *interior*, 221.
centre, 223.
mind, 450.
will, 600.
affections, 820.
courage, 861.
love, 897.
Heart-ache, *pain*, 828.
Heart-breaking, *painful*, 830.
Heart-broken, *pain*, 828.
Heart-burning, *resentment*, 900.
Hearten, *inspirit*, 824, 861.
Heart-felt, *feeling*, 821.
Hearth, *abode*, 189.
Heartiness, *feeling*, 821.
sociality, 892.
Heartless, *malevolent*, 945.
Heart-rending, *painful*, 830.
Heart-sick, *dejected*, 837.
Heart-sinking, *fear*, 860.
Heart-strings, *affections*, 820.

Heart-swelling, *resentment*, 900.
Heart-whole, *free*, 748.
Hearty, *healthy*, 654.
willing, 602.
feeling, 821.
cheerful, 831, 836.
Heat, *warmth*, 382.
calefaction, 384.
contest, 720.
violence, 173.
excitement, 825.
Heat, dead, *equality*, 27.
Heath, *plain*, 344.
Heathen, *pagan*, 984.
irreligious, 988.
Heathenish, *vulgar*, 851.
Heave, *raise*, 307.
pant, 821.
throw, 284.
Heave in sight, *visibility*, 446.
Heave-to, *stop*, 265.
Heaven, *paradise*, 981.
bliss, 827.
Heaven-born, *virtue*, 944.
Heaven-directed, *wisdom*, 498.
Heavenly, *divine*, 976.
rapturous, 829.
celestial, 318.
Heavens, *world*, 318.
Heaviness, *inertia*, 172.
dejection, 837.
dullness, 843.
Heavy, *weighty*, 319.
inert, 172, 682.
slow, 275.
stupid, 499.
rude, 851.
large, 31.
Hebdomadal, *period*, 108.
Hebe, *beauty*, 845.
Hebetate, *insensible*, 823.
Hecate, *hag*, 846.
Heckle, *question*, 461.
Hectic, *fever*, 382.
flush, 821.
Hector, *courage*, 861.
bully, 885.
Hedge, *enclosure*, 232.
to shuffle, 544.
to compensate, 30.
Hedgehog, *sharpness*, 253.
Hedge in, *enclose*, 231.
safe, 664.
Hedonism, *intemperance*, 954.
Heed, *attend*, 457.
care, 459.
caution, 864.
Heedless, *inattentive*, 458.
neglectful, 460.
Heel, *circuition*, 311.
slope, 217.
Heel-piece, *improvement*, 658.
Heel-tap, *remainder*, 40.
Heels, *rear*, 235.
Heels over head, *reckless*, 460.
Heft, *handle*, 633.
exertion, 686.
Hegemony, *authority*, 737.
Hegira, *departure*, 293.
Heigh-ho! *lamentation*, 839.
Height, *altitude*, 206.
degree, 26.
Height, at its, *superiority*, 33.
Heighten, *increase*, 35.
exalt, 206.
aggravate, 835.
Heinous, *vice*, 945.
Heir, *possessor*, 779.
futurity, 121.
Heir-apparent, *futurity*, 121.
Heir-presumptive, *futurity*, 121.
Heirloom, *property*, 780.
Heliacal, *morning*, 125.
Helicopter, *flying ship*, 273.
Heliograph, *signal*, 550.
Heliotype, *picture*, 556.
Helix, *convolution*, 248.
Hell, *gehenna*, 982.
abyss, 208.
Hell-born, *vice*, 945.
Hell broke loose, *disorder*, 59.
Hellebore, *bane*, 663.
Hell-hound, *miscreant*, 949.
ruffian, 913.
Hellish, *bad*, 649.
malevolent, 907.
vicious, 945.
Helm, *handle*, 633.
authority, 737.
sceptre, 747.
Helmet, *dress*, 225.
defence, 717.
Helot, *servant*, 746.
Help, *aid*, 707.
auxiliary, 711.
utility, 644.
remedy, 662.
(not to), 601.
Helpless, *weak*, 160.
incapable, 158.
irremediable, 659.
exposed, 665.
Helpmate, *auxiliary*, 711.
wife, 903.
Helter-skelter, *disorder*, 59.
haste, 684.
Hem, *edge*, 230.
to stammer, 583.

Hem in, *enclose*, 231.
restrain, 751.
Hemlock, *bane*, 663.
Henbane, *bane*, 663.
Hence, *arising from*, 155.
deduction, 476.
motive, 615.
Henceforth, *futurity*, 121.
Henchman, *servant*, 746.
Hen-pecked, *obedience*, 743.
Heptad, *seven*, 98.
Herald, *messenger*, 534.
omen, 512.
to predict, 511.
to proclaim, 531.
Herb, *plant*, 367.
*Herbarium (L.), *plant*, 367.
Herculean, *strength*, 159.
difficulty, 704.
Herd, *animal*, 366.
flock, 72, 102.
Here, *present*, 186.
Hereabouts, *nearness*, 197.
Hereafter, *futurity*, 121.
Hereditament, *property*, 780.
Hereditary, *derivative*, 154.
habit, 613.
intrinsic, 5.
Heredity, *paternity*, 166.
Heresy, *error*, 495.
religious, 984.
Heretic, *dissent*, 489.
Heretofore, *preterition*, 122.
Herewith, *accompaniment*, 88.
Heritage, *futurity*, 121.
possession, 777.
Heritor, *possessor*, 779.
Hermaphrodite, *incongruity*, 83.
Hermeneutic, *interpretation*, 522.
Hermetically, *closure*, 261.
Hermit, *seclusion*, 893.
Hermitage, *abode*, 189.
Hero, *brave*, 861.
saint, 948.
Heroic, *brave*, 861.
glorious, 873.
magnanimous, 942.
verse, 597.
Heroics, *exaggeration*, 549.
Hesitate, *reluctant*, 603.
irresolute, 605.
uncertainty, 475.
fearful, 860.
sceptical, 485.
to stammer, 583.
*Hetæra (Gr.), *courtesan*, 962.
Heteroclite, *incongruity*, 83.
Heterodox, *heterodoxy*, 984.
Heterogeneous, *mixed*, 10, 15, 41.
multiform, 81.
exceptional, 83.
Heteromorphic, *difference*, 15.
Heuristic, *inquiry*, 461.
Hew, *cut*, 44.
shorten, 201.
fashion, 240.
Hexachord, *melody*, 413.
Hexagon, *numbers*, 98.
Heyday, *wonder*, 870.
success, 731.
exultation, 836.
youth, 127.
Hiatus, *interval*, 198.
opening, 260.
unsubstantiality, 4.
discontinuity, 70.
Hibernal, *cold*, 383.
Hibernate, *sleep*, 683.
Hibernicism, *absurdity*, 497.
Hid, *invisible*, 447.
concealed, 528.
*Hidalgo (Sp.), *master*, 875.
Hide, *conceal*, 528.
skin, 222.
Hideous, *ugly*, 846.
Hiding-place, *refuge*, 666.
ambush, 530.
Hie, *go*, 264, 266, 274.
Hiemal, *cold*, 383.
Hierarchy, *churchdom*, 995.
order, 58.
Hieroglyphic, *letter*, 561.
representation, 554.
unintelligible, 519.
Hierogram, *revelation*, 985.
Hierography, *theology*, 983.
Hieromancy, *prediction*, 511.
Hierophant, *churchman*, 996.
Hieroscopy, *prediction*, 511.
Higgle, *chaffer*, 794.
bargain, 769.
Higgledy-piggledy, *disorder*, 59.
Higgler, *merchant*, 797.
High, *lofty*, 206.
pungent, 392.
proud, 878.
magnanimous, 942.
High-born, *master*, 875.
Higher, *superiority*, 33.
Highfalutin, *exaggeration*, 549.
High-flown, *proud*, 878.
vain, 880.
insolent, 885.
exaggerated, 549.
High-flier, *imagination*, 515.
pride, 878.
High-handed, *insolent*, 885.
Highland, *land*, 342.

High life, *fashion*, 852.
Highly, *great*, 31.
High-mettled, *spirited*, 861.
High-minded, *proud*, 878.
generous, 942.
honourable, 940.
Highness, *title*, 877.
prince, 745.
High-priced, *dear*, 814.
High-seasoned, *pungent*, 392.
obscene, 961.
High-spirited, *courageous*, 861.
High-strung, *excitable*, 825.
Hight, *nomenclature*, 564.
Highway, *road*, 627.
Highwayman, *thief*, 792.
High-wrought, *perfect*, 650.
finished, 729.
excited, 825.
Hilarity, *cheerfulness*, 836
Hill, *height*, 206.
Hillock, *height*, 206.
Hilt, *instrument*, 633.
Hind, *back*, 235.
clown, 876.
Hinder, *back*, 235.
end, 67.
to impede, 179.
obstruct, 706.
prohibit, 761.
Hindrance, *obstruction*, 706.
Hinge, *depend upon*, 154.
cause, 153.
rotate, 312.
fastening, 43, 45.
Hinny, *beast of burden*, 271.
Hint, *suggest*, 505.
inform, 527.
suppose, 514.
Hinterland, *interior*, 221.
Hip, *side*, 236.
Hipped, *dejection*, 837.
Hippocentaur, *incongruity*, 83.
Hippodrome, *arena*, 728.
Hippogriff, *incongruity*, 83.
*Hiraeth (W.), *love*, 897.
Hire, *commission*, 755.
purchase, 795.
Hireling, *servant*, 746.
Hirsute, *rough*, 256.
Hispid, *rough*, 256
Hiss, *sound*, 409.
disapprobation, 932.
disrespect, 929.
Histology, *texture*, 329.
Historian, *recorder*, 553, 594.
Historic, *indication*, 550.
History, *record*, 551.
narrative, 594.
Histrionic, *the drama*, 599.
ostentatious, 882.
Hit, *strike*, 276.
punish, 972.
succeed, 731.
chance, 156, 621.
reach, 292.
agree, 23.
Hit off, *imitate*, 19, 554.
Hit upon, *find*, 480.
Hitch, *difficulty*, 704.
jerk, 315.
hang, 43, 214.
Hither, *arrival*, 292.
Hitherto, *preterition*, 122.
Hive, *workshop*, 691.
multitude, 102.
dwelling, 186.
Hoar, *white*, 430.
aged, 128.
Hoar-frost, *cold*, 383.
Hoard, *store*, 636.
assemblage, 72.
Hoarding, *screen*, 530.
Hoarse, *sound*, 405, 410.
voice, 581.
Hoary, *white*, 430.
aged, 128.
Hoax, *deception*, 545.
Hob, *support*, 215.
Hobble, *limp*, 275.
difficulty, 704.
lame, 732.
awkward, 699.
Hobbledehoy, *youth*, 129.
Hobby, *pursuit*, 622.
desire, 865.
Hobgoblin, *demon*, 980.
Hob-nob, *courtesy*, 894.
Hobson's choice, *necessity*, 601.
Hocus, *deceive*, 545.
stupefy, 376.
Hocus-pocus, *cheat*, 545.
conjuration, 992.
Hod, *receptacle*, 191.
vehicle, 272.
Hodge, *clown*, 876.
Hodge-podge, *mixture*, 41.
confusion, 59.
Hog, *sensuality*, 954.
gluttony, 957.
Hog, to go the whole, *completeness*, 52.
Hog-wash, *uncleanness*, 653.
Hoist, *elevate*, 307.
Hoity-toity! *wonder*, 870.
Hold, *possess*, 777.
believe, 484.
retain, 781.

Hookah, *tobacco-pipe*, 351.
Hooker, *ship*, 273.
Hooligan, *ruffian*, 913, 949.
Hooliganism, *brutality*, 907.
Hoop, *circle*, 247.
Hoot, *cry*, 411.
deride, 929, 930.
scout, 932.
Hooter, *indication*, 550.
Hop, *leap*, 305, 309.
dance, 840.
Hop the twig, *move off*, 287.
die, 360.
Hope, *hope*, 858.
Hopeful, *probable*, 472.
Hopeless, *desperate*, 859.
impossible, 471.
irreparable, 659.
Horde, *assemblage*, 72.
Horizon, *distance*, 196.
view, 441.
futurity, 121.
Horizontal, *horizontality*, 213.
Horn, *sharpness*, 253.
(French), *musical*, 417.
Horn-book, *school*, 542.
Horn-mad, *jealousy*, 920.
Horn of plenty, *sufficient*, 639.
Hornet, *bane*, 663, 830.
Hornpipe, *dance*, 840.
Hornwork, *defence*, 717.
Horny, *hard*, 323.
Horology, *chronometry*, 114.
Horoscope, *prediction*, 511.
Horrible, *great*, 31.
fearful, 860.
Horrid, *noxious*, 649.
ugly, 846.
dire, 830.
vulgar, 851.
fearful, 860.
hateful, 898.
Horripilation, *cold*, 383.
terror, 860.
Horror, *dislike*, 867.
hate, 898.
terror, *fear*, 860.
*Hors de combat (Fr.), *impotence*, 158.
disease, 655.
*Hors d'œuvre (Fr.), *food*, 298.
Horse, *animal*, 271.
cavalry, 726.
stand, 215.
Horse-laugh, *laugh*, 838.
Horseman, *traveller*, 268.
Horse-play, *violence*, 173.
Horse-sense, *wisdom*, 498.
Horseshoe, *curvature*, 245.
Horsewhip, *punishment*, 972.
Hortation, *advice*, 615, 695.
Horticulture, *agriculture*, 371.
*Hortus siccus (L.), *plant*, 367.
Hosanna, *worship*, 990.
Hose, *dress*, 225.
conduit, 350.
Hospice, *abode*, 189.
Hospitable, *social*, 892.
liberal, 816.
Hospital, *remedy*, 662.
Hospodar, *master*, 745.
Host, *multitude*, 100.
collection, 72.
friend, 890.
religious, 999.
Hostage, *security*, 771.
Hostel, *inn*, 189.
Hostilities, *warfare*, 722.
Hostility, *enmity*, 889.
Hot, *warm*, 382.
pungent, 392.
irascible, 901.
Hot-bed, *workshop*, 691.
cause, 153.
Hotchpotch, *mixture*, 41.
confusion, 59.
Hotel, *inn*, 189.
Hot-brained, *rash*, 863.
excited, 825.
Hot-headed, *rash*, 863.
excited, 825.
Hothouse, *conservatory*, 386.
workshop, 691.
Hotspur, *rashness*, 863.
courage, 861.
Hottentot, *boor*, 876.
Hot water, *difficulty*, 704.
Hough, *maltreat*, 649.
Hound, *pursue*, 281, 622.
wretch, 949.
Hour, *period*, 108.
Hour-glass, *time*, 114.
form, 203.
Houri, *beauty*, 845.
House, *abode*, 189.
to locate, 184.
safety, 664.
party, 712.
senate, 696.
partnership, 797.
House-boat, *abode*, 189.
Housebreaker, *thief*, 792.
Household, *abode*, 189.
conformity, 82.
property, 780.
Housekeeper, *director*, 694.
Housekeeping, *conduct*, 692.
Houseless, *displacement*, 185.

Housemaid, *servant*, 746.
House-warming, *sociality*, 892.
Housewife, *activity*, 682.
Housewifery, *conduct*, 692.
economy, 817.
Housing, *lodging*, 189.
Hovel, *abode*, 189.
Hover, *soar*, 267.
rise, 305.
high, 206.
How, *in what way*, 627.
by what means, 632.
Howbeit, *counteraction*, 179.
Howdah, *seat*, 215.
How-d'ye-do, *difficulty*, 704.
However, *except*, 83.
notwithstanding, 179.
degree, 23.
compensation, 30.
Howitzer, *arms*, 727.
Howl, *ululation*, 411, 412, 839.
Howsoever, *degree*, 26.
Hoy, *ship*, 273.
Hoyden, *vulgarity*, 851.
Hub, *centre*, 223.
Hubble-bubble, *tobacco-pipe*, 351.
Hubbub, *noise*, 402.
discord, 713.
Huckster, *merchant*, 797.
Huddle, *mix*, 41.
disorder, 59.
derange, 61.
collect, 72.
don, 225.
nearness, 197.
Hue, *colour*, 428.
Hue and cry, *noise*, 404.
outcry, 931.
proclamation, 531.
Hueless, *achromatism*, 429.
Huff, *anger*, 900.
insolence, 885.
Huffiness, *irascibility*, 901.
Hug, *cohere*, 46.
retain, 781.
endearment, 894, 902.
Hug the shore, *approach*, 286.
Huge, *in degree*, 31.
in size, 192.
Hugger-mugger, *confusion*, 59.
Hulk, *whole*, 50.
ship, 273.
Hulking, *big*, 192.
awkward, 853.
Hull, *whole*, 50.
Hullabaloo, *noise*, 404.
cry, 411.
Hum, *faint sound*, 405.
continued sound, 407, 412.
Hum, *to sing*, 415.
deceive, 545.
Hum and ha, *hesitate*, 583.
demur, 605.
Human, *mankind*, 372.
Humane, *benevolent*, 906.
philanthropic, 910.
Humanism, *knowledge*, 490.
Humanist, *scholar*, 492.
Humanitarian, *philanthropist*, 906.
Humanities, *letters*, 560.
Humanity, *human nature*, 372.
benevolence, 906.
Humanise, *courtesy*, 894.
Humble, *meek*, 879.
modest, 881.
to abash, 874.
pious, 987.
Humbug, *deception*, 545.
falsehood, 544.
Humdrum, *dull*, 843.
Humectate, *moisten*, 339.
Humid, *moist*, 339.
Humiliate, *humble*, 879.
shame, 874.
worship, 990.
Humility, *piety*, 987.
Humming-top, *musical*, 417.
Hummock, *height*, 206, 250.
Hum-note, *melody*, 413.
Humoresque, *music*, 415.
Humorist, *humorist*, 844.
Humour, *essence*, 5.
liquid, 333.
disposition, 602.
caprice, 608.
indulge, 760.
affections, 820.
to please, 829.
wit, 842.
Humoursome, *capricious*, 608.
discourteous, 895.
Hump, *convexity*, 250.
Humpbacked, *distortion*, 243.
ugliness, 846.
Humph! *wonder*, 870.
Humus, *soil*, 342.
Hun, *evil-doer*, 913.
Hunch, *convexity*, 250.
Hundred, *number*, 99.
Hunger, *desire*, 865.
Hungry, *sterile*, 169.
Hunks, *parsimony*, 819.
Hunnish, *malevolent*, 907.
Hunt, *follow*, 281.
pursue, 622.
inquire, 461.
Hunter, *carrier*, 271.
Hurdle, *fence*, 232.

Hurdy-gurdy, *musical*, 417.
Hurl, *propel*, 284.
Hurly-burly, *confusion*, 59.
turmoil, 315.
Hurrah! *cheerfulness*, 836.
Hurricane, *tempest*, 349.
violence, 173.
Hurried, *excitability*, 825.
Hurry, *haste*, 684.
swiftness, 274.
earliness, 132.
to urge, 615.
to excite, 824.
Hurst, *plant*, 367.
Hurt, *evil*, 619.
physical pain, 378.
moral pain, 828.
to injure, 649, 907.
to molest, 830.
Hurtful, *badness*, 649.
Hurtle, *impulse*, 276.
Husband, *spouse*, 903.
to store, 636.
Husbandman, *agriculture*, 371.
Husbandry, *agriculture*, 371.
conduct, 692.
economy, 817.
Hush, *silence*, 403.
moderate, 174.
assuage, 826.
pacify, 723.
Hush-boat, *deception*, 545.
Hush up, *conceal*, 528.
Hush-money, *bribe*, 809.
Husk, *covering*, 222.
to strip, 226.
Husky, *dry*, 340.
faint sound, 405, 501.
Hussar, *combatant*, 726.
Hussy, *libertine*, 962.
impertinent, 887.
Hustings, *tribunal*, 966.
platform, 542.
Hustle, *push*, 276.
disarrange, 61.
agitate, 315.
bustle, 682.
Hut, *abode*, 189.
Hutch, *cage*, 191.
Huzza! *cheerfulness*, 836.
Hyaline, *transparency*, 425.
Hybrid, *mixture*, 41.
nondescript, 83.
Hydra, *unconformity*, 83.
Hydraulics, *fluids*, 348.
Hydrology, *water*, 333.
Hydromancy, *prediction*, 511.
Hydromel, *sweetness*, 396.
Hydrometer, *density*, 321.
Hydropathy, *remedy*, 662.
Hydrophobia, *dislike*, 867.
Hydroplane, *ship*, 273.
Hydrostatics, *water*, 333.
Hyena, *evil-doer*, 913.
Hygiene, *salubrity*, 656.
Hymen, *marriage*, 903.
Hymn, *worship*, 990.
Hyperæsthesia, *excitability*, 825.
Hyperbole, *exaggeration*, 549.
Hyperborean, *cold*, 383.
Hypercritical, *disapprobation*, 932.
Hyperion, *beauty*, 845.
Hypermetropia, *vision*, 443.
Hypersensitive, *sensitive*, 375, 825.
Hypertrophy, *size*, 192.
Hyphen, *vinculum*, 45.
Hypnosis, *inactivity*, 683.
Hypnotise, *entrance*, 992.
Hypocaust, *furnace*, 386.
Hypochondriac, *dejection*, 837.
Hypocrisy, *deception*, 545.
religious, 989.
Hypocrite, *deceiver*, 548.
Hypocritical, *falsehood*, 544.
Hypostasis, *substantiality*, 3.
Hypostatic, *Deity*, 976.
Hypothecation, *lending*, 787.
Hypothesis, *supposition*, 514.
Hysterical, *violence*, 173.
excitement, 825.
*Hysteron proteron (Gr.), *inversion* 218.

I

Icarus, *ascent*, 305.
Ice, *cold*, 383.
Ice-house, *refrigeratory*, 387.
Ichnography, *representation*, 554.
Ichor, *liquidity*, 333.
Ichthyomancy, *prediction*, 511.
Icicle, *cold*, 383.
Icy, *discourteous*, 895.
*Incognito (It.), *secrecy*, 528.
Icon, *representation*, 554.
Idea, *notion*, 453.
belief, 484.
knowledge, 490.
small degree, 32.
small quantity, 192.
inexistence, 2.
Ideal, *erroneous*, 495.
unreal, 2, 515.
pleasurable, 829.
Ideality, *intellect*, 450.
imagination, 515.
Ideate, *imagine*, 515.
apprehend, 490.

*Idée fixe (Fr.), *misjudgment*, 481.
Identify, *comparison*, 464.
Identity, *identity*, 13.
Ideologist, *doctrinaire*, 493.
Ideology, *intellect*, 450.
*Id est (L.), *interpretation*, 522.
Idiocy, *folly*, 499.
Idiom, *phrase*, 566.
style, 569.
Idiosyncrasy, *essence*, 5.
speciality, 79.
temperament, 820.
Idiot, *imbecile*, 501.
foolish, 499.
Idle, *slothful*, 683.
trivial, 643.
Ido, *language*, 560.
Idol, *favourite*, 899.
Idolatry, *superstition*, 984.
impious worship, 991.
love, 897.
Idolise, *love*, 897.
impiety, 989.
Idyll, *poetry*, 597.
If, *supposition*, 514.
qualification, 469.
Igneous, *heat*, 382.
*Ignis fatuus (L.), *light*, 420.
phantom, 515.
unsubstantial, 4.
dim sight, 443.
error, 495.
Ignite, *calefaction*, 384.
Ignition, *heat*, 382.
Ignoble, *base*, 876.
Ignominy, *dishonour*, 940.
shame, 874.
Ignoramus, *ignoramus*, 493.
Ignorant, *ignorance*, 491.
Ignore, *repudiate*, 773.
dissent, 489.
Ilk, *identity*, 13.
Ill, *sick*, 655.
evil, 619.
Ill-advised, *foolish*, 499, 699.
Ill-assorted, *disagreement*, 24.
Illation, *judgment*, 480.
Ill-bred, *discourtesy*, 895.
Ill-conditioned, *discourteous*, 895.
malevolent, 907.
vicious, 945.
Ill-advised, *folly*, 499.
Illegal, *illegality*, 964.
Illegible, *unintelligibility*, 519.
Illegitimate, *undue*, 925.
illegal, 964.
erroneous, 495.
Ill-favoured, *ugliness*, 846.
Ill-flavoured, *unsavouriness*, 395.
Illiberal, *selfish*, 943.
stingy, 819.
Illlicit, *illegality*, 964.
Illimitable, *infinite*, 105.
great, 31.
Illiterate, *ignorance*, 491.
Ill-looking, *ugliness*, 846.
Ill-natured, *malevolence*, 907.
Illness, *disease*, 655.
Ill-judged, *foolish*, 492, 499.
ill-advised, 699.
Ill off, *adversity*, 735.
Illogical, *sophistical*, 477.
erroneous, 495.
Ill-sorted, *disagreement*, 24.
Ill-omened, *evil*, 649.
disagreeable, 858.
Ill-starred, *adversity*, 735.
Ill-temper, *discourtesy*, 895.
irascibility, 901.
Ill-timed, *inappropriate*, 24.
untimely, 135.
Ill-treat, *injure*, 649, 907.
Ill-turn, *evil*, 619.
Illuminate, *enlighten*, 420.
colour, 428.
*Illuminati (It.), *scholar*, 492.
Illumination, *drawing*, 556.
ornament, 847.
Illusion, *error*, 495.
deceit, 545.
Illusionist, *conjuror*, 548.
Illusive, *erroneous*, 495.
sophistical, 477.
deceitful, 544.
Illusory, *see* Illusive.
Illustration, *interpretation*, 522.
drawing, 556.
ornament, 847.
example, 82.
Illustrious, *repute*, 873.
Ill will, *malevolence*, 907.
Image, *representation*, 554.
idea, 453.
statue, 557.
likeness, 17.
Imagery, *metaphor*, 521.
fancy, 515.
Imaginary, *non-existing*, 2.
erroneous, 495.
quantity, 84.
Imagination, *fancy*, 515.
wit, 842.
Imam, *clergy*, 996.
Imbecile, *foolish*, 477, 499.
weak, 160.
incapable, 158.
Imbibe, *receive*, 296.
learn, 539.

Imbricated, *covering*, 222.
Imbroglio, *unintelligibility*, 519.
discord, 713.
Imbrue, *moisten*, 339.
impregnate, 300.
Imbue, *mix*, 41.
tinge, 428.
impregnate, 300.
moisten, 339.
teach, 537.
feel, 821.
Imitate, *to copy*, 19.
repetition, 104.
to represent, 554.
Imitation, *copy*, 21.
Immaculate, *excellent*, 648.
spotless, 652.
faultless, 650.
innocent, 946.
Immanent, *inherent*, 5.
Immanity, *malevolence*, 907.
Immaterial, *unsubstantial*, 4.
spiritual, 317.
mental, 450.
trifling, 643.
Immature, *new*, 123.
unprepared, 674.
Immeasurable, *infinite*, 105.
great, 31.
Immediate, *transient*, 111.
Immedicable, *incurable*, 655, 659.
Immemorial, *old*, 124.
Immense, *in degree*, 31.
in size, 192.
Immerse, *introduce*, 300.
dip, 337.
Immethodical, *disorder*, 59.
Immigration, *migration*, 266.
entrance, 294.
Imminent, *futurity*, 121.
Immiscibility, *incoherence*, 47.
Immission, *reception*, 296.
Immitigable, *ire*, 900.
violence, 173.
ruin, 659.
Immobility, *immutability*, 150.
quiescence, 265.
resolution, 604.
Immoderately, *greatness*, 31.
Immodest, *impurity*, 961.
Immolate, *destroy*, 162.
kill, 361.
offer, 763.
Immolation, *sacrifice*, 991.
Immoral, *vicious*, 945.
wrong, 923.
Immortal, *perpetual*, 112.
glorious, 873.
celebrated, 883.
Immovable, *unchangeable*, 150.
resolved, 604.
Immunity, *exemption*, 927.
right, 924.
freedom, 748.
Immure, *enclose*, 231.
imprison, 751.
Immutable, *immutability*, 150.
Imp, *demon*, 980.
ruffian, 913.
wretch, 943.
Impact, *contact*, 43.
impulse, 276.
insertion, 300.
Impair, *deterioration*, 659.
Impale, *transfix*, 260.
pierce, 302.
execute, 972.
Impalpable, *small*, 193.
powder, 330.
intangible, 381.
Impanation, *rite*, 998.
Imparity, *inequality*, 28.
Impart, *give*, 784.
inform, 527.
Impartial, *just*, 922.
honourable, 939.
Impassable, *closed*, 261, 704.
Impasse, *hindrance*, 706.
difficulty, 704.
Impassible, *insensible*, 376, 823.
Impassion, *excite*, 824.
Impassive, *insensible*, 823.
Impasto, *painting*, 556.
Impatient, *excitable*, 825.
Impawn, *lending*, 787.
Impeach, *accuse*, 938.
Impeccability, *perfection*, 650.
Impede, *hindrance*, 706.
Impedimenta, *hindrance*, 706.
baggage, 635.
Impel, *push*, 276, 284.
induce, 615.
Impend, *future*, 121.
height, 206.
destiny, 152.
Impenetrable, *latent*, 526.
hidden, 528.
Impenitence, *impenitence*, 951.
Imperative, *authority*, 737.
*Imperator (L.), *master*, 745.
Imperceptible, *invisible*, 447.
minute, 193.
Impercipient, *insensibility*, 376.
Imperfect, *incomplete*, 53.
failing, 651.
vicious, 945.
small, 32.
Imperforate, *closure*, 261.

Imperial, *authority*, 737.
beard, 256.
Imperil, *endanger*, 665.
Imperious, *stern*, 739.
insolent, 885.
Imperishable, *external*, 112, 150.
glorious, 873.
Impermanent, *transitory*, 111.
Impermeable, *closed*, 261.
dense, 321.
Impersonal, *generality*, 78.
Impersonate, *represent*, 554.
imitate, 19.
Impertinence, *inexpedience*, 647.
Impertinent, *irrelevant*, 10.
disagreeing, 24.
insolent, 885.
Imperturbable, *unruffled*, 823, 826.
Impervious, *closure*, 261.
Impetrate, *beseech*, 765.
Impetuous, *boisterous*, 173.
hot, 825.
hasty, 684.
eager, 865.
Impetus, *impulse*, 276.
Impiety, *impiety*, 899.
Impignorate, *lending*, 787.
Impinge, *impulse*, 276.
Impish, *supernatural*, 980.
Implacable, *hatred*, 898.
wrath, 900.
unforgiving, 919.
Implanted, *adventitious*, 6.
Implant, *insert*, 300.
teach, 537.
Implement, *instrument*, 633.
Impletion, *sufficiency*, 639.
Implicate, *accuse*, 938.
involve, 54.
Implication, *inference*, 521.
Implicit, *understood*, 516.
metaphorical, 521.
trust, 484.
Implore, *beseech*, 765.
pray, 990.
pity, 914.
Imply, *mean*, 516.
latent, 526.
evidence, 467.
metaphor, 521.
Impolite, *rude*, 895.
vulgar, 851.
Impolitic, *folly*, 499.
Imponderable, *light*, 320.
Import, *ingress*, 294.
transfer, 270.
insert, 300.
mean, 516.
be of consequence, 642.
Import, *receive*, 296.
Importance, *greatness*, 31.
Important, *importance*, 642.
Importunate, *painfulness*, 830.
Importune, *ask*, 765.
pester, 830.
Impose, *order*, 741.
cheat, 545.
be unjust, 923.
palm upon, 486.
Imposing, *grand*, 873.
Impossible, *incredible*, 471.
impracticable, 704.
Impost, *price*, 812.
Impostor, *deceiver*, 548.
Imposture, *deception*, 545.
Impotence, *impotence*, 158.
Impound, *enclose*, 231.
imprison, 751.
Impoverish, *drain*, 638.
render poor, 804.
Impracticable, *difficult*, 704.
impossible, 471.
obstinate, 606.
Imprecation, *request*, 765.
malediction, 908.
Impregnable, *safety*, 664.
Impregnate, *insert*, 300.
mix, 41.
teach, 537.
Impresario, *drama*, 599.
Imprescriptible, *dueness*, 924.
Impress, *mark*, 550.
memory, 505.
excite, 375, 824.
compel, 744.
Impressible, *sensibility*, 822.
Impression, *belief*, 375, 484.
idea, 453.
feeling, 821.
engraving, 558.
Impressive, *exciting*, 824.
notable, 642.
Impressionist, *artist*, 559.
*Imprimatur (L.), *sanction*, 924.
*Imprimis (L.), *beginning*, 66.
Imprint, *indication*, 550.
Imprison, *shut up*, 751.
circumscribe, 231.
Improbable, *improbability*, 473.
Improbity, *improbity*, 940.
Impromptu, *impulse*, 612.
music, 415.
Improper, *wrong*, 923, 925.
inexpedient, 499, 647.
incongruous, 24.
unseemly, 961.
Impropriate, *take*, 789.
possess, 777.

Improve, *improvement*, 658.
Improvident, *careless*, 460.
not preparing, 674, 863.
Improvise, *impulse*, 612.
Imprudent, *rash*, 863.
unwise, 699.
neglectful, 460.
Impudent, *insolence*, 885.
Impudicity, *impurity*, 961.
Impugn, *blame*, 932.
deny, 536.
Impuissance, *impotence*, 158.
Impulse, *push*, 276.
unpremeditation, 612.
necessity, 601.
Impulsive, *instinctive*, 477.
motive, 615.
Impunity, *acquittal*, 970.
Impure, *foul*, 653.
licentious, 961.
Impute, *ascribe*, 155.
accuse, 938.
Inability, *want of power*, 158.
want of skill, 699.
Inaccessible, *distance*, 196.
Inaccurate, *error*, 495, 568.
Inaction, *inaction*, 681.
Inactivity, *inactivity*, 172, 683.
Inadaptability, *disagreement*, 24.
Inadequate, *insufficient*, 640, 645.
imperfect, 651.
weak, 158, 160.
Inadmissible, *inexpedient*, 647.
incongruous, 24.
excluded, 55.
Inadvertence, *inattention*, 458.
Inalienable, *right*, 924.
possession, 777.
*Inamorata (It.), *love*, 897.
Inane, *trivial*, 643.
void, 4.
Inanimate, *dead*, 360.
inorganic, 358.
Inanition, *insufficiency*, 640.
Inanity, *inutility*, 645.
insignificance, 643.
Inappetence, *indifference*, 866.
Inapplicable, *irrelation*, 10.
disagree, 24.
Inapposite, *disagree*, 24.
Inappreciable, *in size*, 193.
in degree, 32.
Inapprehensible, *unknowable*, 519.
Inappropriate, *discordant*, 24.
inexpedient, 647.
Inapt, *inexpedient*, 647.
incongruous, 24.
Inaptitude, *impotence*, 158.
Inarticulate, *stammering*, 583.
Inartistic, *unskilled*, 699.
imperfect, 651.
Inartificial, *artlessness*, 703.
Inattention, *indifference*, 458.
Inaudible, *silent*, 403, 405.
mute, 581.
Inaugurate, *begin*, 66.
celebrate, 883.
Inauguration, *commission*, 755.
Inauspicious, *hopeless*, 859.
untimely, 135.
untoward, 649.
Inbeing, *intrinsicality*, 5.
Inborn, *intrinsic*, 5, 820.
habitual, 613.
Inbred, *intrinsic*, 5, 820.
Incalculable, *infinite*, 105.
much, 31.
Incalescence, *heat*, 382.
Incandescence, *heat*, 382.
light, 420.
Incantation, *invocation*, 765.
spell, 993.
Incapable, *weak*, 160.
unable, 158.
Incapacity, *impotence*, 158.
weakness, 160.
stupidity, 499.
indocility, 538.
Incarcerate, *imprison*, 751.
surround, 231.
Incarnadine, *red*, 434.
Incarnation, *intrinsic*, 5.
Incautious, *neglectful*, 460.
rash, 863.
Incendiary, *evil-doer*, 913.
Incense, *fragrance*, 400.
to provoke, 900.
hatred, 898.
flattery, 933.
worship, 990.
Incentive, *motive*, 615.
Inception, *beginning*, 66.
Inceptor, *learner*, 541.
Incertitude, *uncertain*, 475.
Incessant, *perpetual*, 112.
frequency, 136.
Incest, *impurity*, 961.
Inch, *littleness*, 193.
Inch by inch, *degree*, 26.
Inchoate, *amorphous*, 241.
Inchoation, *beginning*, 66.
Incidence, *direction*, 278.
Incident, *event*, 151.
Incidental, *extrinsic*, 6, 8.
irrelative, 10.
liable, 177.
casual, 156, 621.
Incinerate, *calefaction*, 384.

Incipient, *beginning*, 66.
style, 574.
Incision, *cut*, 44.
Incisive, *style*, 574.
Incite, *urge*, 615.
exasperate, 173.
Incivility, *rudeness*, 895.
Incivism, *misanthropy*, 911.
Inclement, *cold*, 383.
severe, 739.
Incline, *slope*, 217.
direction, 278.
tendency, 176.
willing, 602.
desire, 862.
love, 897.
induce, 615.
Inclusive, *in a compound*, 54.
in a class, 76.
Incogitable, *incogitancy*, 452.
Incognisable, *unknowable*, 519.
Incognisance, *ignorance*, 491.
*Incognito (It.), *concealment*, 528.
Incoherent, *physical*, 47.
mental, 503.
meaning, 519.
Incombustible, *cold*, 383.
Income, *receipt*, 810.
wealth, 803.
Incommensurable, *quantity*, 84.
irrelation, 10.
disagreeing, 24.
Incommode, *to hinder*, 706.
annoy, 830.
Incommodious, *inconvenient*, 647.
Incommunicable, *retention*, 781.
Incommutable, *unchangeable*, 150.
Incomparable, *goodness*, 648.
Incompatible, *disagree*, 24.
Incompetence, *inability*, 158.
incapacity, 499.
insufficiency, 640.
unskilfulness, 699.
Incomplete, *defective*, 53.
not completed, 730.
Incomprehensible, *unintelligible*, 519.
Incomprehension, *ignorance*, 491.
Incompressible, *density*, 321.
Inconceivable, *unintelligible*, 519.
incredible, 485.
Inconclusive, *sophistry*, 477.
Incondite, *inelegant*, 579.
Incongruous, *disagreement*, 24.
Inconsecutive, *discontinuous*, 70.
Inconsiderable, *in size*, 193.
in degree, 32.
Inconsiderate, *thoughtless*, 452.
heedless, 460.
foolish, 699.
Inconsistent, *contrary*, 14.
disagreeing, 24.
absurd, 497.
capricious, 608.
Inconsolable, *pain*, 828.
Inconsonance, *disagreement*, 24.
Inconspicuous, *invisible*, 447.
latent, 526.
Inconstant, *irresolution*, 605.
Incontestable, *certainty*, 474.
Incontinent, *impurity*, 961.
Incontinently, *transient*, 111.
Incontrovertible, *certainty*, 474.
Inconvenient, *inexpedient*, 647.
Inconvertible, *immutable*, 150.
Inconvincible, *incredulity*, 487.
Incorporate, *combination*, 48.
Incorporeal, *immaterial*, 317.
Incorrect, *erroneous*, 495, 568.
sophistical, 477.
Incorrigible, *vicious*, 945.
impenitent, 951.
irremediable, 649.
Incorruptible, *honourable*, 939.
pure, 942.
Incorruption, *health*, 654.
innocence, 946.
Incrassate, *thickness*, 202.
density, 321.
Increase, *in degree*, 35.
in size, 194.
Incredible, *impossible*, 471.
improbable, 473, 485.
much, 31.
wonderful, 870.
Incredulity, *unbelief*, 487.
religious, 988.
Increment, *increase, in degree*, 35.
in size, 194.
addition, 39.
Incrustation, *covering*, 222.
Incubation, *preparation*, 673.
Incubus, *hindrance*, 706.
Inculcate, *teach*, 537.
Inculpate, *accuse*, 938.
Incumbent, *height*, 206.
weight, 319.
duty, 926.
clergyman, 996.
*Incunabula (L.), *beginning*, 66.
book, 591.
Incur, *liable*, 177.
Incurable, *disease*, 655.
Incuriosity, *incurious*, 456.
Incursion, *ingress*, 294.
Incurvation, *curvature*, 245.
Indebted, *owing*, 806.
duty, 926.
gratitude, 916.

Indecent, *impure*, 961.
Indecision, *irresolute*, 605.
Indecisive, *uncertain*, 475.
inconclusive, 477.
Indeclinable, *immutable*, 150.
Indecorum, *vice*, 945.
impurity, 961.
vulgarity, 851.
Indeed, *very*, 31.
wonder, 870.
truth, 494.
assertion, 535.
Indefatigable, *activity*, 682.
Indefeasible, *dueness*, 150, 924.
Indefectible, *perfection*, 650.
Indefensible, *wrong*, 945.
inexcusable, 938.
weak, 160, 725.
Indefinite, *vague*, 447, 519.
uncertain, 475.
inexact, 495.
infinite, 105.
in degree, 31.
Indelible, *mark*, 550.
condition, 150.
memory, 505.
feeling, 821.
Indelicate, *impurity*, 961.
Indemnify, *reward*, 973.
compensate, 30.
Indentation, *notch*, 252, 257.
Indenture, *record*, 551.
security, 771.
evidence, 467.
compact, 769.
Independence, *irrelation*, 10.
wealth, 803.
freedom, 748.
Indescribable, *wonder*, 870.
Indestructible, *perpetual*, 112.
Indeterminate, *uncertain*, 475.
chance, 156.
Indetermination, *irresolution*, 605.
Index, *sign*, 550.
list, 86, 562.
numerical exponent, 84.
India-rubber, *elasticity*, 325.
Indicate, *point out*, 550.
manifest, 525.
evidence, 467.
Indict, *arraign*, 969.
accuse, 938.
Indictable, *criminal*, 945.
Indifference, *unconcern*, 866.
coldness, 823.
unwillingness, 603.
unimportance, 643.
imperfect, 651.
Indigene, *inhabitant*, 188.
Indigenous, *intrinsic*, 5.
Indigent, *poor*, 804.
insufficient, 640.
Indignation, *resentment*, 900.
Indignity, *insult*, 929.
affront, 900.
outrage, 830.
Indigo, *blueness*, 438.
Indirect, *obliquity*, 217.
Indiscernible, *invisible*, 447.
Indiscerptible, *unity*, 50.
whole, 87.
dense, 321.
Indiscreet, *unskilful*, 699.
blamable, 945.
neglectful, 460.
foolish, 499.
Indiscretion, *guilt*, 947.
Indiscriminate, *multiform*, 81.
unarranged, 59.
casual, 621.
Indiscrimination, *neglect*, 460.
indistinction, 465A.
Indispensable, *requirement*, 630.
Indisposed, *disincline*, 603.
to dissuade, 616.
sick, 655.
Indisputable, *certainty*, 474.
Indissoluble, *whole*, 50.
dense, 321.
united, 43.
unchangeable, 150.
Indistinct, *vague*, 519.
dim, 447.
Indistinguishable, *minute*, 447.
identical, 13.
Indite, *write*, 509.
Individual, *special*, 79.
unity, 87.
whole, 50.
style, 574.
Indivisible, *whole*, 50.
dense, 321.
Indocility, *obstinacy*, 606.
incapacity, 538.
Indoctrinate, *teach*, 484, 537.
Indolence, *inactivity*, 683.
Indomitable, *resolution*, 604.
courage, 861.
unyielding, 719.
Indraught, *current*, 348.
Indubitable, *certainty*, 474.
Induce, *motive*, 615.
cause, 153,
produce, 161.
Induction, *investigation*, 461.
reasoning, 476.
of a priest, 995.
appointment, 755.

Indulge, *allow*, 760.
give, 784.
lenity, 740.
pleasure, 827.
pleasing, 829.
intemperance, 954.
satisfy, 831.
Induration, *hardening*, 323.
impenitence, 951.
Industry, *activity*, 682.
business, 625.
Indweller, *inhabitant*, 188.
Inebriety, *drunkenness*, 959.
Inedible, *unsavoury*, 395.
Ineffable, *wonder*, 870.
Ineffably, *greatness*, 31.
Ineffaceable, *memory*, 505.
feeling, 821.
Ineffectual, *incapable*, 158.
weak, 160.
useless, 645.
failing, 732.
Inefficacious, *see* Ineffectual.
Inefficient, *see* Ineffectual.
Inelastic, *not elastic*, 326.
soft, 324.
Inelegant, *ugly*, 846.
in style, 579.
Ineligible, *inexpedience*, 647.
Ineluctable, *destiny*, 152.
Inept, *incapable*, 158, 699.
useless, 645.
Inequality, *inequality*, 28.
Inequitable, *wrong*, 923.
Inerrable, *innocence*, 946.
Inert, *physically*, 172, 683.
morally, 823.
Inertia, *inertness*, 172.
Inestimable, *goodness*, 648.
Inevitable, *destiny*, 152, 601.
certain, 474.
Inexact, *error*, 495.
Inexcitability, *inexcitability*, 826.
Inexcusable, *vice*, 938, 945.
Inexecution, *non-completion*, 730.
Inexhaustible, *sufficiency*, 639.
Inexistence, *inexistence*, 2.
Inexorable, *resolved*, 604.
stern, 739.
compelling, 744.
wrathful, 900.
relentless, 907.
Inexpectation, *inexpectation*, 508.
Inexpedient, *inexpedience*, 647.
Inexpensive, *cheapness*, 815.
Inexperience, *ignorance*, 491.
disqualification, 699.
Inexpert, *unskilfulness*, 699.
Inexpiable, *vice*, 945.
Inexplicable, *unintelligible*, 519.
wonderful, 870.
Inexpressible, *unmeaning*, 517.
wonder, 870.
great degree, 31.
Inexpressive, *unmeaning*, 517.
Inexpugnable, *safety*, 664.
*In extenso (L.), *whole*, 50.
diffuse, 573.
*In extremis (L.), *death*, 360.
Inextinguishable, *immutable*, 150.
energetic, 157.
Inextricable, *difficult*, 704.
disorder, 59.
Infallible, *certainty*, 474.
Infamy, *dishonour*, 940.
shame, 874.
vice, 945.
Infancy, *beginning*, 66.
youth, 127.
Infant, *infant*, 129.
*Infanta (Sp.), *master*, 745.
Infantile, *puerile*, 643.
foolish, 499.
Infantry, *combatant*, 726.
Infatuation, *folly*, 499.
obstinacy, 606.
credulity, 486.
passion, 825.
love, 897.
Infeasible, *impossible*, 471.
difficult, 704.
Infection, *disease*, 655.
contamination, 659.
excitation, 824.
Infectious, *insalubrity*, 657.
Infecund, *unproductiveness*, 169.
Infelicity, *unhappiness*, 828.
inexpertness, 699.
Infer, *judgment*, 480.
Inference, *judgment*, 480.
interpretation, 522.
Inferior, *less*, 34.
imperfect, 651.
Infernal, *bad*, 649.
wicked, 945.
malevolent, 907.
Infertility, *unproductiveness*, 169.
Infest, *annoy*, 649, 830.
Infibulation, *junction*, 43.
Infidelity, *dishonour*, 940.
irreligion, 988.
Infiltrate, *intervene*, 228.
imbue, 339.
teach, 537.
mixture, 41.
Infiltration, *ingress*, 294, 302.
Infinite, *in quantity*, 105.
in degree, 31.

Infinite, *in size*, 192.
Infinitesimal, *in degree*, 32.
in quantity, 193.
Infirm, *weak*, 160.
irresolute, 605.
vicious, 945.
Infirmary, *remedy*, 662.
Infirmity, *weakness*, 160.
disease, 655.
failing, 945.
Infix, *teaching*, 537.
Inflame, *burn*, 384.
stir up, 173.
incense, 900.
incite, 615.
Inflate, *expand*, 194.
rarefy, 322.
blow, 349.
style, 573, 577.
ridiculous, 853.
vanity, 880.
Inflect, *curvature*, 245.
grammar, 567.
Inflexible, *hard*, 323.
resolved, 604.
stern, 739.
Inflexion, *curvature*, 245.
grammar, 567.
Inflict, *condemn*, 971.
act upon, 680.
give pain, 830.
Influence, *physical*, 175.
authority, 737.
inducement, 615.
importance, 642.
Influential, *important*, 642.
Influx, *ingress*, 294.
Inform, *information*, 527.
Inform against, *accusation*, 938.
Informal, *irregular*, 83.
lawless, 964.
Information, *knowledge*, 490.
communication, 527.
Infraction, *non-observance*, 773.
unconformity, 83.
exemption, 927.
disobedience, 742.
violation, 614.
*Infra dignitatem (L.), *disrepute*, 874.
Infrangible, *coherence*, 46, 321.
Infrequency, *infrequency*, 137.
Infringe, *transgress*, 303.
violate, 773, 925, 927.
break through, 614.
Infundibular, *concavity*, 252.
Infuriate, *wrathful*, 900.
violent, 173.
Infuse, *mix*, 41.
Infuse, *insert*, 300.
teach, 537.
Ingeminate, *duplication*, 90.
Ingenious, *skill*, 698.
*Ingénue (Fr.), *actress*, 599.
Ingenuous, *artless*, 703.
sincere, 543.
guileless, 939.
Ingest, *absorb*, 296.
Ingle, *fuel*, 388.
Inglorious, *disrepute*, 874.
Ingoing, *ingress*, 294.
Ingot, *money*, 800.
Ingraft, *see* Engraft.
Ingratiate, *love*, 897.
Ingratitude, *ingratitude*, 917.
Ingredient, *component*, 56.
Ingress, *ingress*, 294.
Ingrowing, *insertion*, 300.
Ingurgitate, *reception*, 296.
Inhabile, *unskilfulness*, 699.
Inhabit, *presence*, 186.
Inhabitant, *inhabitant*, 188.
Inhale, *reception*, 296.
Inharmonious, *discordant*, 414.
incongruity, 24.
Inherence, *intrinsicality*, 5.
Inherit, *acquire*, 775.
possess, 777.
Inhesion, *intrinsicality*, 5.
Inhibit, *prohibit*, 761.
dissuade, 616.
hinder, 706.
Inhospitable, *seclusion*, 893.
Inhuman, *malevolence*, 907.
Inhume, *interment*, 363.
Inimical, *hostile*, 889.
unfavourable, 706.
Inimitable, *perfect*, 650.
good, 648.
Iniquity, *wrong*, 923.
vice, 945.
Initiate, *begin*, 66.
teach, 537.
Initiated, *skilful*, 698.
Initiative, *enterprise*, 676.
beginning, 66.
Inject, *insertion*, 300.
Injudicious, *folly*, 499.
Injunction, *command*, 741.
advice, 695.
decree, 963.
Injure, *to damage*, 659.
malevolence, 907.
Injury, *harm*, 649.
Injustice, *wrong*, 923.
Ink, *blackness*, 431.
Inkling, *information*, 527.
knowledge, 490.

Inlaid, *variegation*, 440.
Inland, *interiority*, 221.
Inlay, *variegation*, 440.
Inlet, *opening*, 260.
way, 627.
beginning, 66.
of the sea, 343.
*In limine (L.), *beginning*, 66.
*In loco (L.), *relation*, 9.
Inly, *interiority*, 221.
Inmate, *inhabitant*, 188.
*In mediis rebus (L.), *middle*, 68.
Inmost, *interiority*, 221.
Inn, *abode*, 189.
Innate, *intrinsicality*, 5.
Innavigable, *difficulty*, 704.
Inner, *interiority*, 221.
Innocence, *innocence*, 946.
Innocuous, *harmless*, 648.
wholesome, 656.
Innominate, *misnomer*, 565.
Innovation, *newness*, 123.
change, 140.
Innoxious, *innocent*, 946.
salubrious, 656.
harmless, 648.
*In nubibus (L.), *inexistence*, 2.
incogitancy, 452.
imagination, 515.
unintelligibility, 519.
Innuendo, *information*, 527.
Innumerable, *infinity*, 105.
Inoculate, *insert*, 300.
teach, 537
Inodorous, *inodorousness*, 399.
Inoffensive, *harmless*, 648, 946.
Inofficious, *malevolence*, 907.
Inoperative, *unproductive*, 169.
useless, 645.
Inopportune, *untimely*, 135.
inexpedient, 647.
Inordinate, *size*, 192.
excessive, 31.
Inorganic, *inorganisation*, 358.
Inosculate, *intersect*, 219.
convoluted, 248.
joined, 43.
*In posse (L.), *being*, 1.
*In propriâ personâ (L.), *speciality*, 79.
*In puris naturalibus (L.), *divestment*, 226.
Inquest, *inquiry*, 461.
jurisdiction, 965.
Inquietude, *uneasiness*, 828.
apprehension, 860.
discontent, 832.
restlessness, 264.
disorder, 59.
Inquiry, *search*, 461.
curiosity, 455.
Inquisition, *inquiry*, 461.
jurisdiction, 965.
*In re (L.), *relation*, 9.
Inroad, *ingress*, 294.
invasion, 716.
devastation, 619.
*In sæcula sæculorum (L.), *perpetuity*, 112.
Insalubrity, *insalubrity*, 657.
Insane, *mad*, 503.
rash, 863.
Insanitary, *insalubrious*, 657.
Insatiable, *desire*, 865.
Inscribe, *write*, 590.
label, 551.
represent, 554.
Inscrutable, *unintelligibility*, 519.
Insculpture, *sculpture*, 557.
Insect, *animal*, 366.
minute, 193.
Insecure, *danger*, 665.
Insensate, *foolish*, 499.
mad, 503.
Insensibility, *physical*, 376.
moral, 823.
Inseparable, *cohering*, 46.
attached, 43.
Insert, *put in*, 300.
locate, 184.
interpose, 228.
enter, 294.
Inseverable, *junction*, 43.
unity, 87.
Inside, *interiority*, 221.
Insidious, *false*, 544.
cunning, 702.
dishonourable, 940.
Insight, *knowledge*, 490.
Insignia, *indication*, 550.
Insignificance, *smallness*, 32.
Insignificant, *unimportance*, 643.
Insincere, *falsehood*, 544.
Insinuate, *intervene*, 228.
ingress, 294.
mean, 516.
suppose, 514.
hint, 527.
blame, 932.
insert, 300.
Insipid, *tasteless*, 391.
indifferent, 866.
Insist, *command*, 741.
Insistent, *importunate*, 830.
Insobriety, *drunkenness*, 959.
Insolence, *insolence*, 885.
Insoluble, *dense*, 321.
unintelligible, 519.

Insolvent, *non-payment*, 808.
Insomnia, *wakefulness*, 680.
Insomuch, *greatness*, 31.
*Insouciance (Fr.), *thoughtlessness*, 458.
supineness, 823.
indifference, 866.
Inspan, *harness*, 43.
Inspect, *look*, 441.
attend to, 457.
Inspector, *spectator*, 444.
director, 694.
Inspiration, *breathing*, 349.
impulse, 612.
prompting, 615.
imagination, 515.
wisdom, 498.
piety, 987.
revelation, 985.
Inspire, *prompt*, 615.
animate, 824.
Inspirit, *urge*, 615.
animate, 824.
courage, 861.
Inspissation, *semiliquidity*, 352.
Instability, *mutability*, 149.
Install, *locate*, 184.
commission, 755.
celebrate, 883.
Instalment, *portion*, 51.
Instance, *example*, 82.
solicitation, 765.
motive, 615.
Instancy, *urgency*, 642.
Instant, *moment*, 113.
present, 118.
future, 121
Instanter, *earliness*, 132.
instantaneity, 113.
*In statu pupillari (L.), *youth*, 127.
learner, 541.
*In statu quo (L.), *permanence*, 142.
restoration, 660.
Instauration, *restoration*, 660.
Instead, *substitution*, 147.
Instigate, *motive*, 615.
Instil, *insert*, 300.
teach, 537.
mix, 41.
Instinct, *intellect*, 450.
intuition, 477.
impulse, 601.
innate, 5.
Instinctive, *habitual*, 613.
Institute, *school*, 542.
beginning, 66.
Institutor, *teacher*, 540.
Instruct, *teach*, 537.
advise, 695.
Instruct, *precept*, 697.
Instructor, *teacher*, 540.
Instrument, *implement*, 633.
record, 551.
security, 771.
Instrumental, *means*, 632.
music, 415.
subservient, 631.
Instrumentality, *medium*, 631.
Insubordinate, *disobedience*, 742.
Insubstantiality, *nothingness*, 4.
Insufferable, *painfulness*, 830.
Insufficient, *insufficiency*, 640.
Insufflation, *wind*, 349.
Insular, *island*, 346.
detach, 44.
single, 87.
Insulate, *separate*, 44.
Insult, *rudeness*, 895.
offence, 900.
Insuperable, *difficulty*, 704.
Insupportable, *painfulness*, 830.
Insuppressible, *violence*, 173.
Insurance, *promise*, 768.
precaution, 664.
Insurgent, *disobedience*, 742.
Insurmountable, *difficulty*, 704.
Insurrection, *disobedience*, 742.
resistance, 719.
Insusceptible, *insensibility*, 823.
Intact, *permanence*, 142.
Intaglio, *concavity*, 252.
sculpture, 557.
Intake, *inlet*, 260.
Intangible, *numbness*, 381.
Integer, *whole*, 50.
Integral calculus, *number*, 84.
Integrant part, *component*, 56.
Integrate, *consolidate*, 50.
complete, 52.
Integration, *number*, 84.
Integrity, *whole*, 50.
virtue, 944.
probity, 939.
Integument, *covering*, 222.
Intellect, *intellect*, 450.
Intelligence, *mind*, 450.
news, 532.
wisdom, 498.
Intelligible, *intelligibility*, 518, 570.
Intemperate, *intemperance*, 954.
Intempestivity, *unseasonableness*, 135.
Intend, design, 620.
Intended, *will*, 600.
Intensify, *energise*, 171.
Intensity, *degree*, 26.
greatness, 31.
energy, 171.

Intent, *active*, 682.
thoughtful, 451, 457.
Intention, *design*, 620.
Intentional, *will*, 600.
Intentness, *attention*, 457.
thought, 451.
Inter, *bury*, 363.
insert, 300.
Interaction, *reciprocal*, 12.
*Inter alia (L.), *conformity*, 82.
Interblend, *mix*, 41.
Interbreed, *mix*, 41.
Intercalate, *insert*, 300.
intervene, 228.
Intercede, *mediate*, 724.
deprecate, 766.
Intercept, *hinder*, 706.
take, 789.
Intercession, *deprecation*, 766.
Interchange, *interchange*, 148.
reciprocate, 12.
barter, 794.
transfer, 783.
Interclude, *hindrance*, 706.
Intercommunicate, *interlocution*, 588.
Intercommunion, *sociality*, 892.
Intercostal, *interiority*, 221.
Intercourse, *interlocution*, 588.
Intercross, *mix*, 41.
Intercurrence, *passage*, 302.
Interdict, *prohibition*, 761.
Interdigitate, *intervene*, 228.
intersect, 219.
Interest, *advantage*, 618.
concern, 9.
curiosity, 455.
attention, 457.
to please, 829.
debt, 806.
Interesting, *style*, 574.
Interfere, *intervene*, 228.
meddle, 682.
disagree, 24.
counteract, 179.
thwart, 706.
mediate, 724.
activity, 682.
Interim, *duration*, 106.
Interim, in the, *synchronism*, 120.
Interior, *interiority*, 221.
Interjacence, *coming between*, 228.
middle, 68.
Interject, *insert*, 300.
interpose, 228.
Interlace, *twine*, 219.
join, 43.
Interlard, *interpose*, 228.
mix, 41.
Interlard, *insert*, 300.
Interleave, *interjacence*, 228.
Interline, *insert*, 228.
write, 590.
Interlink, *junction*, 43.
Interlocation, *interjacence*, 228.
Interlock, *cross*, 219.
join, 43.
Interlocution, *interlocution*, 588.
Interloper, *intervene*, 228.
obstruct, 706.
extraneous, 57.
Interlude, *dramatic*, 599.
time, 106.
Intermarriage, *marriage*, 903.
Intermeddle, *hinder*, 706.
interfere, 782.
Intermeddling, *mediation*, 724.
Intermediate, *mean*, 29.
middle, 68.
intervening, 228.
Intermedium, *link*, 45.
instrument, 631.
intervention, 228.
Interment, *interment*, 300, 363.
*Intermezzo (It.), *interlude*, 106.
music, 415.
Interminable, *infinite*, 105.
eternal, 112.
long, 200.
Intermingle, *mixture*, 41.
Intermission, *discontinuance*, 142.
Intermit, *interrupt*, 70.
discontinue, 141.
recur, 138.
suspend, 265.
in time, 106.
Intermix, *mixture*, 41.
Intern, *restrain*, 751.
Internal, *interior*, 221.
intrinsic, 5.
International, *reciprocal*, 12.
law, 963.
Internecine, *slaughter*, 361.
war, 722.
Internuncio, *messenger*, 534.
consignee, 758.
Interpellation, *inquiry*, 461.
address, 586.
appeal, 765.
summons, 741.
Interpenetration, *passage*, 302.
ingress, 294.
Interpolate, *intervene*, 228.
mix, 41.
analytical, 85.
Interpose, *intervene*, 228.
mediate, 724.
mix, 41.

Interpose, *act*, 682.
hinder, 706.
Interpret, *explain*, 522.
answer, 462.
Interpreter, *interpretation*, 524.
Interregnum, *laxity*, 738.
intermission, 106.
transient, 111.
cessation, 141.
discontinuity, 70.
Interrogate, *inquiry*, 461.
*In terrorem (L.), *threat*, 909.
Interrupt, *discontinuity*, 70.
hindrance, 706.
cessation, 141.
pause, 265.
Intersect, *crossing*, 219.
Interspace, *interval*, 198.
interior, 221.
Intersperse, *diffuse*, 73.
mix, 41.
intervene, 228.
Interstice, *interval*, 198.
Interstitial, *interjacent*, 228.
internal, 221.
Intertexture, *tissue*, 329.
intersection, 219.
Intertwine, *cross*, 219.
Intertwist, *unite*, 43, 219.
Interval, *of space*, 198.
of order, 70.
of time, 106.
Intervene, *in space*, 228, 300.
in time, 106.
in order, 68.
Intervention, *mediation*, 724.
instrumentality, 170, 631.
Interview, *conference*, 588.
society, 892.
Intervolved, *junction*, 43.
Interweave, *crossing*, 219.
Intestate, *obliteration*, 552.
Intestine, *interiority*, 221.
Intimate, *to tell*, 527.
friendly, 888.
close, 197.
Intimidate, *frighten*, 860.
insolence, 885.
threat, 909.
Intolerable, *painfulness*, 830.
Intolerant, *impatient*, 825.
insolent, 885.
prejudice, 481.
Intonation, *sound*, 402.
voice, 580.
Intone, *recite*, 582.
*In toto (L.), *whole*, 50.
greatness, 31.
Intoxicate, *excite*, 824, 825.
Intoxicate, *inebriate*, 959.
Intractable, *difficult*, 704.
obstinate, 606.
discourteous, 895.
Intramural, *interiority*, 221.
Intransient, *diuturnity*, 110.
Intransigent, *discordant*, 24.
Intransitive, *diuturnity*, 110.
*In transitu (L.), *transient*, 111.
conversion, 144.
motion, 264.
transference, 270.
method, 627.
Intransmutable, *diuturnity*, 110.
Intraregarding, *interiority*, 221.
Intrepid, *courage*, 861.
Intricate, *difficult*, 704.
confused, 59.
perplexed, 519.
*Intrigant (Fr.), *activity*, 682.
libertine, 962.
Intrigue, *plot*, 626.
cunning, 702.
activity, 682.
licentiousness, 961.
Intrinsic, *intrinsicality*, 5.
Introduction, *addition*, 37.
ingress, 294.
insertion, 300.
precursor, 64.
acquaintance, 888.
presentation, 894.
musical, 415.
Introductory, *preceding*, 62.
precursory, 116.
beginning, 66.
Introgression, *ingress*, 294.
Introit, *music*, 415.
Intromit, *receive*, 294, 296.
discontinue, 141.
Introspection, *look into*, 441.
thought, 451.
attend to, 457.
Introvert, *invert*, 140, 218.
evolve, 313.
Intrude, *intervene*, 228.
enter, 294.
inopportune, 135.
interfere, 24.
Intruder, *extraneous*, 57, 228.
Intrusion, *mixture*, 41.
Intuition, *mind*, 450.
instinct, 477.
knowledge, 490.
Intuitive, *instinctive*, 477.
Intumescence, *expansion*, 194.
convexity, 250.
Inunction, *covering*, 222.
Inundate, *effusion*, 337.

Inundate, *flow*, 348.
redundance, 641.
Inurbanity, *discourteous*, 895.
Inure, *habituate*, 613.
train, 673.
harden, 823.
Inutility, *inutility*, 645.
Invade, *ingress*, 294.
attack, 716.
Invalid, *disease*, 655.
Invalidate, *disable*, 158.
disentitle, 925.
confute, 479.
rebut, 468.
Invalidity, *confutation*, 479.
Invaluable, *goodness*, 648.
Invariable, *intrinsic*, 5.
immutability, 150.
Invasion, *ingress*, 294.
attack, 716.
Invective, *accusation*, 938.
Inveigh, *blame*, 932.
Inveigle, *deceive*, 546.
seduce, 615.
Invent, *imagine*, 515.
devise, 626.
falsehood, 544.
Inventive, *skilful*, 698.
Inventory, *list*, 86.
Inversion, *reversion*, 145.
of position, 218, 237.
of relation, 14.
of order, 59, 61.
Invertebrate, *feeble*, 160, 575.
irresolute, 605.
Invest, *give*, 784.
lend, 787.
empower, 157, 755.
ascribe, 155.
clothe, 225.
besiege, 716.
Investigate, *inquiry*, 461.
Investiture, *see* Invest.
Investment, *see* Invest.
Inveterate, *habit*, 613.
old, 124.
belief, 484.
Invidious, *envy*, 921.
hatred, 898.
unfair, 923.
Invigoration, *strength*, 159.
Invincible, *strength*, 159.
Inviolable, *right*, 924.
honour, 939.
concealment, 528.
Invisible, *not to be seen*, 447.
small, 193.
concealed, 526.
Invite, *ask*, 765.
Invite, *offer*, 763.
induce, 615.
Inviting, *pleasing*, 899.
alluring, 615.
Invoke, *implore*, 765.
pray, 990.
address, 586.
curse, 908.
Invoice, *list*, 86.
Involuntary, *compulsory*, 601.
Involution, *disorder*, 59.
convolution, 248.
numerical, 85.
style, 571.
Involve, *derange*, 61.
include, 54.
wrap, 225.
evidence, 467.
meaning, 516.
Involved, *disorder*, 59.
Invulnerable, *safety*, 664.
Inward, *interiority*, 221.
Inweave, *crossing*, 219.
*Iota (Gr.), *particle*, 32.
minute, 193.
*Ipsissimis verbis (L.), *word*, 562.
*Ipso facto (L.), *being*, 1.
truth, 494.
Irascible, *anger*, 901.
Irate, *resentment*, 900.
Ire, *resentment*, 900.
Iridescent, *variegation*, 440.
Iris, *variegation*, 440.
Irishism, *absurdity*, 497.
Irk, *oppress*, 830.
Irksome, *tiresome*, 688.
tedious, 841.
oppressive, 830.
Iron, *strength*, 159.
hardness, 323.
to smooth, 255.
Ironclad, *ship*, 273.
Iron-hearted, *malevolence*, 907.
Irony, *ridicule*, 856.
untruth, 544, 546.
Irradiate, *light*, 420.
Irrational, *number*, 84.
silly, 477, 499.
Irreclaimable, *degenerate*, 659.
vile, 945.
impenitent, 951.
Irreconcilable, *discordant*, 24.
unrelated, 10.
Irrecoverable, *lost*, 776.
past, 122.
hopeless, 659.
Irredeemable, *degenerate*, 659.
impenitent, 951.
Irreducible, *out of order*, 59.

Irreducible, *discordant*, 24.
derangement, 61.
fixed, 150.
Irrefragable, *certain*, 475.
proved, 478.
Irrefutable, *certain*, 475.
proved, 467, 478.
Irregular, *out of order*, 59.
against rule, 83
in time, 139.
distorted, 243.
multiform, 81.
Irrelation, *unrelated*, 10.
Irrelevant, *unrelated*, 10.
unaccordant, 24.
sophistical, 477.
Irreligion, *atheism*, 988.
Irremediable, *lost*, 776.
spoiled, 659.
bad, 649.
Irremissible, *vice*, 945.
Irremovable, *immutable*, 150.
quiescence, 265.
Irreparable, *loss*, 776.
bad, 649.
incurable, 659.
Irreplaceable, *indispensable*, 630.
Irrepressible, *violent*, 173.
excitement, 825.
free, 748.
Irreproachable, *innocence*, 946.
Irresistible, *strength*, 159.
compulsory, 601.
evidence, 467.
Irresolute, *irresolution*, 149, 605.
Irresolvable, *unity*, 87.
Irrespective, *irrelation*, 10.
Irrresponsible, *exempt*, 927.
arbitrary, 964.
Irretrievable, *unalterable*, 776.
remediless, 659.
lost, 776.
Irreverence, *disrespect*, 929.
impiety, 989.
Irreversible, *past*, 122.
immutable, 150.
Irrevocable, *immutable*, 150, 601, 604.
Irrigate, *water*, 337.
Irritable, *excitable*, 825.
irascible, 901.
Irritate, *provoke*, 898.
incense, 900.
fret, 828.
pain, 830.
excite, 171.
Irruption, *ingress*, 294.
invasion, 716.
Isis, *deity*, 979.
Island, *island*, 346.
Isochronous, *synchronism*, 120.
Isolation, *singleness*, 87.
seclusion, 893.
detachment, 44.
irrelation, 10.
Isomeric, *part*, 51.
Isomorphism, *form*, 240.
Isothermal, *heat*, 382.
Issue, *effect*, 154.
event, 151.
end, 67.
posterity, 167.
depart, 293.
egress, 295.
stream, 347.
distribute, 73.
(to join) 476.
Issueless, *unproductive*, 169.
Isthmus, *narrowness*, 203.
connection, 45.
Italicise, *emphasise*, 642.
Italics, *indication*, 550.
Itch, *desire*, 865.
titillation, 380.
Item, *addition*, 37.
speciality, 79.
adjunct, 39.
part, 51.
Iteration, *repetition*, 90, 104.
Itinerant, *moving*, 266.
traveller, 268.
Itinerary, *description*, 594.
guide, 695.
Ivory, *whiteness*, 430.

J

Jab, *stab*, 260.
poke, 276.
Jabber, *chatter*, 584.
stammer, 583.
*Jabot (Fr.), *frill*, 230.
Jacent, *horizontal*, 213.
Jack, *instrument*, 633.
ensign, 550.
Jack-a-dandy, *fop*, 854.
Jackal, *provision*, 637.
Jackanapes, *fop*, 854.
blusterer, 887.
Jackass, *carrier*, 271.
Jacket, *dress*, 225.
Jack-in-office, *blusterer*, 887.
Jack-o'-lantern, *vision*, 515.
light, 420.
Jack-pudding, *buffoon*, 844.
*Jacquerie (Fr.), *tumult*, 719.

*Jacquerie (Fr.), *attack*, 716.
Jactitation, *tossing*, 315.
Jade, *to fatigue*, 688.
woman, 374.
horse, 271.
Jagged, *angular*, 244.
notched, 257.
Jail, *prison*, 752.
Jailer, *keeper*, 753.
Jam, *to squeeze*, 43.
confection, 396.
Jangle, *sound*, 410.
discord, 713.
Janitor, *stopper*, 263.
Janizary, *combatant*, 726.
Janus, *deceiver*, 548.
Janus-headed, *duality*, 89.
Japan, *varnish*, 222.
beautify, 845.
ornament, 847.
Jape, *jest*, 842.
Jar, *vessel*, 191.
stridor, 410.
discord, 414, 713.
agitation, 315.
clash, 24.
Jargon, *unmeaning*, 519.
absurdity, 497.
Jasper-coloured, *green*, 435.
Jaundiced, *prejudiced*, 481.
jealous, 920.
dejected, 837.
Jaunt, *journey*, 266.
Jaunty, *fashionable*, 852.
pretty, 845.
showy, 882.
Javelin, *arms*, 727.
Jaw, *mouth*, 230.
loquacity, 584.
to scold, 932.
Jaw-breaker, *neology*, 563.
Jaws of death, *death*, 360.
Jay, *loquacity*, 584.
Jazz, *melody*, 413.
Jealousy, *envy*, 920.
Jeer, *banter*, 856.
flout, 929.
joke, 842.
Jehovah, *Deity*, 976.
Jejune, *scanty*, 640.
style, 575.
Jelly, *pulpiness*, 354.
Jeopardy, *danger*, 665.
Jeremiad, *accusation*, 938.
invective, 932.
lamentation, 839.
Jerk, *throw*, 146, 284.
draw, 285.
agitate, 315.
Jerry, *flimsy*, 643.
Jest, *wit*, 842.
trifle, 643.
Jester, *humorist*, 844.
buffoon, 857.
Jesuit, *deceiver*, 548.
Jesuitry, *deception*, 544.
sophistry, 477.
JESUS, *Deity*, 976.
Jet, *water*, 347.
stream, 348.
blackness, 431.
Jetsam, *fragments*, 51.
Jetty, *convexity*, 250.
*Jeu d'esprit (Fr.), *wit*, 842.
*Jeu de mots (Fr.), *neology*, 563.
*Jeu de théâtre (Fr.), *appearance*, 448.
Jew, *heterodoxy*, 984.
Jew's-harp, *musical*, 417.
Jewel, *gem*, 650.
ornament, 847.
favourite, 899.
Jezebel, *wretch*, 949.
courtesan, 962.
Jib, *deviation*, 279.
demur, 603.
Jiffy, *instant*, 113.
Jig, *dance*, 840.
Jilt, *deception*, 545.
Jingle, *resonance*, 408.
vehicle, 272.
Jingo, *warlike*, 722.
Jinnee, *demon*, 980.
Jiu-jitsu, *contention*, 720.
Job, *business*, 625.
action, 680.
unfairness, 940.
Jobation, *upbraiding*, 932.
Jobber, *merchant*, 797.
agent, 690.
trickster, 943.
Jobbernowl, *fool*, 501.
Jobbing, *skill*, 698.
barter, 794.
Jockey, *horseman*, 268.
servant, 746.
to deceive, 545.
deceiver, 548.
Jocose, *witty*, 836, 840, 842.
Jocular, *gay*, 836.
amusing, 840.
Jocund, *cheerful*, 836.
Joe Miller, *wit*, 844.
Jog, *push*, 276.
shake, 315.
Jog on, *advance*, 282.
slowness, 275.
trudge, 266.

Joggle, *agitation*, 315.
Jog-trot, *routine*, 613.
Johnsonian, *style*, 577.
Join, *junction*, 43.
Joint, *part*, 51.
junction, 43.
flexure, 258.
accompanying, 88.
Joint-stock, *share*, 778.
Jointure, *receipt*, 810.
Joist, *support*, 215.
Joke, *wit*, 842.
trifle, 643.
Jollity, *amusement*, 840.
Jolly, *gay*, 836.
plump, 192.
Jolly-boat, *ship*, 273.
Jolt, *impulse*, 276.
agitation, 315.
Jolthead, *fool*, 501.
Jorum, *receptacle*, 191.
Joskin, *clown*, 876.
Joss-house, *temple*, 1000.
Jostle, *clash*, 24.
push, 276.
agitate, 315.
Jot, *small quantity*, 32.
particle, 193.
to record, 551.
Jotting, *writing*, 590.
Jounce, *agitation*, 315.
Journals, *annals*, 114.
record, 551.
description, 594.
book, 593.
Journalese, *style*, 573.
Journalism, *publication*, 531.
Journalist, *recorder*, 553.
writer, 590.
Journey, *journey*, 266.
Journeyman, *agent*, 690.
servant, 746.
Joust, *contention*, 720.
Jove, *Jupiter*, 979.
Jovial, *gay*, 836.
amusement, 840.
Jowl, *laterality*, 236.
Joy, *pleasure*, 827.
Joyful, *cheerful*, 836.
Joyless, *dejection*, 830, 837.
Joyous, *cheerful*, 836.
Joy-ride, *journey*, 266.
Jubilant, *joyous*, 836.
boastful, 884.
Jubilee, *rejoicing*, 836, 838.
festival, 840.
celebration, 883.
Judaism, *heterodoxy*, 984.
Judge, *arbitrator*, 967.
Judge, *master*, 745.
taste, 850.
Judgmatic, *wisdom*, 498.
Judgment, *decision*, 480.
intellect, 450.
belief, 484.
wisdom, 498.
sentence, 969.
Judgment-seat, *tribunal*, 966.
Judicature, *law*, 965.
Judicial, *discriminative*, 465.
impartial, 922.
Judicious, *wisdom*, 498.
Jug, *receptacle*, 191.
Juggernaut, *idol*, 991.
Juggle, *deception*, 545.
Juice, *liquid*, 333.
Juicy, *moist*, 339.
style, 574.
Ju-ju, *idol*, 991.
Julep, *sweet*, 396.
Jumble, *confusion*, 59.
derangement, 61.
mixture, 41.
Jump, *rise*, 305.
leap, 146, 309.
dance, 840.
Jump at, *seize*, 789.
pursue, 622.
desire, 865.
conclusion, 480.
Jump over, *neglect*, 460.
Jumpy, *fear*, 860.
Junction, *join*, 43.
Juncture, *period*, 134.
circumstance, 8.
junction 43.
Jungle, *plant*, 367.
Junior, *youth*, 127.
Junk, *ship*, 273.
Junket, *merry-making*, 840.
dish, 298.
*Junta (Sp.), *party*, 712.
council, 696.
Jupiter, *Jupiter*, 979.
*Jure divino (L.), *dueness*, 624.
Jurisconsult, *lawyer*, 968.
Jurisdiction, *law*, 965.
Jurisprudence, *law*, 963.
Jurist, *lawyer*, 968.
Jury, *judge*, 967.
Jury-mast, *substitute*, 634.
resource, 666.
*Jus gentium (L.), *legality*, 963.
Just, *accurate*, 494.
reasonable, 476.
right, 922.
equitable, 939.
Just as, *similarity*, 17.

Just so, *assent*, 488.
*Juste milieu (Fr.), *mean*, 29.
Justice, *right*, 922.
magistrate, 967.
Justification, *religious*, 987.
vindication, 937.
Justify, *deity*, 976.
Jut out, *convexity*, 250.
Juvenescence, *youth*, 127.
Juvenile, *youth*, 127.
Juxtaposition, *contiguity*, 199.

K

Kadi, *judge*, 967.
Kaleidoscope, *optical*, 445.
Karma, *effect*, 154.
Katabolism, *dissolution*, 360.
Kavass, *authority*, 745.
jurisdiction, 965.
Keck, *ejection*, 297.
Kedge, *anchor*, 666.
ship, 273.
Kelpie, *fabulous being*, 979.
Keel, *base*, 211.
Keen, *sharp*, 253.
energetic, 171.
poignant, 821.
desirous, 865.
to cry, 839.
Keen-witted, *wisdom*, 498.
Keep, *retain*, 781.
custody, 751.
prison, 752.
to observe, 772.
to celebrate, 883.
to persist, 142.
to continue, 143.
food, 298.
provision, 637.
Keep back, *conceal*, 528.
disuse, 678.
dissuade, 616.
Keep from, *refrain*, 603.
Keep off, *distance*, 196.
Keep on, *continue*, 143.
Keep pace with, *equality*, 27.
Keep under, *restrain*, 751.
Keep up, *continue*, 143.
Keeper, *keep*, 753.
Keeping, in, *congruity*, 23.
Keeping, out of, *incongruity*, 24.
Keepsake, *memory*, 505.
Keg, *receptacle*, 191.
Ken, *knowledge*, 490.
Kennel, *ditch*, 259.
conduit, 350.
hovel, 189.
Kerb-stone, *limit*, 233.
Kerchief, *dress*, 225.
*Kermis (Dutch), *amusement*, 840.
Kern, *commonalty*, 876.
Kernel, *central*, 223.
Ketch, *ship*, 273.
Kettle, *vessel*, 191.
caldron, 386.
Kettle-drum, *musical*, 417.
Key, *interpretation*, 522.
answer, 462.
music, 413.
cause, 153.
instrument, 631.
Keyhole, *opening*, 260.
Keynote, *music*, 413.
model, 22.
rule, 80.
Key up, *stimulate*, 615.
Keystone, *support*, 215.
Khaki, *brown*, 433.
Khan, *master*, 745.
Khedive, *master*, 745.
Khidmutgar, *servant*, 746.
Kibitka, *vehicle*, 272.
Kick, *strike*, 276.
attack, 716.
disobey, 742.
resist, 719.
punish, 972.
Kickshaw, *unimportance*, 643.
Kid, *child*, 129.
to hoax, 545.
Kidnap, *stealing*, 789, 791.
Kidney, *class*, 75.
Kilderkin, *receptacle*, 191.
Kill, *kill*, 361.
Killing, *charming*, 829.
funny, 842.
Kiln, *furnace*, 386.
Kilt, *dress*, 225.
Kimono, *dress*, 225.
Kin, *class*, 75.
Kind, *class*, 75.
benevolent, 906.
Kindle, *set fire to*, 384.
cause, 153.
quicken, 171.
incite, 615.
excite, 824.
incense, 900.
Kindred, *consanguinity*, 11.
Kinematics, *motion*, 264.
Kinematograph, *show*, 448.
King, *master*, 745.
Kingcraft, *authority*, 737.
Kingdom, *property*, 780.
region, 181.
Kingly, *majestic*, 873.

Kingship, *authority*, 737.
Kink, *distortion*, 243.
angle, 244.
caprice, 608.
Kinsfolk, *consanguinity*, 11.
Kinsman, *consanguinity*, 11.
Kipper, *preservation*, 670.
Kirk, *temple*, 1000.
Kirtle, *dress*, 225.
Kismet, *destiny*, 152.
Kiss, *endearment*, 902.
courtesy, 894.
Kit, *bag*, 191.
accoutrements, 225.
fiddle, 417.
Kit-cat, *painting*, 556.
Kitchen, *workshop*, 691.
room, 191.
Kite, *flying*, 273.
bill, 800.
Kith and kin, *consanguinity*, 11.
Knack, *skill*, 698.
toy, 840.
Knap, *ridge*, 206.
to break, 44.
Knapsack, *receptacle*, 191.
Knave, *deceiver*, 548.
rogue, 941.
dishonour, 949.
Knavish, *improbity*, 940.
Knead, *mix*, 41.
soften, 324.
Knee, *angularity*, 244.
Kneel, *beg*, 765.
respect, 928.
pray, 990.
servility, 886.
Knell, *interment*, 363.
Knick-knack, *unimportant*, 643.
Knife, *sharpness*, 253.
Knight, *noble*, 875.
Knight-errant, *defence*, 717.
rash, 863.
Knighthood, *title*, 877.
Knit, *junction*, 43.
Knob, *protuberance*, 250.
ball, 249.
Knobkerrie, *arms*, 727.
Knock, *blow*, 276.
sound, 406.
beat, 972.
Knock about, *maltreat*, 649.
wander, 266.
boisterous, 173.
Knock down, *destroy*, 162.
overthrow, 308.
Knock off, *finish*, 729.
Knock out, *beating*, 972.
combine, 778.
Knock under, *yield*, 725.
obey, 743.
Knock up, *fatigue*, 688.
Knock-kneed, *curved*, 245.
Knoll, *height*, 206.
Knot, *ligature*, 45.
to fasten, 43.
entanglement, 59.
group, 72.
intersection, 219.
difficulty, 704.
ornament, 847.
Knotted, *crossing*, 219.
Knotty, *difficult*, 704.
dense, 321.
Knout, *scourge*, 972, 975.
Know no bounds, *greatness*, 31.
Knowing, *skill*, 698.
cunning, 702.
Knowledge, *know*, 490.
Knuckle, *angularity*, 244.
Knuckle-duster, *arms*, 727.
Knuckle under, *submit*, 725.
humble, 879.
Kobold, *gnome*, 980.
Koran, *pseudo-revelation*, 986.
Kotow, *bow*, 894.
respect, 928.
obedience, 743.
Kraal, *abode*, 189.
Kraken, *unconformity*, 83.
Kris, *knife*, 727.
Kudos, *repute*, 873, 931.
Ku Klux Klan, *illegality*, 964.
Kukri, *arms*, 727.
Kyanise, *preserve*, 670.

L

Laager, *defence*, 717.
Label, *indication*, 550.
Laboratory, *workshop*, 691.
Labour, *exertion*, 686.
work, 680.
difficulty, 704.
Labourer, *agent*, 690.
Labyrinth, *secret*, 533.
difficulty, 704.
convolution, 248.
Lace, *tie*, 43.
net, 219.
to beat, 972.
Lacerate, *disjunction*, 44.
pain, 830.
Laches, *neglect*, 460.
omission, 773.
Lachrymation, *lamentation*, 839.
Lack, *insufficiency*, 640.

Lack, *destitution*, 804.
requisition, 630.
number, 98.
Lackadaisical, *affected*, 855.
Lacker, *see* Lacquer.
Lackey, *servant*, 746.
Lack-brain, *fool*, 501.
Lack-lustre, *dim*, 423.
discoloured, 429.
Laconic, *conciseness*, 572.
Lacquer, *varnish*, 22.
adorn, 845.
*Lacuna (L.), *orifice*, 260.
pit, 252.
interval, 198.
Lacustrine, *lake*, 343.
Lad, *infant*, 129.
Ladder, *method*, 627.
Lade, *transfer*, 270.
Laden, *charged*, 639.
La-di-da, *foppish*, 855.
Lading, *cargo*, 190, 635.
baggage, 780.
Ladle, *spoon*, 272.
vessel, 191.
Lady, *woman*, 374.
Lady-like, *fashion*, 852.
courteous, 894.
Lag, *linger*, 275.
follow, 281.
dawdle, 683.
imprison, 751.
prisoner, 754.
Laggard, *slack*, 603, 683.
Lagoon, *lake*, 343.
Laical, *laity*, 997.
Lair, *den*, 189.
stye, 653.
*Laissez aller (Fr.), *inactivity*, 683.
*Laissez faire (Fr.), *inactivity*, 683.
Laity, *laity*, 997.
Lake, *lake*, 343.
Lama, *priest*, 996.
Lamarckism, *causation*, 153.
Lamb, *innocent*, 946.
Saviour, 976.
saint, 948.
Lambent flame, *light*, 420.
Lamb-like, *innocent*, 946.
Lame, *weak*, 160.
bad, 649.
failing, 732.
laxity, 738.
Lamella, *layer*, 204.
Lament, *complain*, 839.
regret, 833.
pity, 914.
Lamentable, *greatness*, 31.
painful, 830.
Lamia, *demon*, 980.
Lamina, *layer*, 204.
part, 51.
Lamp, *luminary*, 423.
Lampoon, *disparage*, 932.
libel, 934.
Lance, *throw*, 284.
javelin, 727.
Lancer, *combatant*, 726.
Lancet, *perforator*, 262.
Lancinate, *pain*, 378.
Land, *ground*, 342.
to arrive, 292.
to stop, 265.
estate, 780.
Landau, *vehicle*, 272.
Landgrave, *master*, 745.
Landing-place, *support*, 215.
destination, 292.
Land-locked, *circumjacent*, 227.
Landlord, *possessor*, 779.
Landlubber, *bungler*, 701.
Landmark, *indicate*, 550.
Landscape, *view*, 448.
delineation, 556.
*Landsturm (Gr.), *combatant*, 726.
*Landwehr (Ger.), *combatant*, 726.
Lane, *street*, 189.
way, 627.
Language, *words*, 560.
Languid, *weak*, 160.
slow, 275.
torpid, 683, 823.
style, 575.
Languish, *desire*, 865.
illness, 655.
Languor, *weakness*, 160.
inactivity, 683.
Lank, *little*, 193.
Lanolin, *oil*, 356.
Lantern, *light*, 423.
Lantern-jawed, *lean*, 193.
Lap, *support*, 215.
interior, 221.
to wrap, 222.
encompass, 227.
drink, 296.
Lapidary, *concise*, 572.
*Lapis lazuli (L.), *blue*, 438.
Lappet, *adjunct*, 39.
Lapse, *of time*, 109, 135.
past time, 122.
fall, 306.
degeneracy, 659.
guilt, 947.
*Lapsus linguæ (L.), *solecism*, 568.
ridicule, 856.
error, 495.
equivocal, 520.

Larboard, *sinistrality*, 239.
Larceny, *theft*, 791.
Lard, *unctuousness*, 353, 256.
Larder, *store*, 636.
food, 298.
Lares and penates, *abode*, 189.
Large, *in quantity*, 31.
in size, 192.
Largess, *giving*, 784, 809.
*Largo (It.), *slowness*, 275, 415.
Lariat, *vinculum*, 45.
Lark, *mount*, 305.
frolic, 840.
Larrikin, *rowdy*, 949.
Larrup, *strike*, 972.
Larva, *youth*, 127.
Lascivious, *impure*, 961.
Lash, *tie together*, 43.
punish, 972.
scourge, 830, 975.
censure, 932.
violence, 173.
Lashings, *plenty*, 639.
Lass, *girl*, 129, 374.
Lassitude, *fatigue*, 688.
weariness, 841.
Lasso, *vinculum*, 45.
Last, *in order*, 67.
endure, 106.
continue, 142.
durable, 110.
model, 22.
Latakia, *tobacco*, 298A.
Latch, *vinculum*, 45.
Latchet, *vinculum*, 45.
Late, *tardy*, 133.
past, 122.
new, 123.
Latent, *concealed*, 526.
implied, 516.
inert, 172.
Later, *posteriority*, 117.
Lateral, *side*, 236.
Lath, *strip*, 205.
Lathe, *instrument*, 633.
Lather, *foam*, 353.
to flog, 972.
Latitude, *scope*, 180.
place, 182, 183.
breadth, 202.
freedom, 748.
Latitudinarian, *heterodoxy*, 984.
Latria, *worship*, 990.
Latter, *sequent*, 63.
past, 122.
Lattice, *crossing*, 219.
Laud, *praise*, 931.
worship, 990.
Laudable, *virtue*, 944.
Laudation, *approval*, 931.
*Laudator temporis acti (L.), *oldness*, 124.
permanence, 142.
discontent, 832.
lamentation, 839.
Laugh, *rejoice*, 838.
Laugh at, *ridicule*, 856.
sneer, 929.
underestimate, 483.
joke, 842.
Laughable, *ridiculous*, 853.
Laughing-stock, *ridicule*, 857.
Laughter, *rejoice*, 836, 838, 840.
Launch, *propel*, 284.
begin, 66.
adventure, 876.
Launch out, *expatiate*, 584.
style, 573.
Laurel, *trophy*, 733.
reward, 973.
glory, 873.
decoration, 877.
Lave, *cleanness*, 652.
Lavender, *colour*, 437.
Lavish, *prodigal*, 818.
profuse, 639, 641.
Lavolta, *dance*, 840.
Law, *rule*, 80.
ordination, 963.
command, 741.
permission, 760.
Lawful, *dueness*, 924.
Lawless, *arbitrary*, 964.
irregular, 83.
Lawn, *plain*, 344.
Lawsuit, *law*, 969.
Lawyer, *lawyer*, 968.
Lax, *incoherent*, 47.
soft, 324.
diffuse, 573.
remiss, 738.
licentious, 945.
Lay, *place*, 184.
assuage physically, 174.
morally, 826.
bet, 151.
poetry, 597.
music, 415.
level, 213.
secular, 997.
Lay aside, *relinquish*, 624.
give up, 782.
reject, 610.
Lay bare, *manifest*, 525.
Lay by, *store*, 636.
economise, 817.
Lay down, *assert*, 535.
renounce, 757.

Lay in, *store*, 636.
Lay into, *thump*, 972.
buffet, 276.
Lay open, *disclose*, 529.
show, 525.
divest, 226.
Lay to, *stop*, 265.
be inactive, 683.
repose, 687.
Lay up, *illness*, 655.
store, 636.
Lay waste, *ravage*, 649.
disorganise, 659.
Lay figure, *prototype*, 22.
effigy, 554.
nonentity, 643.
Layer, *layer*, 204.
Layman, *laity*, 997.
Laystall, *unclean*, 653.
Lazaretto, *remedy*, 662.
Lazy, *inactive*, 683.
slow, 275.
Lea, *plain*, 342, 344.
Lead, *to precede in order*, 62.
precede in motion, 280.
to tend, 176.
to direct, 693.
to induce, 615.
authority, 737.
heaviness, 319.
Lead, the, *precedence*, 62.
Lead off, *begin*, 66.
precursor, 64.
Leader, *master*, 745.
dissertation, 595.
Leading, *important*, 642.
Leading-strings, *reins*, 747.
subjection, 749.
Leaf, *part*, 51.
layer, 204.
of a book, 593.
Leaflet, *part*, 51.
League, *party*, 712.
Leak, *dribble*, 295.
waste, 638.
Lean, *thin*, 193.
narrow, 203.
oblique, 217.
recline, 215.
Leaning, *direction*, 278.
willingness, 602.
Lean-to, *building*, 189.
Leap, *ascent*, 305, 309.
Leap to, *change*, 140.
Learned, *knowledge*, 490.
Learner, *learner*, 541.
Learning, *acquiring*, 539.
erudition, 490.
Lease, *sale*, 796.
Leash, *tie*, 43.
three, 92.
Least, *inferiority*, 34.
Least, to say the, *greatness*, 31.
Leat, *conduit*, 350.
Leather, *to beat*, 972.
Leave, *quit*, 293.
vacate, 185.
relinquish, 624.
permission, 760.
bequeath, 784.
Leave off, *cessation*, 141, 614, 624.
Leave out, *exclusion*, 55.
Leave over, *postpone*, 133.
Leaven, *cause*, 153.
bane, 663.
dirt, 153.
to spoil, 659.
Leavings, *remainder*, 40.
Lecher, *libertine*, 962.
Lechery, *impurity*, 961.
Lecture, *teach*, 537.
censure, 932.
discourse, 582.
Lecturer, *learner*, 541.
Ledge, *support*, 215.
Ledger, *accounts*, 811.
list, 86.
Lee, *laterality*, 236.
Leech, *suck*, 789.
physician, 695.
Lee-shore, *pitfall*, 667.
Lee-way, *shortcoming*, 304.
Leer, *vision*, 441.
Lees, *uncleanness*, 653.
Left, *remaining*, 40.
sinistral, 239.
Left-handed, *unskilful*, 699.
equivocal, 520.
sinister, 649.
Legacy, *gift*, 784.
acquisition, 775.
Leg, *swindler*, 548.
Legal, *legitimate*, 924.
relating to law, 963.
Legate, *consignee*, 750.
messenger, 534.
deputy, 759.
Legation, *commission*, 755.
Legend, *narrative*, 594.
record, 551.
Legerdemain, *trick*, 545, 702.
cunning, 702.
*Legèreté (Fr.), *irresolution*, 605.
Legging, *dress*, 225.
Legible, *intelligible*, 518.
Legion, *army*, 726.
multitude, 102.
assemblage, 72.

Legislate, *legality*, 963.
Legislature, *legality*, 963.
Legitimate, *true*, 494.
just, 922.
due, 924.
legal, 963.
Legs, *journey*, 266.
Leisure, *unoccupied*, 685.
opportunity, 134.
Leisurely, *slowly*, 133, 275.
*Leit-motiv (Ger.), *music*, 415.
Leman, *favourite*, 899.
Lemma, *evidence*, 467.
maxim, 496.
Lemon colour, *yellow*, 430.
Lend, *lending*, 787.
Length, *length*, 200.
Lengths, all, *greatness*, 31.
Lengthy, *diffuse*, 573.
Lenient, *compassionate*, 914.
moderate, 174.
mild, 740.
Lenify, *moderate*, 174.
Lenitive, *remedy*, 662.
relief, 834.
Lenity, *lenity*, 740.
Lens, *optical instrument*, 445.
Lent, *fasting*, 956.
Lenticular, *curvature*, 245.
Lentor, *inertness*, 172.
inactivity, 683.
Lentous, *viscid*, 352.
Leopard, *variegation*, 440.
Leprechaun, *sprite*, 980.
Leprosy, *disease*, 655.
*Lèse-majesté (Fr.), *disobedience*, 742.
Less, *inferior*, 34.
subduction, 38.
Lessee, *debt*, 806.
Lessen, *in quantity or degree*, 36.
in size, 195.
Lesson, *teaching*, 537.
warning, 668.
Lessor, *credit*, 805.
Lest, *avoidance*, 623.
Let, *hindrance*, 706.
sell, 796.
permit, 760.
Let down, *depress*, 308.
disappoint, 509.
Let fall, *depression*, 308.
Let fly, *propulsion*, 284.
Let go, *liberate*, 750.
relinquish, 782.
unclutch, 790.
Let in, *admit*, 296.
insert, 300.
Let loose, *release*, 750.
Let off, *exempt*, 927.
forgive, 918.
explode, 173.
Let out, *eject*, 297.
release, 750.
disclose, 529.
Let slip, *lose*, 776.
Lethal, *deadly*, 361.
pernicious, 649.
Lethargy, *insensibility*, 823.
inactivity, 683.
Lethe, *oblivion*, 506.
Letter, *character*, 561.
epistle, 592.
Lettered, *knowledge*, 490.
Letterpress, *printing*, 591.
Letters, *language*, 560.
*Lettre de cachet (Fr.), *restraint*, 751.
Levant, *abscond*, 671.
Levee, *sociality*, 892.
Level, *horizontal*, 213.
flat, 251.
smooth, 16, 255.
to equalise, 27.
to direct, 278.
to lower, 308.
to raze, 649.
Level at, *intention*, 620.
Lever, *instrument*, 633.
Leverage, *influence*, 175.
Leviathan, *size*, 192.
Levigate, *pulverulence*, 330.
Levite, *clergy*, 996.
Levity, *lightness*, 320.
trifle, 643.
irresolution, 605.
jocularity, 836.
Levy, *demand*, 812.
assemblage, 72.
distrain, 789.
conscription, 744.
Lewd, *impurity*, 961.
Lexicography, *word*, 562.
Lexicon, *word*, 562.
*Lex non scripta (L.), *legality*, 963.
*Lex talionis (L.), *right*, 922.
Liable, *subject to*, 177.
debt, 806.
duty, 926.
*Liaison (Fr.), *impurity*, 961.
Liar, *deceiver*, 548.
Libation, *potation*, 296.
worship, 990.
Libel, *detraction*, 934.
censure, 932.
Liberal, *generous*, 816.
disinterested, 942.
ample, 639.
reformer, 658.

Liberate, *release*, 750.
disjoin, 44.
Libertarianism, *will*, 600.
Libertinage, *impurity*, 961.
Libertine, *libertine*, 962.
Libertinism, *impurity*, 961.
Liberty, *freedom*, 748.
right, 924.
exemption, 927.
permission, 760.
Libidinous, *impurity*, 961.
Library, *book*, 593.
room, 191.
Librate, *oscillation*, 314.
Libretto, *poetry*, 597.
Licence, *permission*, 760.
laxity, 738.
right, 924.
exemption, 927.
toleration, 750.
License, *permit*, 760.
exempt, 927.
Licentious, *dissolute*, 954.
debauched, 961.
Lichen, *plant*, 367.
Licit, *dueness*, 924.
Lick, *beat*, 972.
Lickerish, *fastidious*, 868.
greedy, 865.
licentious, 961.
Lickspittle, *flatterer*, 935.
servile, 886.
Lictor, *law*, 965.
Lid, *cover*, 263.
integument, 22.
Lie, *place*, 186.
position, 183.
exist, 1.
recline, 213, 215.
descend, 306.
to deceive, 545.
untruth, 546.
contradict, 489.
Lie by, *inaction*, 681.
Lie in wait, *ambush*, 530.
Lie low, *concealment*, 528.
Lie over, *postpone*, 133.
future, 121.
Lie to, *quiescence*, 265.
*Lied (Ger.), *music*, 415.
Lief, *willingness*, 602.
Liege, *master*, 745.
Lien, *dueness*, 924.
Lieu, *place*, 182.
Lieutenant, *officer*, 745.
deputy, 759.
Life, *vitality*, 359.
events, 151.
Life and death, *important*, 642.
Life-blood, *life*, 359.
Life-boat, *boat*, 273.
safety, 666.
Lifeless, *dead*, 360.
inert, 172.
Life-like, *similarity*, 17.
Life-weary, *weariness*, 841.
Lift, *raise*, 307.
way, 627.
aid, 707.
steal, 791.
Ligament, *vinculum*, 45.
Ligature, *vinculum*, 45.
Light, *luminosity*, 420.
levity, 320.
to kindle, 384.
luminary, 423.
small, 32.
trifling, 643.
gay, 836.
idea, 453.
knowledge, 490.
to arrive, 292.
loose, 961.
Light up, *illuminate*, 420.
cheer, 836.
awaken, 615.
Light upon, *find*, 480.
arrive, 292.
Lighten, *render easy*, 705.
Lighter, *ship*, 273.
Light-fingered, *stealing*, 791.
Light-footed, *swift*, 274.
active, 682.
Light-headed, *delirious*, 503.
foolish, 499.
Light-hearted, *cheerful*, 836.
Lighthouse, *beacon*, 668.
luminary, 423.
Light-legged, *velocity*, 274.
Light-minded, *irresolution*, 605.
Lightness, *see* Light.
Lightning, *velocity*, 274.
luminousness, 420.
Lightsome, *cheerful*, 836.
fickle, 605.
Likable, *attractive*, 829.
Like, *similar*, 17.
to relish, 394.
will, 600.
enjoy, 827.
Likelihood, *probable*, 472.
Likely, *probable*, 472.
Likeness, *similitude*, 17.
copy, 21.
representation, 554.
portrait, 556.
Likewise, *addition*, 37.
Liking, *love*, 897.

Liking, *desire*, 865.
Lilac, *purple*, 437.
Lilliputian, *little*, 193.
Lilt, *music*, 415.
cheerful, 836.
Lily, *whiteness*, 430.
Lily-hearted, *coward*, 862.
Lily-livered, *coward*, 862.
Limature, *pulverulence*, 330, 331.
Limb, *member*, 51.
component, 56.
instrument, 633.
Limber, *flexible*, 324.
Limbo, *incarceration*, 751.
purgatory, 982.
Lime, *deception*, 545.
Limelight, *publicity*, 531.
Limerick, *absurdity*, 497.
Limit, *boundary*, 233.
to circumscribe, 231.
qualify, 469.
prohibit, 761.
Limitless, *infinity*, 105.
space, 180.
Limn, *painting*, 556.
Limner, *artist*, 559.
Limousine, *vehicle*, 272.
Limp, *halt*, 275.
fail, 732.
weak, 160.
inert, 172, 683.
soft, 324.
Limpid, *transparent*, 425.
Line, *length*, 200.
filament, 205.
to coat, 224.
band, 45.
order, 58.
contour, 229.
continuity, 69.
direction, 278.
feature, 550.
appearance, 448.
posterity, 167.
Lineage, *posterity*, 167.
series, 69.
kindred, 11.
Lineament, *appearance*, 448.
mark, 550.
Linear, *length*, 200.
Linger, *loiter*, 275.
delay, 133.
protract, 110.
Lingo, *language*, 560.
*Lingua franca (It.), *neology*, 563.
Linguist, *scholar*, 492.
Liniment, *unctuous*, 355.
remedy, 662.
Lining, *lining*, 224.
Link, *relation*, 9.
connecting, 45.
to connect, 43.
part, 51.
term, 71.
flambeau, 423.
Linotype, *printing*, 591.
Linsey-woolsey, *mixed*, 41.
Lion, *courage*, 861.
prodigy, 872.
celebrity, 873.
Lip, *edge*, 230.
beginning, 66.
prominence, 250.
impudence, 885.
Lip-devotion, *impiety*, 989.
Lipogram, *misnomer*, 565.
Lippitude, *dim sight*, 443.
Lip-salve, *ornament*, 847.
Lip-service, *insincerity*, 544.
Lip-wisdom, *folly*, 499.
Liquation, *calefaction*, 384.
Liquefaction, *soluble*, 335.
calefaction, 384.
Liquescence, *calefaction*, 384.
Liquescent, *soluble*, 335.
Liquid, *fluid*, 333.
sound, 405.
Liquidate, *pay*, 807.
Liquor, *liquid*, 333.
potable, 299.
Lisp, *stammering*, 583.
Lissom, *soft*, 324.
List, *catalogue*, 86.
strip, 205.
fringe, 230.
to hear, 418.
will, 600.
choose, 609.
Lists, *arena*, 728.
Listed, *variegation*, 440.
Listen, *hearing*, 418.
Listless, *inattentive*, 458.
inactive, 683.
indifferent, 866.
Litany, *rite*, 998.
*Literæ humaniores (L.), *language*, 560.
Literal, *exact*, 19.
meaning, 516.
unimaginative, 843.
Literate, *knowledge*, 491.
*Literati (It.), *scholar*, 492.
*Literatim (L.), *imitation*, 19.
word, 562.
Literature, *learning*, 490.
language, 560.
Lithe, *softness*, 324.
Lithograph, *engraving*, 558.

Lithomancy, *prediction*, 511.
Litigant, *combatant*, 726.
Litigate, *discord*, 713.
Litigious, *discord*, 713.
Litter, *disorder*, 59.
to derange, 61.
trash, 643.
useless, 645.
vehicle, 272.
*Littérateur (Fr.), *scholar*, 492.
Little, *in degree*, 32.
in size, 193.
Littoral, *land*, 342.
Liturgy, *rite*, 998.
Live, *exist*, 1.
continue, 142.
dwell, 186.
fame, 873.
Livelihood, *wealth*, 803.
Livelong, *perpetuity*, 110.
Lively, *sprightly*, 836.
acute, 821.
sensitive, 375, 822.
active, 682.
style, 574.
Liver-coloured, *brown*, 433.
Livery, *badge*, 550, 877.
colour, 428.
suit, 225.
Livid, *dark*, 431.
purple, 437.
Living, *life*, 359.
benefice, 995.
Lixiviate, *cleanness*, 652.
Lixivium, *liquidity*, 333.
Llama, *carrier*, 271.
Llano, *plain*, 344.
Llyn, *lake*, 343.
Lo! *see*, 441.
wonder, 870.
Load, *weight*, 319.
cargo, 190.
quantity, 31.
redundance, 641.
hindrance, 706.
anxiety, 828.
to oppress, 830.
Loadstone, *attraction*, 289.
motive, 615.
Loam, *soil*, 342.
Loan, *lending*, 787.
Loathe, *dislike*, 867.
hate, 898.
Loathsome, *hateful*, 649, 898.
abhorrent, 867.
nauseous, 395.
Loathing, *nausea*, 841.
Lob, *toss*, 284.
Lobby, *room*, 191.
Lobe, *part*, 51.
Lobster, *red*, 434.
Local, *situation*, 183.
Locality, *place*, 182.
Localise, *location*, 184.
limit, 231.
Locate, *location*, 184.
Loch, *lake*, 343.
Lock, *fasten*, 43.
confine, 229.
rest, 265.
enclose, 232.
barrier, 706.
canal, 350.
tuft, 256.
Locker, *receptacle*, 191.
Lock up, *concealment*, 528.
restraint, 751.
Lock-up, *jail*, 752.
Loafer, *idler*, 683.
*Loco, in (L.), *agreement*, 23.
Locomotion, *motion*, 264.
Locomotive, *traction*, 285.
*Locum-tenens (L.), *deputy*, 759.
*Locus standi (L.), *influence*, 175.
support, 215.
repute, 873.
Lode, *conduit*, 350.
mine, 636.
Lodestar, *beacon*, 289, 550.
guide, 695.
Lodge, *presence*, 186.
dwelling, 189.
receptacle, 191.
place, 184.
Lodger, *inhabitant*, 188.
Loft, *garret*, 191.
toss, 184.
Lofty, *high*, 206.
proud, 878.
sublime, 574.
magnanimous, 942.
Log, *measure*, 466.
record, 551.
Logarithm, *number*, 84.
Log-book, *dissertation*, 594.
Loggerhead, *fool*, 501.
Loggerheads, *quarrel*, 713, 889.
*Loggia (It.), *place*, 191.
Logic, *reasoning*, 476.
Logogriph, *secret*, 533.
Logomachy, *words*, 588.
dispute, 720.
reasoning, 476.
Logometer, *numeration*, 85.
Loin, *laterality*, 236.
Loiter, *slow*, 275.
inactive, 683.

Loiter, *tardy*, 133.
linger, 110.
Loll, *recline*, 215.
lounge, 683.
sprawl, 213.
Lollipop, *sweetness*, 396.
Lone, *unity*, 87.
unwedded, 904.
Lonesome, *seclusion*, 893.
Long, *in space*, 200.
in time, 110.
Longanimity, *inexcitability*, 826.
Long-boat, *ship*, 273.
Long dozen, *thirteen*, 78.
Longeval, *diuturnity*, 110.
Long-headed, *wisdom*, 498.
Longing, *desire*, 865.
Longitude, *length*, 200.
Long-lived, *diuturnity*, 110.
*Longo intervallo (L.), *discontinuity*, 7.
Long-sighted, *sagacious*, 498.
presbyopic, 443.
Longsome, *long*, 200.
Long-sufferance, *inexcitable*, 826.
Long-winded, *diffuse*, 573.
protracted, 110.
loquacious, 584.
Looby, *clown*, 876.
fool, 501.
Look, *see*, 441.
appearance, 448.
Look after, *attention*, 457.
Look for, *seek*, 461.
expect, 507.
Look forward, *expect*, 507.
foresee, 510.
Look into, *examine*, 461.
Look out, *prospect*, 448.
Look out for, *expect*, 507.
Look over, *examine*, 461.
Look upon, *belief*, 484.
Looker-on, *spectator*, 444.
Looking-glass, *optical*, 445.
Loom, *dim*, 422.
come in sight, 446.
weaver's, 691.
future, 121.
Loon, *clown*, 876.
fool, 501.
Loop, *curve*, 245.
circle, 247.
Loophole, *opening*, 260.
vista, 441.
plea, 617.
refuge, 666.
escape, 671.
feint, 545.
Loose, *detach*, 44.
Loose, *free*, 748.
liberate, 750.
incoherent, 47.
Loose, *vague*, 519.
style, 573.
lax, 738.
dissolute, 961.
Loosen, *disjoin*, 47, 750.
Loot, *stealing*, 791.
booty, 793.
Lop, *retrench*, 38.
shorten, 53, 201.
Lope, *velocity*, 274.
Loquacity, *talk*, 584.
Lord, *nobleman*, 875.
ruler, 745.
GOD, 976.
Lord it over, *insolence*, 885.
Lordling, *bluster*, 875.
Lordly, *proud*, 878.
grand, 873.
Lordship, *title*, 877.
Lore, *knowledge*, 490.
Lorn, *seclusion*, 893.
Lorry, *vehicle*, 272.
Lose, *opportunity*, 135.
property, 776.
time, 683.
Loss, *privation*, 776.
evil, 619.
Lost, *invisible*, 449.
non-existing, 2.
bewildered, 491.
inattentive, 458.
demoralised, 945.
Lot, *destiny*, 152.
chance, 156, 621.
group, 72.
allotment, 786.
quantity, 25.
Lotion, *remedy*, 662.
Lottery, *chance*, 156, 621.
Lotus-eater, *inactivity*, 683.
Loud, *loudness*, 404.
showy, 428, 851.
Lough, *lake*, 343.
Lounge, *inactive*, 683.
to loiter, 275.
seat, 215.
Lour, *darken*, 422.
mope, 837.
frown, 895.
threaten, 511.
resent, 900.
Lout, *clown*, 876.
fool, 501.
to stoop, 306.
Love, *attachment*, 897.
favourite, 899.

Love-lorn, *love-sick*, 897.
rejected, 898.
Lovely, *dear*, 897.
pleasing, 829.
beautiful, 845.
Lover, *love*, 897.
Low, *depressed*, 207.
debased, 940.
vulgar, 876.
cry, 412.
price, 815.
sound, 403.
smallness, 32.
Lower, *depress*, 308.
decrease, 36.
inferior, 34.
Lowlands, *lowness*, 207.
Lowly, *humility*, 879.
Lowness, *lowness*, 207. *See* Low.
Low-thoughted, *improbity*, 940.
Loyal, *probity*, 939.
Lozenge, *angularity*, 244.
Lubber, *slow*, 683.
awkward, 699.
fool, 501.
big, 192.
Lubricate, *smooth*, 255, 332.
facilitate, 705.
Lubricity, *slippery*, 255.
impurity, 961.
Lucid, *luminous*, 420.
intelligible, 518.
style, 570.
sane, 502.
Lucifer, *Satan*, 978.
match, 388.
Luck, *chance*, 621.
good, 618.
success, 731.
prosperity, 734.
Luckless, *failure*, 732.
adversity, 735.
distressed, 828.
Lucky, *prosper*, 134, 734.
Lucrative, *receipt*, 810.
Lucre, *gain*, 775.
wealth, 803.
Lucubration, *thought*, 451.
Luculent, *light*, 420.
Ludicrous, *laughable*, 838.
ridiculous, 853.
witty, 842.
Lug, *traction*, 285.
Luggage, *baggage*, 780.
materials, 635.
Lugger, *ship*, 273.
Lugubrious, *dejection*, 837.
Lukewarm, *temperate*, 382.
unwilling, 603.
Lukewarm, *indifferent*, 866.
torpid, 823.
Lull, *assuage*, 174.
mitigate, 826.
silence, 403.
quiescence, 265.
Lullaby, *soothing*, 174.
song, 415.
relief, 834.
Lumber, *useless*, 645.
slow, 275.
trash, 643.
disorder, 59.
hindrance, 647, 706.
Lumber-room, *receptacle*, 191, 636.
Luminary, *light*, 423.
sage, 500.
Luminous, *light*, 420.
Lump, *mass*, 192.
density, 321.
concrete, 46.
totality, 50.
to amass, 72.
Lump, in the, *whole*, 50.
Lumpish, *heavy*, 319.
massive, 192.
sluggish, 683.
awkward, 853.
Lunacy, *insanity*, 503.
Lunar, *world*, 318.
Lunatic, *madman*, 504.
Luncheon, *food*, 298.
Lunette, *curvature*, 245.
Lunge, *impulse*, 276.
Lungs, *loudness*, 404.
Lurch, *sink*, 306.
difficulty, 704.
failure, 732.
deception, 545.
oscillation, 314.
slope, 217.
Lure, *entice*, 615.
deception, 545.
Lurid, *dim*, 422.
dark, 421.
yellow, 436.
sensational, 549.
Lurk, *latent*, 526.
concealed, 528.
hide, 530.
unseen, 447.
Luscious, *savoury*, 394, 396.
grateful, 829.
style, 577.
Lush, *succulent*, 333.
luxuriant, 639.
Lushy, *drunkenness*, 959.
Lusk, *inactivity*, 683.
Lust, *desire*, 865.

Lust, *concupiscence*, 961.
Lustration, *purification*, 652.
atonement, 952.
Lustre, *brightness*, 420.
chandelier, 423.
*Lustrum (L.), *period*, 108.
Lusty, *size*, 192.
*Lusus naturæ (L.), *unconformity*, 83.
Lute, *cement*, 45.
to cement, 46.
guitar, 417.
Luxation, *disjunction*, 44.
Luxuriant, *sufficiency*, 639.
Luxuriate, *pleasure*, 827.
Luxurious, *pleasurableness*, 829.
Luxury, *physical*, 377.
enjoyment, 827.
sensuality, 954.
Lying, *decumbent*, 213.
deceptive, 546.
Lyke-wake, *interment*, 363.
Lymph, *water*, 337.
Lymphatic, *inert*, 172.
soft, 324.
Lyceum, *school*, 542.
Lynch, *punish*, 972.
kill, 361.
Lynch-law, *illegality*, 964.
Lynx-eyed, *vision*, 441.
Lyre, *musical instrument*, 417.
Lyrics, *poetry*, 597.

M

Mab, *fairy*, 979.
*Macabre (Fr.), *gruesome*, 846.
Macadam, *smoothness*, 255.
Macaroni, *fop*, 854.
Macaronic, *poetry*, 597.
Mace, *club*, 633.
weapon, 727.
sceptre, 747.
Mace-bearer, *jurisprudence*, 965.
Macerate, *water*, 337.
Maceration, *asceticism*, 955.
atonement, 952.
Machiavellian, *falsehood*, 544.
Machiavellism, *cunning*, 702.
Machicolation, *embrasure*, 257.
Machination, *plan*, 626.
Machine, *instrument*, 633.
Machinist, *agent*, 690.
Mackintosh, *dress*, 225.
Macrocosm, *world*, 318.
*Macula (L.), *blemish*, 848.
Maculated, *variegation*, 440.
Maculation, *ugliness*, 846.
Mad, *insane*, 503.
Mad, *violent*, 173.
Madcap, *caprice*, 608.
Madden, *excite*, 824.
Madefaction, *moisture*, 339.
Made of, *composition*, 54.
Madhouse, *hospital*, 662.
Madman, *madman*, 504.
Madness, *insanity*, 503.
Madrigal, *poetry*, 597.
Maelstrom, *whirlpool*, 312.
turmoil, 59.
Mænad, *violence*, 173.
Magazine, *store*, 636.
book, 593.
Mage, *sorcerer*, 994.
Magenta, *purple*, 437.
Maggot, *whim*, 608.
desire, 865.
Maggoty, *uncleanness*, 653.
Magi, *sage*, 500.
saint, 948.
Magic, *sorcery*, 992.
Magic lantern, *optical*, 445.
Magician, *sorcerer*, 994.
Magisterial, *pride*, 878.
Magistracy, *authority*, 737.
jurisdiction, 965.
Magistrate, *justiciary*, 967.
ruler, 745.
Magistrature, *authority*, 737.
Magma, *mixture*, 41.
Magnanimity, *disinterestedness*, 942.
Magnate, *nobility*, 875.
Magnet, *desire*, 865.
attractive, 829.
Magnificent, *grand*, 882.
fine, 845.
magnanimous, 942.
*Magnifico (Sp.), *nobility*, 875.
Magnifier, *optical instrument*, 445.
Magnify, *increase*, 35.
enlarge, 194.
praise, 990.
approve, 931.
Magniloquent, *ornament*, 577.
speech, 582.
Magnitude, *quantity*, 25.
size, 192.
Magpie, *loquacity*, 584.
Maharajah, *master*, 745.
Mahatma, *sorcerer*, 994.
Mahogany colour, *brown*, 433.
Mahomet, *pseudo-revelation*, 986.
Mahometanism, *heterodoxy*, 984.
Maiden, *girl*, 129, 374.
servant, 746.
spinster, 904.
guillotine, 975.
first, 66.

Mail, *letters*, 592.
defence, 717.
armoury, 727.
Maim, *injure*, 649.
weaken, 160.
Main, *whole*, 50.
tunnel, 260.
conduit, 350.
ocean, 341.
principal, 642.
Mainly, *greatness*, 31.
Mainland, *land*, 342.
Mainspring, *cause*, 153.
motive, 615.
Mainstay, *instrument*, 631.
refuge, 666.
hope, 858.
Maintain, *continue*, 143.
preserve, 670.
sustain, 170.
assert, 535.
*Maison de santé (Fr.), *remedy*, 662.
Majestic, *repute*, 873.
*Maintien (Fr.), *conduct*, 692.
Majesty, *king*, 745.
rank, 873.
Deity, 976.
Major, *greater*, 33.
officer, 745.
Major-domo, *director*, 694.
commissary, 746.
Majority, *age*, 131.
greater number, 102.
dead, 362.
Majuscules, *printing*, 591.
Make, *produce*, 161.
constitute, 54.
form, 240.
arrive at, 292.
price, 812.
Make-believe, *untruth*, 546.
Make fast, *vinculum*, 43.
Make for, *tend*, 176.
Make good, *compensation*, 30.
Make it up, *forgive*, 918.
Make known, *information*, 527.
Make loose, *incoherence*, 47.
Make out, *decipher*, 522.
discover, 480.
Make over, *transfer*, 783.
Make up, *complete*, 52.
compose, 54.
imagine, 515.
invent, 544.
Make up for, *compensate*, 30.
Make up to, *accost*, 586.
approach, 286.
Make way, *progress*, 282.
improve, 658.
Maker, *artificer*, 690.
Deity, 976.
Makeshift, *substitute*, 147.
plan, 626.
plea, 617.
Makeweight, *compensate*, 30.
equality, 27.
completeness, 52.
Malachite, *green*, 435.
*Maladie du pays (Fr.), *discontent*, 832.
dejection, 837.
*Malade imaginaire (Fr.), *madman*, 504.
dejection, 837.
Maladministration, *unskilful*, 699.
Maladroit, *unskilful*, 699.
Malady, *disease*, 655.
*Mala fide (L.), *improbity*, 940.
Malaise, *pain*, 828.
Malapert, *jackanapes*, 887.
insolent, 885.
Malaprop, *misnomer*, 565.
Malapropos, *irrelevant*, 10.
discordant, 24.
inopportune, 135.
Malaria, *disease*, 657.
Malcontent, *discontent*, 832.
Male, *strength*, 159.
Malediction, *curse*, 908.
Malefactor, *evil-doer*, 949.
Maleficent, *malevolence*, 907.
Malevolent, *malevolence*, 907.
Malfeasance, *guilt*, 947.
Malformation, *ugliness*, 846.
Malice, *spite*, 907.
hate, 898.
Malign, *detraction*, 934.
Malignant, *malevolent*, 907.
pernicious, 649.
Malignity, *violence*, 173.
Malinger, *falsehood*, 544.
Mall, *club*, 633.
street, 189.
Malleable, *soft*, 324.
facile, 705.
Mallet, *hammer*, 276.
instrument, 633.
Malodorous, *fetor*, 401.
Malpractice, *guilt*, 947.
Maltreat, *injure*, 649.
aggrieve, 830.
molest, 907.
Malversation, *prodigality*, 818.
Mamilla, *convexity*, 250.
Mamilliform, *convexity*, 250.
Mammal, *animal*, 366.
Mammet, *representation*, 554.
Mammon, *wealth*, 803.

Mammoth, *size*, 192.
Man, *mankind*, 372.
person, 373.
to arm, 673.
Man, to a, *generality*, 78.
Manacle, *shackle*, 752.
to fetter, 43.
Manage, *direction*, 693.
Manageable, *facility*, 705.
Management, *skill*, 698.
Manager, *director*, 694.
Managing, *active*, 682.
Mancipation, *liberation*, 750.
Mandamus, *command*, 741.
Mandarin, *master*, 745.
Mandate, *command*, 741.
Mandolin, *musical instrument*, 417.
Manducation, *feeding*, 296.
Mane, *rough*, 256.
*Manège (Fr.), *cicuration*, 370.
*Manes (L.), *corpse*, 362.
Manful, *strong*, 159.
brave, 861.
Mangle, *disjunction*, 44.
Mangy, *disease*, 655.
Man-handle, *maltreat*, 649.
Manhood, *virility*, 131, 373.
bravery, 861.
Mania, *insanity*, 503.
desire, 865.
Maniac, *mad*, 504.
Manichæism, *Satan*, 978.
Manifest, *visible*, 446.
obvious, 518.
to show, 525.
to appear, 448.
Manifesto, *publication*, 531.
Manifold, *multitude*, 102.
Manikin, *image*, 554.
dwarf, 193.
Manila, *tobacco*, 298A.
Manipulate, *handle*, 379.
conduct, 692.
Mankind, *man*, 372.
Manlike, *strength*, 159.
Manly, *adolescent*, 131.
resolute, 604.
brave, 861.
Manna, *sweetness*, 396.
*Mannequin (Fr.), *image*, 554.
Manner, *intrinsic*, 5.
way, 627.
conduct, 692.
kind, 75.
Mannerism, *singularity*, 79.
phrase, 566.
ornament, 577.
affectation, 855.
vanity, 880.
Mannerly, *courtesy*, 894.
Manners, *breeding*, 852.
politeness, 894.
Manœuvre, *scheme*, 626.
operation, 680.
skill, 698.
stratagem, 545, 702.
Man-of-war, *ship*, 273.
Manor, *property*, 780.
Manse, *temple*, 1000.
Mansion, *abode*, 189.
Mansuetude, *courtesy*, 894.
Mantel, *support*, 215.
Mantilla, *dress*, 225.
Mantle, *cloak*, 225.
kindle, 900.
spread, 194.
Mantology, *prediction*, 511.
Mantlet, *dress*, 225.
Manual, *book*, 542, 593.
reference, 695.
Manufactory, *workshop*, 691.
Manufacture, *production*, 161.
Manufacturer, *agent*, 690.
Manumit, *liberate*, 750.
Manure, *unclean*, 653.
Manuscript, *writing*, 590.
Many, *multitude*, 102.
Many-coloured, *variegation*, 440.
Many-sided, *accomplished*, 698.
Map, *representation*, 554.
Mar, *spoil*, 649.
obstruct, 706.
*Maranatha (Syriac), *malediction*, 908
*Marasmus (L.), *atrophy*, 655.
shrinking, 195.
Marauder, *thief*, 792.
Marauding, *stealing*, 791.
Marble, *ball*, 249.
hard, 323.
sculpture, 557.
Marbled, *variegated*, 440.
Marble-hearted, *malevolence*, 907.
March, *journey*, 266.
Marches, *limit*, 233.
Marchpane, *sweet*, 396.
Marconigram, *message*, 532.
Mare, *carrier*, 271.
Mare's nest, *absurdity*, 497.
failure, 732.
*Maréchal (Fr.), *master*, 745.
Margin, *edge*, 230.
latitude, 748.
Marginalia, *commentary*, 522.
Margrave, *master*, 745.
Marinade, *pickle*, 670.
Marine, *oceanic*, 341.
fleet, 273.

Marine, *soldier*, 726.
Marish, *marsh*, 345.
Marital, *marriage*, 903.
Maritime, *oceanic*, 341.
Mark, *indication*, 550.
record, 551.
object, 620.
degree, 26.
observe, 441.
attend to, 457.
Market, *mart*, 799.
Marksman, *proficient*, 700.
Marl, *land*, 342.
Maroon, *seclusion*, 893.
Marplot, *bungler*, 701.
obstacle, 706.
malicious, 913.
Marquee, *tent*, 189.
Marquetry, *mixture*, 41.
variegation, 440.
Marquis, *master*, 875.
Marriage, *marry*, 903.
union, 41.
Marriageable, *adolescence*, 131.
Marrow, *essence*, 5.
interior, 221.
whole, 50.
gist, 516.
essential, 642.
Marsh, *marsh*, 345.
Marshal, *arrange*, 60.
officer, 745.
in law, 968.
messenger, 534.
Mart, *mart*, 799.
*Martellato (It.), *music*, 415.
Martial, *contention*, 720.
Martinet, *tyrant*, 739.
teacher, 540.
Martingale, *bridle*, 752.
Martyr, *pain*, 828.
Martyrdom, *torture*, 378.
agony, 828.
asceticism, 955.
Marvel, *wonder*, 870.
prodigy, 872.
Marvellous, *great*, 31.
impossible, 471.
Marzipan, *sweet*, 396.
Mascot, *talisman*, 993.
Masculine, *strength*, 159.
man, 373.
Mash, *mix*, 41.
knead, 324.
Masher, *fop*, 854.
Mask, *concealment*, 528.
ambush, 530.
untruth, 546.
shade, 424.
Mask, *dress*, 225.
Masked, *invisible*, 447.
Masorah, *revelation*, 985.
Masque, *drama*, 599.
Masquerade, *frolic*, 840.
concealment, 528.
ambush, 530.
deception, 546.
Mass, *quantity*, 25.
degree, 31.
whole, 50.
heap, 72.
size, 192.
weight, 319.
density, 321.
rites, 998.
Massacre, *killing*, 361.
Massage, *friction*, 331.
Massive, *huge*, 192.
heavy, 319.
dense, 321.
Master, *ruler*, 745.
director, 694.
proficient, 700.
teacher, 540.
to succeed, 731.
possessor, 779.
to learn, 539.
to understand, 518.
to overpower, 824.
Mastered, *failure*, 732.
Masterful, *domineering*, 736.
Master-hand, *skilled*, 698.
Master-key, *explanation*, 462.
instrumentality, 631.
Masterly, *skill*, 698.
Masterpiece, *perfection*, 650, 698.
Mastership, *authority*, 737.
Master-stroke, *plan*, 626.
skill, 698.
Mastery, *authority*, 737.
success, 731.
Masticate, *eat*, 296.
Mat, *network*, 219.
colourless, 429.
Match, *equal*, 27.
similar, 17.
to copy, 19.
agreement, 23.
fuel, 388.
marriage, 903.
Matchless, *good*, 648.
perfect, 650.
virtuous, 944.
greatness, 31.
Matchlock, *arms*, 727.
Mate, *similar*, 17.
equal, 27.
friend, 890.

Mate, *wife*, 903.
Materfamilias, *paternity*, 166.
*Materia medica (L.), *remedy*, 662.
Material, *substance*, 3, 316.
important, 642.
embody, 316.
Materialise, *appear*, 448.
Materialism, *intellect*, 450.
Materiality, *corporality*, 316.
Materials, *materials*, 635.
Maternity, *paternity*, 166.
Mathematical, *exact*, 494.
Mathematics, *quantity*, 25.
Matinée, *drama*, 599.
Matins, *rite*, 998.
Matriarchy, *authority*, 737.
Matriculation, *learner*, 541.
Matrimony, *wedlock*, 903.
mixture, 41.
Matrix, *mould*, 22.
workshop, 691.
Matron, *woman*, 374.
old, 130.
adolescent, 131.
superintendent, 694.
Matted, *crossing*, 219.
Matter, *substance*, 3.
material world, 316.
topic, 454.
meaning, 516.
importance, 642.
Matter of course, *conformity*, 82.
Matter of fact, *being*, 1.
Matter-of-fact, *prosaic*, 843.
Mattock, *instrument*, 633.
Mattress, *support*, 215.
Mature, *ripe*, 144, 673.
scheme, 626.
old, 124.
adolescent, 131.
Matutinal, *early*, 125, 132.
Maudlin, *drunk*, 959.
spurious sensibility, 823.
Maugre, *counteraction*, 179.
Maul, *maltreat*, 649.
Maunder, *lamentation*, 839.
Mausoleum, *interment*, 363.
*Mauvaise honte (Fr.), *modesty*, 881.
*Mauvaise plaisanterie (Fr.), *vulgarity*, 852.
*Mauvais sujet (Fr.), *bad man*, 949.
Maw, *receptacle*, 191.
Mawkish, *insipid*, 391.
indifferent, 866.
Maxim, *maxim*, 496, 697.
Maximum, *greatness*, 33.
May, *possible*, 470.
chance, 156.
supposition, 514.
*Maya (Sanscrit), *illusion*, 495.
May be, *possible*, 470.
chance, 156.
supposition, 514.
Mayhap, *possible*, 470.
chance, 156.
supposition, 514.
Mayor, *master*, 745.
Maypole, *height*, 206.
Mazarine, *blue*, 438.
Maze, *convolution*, 248.
bewilderment, 491.
enigma, 533.
Mazurka, *dance*, 840.
music, 415.
*Mea culpa (L.), *penitence*, 950.
Mead, *plain*, 344.
Meadow, *plain*, 344.
Meagre, *thin*, 193.
narrow, 203.
scanty, 640.
style, 575.
Meal, *powder*, 330.
repast, 298.
Mealy-mouthed, *false*, 544.
servile, 886.
Mean, *average*, 29.
middle, 68, 628.
small, 32.
contemptible, 643.
shabby, 874.
base, 940.
humble, 879.
sneaking, 886.
selfish, 943.
stingy, 819.
intend, 620.
to signify, 516.
Meander, *circuition*, 311.
convolution, 248.
river, 348.
wander, 279, 629.
Means, *appliances*, 632.
fortune, 803.
Meantime, *duration*, 106, 120.
Meanwhile, *duration*, 106, 120.
Measure, *extent*, 25.
degree, 26.
moderation, 639.
to compute, 466.
proceeding, 626.
to apportion, 786.
in music, 413.
in poetry, 597.
Measure, in a great, *greatness*, 31.
Measure for measure, *compensation*, 30.
Meat, *food*, 298.
Meaty, *savoury*, 394.

Mechanic, *agent*, 690.
Mechanical, *automatic*, 601.
style, 575.
imitative, 19.
Mechanics, *force*, 159.
machinery, 632.
Mechanism, *means*, 632.
Medal, *reward*, 973.
palm, 733.
decoration, 877.
Medallion, *sculpture*, 557.
Meddle, *interpose*, 682.
act, 680.
Meddlesome, *interpose*, 682.
Mediæval, *oldness*, 124.
Medial, *middle*, 68.
Mediation *mediation*, 724.
Mediator, *Saviour*, 976.
Medicament, *remedy*, 662.
Medicaster, *deceiver*, 548.
Medicate, *heal*, 660.
compound, 41.
Medicine, *remedy*, 662.
Mediocrity, *moderate*, 32.
of fortune, 736.
imperfect, 648, 651.
Meditate, *think*, 451.
purpose, 620.
Mediterranean, *middle*, 68.
interjacent, 228.
Medium, *mean*, 29.
instrument, 631.
spiritualist, 994.
Medley, *mixture*, 41.
Meed, *reward*, 973.
gift, 784.
praise, 931.
Meek, *humble*, 879.
gentle, 826.
Meerschaum, *tobacco-pipe*, 351.
Meet, *contact*, 199, 292.
agreement, 23.
converge, 290.
assemble, 72.
expedient, 646.
proper, 926.
fulfil, 772.
Meet with, *find*, 480.
happen, 151.
Meeting-place, *focus*, 74.
Megalomania, *insanity*, 503.
vanity, 880.
Megalomaniac, *madman*, 504.
Megaphone, *loudness*, 404.
Megascope, *optical instrument*, 445.
Megrims, *dejection*, 837.
*Me judice (L.), *belief*, 484.
Melancholy, *distressing*, 830.
dejection, 837.
*Mélange (Fr.), *mixture*, 41.
*Mêlée (Fr.), *contention*, 720.
disorder, 59.
Meliorate, *improve*, 658.
Mellifluous, *sound*, 405.
melody, 413.
style, 578.
Mellow, *sound*, 413, 580.
mature, 144, 673.
soft, 324.
tipsy, 959.
Melodrama, *the drama*, 599.
Melody, *music*, 413.
Melpomene, *the drama*, 599.
Melt, *liquefy*, 335.
fuse, 384.
change, 144.
disappear, 449.
pity, 914.
Melt away, *disappear*, 2, 449.
Member, *part*, 51.
component, 56.
Membrane, *layer*, 204.
Memento, *memory*, 505.
*Memento mori (L.), *interment*, 363.
Memoir, *description*, 594.
dissertation, 595.
*Memorabilia (L.), *memory*, 505.
Memorable, *importance*, 642.
Memorandum, *memory*, 505.
record, 551.
Memorial, *record*, 551.
*Memoriter [L.], *memory*, 505.
Memory, *reminiscence*, 505.
fame, 873.
Menace, *threat*, 908.
*Ménage (Fr.), *conduct*, 692.
Menagerie, *of animals*, 366.
collection, 72.
store, 636.
Mend, *improve*, 658.
Mendacity, *falsehood*, 544.
Mendelism, *production*, 161.
Mendicant, *beggar*, 767.
monk, 996.
Mendicity, *beggar*, 804.
Menial, *servant*, 746.
servile, 876.
Mental, *intellect*, 450.
Mention, *information*, 527.
Mention, not to, *addition*, 37.
Menstrual, *period*, 108.
Mensuration, *measure*, 466.
Mentor, *adviser*, 695.
teacher, 540.
*Menu (Fr.), *list*, 86.
Mephistopheles, *Satan*, 978.
miscreant, 949.
Mephitic, *fetid*, 401.

Mephitic, *pernicious*, 649.
deleterious, 657.
Mercantile, *merchant*, 794.
Mercenary, *parsimonious*, 819.
servant, 746.
self-seeking, 943.
Merchandise, *goods*, 798.
Merchant, *merchant*, 797.
Merchantman, *ship*, 273.
Merciful, *pity*, 914.
Merciless, *malevolence*, 907.
Mercurial, *excitable*, 825.
mobile, 264.
quick, 274.
Mercury, *messenger*, 534.
Mercy, *mercy*, 914.
Mercy-seat, *tribunal*, 966.
Mere, *simple*, 32.
lake, 343.
Meretricious, *false*, 495.
vulgar, 851.
licentious, 961.
Merge, *plunge*, 337.
insert, 300.
include, 76.
combine, 48.
midst, 68.
Meridian, *summit*, 210.
noon, 125.
Merit, *desert*, 944.
to deserve, 922, 924.
usefulness, 644.
Mermaid, *ocean*, 341.
Merry, *cheerful*, 836.
Merry-andrew, *humorist*, 844.
Merry-go-round, *rotation*, 312.
Merry-making, *amuse*, 836, 840.
sociality, 892.
*Merum sal (L.), *wit*, 842.
*Mésalliance, (Fr.), *ill-assorted*, 24.
marriage, 904.
Meseems, *belief*, 484.
Mesh, *crossing*, 219.
interval, 198.
Mesmerism, *occult arts*, 992.
Mess, *mixture*, 41.
disorder, 59.
dirt, 653.
failure, 732.
meal, 298.
Message, *command*, 741.
intelligence, 532.
Messenger, *message*, 534.
Messiah, *Deity*, 976.
Messmate, *friend*, 890.
Messuage, *abode*, 189.
Metabolism, *change*, 140.
life, 369.
Metachronism, *anachronism*, 115.
Metal, *material*, 635.
Metallurgy, *inorganisation*, 358.
Metamorphosis, *change*, 140.
Metaphor, 521.
comparison, 464.
analogy, 17.
Metaphorical, *style*, 557.
Metaphrase, *interpret*, 522.
Metaphysics, *intellect*, 450.
Metastasis (Gr.), *change*, 140.
Metathesis, *transference*, 270.
Mete, *measure*, 466.
give, 784.
distribute, 786.
Metempsychosis, *change*, 140.
Meteor, *luminary*, 423.
light, 420.
Meteoric, *violent*, 173.
refulgent, 420.
transient, 111.
Meteorology, *air*, 338.
Methinks, *belief*, 484.
Method, *order*, 58.
way, 627.
Methodise, *arrange*, 60.
Meticulous, *careful*, 459.
*Métis (Fr.), *unconformity*, 83.
Metonymy, *metaphor*, 521.
substitution, 147.
Metoposcopy, *interpret*, 522.
Metre, *poetry*, 597.
Metrical, *measurement*, 466.
Metropolis, *abode*, 189.
Mettle, *spirit*, 820.
courage, 861.
Mettlesome, *excitable*, 822, 825.
brave, 861.
Mew, *enclose*, 231.
restrain, 751.
complain, 839.
Mewl, *ululation*, 412.
*Mezzo rilievo (It.), *sculpture*, 557.
*Mezzo-soprano (It.), *melody*, 413.
*Mezzo termine (It.), *middle*, 68.
mid-course, 628.
Mezzotint, *engraving*, 558.
Miasma, *bane*, 663.
Miasmal, *morbific*, 649.
Microbe, *bane*, 663.
Microcosm, *little*, 193.
Microphone, *loudness*, 404.
Microscope, *optical*, 445.
Microscopic, *little*, 193.
Mid, *middle*, 68.
Midas, *wealth*, 803.
Mid-course, *middle*, 628.
Midday, *course*, 125.
Midden, *uncleanness*, 653.
Middle, *in order*, 68.

Middle, *in degree*, 29.
in space, 223.
Middleman, *agent*, 690.
salesman, 797.
Middling, *imperfect*, 651.
Midland, *land*, 342.
Midnight, *evening*, 126.
darkness, 421.
Midst, *central*, 223.
Midst, in the, *mixture*, 41.
Midway, *middle*, 68.
Mien, *appearance*, 448.
Miff, *resentment*, 900.
Might, *power*, 157.
degree, 26.
violence, 173.
Mighty, *much*, 31.
large, 192.
powerful, 159.
haughty, 878.
Migrate, *journey*, 266.
Mikado, *master*, 745.
Milch-cow, *store*, 636.
Mild, *moderate*, 174.
insipid, 391.
lenient, 740.
calm, 826.
courteous, 894.
warm, 382.
Mildew, *unclean*, 653.
Mileage, *measurement*, 466.
Militant, *contention*, 720.
Militarism, *warfare*, 722.
authority, 737.
Military, *combatant*, 726.
Militate, *opposition*, 608.
Militia, *combatant*, 726.
Milk, *moderation*, 174.
to despoil, 789.
Milk-and-water, *imperfect*, 651.
Milk-livered, *coward*, 862.
Milksop, *coward*, 862.
Milk-white, *whiteness*, 430.
Milky, *semitransparent*, 427.
emulsive, 252.
Milky Way, *world*, 318.
Mill, *machine*, 330, 633.
workshop, 691.
Millennium, *period*, 108.
futurity, 121.
Utopia, 515.
hope, 858.
Millesimal, *number*, 99.
Millet-seed, *littleness*, 193.
Million, *number*, 98.
Millionaire, *wealth*, 803.
Mill-pond, *store*, 636.
Mill-stone, *incubus*, 706.
weight, 319.
Miltonic, *sublime*, 574.
Mime, *player*, 599.
buffoon, 856.
Mimeograph, *imitation*, 19.
Mimesis, *imitation*, 19.
Mimic, *imitation*, 19.
repeat, 104.
Minacity, *threat*, 909.
Minaret, *height*, 206.
Minatory, *threatening*, 909.
dangerous, 665.
*Minauderie (Fr.), *affected*, 855.
Mince, *disjoin*, 44.
Mincing, *slow*, 275.
affected, 855.
Mind, *intellect*, 450.
will, 600.
desire, 865.
purpose, 620.
to attend to, 457.
believe, 484.
remember, 505.
Minded, *willing*, 602.
Mindful, *attentive*, 457.
remembering, 505.
Mindless, *inattentive*, 458.
forgetful, 506.
Mine, *store*, 636.
abundance, 639.
to hollow, 252.
open, 260.
sap, 162.
damage, 659.
Mineral, *inorganic*, 358.
Mineralogy, *inorganic*, 358.
Mingle, *mix*, 41.
Mingled yarn, a, *mixture*, 41.
Miniature, *portrait*, 556.
small, 193.
Minikin, *small*, 193.
Minim, *small*, 193.
Minimise, *moderate*, 174.
underestimate, 483.
Minimum, *small*, 32, 193.
Mining, *opening*, 260.
Minion, *favourite*, 899.
Minister, *deputy*, 759.
director, 694.
to aid, 707.
rites, 998.
Ministry, *direction*, 693.
church, 995.
Minnow, *littleness*, 193.
Minor, *inferior*, 34.
infant, 129.
Minority, *fewness*, 103.
Minotaur, *unconformity*, 83.
Minster, *temple*, 1000.
Minstrel, *music*, 416.

Minstrelsy, *musician*, 415.
Mint, *workshop*, 691.
mould, 22.
wealth, 803.
Minuet, *dance*, 840.
music, 415.
*Minus (L.), *less*, 38.
in debt, 806.
deficient, 304.
Minuscules, *printing*, 591.
Minute, *in quantity*, 32.
in size, 193.
of time, 108.
instant, 113.
compendium, 596.
record, 551.
in style, 573.
Minutest, *inferior*, 34.
Minutiæ, (L.), *small*, 32.
little, 193.
unimportant, 643.
Minx, *impertinent*, 887.
*Mirabile dictu (L.), *wonder*, 870.
Miracle, *prodigy*, 872.
Miraculous, *wonder*, 870.
*Mirage (Fr.), *dim sight*, 443.
appearance, 448.
shadow, 4.
Mire, *uncleanness*, 653.
Mirror, *reflector*, 445.
perfection, 650.
saint, 948.
glory, 873.
Mirth, *cheerful*, 836.
Mirthless, *dejected*, 837.
Misadventure, *failure*, 732.
misfortune, 830.
Misanthrope, *recluse*, 893, 911.
Misapply, *misuse*, 679.
misinterpret, 523.
mismanage, 699.
Misapprehend, *mistake*, 495.
misinterpret, 523.
Misappropriate, *misuse*, 679.
Misarrange, *derange*, 61.
Misbecome, *vice*, 945.
Misbegotten, *vice*, 945.
Misbehaviour, *discourtesy*, 895.
guilt, 947.
Misbelief, *doubt*, 495.
Miscalculate, *sophistry*, 477.
disappoint, 509.
Miscall, *misnomer*, 565.
Miscarriage, *failure*, 732.
Miscegenation, *mixture*, 41.
Miscellany, *mixture*, 41.
collection, 72.
generality, 78.
Mischance, *misfortune*, 830.
Mischance, *failure*, 732.
Mischief, *evil*, 619.
Mischievous, *badness*, 649.
Miscible, *mix*, 41.
Miscompute, *mistake*, 495.
Misconceive, *mistake*, 495.
misinterpret, 523.
Misconduct, *guilt*, 947.
bungling, 699.
Misconstrue, *misinterpret*, 523.
Miscount, *error*, 495.
Miscreant, *wretch*, 949.
apostate, 941.
Miscreated, *vice*, 945.
Miscue, *unskilfulness*, 699.
Misdate, *anachronism*, 115.
Misdeed, *guilt*, 947.
Misdeem, *misinterpret*, 523.
Misdemean, *vice*, 945.
Misdevotion, *impiety*, 989.
Misdirect, *misteaching*, 538.
Misdoing, *guilt*, 947.
Misemploy, *misuse*, 679.
Miser, *parsimony*, 819.
Miserable, *contemptible*, 643.
unhappy, 828.
small, 32.
Miserly, *parsimony*, 819.
Misery, *pain*, 828.
Misestimate, *error*, 495.
Misfit, *disparity*, 24.
Misfortune, *evil*, 619.
failure, 732.
unhappiness, 830.
Misgiving, *fear*, 860.
doubt, 485.
Misgovern, *unskilful*, 699.
Misguide, *misteaching*, 538.
Misguided, *foolish*, 699.
Mishandle, *maltreat*, 649.
Mishap, *evil*, 619.
failure, 732.
disaster, 830.
Mishmash, *mixture*, 41.
Misinform, *misteach*, 538.
Misintelligence, *misteach*, 538.
Misinterpret, *misinterpret*, 523.
Misjoined, *disagreement*, 24.
Misjudge, *err*, 495.
sophistry, 477.
Mislay, *lose*, 776.
derange, 61.
Mislead, *deceive*, 477, 545.
misteach, 538.
error, 495.
Mislike, *dislike*, 867.
Mismanage, *unskilful*, 699.
Mismatch, *difference*, 15.
Mismatched, *disagreement*, 24.

Misname, *misnomer*, 565.
Misnomer, *misnomer*, 565.
Misogamy, *celibacy*, 904.
Misplace, *disorder*, 59.
unconformity, 83.
Misprint, *error*, 495.
Mispronounce, *speech*, 583.
Misproportioned, *ugliness*, 846.
Misquote, *misinterpret*, 523.
Misreckon, *error*, 495.
Misrelate, *error*, 495.
Misremember, *error*, 495.
Misreport, *err*, 495.
falsify, 544.
Misrepresent, *untruth*, 546.
Misrepresentation, *perversion* 523.
falsehood, 544.
caricature, 555.
Misrule, *misconduct*, 699.
laxity, 738.
Miss, *lose*, 776.
fail, 732.
inattention, 458.
want, 865.
girl, 374.
Missal, *rite*, 998.
Missay, *stammer*, 583.
misnomer, 565.
Misshapen, *ugliness*, 846.
Missile, *thing thrown*, 284.
arms, 727.
Missing, *absence*, 187.
Mission, *commission*, 755.
business, 625.
Missive, *correspond*, 592.
Misspell, *misinterpret*, 523.
Misspend, *prodigal*, 818.
Misstate, *misinterpret*, 523.
falsify, 544.
Misstatement, *error*, 495.
falsehood, 544.
untruth, 546.
perversion, 523.
Mist, *dimness*, 422.
Mistake, *error*, 495.
failure, 732.
mismanagement, 699.
misconstrue, 523.
Misteach, *misteach*, 538.
Misterm, *misnomer*, 565.
Misthink, *error*, 495.
Mistime, *intempestivity*, 135.
Mistral, *wind*, 349.
Mistranslate, *misinterpret*, 523
Mistress, *lady*, 374.
concubine, 962.
Mistrust, *doubt*, 485.
Misty, *opaque*, 426.
dim, 422.
Misty, *invisible*, 447.
Misunderstanding, *error*, 495.
misinterpretation, 523.
discord, 713.
Misuse, *misuse*, 679.
Mite, *small*, 193.
bit, 32.
money, 800.
Mitigate, *abate*, 36, 174.
relieve, 834.
calm, 826.
improve, 658.
*Mitrailleuse (Fr.), *gun*, 727.
Mitre, *canonicals*, 999.
joint, 43.
Mitten, *dress*, 225.
Mittimus, *command*, 741.
Mix, *mix*, 41.
Mixed, *disorder*, 59.
Mixture, *mix*, 41.
Mizzle, *rain*, 348.
Mnemonics, *memory*, 505.
Mnemosyne, *memory*, 505.
Moan, *lamentation*, 839, 411.
Moat, *enclosure*, 232.
ditch, 350.
Mob, *crowd*, 72.
vulgar, 876.
to scold, 932.
Mob-law, *illegal*, 964.
Mobile, *movable*, 264.
sensible, 822.
inconstant, 607.
Mobilisation, *warfare*, 722.
Mobility, *commonalty*, 876.
Mobocracy, *authority*, 737.
Moccasin, *dress*, 225.
Mock, *imitate*, 17.
repeat, 104.
erroneous, 495.
false, 544.
to ridicule, 483, 856.
laugh at, 838.
Modal, *extrinsic*, 6.
state, 7.
Mode, *fashion*, 852.
Model, *prototype*, 22.
to change, 140, 144.
rule, 80.
example, 82.
to copy, 19.
sculpture, 557.
perfection, 650.
saint, 948.
Modeller, *artist*, 559.
Moderate, *small*, 32.
to allay, 174.
to assuage, 826.
temperate, 953.

Moderate, *cheap*, 815.
*Moderato (It.), *music*, 415.
Moderator, *master*, 745.
Modern, *newness*, 123.
Modernise, *change*, 140.
Modesty, *humility*, 881.
purity, 960.
Modicum, *little*, 33.
allotment, 786.
Modification, *difference*, 15.
variation, 20.
change, 140.
qualification, 469.
Modify, *convert*, 144.
Modish, *fashion*, 852.
Modulation, *change*, 140.
harmony, 413.
*Modus operandi (L.), *method*, 627.
conduct, 692.
*Modus vivendi (L.), *arrangement*, 723.
compromise, 774.
Mohock, *roisterer*, 949.
Moiety, *bisection*, 91.
Moil, *action*, 680.
Moist, *wet*, 337.
humid, 339.
Moither, *inattention*, 458.
Molasses, *sweetness*, 396.
Mole, *mound*, 206.
defence, 717.
refuge, 666.
Molecule, *small*, 32, 193.
Molehill, *lowness*, 207.
trifling, 643.
Molestation, *evil*, 619.
damage, 649.
malevolence, 907.
Mollify, *allay*, 174.
soften, 324.
assuage, 826.
Molly-coddle, *pamper*, 954.
Mollusc, *animal*, 366.
Moloch, *slaughter*, 361.
tyranny, 739.
divinity, 979.
Molten, *liquid*, 335.
Moment, *of time*, 113.
importance, 642.
Momentum, *impulse*, 276.
Momus, *rejoicing*, 838.
Monachism, *church*, 995.
Monad, *littleness*, 193.
Monarch, *master*, 745.
Monarchy, *authority*, 737.
Monastery, *temple*, 1000.
Monastic, *churchdom*, 995.
Monetary, *money*, 800.
Money, *money*, 800.
Money-bag, *treasury*, 802.
Moneyed, *wealth*, 803.
Moneyer, *treasurer*, 801.
Money-grubber, *miser*, 819.
Moneyless, *poverty*, 804.
Monger, *merchant*, 797.
Mongrel, *mixture*, 41.
anomalous, 83.
Moniliform, *circular*, 247.
Monism, *unity*, 87.
Monition, *advice*, 695.
information, 527.
omen, 512.
Monitor, *teacher*, 540.
director, 694.
Monitory, *prediction*, 511.
Monk, *clergy*, 996.
Monkery, *churchdom*, 995.
Monkey, *imitative*, 19.
engine, 276, 633.
ridiculous, 856.
laughing-stock, 857.
to play the fool, 499.
Monkish, *clergy*, 995.
Monochord, *musical*, 417.
Monody, *lamentation*, 839.
Monogamy, *marriage*, 903.
Monogram, *word*, 562.
cipher, 533.
diagram, 554.
Monograph, *dissertation*, 595.
Monolith, *record*, 551.
Monologue, *soliloquy*, 589.
Monomania, *insanity*, 503.
error, 495.
obstinacy, 606.
Monomaniac, *madman*, 504.
Monometallism, *money*, 800.
Monoplane, *airship*, 273.
Monopolise, *possess*, 777.
engross, 457.
Monosyllable, *letter*, 561.
Monotheism, *theology*, 983.
Monotony, *identity*, 13.
uniformity, 16.
repetition, 104, 841.
in style, 575.
Monotype, *printing*, 591.
Monsoon, *wind*, 349.
Monster, *exception*, 83.
prodigy, 872.
size, 192.
ugly, 846.
evil-doer, 913.
ruffian, 949.
Monstrous, *greatness*, 31.
huge, 192.
wonderful, 870.
ugly, 846.

Monstrous, *ridiculous*, 853.
*Mont de piété (Fr.), *lending*, 787.
Montgolfier, *airship*, 273.
Month, *period*, 108.
Monticule, *height*, 206.
Monument, *record*, 551.
tallness, 206.
Monumental, *great*, 31.
Mood, *nature*, 5.
state, 7.
temper, 820.
will, 600.
disposition, 602.
variation, 20.
change, 140.
Moody, *sullen*, 895.
fretful, 900.
furious, 825.
Moon, *inaction*, 681.
Mooncalf, *fool*, 501.
Moon-eyed, *dim sight*, 443.
Moonshine, *nonsense*, 497.
excuse, 617.
trumpery, 643.
Moonstruck, *insanity*, 503.
Moony, *dreamy*, 458.
foolish, 499.
listless, 683.
Moor, *open space*, 180.
plain, 344.
locate, 184.
rest, 265.
Moorland, *plain*, 344.
Moot, *inquire*, 461.
argue, 476.
Moot point, *topic*, 454, 461.
Mop, *clean*, 652.
Mope, *dejection*, 837.
Mope-eyed, *dim sight*, 443.
Mopus, *money*, 800.
Moraine, *débris*, 330.
Moral, *right*, 922.
duty, 926.
virtuous, 944.
maxim, 496.
Morale, *state*, 7.
Moralise, *reason*, 476.
teach, 537.
Morality, *drama*, 599.
Morass, *marsh*, 345.
Morbid, *bad*, 649.
diseased, 655.
noxious, 657.
Morbific, *bad*, 649.
diseased, 655.
noxious, 657.
Mordacity, *malevolence*, 907.
Mordant, *pungent*, 392.
Mordant, *keen*, 171.
sarcastic, 932.
Mordent, *grace-note*, 415.
More, *addition*, 37.
superiority, 33.
More or less, *smallness*, 32.
equality, 27.
Moreover, *addition*, 37.
accompaniment, 88.
*More suo (L.), *conformity*, 82.
Morganatic, *marriage*, 904.
*Morgue (Fr.), *pride*, 878.
dead-house, 363.
Moribund, *dying*, 360.
sick, 655.
Mormon, *polygamist*, 903.
Morning, *morning*, 125.
Morose, *discourtesy*, 895.
Morphology, *form*, 240.
Morris-dance, *dance*, 840.
Morrow, *futurity*, 121.
morning, 125.
Morsel, *small quantity*, 32.
portion, 51.
Mortal, *man*, 373.
fatal, 361.
bad, 649.
wearisome, 841.
Mortality, *death*, 360.
evanescence, 111.
mankind, 372.
Mortar, *cement*, 45.
artillery, 727.
pulverisation, 330.
Mortgage, *sale*, 796.
lend, 787.
security, 771.
Mortgagee, *credit*, 805.
Mortgagor, *debt*, 806.
Mortify, *pain*, 828.
to vex, 830.
to discontent, 832.
to humiliate, 874.
asceticism, 955.
Mortise (or Mortice), *unite*, 43.
insert, 300.
intersect, 219.
Mortuary, *interment*, 363.
Mosaic, *mixture*, 41.
variegation, 440.
painting, 556.
Mosque, *temple*, 1000.
Moss, *marsh*, 345.
tuft, 256.
Moss-grown, *deterioration*, 659.
Moss-trooper, *thief*, 792.
Most, *greatness*, 31.
Most part, for the, *general*, 78.
conformity, 82.

Mote, *particle*, 193.
light, 320.
Motet, *music*, 415.
Moth, *decay*, 659.
Mother, *parent*, 166.
mould, 653.
Mother-of-pearl, *variegation*, 440.
Mother-tongue, *language*, 560.
Mother wit, *wisdom*, 498.
*Motif (F.), *music*, 415.
Motion, *change of place*, 264.
proposition, 514.
topic, 454.
request, 765.
offer, 763.
Motionless, *quiescence*, 265.
Motive, *reason*, 615.
music, 415.
Motley, *multiform*, 81.
variegated, 440.
Motor, *machine*, 633.
Motor-car, *vehicle*, 272.
Mottled, *variegated*, 440.
Motto, *device*, 550.
maxim, 496.
phrase, 566.
Mouch, *inactivity*, 688.
Mould, *form*, 240, 329.
condition, 7.
earth, 342.
to model, 554.
carve, 557.
mildew, 653.
matrix, 22.
Moulder, *deterioration*, 659.
Moulding, *ornament*, 847.
Mouldy, *decayed*, 653.
fetid, 401.
Moult, *divestment*, 226.
Mound, *defence*, 717.
hillock, 206.
Mount, *to rise*, 305.
hillock, 206, 250.
support, 215.
to prepare, 673.
Mountain, *hill*, 206.
size, 192.
weight, 319.
Mountaineer, *climber*, 305.
Mountebank, *quack*, 548.
buffoon, 844, 857.
Mourn, *grieve*, 828.
lament, 839.
Mournful, *sad*, 837.
afflicting, 830.
Mouse, *little*, 193.
to search, 461.
Mouse-coloured, *grey*, 432.
Mouse-hole, *opening*, 260.
*Mousseux (Fr.), *bubble*, 353.
Moustache, *hair*, 256.
Mouth, *entrance*, 66.
opening, 260.
brink, 230.
voice, 580.
Mouthful, *portion*, 51, 193.
Mouthpiece, *speaker*, 524, 540.
speech, 582.
Mouth-watering, *desire*, 865.
Mouthy, *style*, 577.
Movable, *transference*, 270.
Movables, *property*, 780.
Move, *be in motion*, 264.
induce, 615.
excite, 824.
act, 680.
undertaking, 676.
propose, 514.
Move off, *recede*, 287.
depart, 293.
Move on, *progression*, 282.
Moved, *impressed*, 827.
Moveless, *quiescence*, 265.
Movement, *motion*, 264.
stir, 682.
Mow, *destruction*, 162.
Much, *greatness*, 31.
Mucilage, *semiliquid*, 352.
Muck, *uncleanness*, 653.
Muckle, *greatness*, 31.
Muckworm, *miser*, 819.
baseborn, 876.
Mucus, *semiliquid*, 352.
Mud, *unclean*, 653.
Muddle, *disorder*, 59.
derange, 61.
bungle, 699.
Muddled, *confused*, 458.
tipsy, 959.
foolish, 499.
Muddy, *opaque*, 426.
moist, 339.
Mudlark, *commonalty*, 876.
Muff, *bungler*, 701.
to bungle, 699.
Muffle, *silent*, 403.
conceal, 528.
taciturn, 585.
wrap, 225.
Mufti, *clergy*, 996.
dress, 225.
Mug, *receptacle*, 191.
fool, 501.
face, 448.
to study, 539.
diligent, 682.
Muggy, *dim*, 422.
moist, 339.

Mulatto, *unconformity*, 83.
mixture, 41.
Mulct, *penalty*, 974.
Mule, *beast*, 271.
mongrel, 83.
obstinate, 606.
fool, 499.
Muliebrity, *woman*, 374.
Mullah, *judge*, 967.
priest, 996.
Mullıgrubs, *depression*, 837.
Multifarious, *multiform*, 81.
various, 15.
Multifid, *divided*, 51.
Multifold, *multiform*, 81.
Multiform, *multiform*, 81.
Multigenerous, *multiform*, 81.
Multipartite, *disjunction*, 44.
Multiple, *numerous*, 102.
product, 84.
Multiplicand, *number*, 84.
Multiplicator, *number*, 84.
Multiplication, *arithmetical*, 85.
reproduction, 163.
Multiplicity, *multitude*, 102.
Multiplier, *number*, 84.
Multitude, *number*, 102.
assemblage, 72.
mob, 876.
Multitudinous, *multitude*, 102.
*Multum in parvo (L.), *contraction*, 195.
conciseness, 572.
Mum, *silence*, 403.
aphony, 581.
secrecy, 528.
Mumble, *eat*, 296.
mutter, 583.
Mumbo-jumbo, *idol*, 991.
Mummer, *the drama*, 599.
Mummery, *absurdity*, 497.
ridicule, 856.
parade, 882.
imposture, 545.
masquerade, 840.
Mummify, *preserve*, 670.
Mummy, *corpse*, 362.
dryness, 340.
Mump, *dejection*, 837.
Mumper, *beggar*, 767.
Mumps, *sullenness*, 895.
Munch, *eat*, 296.
Munchausen, *exaggerate*, 549.
Mundane, *world*, 318.
selfishness, 943.
irreligion, 988.
Municipal, *law*, 965.
distinct, 189.
Munificent, *liberality*, 816.
Muniment, *record*, 551.
defence, 717.
refuge, 666.
Munition, *material*, 635.
Murder, *killing*, 361.
to bungle, 699.
Murex, *purple*, 437.
Muricate, *sharpness*, 253.
Murky, *darkness*, 421.
Murmur, *sound*, 405.
complaint, 839.
Murrain, *disease*, 655.
Murrey, *redness*, 434.
Muscle, *strength*, 159.
Muscular, *strength*, 159.
Muse, *to reflect*, 451.
poetry, 597.
language, 560.
Musette, *musical instrument*, 415.
Museum, *store*, 636.
collection, 72.
focus, 74.
Mushroom, *small*, 193.
newness, 123.
low-born, 876.
upstart, 734.
Music, *music*, 415.
Musical, *melodious*, 413.
Music-hall, *theatre*, 599.
Musician, *music*, 416.
Musk, *fragrance*, 400.
Musket, *arms*, 727.
Musketeer, *combatant*, 726.
Mussulman, *heterodoxy*, 984.
Must, *mucor*, 653.
necessity, 152.
obligation, 926.
compulsion, 744.
Mustard, *condiment*, 393.
Mustard-seed, *little*, 193.
Muster, *collect*, 72.
numeration, 85.
(to pass), 651.
Muster-roll, *record*, 551.
list, 86.
Musty, *foul*, 653.
rank, 401.
Mutable, *changeable*, 149.
irresolute, 605.
Mutation, *change*, 140.
*Mutatis mutandis (L.), *reciprocalness*, 12.
substitution, 147.
*Mutato nomine (L.), *substitution*, 147.
Mute, *silent*, 403.
silencer, 417.
speechless, 581.
taciturn, 585.

Mutilate, *retrench*, 38.
deform, 241.
garble, 651.
incomplete, 53.
injure, 649.
spoliation, 619.
Mutineer, *disobey*, 742.
Mutiny, *disobey*, 742.
revolt, 719.
Mutter, *speak*, 583.
murmur, 405.
threaten, 909.
Mutual, *reciprocal*, 12, 148.
Muzzle, *opening*, 260.
edge, 230.
to silence, 403, 581.
taciturn, 585.
to incapacitate, 158.
restrain, 751.
imprison, 752.
Muzzy, *confused*, 458.
in liquor, 959.
Myomancy, *prediction*, 511.
Myopic, *dim sight*, 443.
Myriad, *number*, 98.
multitude, 102.
Myrmidon, *troop*, 726.
swarm, 72.
Myrrh, *fragrance*, 400.
Myrtle, *love*, 897.
Mysterious, *concealed*, 528.
obscure, 519.
Mystery, *secret*, 533.
concealment, 528.
craft, 625.
drama, 599.
Mystic, *concealed*, 528.
obscure, 519.
Mystify, *to deceive*, 545.
hide, 528.
falsify, 477.
misteach, 538.
Myth, *imagination*, 515.
Mythological, deities, *Jupiter*, 979.
Mythology, *heterodoxy*, 984.

N

Nab, *seize*, 789.
Nabob, *wealth*, 803.
Nacreous, *variegation*, 440.
Nadir, *base*, 211.
Nag, *carrier*, 271.
to scold, 932.
Naiad, *mythological*, 979.
Nail, *to fasten*, 43.
fastening, 45.
*Naïveté (Fr.), *artless*, 703.
Naked, *denuded*, 226.
visible, 446.
Namby-pamby, *affected*, 855.
insipid, 866.
style, 575.
Name, *appellation*, 564.
fame, 873.
to appoint, 755.
Nameless, *anonymous*, 565.
obscure, 874.
Namely, *conformity*, 82.
Namesake, *nomenclature*, 564.
Nap, *sleep*, 683.
down, 256.
texture, 329.
Napping, *inattentive*, 458.
Nappy, *frothy*, 353.
Narcissus, *beauty*, 845.
Narcotic, *noxious*, 649.
somniferous, 683.
Narrate, *description*, 594.
Narghile, *tobacco-pipe*, 351.
Narrow, *thinness*, 203.
Narrow-minded, *bigoted*, 499.
prejudiced, 481.
selfish, 943.
Nasal, *accent*, 583.
Nascent, *begin*, 66.
new, 123.
Nasty, *foul*, 653.
unsavoury, 395.
offensive, 830.
ugly, 846.
Natal, *beginning*, 66.
Natation, *navigation*, 267.
Nathless, *counteraction*, 179.
Nation, *mankind*, 372.
Nationality, *philanthropy*, 910.
Native, *inhabitant*, 188.
artless, 703.
Nativity, *prediction*, 511.
Natty, *spruce*, 845.
Natural, *intrinsic*, 5.
regular, 82.
true, 543.
artless, 703.
a fool, 501.
style, 578.
Natural history, *organise*, 357.
Natural philosophy, *materiality*, 316.
Naturalised, *habitual*, 613.
established, 82.
Naturalistic, *description*, 594.
Nature, *essence*, 5.
world, 318.
organisation, 357.
affections, 820.
reality, 494.
rule, 82.

Nature, *artlessness*, 703.
unfashioned, 674.
spontaneous, 612.
style, 578.
Naught, *nothing*, 4.
zero, 101.
Naughty, *vicious*, 945.
disobedient, 742.
perverse, 895.
*Naumachia (Gr.), *contention*, 720.
Nausea, *disgust*, 867.
weariness, 841.
hatred, 898.
unsavoury, 395.
Nautch-girl, *dancer*, 599.
Nautical, *navigation*, 267.
Nave, *middle*, 68.
centre, 223.
church, 1000.
Navel, *middle*, 68.
Navigation, *ship*, 267.
Navigator, *mariner*, 269.
Navvy, *workman*, 690.
Navy, *ship*, 273.
Nawaub, *master*, 745.
Nay, *negation*, 536.
Neap, *lowness*, 207.
Near, *in space*, 197.
in time, 121.
approach, 286.
stingy, 817.
likeness, 17.
Near side, *sinistrality*, 239.
Near-sighted, *dim sight*, 443.
Nearly, *small*, 32.
Neat, *spruce*, 845.
clean, 652.
in writing, 576.
Neb, *convexity*, 250.
Nebula, *stars*, 318.
dimness, 422.
invisible, 447.
obscure, 519.
Nebulosity, *see* Nebula.
Necessitate, *evidence*, 467.
Necessity, *fate*, 601.
indigence, 804.
requirement, 630.
Neck, *contraction*, 195.
narrow, 203.
Neck and crop, *whole*, 50.
Necklace, *circularity*, 247.
Neck-cloth, *dress*, 225.
Necrology, *description*, 594.
Necromancer, *sorcerer*, 994.
Necromancy, *sorcery*, 992.
Nectar, *sweet*, 394, 396.
Need, *requirement*, 630.
insufficiency, 640.
Need, *indigence*, 804.
desire, 865.
Needle, *sharpness*, 253.
perforator, 262.
Needless, *redundance*, 641.
Needs, *necessity*, 601.
Nefarious, *vice*, 945.
Negation, *negation*, 536.
Negative, *inexisting*, 2.
contrariety, 14.
quantity, 84.
denial, 536.
refusal, 764.
prototype, 22.
Neglect, *disregard*, 460.
disuse, 678.
non-observance, 773.
to leave undone, 730.
to slight, 929.
to evade, 927.
Negotiate, *bargain*, 769.
traffic, 794.
mediate, 724.
Negro, *black*, 431.
Neigh, *cry*, 412.
Neighbour, *friend*, 890.
Neighbourhood, *nearness*, 197.
Neighbourly, *social*, 892.
friendly, 888.
Neither, *rejection*, 610.
*Nem. con. (L.), *assent*, 488.
Nemesis, *right*, 922.
*Nemine contradicente (L.), *assent*, 488.
Nemine discrepante (L.), *agreement*, 23.
assent, 488.
*Nemo (L.), *zero*, 101.
*Nenia (L.), *dirge*, 415.
Neolithic, *oldness*, 124.
Neology, *language*, 563.
Neophyte, *learner*, 541.
Neoteric, *newness*, 123.
Nephelology, *clouds*, 353.
*Ne plus ultra (L.), *complete*, 52.
greatness, 31.
end, 67.
distance, 196.
superiority, 33.
goodness, 648.
perfection, 650.
Nepotism, *relation*, 11.
sociality, 892.
Neptune, *ocean*, 341.
Nereid, *ocean*, 341.
Nerve, *strength*, 159.
courage, 861.
Nerveless, *weakness*, 160.
Nervous, *weak*, 160.

Nervous, *timid*, 860.
concise style, 572.
vigorous style, 574.
Nescience, *ignorance*, 491.
Nest, *lodging*, 189.
cradle, 153.
Nestle, *lodge*, 186.
safety, 664.
endearment, 902.
Nestling, *infant*, 129.
Nestor, *veteran*, 130.
Net, *intersection*, 219.
snare, 667, 702.
to capture, 789.
difficulty, 704.
remainder, 40.
Nether, *lowness*, 207.
Nettle, *to sting*, 830.
incense, 900.
Network, *crossing*, 219.
Neurasthenia, *weakness*, 160.
Neurotic, *sensitive physically*, 375.
morally, 822.
Neutral, *mean*, 29.
non-interference, 681.
Neutralise, *counteract*, 179.
compensate, 30.
Never, *neverness*, 107.
Nevertheless, *counteraction*, 179.
compensation, 30.
New, *newness*, 123.
New-born, *newness*, 123.
New-comer, *extraneous*, 57.
New-fangled, *new*, 123.
strange, 83.
barbarous, 851.
New-fashioned, *newness*, 123.
News, *news*, 532.
Newspaper, *record*, 551.
Next, *following*, 63.
later, 117.
*Niais (Fr.), *fool*, 501.
*Niaiserie (Fr.), *absurd*, 497.
Nib, *point*, 253.
summit, 210.
disjunction, 44.
end, 67.
Nibble, *carp at*, 932.
eat, 296.
Niblick, *club*, 276.
Nice, *savoury*, 394.
good, 648.
exact, 494.
pleasing, 829.
honourable, 939.
fastidious, 868.
Nicely, *greatness*, 31.
Nicety, *taste*, 850, 868.
exactness, 94.
Niche, *recess*, 182.
receptacle, 191.
Nick, *notch*, 257.
mark, 550.
deceive, 545.
of time, 134.
Nicker, *animal sound*, 412.
Nickname, *misnomer*, 565.
Nicotian, *tobacco*, 298A.
Nictitate, *blind*, 442.
dim sight, 443.
Nidification, *abode*, 189.
*Nidus (L.), *nest*, 189.
cradle, 153.
Niggard, *parsimony*, 819.
Nigger, *blackness*, 431.
Niggle, *trifle*, 643.
depreciate, 483.
Nigh, *nearness*, 197.
Night, *darkness*, 421.
Nightfall, *evening*, 126.
Nightingale, *music*, 416.
Nightmare, *pain*, 378, 828.
hindrance, 706.
Nightshade, *bane*, 663.
Nigrification, *black*, 431.
Nihility, *unsubstantiality*, 4.
Nihilism, *non-existence*, 1.
scepticism, 487.
anarchism, 738.
*Nil admirari (L.), *expectance*, 871.
*Nil desperandum (L.), *hope*, 858.
*Nil ultra (L.), *superiority*, 33.
Nimble, *swift*, 274.
active, 682.
skilful, 698.
Nimiety, *redundance*, 641.
Niminy-piminy, *affection*, 855.
*N'importe (Fr.), *unimportance*, 643
Nincompoop, *fool*, 501.
Nine, *number*, 98.
Nine days' wonder, *transientness*, 111.
Ninny, *fool*, 501.
Ninnyhammer, *fool*, 501.
Niobe, *lament*, 839.
Nip, *cut*, 44.
destroy, 162.
Nip up, *taking*, 789.
Nipper, *youngster*, 129.
Nipping, *cold*, 383.
Nipple, *convexity*, 250.
Nirvana, *extinction*, 2.
happiness, 827.
heaven, 979.
Nixie, *fairy*, 980.
Nizam, *master*, 745.
No, *dissent*, 489.
negation, 536.

Nob, *summit*, 210.
nobility, 875.
Nobble, *deceive*, 545.
tamper with, 682.
circumvent, 702.
Nobility, *nobleness*, 875.
Noble, *rank*, 873.
generous, 942.
virtue, 944.
Nobleman, *nobleness*, 875.
*Noblesse (Fr.), *nobility*, 875.
Nobody, *absence*, 187.
zero, 101.
unimportant, 643.
ignoble, 876.
Nocturnal, *dark*, 421.
black, 431.
Nocturne, *music*, 415.
picture, 556.
Nod, *sleep*, 683.
signal, 550.
assent, 488.
order, 741.
information, 527.
bow, 894.
to wag, 314.
Noddle, *head*, 450.
summit, 210.
Noddy, *fool*, 501.
Node, *convexity*, 250.
Nodosity, *roughness*, 256.
tuberosity, 250.
Nodule, *convexity*, 250.
Noetic, *intellect*, 450.
Noggin, *receptacle*, 191.
Noise, *sound*, 402.
Noiseless, *silence*, 403.
Noisome, *fetor*, 401.
Noisy, *showy*, 428.
*Noli me tangere (L.), *excitability*, 825.
*Nolens volens (L.), *compulsion*, 744.
*Nom de guerre (Fr.), *misnomer*, 565.
*Nom de plume (Fr.), *misnomer*, 565.
Nomad, *vagrant*, 264.
traveller, 268.
locomotive, 266.
Nomancy, *prediction*, 511.
Nomenclature, *name*, 564.
Nominate, *commission*, 755.
Nominee, *consignee*, 758.
Non-admission, *exclusion*, 55.
Nonage, *youth*, 127.
Non-attendance, *absence*, 187.
Non-appearance, *invisible*, 447.
Nonce, *present time*, 118.
Nonchalance, *neglect*, 460.
indifference, 823.
unwillingness, 603.
Non-coincidence, *contrariety*, 14.
Non-combatant, *non-combatant*, 726A.
Non-committal, *cautious*, 864.
Non-completion, *non-complete*, 730.
Non-compliance, *disobey*, 742.
Nonconformity, *dissent*, 489.
sectarianism, 984.
*Non constat (L.), *sophistry*, 477.
Nondescript, *unconformity*, 83.
None, *zero*, 101.
Non-effective, *non-combatant*, 726A.
Nonentity, *inexistence*, 2.
unimportance, 643.
Non-essential, *unimportance*, 643.
Nonesuch, *perfection*, 650.
unconformity, 83.
Non-existence, *inexistence*, 2.
Non-expectance, *inexpectation*, 508.
Non-intervention, *inaction*, 681.
Non-observance, *non-observe*, 773.
*Non obstante (L.), *counteraction*, 179.
*Nonpareil (Fr.), *perfection*, 650.
Non-payment, *non-payment*, 808.
Non-performance, *non-complete*, 730.
Nonplus, *difficulty*, 704.
Non-preparation, *non-prepare*, 674.
Non-residence, *absence*, 187.
Non-resistance, *submission*, 725.
obedience, 743.
Nonsense, *unmeaningness*, 517.
absurdity, 497.
folly, 499.
trash, 643.
*Non sequitur (L.), *sophistry*, 477.
Nonsuch, *see* Nonesuch.
Nonsuit, *to cast*, 731.
to fail, 732.
Noodle, *fool*, 501.
Nook, *place*, 182.
receptacle, 191.
Noon, *mid-day*, 125.
light, 420.
Noose, *ligature*, 45.
loop, 247.
snare, 665, 667.
Norm, *type*, 80.
Normal, *regular*, 82.
vertical, 212.
Northern lights, *light*, 420.
Nose, *smell*, 398.
prominence, 250.
Nosegay, *fragrance*, 400.
ornament, 847.
Nose out, *detect*, 480.
Nosology, *disease*, 655.
Nostalgia, *discontent*, 832.
Nostril, *air-pipe*, 351.

Nostrum, *remedy*, 662.
Nosy, *curiosity*, 455.
Not, *dissent*, 489.
*Nota bene (L.), *care*, 457.
Notability, *personage*, 642, 875.
Notable, *visible*, 446.
important, 642.
active, 682.
famous, 873.
Notably, *greatness*, 31.
Notary, *recorder*, 553.
lawyer, 968.
Notch, *nick*, 257.
mark, 550.
Note, *sign*, 550.
record, 551.
letter, 592.
precursor, 64.
music, 413.
fame, 873.
notice, 457.
minute, 596.
money, 800.
Note-book, *compendium*, 596.
Nothing, *nihility*, 4.
zero, 101.
trifle, 643.
Nothing of the kind, *dissimilarity*, 18.
Nothing of, to say, *addition*, 37.
Notice, *observe*, 457.
mark, 550.
warning, 668.
Notify, *inform*, 527.
publish, 531.
Notion, *idea*, 453.
belief, 484.
knowledge, 490.
Notoriety, *disrepute*, 874.
publication, 531.
Notorious, *known*, 490.
seen, 446.
Notwithstanding, *counteraction*, 179.
compensation, 30.
Noumenal, *intellect*, 450.
Noun, *nomenclature*, 564.
Nourish, *aid*, 707.
*Nouveau riche (Fr.), *newness*, 123.
prosperity, 734.
*Nous (Gr.), *intellect*, 450.
wisdom, 498.
*Nous verrons (Fr.), *expectation*, 507.
Novel, *new*, 18, 123.
fiction, 515.
description, 594.
unknown, 491.
false, 546.
Novice, *learner*, 541.
ignoramus, 493.
Novice, *bungler*, 701.
religious, 996.
Novitiate, *learner*, 541.
training, 674.
*Novus homo (L.), *extraneous*, 57.
commonalty, 876.
Now, *present time*, 118.
Now or never, *occasion*, 134.
Nowadays, *present time*, 118.
Noways, *in no degree*, 32.
Nowhere, *absence*, 187.
Nowise, *in no degree*, 32.
dissent, 489.
Noxious, *badness*, 649.
*Noyade (Fr.), *killing*, 361.
Nozzle, *projection*, 250.
air-pipe, 351.
opening, 260.
*Nuance (Fr.), *difference*, 15.
Nubble, *lump*, 150.
Nubile, *adolescence*, 131.
Nucleus, *centre*, 223.
middle, 68.
cause, 153.
Nudge, *indication*, 550.
Nudity, *divestment*, 226.
*Nugæ (L.), *unmeaning*, 517.
unimportant, 643.
Nugatory, *inexistence*, 2.
useless, 645.
inoperative, 158.
Nugget, *lump*, 321.
Nuisance, *annoyance*, 830.
evil, 619.
Null, *unsubstantiality*, 4.
*Nulli secundus (L.), *superiority*, 33.
goodness, 648.
Nullibiety, *absence*, 187.
Nullify, *counteract*, 179.
repudiate, 773.
Numb, *morally*, 823.
physically, 381.
Number, *abstract*, 84.
plurality, 100.
publication, 593.
to count, 85.
Numberless, *infinity*, 105.
Numbers, *poetry*, 597.
Numbness, *physical*, 381.
moral, 823.
Numeral, *number*, 84.
Numeration, *numeration*, 85.
Numerator, *number*, 84.
Numerous, *multitude*, 102.
Numismatics, *money*, 800.
Numskull, *fool*, 501.
Nun, *clergy*, 996.
Nuncio, *messenger*, 534.
consignee, 758.

Nuncupatory, *naming*, 564.
informing, 527.
Nunnery, *temple*, 1000.
seclusion, 893.
Nuptials, *marriage*, 903.
Nurse, *servant*, 746.
to help, 707.
Nursery, *school*, 542.
workshop, 691.
for plants, 367.
Nurseryman, *horticulture*, 371.
Nursling, *infant*, 129i
Nurture, *food*, 298.
to support, 707.
prepare, 673.
Nut, *head*, 450.
fop, 854.
Nutation, *oscillation*, 314.
Nut-brown, *brown*, 433.
Nutriment, *food*, 298.
Nutrition, *aid*, 707.
Nutshell, *littleness*, 193.
compendium, 596.
Nuzzle, *endearment*, 902.
Nymph, *woman*, 374.

O

Oaf, *fool*, 501.
Oak, *strength*, 159.
Oar, *instrument*, 633.
paddle, 267.
Oasis, *land*, 342.
Oath, *promise*, 768.
assertion, 535.
expletive, 641.
*Obbligato (It.), *music*, 415.
Obduracy, *sin*, 945.
impenitence, 931.
obstinacy, 606.
Obeah, *occult arts*, 992.
Obedience, *obedience*, 743.
Obeisance, *bow*, 894.
reverence, 928.
worship, 990.
fealty, 743.
Obelise, *indicate*, 550.
Obelisk, *monument*, 551.
tall, 206.
Oberon, *sprite*, 980.
Obesity, *size*, 192.
Obey, *obedience*, 743, 749.
Obfuscate, *darken*, 421.
bewilder, 458.
Obit, *death*, 360.
*Obiter dictum (L.), *irrelation*, 10.
Obituary, *description*, 594.
Object, *thing*, 3.
Object, *intention*, 620.
ugly, 846.
to disapprove, 932.
Objectify, *existence*, 1.
Objective, *extrinsic*, 6.
material, 316.
Object-lesson, *explanation*, 522.
Objurgate, *disapprobation*, 932.
Oblate, *shortness*, 201.
monk, 996.
Oblation, *gift*, 789.
proffer, 763.
(religious), 990.
Obligation, *duty*, 926.
promise, 768.
debt, 806.
gratitude, 916.
Oblige, *compel*, 744.
benefit, 707.
Obliging, *kind*, 906.
courteous, 894.
Oblique, *obliquity*, 217.
Obliquity, *vice*, 945.
Obliterate, *efface*, 552.
Oblivion, *oblivion*, 506.
Oblong, *length*, 200.
Obloquy, *censure*, 932.
disgrace, 874.
Obmutescence, *aphony*, 581.
Obnoxious, *hateful*, 898.
unpleasing, 830.
pernicious, 649.
liable, 177.
Oboe, *musical instrument*, 417.
Obscene, *impurity*, 961.
Obscurantist, *ignoramus*, 493.
Obscure, *dark*, 421.
unseen, 447.
unintelligible, 519.
style, 571.
to eclipse, 874.
*Obscurum per obscurius (L.), *unintelligibility*, 519.
misteaching, 538.
Obsecration, *request*, 765.
Obsequies, *interment*, 363.
Obsequious, *respectful*, 928.
courteous, 894.
servile, 886.
Observe, *note*, 457.
conform, 926.
remark, 535.
Observance, *fulfilment*, 772.
rule, 82.
habit, 613.
practice, 692.
rites, 998.
Observer, *spectator*, 444.
Obsess, *preoccupy*, 457.

Obsess, *worry*, 830.
haunt, 860.
Obsession, *misjudgment*, 481.
Obsolete, *old*, 124.
effete, 645.
vulgar, 851.
Obstacle, *physical*, 179.
moral, 706.
Obstinate, *stubborn*, 606.
prejudiced, 481.
Obstreperous, *violent*, 173.
loud, 404.
Obstruct, *hinder*, 706.
close, 261.
Obtain, *exist*, 1.
acquire, 775.
Obtainable, *possibility*, 470.
Obtestation, *entreaty*, 765.
injunction, 695.
Obtrude, *intervene*, 228.
insert, 300.
obstruct, 706.
Obtund, *blunt*, 254.
deaden, 376.
paralyse, 826.
Obtuse, *blunt*, 254.
stupid, 499.
dull, 823.
Obverse, *front*, 234.
Obviate, *hindrance*, 706.
Obvious, *visible*, 446.
clear, 516, 518.
Ocarina, *musical instrument*, 417.
Occasion, *juncture*, 8.
opportunity, 134.
cause, 153.
Occasionally, *frequency*, 136.
Occidental, *lateral*, 236.
Occlusion, *closure*, 261.
Occult, *latent*, 526.
hidden, 528.
supernatural, 992.
Occupancy, *presence*, 186.
property, 780.
possession, 777.
Occupant, *dweller*, 188.
proprietor, 779.
Occupation, *business*, 625.
presence, 186.
Occupier, *dweller*, 188.
possessor, 779.
Occupy, *station*, 71.
place, 186.
attention, 457.
Occur, *exist*, 1.
happen, 151.
be present, 186.
to the mind, 451.
Ocean, *ocean*, 341.
Ochlocracy, *authority*, 737.
O'clock, *time*, 114.
Octad, *number*, 98.
Octofid, *number*, 99.
Octoroon, *mixture*, 41.
***Octroi** (Fr.), *tax*, 812.
Octuple, *number*, 98.
Ocular, *vision*, 441.
Odalisque, *concubine*, 962.
Odd, *exception*, 83.
single, 87.
remaining, 40.
eccentric, 499.
ludicrous, 853.
vulgar, 851.
Oddity, *folly*, 499.
laughing-stock, 857.
Oddments, *part*, 51.
Odds, *inequality*, 28.
chance, 156.
discord, 713.
Odds, at, *disagreement*, 24.
Odds and ends, *portions*, 51.
dispersion, 73.
mixture, 41.
Ode, *poetry*, 597.
Odin, *deity*, 979.
Odious, *ugly*, 846.
hateful, 898.
offensive, 830.
Odium, *blame*, 932.
disgrace, 874.
hatred, 898.
Odour, *odour*, 398.
Odourless, *inodorous*, 399.
Odyssey, *journey*, 266.
Œcology, *organisation*, 357.
Œcumenical, *generality*, 78.
Œdematous, *soft*, 324.
swollen, 192.
Œdipus, *expounder*, 524.
answer, 462.
O'ertop, *expansion*, 194.
Off, *distance*, 196.
Offal, *uncleanness*, 653.
Off-chance, *chance*, 621.
Offend, *affront*, 900.
Offence, *attack*, 716.
guilt, 947.
Offensive, *unsavoury*, 395.
fetid, 401.
foul, 653.
displeasing, 830.
distasteful, 867.
obnoxious, 898.
Offer, *proposal*, 763.
gift, 784.
Offering, *worship*, 990.
Offhand, *spontaneous*, 612, 674.

Offhand, *careless*, 460.
Office, *function*, 644.
duty, 926.
business, 625.
mart, 799.
room, 191.
bureau, 691.
authority, 737.
Officer, *director*, 694.
constable, 965.
master, 745.
Official, *authoritative*, 474, 737.
business, 625.
authorised, 924.
Officiate, *conduct*, 692.
act, 680.
religious, 998.
Officious, *activity*, 682.
Offing, *distance*, 196.
Offish, *unsocial*, 893.
discourteous, 895.
Offscourings, *remains*, 40.
dirt, 653.
trash, 643.
Offset, *compensation*, 30.
ridge, 250.
Offshoot, *part*, 51.
posterity, 167.
Offspring, *posterity*, 167.
Often, *frequency*, 136.
Ogee, *curve*, 245.
Ogham, *writing*, 590.
Ogle, *vision*, 441.
Ogre, *demon*, 980.
bugbear, 860.
Oil, *unctuosity*, 355, 356.
smooth, 255.
flattery, 933.
bland, 894.
relief, 834.
to assuage, 174.
Old, *oldness*, 124.
Old-fashioned, *obsolete*, 851.
quaint, 83.
Oleaginous, *unctuousness*, 355.
Olfactory, *odour*, 398.
Olid, *fetor*, 401.
Oligarchy, *authority*, 737.
Olio (Sp.), *mixture*, 41.
Olive, *brown*, 433.
Olive-branch, *pacification*, 723.
Olive-green, *greenness*, 435.
*Olla podrida (Sp.), *mixture*, 41.
Olympus, *heaven*, 981.
Omega, *end*, 67.
Omelet, *food*, 298.
Omen, *omen*, 512.
Ominous, *prediction*, 511.
danger, 665.
Omission, *neglect*, 460.
exclusion, 55.
incomplete, 53.
non-fulfilment, 773.
guilt, 947.
Omnibus, *vehicle*, 272.
*Omnibus rebus, de (L.), *multiformity*, 81.
Omnifarious, *multiformity*, 81.
Omnipotence, *Deity*, 976.
Omnipresence, *presence*, 186.
Deity, 976.
Omniscience, *knowledge*, 490.
divine, 976.
Omnium gatherum, *mixture*, 41.
confusion, 59.
assemblage, 72.
Omphalos, *middle*, 68.
centre, 223.
On, *forwards*, 282.
*On dit (Fr.), *publication*, 531.
news, 532.
interlocution, 588.
On end, *verticality*, 212.
Once, *preterition*, 122.
infrequency, 137.
Once for all, *end*, 67, 137.
Once upon a time, *different time*, 119.
period, 108.
One, *unity*, 87.
One by one, *disjunction*, 44.
unity, 87.
One-ideaed, *folly*, 499.
Oneiromancy, *prediction*, 511.
Oneness, *unity*, 87.
identity, 13.
Onerous, *difficulty*, 704.
One-sided, *prejudiced*, 481.
partial, 940.
incorrect, 495.
One-step, *dance*, 840.
Onomancy, *prediction*, 511.
Onset, *attack*, 716.
beginning, 66.
Onslaught, *attack*, 716.
Ontology, *existence*, 1.
Onus, *duty*, 926.
*Onus probandi (L.), *reasoning*, 476.
Onychomancy, *prediction*, 511.
Onward, *progression*, 282.
Ooze, *distil*, 295, 297.
river, 348.
sea, 341.
transpire, 529.
Opacity, *opacity*, 426.
Opalescent, *variegation*, 440.
Opaque, *opacity*, 426.
Open, *begin*, 66.
expand, 194.

Open, *unclose*, 260.
manifest, 518, 525.
reveal, 529.
frank, 543.
artless, 703.
Open-eyed, *attention*, 457.
Open-handed, *liberal*, 816.
Open-hearted, *sincere*, 543.
frank, 703.
honourable, 939.
Opening, *aperture*, 198, 260.
occasion, 134.
beginning, 66.
Open-minded, *intelligence*, 498.
Open-mouthed, *loud*, 404.
loquacious, 584.
gaping, 865.
Open sesame, *interpretation*, 522.
Operà, *drama*, 599.
music, 415.
*Opéra bouffe (Fr.), *drama*, 599.
Operate, *incite*, 615.
work, 170, 680.
Operative, *agent*, 690.
Operator, *agent*, 690.
Operculum, *covering*, 222.
stopper, 263.
Operose, *difficult*, 704.
active, 683.
exertive, 686.
Ophicleide, *musical*, 417.
Opiate, *remedy*, 174.
sedative, 174.
Opine, *belief*, 484.
*Opiniâtre (Fr.), *obstinacy*, 606.
Opinion, *belief*, 484.
Opinionative, *obstinacy*, 606.
Opium, *moderation*, 174.
Oppilation, *hindrance*, 706.
Opponent, *antagonist*, 710.
enemy, 891.
Opportune, *well-timed*, 134.
expedient, 646.
Opportunism, *cunning*, 702.
Opportunist, *time-server*, 607, 943.
Opportunity, *occasion*, 134.
Oppose, *antagonise*, 179.
clash, 708.
evidence, 468.
Opposite, *contrary*, 14.
antiposition, 237.
Oppress, *molest*, 649.
Oppression, *injury*, 619.
dejection, 837.
Opprobrium, *disrepute*, 874.
Optics, *light*, 420.
sight, 441.
*Optimates (L.), *nobility*, 875.
Optimism, *hope*, 858.
Option, *choice*, 609.
Opulence, *wealth*, 803.
*Opus (L.), *music*, 415.
Opuscule, *book*, 593.
Oracle, *prophet*, 513.
sage, 500.
Oracular, *wise*, 498.
prophetic, 511.
Oral, *voice*, 580.
Orange, *orange*, 439.
Oration, *speech*, 582.
Orator, *speaker*, 582.
teacher, 540.
Oratorio, *music*, 415.
Oratory, *speech*, 582.
Orb, *circle*, 247.
region, 181.
luminary, 423.
sphere of action, 625.
Orbicular, *circularity*, 247.
Orbit, *path*, 627.
Orchestration, *music*, 415.
Orchestra, *musician*, 416.
Orchestrion, *musical*, 417.
Ordain, *command*, 741, 976.
churchdom, 976.
Ordained, *prescribed*, 924.
Ordeal, *experiment*, 463.
sorcery, 992.
Order, *regularity*, 58.
subordinate class, 75.
law, 963.
precept, 697.
command, 741.
rank, 873, 875.
of the day, 82.
Orderless, *disorder*, 59.
Orderly, *conformity*, 82.
Orders, holy, *churchdom*, 995.
Ordinance, *command*, 741.
law, 963.
rite, 998.
Ordinary, *usual*, 82.
mean, 29.
ugly, 846.
Ordination, *command*, 741.
arrangement, 60.
Ordure, *uncleanness*, 653.
Ore, *materials*, 635.
*Ore rotundo (L.), *ornament*, 577.
speech, 582.
Organ, *instrument*, 633.
music, 417.
Organic, *state*, 7.
animal, 366.
Organism, *state*, 7.
structure, 329.
Organist, *musician*, 416.
Organisation, *structure*, 329.

Organise, *arrange*, 60.
plan, 626.
prepare, 673.
produce, 161.
Organised, *organisation*, 357.
Orgasm, *violence*, 173.
Orgy, *intemperance*, 954.
Orient, *light*, 420.
Orientate, *direction*, 278.
Orifice, *opening*, 66, 260.
Oriflamme, *indication*, 550.
Origin, *cause*, 153.
beginning, 66.
Original, *model*, 22.
oddity, 857.
invented, 515.
Originate, *cause*, 153.
begin, 66.
invent, 515.
Originator, *producer*, 164.
Orison, *request*, 765.
prayer, 990.
Ormuzd, *deity*, 979.
Ornament, *ornament*, 847.
glory, 873.
style, 577.
Ornate, *ornament*, 847.
style, 577.
Ornithomancy, *prediction*, 511.
Orography, *height*, 206.
Orotund, *style*, 577.
Orphan, *weakness*, 160.
Orthodox, *true*, 494.
conformity, 82.
in religion, 983.
Orthoepy, *voice*, 580.
Orthogenesis, *causation*, 153.
Orthography, *writing*, 590.
Orthometry, *measurement*, 466.
Orts, *remnants*, 40.
refuse, 643.
useless, 645.
Oscillation, *oscillation*, 314.
Osculate, *contiguity*, 199.
kiss, 902.
Osmosis, *percolation*, 302.
Ossification, *hardness*, 323.
Ossuary, *interment*, 363.
Ostensible, *visible*, 446.
probable, 472.
plea, 617.
explicit, 576.
Ostentation, *ostentation*, 882.
Osteopathy, *remedy*, 662.
Ostracise, *exclude*, 55.
displace, 185.
seclude, 893.
censure, 932.
Other, *difference*, 15.
Otherwise, *difference*, 15.
Other-worldliness, *piety*, 987.
O'Trigger, *blusterer*, 887.
Otto, *see* Attar.
Ottoman, *support*, 215.
*Oubliette (Fr.), *prison*, 752.
Ought, *duty*, 926.
*Oui-dire (Fr.), *news*, 532.
Oust, *displace*, 185.
deprive, 789.
dismiss, 756.
Out, *exteriority*, 220.
Out and out, *greatness*, 31.
Outbalance, *superiority*, 28, 33.
Outbid, *barter*, 794.
Outbrave, *insolence*, 885.
Outbrazen, *insolence*, 885.
Outbreak, *violence*, 173.
contest, 720.
passion, 825.
Outburst, *violence*, 173.
passion, 825.
Outcast, *secluded*, 893.
sinner, 949.
apostate, 941.
Outclass, *superiority*, 33.
Outcome, *result*, 154.
Outcry, *noise*, 411.
complaint, 839.
censure, 932.
Outdo, *activity*, 682.
superiority, 33.
Outdoor, *exteriority*, 220.
Outer, *exteriority*, 220.
Outface, *insolence*, 885.
Outfit, *preparation*, 673.
Outflank, *baffle*, 731.
Outgeneral, *success*, 731.
Outgo, *transgress*, 303.
distance, 196.
Outgoings, *expenditure*, 809.
Outgrow, *expansion*, 194.
Out-herod, *bluster*, 173.
exaggerate, 549.
Outhouse, *abode*, 189.
Outlandish, *irregular*, 83.
foreign, 10.
barbarous, 851.
Outlast, *diuturnity*, 110.
Outlaw, *reprobate*, 949.
Outlawry, *illegality*, 964.
Outlay, *expenditure*, 809.
Outleap, *transcursion*, 303.
Outlet, *egress*, 295.
opening, 260.
Outline, *contour*, 229.
sketch, 554.
features, 448.
plan, 626.

Outlive, *survive*, 110.
  continue, 142.
Outlook, *insolence*, 885.
  futurity, 121.
  view, 448.
Outlying, *exteriority*, 220.
  remainder, 40.
Outmanœuvre, *success*, 731.
Outmatch, *inequality*, 28.
Outnumber, *multitude*, 102.
Out of bounds, *transcursion*, 303.
Out of date, *old*, 124.
  past, 122.
  obsolete, 851.
Out of place, *disorder*, 59.
  unconformity, 83.
Outpace, *velocity*, 274.
  transcursion, 303.
Outpost, *distance*, 196.
  circumjacent, 227.
  front, 234.
Outpouring, *information*, 527.
Outrage, *evil*, 619.
  grievance, 830.
Outrageous, *excessive*, 31.
  violence, 173.
*Outré (Fr.), *ridiculous*, 853.
  unconformity, 83.
  exaggerated, 549.
Outreach, *deception*, 545.
Outreckon, *overestimation*, 482.
Outrider, *precursor*, 64.
Outrigger, *support*, 215.
  boat, 273.
Outright, *greatness*, 31.
  completeness, 52.
Outrun, *velocity*, 274, 303.
Outset, *beginning* 66.
  departure, 293.
Outshine, *glory*, 873.
  eclipse, 874.
Outside, *exteriority*, 220.
Outsider, *extraneous*, 57.
  upstart, 876.
Outskirt, *environs*, 227.
  distance, 196.
Outspoken, *speech*, 582.
  candour, 703.
Outspread, *thickness*, 202.
Outstanding, *remainder*, 40.
  salient, 642.
  unpaid, 806.
Outstep, *go beyond*, 303.
  distance, 196.
Outstretched, *length*, 200.
  breadth, 202.
Outstrip, *velocity*, 274.
Out-talk, *loquacity*, 584.
Outvie, *contend*, 720.
Outvie, *shine*, 873.
Outvote, *success*, 731.
Outward, *exteriority*, 220.
Outweigh, *exceed*, 33.
  preponderate, 28.
  predominate, 175.
Outwit, *deceive*, 545.
  succeed, 731.
Outwork, *refuge*, 666.
  defence, 717.
Oval, *circularity*, 247.
Ovary, *receptacle*, 191.
Ovate, *circularity*, 247.
Ovation, *triumph*, 733.
  celebration, 883.
Oven, *furnace*, 386.
Over, *more*, 33.
  past time, 122.
  above, 206.
Over head and ears, *greatness*, 31.
Over and above, *remainder*, 40.
Over and over, *repetition*, 104.
Overabound, *redundance*, 641.
Over against, *antiposition*, 237.
Over-act, *act*, 680.
  bustle, 682.
  affect, 855.
Overalls, *dress*, 225.
Over-anxiety, *desire*, 865.
Overawe, *intimidate*, 860.
  authority, 737.
Overbalance, *inequality*, 28, 33.
  compensation, 30.
Overblown, *deterioration*, 659.
Overboard (to throw), *disuse*, 678.
Overbold, *rashness*, 863.
Overburden, *fatigue*, 688.
  redundant, 641.
Overcast, *dark*, 421.
  dim, 422.
Overcharge, *exaggerate*, 549.
  redundance, 641.
  dearness, 814.
  style, 577.
Overcolour, *exaggeration*, 549.
Overcome, *conquer*, 731.
  subdued, 732.
  shock, 824.
  tipsy, 959.
Overdo, *activity*, 682.
  exaggerate, 549.
Overdose, *redundance*, 641.
Overdue, *anachronism*, 115.
Overestimate, *overestimation*, 482.
Overfed, *gluttony*, 957.
Overflow, *stream*, 348.
  redundance, 641.
Overgo, *transcursion*, 303.
Overgrown, *size*, 31, 192.

Overhang, *height*, 206.
jut out, 250.
impend, 121.
Overhaul, *inquire*, 461.
attend to, 457.
number, 85.
overtake, 292.
Overhead, *height*, 206.
Overhear, *hear*, 418.
learn, 539.
Overjoyed, *pleasure*, 827.
Overjump, *transcursion*, 303.
Overland, *journey*, 266.
Overlap, *cover*, 222.
go beyond, 303.
Overlay, *excess*, 641.
oppress, 649.
hinder, 706.
style, 577.
Overleap, *transcursion*, 303.
Overload, *excess*, 641.
obstruct, 706.
Overlook, *disregard*, 458.
neglect, 460.
superintend, 693.
forgive, 918.
slight, 929.
Overlooker, *director*, 694.
Overmatch, *inequality*, 28, 149.
Overmuch, *redundance*, 641.
Overnight, *preterition*, 122.
Over-officious, *activity*, 682.
Overpass, *exceed*, 33.
transgress, 303.
Overplus, *excess*, 641.
remainder, 40.
Overpower, *subdue*, 731.
emotion, 824.
Overpowered, *failure*, 732.
Overpowering, *excitability*, 825.
Overprize, *overestimation*, 482.
Overrate, *overestimation*, 482.
Overreach, *pass*, 303, 305.
deceive, 545.
baffle, 731.
Override, *pass*, 303.
be superior, 33.
Over-righteous, *impiety*, 989.
Overrule, *control*, 737.
cancel, 736.
Overrun, *ravage*, 649.
pass, 303.
excess, 641.
Overseas, *extraneous*, 57.
Overseer, *director*, 694.
Overset, *level*, 308.
invert, 218.
subvert, 731.
Overshadow, *darkness*, 421.
superiority, 33.
Overshoe, *dress*, 225.
Overshoot, *transcursion*, 303.
Oversight, *error*, 495.
failure, 732.
Overspread, *cover*, 222.
pervade, 73, 186.
Overstate, *exaggeration*, 549.
Overstep, *transcursion*, 303.
Overstrain, *overrate*, 482.
fatigue, 688.
Overstrung, *excitability*, 825.
Overt, *visible*, 446.
plain, 516.
Overtake, *arrive*, 292.
Overtaken, *tipsy*, 959.
Overtask, *fatigue*, 688.
Overtax, *fatigue*, 688.
Overthrow, *destroy*, 162.
level, 308.
confute, 479.
vanquish, 731, 732.
Overtone, *melody*, 413.
Overtop, *surpass*, 33.
height, 206.
perfection, 650.
Overture, *beginning*, 66.
offer, 763.
music, 415.
request, 765.
Overturn, *destroy*, 162.
level, 308.
confute, 571.
invert, 218.
Overvalue, *overestimation*, 482.
Overweening, *conceit*, 880.
pride, 878.
Overweigh, *overrate*, 482.
exceed, 33.
influence, 175.
Overwhelm, *destroy*, 162.
affect, 824.
Overwhelming, *excitability*, 825.
Overwork, *fatigue*, 688.
Overwrought, *excited*, 825.
Over-zealous, *excitability*, 825.
Ovoid, *rotundity*, 249.
Ovule, *circularity*, 247.
Owe, *debt*, 806.
Owing to, *attribution*, 155.
Owl-light, *dimness*, 422.
Own, *assent*, 488, 535.
divulge, 529.
possess, 777.
Owner, *possessor*, 779.
Ownership, *property*, 780.
Oxygenate, *air*, 338.

P

Pabulum, *food*, 298.
Pace, *speed*, 274.
step, 266.
measure, 466.
Pace with, keep, *equality*, 27.
Pacific, *concord*, 714, 721.
Pacifism, *pacification*, 723.
Pacifist, *non-combatant*, 726A.
Pacify, *allay*, 174.
compose, 826.
give peace, 723.
forgive, 918.
Pachydermatous, *insensible*, 823.
Pack, *to join*, 43.
arrange, 60.
bring close, 197.
locate, 184.
assemblage, 72.
Pack off, *depart*, 293.
recede, 287.
decamp, 671.
Pack up, *circumscription*, 231.
Package, *parcel*, 72.
Packet, *parcel*, 72.
ship, 273.
Pack-horse, *carrier*, 271.
Packing-case, *receptacle*, 191.
Packthread, *vinculum*, 45.
Pact, *agreement*, 769.
Pactolus, *wealth*, 803.
Pad, *carrier*, 271.
to expand, 194.
Paddle, *oar*, 267, 633.
to bathe, 337.
Paddock, *arena*, 181.
enclosure, 232, 752.
Padlock, *fastening*, 45.
fetter, 752.
Pæan, *thanks*, 916.
rejoicing, 836.
Paganism, *heterodoxy*, 984.
Page, *attendant*, 746.
of a book, 593.
Pageant, *spectacle*, 448.
the drama, 599.
show, 882.
Pagoda, *temple*, 1000.
Pail, *receptacle*, 191.
*Paillard (Fr.), *libertine*, 962.
Pain, *physical*, 378.
moral, 828.
penalty, 974.
Painful, *painfulness*, 830.
Pains, *exertion*, 686.
Painstaking, *active*, 682.
laborious, 686.
Paint, *coat*, 222.
Paint, *colour*, 428.
delineate, 556.
describe, 594.
Painter, *artist*, 559.
Painting, *painting*, 556.
Pair, *couple*, 89.
similar, 17.
Pair off, *average*, 29.
Pal, *friend*, 890.
Palace, *abode*, 189.
Palæography, *interpretation*, 522.
Palæolithic, *oldness*, 142.
Palæology, *preterition*, 122.
Palæontology, *zoology*, 368.
*Palæstra (L.), *school*, 542.
arena, 728.
training, 673.
Palæstric, *exertion*, 686.
Palankeen, *vehicle*, 272.
Palatable, *savoury*, 394.
pleasant, 829.
Palate, *taste*, 390.
Palatine, *master*, 745.
Palaver, *speech*, 582.
colloquy, 588.
council, 696.
nonsense, 497.
loquacity, 584.
Pale, *dim*, 422.
colourless, 429.
enclosure, 232.
Palfry, *carrier*, 271.
Palimpsest, *substitution*, 147.
Palindrome, *neology*, 563.
Palinode, *denial*, 536.
recantation, 607.
Paling, *prison*, 752.
enclosure, 232.
Palisade, *prison*, 752.
enclosure, 232.
Pall, *funeral*, 363.
disgust, 395.
satiate, 869.
Palladium, *defence*, 717.
Pallet, *support*, 215.
Palliasse, *support*, 215.
Palliate, *mend*, 658.
relieve, 834.
extenuate, 937.
Pallid, *achromatism*, 429.
Palling, *unsavouriness*, 395.
Pallium, *dress*, 225.
canonicals, 999.
Palm, *trophy*, 733.
glory, 873.
laurel, 877.
deceive, 545.
impose upon, 486.
Palmer, *traveller*, 268.

Palmist, *fortune-teller*, 513.
Palmistry, *prediction*, 511.
Palmy, *prosperous*, 734.
halcyon, 827, 829.
Palpable, *tactile*, 379.
obvious, 446, 525.
intelligible, 518.
Palpitate, *tremble*, 315.
emotion, 821.
fear, 860.
Palsy, *disease*, 655.
weakness, 160.
insensibility, 823.
Palter, *falsehood*, 544.
shift, 605.
elude, 773.
Paltry, *mean*, 940.
despicable, 643.
little, 32.
Paludal, *marsh*, 345.
Pampas, *plain*, 344.
Pamper, *indulge*, 954.
gorge, 957.
Pampero, *wind*, 349.
Pamphlet, *book*, 593.
Pamphleteer, *writing*, 590.
Pan, *receptacle*, 191.
Panacea, *remedy*, 662.
Panache, *plume*, 256.
ornament, 847.
Pandect, *code*, 963.
compendium, 596.
erudition, 490.
Pandemic, *insalubrity*, 657.
Pandemonium, *hell*, 982.
disorder, 59.
Pander, *flatter*, 933.
indulge, 954.
help, 707.
Pandora, *evil*, 619.
Paned, *variegation*, 440.
Panegyric, *approbation*, 931.
Panel, *list*, 86.
partition, 228.
legal, 967.
•Panem et circenses (L.), *giving*, 784.
Pang, *physical*, 378.
moral, 828.
Panic, *fear*, 860.
Pannier, *receptacle*, 191.
Panoply, *defence*, 717.
Panopticon, *prison*, 752.
Panorama, *view*, 448.
painting, 556.
Pansophy, *knowledge*, 490.
Pant, *breathless*, 688.
desire, 865.
agitation, 821.
Pantaloon, *buffoon*, 844.
dress, 225.
Pantechnicon, *vehicle*, 272.
Pantheism, *heterodoxy*, 984.
Pantheon, *temple*, 1000.
Pantograph, *imitation*, 19.
Pantomime, *sign*, 550.
language, 560.
drama, 599.
Pantry, *receptacle*, 191.
Pap, *pulp*, 354.
teat, 250.
Paper, *writing*, 590.
book, 593.
record, 551.
white, 430.
Papilla, *convexity*, 250.
Papoose, *infant*, 129.
Pappy, *semiliquidity*, 352.
Par, *equality*, 27.
Par, above, *greatness*, 31.
Parable, *metaphor*, 521.
story, 594.
Parabolic, *metaphor*, 521.
curve, 245.
Parachronism, *anachronism*, 115.
Parachute, *refuge*, 666.
Paraclete, *Deity*, 976.
Parade, *walk*, 189.
ostentation, 882.
Paradigm, *prototype*, 22.
example, 80.
Paradise, *heaven*, 981.
bliss, 827.
Paradox, *obscurity*, 519.
absurdity, 497.
mystery, 528.
enigma, 533.
Paragon, *perfection*, 650.
saint, 948.
glory, 873.
Paragraph, *phrase*, 566.
part, 51.
article, 593.
Paralipsis, *neglect*, 460.
Parallax, *distance*, 196.
Parallel, *position*, 216.
similarity, 17.
to imitate, 19.
agreement, 23.
Parallel, without, *superiority*, 33.
Parologism, *sophistry*, 477.
Paralyse, *weaken*, 160.
benumb, 381.
deaden, 823.
insensibility, *physical*, 376.
moral, 823.
disqualify, 158.
disease, 655.

Paramount, *essential*, 642.
in degree, 33.
Paramour, *love*, 897.
Paranoia, *insanity*, 503.
Parapet, *defence*, 717.
Paraph, *writing*, 590.
Paraphernalia, *machinery*, 633.
materials, 635.
property, 780.
Paraphrase, *interpretation*, 522.
phrase, 566.
imitation, 19, 21.
Parasite, *flatterer*, 935.
servile, 886.
follow, 88.
Parboil, *calefaction*, 384.
Parcel, *group*, 72.
portion, 51.
Parcel out, *arrange*, 60.
allot, 786.
Parch, *dry*, 340.
bake, 384.
Parchment, *manuscript*, 590.
record, 551.
Pardon, *forgiveness*, 918.
Pardonable, *vindication*, 937.
Pare, *scrape*, 38, 226, 331.
shorten, 201.
decrease, 36.
Paregoric, *salubrity*, 656.
Parenchyma, *texture*, 329.
Parent, *paternity*, 166.
Parentage, *kindred*, 11.
Parenthesis, *interjacence*, 228.
discontinue, 70.
Parenthetically, *irrelation*, 10.
*Par excellence (Fr.), *greatness*, 31.
superiority, 33.
*Par exemple (Fr.), *example*, 82.
Pariah, *commonalty*, 876.
outcast, 892.
Paring, *part*, 51. *See* Pare.
smallness, 32.
*Pari passu (L.), *equality*, 27.
Parish, *region*, 181.
Parishioner, *laity*, 997.
Parity, *equality*, 27.
Park, *plain*, 344.
vegetation, 367.
artillery, 727.
Parlance, *speech*, 582.
*Parlementaire (Fr.), *messenger*, 534.
Parley, *talk*, 588.
mediation, 724.
Parliament, *council*, 696.
Parlour, *receptacle*, 191.
Parlour, *room*, 191.
Parnassus, *poetry*, 597.
Parody, *imitation*, 19.
copy, 21.
travesty, 856.
misinterpret, 523.
Parole, *promise*, 768.
Paronomasia, *pun*, 563.
Paronymous, *word*, 562.
Paroxysm, *violence*, 173.
emotion, 825.
anger, 900.
*Par parenthèse (Fr.), *occasion*, 134.
Parrot, *imitation*, 19.
loquacity, 584.
repetition, 104.
Parry, *avert*, 623.
defend, 717.
Parse, *grammar*, 567.
Parsee, *heterodoxy*, 984.
Parsimony, *parsimony*, 819.
Parson, *clergy*, 996.
Parsonage, *temple*, 1000.
Part, *portion*, 51.
component, 56.
to diverge, 291.
to divide, 44.
business, 625.
function, 644.
Part, in, *smallness*, 32.
Part with, *relinquish*, 782.
give, 784.
Partake, *participation*, 778.
*Parterre (Fr.), *plant*, 367.
*Parti (Fr.), *adolescence*, 131.
Partial, *unequal*, 28.
special, 79.
one-sided, 481.
unjust, 923.
love, 897.
desire, 865.
erroneous, 495.
smallness, 32.
harmonic, 413.
*Particeps criminis (L.), *auxiliary*, 711.
bad man, 949.
Participation, *participation*, 778.
Particle, *quantity*, 32.
size, 193.
Parti-coloured, *variegation*, 440.
Particular, *special*, 79.
event, 151.
careful, 459.
capricious, 608.
fastidious, 868.
item, 51.
detail, 79.
Particularly, *greatness*, 31.
Parting, *disjunction*, 44.
*Parti pris (Fr.), *prejudgment*, 481.

Partisan, *auxiliary*, 711.
Partition, *allot*, 51, 786.
wall, 228.
Partner, *auxiliary*, 711.
Partnership, *participation*, 778.
company, 797.
companionship, 88.
Parts, *intellect*, 450.
wisdom, 498.
talents, 698.
Party, *assemblage*, 72.
association, 712.
society, 892.
special, 79.
Party-wall, *interjacence*, 228.
*Parvenu (Fr.), *upstart*, 876.
successful, 734.
*Pas (Fr.), *rank*, 873.
precedence, 62.
term, 71.
Pasha, *master*, 745.
Pasquinade, *satire*, 932.
Pass, *move*, 264.
move out, 295.
move through, 302.
exceed, 303.
be superior, 33.
happen, 151.
lapse, 122.
vanish, 449.
passage, 260.
defile, 203.
way, 627.
difficulty, 704.
conjuncture, 8.
forgive, 918.
thrust, 716.
passport, 760.
time, 106.
Pass away, *cease*, 2, 141.
Pass by, *disregard*, 929.
Pass for, *falsehood*, 544.
Pass in the mind, *thought*, 451.
Pass over, *disregard*, 458.
neglect, 460.
forgive, 918.
exclude, 55.
traverse, 302.
Pass the time, *duration*, 106.
Pass through, *experience*, 151.
Passable, *imperfection*, 651.
Passage, *motion*, 264.
opening, 260.
passage, 302.
eventuality, 151.
method, 627.
transfer, 270.
text, 593.
act, 680.
Passage, *assault*, 720.
See Pass.
*Passage d'armes (Fr.), *contention*, 720.
*Passé (Fr.), *age*, 128.
deterioration, 659.
Passenger, *traveller*, 268.
*Passe-partout (Fr.), 462.
instrumentality, 631.
*Passim (L.), *dispersion*, 73.
situation, 183.
Passing, *exceeding*, 33.
transient, 111.
greatness, 31.
Passion, *emotion*, 820, 821.
desire, 865.
love, 987.
anger, 900.
Passionate, *warm*, 825.
irascible, 901.
Passionless, *insensibility*, 823.
Passive, *inert*, 172.
submissive, 743.
Passive resister, *non-combatant*, 726A.
Passport, *permit*, 760.
instrument, 631.
order, 741.
Password, *sign*, 550.
Past, *preterition*, 122.
Paste, *cement*, 45.
to cement, 46.
pulp, 354.
Pasteurise, *inject*, 300.
*Pasticcio (It.), *mixture*, 41.
Pastime, *amusement*, 840.
Pastor, *clergy*, 996.
Pastoral, *agricultural*, 371.
poem, 597.
religious, 995.
Pasturage, *plain*, 344.
Pasture, *food*, 298.
materials, 635.
Pasty, *semiliquid*, 352.
colourless, 429.
Pat, *expedient*, 646.
pertinent, 9.
to strike, 276.
Patagonian, *height*, 206.
Patch, *region*, 181.
smallness, 193.
repair, 658.
Patchwork, *mixture*, 41.
variegation, 440.
Patchy, *imperfect*, 53.
Pate, *head*, 450.
Patent, *open*, 260.
visible, 446.
privilege, 924.

Patera, *plate*, 191.
church, 1000.
Paternity, *paternity*, 155, 166.
Path, *way*, 627.
direction, 278.
Pathetic, *painful*, 830.
affecting, 824.
Pathless, *closure*, 261.
difficult, 704.
spacious, 180.
Pathognomonic, *indication*, 550.
Pathology, *disease*, 655.
Pathos, *feeling*, 821.
Pathway, *way*, 627.
Patience, *endurance*, 826.
content, 831.
perseverance, 682.
Patient, *invalid*, 655.
*Patois (Fr.), *language*, 560.
Patriarch, *veteran*, 130.
Patriarchy, *authority*, 737.
Patrician, *nobility*, 875.
Patrimony, *property*, 780.
Patriot, *philanthropy*, 910.
Patrol, *safeguard*, 664.
warning, 668.
Patronage, *aid*, 707.
Patronise, *aid*, 707.
Patronising, *condescending*, 878.
Patronymic, *nomenclature*, 564.
Patter, *to strike*, 276.
step, 266.
sound, 407.
chatter, 584.
patois, 560.
Pattern, *model*, 22.
type, 80.
perfection, 650.
saint, 948.
Patulous, *opening*, 260.
Paucity, *fewness*, 103.
scantiness, 640.
smallness, 32.
Paul Pry, *curiosity*, 455.
Paunch, *receptacle*, 191.
Pauperism, *poverty*, 804.
Pause, *stop*, 265.
discontinuance, 141.
rest, 687.
disbelief, 485.
Pavane, *dance*, 840.
Pave, *prepare*, 673.
cover, 222.
Pavement, *base*, 311.
footway, 627.
Pavilion, *abode*, 189.
Paving, *base*, 211.
Paw, *touch*, 379.
finger, 633.
Pawn, *security*, 771.
lending, 787.
*Pax vobiscum (L.), *courtesy*, 894.
Pay, *expend*, 809.
defray, 807.
condemn, 971.
punish, 972.
Paymaster, *treasury*, 801.
Paynim, *heterodoxy*, 984.
Pea, *rotundity*, 249.
Peace, *silence*, 403.
amity, 721.
concord, 714.
Peaceable, *gentle*, 174.
Peace-offering, *pacification*, 723.
atonement, 952.
Peach, *disclosure*, 529.
Peach-colour, *redness*, 434.
Peacock, *variegation*, 440.
beauty, 845.
boaster, 884.
Pea-green, *greenness*, 435.
Peak, *summit*, 210.
Peaked, *sharpness*, 253.
Peal, *loudness*, 404.
laughter, 838.
Pearl, *gem*, 650.
glory, 873.
Pearly, *nacreous*, 440.
semitransparent, 427.
white, 439.
Pear-shaped, *rotundity*, 249.
Peasant, *commonalty*, 876.
Pea-shooter, *propulsion*, 284.
Peat, *fuel*, 388.
Pebble, *hardness*, 323.
trifle, 643.
Peccability, *vice*, 945.
Peccadillo, *guilt*, 947.
Peccancy, *disease*, 655.
imperfection, 651.
badness, 649.
Peccant, *wrong*, 945.
Peccavi (L.), *penitence*, 950.
Peck, *quantity*, 31.
eat, 296.
Peckish, *desire*, 865.
Pecksniff, *hypocrite*, 548.
Pectinated, *sharpness*, 253.
Peculate, *stealing*, 791.
Peculator, *thief*, 792.
Peculiar, *special*, 5, 79.
exceptional, 83.
Peculiarly, *greatness*, 31, 33.
Pecuniary, *money*, 800.
Pedagogue, *scholar*, 492.
teacher, 540.
Pedant, *scholar*, 492.
affected, 855.

Pedant, *teacher*, 540.
Pedantic, *affected*, 855.
half-learned, 491.
style, 577.
Peddle, *trifle*, 683.
sell, 796.
Pedestal, *support*, 215.
Pedestrian, *traveller*, 268.
dull, 843.
style, 573.
Pedicel, *pendency*, 214.
Pedigree, *ancestry*, 155, 166.
continuity, 69.
Pediment, *capital*, 210.
base, 215.
Pedlar, *merchant*, 797.
Peduncle, *pendency*, 214.
Peel, *skin*, 222.
to uncover, 226.
Peep, *vision*, 441.
Peep out, *visibility*, 446.
Peer, *equal*, 27.
nobleman, 875.
pry, 441.
inquire, 461.
appear, 446.
Peerage, *list*, 86.
Peerless, *perfect*, 650.
excellent, 648, 873.
virtuous, 944.
Peevish, *cross*, 895.
irascible, 901.
Peg, *degree*, 26.
project, 250.
hang, 214.
jog on, 266.
drink, 298.
Pegasus, *imagination*, 515.
Peg away, *persist*, 143.
Pegomancy, *prediction*, 511.
*Peine forte et dure (Fr.), *punishment*, 972.
Pejoration, *deterioration*, 659.
Pelagic, *ocean*, 341.
Pelerine, *dress*, 225.
Pelf, *money*, 803.
materials, 635.
gain, 775.
Pellet, *rotundity*, 249.
Pellicle, *film*, 205.
skin, 222.
Pell-mell, *disorder*, 59.
Pellucid, *transparency*, 425.
Pelt, *skin*, 222.
throw, 276.
attack, 716.
beat, 972.
Pen, *surround*, 231.
enclose, 232.
Pen, *restrain*, 751.
imprison, 752.
draw, 559.
write, 590.
Penalty, *penalty*, 974.
Penance, *atonement*, 952.
penalty, 974.
*Penchant (Fr.), *inclination*, 865.
love, 897.
Pencil, *bundle*, 72.
of light, 420.
artist, 556, 559, 590.
Pen-craft, *writing*, 590.
Pendant, *adjunct*, 39.
flag, 550.
pendency, 214.
match, 17.
Pendent, *during*, 106.
hanging, 214.
uncertain, 485.
*Pendente lite (L.), *warfare*, 722.
law-suit, 969.
Pending, *duration*, 106.
uncertain, 475.
Pendulous, *pendency*, 214.
Pendulum, *clock*, 114.
oscillation, 314.
*Penetralia (L.), *interiority*, 221.
secret, 533.
Penetrating, *affecting*, 821.
Penetration, *ingress*, 294.
passage, 302.
discernment, 441.
sagacity, 498.
Penfold, *enclosure*, 232.
Peninsula, *land*, 342.
Penitent, *penitence*, 950.
Penitentiary, *prison*, 752.
Penman, *writing*, 590.
Penmanship, *writing*, 590.
Pen-name, *misnomer*, 565.
Penniless, *poverty*, 804.
Pennon, *indication*, 550.
Penny-a-liner, *writer*, 590.
Pennyworth, *price*, 812.
*Penseroso (It.), *dejection*, 837.
Pensile, *pendency*, 214.
Pension, *wealth*, 803, 810.
Pensioner, *servant*, 746.
Pensive, *thoughtful*, 451.
sad, 837.
Pentatonic, *melody*, 413.
Penthouse, *building*, 189.
Penultimate, *end*, 67.
Penumbra, *darkness*, 421, 424.
Penurious, *parsimony*, 819.
Penury, *poverty*, 804.
scantiness, 640.
People, *man*, 373.

People, *commonalty*, 876.
to colonise, 184.
Pepper, *hot*, 171.
pungent, 392.
condiment, 393.
attack, 716.
Peppercorn, *unimportance*, 643.
Peppery, *irascibility*, 901.
Peradvanture, *chance*, 156.
uncertainty, 475.
Perambulate, *journey*, 266.
Percentage, *proportion*, 84.
discount, 813.
Perception, *idea*, 453.
of touch, 380.
Perceptible, *visibility*, 446.
smallness, 32.
Perceptivity, *sensibility*, 375.
Perch, *support*, 215.
to alight, 186.
tall, 206.
habitation, 189.
Perchance, *chance*, 156.
Percipience, *intellect*, 450.
Percolate, *distil*, 295.
Percolation, *passage*, 302.
*Per contra (L.), *contrariety*, 14.
opposition, 708.
Percussion, *impulse*, 276.
Perdition, *ruin*, 732.
loss, 776.
*Perdu (Fr.), *concealment*, 528.
Perdurable, *permanence*, 142.
Peregrination, *journey*, 266.
Peremptory, *assertion*, 535.
denial, 536.
firm, 604.
rigorous, 739.
authoritative, 737.
compulsory, 744.
order, 740, 741.
Perennial, *diuturnity*, 110, 150.
Perfect, *entire*, 52.
complete, 729.
excellent, 650.
Perfectly, *greatness*, 31.
Perfidy, *improbity*, 940.
Perforate, *opening*, 260.
Perforator, *perforator*, 263.
Perforce, *compulsion*, 744.
Perform, *do*, 170, 680.
achieve, 729.
produce, 161.
act, 599.
fulfil, 772.
duty, 926.
Performable, *facility*, 705.
Performance, *effect*, 154.
Performer, *musician*, 416.
Performer, *actor*, 599.
workman, 164.
agent, 690.
Perfume, *fragrance*, 400.
Perfunctory, *neglect*, 460.
Perhaps, *possibly*, 470.
chance, 156.
supposition, 514.
Peri, *fairy*, 979.
Periapt, *spell*, 993.
Perihelion, *nearness*, 197.
Peril, *danger*, 665.
Perimeter, *outline*, 229.
Period, *end*, 67.
of time, 106, 108.
point, 71.
recurrence, 138.
Periodical, *book*, 593.
Peripatetic, *traveller*, 268.
ambulatory, 266.
Periphery, *outline*, 229.
Periphrasis, *phrase*, 566.
diffuseness, 573.
Perique, *tobacco*, 298A.
Periscope, *vision*, 441.
optical instrument, 445.
Perish, *vanish*, 2.
die, 360.
decay, 659.
Peristaltic, *convolution*, 248.
Periwig, *dress*, 225.
Perjured, *false*, 940.
Perjury, *falsehood*, 544.
untruth, 546.
Perk, *lift*, 307.
smarten, 845.
Perky, *saucy*, 885.
Perlustration, *vision*, 441.
Permanent, *unchanged*, 142.
unchangeable, 150.
lasting, 106, 110.
Permeable, *opening*, 260.
Permeate, *pervade*, 186.
insinuate, 228.
pass through, 302.
Permissible, *dueness*, 924.
Permission, *permission*, 760.
Permit, *permission*, 760.
Permutation, *change*, 140.
numerical, 84.
Pernicious, *badness*, 649.
Pernickety, *fastidious*, 868.
difficult, 704.
Peroration, *end*, 67.
Perpend, *thought*, 451.
Perpendicular, *verticality*, 212.
Perpetrate, *action*, 680.
Perpetual, *perpetuity*, 112.
duration, 106.

Perpetual, *frequent*, 136.
Perplex, *to derange*, 61.
bewilder, 458, 519.
bother, 830.
embarrass, 475.
puzzle, 528.
Perplexity, *disorder*, 59.
difficulty, 704.
ignorance, 491.
doubt, 475.
unintelligibility, 519.
maze, 533.
Perquisite, *receipt*, 810.
Perquisition, *inquiry*, 461.
*Per saltum, (L.), *discontinuity*, 70.
transientness, 111.
instantaneity, 113.
*Per se (L.), *unity*, 87.
Persecute, *worry*, 830, 907.
oppress, 619, 649.
Perseverance, *firmness*, 604.
activity, 682.
continuance, 143.
*Persiflage, (Fr.), *ridicule*, 856.
Persist, *endure*, 106, 143, 606.
Persistence, *continuance*, 110, 142.
activity, 682.
Person, *man*, 373.
Personable, *beauty*, 845.
Personage, *nobility*, 875.
important, 642.
*Persona grata (L.), *favourite*, 899.
Personal, *special*, 79, 317, 372.
Personate, *imitate*, 17.
act, 554.
Personify, *metaphor*, 521.
Perspective, *view*, 448.
futurity, 121.
sagacity, 498.
sight, 441.
Perspicacious, *foreseeing*, 510.
Perspicacity, *intelligence*, 498.
Perspicuity, *perspicuity*, 570.
Perspiration, *excretion*, 299.
Perstringe, *attention*, 457.
Persuade, *induce*, 609, 615.
teach, 537.
advise, 695.
Persuasible, *learning*, 539.
Persuasion, *opinion*, 484.
creed, 983.
Pert, *vain*, 880.
saucy, 885.
discourteous, 895.
Pertain, *belong*, 76, 777.
relate to, 9.
behove, 926.
Pertinacious, *obstinacy*, 606.
Pertinent, *relative*, 9.
Pertinent, *congruous*, 23.
relevant, 476.
applicable, 646.
Perturb, *derange*, 61.
agitate, 315.
emotion, 821.
ferment, 171.
Peruke, *dress*, 225.
Peruse, *learning*, 539.
examine, 461.
Pervade, *extend*, 186.
affect, 821.
Perverse, *crotchety*, 608.
difficult, 704.
wayward, 895.
Perversion, *injury*, 659.
sophistry, 477.
falsehood, 544.
misinterpretation, 523.
misteaching, 538.
Pervert, *apostate*, 941.
Pervicacious, *obstinacy*, 606.
*Pervigilium (L.), *activity*, 682.
Pervious, *opening*, 260.
Pessimism, *dejection*, 837.
hopelessness, 859.
Pessomancy, *prediction*, 511.
Pest, *bane*, 663.
Pester, *painfulness*, 830.
Pest-house, *remedy*, 662.
Pestiferous, *insalubrity*, 657.
Pestilent, *badness*, 649.
Pestle, *pulverulence*, 330.
Pet, *plaything*, 840.
favourite, 899.
passion, 900.
to love, 897.
to fondle, 902.
Petard, *arms*, 727.
Peter out, *end*, 67.
Petition, *ask*, 765.
pray, 990.
Petitioner, *petitioner*, 767.
*Petitio principii (L.), *sophistry*, 477.
*Petit-maître (Fr.), *fop*, 854.
*Petits soins (Fr.), *courtesy*, 894.
courtship, 903.
*Pétri (Fr.), *feeling*, 821.
Petrify, *dense*, 321.
hard, 323.
affright, 860.
astonish, 870.
thrill, 824.
Petroleum, *oil*, 356.
Petronel, *arms*, 727.
Petticoat, *dress*, 225.
Pettifogger, *lawyer*, 968.
Pettifogging, *discord*, 713.
Pettish, *irascibility*, 895, 901.

Petty, *in degree*, 32.
in size, 193.
Petulant, *insolent*, 885.
snappish, 895.
angry, 900.
irascible, 901.
Pew, *temple*, 1000.
Phaeton, *carriage*, 272.
Phalanx, *army*, 726.
party, 712.
assemblage, 72.
Phantasm, *unreal*, 4.
appearance, 448.
delusion, 443.
Phantasmagoria, *optical*, 445.
Phantom, *vision*, 448.
unreal, 4.
imaginary, 515.
Pharisaical, *falsehood*, 544.
Pharisee, *deceiver*, 548.
Pharmacology, *remedy*, 662.
Pharmacy, *remedy*, 662.
Pharos, *warning*, 668.
indication, 550.
Phase, *aspect*, 8.
appearance, 448.
change, 144.
form, 240.
Phenomenal, *great*, 31.
apparent, 448.
wonderful, 870.
Phenomenon, *appearance*, 448.
event, 151.
prodigy, 872.
Phial, *receptacle*, 191.
Phidias, *artist*, 559.
Philanthropy, *philanthropy*, 910.
Philatelist, *collector*, 775.
Philippic, *disapprobation*, 932.
Philistine, *uncultured*, 491, 493.
Philology, *grammar*, 567.
Philomath, *scholar*, 492.
sage, 500.
Philomel, *musician*, 416.
Philosopher, *scholar*, 492.
Philosophy, *calmness*, 826.
knowledge, 490.
Philter, *charm*, 993.
love, 897.
Phiz, *appearance*, 448.
Phlegm, *insensibility*, 823.
Phœnix, *prodigy*, 872.
exception, 83.
paragon, 650.
saint, 948.
renovation, 163, 660.
Phonetics, *sound*, 402.
speech, 580.
Phonograph, *musical instrument*, 417.
Phosphorescent, *light*, 420, 423.
Photograph, *copy*, 21.
Photography, *painting*, 556.
Photology, *light*, 420.
Photometer, *optical instrument*, 445.
Phrase, *phrase*, 566.
Phraseology, *style*, 569.
Phratry, *class*, 75.
Phrenetic, *see* Frantic.
Phylactery, *spell*, 993.
Physic, *remedy*, 662.
to cure, 660.
Physical, *materiality*, 316.
Physician, *advice*, 695.
Physics, *materiality*, 316.
Physiognomy, *appearance*, 448.
face, 234.
Physiology, *life*, 359.
Physique, *substance*, 3.
Phytography, *botany*, 369.
Phytology, *botany*, 369.
Piacular, *atonement*, 952.
Pianist, *musician*, 416.
*Pianissimo (L.), *faintness*, 405.
*Piano (It.), *slowly*, 275.
faint sound, 405.
instrument, 417.
Pianola, *instrument*, 417.
*Piazza (It.), *street*, 189.
Pibroch, *music*, 415.
Picaroon, *thief*, 792.
Piccaninny, *child*, 129.
Piccolo, *musical instrument*, 417.
Pick, *select*, 609.
extract, 301.
eat, 296.
clean, 652.
Pick up, *learn*, 539.
improve, 658.
acquire, 775.
Picket, *join*, 43.
tether, 265.
fence, 231.
guard, 664.
imprison, 752.
torture, 972.
Pickings, *part*, 51.
booty, 793.
Pickle, *state*, 7.
difficulty, 704.
condition, 8.
preserve, 670.
pungent, 392.
macerate, 337.
Pickle-herring, *humorist*, 844.
Pick-me-up, *stimulant*, 615.
Pickpocket, *thief*, 792.
Pick-thank, *flatterer*, 935.

Picnic, *food*, 298.
Picture, *painting*, 556.
fancy, 515.
Picture of, the, *similarity*, 17.
Picturesque, *beautiful*, 845.
graphic, 556.
Piddling, *paltry*, 643.
Pidgin-English, *language*, 560.
Pie, *type*, 591.
Piebald, *variegation*, 440.
Piece, *bit*, 51.
cannon, 727.
drama, 599.
*Pièce justificative (Fr.), *evidence*, 467.
Piece, of a, *agreement*, 23.
Piecemeal, *part*, 51.
Piece out, *completeness*, 42.
Pied, *variegation*, 440.
*Pied à terre (Fr.), *abode*, 189.
Pier, *refuge*, 666.
Pierce, *perforate*, 302.
pain, 378, 830.
affect, 824.
Piercing, *cold*, 383.
sound, 404.
sagacious, 498.
feeling, 821.
sight, 441.
Pier-glass, *optical instrument*, 445.
Pierrot, *actor*, 599.
Pietism, *impiety*, 989.
Piety, *piety*, 987.
Piffle, *absurdity*, 497.
Pig, *sensual*, 954.
Pigeon-hearted, *cowardice*, 862.
Pigeon-hole, *receptacle*, 191.
aperture, 260.
Piggish, *intemperance*, 954.
Pigheaded, *prejudiced*, 481.
obstinate, 606.
stupid, 499.
Pigment, *colour*, 428.
Pigmy, *see* Pygmy.
Pig-sty, *uncleanness*, 653.
Pig-tail, *pendant*, 214.
Pike, *javelin*, 727.
hill, 206.
Pikestaff, *height*, 206.
Pilaster, *height*, 206.
Pile, *heap*, 72.
nap, 256.
building, 189.
store, 636.
wealth, 803.
Pile-driver, *hammer*, 276.
Pilfer, *stealing*, 791.
Pilgrim, *traveller*, 268.
Pilgrimage, *journey*, 266.
Pill, *rotundity*, 249.
remedy, 662.
Pillage, *rob*, 971.
rapine, 619.
devastation, 649.
Pillar, *support*, 150, 215.
monument, 551.
lofty, 206.
Pillion, *support*, 215.
Pillory, *scourge*, 975.
to ridicule, 856.
Pillow, *support*, 215, 265.
soft, 324.
ease, 831.
Pilot, *director*, 694.
to guide, 693.
balloon, 273.
trial, 463.
Pilous, *roughness*, 256.
Pimp, *libertine*, 962.
Pimple, *tumour*, 250.
blemish, 848.
Pin, *fastening*, 45.
to fasten, 43.
axis, 312.
sharp, 253.
trifle, 643.
Pin down, *restrain*, 751.
compel, 744.
Pinafore, *dress*, 225.
Pinch, *emergency*, 8.
to contract, 195.
narrow, 203.
chill, 385.
pain, 378.
stint, 640, 819.
to hurt, 830.
to steal, 791.
Pinched, *chilled*, 383.
indigent, 804.
Pinchbeck, *spurious*, 544.
Pinching, *miserly*, 819.
Pine, *desire*, 865.
grieve, 828.
droop, 837.
Ping, *sound*, 406.
Pinguid, *unctuousness*, 355.
Pin-hole, *opening*, 260.
Pinion, *instrument*, 633.
wing, 267.
fetter, 752.
to fasten, 43.
to restrain, 751.
Pink, *colour*, 434.
perfection, 650.
beauty, 845.
glory, 873.
to pierce, 260.
Pinnace, *ship*, 273.

Pinnacle, *summit*, 210.
Pin-pricks, *annoyance*, 830.
Pioneer, *precursor*, 64.
preparer, 673.
teacher, 540.
Pious, *piety*, 987.
Pipe, *conduit*, 350.
vent, 351.
tobacco, 351.
tube, 160.
sound, 510.
cry, 411.
music, 415.
instrument, 417.
Piper, *musician*, 416.
Piping, *sound*, 410.
hot, 382.
Pipkin, *receptacle*, 191.
*Piquant (Fr.), *pungent*, 392.
style, 574.
motive, 615.
feeling, 821.
Pique, *umbrage*, 889.
hate, 898.
anger, 900.
to stimulate, 615.
Pique oneself, *pride*, 878.
Pirate, *thief*, 792.
to steal, 791.
Pirouette, *rotation*, 312.
*Pis-aller (Fr.), *substitute*, 634.
necessity, 601.
plan, 626.
Piscatory, *animal*, 366.
*Piste (Fr.), *track*, 551.
Pistol, *arms*, 727.
Piston, *stopper*, 264.
Pit, *hole*, 252.
opening, 260.
deep, 208.
grave, 363.
hell, 982.
Pit against, *opposition*, 708.
Pit-a-pat, *feeling*, 821.
Pitch, *degree*, 26.
term, 51.
station, 182.
height, 206.
descent, 306.
summit, 210.
musical note, 413.
dark, 421.
black, 431.
to throw, 294.
to reel, 314.
to place, 184.
Pitch tent, *settle*, 184, 265.
Pitch upon, *choose*, 609.
reach, 292.
Pitcher, *receptacle*, 191.
Pitch-pipe, *musical*, 417.
Piteous, *painfulness*, 830.
greatness, 31.
Pitfall, *pitfall*, 667.
Pith, *gist*, 4.
strength, 159.
interior, 221.
essential, 50.
important, 642.
meaning, 516.
Pithy, *significant*, 516.
concise, 572.
Pitiable, *unimportance*, 643.
Pitiful, *unimportant*, 643.
compassionate, 914.
paltry, 940.
Pitiless, *malevolent*, 907.
revengeful, 900, 919.
Pittance, *allotment*, 786.
Pity, *compassion*, 914.
regret, 833.
Pivot, *cause*, 153.
axis, 312.
Pix, *see* Pyx.
Pixy, *sprite*, 980.
*Pizzicato (It.), *music*, 415.
Placable, *forgiveness*, 918.
Placate, *pacify*, 826.
Placard, *notice*, 550.
to publish, 531.
Place, *situation*, 182, 183.
circumstances, 8.
rank, 873.
term, 71.
in order, 58.
abode, 189.
to locate, 184.
substitution, 147.
office, 625.
Place, out of, *disagreement*, 24.
Placeman, *consignee*, 758.
*Placet (L.), *command*, 741.
Placid, *calm*, 826.
Placket, *dress*, 225.
Plagiarism, *stealing*, 791.
borrowing, 788.
imitation, 19.
Plagiarist, *thief*, 792.
Plagioclastic, *oblique*, 217.
Plague, *disease*, 655.
pain, 828.
to worry, 830.
evil, 619.
Plaid, *dress*, 225.
Plain, *horizontal*, 213.
country, 344.
obvious, 446.
meaning, 518.

Plain, *simple*, 849.
artless, 703.
ugly, 846.
style, 576.
Plain-dealing, *veracity*, 543.
Plain-song, *worship*, 990.
music, 415.
Plain-speaking, *veracity*, 543.
perspicuity, 570.
Plain-spoken, *veracity*, 543.
Plaint, *cry*, 411.
lamentation, 839.
Plaintiff, *prosecutor*, 967.
Plaintive, *lamentation*, 839.
Plait, *fold*, 258.
to mat, 219.
Plan, *project*, 626.
order, 58.
diagram, 554.
Planchette, *writing*, 590.
Plane, *flat*, 251.
smooth, 255.
horizontal, 213.
to soar, 305.
Planet-struck, *failure*, 732.
Plangent, *loud*, 404.
Plank, *board*, 204.
safety, 666.
Plant, *vegetable*, 367.
to insert, 300.
place, 184.
stop, 265.
swindle, 545.
equipment, 633.
Plantation, *plant*, 367.
Plash, *lake*, 343.
Plashy, *marshy*, 345.
Plasm, *prototype*, 22.
Plasmic, *form*, 240.
Plaster, *cement*, 45.
remedy, 662.
mend, 658.
cover, 222.
Plastic, *soft*, 324.
form, 240.
mutable, 149.
Plat, *crossing*, 219.
Plate, *layer*, 204.
engraving, 558.
to cover, 222.
Plateau, *horizontality*, 213.
height, 206.
Platform, *support*, 215.
stage, 542.
horizontal, 213.
Platitude, *absurdity*, 497.
Platitudinous, *feeble*, 575.
Platonic, *contemplative*, 451.
cold, 823.
Platonic, *chaste*, 960.
Platoon, *army*, 726.
assemblage, 72.
Platter, *receptacle*, 191.
layer, 204.
Plaudit, *approbation*, 931.
Plausible, *probable*, 472.
sophistical, 477.
false, 544.
specious, 937.
Play, *operation*, 170.
scope, 180, 748.
chance, 186.
drama, 599.
amusement, 840.
music, 415.
oscillation, 314.
to act, 680.
Play a part, *falsehood*, 544.
Play of colours, *variegation*, 440.
Play upon, *deception*, 545.
Play with, *deride*, 483.
Played out, *fatigue*, 688.
Player, *actor*, 599.
deceiver, 548.
musician, 416.
Playfellow, *friend*, 890.
Playful, *cheerfulness*, 836.
Playhouse, *the drama*, 599.
Playmate, *friend*, 890.
Plaything, *toy*, 840.
trifle, 643.
dependence, 749.
Plea, *excuse*, 617.
vindication, 937.
falsehood, 546.
in law, 969.
Plead, *argue*, 467.
encourage, 615.
vindicate, 937.
Pleader, *lawyer*, 968.
Pleasant, *agreeable*, 829.
witty, 842.
amusing, 840.
Please, *pleasurableness*, 829.
Pleasurable, *pleasurableness*, 829.
Pleasure, *will*, 600.
physical, 377.
moral, 827.
Plebeian, *commonalty*, 876.
Plebiscite, *verdict*, 969.
Pledge, *security*, 771.
promise, 768.
to borrow, 788.
drink to, 894.
Plenary, *full*, 31.
complete, 52.
abundant, 639.
Plenipotentiary, *consignee*, 758.

Plenitude, *sufficiency*, 639.
Plenty, *sufficiency*, 639.
*Plenum (L.), *substantiality*, 3.
Pleonasm, *diffuseness*, 573.
Pleonastic, *diffuseness*, 573.
Plethora, *redundance*, 641.
*Plexus (L.), *crossing*, 219.
Pliable, *softness*, 324.
Pliant, *soft*, 324.
facile, 705.
irresolute, 605.
Plication, *fold*, 258.
Plight, *state*, 7.
predicament, 8.
to promise, 768.
security, 771.
Plinth, *base*, 211.
rest, 215.
Plod, *trudge*, 275.
work, 682.
Plodding, *dull*, 843.
Plop, *plunge*, 310.
sound, 406.
Plot, *plan*, 626.
of ground, 181.
Plough, *preparation*, 673.
to furrow, 259.
Plough in, *insertion*, 300.
Ploughman, *commonalty*, 876.
Pluck, *take*, 789.
cheat, 545.
extract, 301.
courage, 861.
resolution, 604.
Plug, *stopper*, 263.
to close, 261.
tobacco, 298A.
Plum, *sweetness*, 396.
money, 800.
Plum-colour, *purple*, 437.
Plumb, *close*, 261.
measure, 466.
Plume, *roughness*, 256.
Plume oneself, *pride*, 878.
Plummet, *measurement*, 466.
Plumose, *roughness*, 256.
Plump, *size*, 192.
Plump down, *descent*, 306.
Plump upon, *arrival*, 292.
Plumper, *choice*, 609.
Plunder, *booty*, 793.
to steal, 791.
ravage, 649.
evil, 619.
Plunge, *dive*, 310.
leap, 146, 309.
insert, 300.
immerse, 208, 337.
precipitate, 308.
Plunge, *gamble*, 621.
adventure, 676.
hurry, 684.
Plurality, *plurality*, 100.
Plus, *addition*, 37.
Plush, *roughness*, 256.
Pluto, *hell*, 982.
Plutocrat, *wealth*, 803.
Pluvial, *river*, 348.
Ply, *use*, 677.
work, 680.
fold, 258.
Pneumatics, *gaseity*, 334.
Pneumatology, *intellect*, 450.
Poach, *steal*, 791, 964.
Poachy, *marsh*, 345.
Pocket, *pouch*, 191.
to place, 184.
take, 789.
endure, 826.
receipts, 810.
treasury, 802.
diminutive, 193.
*Pococurante (It.), *indifferent*, 603.
Podgy, *size*, 192.
Poem, *poetry*, 597.
Poet, *poetry*, 597.
Poetic, *metrical*, 597.
style, 574.
Poignant, *physical*, 171.
moral, 821.
Point, *condition*, 8.
degree, 26.
term, 71.
place, 182.
question, 461.
topic, 454.
prominence, 250.
mark, 550.
intention, 620.
wit, 842.
style, 574.
punctilio, 939.
speck, 193.
poignancy, 171.
sharp, 253.
*Point d'appui (Fr.), *influence*, 175.
Point of view, *aspect*, 441.
idea, 453.
relation, 9.
Point to, *indicate*, 550.
show, 525.
mean, 516.
predict, 511.
Point-blank, *direction*, 278.
Pointed, *explicit*, 535.
Pointer, *index*, 550.
Pointillist, *artist*, 559.
Pointless, *dullness*, 843.

Point-to-point, *direction*, 278.
Poise, *balance*, 27.
measure, 466.
Poison, *bane*, 663.
to injure, 659.
Poisonous, *deleterious*, 657.
injurious, 649.
Poke, *push*, 276.
project, 250.
pocket, 191.
Poker, *stiff*, 323.
Polacca (or Polacre), *ship*, 273.
Polar, *summit*, 210.
Polariscope, *optical*, 445.
Polarity, *duality*, 89.
antagonism, 179, 237.
Pole, *lever*, 633.
axis, 223.
summit, 210.
tallness, 206.
Poleaxe, *arms*, 727.
Polecat, *fetor*, 401.
Polemics, *discussion*, 476.
discord, 713.
Polemoscope, *optical*, 445.
Pole-star, *indication*, 550.
guide, 695.
Police, *jurisdiction*, 965.
constable, 968.
Policy, *plan*, 626.
conduct, 692.
skill, 698.
Polish, *smooth*, 255.
to rub, 331.
urbanity, 894.
furbish, 658.
beauty, 845.
ornament, 847.
taste, 850.
Politeness, *manners*, 852.
urbanity, 894.
Politic, *wise*, 498.
skilful, 698.
cunning, 702.
Politician, *tactician*, 700.
statesman, 745.
Politics, *government*, 693.
Polity, *plan*, 626.
conduct, 692.
community, 372.
Polka, *dance*, 840.
Poll, *count*, 85.
crop, 201.
parrot, 584.
Pollute, *corrupt*, 659.
soil, 653.
disgrace, 874.
dishonour, 940.
Pollution, *vice*, 945.
Pollution, *disease*, 655.
*Poltergeist (Ger.), *demon*, 980.
Poltroon, *cowardice*, 862.
Polychord, *musical*, 417.
Polychromatic, *variegation*, 440.
Polygamy, *marriage*, 903.
Polyglot, *word*, 562.
Polygon, *figure*, 244.
buildings, 189.
Polygraphy, *writing*, 590.
Polymorphic, *multiformity*, 81.
Polyphonism, *voice*, 580.
Polyphony, *melody*, 413.
Polysyllable, *letter*, 561.
Polytechnic, *school*, 542.
Polytheism, *heterodoxy*, 984.
Pomade, *oil*, 356.
Pomatum, *oil*, 356.
Pommel, *rotundity*, 249.
Pomp, *ostentation*, 882.
Pomposity, *pride*, 878.
style, 577.
Poncho, *dress*, 225.
Pond, *lake*, 343.
Ponder, *thought*, 451.
Ponderation, *judgment*, 480.
Ponderous, *gravity*, 319.
style, 577.
Poniard, *arms*, 727.
*Pons asinorum (L.), *difficulty*, 704.
Pontiff, *clergy*, 996.
Pontifical, *churchdom*, 995.
Pontificals, *dress*, 225.
Pony, *carrier*, 271.
Pooh-pooh, *unimportance*, 643.
contempt, 930.
to make light of, 483.
Pool, *lake*, 343.
participation, 778.
Poop, *rear*, 235.
Poor, *indigent*, 804.
weak, 160.
insufficient, 640.
trifling, 643.
contemptible, 930.
style, 575.
Poorly, *disease*, 655.
Poor-spirited, *cowardice*, 862.
Pop, *noise*, 406.
unexpected, 508.
Pop upon, *arrive*, 292.
find, 480.
Pope, *clergy*, 996.
Pop-gun, *snap*, 406.
Popinjay, *fop*, 854.
Populace, *commonalty*, 876.
Popular, *current*, 484.
favourite, 897.
celebrated, 873.

Popularise, *facilitate*, 705.
Populate, *to stock*, 184.
Population, *mankind*, 373.
inhabitants, 188.
Populous, *crowded*, 72.
Porch, *entrance*, 66.
opening, 260.
mouth, 230.
way, 627.
receptacle, 191.
Porcupine, *sharpness*, 253.
Pore, *opening*, 260.
conduit, 350.
look, 441.
apply the mind, 457.
Pornography, *impurity*, 961.
Porous, *foraminous*, 260.
light, 322.
Porpoise, *size*, 192.
Porringer, *receptacle*, 191.
Port, *harbour*, 666.
gait, 264.
resting-place, 265.
arrival, 292.
carriage, 448.
demeanour, 852.
Portable, *movable*, 268, 270.
light, 320.
little, 193.
Portage, *transference*, 270.
Portal, *entrance*, 66.
mouth, 230.
opening, 260.
way, 627.
Portative, *transference*, 270.
small, 193.
Portcullis, *defence*, 706, 717.
*Porte-monnaie (Fr.), *purse*, 802.
Portend, *prediction*, 511.
Portent, *omen*, 512.
prodigy, 872.
Portentous, *prophetic*, 511.
fearful, 860.
Porter, *carrier*, 271.
janitor, 263.
Porterage, *transference*, 270.
Portfolio, *record*, 551.
miscellany, 72.
receptacle, 191.
badge, 747.
Port-hole, *opening*, 260.
Portico, *entrance*, 66.
room, 191.
Portion, *piece*, 51, 41.
allotment, 786.
Portly, *size*, 192.
Portmanteau, *receptacle*, 191.
Portrait, *painting*, 556.
copy, 21.
Portray, *describe*, 594.
paint, 556.
Pose, *puzzle*, 485.
hide, 528.
difficulty, 704.
affirm, 535.
embarrassment, 491.
attitude, 240.
affectation, 855.
Poser, *secret*, 533.
*Poseur (Fr.), *affectation*, 855.
*Poses plastiques (Fr.), *form*, 240.
Posit, *locate*, 184.
assume, 467, 514.
affirm, 535.
Position, *circumstance*, 8.
situation, 183.
assertion, 535.
degree, 26.
Positive, *certain*, 474.
real, 1.
true, 494.
meaning, 516.
unequivocal, 518.
absolute, 739.
obstinate, 481, 606.
assertion, 535.
quantity, 84.
Positively, *great*, 31.
Positivism, *materiality*, 316.
*Posse (L.), *collection*, 72.
party, 712.
*Posse comitatus (L.), *assemblage*, 72.
Possess, *have*, 777.
feel, 821.
Possessed, *insane*, 503.
Possession, *property*, 780.
Possessor, *possessor*, 779.
Possible, *contingent*, 470, 705.
casual, 156, 621.
Post, *support*, 215.
place, 184.
beacon, 550.
swift, 274.
employment, 625.
office, 926.
to record, 551.
accounts, 811.
mail, 592.
to stigmatise, 874.
inform, 527.
Post-date, *anachronism*, 115.
Postdiluvian, *posterity*, 117.
Poster, *notice*, 531.
Posterior, *in time*, 117.
in order, 63.
in space, 235.
Posterity, *in time*, 117, 121.

Posterity, *descendants*, 167.
Postern, *back*, 235.
portal, 66.
Post-existence, *futurity*, 121.
Post-haste, *fast*, 274.
precipitate, 863.
*Post hoc (L.), *sophistry*, 477.
Posthumous, *late*, 133.
subsequent, 117.
*Postiche (Fr.), *artificial*, 544.
Postilion, *director*, 694.
Post-impressionist, *artist*, 559.
Postlude, *music*, 415.
*Post-mortem (L.), *death*, 360.
*Post-obit (L.), *death*, 360.
Postpone, *lateness*, 133.
Postscript, *sequel*, 65.
appendix, 39.
Postulant, *petitioner*, 767.
Postulate, *supposition*, 514.
evidence, 467.
reasoning, 476.
Postulation, *request*, 765.
Posture, *circumstance*, 8.
attitude, 240.
Posture-master, *buffoon*, 844.
mountebank, 548.
Posy, *motto*, 550.
poem, 597.
flowers, 847.
Pot, *mug*, 191.
ruin, 732.
Potable, *drinkable*, 298.
Potation, *drink*, 296.
Pot-companion, *friend*, 890.
Potency, *power*, 157.
Potentate, *master*, 745.
Potential, *virtual*, 2.
possible, 470.
power, 157.
Pother, *to worry*, 830.
confusion, 59.
Pot-hooks, *writing*, 590.
Pot-hunting, *acquisition*, 775.
Pot-luck, *food*, 298.
*Pot-pourri (Fr.), *mixture*, 41.
fragrance, 400.
music, 415.
Pottage, *food*, 298.
Potter, *idle*, 683.
Pottle, *receptacle*, 191.
Pot-valiant, *drunkenness*, 959.
Pouch, *receptacle*, 191.
Poultice, *soft*, 354.
remedy, 662.
Pounce upon, *taking*, 789.
Pound, *bruise*, 330.
mix, 41.
enclose, 232.
Pound, *imprison*, 752.
Poundage, *discount*, 813.
Pounds, *money*, 800.
Pour, *egress*, 295.
Pour out, *eject*, 185, 297, 348.
*Pourboire (Fr.), *giving*, 784.
expenditure, 809.
*Pourparler (Fr.), *discussion*, 476.
*Pour rire (Fr.), *ridicule*, 853.
*Pou sto (Gr.), *influence*, 175.
Pout, *sullen*, 895.
sad, 837.
Poverty, *indigence*, 804.
scantiness, 640.
trifle, 643.
Powder, *pulverulence*, 330.
ornament, 845, 847.
Powder-box, *receptacle*, 191.
Power, *efficacy*, 157.
authority, 737.
much, 31.
numerical, 84.
of style, 574.
Powerful, *strength*, 159.
Powerless, *weakness*, 160.
Pow-wow, *conference*, 588.
Pox, *disease*, 655.
Praam, *ship*, 273.
Practicable, *possible*, 470.
easy, 705.
Practical, *activity*, 682.
Practice, *act*, 680.
conduct, 692.
use, 677.
habit, 613.
rule, 80.
proceeding, 626.
Practise, *deceive*, 645.
Practised, *skill*, 698.
Practitioner, *agent*, 690.
*Præcognita (L.), *evidence*, 467.
*Prænomen (L.), *nomenclature*, 564.
Pragmatical, *pedantic*, 855.
vain, 880.
Prairie, *plain*, 344.
Praise, *commendation*, 931.
thanks, 916.
worship, 990.
Praiseworthy, *commendable*, 931.
virtuous, 944.
Prance, *dance*, 315.
move, 266.
Prank, *caprice*, 608.
amusement, 840.
vagary, 856.
to adorn, 845.
Prate, *babble*, 584, 588.
Prattle, *talk*, 582, 588.
Pravity, *badness*, 649.

Pray, *request*, 765.
Prayer, *request*, 765.
worship, 990.
Preach, *teach*, 537.
predication, 998.
Preacher, *clergy*, 996.
Preachify, *speech*, 582.
Pre-Adamite, *veteran*, 130.
Preamble, *precursor*, 64.
Preapprehension, *misjudgment*, 481.
Prebendary, *clergy*, 996.
Prebendaryship, *churchdom*, 995.
Precarious, *uncertain*, 475.
perilous, 665.
Precatory, *request*, 764.
Precaution, *care*, 459.
safety, 664.
expedient, 626.
preparation, 673.
Precede, *in order*, 62.
in time, 116.
lead, 280.
Precedent, *rule*, 80.
Precentor, *clergy*, 996.
Precept, *maxim*, 697.
order, 741.
permit, 760.
decree, 963.
Preceptor, *teacher*, 540.
Precession, *in order*, 62.
in motion, 280.
*Précieuse ridicule (Fr.), *affectation*, 855.
style, 577.
Precincts, *environs*, 227.
boundary, 233.
region, 181.
place, 182.
Preciosity, *affectation*, 855.
Precious, *excellent*, 648.
valuable, 814.
beloved, 897.
Precipice, *slope*, 217.
vertical, 212.
Precipitancy, *haste*, 274, 684.
Precipitate, *rash*, 863.
early, 132.
transient, 111.
to sink, 308.
refuse, 653.
consolidate, 321.
swift, 274.
Precipitous, *obliquity*, 217.
*Précis (Fr.), *compendium*, 596.
Precise, *exact*, 494.
definite, 516, 518.
Precisely, *assent*, 488.
Precisian, *formalist*, 855.
Preclude, *hindrance*, 706.
Precocious, *early*, 132.
immature, 674.
Precognition, *foresight*, 510.
knowledge, 490.
Preconception, *misjudgment*, 481.
Preconcert, *preparation*, 673.
Preconcerted, *will*, 600.
Precursor, *forerunner*, 64.
harbinger, 512.
Precursory, *in order*, 62.
in time, 116.
Predacious, *stealing*, 791.
Predatory, *stealing*, 791.
Predecessor, *in order*, 64.
in time, 116.
Predeliberation, *care*, 459.
Predestination, *fate*, 152.
necessity, 601.
Predetermination, *predetermination*, 611.
Predetermined, *will*, 600.
predetermination, 611.
Predial, *property*, 780.
Predicament, *situation*, 8.
class, 75.
Predicate, *affirmation*, 535.
Predication, *rite*, 998.
Prediction, *prediction*, 511.
Predilection, *love*, 897.
desire, 865.
choice, 609.
inclination, 602.
Predisposition, *proneness*, 602.
motive, 615.
affection, 820.
preparation, 673.
Predominance, *influence*, 175.
inequality, 28.
Pre-eminent, *celebrated*, 873.
superior, 31, 33.
Pre-emption, *purchase*, 795.
Preen, *adorn*, 845.
Pre-establish, *preparation*, 673.
Pre-examine, *inquiry*, 461.
Pre-exist, *priority*, 116.
past, 122.
Preface, *precedence*, 62.
precursor, 64.
front, 234.
Prefatory, *in order*, 62.
in time, 106.
Prefect, *ruler*, 745.
deputy, 759.
Prefecture, *authority*, 737.
Prefer, *choose*, 609.
a petition, 765.
Preferment, *improvement*, 658.
ecclesiastical, 995.
Prefiguration, *indication*, 550.

Prejiguration, *prediction*, 510.
Prefix, *precedence*, 62.
precursor, 64.
Pregnant, *productive*, 168.
predicting, 511.
important, 642.
Prehension, *taking*, 789.
Prehistoric, *preterition*, 122.
old, 124.
Prejudge, *misjudgment*, 481.
Prejudice, *evil*, 619.
detriment, 649.
Prelacy, *churchdom*, 995.
Prelate, *clergy*, 996.
Prelection, *teaching*, 537.
Prelector, *teacher*, 540.
Preliminary, *preceding*, 62.
precursor, 64.
priority, 116.
Prelude, *preceding*, 62.
precursor, 64.
priority, 116.
music, 415.
Prelusory, *preceding*, 62.
precursor, 64.
priority, 116.
Premature, *earliness*, 132.
Premeditate, *intend*, 630.
predetermine, 611.
Premeditated, *will*, 600.
*Prémices (Fr.), *effect*, 154.
Premier, *director*, 694, 759.
Premiership, *authority*, 737.
Premise, *prefix*, 62.
announce, 511.
Premises, *ground*, 182.
evidence, 467.
Premium, *reward*, 973.
receipt, 810.
Premonition, *warning*, 668.
Prenticeship, *preparation*, 673.
Preoccupied, *inattentive*, 458.
Preoccupy, *possess*, 777.
the attention, 457.
Preoption, *choice*, 609.
Preordain, *necessity*, 601.
Preordination, *destiny*, 152.
Preparatory, *precedence*, 62.
Prepare, *mature*, 673.
plan, 626.
instruct, 537.
Prepared, *ready*, 698.
Prepay, *expenditure*, 809.
Prepense, *advised*, 611.
spontaneous, 600.
intended, 620.
Prepollence, *power*, 157.
Preponderant, *unequal*, 28.
important, 642.
Prepossessing, *pleasurableness*, 829.
Prepossession, *misjudgment*, 481.
Preposterous, *in degree*, 31.
in size, 192.
ridiculous, 853.
absurd, 499.
Prepotency, *power*, 157.
Pre-Raphaelite, *artist*, 559.
Prerequisite, *requirement*, 630.
Prerogative, *right*, 924.
authority, 737.
Presage, *omen*, 512.
to predict, 511.
Presbyopic, *dim-sightedness*, 443.
Presbytery, *parsonage*, 1000.
Prescient, *foresight*, 510.
Prescribe, *order*, 741.
entitle, 924.
duty, 926.
Prescript, *decree*, 741.
precept, 697.
law, 963.
Prescription, *remedy*, 662.
Prescriptive, *dueness*, 924.
Presence, *in space*, 186.
appearance, 448.
carriage, 852.
Presence of mind, *caution*, 864.
Present, *in time*, 118.
in place, 186.
in memory, 505.
give, 784.
offer, 763.
introduce, 894.
to the mind, 451.
Presentable, *fashion*, 852.
Presentation, *offer*, 763.
gift, 784.
Presentiment, *prejudgment*, 481.
instinct, 477.
foresight, 510.
Presently, *soon*, 111, 132.
Preservation, *continuance*, 142.
conservation, 670.
Preside, *command*, 737.
direct, 693.
Presidency, *authority*, 737.
President, *master*, 694, 745.
Press, *hasten*, 132, 684.
beg, 765.
compel, 744.
offer, 763.
weigh, 319.
solicit, 615.
crowd, 72.
closet, 191.
velocity, 274.
Press in, *insertion*, 300.
Pressing, *urgent*, 642.

Pressman, *writer*, 590.
printer, 591.
Pressure, *weight*, 319.
influence, 175.
urgency, 642.
affliction, 830.
Prestidigitation, *deception*, 545.
Prestige, *attractiveness*, 829.
wonder, 870.
*Prestissimo (It.), *music*, 415.
*Presto (It.), *transientness*, 111.
velocity, 274.
music, 415.
Presume, *suppose*, 514.
hope, 858.
prejudge, 481.
take liberties, 885.
Presumption, *probable*, 472.
right, 924.
rashness, 863.
insolence, 885.
Presumptive, *conjectural*, 514.
rightful, 924.
probable, 472.
indicative, 467.
Presumptuous, *rash*, 863.
insolent, 885.
Presuppose, *prejudge*, 481.
conjecture, 514.
Presurmise, *prejudge*, 481.
conjecture, 514.
Pretence, *untruth*, 546.
excuse, 617.
Pretend, *simulate*, 544.
assert, 535.
Pretender, *boaster*, 884.
deceiver, 548.
Pretension, *claim*, 924.
affectation, 855.
vanity, 880, 884.
Preterition, *preterition*, 122.
Preterlapsed, *preterition*, 122.
Pretermit, *omit*, 460.
Preternatural, *irregular*, 83.
Pretext, *excuse*, 617.
falsehood, 546.
Pretty, *beauty*, 845.
Pretty well, *much*, 31.
imperfect, 651.
Prevail, *influence*, 175.
be general, 78.
exist, 1.
Prevail upon, *motive*, 615.
Prevailing, *preponderating*, 28.
usual, 82.
Prevalence, *influence*, 175.
usage, 613.
superiority, 33.
Prevalent, *see* Prevail.
Prevaricate, *falsehood*, 544.
equivocate, 520.
*Prévenance, (Fr.), *courtesy*, 894.
Prevenient, *precedence*, 62.
Prevention, *hindrance*, 706.
prejudice, 481.
Previous, *in order*, 62.
in time, 116.
Prevision, *foresight*, 510.
Prey, *food*, 298.
booty, 793.
object, 620.
victim, 828.
Price, *money*, 812.
value, 648.
Priceless, *goodness*, 648.
Prick, *sharpness*, 253.
to incite, 615.
to sting, 615.
pain, 830.
Prick off, *weed*, 103.
Prick up, *raise*, 212.
Prickle, *sharpness*, 253.
Pride, *loftiness*, 878.
ornament, 847.
Priest, *clergy*, 996.
Priestcraft, *churchdom*, 995.
Priesthood, *clergy*, 996.
Priest-ridden, *impiety*, 989.
Prig, *puppy*, 854.
to steal, 791.
Priggish, *affectation*, 855.
Prim, *affectation*, 855, 878.
Primacy, *churchdom*, 995.
pre-eminence, 33.
*Prima donna (It.), *the drama*, 599.
repute, 873.
*Prima facie (L.), *appearance*, 448.
meaning, 516.
Primary, *importance*, 642.
Primate, *clergy*, 996.
nobility, 875.
Prime, *early*, 132.
primeval, 124.
excellent, 648, 650.
important, 642.
to prepare, 673.
teach, 537.
number, 84.
Primed, *prepared*, 698.
Primer, *school*, 542.
Primeval, *oldness*, 124.
Primigenial, *beginning*, 66.
Primitive, *old*, 124.
simple, 849.
Primogeniture, *posterity*, 167.
Primordial, *oldness*, 124.
Primrose-colour, *yellowness*, 436.
*Primum mobile (L.), *cause*, 153.

Prince, *master*, 745.
Princely, *authoritative*, 737.
liberal, 816.
generous, 942.
noble, 873, 975.
Principal, *importance*, 642.
money, 800.
Principality, *property*, 780.
Principle, *element*, 316.
cause, 153.
truth, 494.
reasoning, 476.
law, 80.
tenet, 484.
motive, 615.
Prink, *adorn*, 845.
show off, 882.
Print, *mark*, 550.
record, 551.
engraving, 558.
letterpress, 591.
Printless, *obliteration*, 552.
Prior, *in order*, 62.
in time, 116.
religious, 996.
Prioress, *clergy*, 996.
Priory, *temple*, 1000.
Prise, *extract*, 301.
Prism, *optical instrument*, 445.
Prismatic, *colour*, 428, 440.
Prison, *prison*, 752.
Prisoner, *captive*, 754.
defendant, 967.
Pristine, *preterition*, 122.
Prithee, *request*, 765.
Prittle-prattle, *interlocution*, 588.
Privacy, *secrecy*, 526.
seclusion, 893.
Private, *special*, 79.
Privateer, *combatant*, 726.
Privation, *loss*, 776.
poverty, 804.
Privative, *taking*, 789.
Privilege, *dueness*, 924.
Privity, *knowledge*, 490.
Prize, *booty*, 793.
success, 731.
palm, 733.
good, 618.
Prize-fighter, *combatant*, 726.
Proa, *ship*, 273.
Probable, *probability*, 471.
Probate, *evidence*, 467.
Probation, *trial*, 463.
essay, 675.
demonstration, 478.
Probationer, *learner*, 541.
*Probatum est (L.), *goodness*, 648.
Probe, *stiletto*, 262.
Probe, *measure*, 466.
investigate, 461.
Probity, *virtue*, 944.
integrity, 939.
Problem, *enigma*, 533.
inquiry, 461.
Problematical, *uncertain*, 475.
hidden, 528.
*Pro bono publico (L.), *utility*, 644.
philanthropy, 910.
Proboscis, *convexity*, 250.
Procedure, *conduct*, 692.
action, 680.
plan, 626.
Proceed, *advance*, 282.
from, 154.
elapse, 109.
happen, 151.
Proceeding, *action*, 680.
event, 151.
plan, 626.
Proceeds, *money*, 800.
receipts, 810.
gain, 775.
Procerity, *height*, 206.
Process, *projection*, 250.
plan, 626.
action, 680.
conduct, 692.
engraving, 558.
time, 109.
Procession, *train*, 69.
ceremony, 882.
*Procès-verbal (Fr.), *compendium*, 596.
Prochronism, *anachronism*, 115.
Proclaim, *publication*, 531.
Proclivity, *disposition*, 602.
proneness, 176, 820.
Proconsul, *deputy*, 759.
Proconsulship, *authority*, 737.
Procrastination, *delay*, 133, 683.
Procreant, *productiveness*, 168.
Procreate, *production*, 161.
Procreator, *paternity*, 166.
Proctor, *officer*, 694.
law, 968.
Proctorship, *direction*, 693.
Procumbent, *horizontality*, 213.
Procuration, *commission*, 755.
pimping, 961.
Procurator, *director*, 694.
Procure, *get*, 775.
cause, 153.
buy, 795.
pimp, 962.
Prod, *poke*, 276.
Prodigal, *extravagant*, 818.
lavish, 641.

Prodigious, *wonderful*, 870.
much, 31.
Prodigy, *prodigy*, 872.
*Prodromus (L.), *compendium*, 596.
Produce, *cause*, 153.
create, 161.
prolong, 200.
show, 525, 599.
evidence, 467.
result, 154.
fruit, 775.
ware, 798.
Product, *effect*, 154.
acquisition, 775.
multiple, 84.
Productive, *productiveness*, 168.
Proem, *precursor*, 64.
Proemial, *preceding*, *in order*, 62.
beginning, 66.
in time, 106.
Profane, *impious*, 989.
desecrate, 679.
laical, 997.
Profess, *affirmation*, 535.
Profession, *business*, 625.
Professor, *teacher*, 540.
Proffer, *offer*, 763.
Proficiency, *skill*, 698.
Proficient, *adept*, 700.
knowledge, 490.
skilful, 698.
Profile, *lateral*, 236.
outline, 229.
appearance, 448.
Profit, *acquisition*, 775.
advantage, 618.
Profitable, *useful*, 644.
gainful, 810.
Profiteer, *acquisition*, 775.
Profitless, *inutility*, 645.
Profligacy, *vice*, 945.
Profluent, *advancing*, 282.
flowing, 348.
*Pro forma (L.), *habit*, 613.
Profound, *deep*, 208.
knowledge, 490.
sagacity, 702.
feeling, 821.
thought, 451.
Profoundly, *great*, 31.
Profuse, *prodigal*, 818.
lavish, 641.
Prog, *food*, 298.
materials, 635.
Progenitor, *paternity*, 166.
Progeny, *posterity*, 167.
Prognostic, *omen*, 512.
Prognosticate, *prediction*, 511.
Programme, *catalogue*, 86.
Programme, *announcement*, 510.
plan, 626.
Progress, *advance*, 282.
speed, 274.
of time, 109.
improvement, 658.
success, 741.
Progression, *series*, 69.
gradation, 58.
numerical, 84.
motion, 282.
*Pro hac vice (L.), *present*, 118.
infrequency, 137.
occasion, 134.
Prohibit, *forbid*, 761.
Prohibition, *sobriety*, 958.
Project, *bulge*, 250.
propel, 284.
plan, 626.
intend, 620.
Projectile, *missile*, 284.
weapon, 727.
Projection, *map*, 554.
*Prolegomena (Gr.), *precursor*, 64.
*Prolepsis (Gr.), *anachronism*, 115.
*Prolétaire (Fr.), *commonalty*, 876.
Proletarian, *commonalty*, 876.
Proliferate, *reproduction*, 161.
Prolific, *productive*, 157, 168.
Prolix, *diffuse*, 573.
Prolocutor, *teacher*, 540.
speaker, 582.
Prologue, *precursor*, 64.
Prolong, *lengthen*, 200.
protract, 110, 133.
Prolusion, *beginning*, 64.
lesson, 537.
dissertation, 595.
Promenade, *journey*, 266.
causeway, 627.
Promethean, *life*, 359.
Prominent, *convex*, 250, 252.
conspicuous, 446, 525.
important, 642.
famous, 873.
Prominently, *great*, 31.
Promiscuous, *irregular*, 59.
casual, 621.
Promise, *engage*, 768.
augur, 507.
hope, 858.
Promontory, *cape*, 206, 342.
projection, 250.
*Pro more (L.), *conformity*, 62.
habit, 613.
Promote, *aid*, 707.
Promotion, *improvement*, 658.
Prompt, *in time*, 111.
early, 132.

Prompt, *quick*, 274.
suggest, 514.
tell, 527.
remind, 505.
induce, 615.
active, 682.
Promptuary, *store*, 636.
Promulgate, *publication*, 531.
Pronation, *inversion*, 218.
Prone, *horizontal*, 213.
tending, 176.
inclined, 602.
disposed, 820.
*Prôner (Fr.), *ostentation*, 882.
Pronounce, *articulate*, 580.
assert, 535.
judge, 480.
sentence, 969.
Pronounced, *great*, 31.
obvious, 518.
emphatic, 535.
*Pronunciamento (Sp.), *revolt*, 719.
Proof, *demonstration*, 478.
test, 463.
copy, 21.
Prop, *support*, 215.
help, 707.
refuge, 666.
Propagable, *productive*, 168.
Propaganda, *publicity*, 531.
teaching, 542.
Propagandism, *teaching*, 537.
proselytism, 484.
Propagate, *produce*, 161.
publish, 531.
Propel, *propulsion*, 284.
Propensity, *tendency*, 176.
disposition, 602.
Proper, *special*, 79.
right, 922, 926.
expedient, 646.
consonant, 23.
handsome, 845.
Property, *possession*, 780.
power, 157.
Prophecy, *prediction*, 511.
scriptural, 985.
Prophesy, *predict*, 511.
Prophet, *oracle*, 513.
Prophylactic, *remedy*, 662.
preservative, 670.
Prophylaxis, *preservation*, 670.
Propinquity, *nearness*, 197.
Propitiate, *conciliate*, 918.
atone, 952.
pity, 914.
religious, 976.
worship, 990.
Propitious, *favouring*, 707.
Propitious, *opportune*, 134.
prosperous, 734.
auspicious, 858.
Proplasm, *prototype*, 22.
Proportion, *relation*, 9.
mathematical, 84.
Proposal, *plan*, 626.
Propose, *offer*, 763.
intend, 620.
suggest, 514.
broach, 535.
ask, 461.
Proposition, *reasoning*, 476.
supposition, 454.
Propound, *broach*, 535.
inquire, 461.
suggest, 514.
*Propria persona (L.), *speciality*, 79.
Proprietary, *possessor*, 779.
Proprietor, *possessor*, 779.
Proprietorship, *possession*, 777.
Propriety, *consonance*, 23.
duty, 922, 926.
*Proprio motu (L.), *will*, 600.
*Propter hoc (L.), *attribution*, 155.
Propulsion, *propulsion*, 284.
*Pro rata (L.), *relation*, 9.
*Pro re nata (L.), *circumstance*, 8.
occasion, 134.
Prorogue, *lateness*, 133.
Prosaic, *dull*, 843.
style, 575, 598.
Proscenium, *front*, 234.
Proscribe, *interdict*, 761.
curse, 908.
condemn, 971.
denounce, 938.
exclude, 77.
Prose, *not verse*, 598.
dullness, 843.
to prate, 584.
to weary, 841.
Prosector, *anatomist*, 44.
Prosecute, *pursue*, 622.
arraign, 969.
Prosecutor, *judge*, 967.
Proselyte, *learner*, 541.
Proselytism, *teaching*, 537.
belief, 484.
Prosody, *poetry*, 597.
Prosopopœia, *metaphor*, 521.
Prospect, *view*, 448.
futurity, 121, 507.
Prospectus, *scheme*, 626.
compendium, 596.
programme, 86.
Prosperity, *success*, 731, 734.
Prostitute, *to corrupt*, 659.
misuse, 679.

Prostitute, *dishonour*, 961, 962.
Prostrate, *low*, 207.
level, 213.
to depress, 308.
weak, 160.
exhausted, 688.
laid up, 655.
dejected, 837.
heart-broken, 830.
Prostration, *ruin*, 619.
servility, 886.
obeisance, 743, 928.
worship, 990.
Prosy, *diffuse*, 573.
dull, 575.
Prosyllogism, *reasoning*, 476.
Protagonist, *leader*, 745.
champion, 711.
*Pro tanto (L.), *greatness*, 31.
smallness, 32.
Protasis, *precursor*, 64.
Protean, *mutable*, 149, 605.
Protect, *shield*, 664.
defend, 717.
Protector, *master*, 745.
Protectorate, *authority*, 737.
*Protégé (Fr.), *servant*, 746.
friend, 890.
*Pro tempore (L.), *temporarily*, 111.
occasion, 134.
Protervity, *petulance*, 901.
Protest, *dissent*, 489.
denial, 536.
affirmation, 535.
refusal, 764.
deprecate, 766.
censure, 932.
non-observance, 773.
non-payment, 808.
Proteus, *change*, 149.
Prothonotary, *recorder*, 553.
Protocol, *document*, 551.
warrant, 771.
Protoplasm, *substance*, 3.
Protoplast, *prototype*, 22.
Prototype, *thing copied*, 22.
Protract, *time*, 110, 133.
length, 200.
Protractor, *angularity*, 244.
Protrude, *convexity*, 250.
Protuberance, *convexity*, 250.
Proud, *lofty*, 878.
dignified, 873.
Prove, *demonstrate*, 85, 478.
try, 463.
turn out, 151.
affect, 821.
Provenance, *cause*, 153.
Provender, *food*, 298.
Provender, *materials*, 635.
Proverb, *maxim*, 496.
Proverbial, *knowledge*, 490.
Provide, *furnish*, 637.
prepare, 673.
Provided, *qualification*, 469.
condition, 770.
conditionally, 8.
Providence, *foresight*, 510.
divine government, 976.
Provident, *careful*, 459.
wise, 498.
prepared, 673.
Province, *region*, 181.
department, 75.
office, 625.
duty, 926.
Provincialism, *language*, 560.
Provision, *supply*, 637.
materials, 635.
preparation, 673.
wealth, 803.
food, 298.
Provisional, *preparing*, 673.
temporary, 111.
conditional, 8.
Proviso, *qualification*, 469.
condition, 770.
Provoke, *incite*, 615.
excite, 824.
vex, 830.
hatred, 898.
anger, 900.
Provost, *master*, 745.
Prow, *front*, 234.
Prowess, *courage*, 861.
Prowl, *journey*, 266.
Proximity, *contiguity*, 199.
*Proximo (L.), *futurity*, 121.
Proxy, *deputy*, 759.
Prude, *affectation*, 855.
Prudent, *cautious*, 864.
careful, 459.
wise, 498.
discreet, 698.
Prudery, *affectation*, 855.
Prune, *shorten*, 201.
purple, 437.
Prunella, *unimportance*, 643.
Prurient, *desire*, 865.
lust, 961.
Pry, *inquire*, 461.
look, 441.
Psalm, *worship*, 990.
Psalmody, *music*, 415.
Psephomancy, *prediction*, 511.
*Pseudo (Gr.), *spurious*, 495.
sham, 544.
Pseudonym, *misnomer*, 565.

Pseudo-revelation, *spurious*, 986.
Pseudoscope, *optical*, 445.
*Psyche (Gr.), *soul*, 450.
Psychical, *immaterial*, 317.
intellectual, 450.
Psychology, *intellect*, 450.
Psychopath, *madman*, 504.
Psychomancy, *prediction*, 511.
divination, 992.
Psychosis, *insanity*, 503.
Ptisan, *remedy*, 662.
Puberty, *youth*, 127.
Public, *people*, 373.
open, 529, 531.
Publication, *promulgation*, 531.
printing, 591.
book, 593.
Public-house, *drink*, 298.
Publicist, *writer*, 593.
lawyer, 968.
Publicity, *publication*, 531.
Public-spirited, *philanthropy*, 910.
Puce-colour, *purple*, 437.
Puck, *imp*, 980.
Pucka, *goodness*, 648.
Pucker, *fold*, 258.
Pudder, *disorder*, 59.
Pudding, *food*, 298.
Puddle, *lakelet*, 343.
lining, 224.
Pudency, *purity*, 960.
Puerile, *boyish*, 127, 129.
trifling, 643.
foolish, 499.
weak, 477.
Puff, *wind*, 349.
vapour, 334.
inflate, 194.
advertisement, 531.
boast, 884.
pant, 688.
Puffed up, *vain*, 770.
proud, 878.
Puffy, *size*, 192.
wind, 349.
Pug, *shortness*, 201.
foot-print, 551.
Pugilism, *contention*, 720.
Pugilist, *combatant*, 726.
Pugnacity, *anger*, 901.
Puissant, *strong*, 157, 159.
Puke, *ejection*, 297.
Pulchritude, *beauty*, 845.
Pule, *cry*, 411, 412.
weep, 839.
Pull, *draw*, 285.
attract, 288.
advantage, 33.
Pull down, *destroy*, 162.
Pull down, *lay low*, 308.
Pull out, *extract*, 301.
Pull together, *concord*, 714.
Pull through, *recover*, 658.
Pull up, *stop*, 265.
accuse, 938.
Pullet, *infant*, 129.
Pulley, *instrument*, 633.
Pullulate, *grow*, 194.
multiply, 168.
Pulp, *pulpiness*, 354.
Pulpiness, *semiliquid*, 352.
Pulpit, *rostrum*, 542.
church, 1000.
Pulsate, *see* Pulse.
Pulse, *oscillate*, 314.
agitate, 315.
periodically, 138.
Pulverise, *maltreat*, 649.
Pulverulence, *powder*, 330.
Pulvil, *fragrance*, 400.
Pummel, *handle*, 633.
beat, 276, 972.
Pump, *inquire*, 461.
reservoir, 636.
Pun, *verbal*, 520, 563.
wit, 842.
Punch, *to perforate*, 260.
perforator, 262.
to strike, 276.
punish, 972.
buffoon, 857.
humorist, 844.
puppet, 599.
nag, 271.
Punctate, *spotted*, 440.
Punctilio, *ostentation*, 882.
Punctilious, *correct*, 494.
observant, 772.
scrupulous, 939.
Punctual, *early*, 132.
periodical, 138.
scrupulous, 939.
Punctuation, *grammar*, 567.
Puncture, *opening*, 260.
Pundit, *scholar*, 462.
sage, 500.
Pungent, *taste*, 392.
caustic, 171.
feeling, 821.
Punic faith, *improbity*, 940.
Punish, *punishment*, 972.
Punk, *prostitute*, 962.
Punka, *fan*, 349.
Punnet, *receptacle*, 191.
Punt, *ship*, 273.
propel, 267, 284.
Puny, *in degree*, 32.
in size, 193.

Pup, *infant*, 129.
Pupil, *learner*, 541.
Puppet, *subjection*, 749.
effigy, 554.
dupe, 547.
little, 193.
Puppet-show, *the drama*, 599.
amusement, 840.
Puppy, *fop*, 854.
blusterer, 887.
braggart, 884.
Purana, *heterodoxy*, 984.
Purblind, *blind*, 442.
undiscerning, 499.
Purchase, *buy*, 795.
leverage, 175.
Pure, *simple*, 42.
true, 494.
good taste, 850.
clean, 652.
truthful, 543.
innocent, 946.
virtuous, 944.
Purely, *smallness*, 32.
greatness, 31.
Purgation, *cleansing*, 652.
atonement, 952.
Purgatory, *suffering*, 828.
atonement, 952.
hell, 982.
Purge, *clean*, 652.
improve, 658.
atone, 952.
subduction, 38.
Purify, *cleanse*, 652.
improve, 658.
Purist, *style*, 578.
taste, 850.
Puritanical, *ascetic*, 955.
pedantic, 855.
Purity, *purity*, 960. *See* Pure.
of style, 578.
Purl, *gargle*, 405.
Purlieus, *suburbs*, 197, 227.
Purloin, *steal*, 791.
Purple, *purple*, 437.
Purport, *meaning*, 516.
intent, 620.
Purpose, *intention*, 620.
Purposeless, *chance*, 621.
Purposely, *will*, 600, 620.
Purr, *animal sound*, 412.
Purse, *money-bag*, 802.
wealth, 803.
to shrivel, 195.
Purse-bearer, *treasurer*, 801.
Purse-proud, *pride*, 878.
Purser, *treasurer*, 801.
Purse-strings, *treasury*, 802.
Pursuant to, *intention*, 620.
Pursue, *follow*, 281.
continue, 143.
aim, 622.
inquire, 461.
Pursuivant, *messenger*, 534.
Pursy, *size*, 192.
Purulent, *unclean*, 653.
Purview, *extent*, 180.
intention, 620.
Purvey, *provision*, 637.
Push, *exigency*, 8.
accelerate, 274.
impel, 276.
propel, 284.
repel, 289.
activity, 682.
Push on, *progression*, 282, 684.
Pusillanimity, *cowardice*, 862.
Pustule, *pimple*, 250.
blemish, 848.
Put, *place*, 184.
a question, 461.
fool, 501.
Put about, *turn back*, 283.
circuition, 311.
Put away, *relinquish*, 624.
Put by, *economy*, 817.
Put down, *destroy*, 162.
coerce, 744.
baffle, 731.
humiliate, 874.
Put forth, *assert*, 535.
suggest, 514.
Put in, *interject*, 228.
Put into, *insert*, 300.
arrive, 292.
Put off, *delay*, 133.
deter, 616.
Put on, *clothe*, 225.
deceive, 544.
Put out, *quench*, 385.
darken, 421.
perplex, 458.
difficulty, 704.
Put up to, *teach*, 537.
Put up with, *feeling*, 821.
Put upon, *deception*, 545.
Putative, *attribution*, 155, 514.
Putid, *improbity*, 940.
Putrefy, *unclean*, 653.
Putrid, *unclean*, 653.
Putt, *impel*, 276.
Puttee, *dress*, 225.
Putty, *vinculum*, 45.
Puzzle, *enigma*, 533.
mystify, 528.
stagger, 485.
bewilder, 491.

Puzzle-headed, *fool*, 499.
Puzzling, *uncertain*, 475.
Pygmy, *little*, 193.
Pylades, *friend*, 890.
Pyramid, *point*, 253.
heap, 72.
Pyre, *interment*, 363.
Pyromancy, *prediction*, 511.
Pyrometer, *thermometer*, 389.
Pyrotechny, *heat*, 382.
Pyrrhonism, *incredulity*, 487.
Pythagorean, *temperance*, 953.
Python, *oracle*, 513.
Pyx, *receptacle*, 191.
assay, 463.
ritual, 998.

Q

Quack, *impostor*, 548.
cry, 412.
Quackery, *deception*, 545.
affectation, 855.
Quacksalver, *deceiver*, 548.
Quadrant, *measure*, 466.
Quadrate with, *agreement*, 23.
Quadratic, *number*, 95.
Quadrifid, *number*, 97.
Quadrille, *dance*, 840.
Quadripartition, *number*, 97.
Quadrisection, *number*, 97.
Quadruped, *animal*, 366.
Quadruple, *number*, 96.
*Quære (L.), *inquiry*, 461.
Quaff, *reception*, 296.
Quagmire, *bog*, 345.
mire, 653.
difficulty, 704.
Quail, *fear*, 800, 862.
Quaint, *odd*, 83.
ridiculous, 853.
pretty, 845.
Quake, *shake*, 315.
fear, 860.
cold, 383.
Qualification, *modification*, 469.
accomplishment, 698.
change, 140.
retractation, 536.
training, 673.
right, 924.
Qualify, *train*, 673.
modify, 469.
change, 140.
teach, 537.
Quality, *power*, 157.
nature, 5.
Quality, *tendency*, 176.
character, 820.
nobility, 875.
Qualm, *fear*, 860.
scruple, 603, 616.
disbelief, 485.
penitence, 950.
Quandary, *difficulty*, 704.
*Quand même (Fr.), *counteraction*, 179.
opposition, 708.
Quantitative, *amount*, 25.
allotment, 786.
Quantity, *amount*, 25.
*Quantum (L.), *amount*, 25.
apportionment, 786.
*Quantum sufficit (L.), *sufficiency*, 639.
*Quaquaversum (L.), *direction*, 278.
Quarantine, *safety*, 664.
confinement, 751.
Quarrel, *discord*, 713.
Quarrelsome, *enemy*, 901.
Quarry, *mine*, 636.
object, 620.
Quarter, *fourth*, 97.
region, 181.
side, 236.
direction, 278.
to place, 184.
mercy, 914.
Quartering, *number*, 97.
Quartermaster, *provision*, 637.
Quarters, *abode*, 189.
Quartet, *number*, 95.
Quash, *destroy*, 162.
annul, 756.
*Quasi (L.), *similarity*, 17.
Quaternal, *number*, 95.
Quaternity, *number*, 95.
Quatrain, *poetry*, 597.
Quaver, *oscillate*, 314.
shake, 315.
sound, 407.
music, 413.
hesitate, 605.
fear, 860.
shiver, 383.
Quay, *abode*, 189.
Quean, *libertine*, 962.
Queasiness, *dislike*, 867.
Queasy, *fastidious*, 868.
Queen, *master*, 745.
Queenly, *majestic*, 873.
Queer, *unconformity*, 83.
sick, 655.
whimsical, 853.
Quell, *destroy*, 162.
hush, 265.

Quell, *calm*, 826.
moderate, 174.
subdue, 732.
Quench, *cool*, 385.
dissuade, 616.
extinguish, 162.
satiate, 869.
Querimonious, *lament*, 839.
Querist, *inquiry*, 461.
Querulous, *complaining*, 839.
quarrelsome, 901.
Query, *inquiry*, 461.
to doubt, 485.
Quest, *inquiry*, 461.
pursuit, 622.
Question, *inquiry*, 461.
topic, 454.
to doubt, 485.
to deny, 536.
Questionable, *uncertainty*, 475.
Questionless, *certainty*, 474.
Questor, *treasurer*, 801.
Queue, *appendix*, 39, 214.
sequel, 65.
row, 69.
Quibble, *sophistry*, 477.
absurdity, 497.
wit, 842.
Quick, *rapid*, 274.
transient, 111.
active, 682.
early, 132.
skilful, 698.
irascible, 901.
feeling, 821, 822.
Quicken, *hasten*, 132.
animate, 163.
operate, 170.
urge, 615.
excite, 824.
promote, 907.
violence, 173.
Quicksand, *pitfall*, 667.
Quick-sighted, *quick-eyed*, 441.
sagacious, 498.
Quicksilver, *velocity*, 274.
Quick-witted, *wit*, 842.
Quid, *tobacco*, 298A.
Quiddity, *essence*, 5.
quibble, 477.
Quidnunc, *curiosity*, 455.
*Quid pro quo (L.), *compensation*, 30.
payment, 807.
exchange, 794.
interchange, 148.
Quiescence, *cessation*, 141.
inertness, 172.
rest, 265.
Quiet, *rest*, 265.
Quiet, *silent*, 403.
calm, 174, 826.
dissuade, 616.
peace, 714.
Quietism, *piety*, 987.
Quietus, *death*, 360.
quiescence, 265.
Quill, *writing*, 590.
Quill-driver, *writing*, 590.
Quinary, *number*, 98.
Quincunx, *number*, 98.
Quinquefid, *number*, 99.
Quinquesection, *number*, 99.
Quint, *number*, 98.
Quintain, *target*, 620.
Quintessence, *essence*, 5.
importance, 642.
Quintuple, *number*, 98.
Quip, *wit*, 842.
amusement, 840.
ridicule, 856.
satire, 932.
Quirk, *caprice*, 608.
evasion, 617.
wit, 842.
Quit, *depart*, 293.
relinquish, 624.
pay, 807.
Quite, *greatness*, 31.
Quits, *equality*, 27.
atonement, 952.
Quittance, *forgiveness*, 918.
atonement, 952.
reward, 952.
observance, 772.
Quiver, *agitate*, 315.
shiver, 383.
fear, 860.
affect, 821.
store, 636.
arm, 727.
Quixotic, *imaginary*, 515.
rash, 863.
enthusiastic, 825.
Quiz, *to ridicule*, 856.
Quizzical, *ridiculous*, 853.
Quodlibet, *sophism*, 477.
subtle point, 454.
enigma, 461.
wit, 842.
Quondam, *preterition*, 122.
Quorum, *assembly*, 72.
Quota, *apportionment*, 786.
Quotation, *imitation*, 19.
citation, 82.
Quote, *cite*, 82, 467.
bargain, 794.
Quotidian, *period*, 108, 138.
Quotient, *number*, 84.

R

Rabbet, *junction*, 43.
Rabbi, *clergy*, 996.
Rabble, *mob*, 876.
assemblage, 72.
Rabelaisian, *coarse*, 961.
Rabid, *insanity*, 503.
headstrong, 606.
Race, *to run*, 274.
contest, 720.
course, 622.
career, 625.
lineage, 11, 69.
kind, 75.
Racial, *ethnic*, 372.
Racer, *horse*, 271.
fleetness, 274.
Race-horse, *horse*, 271.
fleetness, 274.
Rack, *frame*, 215.
physical pain, 378.
moral pain, 828.
to torture, 830.
punish, 975.
purify, 652.
refine, 658.
cloud, 353.
Racket, *noise*, 402.
roll, 407.
bat, 633.
*Raconteur (Fr.), *narrator*, 594.
Racy, *strong*, 171.
pungent, 392.
feeling, 821.
style, 574.
Raddle, *weave*, 219.
twist, 311.
red, 434.
Radiant, *diverging*, 291.
light, 420.
beauty, 845.
glory, 873.
Radical, *cause*, 153.
algebraic root, 84.
complete, 52.
reformer, 658.
Radically, *thorough*, 31.
Radioactivity, *light*, 420.
Radius, *length*, 200.
*Radix (L.), *cause*, 153.
Raff, *refuse*, 653.
rabble, 876.
miscreant, 949.
Raffia, *tape*, 45.
Raffle, *chance*, 156, 621.
Raft, *ship*, 273.
Rafter, *support*, 215.
Rag, *shred*, 51.
Rag, *clothes*, 225.
escapade, 497.
to tease, 830.
joke, 842.
revile, 932.
Rage, *violence*, 173.
fury, 825.
desire, 865.
wrath, 900.
Ragged, *bare*, 226.
*Ragoût (Fr.), *food*, 298.
Ragtag, *commonalty*, 876.
Raid, *attack*, 716.
Rail, *enclosure*, 232.
fence, 666.
imprison, 752.
Rail at, *disapprove*, 932.
Rail in, *circumscribe*, 231.
Raillery, *ridicule*, 856.
Railway, *road*, 627.
Raiment, *dress*, 225.
Rain, *river*, 348.
Rainbow, *variegation*, 440.
Raise, *elevate*, 307.
increase, 35.
produce, 161.
excite, 824.
*Raison d'être (Fr.), *cause*, 153.
motive, 615.
Raj, *authority*, 737.
Rajah, *master*, 745.
Rakehell, *intemperate*, 954.
Rake up, *collect*, 72.
extract, 301.
recall, 504.
excite, 824.
Rakish, *intemperate*, 954.
licentious, 961.
Rally, *ridicule*, 856.
recover, 658.
stand by, 707.
pluck up courage, 861.
Ram, *impel*, 276.
press in, 261.
insert, 300.
Ram down, *condense*, 321.
fill up, 261.
Ramadan, *fasting*, 956.
Ramble, *stroll*, 266.
wander, 279.
diffuse, 572.
delirium, 503.
folly, 499.
Rambler, *journey*, 268.
Ramification, *branch*, 51, 256.
posterity, 167.
Rammer, *plug*, 263.
impeller, 276.
Ramp, *ascend*, 305.

Rampage, *violence*, 173.
excitement, 825.
Rampant, *violent*, 173.
vehement, 825.
licentious, 961.
free, 748.
rising, 305.
Rampart, *defence*, 717.
Ramrod, *stopper*, 263.
Ramshackle, *imperfect*, 651.
Ranch, *farm*, 780.
Rancid, *fetid*, 401.
Rancour, *malevolence*, 907.
revenge, 919.
Random, *casual*, 156, 621.
uncertain, 475.
Range, *space*, 180.
extent, 26.
draw up, 58.
to collocate, 60.
roam, 266.
direction, 278.
series, 69.
term, 71.
class, 75.
freedom, 748.
Rank, *degree*, 26.
thorough, 31.
collocate, 60.
row, 69.
term, 71.
fetid, 401.
bad, 649.
to estimate, 480.
nobility, 875.
glory, 873.
Rankle, *animosity*, 505, 900.
to corrupt, 959.
Ransack, *seek*, 461.
plunder, 791.
Ransom, *price*, 812.
liberation, 750.
Rant, *nonsense*, 497.
speech, 582.
acting, 599.
style, 573, 577.
Rantipole, *fool*, 499, 501.
Rap, *knock*, 276.
beat, 972.
Rap out, *voice*, 580.
Rapacious, *avaricious*, 819.
greedy, 865.
predatory, 789.
Rape, *violation*, 961.
seizure, 791.
Rapid, *velocity*, 274.
Rapids, *river*, 348.
Rapier, *arms*, 727.
Rapine, *spoliation*, 791.
Rapine, *evil*, 791.
Rapparee, *thief*, 792.
Rappee, *tobacco*, 298A.
*Rapport, en (Fr.), *agreement*, 23.
Rapscallion, *sinner*, 949.
Rapt, *thought*, 451.
pleasure, 827.
Rapture, *emotion*, 821.
bliss, 827.
*Rara avis (L.), *unconformity*, 83.
Rare, *infrequent*, 137.
light, 103.
few, 103.
exceptional, 83.
excellent, 648.
Raree-show, *sight*, 448.
amusement, 840.
Rarefy, *expand*, 194.
render light, 322.
Rascal, *sinner*, 949.
Rascality, *vice*, 945.
Rase, *see* Raze.
Rash, *reckless*, 863.
careless, 460.
Rasher, *layer*, 204.
Rasp, *grate*, 330, 331.
Rat, *tergiversation*, 607.
Rataplan, *roll*, 407.
Ratchet, *sharpness*, 253.
Rate, *degree*, 26.
speed, 274.
measure, 466.
estimation, 480.
price, 812.
to abuse, 932.
Rath, *early*, 132.
Rather, *somewhat*, 32.
choice, 609.
Ratify, *consent*, 762.
affirm, 488.
compact, 769.
Ratio, *relation*, 9.
proportion, 84.
degree, 26.
Ratiocination, *reasoning*, 476.
Ration, *apportion*, 786.
Rations, *food*, 298.
Rational, *sane*, 502.
judicious, 480, 498.
Rationale, *cause*, 153.
attribution, 155.
answer, 462.
interpretation, 522.
Rationalist, *sceptic*, 988.
Rattan, *scourge*, 975.
Ratting, *tergiversation*, 607.
Rattle, *noise*, 407.
prattle, 584.
Rattle off, *speech*, 582.

Rattlesnake, *bane*, 663.
Rattletrap, *imperfect*, 651.
Raucous, *hoarse*, 581.
Ravage, *destroy*, 162.
evil, 619.
despoil, 649.
Rave, *madness*, 503.
excitement, 825.
Ravel, *entangle*, 219.
convolution, 248.
difficulty, 704.
untwist, 44, 61.
Raven, *black*, 431.
gorge, 296.
Ravenous, *desire*, 789, 865.
Raver, *madman*, 504.
Ravine, *pass*, 198, 203.
dike, 259.
Raving, *mad*, 503.
violent, 825.
Ravish, *emotion*, 824.
ecstasy, 829.
Raw, *immature*, 123.
unprepared, 674.
unskilful, 699.
cold, 383.
sensitive, 378.
Raw-boned, *gaunt*, 193, 203.
ugly, 846.
Ray, *light*, 420.
Rayless, *darkness*, 421.
Raze, *level*, 308.
obliterate, 552.
demolish, 649.
Razor, *sharp*, 253.
Razzle-dazzle, *frolic*, 840.
Reabsorb, *reception*, 296.
Reach, *length*, 200.
degree, 26.
distance, 196.
fetch, 270.
arrive at, 292.
grasp, 737.
React, *recoil*, 277.
revert, 145.
counteract, 179.
sensibility, 375.
relapse, 661.
Reactionary, *conservative*, 670.
Read, *interpret*, 522.
learn, 539.
Readable, *intelligible*, 518.
Reader, *teacher*, 540.
Reading, *meaning*, 516.
Readjust, *equality*, 27.
Readmit, *reception*, 296.
Ready, *prepared*, 673.
capable, 157.
willing, 602.
Ready, *eager*, 682.
dexterous, 698.
early, 132.
cash, 800.
Ready money, *payment*, 807.
Reagent, *criterion*, 467.
Real, *existing*, 1.
true, 494.
Realise, *attribute*, 155.
produce, 161.
substantiate, 494.
imagine, 515.
price, 812.
Realistic, *description*, 594.
Reality, in, *existence*, 1.
Really, *very*, 31.
indeed, 870.
Realm, *region*, 181.
property, 780.
land, 372.
Reanimate, *revivify*, 163.
reinstate, 660.
Reap, *acquire*, 775.
succeed, 731.
take, 789.
Reappear, *repetition*, 104, 163.
frequency, 136.
Rear, *back*, 67, 235.
erect, 161, 307.
sequel, 65.
bring up, 537.
Rearrange, *arrangement*, 60.
Reason, *cause*, 153.
motive, 615.
intellect, 450.
evidence, 467.
argue, 476.
wisdom, 498.
moderation, 174.
Reasonable, *judicious*, 498.
right, 922.
equitable, 924.
probable, 472.
sane, 502.
moderate, 174.
cheap, 815.
Reasoning, *logic*, 476.
Reasonless, *fool*, 499.
Reassemble, *gather*, 72.
Reassure, *hope*, 858.
Reasty, *foul*, 653.
fetid, 401.
Rebate, *moderate*, 174, 813.
Rebeck, *musical instrument*, 417.
Rebel, *disobey*, 742.
Rebellion, *resistance*, 719.
Rebellow, *ululation*, 412.
Rebound, *recoil*, 277, 283.
revert, 144.

Rebound, *react*, 179.
*Rebours (Fr.), *regression*, 283.
Rebuff, *refuse*, 764.
repulse, 732.
resist, 719.
recoil, 277, 325.
Rebuild, *reconstruct*, 163.
restore, 660.
Rebuke, *disapprove*, 932.
Rebus, *secret*, 533.
Rebut, *answer*, 462.
confute, 479.
deny, 536.
counter-evidence, 468.
Recalcitrate, *resist*, 276, 719
Recall, *recollect*, 505.
cancel, 756.
Recant, *retract*, 607.
deny, 536.
resign, 757.
Recapitulate, *summary*, 596.
describe, 594.
enumerate, 85.
Recast, *plan*, 626, 660.
Recede, *move back*, 283.
move from, 287.
decline, 659.
Receipt, *money*, 810.
recipe, 697.
Receive, *admit*, 296.
take in, 785.
acquire, 775.
learn, 539.
welcome, 892, 894.
money, 810.
Received, *ordinary*, 82.
Recension, *revision*, 457.
improvement, 658.
Recent, *past*, 122.
new, 123.
Receptacle, *recipient*, 191.
magazine, 636.
Reception, *arrival*, 292.
comprehension, 54.
ingestion, 296.
conference, 588.
admission, 785.
visit, 892, 894.
Receptive, *intelligent*, 498.
Recess, *place*, 182.
regression, 283.
ambush, 530.
holiday, 685.
retirement, 893.
Recession, *motion from*, 287.
*Réchauffé (Fr.), *copy*, 21.
improve, 658.
*Recherché (Fr.), *goodness*, 648.
Recidivism, *relapse*, 661.
Recidivist, *criminal*, 949.
Recipe, *remedy*, 662.
precept, 697.
Recipient, *receptacle*, 191.
receiving, 785.
Reciprocal, *mutual*, 12.
quantity, 84.
interchange, 148.
Reciprocation, *retaliation*, 718.
Recital, *music*, 415.
Recitative, *music*, 415.
Recite, *narrate*, 594.
speak, 582.
enumerate, 85.
Reckless, *rash*, 863.
careless, 460.
Reckon, *count*, 85.
measure, 466.
believe, 484.
Reckon upon, *expect*, 507.
Reckoning, *accounts*, 811.
price, 812.
Reclaim, *restoration*, 660.
*Réclame (Fr.), *advertisement*, 531.
self-advertisement, 884.
Recline, *lie flat*, 213.
rest upon, 215.
repose, 687.
descend, 306.
Recluse, *seclusion*, 893, 955.
Recognisable, *visible*, 446.
Recognisance, *security*, 771.
Recognise, *see*, 441.
know, 490.
assent, 488.
remember, 505.
discover, 480.
acknowledge, 535.
Recognised, *received*, 82.
Recoil, *repercussion*, 277, 325.
revert, 145.
shun, 623.
reluctance, 603.
dislike, 867.
hate, 898.
reaction, 179.
Recollect, *remember*, 505.
Recommence, *repetition*, 104.
Recommend, *advise*, 695.
approve, 931.
induce, 615.
Recompense, *reward*, 973.
payment, 809.
Reconcile, *agree*, 23.
content, 831.
pacify, 723.
forgive, 918.
Recondite, *obscure*, 519.
hidden, 529.

Reconnaissance, *survey*, 441.
Reconnoitre, *see*, 441.
inquire, 461.
Reconsideration, *thought*, 451.
Reconstitute, *restore*, 660.
Reconstruct, *reproduce*, 164.
restore, 660.
Reconvert, *restore*, 660.
Record, *note*, 551.
list, 86.
Record, break the, *superiority*, 33.
Recorder, *recorder*, 553.
Recount, *description*, 594.
Recoup, *restore*, 660.
reward, 973.
Recourse, *use*, 677.
Recovery, *reinstatement*, 660.
improvement, 658.
recruit, 689.
Recreant, *coward*, 862.
base, 940, 945.
apostate, 941.
wretch, 949.
Recreation, *amusement*, 840.
Recrement, *unclean*, 653.
Recrimination, *accusation*, 938.
retaliation, 718.
Recrudescence, *recurrence*, 104, 136.
Recruit, *refresh*, 689.
reinstate, 660.
repair, 658.
aid, 707.
provide, 637.
strengthen, 159.
Rectify, *straighten*, 246.
improve, 658.
re-establish, 660.
Rectilinear, *straightness*, 246.
Rectitude, *virtue*, 944.
Recto, *dextrality*, 228.
Rector, *clergy*, 996.
Rectory, *office*, 995.
house, 1000.
*Reculons (Fr.), *regression*, 283.
Recumbent, *horizontal*, 213.
oblique, 217.
Recuperation, *restitution*, 790.
improvement, 658.
Recur, *repeat*, 104.
frequent, 136.
periodic, 138.
Recurvation, *curvature*, 245.
Recusant, *denying*, 536.
dissenting, 489.
unwilling, 603.
refusing, 764.
heterodox, 984.
impenitent, 951.
Red, *redness*, 434.
Redaction, *publication*, 531.
improvement, 658.
Redargue, *confute*, 479.
Red-book, *list*, 86.
Red-coat, *combatant*, 726.
Reddition, *restoration*, 790.
Redeem, *reinstate*, 660.
deliver, 672.
liberate, 750.
fulfil, 772.
atone, 952.
compensate, 30.
restore, 790.
Redemption, *salvation*, 976.
Red-hot, *heat*, 382.
Redintegrate, *reinstate*, 660.
renovate, 658.
Red letter, *indication*, 550.
Redolence, *odour*, 398.
fragrance, 400.
Redouble, *duplication*, 90.
repeat, 104.
increase, 35.
Redoubt, *defence*, 717.
Redoubtable, *fear*, 860.
Redound, *conduce*, 176.
Redress, *remedy*, 662.
rectify, 658.
restore, 660.
reward, 873.
Red-tape, *custom*, 613.
Red-tapist, *director*, 695.
Reduce, *lessen*, 36.
contract, 195.
shorten, 201.
lower, 308.
weaken, 160.
convert, 144.
subdue, 731.
impoverish, 804.
in number, 103.
*Reductio ad absurdum (L.), *confutation*, 479.
Reduction, *arithmetical*, 85.
Redundant, *ample*, 641.
diffuse, 573.
remaining, 40.
Reduplication, *imitation*, 19.
doubling, 90.
Re-echo, *imitate*, 19.
repeat, 104.
reduplication, 90.
sound, 404.
Reechy, *uncleanness*, 653.
Reed, *musical instrument*, 417.
Reef, *slacken*, 275.
shoal, 346.
danger, 667.
Reek, *hot*, 382.

Reek, *fume*, 334.
Reel, *rock*, 314.
agitate, 315.
rotate, 312.
dance, 840.
Re-embody, *combination*, 43.
junction, 48.
Re-entrant, *angle*, 244.
Re-establishment, *restoration*, 145, 660.
Refection, *refreshment*, 689.
meal, 298.
Refectory, *room*, 191.
Refer, *attribute*, 155.
relate, 9.
Referee, *judge*, 480, 967.
adviser, 695.
Referendum, *vote*, 609.
Refinement, *elegance*, 845.
fashion, 852.
taste, 850.
improvement, 658.
wisdom, 498.
sophistry, 477.
Refit, *repair*, 658.
reinstate, 660.
Reflect, *think*, 451.
imitation, 19.
Reflect upon, *blame*, 932.
Reflecting, *thoughtful*, 498.
Reflection, *maxim*, 496.
likeness, 21.
blame, 932.
Reflector, *optical instrument*, 445.
*Reflet (Fr.), *variegation*, 440.
Reflex, *regress*, 283.
thought, 451.
Reflux, *regress*, 283.
recoil, 277.
Refocillate, *refresh*, 689.
restore, 660.
Reform, *improve*, 658.
change, 140.
Refraction, *deviation*, 279.
angularity, 244.
Refractory, *resisting*, 719.
obstinate, 606.
disobedient, 742.
difficult, 704.
Refractor, *optical instrument*, 445.
Refrain, *avoid*, 623.
reject, 610.
unwilling, 603.
abstain, 616, 681.
temperance, 953.
repetition, 104, 415.
Refresh, *cool*, 385.
relieve, 834.
refit, 658.
Refresh, *restore*, 660.
strengthen, 159.
Refresher, *fee*, 809.
Refreshing, *pleasing*, 829.
Refreshment, *food*, 298.
recruiting, 689.
Refrigeration, *refrigerate*, 385.
Refrigeratory, *cold*, 387.
Reft, *disjoin*, 44.
Refuge, *refuge*, 666.
Refugee, *escape*, 671.
Refulgence, *light*, 420.
Refund, *restore*, 790.
pay, 807.
Refurbish, *improve*, 658.
Refuse, *decline*, 764.
reject, 610.
remains, 40.
offscourings, 643.
Refute, *confute*, 479.
Regain, *acquisition*, 775.
Regal, *authority*, 737.
Regale, *feast*, 298.
enjoyment, 827.
pleasing, 377, 829.
amusement, 840.
Regalia, *sceptre*, 747.
Regard, *esteem*, 931.
love, 897.
view, 441.
judge, 480.
conceive, 484.
credit, 873.
Regarding, *relation*, 9.
Regardless, *inattention*, 458.
Regatta, *amusement*, 840.
Regency, *commission*, 755.
Regenerate, *reproduce*, 163.
restore, 660.
piety, 987.
Regent, *deputy*, 759.
governor, 745.
*Régime (Fr.), *authority*, 737.
circumstance, 8.
conduct, 692.
Regimen, *diet*, 298.
remedy, 662.
Regiment, *army*, 726.
assemblage, 72.
Regimentals, *dress*, 225.
Region, *region*, 181.
Register, *record*, 551.
list, 86.
to arrange, 60.
range, 26.
to coincide, 199.
ventilator, 351.
fire-place, 386.
Registrar, *recorder*, 553.

Regorge, *restitution*, 790.
Regrater, *merchant*, 797.
Regress, *regression*, 283.
Regret, *sorrow*, 833.
penitence, 950.
Regular, *orderly*, 58.
according to rule, 82.
symmetric, 242.
periodic, 138.
Regulation, *arrangement*, 60.
direction, 693.
usage, 80.
order, 741.
law, 963.
Regurgitate, *return*, 283.
flow, 348.
restore, 790.
Rehabilitate, *reinstate*, 660.
restore, 790.
Rehash, *repetition*, 104.
Rehearse, *repeat*, 104.
describe, 594.
dramatic, 599.
Reign, *authority*, 175, 737.
Reimburse, *restore*, 790.
pay, 807.
Rein, *moderate*, 174.
check, 179.
slacken, 275.
restrain, 616.
hold, 737.
curb, 747.
Reincarnation, *reproduction*, 163.
Reinforce, *strengthen*, 159.
aid, 707.
add, 37, 39.
Reinforcement, *supplies*, 635, 637.
Reinstate, *restore*, 660.
Reis Effendi, *deputy*, 759.
Reiterate, *frequent*, 136.
repeat, 104, 535.
multitude, 102.
Reject, *decline*, 610.
refuse, 764.
exclude, 55.
eject, 297.
Rejoice, *exult*, 838.
gratify, 829.
cheer, 836.
amuse, 840.
Rejoinder, *answer*, 462.
evidence, 468.
Rejuvenate, *restore*, 660.
Rekindle, *motive*, 615.
Relapse, *reversion*, 145.
retrogression, 661.
Relate, *narrate*, 594.
refer, 9.
Relation, *relation*, 9.
Relative, *consanguinity*, 11.
Relax, *weaken*, 160.
soften, 324.
slacken, 275.
unbend the mind, 452.
repose, 687.
amuse, 840.
lounge, 683.
loose, 47.
misrule, 738.
relent, 914.
Relay, *materials*, 635.
Release, *liberate*, 750.
discharge, 970.
restore, 790.
exempt, 927.
repay, 807.
death, 360.
Relegate, *transfer*, 270.
remove, 185.
banish, 55.
Relent, *moderate*, 174.
pity, 914.
relax, 324.
Relentless, *malevolent*, 907.
wrathful, 900.
revengeful, 919.
flagitious, 945.
impenitent, 951.
Relevancy, *pertinence*, 9.
congruity, 23.
Reliable, *believable*, 484.
trustworthy, 939.
Reliance, *confidence*, 484.
hope, 858.
Relic, *remainder*, 40.
reminiscence, 505.
token, 551.
sacred, 998.
Relict, *widow*, 905.
Relief, *see* Relieve.
convexity, 250.
Relieve, *comfort*, 834.
refresh, 689.
help, 707.
improve, 658.
Religion, *theology*, 983.
piety, 987.
Religiosity, *sanctimony*, 989.
Religious, *exact*, 494.
pious, 987.
Relinquish, *a purpose*, 607, 624.
property, 782.
to discontinue, 141.
Reliquary, *rite*, 998.
Relish, *like*, 377, 827.
savoury, 394.
desire, 865.
Relucent, *luminous*, 420.

Relucent, *transparent*, 425.
Reluctance, *dislike*, 867.
unwillingness, 603.
dissuasion, 616.
Reluctation, *resistance*, 719.
Rely, *confidence*, 484.
expectation, 507.
hope, 858.
Remain, *endure*, 106.
to be left, 40.
rest, 265.
continue, 142.
Remainder, *left*, 40.
Remains, *corpse*, 362.
vestige, 551.
Remand, *restraint*, 751.
Remark, *observe*, 457.
assert, 535.
Remarkable, *important*, 642.
Remarkably, *greatness*, 31.
Remedy, *cure*, 662.
salubrious, 656.
to restore, 660, 834.
Remember, *recollect*, 505.
Remembrancer, *recorder*, 553.
Remigration, *egress*, 295.
Remind, *recollect*, 505.
Reminiscence, *remember*, 505.
Remiss, *neglectful*, 460.
idle, 683.
reluctant, 603.
laxity, 738.
Remission, *see* Remit.
Remit, *relax*, 174.
forgive, 918.
discontinue, 141.
pay, 807.
Remnant, *remainder*, 40.
Remodel, *conversion*, 140, 144.
Remonstrate, *dissuade*, 616.
expostulate, 932.
Remorse, *penitence*, 950.
Remorseless, *resentment*, 900.
Remote, *distant*, 196.
not related, 10.
Remotion, *see* Remove.
Remove, *displace*, 185.
removal, 185.
retrench, 38.
depart, 293.
recede, 287.
transfer, 270.
extract, 301.
term, 71.
Remunerate, *reward*, 973.
pay, 810.
Renaissance, *revival*, 660.
Renascent, *reproduction*, 163.
*Rencontre (Fr.), *meeting*, 197, 292.
Rencounter, *fight*, 720.
meeting, 292.
Rend, *disjoin*, 44.
Render, *give*, 784.
restore, 790.
interpret, 522.
music, 415.
Rendezvous, *focus*, 74.
assemblage, 72.
Rending, *loud*, 404.
painful, 830.
Rendition, *surrender*, 782.
interpretation, 522.
Renegade, *apostate*, 941.
turncoat, 607.
Renew, *repeat*, 104.
frequent, 136.
repair, 658.
Reniform, *curvature*, 245.
Renounce, *relinquish*, 624.
property, 782.
recant, 607.
resign, 757.
deny, 536.
repudiate, 927.
Renovate, *reproduce*, 163.
restore, 660.
Renown, *repute*, 873.
Rent, *fissure*, 44, 198.
hire, 794.
receipt, 810.
*Rentier (Fr.), *wealth*, 803.
Renunciation, *see* Renounce.
Reorganise, *conversion*, 144.
Repair, *mend*, 658.
refresh, 689.
restore, 790.
atone, 952.
Repair to, *journey*, 266.
Reparation, *compensation*, 973.
Repartee, *wit*, 842.
answer, 462.
Repast, *food*, 298.
Repatriation, *egress*, 295.
Repay, *payment*, 807.
Repeal, *abrogation*, 756.
Repeat, *iterate*, 104, 143.
imitate, 19.
duplication, 90.
frequent, 136.
multiplied, 102.
Repel, *repulse*, 289.
defend, 717.
resist, 719.
disincline, 867.
shock, 898.
refuse, 764.
deter, 616.
Repellent, *unpleasant*, 830.

Repent, *penitence*, 950.
Repercussion, *recoil*, 277.
counteraction, 179.
Repertoire, *store*, 636.
Repertory, *store*, 636.
Repetend, *iteration*, 104.
arithmetical, 84.
Repetition, *iteration*, 90, 104.
copy, 21.
imitation, 19.
Repine, *discontent*, 832.
regret, 833.
repent, 950.
Replace, *restore*, 660.
supersede, 147.
Replant, *restore*, 660.
Replenish, *fill*, 637.
complete, 52.
Repletion, *filling*, 637.
satiety, 869.
Replevin, *restore*, 790.
borrow, 788.
Replica, *copy*, 21.
Reply, *answer*, 462.
Report, *noise*, 406.
record, 551.
inform, 527.
publish, 531.
rumour, 532.
statement, 594.
law, 969.
Repose, *quiescence*, 265.
rest, 685, 687.
Repose on, *support*, 215.
Reposit, *location*, 184.
Repository, *store*, 636.
focus, 74.
*Repoussé (Fr.), *convexity*, 250.
Reprehend, *disapprove*, 932.
Represent, *delineate*, 554.
imitate, 19.
simulate, 17.
describe, 594.
denote, 550.
commission, 755.
Representative, *consignee*, 758.
typical, 82.
Repress, *quiet*, 174.
calm, 826.
control, 179.
Reprieve, *pardon*, 918.
deliverance, 671.
respite, 970.
Reprimand, *disapprove*, 932.
Reprint, *copy*, 21.
Reprisal, *retaliation*, 718.
Reproach, *blame*, 932.
disgrace, 874.
Reprobate, *blame*, 932.
Reprobate, *sinner*, 949.
impious, 989.
Reproduce, *repeat*, 104.
copy, 19.
renovate, 163.
Reprove, *disapprove*, 932.
Reptile, *animal*, 366.
servile, 886.
base, 940.
apostate, 941.
miscreant, 949.
Republic, *man*, 373.
Repudiate, *exclude*, 55.
reject, 610.
violate, 773.
evade, 927.
non-payment, 808.
Repugn, *resistance*, 719.
Repugnance, *dislike*, 876.
reluctance, 603.
hate, 898.
incongruity, 24.
Repulse, *see* Repel, 719.
Repulsive, *disagreeable*, 830, 898.
ugly, 846.
Repurchase, *purchase*, 795.
Reputable, *repute*, 873.
Request, *request*, 765.
Requiem, *funereal*, 363.
dirge, 415.
Require, *need*, 630.
insufficient, 640.
to exact, 741.
charge, 812.
Requisition, *command*, 741.
requirement, 630.
Requital, *reward*, 973.
gratitude, 916.
punishment, 972.
Rescind, *cut off*, 44.
abrogate, 756.
refuse, 764.
Rescission, *see* Rescind.
Rescript, *order*, 741.
letter, 592.
answer, 462.
Rescue, *deliver*, 672.
preserve, 670.
Research, *inquiry*, 461.
Reseat, *restore*, 660.
Resection, *disjunction*, 44.
Resemblance, *similarity*, 17.
Resent, *resentment*, 900.
Reservation, *concealment*, 528.
silence, 585.
shyness, 881.
store, 636.
Reserve, *concealment*, 528.
silence, 585.

Reserve, *shyness*, 881.
caution, 864.
store, 636.
Reservoir, *store*, 636.
receptacle, 191.
Reside, *inhabit*, 184, 186.
Residence, *abode*, 189.
location, 184.
Resident, *inhabitant*, 188.
Residue, *remainder*, 40.
Resign, *give up*, 757.
relinquish, 782.
submit, 743.
Resignation, *endurance*, 826.
content, 831.
abdication, 757.
humility, 743, 879.
renunciation, 872.
Resilient, *elasticity*, 325.
Resist, *withstand*, 719.
disobey, 742.
refuse, 764.
oppose, 179.
tenacity, 327.
Resistless, *strength*, 159.
Resolute, *determined*, 604.
brave, 861.
Resolution, *decomposition*, 49.
investigation, 461.
solution, 462.
topic, 454.
determination, 604.
courage, 861.
Resolve, *purpose*, 620.
to liquefy, 335.
decompose, 49.
investigate, 461.
interpret, 522.
Resonant, *sonorous*, 402.
ringing, 408.
Resorb, *reception*, 296.
Resort, *employ*, 677.
converge, 290.
focus, 74.
assemble, 72.
move, 266.
dwell, 189.
Resound, *be loud*, 402, 404.
ring, 408.
praises, 931.
Resourceful, *skill*, 698.
Resourcelesss, *inactive*, 683.
Resources, *means*, 632.
wealth, 803.
Respect, *deference*, 928.
fame, 873.
salutation, 894.
reference, 9.
Respectable, *repute*, 873.
Respectable, *tolerable*, 651.
Respecting, *relation*, 9.
Respective, *speciality*, 79.
Respectless, *inattention*, 458.
Respire, *breathe*, 359.
repose, 687.
Respite, *pause*, 265.
intermission, 106.
rest, 141, 687.
escape, 671.
reprieve, 970.
Resplendent, *luminous*, 420.
splendid, 845.
Respond, *agree*, 23.
sensibility, 375, 822.
Response, *answer*, 462.
verbal, 587.
rites, 998.
Responsible, *duty*, 926.
Responsive, *see* Respond.
Rest, *quiescence*, 265.
repose, 687.
remainder, 40.
pause, 141.
satisfaction, 831.
recumbence, 215.
Restaurant, *food*, 298.
Rest on, *support*, 215.
Restful, *soothing*, 174.
Resting-place, *support*, 215.
quiescence, 165.
arrival, 292.
Restitution, *restitution*, 790.
Restive, *obstinate*, 606.
disobedient, 742.
impatient, 825.
Restless, *moving*, 264.
agitated, 315.
active, 682.
excited, 825.
fearful, 860.
Restorative, *remedial*, 662.
salubrious, 656.
relieving, 834.
Restore, *reinstate*, 145, 660.
improve, 658.
refresh, 689.
return, 790.
meaning, 522.
Restrain, *moderate*, 174.
emotion, 826.
check, 706.
curb, 751.
prohibit, 761.
circumscribe, 231.
dissuade, 616.
Restrict, *moderate*, 174.
emotion, 826.
check, 706.

Restrict, *curb*, 751.
prohibit, 761.
circumscribe, 231.
dissuade, 616.
Result, *effect*, 154, 476.
remainder, 40.
Resume, *taking*, 789.
Résumé, *compendium*, 596.
Resurrection, *reproduction*, 163.
Resuscitate, *reanimate*, 163.
reinstate, 660.
Retail, *sell*, 796.
particularise, 594.
Retailer, *merchant*, 797.
Retain, *keep in place*, 150.
keep possession, 781.
enlist, 615.
Retainer, *servant*, 746.
Retaliate, *retort*, 718.
revenge, 919.
Retard, *hinder*, 706.
slacken, 275.
Retch, *rejection*, 297.
Retention, *keeping*, 781.
in the memory, 505.
Retentive, *retention*, 781.
*Retenue (Fr.), *reserve*, 881.
Reticence, *latency*, 526.
Reticle, *crossing*, 219.
Reticulate, *crossing*, 219.
Reticule, *receptacle*, 191.
Retiform, *crossing*, 219.
Retinue, *followers*, 65.
suite, 69.
servants, 746.
Retire, *recede*, 287.
depart, 293.
resign, 757.
Retirement, *seclusion*, 893.
privacy, 526.
Retort, *answer*, 462.
confutation, 479.
retaliation, 718.
wit, 842.
vessel, 191.
Retouch, *improve*, 658.
Retrace, *memory*, 505.
Retrace steps, *recede*, 283.
Retract, *deny*, 536.
recant, 607.
abjure, 757.
annul, 756.
violate, 773.
Retreat, *recede*, 287, 725.
abode, 189.
asylum, 666.
escape, 671.
hiding-place, 530.
Retrench, *subduct*, 38.
Retrench, *shorten*, 201.
lose, 789.
economise, 817.
Retribution, *retaliation*, 718.
payment, 807.
punishment, 972.
Retrieve, *restore*, 660.
Retroaction, *recoil*, 277.
regression, 283.
counteraction, 179.
Retrocession, *recession*, 287.
Retrograde, *motion*, 283.
declension, 659.
relapse, 661.
Retrogression, *see* Retrograde.
Retrospect, *memory*, 505.
thought, 451.
past, 122.
Retroversion, *inversion*, 218.
Return, *regression*, 283.
arrival, 292.
frequency, 136.
to restore, 790.
reward, 973.
report, 551.
appoint, 755.
profit, 775.
proceeds, 810.
Reunion, *junction*, 43.
assemblage, 72.
Reveal, *disclosure*, 529.
Revel, *enjoy*, 827.
amuse, 840.
dissipation, 954.
Revelation, *disclosure*, 529.
theological, 985.
Revelry, *cheerful*, 836.
*Revenant (Fr.), *ghost*, 980.
Revendication, *claim*, 765.
recovery, 660.
Revenge, *revenge*, 919.
Revenue, *wealth*, 803.
receipts, 810.
Reverberate, *sound*, 408.
recoil, 277.
Reverberatory, *furnace*, 386.
Reverence, *respect*, 928.
salutation, 894.
piety, 987.
title, 877.
Reverie, *train of thought*, 451.
imagination, 515.
Reverse, *antiposition*, 237.
contrary, 14.
change, 140.
evolution, 313.
inversion, 218.
misfortune, 830.
adversity, 735.

Revert, *recur*, 136.
go back, 283.
deteriorate, 659.
Review, *consider*, 457.
judge, 480.
criticism, 595.
Reviewer, *writer*, 590.
Revile, *abuse*, 932.
blaspheme, 989.
Revise, *consider*, 457.
improve, 658.
Revisit, *presence*, 186.
Revive, *live*, 359.
restore, 660.
refresh, 689.
Revivify, *reproduction*, 163.
Revoke, *recant*, 607.
deny, 536.
cancel, 756.
refuse, 754.
Revolt, *resist*, 719.
disobey, 742.
shock, 830.
Revolting, *vulgar*, 851.
Revolution, *rotation*, 312.
change, 140, 146.
periodicity, 138.
Revolve, *meditate*, 451.
Revolver, *arms*, 727.
Revue, *drama*, 599.
Revulsion, *recoil*, 277.
Reward, *reward*, 973.
Rhabdomancy, *prediction*, 511.
Rhadamanthine, *severity*, 739.
Rhapsody, *discontinuity*, 70.
nonsense, 497.
fancy, 515.
music, 415.
Rhetoric, *speech*, 582.
Rhetorical, *ornament*, 577.
Rheum, *humour*, 333.
water, 337.
Rhine, *ditch*, 350.
Rhino, *money*, 800.
Rhomb, *angularity*, 244.
Rhumb, *direction*, 278.
Rhyme, *poetry*, 597.
Rhymeless, *prose*, 598.
Rhythm, *harmony*, 413.
regularity, 138.
Rib, *ridge*, 250.
wife, 903.
Ribald, *vile*, 874, 961.
Ribbed, *furrow*, 259.
Ribbon, *filament*, 205.
tie, 45.
decoration, 877.
Rich, *wealthy*, 803.
abundant, 639.
Rich, *savoury*, 394.
style, 577.
Richly, *great*, 31.
Rick, *store*, 636.
accumulation, 72.
Rickety, *weak*, 160.
imperfect, 651.
ugly, 846.
Rickshaw, *vehicle*, 272.
*Ricochet (Fr.), *recoil*, 277.
revolution, 146.
Rid, *loss*, 776.
relinquish, 782.
abandon, 624.
deliver, 672.
Riddance, *see* Rid.
Riddle, *enigma*, 533.
question, 461.
sieve, 260.
arrange, 60.
Ride, *move*, 266.
get above, 206.
road, 627.
Rider, *equestrian*, 268.
appendix, 39.
Ridge, *narrowness*, 203.
projection, 250.
Ridicule, *deride*, 856.
depreciate, 483.
disrespect, 929.
Ridiculous, *grotesque*, 853.
silly, 499.
trifing, 643.
*Ridotto (It.), *gala*, 840.
rout, 892.
*Rifacimento (It.), *recast*, 660.
Rife, *ordinary*, 82.
frequent, 132.
prevailing, 175.
Riff-raff, *vulgar*, 876.
dirt, 653.
Rifle, *to plunder*, 791.
musket, 726.
Rifleman, *combatant*, 727.
Rift, *separation*, 44.
fissure, 198.
Rig, *dress*, 225.
prepare, 673.
frolic, 840.
deception, 545.
adorn, 845.
Rigadoon, *dance*, 840.
Rigescence, *hardness*, 323.
Rigging, *gear*, 225.
cordage, 45.
Right, *just*, 922.
privilege, 924.
duty, 926.
honour, 939.

Right, *straight*, 246.
suitable, 646.
Righteous, *virtuous*, 944.
just, 922.
Rigid, *hard*, 323.
exact, 494.
strict, 772.
severe, 739.
stubborn, 606.
regular, 82.
Rigmarole, *nonsense*, 497.
unintelligible, 519.
Rigour, *severity*, 739.
compulsion, 744.
exactness, 494.
Rile, *irritate*, 900.
Rill, *river*, 348.
Rim, *edge*, 230.
Rime, *cold*, 383.
Rind, *covering*, 222.
Ring, *circle*, 247.
sound, 408.
arena, 728.
syndicate, 778.
Ringleader, *master*, 745.
Ringlet, *circle*, 247.
Rinse, *cleanness*, 652.
Riot, *violence*, 173.
revolt, 719, 742.
confusion, 59.
luxuriate, 377, 827.
Rip, *tear*, 44.
rush, 274.
rascal, 949.
Riparian, *land*, 342.
Ripe, *preparation*, 673.
Ripost, *answer*, 462.
Ripping, *excellent*, 648.
delightful, 827.
Ripple, *shake*, 315.
murmur, 405.
wave, 348.
Rise, *ascend*, 206, 305.
slope, 217.
resist, 719.
revolt, 742.
spring, 154.
grow, 35.
Risible, *laughable*, 828.
ridiculous, 853.
witty, 842.
Risk, *danger*, 665.
chance, 621.
Risky, *improper*, 961.
Rite, *law*, 963.
religious, 998.
*Ritornello (It.), *frequency*, 136.
Ritual, *rite*, 998.
Rival, *emulate*, 720.
Rival, *envy*, 921.
oppose, 708.
competitor, 710, 726.
Rive, *disjoin*, 44.
Rivel, *fold*, 258.
River, *water*, 348.
Rivet, *to fasten*, 43, 150.
fastening, 45.
Rivulet, *water*, 348.
Road, *way*, 189, 627.
direction, 278.
Roadstead, *anchorage*, 189.
refuge, 666.
Roadster, *carrier*, 271.
Roadway, *way*, 627.
Roam, *journey*, 266.
Roan, *variegation*, 271.
Roar, *sound*, 404.
cry, 411.
weep, 839.
Roast, *heat*, 384.
ridicule, 856.
censure, 932.
Rob, *plunder*, 791.
pulp, 354.
Robber, *thief*, 792.
Robe, *dress*, 225.
Robin Goodfellow, *imp*, 980.
Robust, *strength*, 159.
Rock, *hardness*, 323.
land, 342.
to oscillate, 314.
pitfall, 667.
Rock-bottom, *base*, 211.
Rocket, *signal*, 550.
arms, 727.
light, 423.
rise, 305.
rapid, 274.
Rocky, *unsteady*, 149.
Rococo, *fantastic*, 853.
Rod, *sceptre*, 747.
scourge, 975.
bane, 663.
measure, 466.
divining, 992.
Rodomontade, *nonsense*, 497.
unintelligible, 519.
boasting, 884.
Rogation, *worship*, 990.
Rogue, *cheat*, 548.
scamp, 949.
Roguery, *vice*, 945.
dishonour, 940.
Roguish, *sportive*, 842.
Roister, *insolence*, 885.
Rôle, *business*, 625.
drama, 599.
Roll, *rotate*, 312.

Roll, *move*, 264.
push, 284.
flow, 348.
sound, 407.
cylinder, 249.
fillet, 205.
record, 551.
list, 86.
Roll-call, *number*, 85.
Roller, *rotundity*, 249.
Rollicking, *frolicsome*, 836.
blustering, 885.
Rolling stone, *traveller*, 268.
Roly-poly, *size*, 192.
Romance, *fiction*, 515.
falsehood, 544.
absurdity, 497.
fable, 594.
Romantic, *sentimental*, 822.
*Rondeau (Fr.), *poem*, 597.
*Rondo (It.), *music*, 415.
Roof, *summit*, 210.
height, 206.
cover, 222.
house, 189.
Roofless, *divestment*, 226.
Rook, *deceiver*, 548.
Rookery, *abode*, 189.
Room, *space*, 180.
occasion, 124.
chamber, 191.
Roomy, *space*, 180.
Roost, *abode*, 186, 189.
Root, *cause*, 153.
base, 211.
algebraic, 84.
to place, 184.
Rooted, *fixed*, 265.
permanent, 142.
old, 124.
habitual, 613.
belief, 484.
Root out, *destroy*, 162.
displace, 185.
eject, 297.
extract, 301.
discover, 480.
Rope, *cord*, 205.
fastening, 45.
Rope-dancer, *proficient*, 700.
Rope-dancing, *skill*, 698.
Ropy, *semiliquidity*, 352.
*Roquelaure (Fr.), *dress*, 225.
Roral, *moisture*, 339.
Rosary, *rite*, 998.
garden, 371.
Roscid, *moisture*, 339.
Rose, *redness*, 434.
Roses, bed of, *pleasure*, 377.
Rosette, *cluster*, 72.
Rosicrucian, *deceiver*, 548.
Roster, *list*, 86
Rostrum, *beak*, 234.
pulpit, 542.
Rosy, *red*, 434.
auspicious, 858.
Rot, *disease*, 655.
decay, 659.
putrefy, 653.
nonsense, 497, 517.
to banter, 856.
Rota, *periodicity*, 138.
Rotate, *rotation*, 312.
Rote, by, *memory*, 505.
Rotten, *foul*, 653.
fetid, 401.
Rotter, *knave*, 949.
Rotunda, *abode*, 189.
Rotundity, *roundness*, 249.
*Roturier (Fr.), *commonalty*, 876.
*Roué (Fr.), *scoundrel*, 949.
sensualist, 954.
Rouge, *red*, 434.
ornament, 847.
*Rouge et noir (Fr.), *chance*, 156.
Rough, *uneven*, 256.
shapeless, 241.
sour, 397.
austere, 395.
violent, 173.
sound, 410.
unprepared, 674.
ugly, 846.
churlish, 895.
to fag, 686.
Rough-and-ready, *transient*, 111.
provisional, 673.
Rough-cast, *unprepared*, 674.
Rough-grained, *texture*, 329.
Rough-hewn, *rugged*, 256.
unprepared, 674.
*Rouleau (Fr.), *cylinder*, 249.
money, 800.
Round, *circular*, 247.
assertion, 535.
periodicity, 138.
fight, 720.
of a ladder, 215.
Roundabout, *circuitous*, 31.
way, 629.
circumlocutory, 566, 573.
Roundelay, *poetry*, 597.
Round-house, *prison*, 752.
Roundlet, *circular*, 247.
Round on, *attack*, 716.
peach, 529.
Round robin, *record*, 551.
Round-up, *assemblage*, 72.
capture, 789.

Roup, *sale*, 796.
Rouse, *stimulate*, 615.
passion, 824.
Rout, *discomfit*, 732.
assembly, 892.
rabble, 876.
Rout out, *destruction*, 162.
Route, *method*, 627.
direction, 278.
Routine, *order*, 58.
cycle, 138.
rule, 60.
custom, 613.
Rove, *wander*, 266.
deviate, 279.
Rover, *traveller*, 268.
Row, *series*, 69.
navigate, 267.
brawl, 713.
riot, 720.
Rowdy, *violent*, 173.
Rowel, *sharpness*, 253.
stimulus, 615.
Royalty, *authority*, 737.
receipt, 810.
Rub, *friction*, 331.
difficulty, 703.
Rub-a-dub, *roll*, 407.
Rub down, *pulverulence*, 330.
Rub out, *disappear*, 449.
efface, 552.
Rub up, *improve*, 658.
Rubber, *elasticity*, 325.
Rubbish, *inutility*, 645.
nonsense, 497, 517.
Rubble, *unimportance*, 643.
Rubefy, *red*, 434.
Rubicon, *limit*, 233.
passage, 303.
undertaking, 676.
Rubicund, *red*, 434.
Rubric, *precept*, 697.
liturgy, 998.
Rubricate, *red*, 434.
Ruby, *red*, 434.
gem, 650.
Ruche, *fold*, 258.
Ruck, *fold*, 258.
*Rucksack (Ger.), *receptacle*, 191.
Rudder, *guidance*, 695.
Ruddy, *red*, 434.
Rude, *violent*, 173.
vulgar, 851.
uncivil, 895.
ugly, 846.
ignorant, 491.
uncivilised, 876.
Rudiment, *beginning*, 66.
cause, 153.
Rudiment, *smallness*, 193.
non-preparation, 674.
Rudiments, *elementary knowledge*, 490.
school, 542.
Rue, *regret*, 833.
repent, 950.
Rueful, *doleful*, 837.
Ruffian, *maleficent*, 913.
scoundrel, 949.
Ruffle, *derange*, 61.
fold, 258.
edge, 230.
discompose, 821.
excite, 824.
anger, 900.
Rufous, *red*, 434.
Rug, *covering*, 222.
Rugged, *rough*, 256.
ugly, 846.
churlish, 895.
style, 579.
Rugose, *wrinkled*, 256.
Ruin, *decay*, 659.
failure, 732.
evil, 619.
impoverish, 804.
adversity, 735.
ruins, 40.
Rule, *regularity*, 80.
length, 200.
measure, 466.
government, 737.
precept, 697.
custom, 613.
law, 963.
to decide, 480.
Ruler, *master*, 745.
Rum, *odd*, 853.
Rumble, *noise*, 407.
Rumbustious, *violent*, 173.
Ruminate, *thought*, 451.
Rummage, *seek*, 461.
Rumour, *publicity*, 531.
report, 532.
Rump, *rear*, 235.
Rumple, *fold*, 258.
derange, 61.
rough, 256.
Rumpus, *confusion*, 59.
violence, 173.
contention, 720.
Run, *move quick*, 274.
move out, 295.
recurrence, 136.
flow, 109, 333.
continue, 143.
operate, 680.
conduct, 692, 693.

Run, *smuggle*, 791.
Run across, *encounter*, 292.
Run after, *pursue*, 622.
Run away, *escape*, 671.
avoid, 623.
from fear, 862.
recede, 287.
Run down, *censure*, 932.
depreciate, 483.
weakness, 160.
Run high, *violence*, 173.
Run in, *insert*, 300.
arrest, 751.
Run into, *become*, 144.
Run low, *decrease*, 36.
Run on, *continue*, 143.
Run out, *elapse*, 122.
waste, 638.
Run over, *redundant*, 641.
describe, 594.
count, 85.
examine, 457, 596.
Run riot, *violence*, 173.
Run through, *peruse*, 539.
squander, 818.
Run up, *expend*, 809.
increase, 35.
Rundle, *circle*, 247.
convolution, 248.
rotundity, 249.
Runlet, *receptacle*, 191.
Runnel, *river*, 348.
Runner, *courier*, 268.
messenger, 534.
Running, *continuously*, 69.
Runt, *littleness*, 193.
Rupture, *break*, 44, 713.
Rural, *country*, 189.
Ruralist, *recluse*, 893.
Ruse, *cunning*, 702.
deception, 545.
Rush, *rapidity*, 274.
to pursue, 622.
trifle, 643.
Rushlight, *light*, 423.
Russet, *red*, 433.
Rust, *decay*, 659.
sluggishness, 683.
canker, 663.
Rustic, *rural*, 189.
clown, 876.
vulgar, 851.
Rustication, *seclusion*, 895.
Rusticity, *inurbanity*, 895.
Rustle, *noise*, 409, 410.
Rusty, *sluggish*, 683.
old, 128.
unserviceable, 645.
dirty, 653.
Rusty, *deteriorated*, 659.
Rut, *groove*, 259.
habit, 613.
Ruth, *pity*, 914.
Ruthless, *pitiless*, 907.
angry, 900.
Rutilant, *light*, 420.
Ruttish, *impurity*, 961.
Ryot, *commonalty*, 876.

S

Sabbatarian, *bigot*, 989.
Sable, *black*, 431.
*Sabot (Fr.), *dress*, 225.
Sabre, *weapon*, 727.
to kill, 361.
Sabretache, *bag*, 191.
Sabulous, *pulverulence*, 330.
Saccharine, *sweet*, 396.
Sacerdotal, *clergy*, 995.
Sachem, *master*, 745.
Sachet, *fragrance*, 400.
Sack, *bag*, 191.
to ravage, 649.
havoc, 619.
plunder, 791.
dismiss, 756.
Sackcloth, *asceticism*, 955.
atonement, 952.
Sacrament, *rite*, 998.
Sacred, *holy*, 976.
pious, 987.
inviolable, 924.
Sacrifice, *destroy*, 162.
offering, 763.
self-denial, 942.
atonement, 952.
worship, 990.
Sacrilege, *irreligion*, 989.
Sacristan, *churchman*, 996.
Sacristy, *temple*, 1000.
Sacrosanct, *inviolable*, 924.
Sad, *dejected*, 837.
bad, 649.
Saddle, *clog*, 706.
add, 37.
Safe, *secure*, 664.
cupboard, 191.
Safe-conduct, *safety*, 664.
Safeguard, *safety*, 664.
Safety-valve, *safety*, 666.
Saffron, *yellowness*, 436.
Sag, *obliquity*, 217.
Saga, *description*, 594.
Sagacious, *intelligent*, 498.
foreseeing, 510.
skilful, 698.

Sagittate, *angular*, 244.
Sahib, *title*, 877.
Saic, *ship*, 273.
Sail, *navigate*, 267.
set out, 293.
Saint, *holy*, 948.
pious, 987.
Saintly, *virtuous*, 944.
pious, 987.
Sake, *cause*, 615.
Salaam, *respect*, 743, 928.
Salacity, *impurity*, 961.
Salad, *mixture*, 41.
Salamander, *furnace*, 386.
Salary, *pay*, 809.
Sale, *merchandise*, 796.
Salesman, *merchant*, 797.
Salient, *projecting*, 250.
sharp, 253.
important, 643.
Saline, *pungent*, 392.
Sallow, *yellow*, 436.
pale, 429.
Sally, *issue*, 293.
attack, 716.
wit, 842.
Salmagundi, *mixture*, 41.
*Salon (Fr.), *room*, 191.
Saloon, *room*, 191.
Salt, *pungent*, 392.
condiment, 393.
wit, 842.
preserve, 670.
Saltation, *dancing*, 309.
Saltatory, *rise*, 305.
leap, 309.
agitation, 315.
*Saltimbanco (It.), *quack*, 548.
Salubrity, *health*, 656.
Salutary, *salubrious*, 656.
remedial, 662.
Salute, *compliment*, 894.
kiss, 902.
address, 586.
firing, 882, 883.
Salvage, *tax*, 812.
discount, 813.
reward, 973.
to save, 672.
Salvation, *deliverance*, 672.
preservation, 670.
religious, 976.
Salve, *to relieve*, 834.
remedy, 662.
Salver, *dish*, 191.
Salvo, *exception*, 83.
condition, 770.
excuse, 937.
plea, 617.
Salvo, *explosion*, 406.
salute, 882.
Samaritan, *benefactor*, 912.
Sambo, *mixture*, 41.
Same, *identity*, 13.
Samiel, *wind*, 349.
Samovar, *vessel*, 191.
Sampan, *ship*, 273.
Sample, *specimen*, 82.
Sanatory, *improvement*, 658.
remedy, 662.
Sanctify, *authorise*, 924.
piety, 987.
Sanctimony, *hypocrisy*, 989.
Sanction, *authority*, 924.
Sanctity, *piety*, 987.
Sanctuary, *refuge*, 666.
altar, 1000.
Sanctum, *holy*, 1000.
room, 191.
Sand, *pulverulence*, 330.
Sand-blind, *dim-sighted*, 443.
Sandal, *dress*, 225.
Sands, *pitfall*, 667.
Sandwich, *interpose*, 228.
Sandy, *pulverulence*, 330.
Sane, *intelligent*, 498.
rational, 502.
*Sang-froid (Fr.), *insensibility*, 823.
inexcitability, 826.
caution, 846.
Sanguinary, *brutal*, 907.
Sanguine, *expectant*, 507.
imagination, 515.
hopeful, 858.
Sanhedrim, *tribunal*, 696.
Sanies, *fluidity*, 333.
Sanitary, *salubrity*, 656.
Sanity, *rationality*, 502.
health, 654.
*Sans (Fr.), *nullibiety*, 187.
*Sans cérémonie (Fr.), *modesty*, 881.
sociality, 892.
friendship, 888.
*Sans-culotte (Fr.), *rebel*, 742.
commonalty, 876.
*Sans façon (Fr.), *modesty*, 881.
sociality, 892.
*Sans pareil (Fr.), *superiority*, 33.
*Sans phrase (Fr.), *frankness*, 543, 566.
*Sans souci (Fr.), *pleasure*, 827.
content, 831.
Santon, *hermit*, 893.
priest, 996.
Sap, *juice*, 333.
to destroy, 162.
damage, 659.
Sapid, *tasty*, 390.

Sapient, *wisdom*, 498.
Sapless, *dry*, 340.
Sapling, *youth*, 129.
Saponaceous, *soapy*, 355.
Sapor, *flavour*, 390.
Sappy, *juicy*, 333.
foolish, 499.
Saraband, *dance*, 840.
Sarcasm, *satire*, 932.
Sarcastic, *irascible*, 901.
Sarcophagus, *interment*, 363.
Sardonic, *contempt*, 838.
Sartorial, *dress*, 225.
Sash, *central*, 247.
Satan, *devil*, 978.
Satanic, *evil*, 649.
vicious, 945.
Satchel, *bag*, 191.
Sate, *see* Satiate.
Satellite, *follower*, 281.
companion, 88.
Satiate, *sufficient*, 639.
redundant, 641.
cloy, 869.
Satiety, *see* Satiate.
Satiny, *smooth*, 255.
Satire, *ridicule*, 856.
censure, 932.
Satisfaction, *duel*, 720.
reward, 973.
Satisfy, *content*, 831.
gratify, 827, 829.
convince, 484.
fulfil a duty, 926.
an obligation, 772.
reward, 973.
pay, 807.
suffice, 639.
satiate, 869.
grant, 762.
Satrap, *ruler*, 745.
deputy, 759.
Saturate, *fill*, 639.
satiate, 869.
Saturated, *greatness*, 31.
Saturnalia, *amusement*, 840.
disorder, 59.
Saturnian, *halcyon*, 734, 829.
Saturnine, *grim*, 837.
Satyr, *ugly*, 846.
demon, 980.
rake, 961.
Sauce, *mixture*, 41.
adjunct, 39.
abuse, 832.
Sauce-box, *impudence*, 887.
Saucer, *receptacle*, 191.
Saucy, *insolent*, 885.
flippant, 895.
Saunter, *ramble*, 266.
dawdle, 275.
*Sauve qui peut (Fr.), *velocity*, 274.
recession, 287.
avoidance, 623.
escape, 671.
cowardice, 862.
Savage, *violent*, 173.
brutal, 876.
angry, 900.
malevolent, 907.
brave, 861.
a wretch, 913.
Savanna, *plain*, 344.
Savant, *scholar*, 492.
wisdom, 500.
Save, *except*, 38, 83.
to preserve, 670.
deliver, 672.
lay by, 636.
economise, 817.
*Savoir faire (Fr.), *tact*, 698.
*Savoir vivre (Fr.), *sociality*, 892.
breeding, 852.
Saviour, *Deity*, 976.
benefactor, 912.
Savour, *taste*, 390.
Savour of, *similarity*, 17.
Savouriness, *palatableness*, 394.
Savourless, *insipid*, 391.
Savoury, *palatable*, 394.
delectable, 829.
Saw, *jagged*, 257.
saying, 496.
Sawder, soft, *flattery*, 933.
Sawdust, *pulverulence*, 330.
Saxophone, *musical instrument*, 417.
Say, *speak*, 582.
assert, 535.
Saying, *assertion*, 535.
maxim, 496.
Sbirro, *jurisdiction*, 965.
Scab, *traitor*, 941.
Scabbard, *receptacle*, 191, 222.
Scabby, *improbity*, 940.
Scabrous, *rough*, 256.
indelicate, 961.
Scaffold, *frame*, 215.
preparation, 673.
way, 627.
execution, 975.
Scald, *burn*, 384.
poet, 597.
Scalding, *hot*, 382.
burning, 384.
Scale, *slice*, 204.
portion, 51.
skin, 222.
order, 58.

Scale, *measure*, 466.
series, 69.
gamut, 413.
to mount, 305.
attack, 716.
Scale, on a large, *greatness*, 31.
Scale, on a small, *smallness*, 32.
Scale, turn the, *superiority*, 33.
Scallop, *convolution*, 248.
Scalp, *trophy*, 733.
to criticise, 932.
Scalpel, *sharpness*, 253.
Scamp, *rascal*, 949.
to neglect, 460.
Scamper, *velocity*, 274.
Scan, *vision*, 441.
metre, 597.
Scandal, *disgrace*, 874.
vice, 945.
news, 532.
Scandalise, *disgust*, 932.
Scandent, *climb*, 305.
Scansion, *metre*, 597.
Scant, *narrowness*, 203.
smallness, 32.
Scantling, *dimensions*, 192.
example, 82.
small quantity, 32.
scrap, 51.
prototype, 22.
Scanty, *smallness*, 32.
few, 103.
insufficient, 640.
Scape, *escape*, 671.
Scapegoat, *blame*, 952.
Scapegrace, *vice*, 949.
Scapulary, *rite*, 998.
Scar, *blemish*, 848.
seam, 43.
Scaramouch, *humorist*, 844.
buffoon, 857.
Scarce, *insufficiency*, 640.
Scarcely, *little*, 32.
rare, 137.
Scare, *frighten*, 860.
Scarecrow, *ugly*, 846.
bugbear, 860.
Scaremonger, *news*, 532.
Scarf, *dress*, 225.
Scarf-skin, *covering*, 222.
Scarify, *torment*, 830.
Scarlet, *red*, 434.
Scarp, *slope*, 217.
Scathe, *evil*, 619.
bane, 663.
badness, 649.
Scatheless, *secure*, 664.
saved, 672.
Scathing, *censorious*, 932.
Scatology, *uncleanness*, 653.
Scatter, *disperse*, 73.
diverge, 291.
derange, 59.
Scatter-brained, *foolish*, 499.
Scattered, *discontinuous*, 70.
Scavenger, *clean*, 652.
Scene, *appearance*, 448.
arena, 728.
painting, 556.
drama, 599.
*Scenario (It.), *plan*, 626.
drama, 599.
Scenery, *vista*, 448.
Scent, *smell*, 398.
knowledge, 490.
trail, 551.
Scent-bag, *smell*, 400.
Scentless, *absence of smell*, 399.
Scepticism, *doubt*, 485, 497.
religious, 988.
Sceptre, *sceptre*, 747.
Schedule, *list*, 86.
record, 551.
draft, 554.
Scheme, *plan*, 626.
draft, 554.
Schemer, *plot*, 626.
*Scherzando (It.), *music*, 415.
*Scherzo (It.), *music*, 415.
Schesis, *state*, 7.
Schism, *discord*, 713.
dissent, 489.
heterodoxy, 984.
Scholar, *learner*, 541.
erudite, 492.
Scholarship, *school*, 490.
learning, 539.
Scholastic, *learning*, 490, 539.
Scholiast, *interpreter*, 524.
Scholium, *interpretation*, 496, 522.
School, *teach*, 537, 542.
Schoolboy, *pupil*, 541.
Schooled, *trained*, 698.
Schoolfellow, *friend*, 890.
Schooling, *teaching*, 538.
Schoolman, *scholar*, 492.
sage, 500.
Schoolmaster, *teacher*, 540.
Schooner, *ship*, 273.
*Schwärmerei (Ger.), *imagination*, 515.
Sciagraphy, *painting*, 556.
Sciamachy, *absurdity*, 497.
Science, *knowledge*, 490.
skill, 698.
Scientific, *exact*, 494.
Scientist, *scholar*, 492.
Scimetar, *arms*, 727.

Scintilla, *small*, 32.
spark, 420.
Sciolism, *smattering*, 491.
Sciolist, *smatterer*, 493.
Sciomancy, *prediction*, 511.
Scion, *child*, 129.
posterity, 167.
*Scire facias (L.), *inquiry*, 641.
Scission, *cut*, 44.
Sclerosis, *hardness*, 323.
Scobs, *pulverulence*, 330.
Scoff, *ridicule*, 856.
deride, 929.
impiety, 989.
Scold, *abuse*, 932.
vixen, 936.
Scollop, *convolution*, 248.
Sconce, *summit*, 210.
mulct, 974.
candlestick, 423.
Scoop, *depth*, 208.
depression, 252.
perforator, 262.
profit, 775.
Scoot, *hurry*, 274, 684.
Scooter, *locomotion*, 266.
Scope, *degree*, 26.
extent, 180.
intention, 620.
freedom, 748.
Scorch, *burn*, 384.
Score, *mark*, 550, 842.
furrow, 259.
motive, 615.
price, 812.
accounts, 805, 811.
twenty, 98.
musical, 415.
to count, 85.
to succeed, 731.
Score, on the — of, *relation*, 9.
*Scoriæ (L.), *unimportance*, 643.
uncleanness, 653.
Scorify, *calefaction*, 384.
Scorn, *contempt*, 930.
Scorpion, *bane*, 663.
painful, 830.
Scotch, *maltreat*, 649.
Scot-free, *gratuitous*, 815.
deliverance, 672.
exemption, 927.
Scotomy, *dim-sightedness*, 443.
Scoundrel, *vice*, 949.
Scour, *rub*, 331.
run, 274.
clean, 652.
Scourge, *whip*, 972, 975.
bane, 663.
painful, 830.
Scourge, *bad*, 649.
Scourings, *refuse*, 643.
Scout, *messenger*, 534.
watch, 664.
to disdain, 930.
deride, 643.
Scowl, *frown*, 895.
complain, 839.
anger, 900.
Scrabble, *fumble*, 379.
Scraggy, *rough*, 256.
narrow, 203.
ugly, 846.
Scramble, *confusion*, 59.
haste, 684.
difficulty, 704.
swift, 274.
mount, 305.
Scrannel, *stridulous*, 410.
meagre, 643.
Scrap, *piece*, 51.
bit, 32.
small portion, 193.
disuse, 678.
contention, 720.
to fight, 722.
Scrap-book, *collection*, 596.
Scrape, *difficulty*, 704.
mischance, 732.
abrade, 330, 331.
bow, 894.
Scrape together, *collect*, 72.
get, 775.
Scratch, *groove*, 259.
mark, 550.
write, 590.
daub, 555.
hurt, 619.
to wound, 649.
Scratch out, *obliteration*, 552.
Scrawl, *write*, 590.
Scream, *cry*, 410.
complain, 839.
Screech, *cry*, 410.
complain, 839.
Screech-owl, *noise*, 412.
Screed, *speech*, 582.
Screen, *concealment*, 528.
asylum, 666, 717.
ambush, 530.
to shield, 664.
sieve, 260.
shade, 424.
drama, 599.
Screened, *safe*, 664.
invisible, 447.
Screw, *fasten*, 43.
joining, 45.
instrument, 267, 633.

Screw, *rotation*, 312
salary, 809.
miser, 819.
Screw up, *strengthen*, 159.
Screwed, *drunk*, 959.
Scribble, *write*, 590.
Scribe, *writer*, 553, 590.
priest, 996.
Scrimp, *shorten*, 201.
stint, 640.
Scrip, *receptacle*, 191.
Script, *writing*, 590.
Scripture, *revelation*, 985.
certain, 474.
Scrivener, *writing*, 590.
Scroll, *record*, 551.
convolution, 248.
Scrub, *clean*, 652.
Scrubby, *vulgar*, 876.
shabby, 940.
bad, 649.
trifling, 643.
small, 193.
rough, 256.
Scrunch, *pulverulence*, 330.
Scrumptious, *pleasurable*, 829.
Scruple, *doubt*, 485.
dissuasion, 616.
smallness, 32.
Scrupulous, *careful*, 459.
incredulous, 487.
exact, 494.
reluctant, 603.
punctilious, 939.
virtuous, 944.
Scrutinise, *examine*, 457, 461.
Scud, *speed*, 274.
sail, 267.
shower, 348.
haze, 353.
Scuffle, *contention*, 720.
Scull, *navigation*, 267.
Scullery, *room*, 191.
Scullion, *servant*, 746.
Sculptor, *artist*, 559.
Sculpture, *carving*, 557.
form, 240.
Scum, *dregs*, 643, 653.
Scupper, *conduit*, 350.
Scurf, *uncleanness*, 653.
Scurrility, *ridicule*, 856.
detraction, 934.
Scurry, *hasten*, 274, 684.
Scurvy, *bad*, 649.
base, 940, 945.
Scut, *tail*, 235.
Scutcheon, *standard*, 550.
honour, 877.
Scuttle, *tray*, 191.
Scuttle, *to destroy*, 162.
hasten, 274, 684.
Scythe, *angularity*, 244.
Sea, *water*, 341.
Seaboard, *edge*, 342.
Sea-green, *green*, 435.
Seal, *to close*, 67, 261.
sigil, 550.
evidence, 467.
record, 551.
compact, 769.
Seals, *authority*, 747.
Seal up, *shut up*, 231.
Seam, *junction*, 43.
Seaman, *mariner*, 269.
Seamanship, *conduct*, 693.
skill, 698.
*Séance (Fr.), *council*, 696.
Sear, *burn*, 384.
deaden, 823.
Search, *seek*, 461.
pursuit, 622.
Searching, *thorough*, 52.
Searchless, *unintelligible*, 519.
Seared, *impenitent*, 951.
Sea-side, *edge*, 342.
Season, *time*, 106.
opportunity, 134.
pungent, 392, 393.
to preserve, 670.
prepare, 673.
accustom, 613.
Seasonable, *opportune*, 134.
expedient, 646.
agreement, 23.
Seasonal, *period*, 108.
Seasoning, *mixture*, 41.
pungency, 171, 393.
Season, out of, *disagreement*, 24.
Seat, *abode*, 189.
position, 183.
to place, 184.
support, 215.
Seaworthy, *useful*, 644.
fit, 673.
Sebaceous, *unctuous*, 355.
Secede, *dissent*, 489.
Seclude, *restrain*, 751.
Seclusion, *retirement*, 526, 893.
Second, *of time*, 108.
instant, 113.
abet, 707.
auxiliary, 711.
Secondary, *following*, 63.
consignee, 758.
deputy, 759.
inferior, 643.
imperfect, 651.
Second-best, *imperfection*, 651.

Second-best, *inferiority*, 34.
Second-hand, *borrowed*, 788.
indifferent, 651.
imitated, 19.
Secondly, *bisection*, 91.
Second-rate, *imperfection*, 651.
inferiority, 34.
Second-sight, *prediction*, 510.
witchcraft, 992.
Secret, *latent*, 526.
hidden, 528.
riddle, 533.
Secretary, *recorder*, 553.
writer, 590.
Secrete, *hide*, 528.
Secretive, *reserved*, 528.
Sect, *division*, 75.
Sectarian, *dissenter*, 984.
Section, *part*, 51.
division, 44.
class, 75.
chapter, 593.
Sector, *part*, 51.
Secular, *number*, 99.
laity, 997.
Secure, *fasten*, 43.
safe, 664.
engage, 768.
gain, 775.
confident, 858.
Security, *pledge*, 771.
warranty, 924.
Sedan, *vehicle*, 272.
Sedate, *thoughtful*, 451.
calm, 826.
grave, 837.
Sedative, *calming*, 174.
remedy, 662.
Sedentary, *quiescence*, 265.
*Sederunt (L.), *council*, 696.
Sediment, *dregs*, 653.
remainder, 40.
Sedition, *disobedience*, 742.
Seduce, *entice*, 615.
love, 897.
Seducer, *libertine*, 962.
Seducing, *charming*, 829.
Seduction, *impurity*, 961.
Seductive, *attractive*, 829, 845, 897.
Sedulous, *active*, 682.
See, *view*, 441.
look, 457.
bishopric, 995.
Seed, *cause*, 153.
posterity, 167.
Seedling, *youth*, 129.
Seedy, *weak*, 160.
ailing, 655.
exhausted, 688.
Seedy, *worn*, 651.
Seek, *inquire*, 461.
pursue, 622.
Seem, *appear*, 448.
Seeming, *semblance*, 448.
Seemly, *expedient*, 646.
proper, 926.
handsome, 845.
Seer, *veteran*, 130.
oracle, 513.
sorcerer, 994.
Seesaw, *oscillation*, 314.
Seethe, *boil*, 382, 384.
Segment, *division*, 51.
Segregate, *exclude*, 55.
separate, 44.
not related, 10.
incoherent, 47.
Seignior, *master*, 745.
Seize, *take*, 789.
rob, 791.
possess, 777.
Seizure, *weakness*, 160.
Seldom, *infrequency*, 137.
Select, *choose*, 609.
good, 648.
Selection, *part*, 51.
Self, *special*, 13.
Self-abasement, *humility*, 879.
Self-admiration, *pride*, 880.
Self-advertisement, *boasting*, 884.
Self-applause, *vanity*, 880.
Self-assertion, *effrontery*, 885.
Self-communing, *thought*, 451.
Self-conceit, *conceit*, 880.
Self-complacency, *conceit*, 880.
Self-confidence, *conceit*, 880.
Self-conquest, *restraint*, 953.
Self-consciousness, *knowledge*, 490.
modesty, 881.
Self-contempt, *humility*, 879.
Self-control, *restraint*, 942.
Self-deceit, *error*, 495.
Self-defence, *defence*, 717.
Self-denial, *disinterestedness*, 942.
temperance, 953.
Self-evident, *clear*, 478.
Self-examination, *thought*, 451.
Self-existing, *existence*, 1.
Self-forgetful, *disinterested*, 942.
Self-importance, *vanity*, 880.
Self-indulgence, *selfishness*, 943.
intemperance, 954.
Selfish, *selfishness*, 943.
Self-love, *selfishness*, 943.
Self-opinionated, *foolish*, 499.
vain, 880.
obstinate, 606.
Self-possession, *caution*, 864.

Self-praise, *vanity*, 880.
Self-regarding, *selfish*, 943.
Self-reliance, *security*, 604.
courage, 861.
Self-reproach, *blame*, 950.
Self-reproof, *blame*, 950.
Self-respect, *virtue*, 944.
Self-restraint, *self-control*, 942.
Self-sacrifice, *unselfishness*, 942.
Self-satisfied, *vanity*, 880.
Self-seeking, *selfishness*, 943.
Self-styled, *pretence*, 544.
Self-sufficient, *vanity*, 880.
Self-supporting, *freedom*, 748.
Self-taught, *knowledge*, 490.
Self-tormentor, *dejection*, 837.
Self-willed, *obstinate*, 606.
Sell, *sale*, 796.
Selvedge, *edge*, 230.
Semaphore, *sign*, 550.
Sematology, *sign*, 550.
Semblance, *likeness*, 19.
copy, 20.
Semi, *half*, 91.
Semicolon, *stop*, 141.
Semifluid, *semiliquidity*, 352.
Semiliquid, *semiliquidity*, 352.
Semilunar, *curvature*, 245.
Seminary, *school*, 542.
Semitransparent, *semitransparency*, 427.
*Semper idem (L.), *identity*, 13.
Sempiternal, *duration*, 112.
Senary, *number*, 98.
Senate, *council*, 696.
Senator, *adviser*, 695.
Send, *propel*, 284.
transfer, 270.
errand, 755.
Send down, *expel*, 893.
Seneschal, *master*, 745.
Seneschalship, *authority*, 737.
Senile, *age*, 128.
Seniority, *age*, 128.
Sensation, *physical*, 375.
affective, 820.
excitement, 824.
Sensational, *exaggerated*, 549.
Sensationalism, *vulgarity*, 851.
Sense, *intellect*, 450.
wisdom, 498.
meaning, 516.
Senseless, *foolish*, 499.
insensible, 376.
unmeaning, 517.
Senses, *feeling*, 375.
Sensibility, *physical*, 375.
moral, 822.
Sensible, *material*, 316.
Sensible, *wise*, 498.
Sensitive, *physically*, 375.
morally, 822.
Sensorium, *intellect*, 450.
Sensual, *intemperance*, 954.
Sensuous, *perception*, 375.
Sentence, *phrase*, 566.
maxim, 496.
judgment, 969.
decision, 480.
Sententious, *concise*, 572.
energetic, 574.
Sentient, *feeling*, 375, 822.
Sentiment, *opinion*, 484.
maxim, 496.
idea, 453.
Sentimental, *sensibility*, 822.
affectation, 855.
Sentinel, *guardian*, 664.
keeper, 753.
watch, 668.
Sentry, *see* Sentinel.
Separate, *simple*, 42.
to disjoin, 44, 91, 198.
exclude, 55.
diverge, 291.
divorce, 905.
Separatist, *heterodoxy*, 984.
Sepoy, *combatant*, 726.
Sept, *class*, 75.
Septet, *number*, 98.
Septic, *insalubrity*, 657.
Septuagint, *revelation*, 985.
*Septum (L.), *partition*, 228.
Sepulchral, *sound*, 408, 410.
Sepulchre, *interment*, 363.
Sepulture, *interment*, 363.
Sequacious, *following*, 63.
servile, 886.
Sequel, *following*, 65.
in time, 117.
addition, 39.
Sequence, *in order*, 63.
in time, 117.
motion, 281.
Sequester, *take*, 789.
hide, 526.
seclude, 893.
confiscate, 974.
Sequestrate, *take*, 789.
confiscate, 974.
Seraglio, *harem*, 961.
Seraph, *angel*, 977.
saint, 948.
Seraphic, *blissful*, 829.
virtuous, 944.
Seraskier, *master*, 745.
Serenade, *music*, 415.
compliment, 902.

Serene, *calm*, 826.
content, 831.
Serf, *clown*, 876.
slave, 746.
Serfdom, *subjection*, 749.
Sergeant, *master*, 745.
Seriatim, *continuity*, 69.
order, 59.
speciality, 79.
continuance, 144.
Series, *sequence*, 69.
book, 593.
Serio-comic, *ridiculous*, 853.
Serious, *great*, 31.
important, 642.
dejected, 837.
resolved, 604.
Sermon, *dissertation*, 595.
lesson, 537.
speech, 582.
pastoral, 998.
Serosity, *fluidity*, 333.
Serpent, *tortuous*, 248.
Satan, 978.
deceiver, 548.
evil, 663.
Serpentine, *convolution*, 248.
Serrated, *angular*, 244.
notched, 257.
Serum, *lymph*, 333.
water, 337.
Servant, *servant*, 711, 746.
Serve, *aid*, 707.
obey, 743, 749.
work, 680.
Serve out, *apportion*, 786.
punish, 972.
Service, *good*, 618.
use, 677.
utility, 644.
worship, 990.
servitude, 749.
warfare, 722.
Serviceable, *useful*, 644.
good, 648.
Servile, *obsequious*, 886.
flattery, 933.
Servitor, *servant*, 746.
Servitude, *subjection*, 749.
Sesqui, *number*, 87.
Sesquipedalian, *long*, 200.
*Sesquipedalia verba (L.), *ornament*, 577.
Sessions, *legal*, 966.
council, 696.
Sestina, *poetry*, 597.
Set, *condition*, 7.
group, 72.
class, 75.
Set, *firm*, 43.
to place, 184.
establish, 150.
prepare, 673.
solidify, 321.
leaning, 278.
gang, 712.
lease, 796.
Set about, *begin*, 676.
Set apart, *disjoin*, 55.
Set aside, *disregard*, 460.
annul, 756.
release, 927.
Set-back, *hindrance*, 706.
relapse, 661.
Set down, *humiliate*, 879.
censure, 932.
slight, 929.
rebuff, 732.
Set fire to, *burn*, 384.
Set foot in, *ingress*, 294.
Set forth, *publish*, 531.
tell, 527.
show, 525.
assert, 535.
describe, 594.
Set forward, *depart*, 293.
Set in, *begin*, 66.
tide, 348.
approach, 286.
Set off, *depart*, 293.
compensate, 30.
adorn, 845.
Set on, *attack*, 615.
Set out, *begin*, 66.
depart, 293.
decorate, 845.
Set right, *reinstate*, 660.
Set sail, *depart*, 293.
Set-to, *combat*, 720.
Set to work, *begin*, 676.
Set up, *raise*, 307.
prosperous, 734.
Set upon, *attack*, 716.
desire, 865.
willing, 602.
determined, 604, 620.
Setaceous, *rough*, 256.
Settee, *support*, 215.
Setting, *surroundings*, 227.
Settle, *decide*, 480.
fixed, 142.
stationary, 265.
dwell, 186.
sink, 306.
arrange, 60.
pacify, 723.
consent, 762.
pay, 807.

Settle, *give*, 784.
bench, 215.
Settlement, *location*, 184.
colony, 188.
dregs, 653.
compact, 762, 769.
Settler, *inhabitant*, 188.
Seven, *number*, 98.
Sever, *disjoin*, 44.
Several, *repetition*, 102.
Severally, *one by one*, 44, 49.
Severe, *harsh*, 739.
energetic, 171.
painful, 830.
unadorned, 576, 849.
critical, 932.
greatness, 31.
Sew, *join*, 43.
Sewer, *drain*, 295, 350.
cloaca, 653.
Sex, *kind*, 75.
women, 374.
Sextet, *number*, 98.
Sexton, *church*, 996.
Sextuple, *number*, 98.
*Sforzando (It.), *music*, 415.
Sgraffito, *see* Graffito.
Shabby, *mean*, 819, 874.
bad, 649.
disgraceful, 940.
trifling, 643.
smallness, 32.
Shackle, *to tie*, 43.
hinder, 706.
restrain, 751.
fetter, 752.
Shade, *darkness*, 421.
shadow, 424.
colour, 428.
degree, 26.
difference, 15, 41.
small quantity, 32.
screen, 530.
manes, 362.
ghost, 980.
decrease, 36.
Shaded, *invisible*, 447.
Shades below, *hell*, 982.
Shading off, *degree*, 26.
Shadow, *darkness*, 421.
shade, 424.
error, 495.
phantom, 4.
little, 193, 203.
small in degree, 32.
part, 51.
sequence, 281.
Shadow forth, *show*, 525.
indicate, 550.
Shadow, *adumbrate*, 521.
describe, 594.
Shadow of doubt, *unbelief*, 485.
Shadow out, *represent*, 554.
Shadowy, *imaginary*, 2.
invisible, 447.
erroneous, 495.
Shady, *umbrageous*, 424.
dishonest, 544.
disreputable, 945.
Shaft, *pit*, 260.
air-pipe, 351.
deep, 208.
frame, 215.
missile, 284.
shank, 633.
weapon, 727.
Shag, *roughness*, 256.
tobacco, 298A.
Shaggy, *hirsute*, 256.
Shah, *master*, 745.
Shake, *agitate*, 315.
fluctuate, 149.
trill, 314, 407.
musical, 415.
dissuade, 616.
injure, 659.
impress, 821.
flutter, 824.
shiver, 383.
Shake-down, *bed*, 215.
Shake off, *ejection*, 297.
Shake up, *agitation*, 315.
Shaken, *weak*, 160.
Shaky, *in danger*, 665.
frail, 149.
Shallop, *ship*, 273.
Shallow, *not deep*, 209.
ignorant, 491.
foolish, 499.
Shallow-brained, *foolish*, 499.
Shallow-pated, *foolish*, 499.
Shallows, *dangers*, 667.
Sham, *humbug*, 544.
Shamble, *shuffle*, 275, 315.
Shambles, *butchery*, 361.
Shame, *disgrace*, 874.
Shamefaced, *abashed*, 881.
Shameful, *disgraceful*, 87.
profligate, 945.
Shameless, *profligate*, 945.
impudent, 885.
Shampoo, *friction*, 331.
Shandrydan, *vehicle*, 272.
Shank, *shaft*, 633.
Shape, *form*, 240.
condition, 7.
to fashion, 144.
aspect, 448.

Shape well, *hopeful*, 858.
Shapeless, *amorphous*, 241.
ugly, 846.
Shapely, *comely*, 845.
symmetrical, 242.
Share, *part*, 51.
participate, 778.
allotted portion, 786.
Share, lion's, *superiority*, 33.
Shark, *thief*, 792.
cheat, 548.
Sharp, *acute*, 253.
musical tone, 410.
pungent, 392, 821.
energetic, 171.
violent, 173.
intelligent, 498.
clever, 698.
cunning, 702.
active, 682.
rude, 895.
censorious, 932.
Sharper, *cheat*, 548.
thief, 792.
Sharpshooter, *combatant*, 726.
Sharp-sighted, *vision*, 441.
Shaster, *pseudo-revelation*, 986.
Shatter, *destroy*, 162.
weaken, 160.
Shave, *cut*, 203.
Shaving, *layer*, 204.
filament, 205.
small part, 32, 51.
Shawl, *dress*, 225.
Sheaf, *assemblage*, 72.
Shear, *subduction*, 38.
Sheath, *receptacle*, 191.
envelope, 222.
Shed, *building*, 189.
to emit, 297.
scatter, 73.
diverge, 291.
Shed tears, *weep*, 839.
Sheen, *light*, 420.
Sheepish, *foolish*, 881.
Sheer, *narrow*, 203.
simple, 42.
smallness, 32.
Sheer off, *departure*, 293.
Sheet, *layer*, 204.
paper, 593.
Sheet-anchor, *refuge*, 666.
Sheik, *ruler*, 745.
priest, 996.
Shelf, *support*, 215.
(on the), *disuse*, 678.
Shell, *cover*, 222.
bomb, 727.
Shelter, *refuge*, 666.
Shelter, *safety*, 664.
Shelty, *horse*, 271.
Shelve, *slope*, 217.
locate, 184.
disuse, 678.
Shepherd, *director*, 694.
pastor, 996.
Sheriff, *jurisdiction*, 965.
Sherlock Holmes, *inquiry*, 461.
Shibboleth, *indication*, 550.
criterion, 467.
Shield, *defend*, 717.
safety, 664.
buckler, 666.
Shift, *move*, 264.
change, 140, 144.
transfer, 270.
expedient, 626, 634.
evasion, 546.
plea, 617.
difficulty, 704.
dress, 225.
Shifting, *transient*, 111.
moving, 270.
Shiftless, *unprepared*, 674.
inhabile, 699.
Shifty, *dishonest*, 544.
Shikar, *pursuit*, 622.
Shillelagh, *club*, 727.
Shilly-shally, *irresolution*, 605.
Shimmer, *lustre*, 420.
Shin, *climb*, 305.
kick, 276.
Shindy, *violence*, 173.
contention, 720.
Shine, *to emit light*, 420.
glory, 873.
beauty, 845.
Ship, *vessel*, 273.
to deliver, 270.
Shipload, *cargo*, 31.
abundance, 639.
Shipment, *transference*, 270.
Shipshape, *order*, 58.
Shipwreck, *failure*, 732.
to defeat, 731.
Shire, *county*, 181.
Shirk, *avoid*, 623.
disobey, 742.
Shirt, *dress*, 225.
Shivaree, *uproar*, 404.
Shive, *slice*, 51, 204.
Shiver, *shake*, 315.
cold, 385.
layer, 204.
fragment, 51.
filament, 205.
to divide, 44.
destroy, 162.

Shoal, *shallow*, 209.
assemblage, 72, 102.
Shoals, *danger*, 667.
Shock, *concussion*, 276.
violence, 173.
sheaf, 72.
contest, 720.
affect, 821.
move, 824.
pain, 830.
dislike, 867.
hate, 898.
scandalise, 932.
Shocking, *bad*, 649.
ugly, 846.
vulgar, 851.
fearful, 860.
painful, 830.
considerable, 31.
Shoe, *dress*, 225.
Shoot, *propel*, 284.
dart, 274.
kill, 361.
grow, 194.
attack, 716.
pain, 378.
grieve, 828.
offspring, 167.
Shoot up, *increase*, 35.
ascend, 305.
prominent, 250.
Shop, *mart*, 799.
Shopkeeper, *merchant*, 797.
Shoplifting, *stealing*, 791.
Shopman, *merchant*, 797.
Shop-walker, *director*, 694.
Shore, *support*, 215.
land, 342.
sewer, 653.
Shoreless, *space*, 180.
Shorn, *deprived*, 776.
reduced, 36.
Short, *not long*, 201.
concise, 572.
incomplete, 53.
unaccomplished, 730.
insufficient, 640.
brittle, 328.
uncivil, 895.
Shortage, *insufficiency*, 640.
Shortcoming, *failing*, 304.
Shorthand, *write*, 590.
Short-lived, *youth*, 111.
Shortly, *soon*, 132.
Short of, *inferiority*, 34.
Short-sighted, *myopic*, 443.
foolish, 499.
Short-tempered, *irascible*, 901.
Short-witted, *foolish*, 499.
Shot, *missile*, 284.
weapon, 727.
variegated, 440.
guess, 514.
Shoulder, *projection*, 250.
support, 215.
to shove, 276.
Shout, *loudness*, 404.
cry, 411.
voice, 580.
Shove, *impulse*, 276.
Shovel, *vehicle*, 272.
to transfer, 270.
receptacle, 191.
Show, *manifest*, 525.
appear, 446, 448.
evince, 467.
demonstrate, 478.
parade, 852, 882.
drama, 599.
Show of, a, *similarity*, 17.
Show up, *accuse*, 938.
Shower, *rain*, 348.
abundance, 639.
assemblage, 72.
Showy, *coloured*, 428.
gaudy, 847, 882.
Shrapnel, *arms*, 727.
Shred, *bit*, 51.
filament, 205.
Shrew, *vixen*, 901.
scold, 932.
Shrewd, *intelligent*, 498.
wise, 490.
clever, 698.
cunning, 702.
Shriek, *ululation*, 411.
Shrill, *noise*, 410.
Shrimp, *little*, 193.
Shrine, *altar*, 1000.
interment, 363.
Shrink, *shrivel*, 195.
narrow, 203.
decrease, 36.
small, 32.
recoil, 287, 898.
avoid, 623.
unwilling, 603.
Shrive, *penitence*, 950.
Shrivel, *decrease*, 36.
shrink, 195.
small, 193.
Shroud, *funeral*, 363.
shelter, 666.
safety, 664.
hide, 528.
Shrub, *plant*, 367.
Shrug, *hint*, 527.
dissent, 489.

Shrunken, *little*, 193.
Shudder, *tremble*, *fear*, 860.
aversion, 867.
hate, 898.
cold, 383.
Shuffle, *mix*, 41.
disorder, 59.
derange, 61.
interchange, 148.
agitate, 315.
toddle, 266, 275.
evasion, 544, 546.
irresolution, 605.
disgrace, 940.
Shuffler, *deceiver*, 548.
Shun, *avoid*, 623.
dislike, 867.
Shunt, *turn aside*, 279.
shelve, 678.
Shut, *close*, 261.
Shut off, *disconnect*, 44.
Shut out, *exclude*, 55.
prohibit, 761.
Shut up, *enclose*, 231.
imprison, 751.
close, 261.
Shuttlecock, *irresolute*, 605.
Shy, *avoid*, 623.
suspicious, 485.
modest, 881.
fearful, 862.
propel, 276, 284.
Shylock, *usurer*, 805.
Sib, *relation*, 111.
Sibilant, *hiss*, 409.
Sibilation, *decry*, 929.
censure, 932.
Sibyl, *oracle*, 513.
ugly, 846.
Sibylline, *prediction*, 511.
*Sic (L.), *imitation*, 19.
word, 562.
Sick, *ill*, 655.
Sicken, *weary*, 841.
nauseate, 395.
fall ill, 655.
disgust, 830, 867.
hate, 898.
Sickle, *instrument*, 244.
Sickly, *ill*, 655.
weak, 160.
Sickness, *disease*, 655.
Side, *laterality*, 236.
party, 712.
affectation, 855.
insolence, 878, 885.
Side with, *aid*, 707.
Sideboard, *receptacle*, 191.
Side-car, *vehicle*, 272.
Side-light, *interpretation*, 522.
Sidelong, *lateral*, 236.
Side-slip, *deviation*, 279.
Sidereal, *world*, 318.
Sideromancy, *prediction*, 511.
Side-track, *set aside*, 678.
Sideways, *oblique*, 217.
lateral, 236.
Sidle, *oblique*, 217.
deviate, 279.
diverge, 291.
lateral, 236.
Siege, *attack*, 716.
Sieve, *perforation*, 260.
to sort, 60.
Siesta, *inactivity*, 683.
Sift, *to sort*, 60.
winnow, 42.
clean, 652.
inquire, 461.
Sigh, *lament*, 839.
Sigh for, *desire*, 865.
Sight, *vision*, 441.
spectacle, 448.
prodigy, 872.
large quantity, 31.
Sightless, *blind*, 442.
invisible, 447.
Sigil, *seal*, 550.
evidence, 467.
Sigmoidal, *convolution*, 248.
Sign, *indication*, 550.
omen, 512.
record, 551.
write, 590.
prodigy, 872.
evidence, 467.
compact, 769.
Sign-board, *indication*, 550.
Sign-manual, *sign*, 550.
Signal, *sign*, 550.
important, 642.
greatness, 31.
Signalise, *celebrate*, 883.
glory, 873.
Signally, *great*, 31.
Signature, *mark*, 550.
writing, 590.
Signet, *evidence*, 467.
signature, 550.
sign of authority, 747.
Significant, *meaning*, 516, 527.
clear, 518.
foreboding, 511.
important, 642.
Signify, *mean*, 516.
inform, 527.
forebode, 511.
Silence, *no sound*, 403.

Silence, *aphony*, 581.
confute, 479.
taciturn, 585.
to check, 731.
Silhouette, *portrait*, 556.
outline, 229.
Silky, *soft*, 255.
Silly, *irrational*, 477.
credulous, 486.
foolish, 499.
Silt, *dirt*, 653.
dregs, 40.
Silver, *money*, 800.
Silver-point, *engraving*, 558.
Silver-toned, *harmony*, 413.
Silvery, *colour*, 430.
voice, 580.
Similar, *relation*, 9.
resembling, 17.
comparison, 464.
Simile, Similitude, *see* Similar.
Simmer, *heat*, 382, 384.
excitement, 824.
Simony, *churchdom*, 995.
Simoom, *blast*, 349.
heat, 382.
Simper, *smile*, 838.
affectation, 855.
Simple, *unmixed*, 42.
unadorned, 576, 849.
small, 32.
credulous, 486.
silly, 499.
true, 543.
Simpleton, *fool*, 501.
Simplify, *meaning*, 518.
Simulate, *resemble*, 17.
imitate, 19.
cheat, 544.
Simultaneous, *contemporary*, 120.
Sin, *guilt*, 947.
vice, 945.
Since, *in order*, 8, 63.
in time, 117.
because, 155, 615.
Sincere, *veracious*, 543.
ingenuous, 703.
Sinecure, *receipt*, 810.
*Sine die (L.), *neverness*, 107.
long duration, 110.
*Sine qua non (L.), *condition*, 770.
importance, 642.
requirement, 630.
Sinewy, *strong*, 159.
*Sinfonietta (It.), *music*, 415.
Sinful, *evil*, 947.
Sing, *music*, 415.
poetry, 597.
cheerful, 836.
Singe, *burn*, 384.
Singer, *musician*, 416.
Single, *unit*, 87.
unmixed, 42.
secluded, 893.
unmarried, 904.
Single-handed, *unaided*, 708.
Single-minded, *honest*, 543.
Single out, *select*, 609.
Singlet, *dress*, 225.
*Singspiel (Ger.), *drama*, 599.
Singsong, *untuneful*, 414.
concert, 415.
Singular, *exceptional*, 79, 83.
one, 87.
remarkable, 31.
Sinister, *left*, 239.
bad, 649.
discourtesy, 895.
vicious, 945.
Sink, *descend*, 306.
lower, 308.
submerge, 310.
deep, 208.
fail, 732.
destroy, 162.
decay, 659.
fatigue, 688.
cloaca, 653.
depressed, 837.
droop, 828.
conceal, 528.
in the memory, 505.
Sinless, *good*, 946.
Sinner, *sinner*, 949.
Sin-offering, *atonement*, 952.
Sinuous, *curved*, 245.
convoluted, 248.
Sinus, *concavity*, 252.
Sip, *drink*, 296.
Siphon, *conduit*, 350.
Sir, *respect*, 877.
Sirdar, *master*, 745.
Sire, *elder*, 166.
Siren, *musician*, 416.
indication, 550.
seducing, 615.
demon, 980.
Sirocco, *wind*, 349.
heat, 382.
Sister, *kindred*, 11.
likeness, 17.
Sisterhood, *assembly*, 72.
party, 712.
Sisyphean, *difficulty*, 704.
Sit, *repose*, 215.
lie, 213.
descend, 306.
Site, *situation*, 183.

Sitting, *consultation*, 696.
Situate, *location*, 184.
Situation, *circumstances*, 8.
place, 183.
business, 625.
Siva, *deity*, 979.
Six, *number*, 98.
Size, *magnitude*, 31, 192.
glue, 45, 352.
quantity, 25.
Size up, *measure*, 466.
estimate, 480.
Sizy, *sticky*, 350.
Sjambok, *scourge*, 975.
Skate, *locomotion*, 266.
Skean, *arms*, 727.
Skedaddle, *escape*, 671.
Skein, *knot*, 219.
disorder, 59.
Skeleton, *corpse*, 362.
frame, 7, 626.
small, 193.
lean, 203.
imperfect, 651.
essential part, 50.
Sketch, *painting*, 556.
description, 594.
plan, 626.
Sketcher, *artist*, 559.
Sketchy, *imperfect*, 651.
Skew, *obliquity*, 217.
Skewbald, *variegation*, 440.
Skewer, *vinculum*, 45.
Ski, *locomotion*, 266.
Skid, *deviation*, 279.
Skiff, *boat*, 273.
Skill, *ability*, 698.
Skim, *move*, 266.
rapid, 274.
attend lightly, 458.
Skimp, *shorten*, 201.
stint, 640.
Skin, *tegument*, 222.
to peel, 226.
Skin-deep, *shallow*, 220.
Skinflint, *miser*, 819.
Skinny, *small*, 193.
slender, 203.
tegumentary, 222.
Skip, *jump*, 309.
ascend, 305.
neglect, 460.
escape, 671.
dance, 840.
Skipjack, *upstart*, 734, 876.
Skirl, *shriek*, 411.
Skirmish, *fight*, 720, 722.
Skirt, *edge*, 230.
appendix, 39.
Skirt, *pendent*, 214.
circumjacent, 227.
Skit, *parody*, 856.
satire, 932.
Skittish, *capricious*, 608.
bashful, 881.
timid, 862.
Skulk, *hide*, 447, 528.
coward, 860.
Skull, *head*, 450.
Skull-cap, *dress*, 225.
Skunk, *fetid*, 401.
bad man, 949.
Sky, *world*, 318.
air, 338.
summit, 210.
Sky-blue, *blue*, 438.
Skylark, *frolic*, 840.
Sky-rocket, *ascent*, 305.
Sky-scraper, *height*, 206.
Slab, *layer*, 204.
Slabber, *ejection*, 297.
Slack, *loose*, 47.
weak, 160.
slow, 275.
inert, 172.
inactive, 683.
unwilling, 603.
laxity, 738.
to moderate, 174.
retard, 706.
calm, 826.
Slacken, *relax*, 687.
Slacks, *dress*, 225.
Slag, *refuse*, 40.
dirt, 653.
Slake, *quench*, 174.
indulge, 954.
gratify, 831, 865.
satiate, 869.
Slam, *shut*, 406.
slap, 276.
Slander, *detraction*, 934.
Slanderer, *detractor*, 936.
Slang, *neology*, 563.
language, 560.
Slant, *obliquity*, 217.
Slap, *to strike*, 276.
hit, 972.
quick, 274.
haste, 684.
Slapdash, *careless*, 460.
reckless, 863.
Slash, *cut*, 44.
Slashing style, *vigour*, 574.
Slat, *strip*, 205.
Slate, *writing-tablet*, 590.
grey, 432.
to criticise, 934.

Slating, *roof*, 210.
Slattern, *negligent*, 460.
awkward, 701.
Slatternly, *vulgar*, 851.
unskilful, 699.
Slaughter, *to kill*, 361.
Slave, *servant*, 746.
to toil, 686.
Slaver, *slobber*, 297.
ship, 273.
Slavery, *servitude*, 749.
Slavish, *imitative*, 19.
Slay, *kill*, 361.
Sledge, *vehicle*, 272.
Sledge-hammer, *impel*, 276.
engine, 633.
Sleek, *smooth*, 255.
pretty, 845.
Sleep, *inactivity*, 683.
Sleeper, *support*, 215.
Sleepless, *active*, 682.
Sleepy, *inactive*, 683, 823.
slow, 275.
weary, 841.
Sleet, *rain*, 383.
Sleight, *cleverness*, 698.
Sleight of hand, *quickness*, 146, 545.
Slender, *narrow*, 203.
small, 32.
trifling, 643.
Sleuth-hound, *inquiry*, 461.
pursuit, 623.
Slice, *layer*, 204.
part, 51.
Slick, *dexterous*, 698.
smooth, 255.
Slide, *pass*, 264.
relapse, 661.
descend, 306.
elapse, 109.
become, 144.
skate, 266.
Slight, *small*, 32.
slender, 203.
trifle, 643.
to neglect, 460, 927.
to dishonour, 929.
Slim, *thin*, 203.
cunning, 702.
Slimy, *viscous*, 352.
dirt, 653.
Sling, *hang*, 214.
project, 284.
weapon, 727.
Slink, *recede*, 287.
escape, 671.
Slip, *descend*, 306.
strip, 205.
part, 51.
Slip, *transfer*, 270.
fail, 732.
liberate, 750.
workshop, 691.
guilt, 947.
smallness, 32.
dress, 225.
scion, 167.
Slip away, *escape*, 287, 671, 750.
Slip cable, *departure*, 293.
Slip of the tongue, *mistake*, 495.
solecism, 568.
Slip on, *dress*, 225.
Slip over, *cover*, 460.
Slipper, *dress*, 225.
Slippery, *smooth*, 255.
uncertain, 475.
changeable, 149.
dangerous, 665.
not trustworthy, 940.
Slipshod, *untidy*, 653.
ungrammatical, 568.
Slipslop, *affected*, 855.
absurd, 497.
style, 573.
Slit, *to divide*, 44.
chink, 198.
Sliver, *part*, 51.
Slobber, *slop*, 337.
emit, 297.
soil, 653.
Sloe, *colour*, 431.
Slog, *hit*, 277.
Slogan, *indication*, 550.
Sloop, *ship*, 273.
Slop, *water*, 337.
emit, 297.
dirt, 653.
Slope, *oblique*, 217.
Sloppy, *wet*, 337.
slovenly, 699.
maudlin, 823.
Slops, *dress*, 225.
Slot, *opening*, 260.
track, 551.
Sloth, *inactivity*, 683.
Slouch, *oblique*, 217.
low, 207.
inactive, 683.
ugly, 846.
Slouch-hat, *dress*, 225.
Slough, *difficulty*, 704.
quagmire, 345.
residuum, 40.
Sloven, *drab*, 653.
careless, 460.
awkward, 699.
bungler, 701.
vulgar, 851.

Slovenly, *style*, 573.
Slow, *sluggish*, 275.
tardy, 133.
dull, 843.
wearisome, 841.
inert, 172.
inactive, 683.
Slubberdegullion, *knave*, 941, 949.
Sludge, *mud*, 653.
Slug, *slow*, 275.
Sluggard, *slow*, 275.
sleepy, 683.
Sluggish, *slow*, 275.
inert, 172.
sleepy, 683.
callous, 823.
Sluice, *conduit*, 350.
river, 348.
to wash, 652.
Slum, *abode*, 189.
Slump, *fall*, 306.
Slur, *stigma*, 874.
gloss over, 937.
reproach, 938.
Slur over, *neglect*, 460.
inattention, 458.
conceal, 528.
exclude, 55.
Slush, *pulp*, 354.
Slut, *hussy*, 962.
Sluttish, *unclean*, 653.
Sly, *cunning*, 702.
false, 544.
Smack, *ship*, 273.
taste, 390.
mixture, 41.
small quantity, 32.
kiss, 902.
Small, *in degree*, 32.
in size, 193.
Smaller, *inferiority*, 34.
Smart, *pain*, 378.
grief, 828.
active, 682.
clever, 698.
cunning, 702.
to feel, 821.
witty, 842.
neat, 845.
fashionable, 852.
Smash, *destroy*, 162.
Smatterer, *ignoramus*, 493.
Smattering, *ignorance*, 491.
Smear, *daub*, 222.
ugly, 846.
Smell, *odour*, 398.
Smelt, *heat*, 384.
Smile, *risible*, 838.
Smile upon, *approve*, 894.
Smirch, *soil*, 653.
Smirk, *grin*, 838.
Smite, *strike*, 276.
punish, 972.
bad, 649.
Smith, *workman*, 690.
Smithereens, *fragments*, 51.
Smitten, *love*, 897.
Smock, *dress*, 225.
Smoke, *cloud*, 334.
dimness, 422.
heat, 382.
trifle, 643.
dirt, 653.
to discover, 480.
suspect, 485.
to end in, *disappoint*, 932.
Smooth, *not rough*, 16, 255.
to calm, 174.
lubricate, 332.
easy, 705.
to flatter, 933.
Smooth-faced, *falsehood*, 544.
Smooth-spoken, *falsehood*, 544.
Smooth-tongued, *falsehood*, 544.
Smother, *kill*, 361.
repress, 174.
calm, 826.
suppress, 528, 585.
Smoulder, *burn*, 382.
inert, 172.
latent, 528.
Smudge, *dirt*, 653.
blemish, 848.
Smug, *affected*, 855.
Smuggle, *contraband*, 791.
introduce, 294.
Smuggler, *thief*, 792.
Smut, *dirt*, 653.
black, 431.
blemish, 848.
impurity, 961.
Snacks, *part*, 51.
participate, 778.
food, 298.
Snaffle, *restraint*, 752.
Snag, *danger*, 667.
sharp, 253.
projection, 250.
Snail, *slow*, 275.
Snake, *miscreant*, 913.
Snaky, *winding*, 248.
Snap, *noise*, 406.
brittle, 328.
break, 44.
snarl, 895.
angry, 900.
seize, 789.
vigour, 574.

Snappy, *concise*, 572.
Snare, *trap*, 667.
Snarl, *growl*, 412.
angry, 900.
rude, 895.
threaten, 909.
Snatch, *to seize*, 789.
opportunity, 134.
part, 51.
Snatches, by, *irregularly*, 139.
Sneak, *servility*, 886.
baseness, 940.
to hide, 528.
retire, 287.
Sneer, *contempt*, 930.
blame, 932.
disparage, 929.
Sneeze, *snuffle*, 409.
blow, 349.
Snick, *part*, 51.
Snickersnee, *weapon*, 727.
Sniff, *odour*, 398.
Sniff at, *despise*, 930.
Sniffy, *contemptuous*, 930.
Snigger, *laugh*, 838.
Snip, *cut*, 44.
Snip-snap, *discord*, 713.
Snivel, *cry*, 839.
Snivelling, *servile*, 886.
Snob, *commonalty*, 876.
Snooze, *sleep*, 683.
Snore, *noise*, 411.
sleep, 683.
Snort, *noise*, 411.
sleep, 683.
Snout, *prominence*, 250.
Snow, *ice*, 383.
white, 430.
Snowball, *collection*, 72.
Snow-shoe, *locomotion*, 266.
Snub, *bluster*, 885.
blame, 932.
short, 201.
Snuff, *odour*, 398.
tobacco, 298A.
Snuff-box, *receptacle*, 191.
Snuff out, *die*, 360.
Shuff up, *inhale*, 296.
Snuffle, *hiss*, 409.
blow, 349.
stammer, 583.
Snug, *comfortable*, 831.
safe, 664.
latent, 526.
secluded, 893.
Snuggery, *room*, 189.
Snuggle, *draw near*, 286.
cuddle, 902.
Soak, *immerse*, 300.
Soak, *water*, 337.
Soaker, *drunkenness*, 959.
Soap, *oil*, 356.
Soapy, *unctuous*, 355.
flattering, 933.
Soar, *rise*, 305.
height, 206.
great, 31.
fly, 267.
Sob, *weep*, 839.
Sober, *moderate*, 174.
temperate, 953.
abstinent, 958.
sane, 502.
wise, 498.
calm, 826.
grave, 837.
Sober-minded, *wise*, 502.
calm, 826.
Sobranje, *council*, 696.
*Sobriquet (Fr.), *misnomer*, 565.
Sociable, *friendly*, 892.
Social, *friendly*, 888, 892.
Socialism, *participation*, 778.
Society, *man*, 372.
friendly, 892.
party, 712.
fashion, 852.
Sociology, *mankind*, 372.
Sock, *stocking*, 225.
drama, 599.
Socket, *receptacle*, 191, 252.
Socratic method, *reasoning*, 461.
Sod, *turf*, 344.
Sodality, *fraternity*, 712.
association, 892.
friendship, 888.
Sodden, *wet*, 339.
overcharged, 641.
Sofa, *support*, 215.
Soft, *not hard*, 324.
moderate, 174.
sound, 405.
smooth, 255.
weak, 160.
silly, 499.
irresolute, 605.
timid, 862.
lenient, 740.
compassionate, 914.
tender, 822.
Soften, *soothe*, 826.
mitigate, 834.
palliate, 937.
subdue, 824.
Soggy, *wet*, 337.
*Soi-disant (Fr.), *deceiver*, 548.
misnomer, 565.
vanity, 800.

*Soi-disant (Fr.), *boaster*, 884.
Soil, *land*, 342.
dirt, 653.
spoil, 659.
deface, 846.
tarnish, 848.
*Soirée (Fr.), *assemblage*, 72.
reception, 892.
Sojourn, *abode*, 189.
inhabit, 186.
settle, 265.
Solace, *relief*, 834.
comfort, 827.
recreation, 840.
Solar, *world*, 318.
Soldan, *master*, 745.
Solder, *cohere*, 46.
cement, 45.
Soldier, *combatant*, 726.
Sole, *alone*, 87.
base, 211.
Solecism, *ungrammatical*, 568.
sophistry, 477.
Solemn, *awful*, 873.
sacred, 987.
grave, 837.
pompous, 882.
positive, 535.
important, 642.
Solemnity, *parade*, 882.
rite, 998.
dullness, 843.
Solemnise, *celebrate*, 883.
Sol-fa, *melody*, 413.
*Solfeggio (It.), *melody*, 413.
Solicit, *induce*, 615.
request, 765.
desire, 865.
Solicitor, *law*, 968.
Solicitude, *anxiety*, 860.
care, 459, 828.
desire, 865.
Solid, *complete*, 52.
dense, 321.
certain, 474.
knowledge, 490.
true, 494.
firm, 604.
wise, 498.
Solidify, *coherence*, 46.
density, 321.
Soliloquy, *speech*, 589.
Solitary, *alone*, 87.
secluded, 893.
Solitude, *see* Solitary.
Solmisation, *melody*, 413.
Solo, *music*, 415.
Soloist, *musician*, 416.
Solomon, *sage*, 500.
Solon, *sage*, 500.
wise, 498.
Soluble, *dissolve*, 335.
Solution, *dissolving*, 335.
explanation, 462.
Solve, *explain*, 462.
Solvency, *wealth*, 803.
Somatics, *material*, 316.
Sombre, *dark*, 421.
grey, 432.
black, 431.
melancholy, 837.
Some, *a few*, 100.
Somebody, *one*, 87.
man, 373.
Somehow, *manner*, 155.
Somerset, *turn*, 218.
Something, *thing*, 3.
small degree, 32.
Sometimes, *frequency*, 136.
Somewhat, *small*, 32.
Somewhere, *place*, 182.
Somnambulism, *imagination*, 515.
Somniferous, *sleepy*, 683.
weary, 841.
Somnolence, *sleepy*, 683.
weary, 841.
Son, *relation*, 167.
Sonata, *music*, 415.
*Sonderbund (Ger.), *compact*, 769.
Song, *music*, 415.
Song, old, *unimportant*, 643.
Songster, *musician*, 416.
Soniferous, *sound*, 402.
Sonnet, *poetry*, 597.
Sonorous, *sound*, 402.
Soon, *early*, 132.
transient, 111.
Soot, *black*, 431.
dirt, 653.
blemish, 846.
Sooth, in, *truth*, 494.
Soothe, *allay*, 174.
calm, 826.
relieve, 834.
Soothsay, *predict*, 511.
Soothsayer, *omen*, 513.
magician, 994.
Sop, *bribe*, 615.
reward, 973.
wet, 337.
Sophism, *bad logic*, 477.
absurdity, 497.
Sophisticate, *mix*, 41.
mislead, 477.
debase, 659.
Sophistry, *false reasoning*, 477.
Soporific, *sleepy*, 683.
boring, 841.

Soprano, *music*, 410, 413.
Sorcerer, *sorcerer*, 994.
Sorcery, *occult arts*, 992.
*Sordes (L.), *uncleanness*, 653.
Sordid, *mean*, 819.
base, 876.
Sordine, *silencer*, 417.
damper, 403.
Sore, *pain*, 376.
grievance, 828.
painful, 830.
angry, 900.
Sorely, *greatness*, 31.
Sorites, *reasoning*, 476.
Sorrel, *redness*, 434.
Sorrow, *pain*, 828.
Sorry, *grieved*, 828.
bad, 649.
mean, 876.
trifling, 643.
smallness, 32.
Sort, *kind*, 75.
degree, 26.
to arrange, 60.
*Sortes (L.), *chance*, 156.
*Sortie (Fr.), *attack*, 716.
Sortilege, *sorcery*, 992.
chance, 621.
Sorting, *arrangement*, 60.
So-so, *imperfection*, 651.
smallness, 32.
*Sostenuto (It.), *music*, 415.
Sot, *fool*, 501.
drunkard, 959.
*Sotto voce (It.), *faintness*, 405.
aphony, 581.
stammering, 583.
Soubrette, *actress*, 599.
Slough, *conduit*, 350.
cloaca, 653.
wind, 349.
Soul, *intrinsic*, 5.
intellect, 450.
affections, 820.
man, 373.
important part, 50, 642.
Soulful, *feeling*, 821.
Soulless, *insensible*, 823.
Sound, *noise*, 402.
healthy, 654.
perfect, 650.
good, 648.
to measure, 466.
to investigate, 461.
true, 494.
wise, 498.
orthodox, 983A.
bay, 343.
greatness, 31.
Soundings, *deep*, 208.
Soundless, *deep*, 208.
silent, 403.
Soundly, *great*, 31.
Soup, *food*, 298.
pulp, 354.
*Soupçon (Fr.), *little*, 32, 193.
mixture, 41.
Sour, *acid*, 397.
uncivil, 895.
misanthropic, 901.
to embitter, 835.
Source, *origin*, 66, 153.
*Sourdine (Fr.), *silencer*, 417.
Souse, *immerse*, 300.
water, 337.
Soutane, *canonicals*, 999.
*Souteneur (Fr.), *libertine*, 962.
Souvenir, *memory*, 505.
Sovereign, *great*, 31.
superiority, 33.
strong, 157.
ruler, 745.
Soviet, *council*, 696.
Sow, *scatter*, 73.
prepare, 673.
Space, *room*, 180.
separate, 44.
Spacious, *roomy*, 180.
Spahee, *combatant*, 726.
Span, *distance*, 196.
nearness, 197.
length, 200.
measure, 466.
time, 106.
Spangle, *spark*, 420.
ornament, 847.
Spaniel, *servile*, 886.
flatterer, 935.
Spanking, *size*, 192.
beating, 972.
Spar, *discord*, 713.
contention, 720, 722.
Spare, *meagre*, 203.
scanty, 642.
to give, 784.
relinquish, 782.
disuse, 678.
refrain, 623.
pity, 914.
frugal, 953.
economic, 817.
in reserve, 636.
Spare time, *leisure*, 685.
Sparing, *temperate*, 953.
small, 32.
economic, 817.
Spark, *light*, 420.
fire, 382.

Spark, *fop*, 854.
Sparkle, *glisten*, 420.
bubble, 353.
Sparse, *scattered*, 73.
few, 103.
*Sparsim (L.), *non-assemblage*, 73.
Spasm, *fit*, 173.
throe, 146.
pain, 378, 828.
Spatial, *space*, 99.
Spatter, *dirt*, 653.
damage, 659.
Spatterdash, *dress*, 225.
Spatula, *layer*, 204.
trowel, 191.
Spawn, *dirt*, 653.
offspring, 167.
Speak, *speech*, 582.
Speak fair, *conciliate*, 615.
Speak to, *allocution*, 586.
Speak out, *disclose*, 529.
Speaker, *speech*, 582.
teacher, 540.
interpreter, 524.
president, 745.
Spear, *lance*, 727.
to pierce, 260.
pass through, 302.
Spearman, *combatant*, 726.
Special, *particular*, 79.
peculiar, 5.
Specialist, *adviser*, 695.
proficient, 700.
Speciality, *intrinsic*, 5.
particular, 79.
Special pleading, *sophistry*, 477.
Specie, *money*, 800.
Species, *kind*, 75.
appearance, 448.
Specific, *special*, 79.
Specify, *name*, 564.
tell, 527.
Specimen, *example*, 82.
Specious, *probable*, 472.
sophistical, 477.
plausible, 937.
Speck, *dot*, 193.
small quantity, 32.
blemish, 848.
Speckle, *variegated*, 400.
blemish, 848.
Spectacle, *appearance*, 448.
show, 882.
prodigy, 872.
Spectacles, *optical instrument*, 445.
Spectator, *spectator*, 444.
Spectre, *vision*, 448.
ugly, 846.
ghost, 980.
Spectroscope, *optical*, 445.
Spectrum, *colour*, 428.
appearance, 448
Speculate, *think*, 451.
venture, 675.
traffic, 794.
view, 441.
Speculum, *optical instrument*, 445.
Speech, *speech*, 582.
Speechify, *speech*, 582.
Speechless, *silence*, 581.
Speed, *velocity*, 274.
activity, 682.
to help, 707.
succeed, 731.
Spell, *interpret*, 522.
read, 539.
period, 106.
charm, 993.
necessity, 601.
motive, 615.
exertion, 686.
Spell-bound, *motive*, 615.
Spelling, *letters*, 561.
Spence, *store*, 636.
Spencer, *dress*, 225.
Spencerism, *causation*, 153.
Spend, *expend*, 809.
waste, 638.
Spendthrift, *prodigal*, 818.
Spent, *exhausted*, 688.
Spermaceti, *oil*, 356.
Spew, *ejection*, 297.
*Sphacelus (L.), *disease*, 655.
Sphere, *ball*, 249.
region, 181.
world, 318.
rank, 26.
business, 625.
Spheroid, *round*, 249.
Spherule, *round*, 249.
Sphinx, *oracle*, 513.
monster, 83.
Spice, *small quantity*, 32.
mixture, 41.
pungent, 392.
condiment, 393.
*Spicilegium (L.), *assembly*, 72, 596.
compendium, 596.
Spick and span, *clean*, 123.
Spicule, *sharp*, 253.
Spidery, *narrowness*, 203.
Spiflicate, *trounce*, 972.
Spike, *to pierce*, 260.
plug, 263.
pass through, 302.
sharp, 253.
Spile, *stopper*, 263.
Spill, *filament*, 205.

Spill, *to shed*, 297.
waste, 638.
splash, 348.
lavish, 818.
misuse, 679.
fall, 306.
Spin, *rotation*, 312.
excursion, 266.
velocity, 274.
Spin out, *prolong*, 200.
protract, 110.
style, 573.
Spindle, *rotation*, 312.
Spindle-shanked, *thin*, 193, 203.
Spindrift, *spray*, 353.
Spine, *sharpness*, 253.
Spinet, *musical instrument*, 417.
Spinster, *celibacy*, 904.
Spiracle, *air-pipe*, 351.
Spiral, *convolution*, 248.
Spire, *peak*, 253.
height, 206.
soar, 305.
Spirit, *essence*, 5.
immateriality, 317.
intellect, 450.
affections, 820.
resolution, 604.
courage, 861.
ghost, 980.
style, 574.
activity, 682.
to stimulate, 824.
Spirited, *brave*, 861.
generous, 942.
Spiritless, *torpid*, 823.
dejected, 837.
timid, 862.
Spirits, *cheerfulness*, 836.
Spiritual, *immaterial*, 317.
mental, 450.
divine, 976.
Spiritualism, *occult arts*, 992.
*Spirituel (Fr.), *witty*, 842.
*Spirituoso (It.), *music*, 415.
Spissitude, *density*, 321, 352.
Spit, *eject*, 297.
pierce, 302.
rain, 348.
bar, 253.
Spite, *malevolence*, 907.
notwithstanding, 179.
Spittoon, *receptacle*, 191.
Splash, *affuse*, 337.
spill, 348.
spatter, 653.
sully, 846.
parade, 882.
Splatter, *affuse*, 337.
Splay, *angularity*, 244.
Spleen, *melancholy*, 837.
hatred, 898.
anger, 900.
discourteous, 895.
Spleenless, *good-natured*, 906.
Splendid, *beautiful*, 845.
glorious, 873.
excellent, 648.
Splenetic, *sad*, 837.
ill-tempered, 895.
irascible, 901.
Splice, *join*, 43.
marry, 903.
Splinter, *divide*, 44.
brittle, 328.
bit, 51, 205.
Split, *divide*, 44, 91.
quarrel, 713.
fail, 732.
laugh, 838.
Split the difference, *compensation*, 30.
Split hairs, *argue*, 465.
sophistry, 477.
Splutter, *stammer*, 583.
haste, 684.
energy, 171.
spitting, 297.
Spoil, *vitiate*, 659.
hinder, 706.
plunder, 791.
booty, 793.
injure, 649.
satiate, 869.
Spoke, *tooth*, 253.
radius, 200.
obstruct, 706.
Spokesman, *interpreter*, 524.
speaker, 582.
Spoliate, *plunder*, 791.
evil, 619.
Sponge, *clean*, 652.
obliterate, 552.
despoil, 791.
porous, 322.
oblivion, 506.
Spongy, *soft*, 324.
Sponsion, *security*, 771.
Sponsor, *security*, 771.
evidence, 467.
Spontaneous, *voluntary*, 600, 602.
impulsive, 612.
Spoof, *deception*, 545.
Spook, *ghost*, 980.
Spoon, *receptacle*, 191.
ladle, 272.
to make love, 902.
Spoonerism, *blunder*, 495.

Spoony, *fool*, 499.
amorous, 897.
Spoor, *track*, 551.
Sporran, *pouch*, 191.
Sport, *amusement*, 840.
gaiety, 836.
wit, 842.
enjoyment, 827.
subjection, 749.
abnormality, 83.
Sportsman, *courage*, 861.
Spot, *place*, 182.
decoloration, 429.
blemish, 848.
to sully, 846.
blot, 874.
disgrace, 940.
to detect, 457, 480.
Spotless, *innocent*, 946.
clean, 652.
good, 648, 650.
fair, 845.
Spotty, *spotted*, 440.
Spouse, *married*, 903.
companion, 88.
Spousals, *marriage*, 903.
Spouseless, *celibacy*, 904.
Spout, *conduit*, 350.
egress, 295.
flow out, 348.
speak, 582.
act, 599.
Sprain, *strain*, 160.
Sprawl, *lie*, 213.
leap, 309.
Spray, *sprig*, 51.
foam, 353.
to sprinkle, 337.
Spread, *enlarge*, 35.
expand, 194.
disperse, 73.
diverge, 291.
expanse, 180.
publish, 531.
Spree, *frolic*, 840.
Sprig, *part*, 51.
scion, 167.
Sprightly, *cheerful*, 836.
Spring, *early*, 125.
cause, 153.
arise from, 154.
ensue, 151.
strength, 159.
velocity, 274.
leap, 309.
rivulet, 348.
instrument, 633.
Spring back, *elastic*, 325.
recoil, 277.
Spring tide, *flow*, 348.
abundance, 639.
Spring up, *grow*, 194.
Springe, *snare*, 667.
deception, 545.
Sprinkle, *add*, 37.
mix, 41.
disperse, 73, 291.
omit, 297.
wet, 337.
Sprinkling, *small quantity*, 32.
little, 193.
Sprint, *velocity*, 480.
Sprite, *ghost*, 980.
Sprocket, *tooth*, 257.
Sprout, *grow*, 35.
expand, 194.
arise from, 154.
offspring, 167.
Spruce, *neat*, 652.
beautiful, 845.
Spry, *active*, 682.
clever, 698.
Spume, *foam*, 353.
Spunk, *courage*, 861.
Spur, *sharp*, 253.
incite, 615.
ridge, 250.
Spurious, *false*, 544.
erroneous, 495.
illegitimate, 925.
Spurn, *disdain*, 866, 930.
Spurt, *impulse*, 612.
haste, 684.
swift, 274.
gush, 348.
Sputter, *emit*, 297.
stammer, 583.
Spy, *see*, 441.
spectator, 444.
emissary, 534.
Spy-glass, *optical instrument*, 445.
Squab, *large*, 192.
broad, 202.
recumbent, 215.
Squabble, *quarrel*, 713.
Squad, *assembly*, 72.
Squadron, *navy*, 273.
army, 726.
assemblage, 72.
Squalid, *dirty*, 653.
unattractive, 846.
Squall, *cry*, 411.
wind, 349.
violence, 173.
Squalor, *see* Squalid.
Squamous, *scaly*, 222.
Squander, *waste*, 638, 818.
Square, *number*, 95.

Square, *buildings*, 189.
congruity, 23.
expedience, 646.
justice, 924.
honour, 939.
form, 244.
to equalise, 27.
to bribe, 795.
Square-toes, *laughing-stock*, 857.
Squash, *destroy*, 162.
throw, 276.
leap, 309.
soft, 324.
water, 337.
Squashy, *pulpy*, 352.
Squat, *to encamp*, 186.
sit, 306.
large, 192.
broad, 202.
flat, 213.
ugly, 846.
Squatter, *inhabitant*, 188.
Squatting, *horizontal*, 213.
Squaw, *marriage*, 903.
Squeak, *cry*, 411, 412.
complain, 839.
Squeal, *cry*, 411, 412.
complain, 839.
Squeamish, *fastidious*, 868.
censorious, 932.
Squeeze, *contract*, 195.
narrow, 203.
condense, 321.
extort, 789.
Squeeze out, *extraction*, 301.
Squib, *sound*, 406.
lampoon, 932.
Squiffy, *drunk*, 959.
Squint, *dim-sighted*, 443.
Squire, *gentry*, 875.
attendant, 746.
Squirm, *wriggle*, 315.
Squirrel, *velocity*, 274.
Squirt, *eject*, 297.
spurt, 348.
Stab, *pierce*, 260.
kill, 361.
injure, 649.
Stable, *house*, 189.
at rest, 265.
immutable, 150.
resolute, 604.
*Staccato (It.), *music*, 415.
Stack, *assembly*, 72.
Stadtholder, *master*, 745.
Staff, *support*, 215.
instrument, 633.
weapon, 727.
sceptre, 747.
Staff, *retinue*, 746.
party, 712.
hope, 858.
Stage, *degree*, 26.
term, 71.
step, 58.
layer, 204.
forum, 542.
vehicle, 272.
arena, 728.
drama, 599.
Stage-effect, *ostentation*, 882.
Stage-play, *the drama*, 599.
Stager, old, *proficient*, 700.
Stagger, *totter*, 314.
slow, 275.
agitate, 315.
doubt, 485.
dissuade, 616.
affect, 824.
astonish, 870.
Stagnant, *quiescent*, 265.
unchanging, 142.
inactive, 683.
Staid, *steady*, 604.
calm, 826.
wise, 498.
grave, 837.
Stain, *colour*, 428.
deface, 846.
blemish, 848.
spoil, 659.
disgrace, 874.
dishonour, 940.
Stainless, *clean*, 652.
innocent, 946.
Stair, *way*, 627.
Stake, *wager*, 621.
danger, 665.
security, 771.
execution, 975.
Stalactite, *lining*, 224.
Stalagmite, *lining*, 224.
Stale, *old*, 124.
vapid, 866.
weary, 841.
Stalemate, *non-completion*, 730.
Stalk, *follow*, 266.
Stalking-horse, *plea*, 617.
deception, 545.
Stall, *lodge*, 189.
mart, 799.
cathedral, 1000.
Stallion, *horse*, 271.
Stalwart, *strong*, 159.
tall, 206.
large, 192.
Stamina, *strength*, 159.
Stammel, *redness*, 434.

Stammer, *stutter*, 583.
Stamp, *character*, 7.
form, 240.
to impress, 505.
mark, 550.
record, 551.
complete, 729.
Stampede, *flight*, 287.
fear, 860, 862.
Stance, *footing*, 175.
Stanch, *dam up*, 348.
stop, 658.
Stanchion, *support*, 215.
Stand, *to be*, 1.
rest, 265.
be present, 186.
to continue, 142, 143.
endure, 110.
station, 58.
rank, 71.
support, 215.
resistance, 719.
Stand against, *resist*, 719.
Stand by, *near*, 197.
be firm, 604.
befriend, 707.
auxiliary, 711.
Stand for, *represent*, 550.
signify, 516.
Stand in with, *participation*, 778.
Stand off, *distance*, 196, 287.
Stand-offish, *unsociable*, 893.
Stand on, *support*, 215.
Stand out, *project*, 250.
opposition, 708.
Stand still, *stop*, 265.
remain, 142.
Stand over, *lateness*, 133.
Stand up, *vertical*, 212.
Stand up for, *vindicate*, 937.
Stand up to, *courage*, 861.
Standard, *rule*, 80.
measure, 466.
degree, 26.
colours, 550.
good, 648.
prototype, 22.
Standard-bearer, *combatant*, 726.
Standardise, *conformity*, 82.
Standing, *footing*, 8.
term, 71.
situation, 183.
degree, 26.
repute, 873.
vertical, 212.
Standpoint, *aspect*, 453.
Stanza, *poetry*, 597.
Staple, *whole*, 50.
peg, 214.
Staple, *sharp*, 253.
mart, 799.
Star, *luminary*, 423.
decoration, 877.
glory, 873.
actor, 599.
Starboard, *dextrality*, 238.
Star-chamber, *jurisprudence*, 966.
Starchy, *stiff*, 323.
proud, 878.
affected, 855.
Stare, *look*, 441.
curiosity, 455.
wonder, 870.
Star-gazer, *astronomer*, 318.
Staring, *visible*, 446.
Stark, *absolute*, 31.
stiff, 323.
stubborn, 606.
Stars, *celestial*, 318.
necessity, 601.
Start, *depart*, 293.
begin, 66.
desultory, 139.
jump, 139.
arise, 151.
suggest, 514.
from fear, 860.
from wonder, 870.
Start up, *project*, 250.
arise, 305.
appear, 446.
Starting-point, *beginning*, 66.
departure, 293.
Startle, *unexpected*, 508.
wonder, 870.
fear, 860.
doubt, 485.
Starve, *fast*, 956.
with cold, 383, 385.
want, 804.
Starved, *lean*, 193.
insufficient, 640.
Starveling, *pinched*, 203.
poor, 804.
famished, 640.
State, *condition*, 7.
nation, 372.
ostentation, 882.
property, 780.
to inform, 527.
describe, 594.
Stately, *pompous*, 882.
proud, 878.
grand, 873.
Statement, *information*, 527.
State-room, *chamber*, 191.
Statesman, *master*, 745.
Statesmanlike, *skill*, 698.

Statesmanship, *direction*, 694.
Statics, *gravity*, 319.
Station, *stage*, 58.
term, 71.
place, 182, 183.
to locate, 184.
stopping-place, 292.
rank, 873.
Stationary, *quiescence*, 265.
Statist, *statesman*, 745.
Statistics, *numeration*, 85.
Statue, *sculpture*, 557.
Stature, *height*, 206.
Status, *standing*, 8.
situation, 183.
order, 58.
rank, 873.
*Status quo (L.), *reversion*, 145.
Statute, *law*, 963.
Staunch, *firm*, 484.
spirited, 604.
healthy, 654.
Stave, *verse*, 597.
Stave in, *open*, 260.
Stave off, *defer*, 133.
Stay, *wait*, 133.
continue, 142.
support, 215.
refuge, 666.
rest, 265.
prevent, 706.
dissuade, 616.
corset, 225.
Stead, *utility*, 644.
Steadfast, *resolved*, 604.
stable, 150.
quiescent, 265.
thought, 451.
belief, 484.
Steady, *resolved*, 604.
cautious, 864.
still, 265.
constant, 138, 150.
normal, 82.
Steal, *rob*, 791.
creep, 275, 528.
Steal away, *evade*, 671.
Stealth, *concealment*, 528.
Steam, *vapour*, 334.
to sail, 267.
Steamboat, *ship*, 273.
Steamer, *ship*, 273.
Stearin, *fat*, 356.
Steed, *horse*, 271.
Steel, *strength*, 159.
inure, 823.
Steeled, *resolved*, 604.
Steelyard, *scale*, 466.
Steep, *slope*, 217.
Steep, *immerse*, 300.
soak, 337.
Steeple, *spire*, 253.
high, 206.
Steeple-chase, *race*, 274.
pursuit, 282, 622.
Steeps, *height*, 206.
Steer, *guide*, 693.
Steer for, *direction*, 278.
Steersman, *director*, 694.
Steganography, *writing*, 590.
*Stele (Gr.), *record*, 551.
Stellar, *heavens*, 318.
Stem, *origin*, 153.
front, 234.
to oppose, 708.
to resist, 718.
Stench, *fetor*, 401.
Stencil, *copy*, 556.
Stenography, *writing*, 590.
Stentorian, *loud*, 404.
Step, *degree*, 26.
station, 58.
term, 71.
near, 197.
support, 215.
motion, 264, 266.
measure, 466.
expedient, 626.
means, 632.
Steppe, *plain*, 344.
Stepping-stone, *link*, 45.
way, 627.
resource, 666.
Stercoraceous, *uncleanness*, 653.
Stereoscope, *optical*, 445.
Stereotype, *printing*, 591.
Stereotyped, *ordinary*, 83.
fixed, 150.
Sterile, *unproductive*, 169.
useless, 645.
Sterling, *true*, 494.
good, 648.
virtuous, 944.
Stern, *back*, 235.
severe, 739.
forbidding, 895.
Sternutation, *sneeze*, 349.
sound, 409.
Stertorous, *sound*, 411.
Stevedore, *workman*, 690, 271.
Stew, *confusion*, 59.
difficulty, 704.
heat, 382.
cook, 384.
perplex, 828.
bagnio, 961.
Steward, *director*, 694.
Stewardship, *charge*, 693.

Stick, *adhere*, 46.
staff, 215.
to stab, 260, 830.
pierce, 302.
difficulty, 704.
fool, 501.
scourge, 975.
Stick at, *demur*, 603.
Stick in, *insert*, 300.
locate, 184.
Stick-in-the-mud, *inactivity*, 683.
Stick out, *project*, 250.
erect, 212.
Stick up, *project*, 250.
erect, 212, 307.
Stickle, *haggle*, 769.
barter, 794.
reluctant, 603.
Stickler, *obstinacy*, 606.
Sticky, *cohering*, 46.
semiliquid, 352.
Stiff, *rigid*, 323.
resolute, 604.
difficult, 704.
restrained, 751.
severe, 739.
dear, 814.
affected, 855.
haughty, 878.
pompous, 882.
ugly, 846.
style, 572, 579.
Stiff-necked, *obstinate*, 606.
resolute, 604.
Stifle, *silence*, 403.
destroy, 162.
kill, 361.
sound, 405.
Stigma, *disgrace*, 874.
blame, 932.
Stiletto, *piercer*, 262.
dagger, 727.
Still, *ever*, 112.
silent, 403.
quiet, 174.
quiescence, 265.
calm, 826.
notwithstanding, 179.
compensation, 30.
Still-born, *failure*, 732.
Stilted, *bombastic*, 577, 853.
Stilts, *support*, 215.
height, 206.
boasting, 884.
Stimulate, *incite*, 615.
violence, 173.
energise, 171.
passion, 824.
Stimulus, *zest*, 615.
Sting, *pain*, 378.
suffering, 824, 830.
provoke, 900.
Stingy, *mean*, 817.
Stink, *fetor*, 401.
Stint, *degree*, 26.
limit, 233.
scanty, 640.
parsimony, 819.
Stipend, *salary*, 809.
Stipendiary, *receiving*, 785.
subjected, 749.
magistrate, 967.
Stippling, *engraving*, 558.
Stipulate, *conditions*, 770.
bargain, 769.
Stir, *move*, 264.
agitation, 315.
activity, 682.
energy, 171.
emotion, 824.
discuss, 476.
Stir up, *mix*, 41.
excite, 615.
violence, 173.
Stitch, *work*, 680.
to join, 43.
pain, 828.
Stithy, *workshop*, 691.
Stiver, *money*, 800.
*Stoa (Ger.), *school*, 542.
Stock, *cause*, 153.
store, 636.
materials, 635.
provision, 637.
property, 780.
money, 800.
merchandise, 798.
collar, 225.
offspring, 166.
relation, 11.
quantity, 25.
Stockade, *defence*, 717.
Stocking, *dress*, 225.
Stocks, *funds*, 802.
punishment, 975.
restraint, 752.
Stock-still, *immovable*, 265.
Stoic, *insensible*, 823.
inexcitable, 826.
disinterested, 942
Stole, *dress*, 225.
Stolid, *dull*, 843.
stupid, 499.
Stomach, *pouch*, 191.
taste, 390.
liking, 865.
Stomacher, *dress*, 225.
Stone, *dense*, 321.

Stone, *hard*, 323.
missile, 284.
weapon, 727.
Stone-blind, *blind*, 442.
Stone-colour, *grey*, 432.
Stony-broke, *insolvent*, 808.
Stony-hearted, *cruel*, 900.
Stook, *assemblage*, 76.
Stool, *support*, 215.
Stool-pigeon, *deceiver*, 548.
Stoop, *lower*, 306.
slope, 217.
humble, 879.
servile, 886.
Stop, *close*, 67, 261.
rest, 265.
prevent, 706.
continue, 142.
discontinue, 141.
Stopcock, *stopper*, 263.
Stop-gap, *shift*, 626.
plug, 263.
Stopper, *stopper*, 263.
Store, *magazine*, 636.
provision, 637.
shop, 799.
the memory, 505.
greatness, 31.
Storehouse, *store*, 636.
στοργή (Gr.), *love*, 897.
Storm, *wind*, 349.
violence, 173.
passion, 825.
convulsion, 146.
anger, 900.
to attack, 716.
assemblage, 72.
Story, *narrative*, 582, **594**.
lie, 546.
layer, 204.
rooms, 191.
Stound, *wonder*, 870.
Stout, *strong*, 159.
lusty, 192.
brave, 861.
Stove, *furnace*, 386.
Stow, *locate*, 184.
Stowage, *space*, 180.
location, 184.
Strabismus, *dim sight*, 443.
Straddle, *sit*, 215.
stride, 266.
trim, 607.
Stradivarius, *violin*, 417.
Strafe, *punish*, 972.
maltreat, 649.
Straggle, *stroll*, 266.
deviate, 279.
disjunction, 44.
Straggle, *disorder*, 59.
Straggler, *rover*, 268.
Straight, *rectilinear*, 246.
vertical, 212.
direction, 278, 628.
Straightforward, *artless*, 703.
honest, 939.
true, 543.
style, 576.
mid-course, 628.
Straightway, *time*, 111.
Strain, *effort*, 686.
violence, 173.
fatigue, 688.
sound, 402.
melody, 413.
to clarify, 658.
percolate, 295.
transgress, 304.
poetry, 597.
voice, 580.
misinterpret, 523.
style, 569.
Strain the eyes, *dim sight*, 441.
Strainer, *sieve*, 260.
Strait, *maritime*, 343.
difficulty, 704.
want, 804.
Strait-laced, *severe*, 739.
censorious, 932.
haughty, 878.
stiff, 751.
fastidious, 868.
Strait-waistcoat, *restraint*, 752.
Strand, *shore*, 342.
Stranded, *difficulty*, 704.
failure, 732.
Strange, *exceptional*, 83.
wonderful, 870.
ridiculous, 853.
Stranger, *extraneous*, 57.
ignorant, 491.
Strangle, *choke*, 361.
Strap, *to tie*, 43.
ligature, 45.
scourge, 975.
Strappado, *punishment*, 972.
Strapping, *large*, 192.
strong, 159.
Stratagem, *plan*, 626.
artifice, 702.
deception, 545.
Strategy, *conduct*, 692.
skill, 698.
warfare, 722.
plan, 626.
Strath, *valley*, 252.
Stratification, *layer*, 204.
Stratocracy, *authority*, 737.

Stratum, *layer*, 204.
Straw, *light*, 320.
trifling, 643.
Straw-colour, *yellow*, 436.
Stray, *wander*, 266.
deviate, 279.
exceptional, 83.
Streak, *colour*, 420.
stripe, 440.
furrow, 259.
narrow, 203.
intersection, 219.
Stream, *flow*, 347.
river, 348.
of light, 420.
of time, 109.
of events, 151.
abundance, 639.
Streamer, *flag*, 550.
Streaming, *incoherent*, 47.
dispersed, 73.
Streamlet, *river*, 348.
Street, *buildings*, 189.
way, 627.
Street-arab, *commonalty*, 876.
Street-walker, *libertine*, 962.
Strength, *vigour*, 159.
greatness, 31.
energy, 171.
tenacity, 327.
degree, 26.
Strengthen, *to increase*, 35.
Strenuous, *active*, 682, 686.
resolved, 604.
*Strepitoso (It.), *music*, 415.
Stress, *weight*, 642.
intonation, 580.
strain, 686.
Stretch, *increase*, 35.
expand, 194.
lengthen, 200.
distance, 196.
exertion, 686.
encroachment, 925.
misinterpret, 523.
exaggeration, 549.
Stretcher, *vehicle*, 272.
Strew, *spread*, 73.
*Stria (L.), *spot*, 440.
furrow, 259.
Striate, *furrowed*, 259.
spotted, 440.
Strict, *severe*, 739.
exact, 494.
Stricture, *disapprobation*, 932.
Stride, *walk*, 266.
Strident, *harsh*, 410.
Stridulous, *shrill*, 410.
Strife, *quarrel*, 713, 720.
Strike, *hit*, 276.
beat, 972, 649.
revolt, 719, 742.
impress, 824.
wonder, 870.
operate, 170.
music, 415.
Strike a balance, *mean*, 29.
Strike off, *exclude*, 55.
Strike out, *invent*, 515.
plan, 626.
efface, 552.
Strike up, *begin*, 66.
String, *continuity*, 69.
to tie, 43.
fibre, 205.
ligature, 45.
to arrange, 60.
*Stringendo (It.), *music*, 415.
Stringent, *severe*, 739.
compulsory, 744.
Stringy, *narrow*, 203.
viscous, 352.
Strip, *to divest*, 226.
rob, 789, 791.
filament, 205.
Stripe, *length*, 200.
blow, 972.
mark, 550.
variegation, 440.
Stripling, *youth*, 129.
Stripped, *poor*, 804.
Strive, *exert*, 686.
endeavour, 676.
contend, 720.
Stroke, *impulse*, 276.
mark, 550.
work, 680.
expedient, 626.
success, 731.
Stroll, *walk*, 266.
Strong, *powerful*, 159.
energetic, 171.
tenacious, 327.
pungent, 392.
cogent, 467.
feeling, 821.
Strong-box, *treasury*, 802.
Stronghold, *defence*, 717.
prison, 752.
Strongly, *great*, 31.
Strong-room, *treasury*, 802.
Strop, *sharpen*, 253.
Strophe, *poetry*, 597.
Structure, *state*, 7.
texture, 329.
building, 189.
Struggle, *contend*, 720.
exert, 686.

Strum, *music*, 415.
Strumpet, *libertine*, 962.
Strut, *parade*, 882.
boast, 884.
pride, 878.
Stub, *part*, 51.
end, 67.
Stubble, *remainder*, 40.
rough, 256.
Stubborn, *obstinate*, 606.
unmanageable, 704.
Stubby, *short*, 201.
ugly, 846.
Stucco, *cement*, 45.
covering, 222.
Stuck fast, *difficulty*, 704.
stopped, 265.
Stuck-up, *vanity*, 880.
Stud, *knob*, 250.
point, 253.
horses, 271.
Studded, *pointed*, 253.
spotted, 440.
Student, *learner*, 541.
Studio, *workshop*, 691.
Studious, *thoughtful*, 451.
docile, 539.
Studiously, *purposely*, 600.
Study, *thought*, 451.
learning, 539.
research, 461.
intention, 620.
copy, 21.
music, 415.
Stuff, *substance*, 3.
matter, 316.
materials, 632.
absurdity, 497.
trifle, 643.
to feed, 296.
to line, 224.
cram, 194.
hoax, 545.
Stuffy, *musty*, 401.
Stultified, *failure*, 732.
Stultify, *counteract*, 708.
Stultiloquy, *absurdity*, 497.
Stumble, *fall*, 306.
fail, 732.
unskilful, 699.
flounder, 315.
Stumble on, *ascertain*, 480.
Stumbling-block, *difficulty*, 704.
hindrance, 706.
Stump, *trunk*, 51.
to step, 266.
Stumpy, *short*, 201.
ugly, 846.
Stun, *stupefy*, 823.
Stun, *affect*, 824.
deafen, 419.
astonish, 865.
loud, 404.
Stung, *pain*, 828.
Stunt, *feat*, 680.
task, 625.
Stunted, *small*, 193.
contracted, 195.
Stupefy, *stun*, 823.
wonder, 870.
Stupendous, *great*, 31.
large, 192.
wonderful, 870.
Stupid, *dull*, 843.
credulous, 486.
foolish, 499.
Stupor, *lethargy*, 823.
Sturdy, *strong*, 157, 159.
Stutter, *stammer*, 583.
Sty, *dirt*, 653.
pen, 189.
Stygian, *infernal*, 982.
dark, 421.
diabolic, 945.
Style, *state*, 7.
time, 114.
fashion, 852.
taste, 850.
to name, 564.
diction, 569.
pencil, 559.
Stylet, *arms*, 727.
Stylish, *fashionable*, 852.
Stylist, *style*, 569.
Stylite, *recluse*, 893.
Stylograph, *writing*, 590.
Stymie, *to hinder*, 706.
Styptic, *remedy*, 662.
Suasion, *persuade*, 615.
Suavity, *courtesy*, 894.
Subacid, *acid*, 397.
Subahdar, *master*, 745.
Subalpine, *height*, 206.
Subaltern, *plebeian*, 876.
inferior, 24.
servant, 746.
officer, 726, 745.
Subaqueous, *depth*, 208.
Subastral, *terrestrial*, 318.
Sub-committee, *committee*, 696.
Subconsciousness, *intellect*, 450.
Sub-contrary, *antiposition*, 237.
Sub-cutaneous, *interiority*, 221.
Sub-dean, *church*, 996.
Subdititious, *substitution*, 147.
Subdivide, *disjoin*, 44.
Subdivision, *part*, 51.
Subdual, *success*, 731.

Subduct, *retrench*, 38.
take, 789.
Subdue, *calm*, 174.
impress, 824.
succeed, 731.
*Subito (L.), *instantaneity*, 113.
Subjacent, *lowness*, 207.
Subject, *topic*, 454.
liable, 177.
to enthral, 749.
musical, 415.
Subjection, *submission*, 743.
dependence, 749.
Subjective, *intrinsic*, 6.
imaginary, 2.
immaterial, 317.
mental, 450.
Subjoin, *addition*, 37.
*Sub judice (L.), *inquiry*, 461.
Subjugate, *subject*, 749.
conquer, 731, 732.
impress, 824.
Subjunction, *addition*, 37.
Sublimate, *to elevate*, 307.
to vaporise, 336.
Sublimated, *ethereal*, 320.
Sublimation, *see* Sublimate.
Sublime, *high*, 206.
beauty, 845.
glory, 873.
lofty, 574.
magnanimous, 942.
Subliminal, *subconscious*, 450.
Sublunary, *world*, 318.
Submarine, *depth*, 208.
ship, 273.
Submerge, *immerse*, 300.
steep, 337.
sink, 208.
plunge, 310.
Submission, *surrender*, 725, 879.
Submissive, *humble*, 725, 879.
enduring, 826.
Submit, *surrender*, 725.
obey, 743.
Subordinate, *inferior*, 34.
unimportant, 643.
servant, 746.
Subordination, *order*, 58.
Suborn, *hire*, 795.
bribe, 784.
Subpœna, *mandate*, 741.
Subscribe, *assent*, 488.
agree to, 769.
give, 707, 784.
Subscription, *donation*, 809.
Subsequent, *in time*, 117.
in order, 63.
Subservient, *utility*, 644.
Subservient, *servility*, 886.
Subside, *sink*, 306.
decrease, 36.
calm down, 826.
Subsidiary, *tending*, 176.
auxiliary, 707.
Subsidy, *pay*, 809.
gift, 784.
Subsist, *existence*, 1.
continuance, 142.
Subsistence, *food*, 298.
livelihood, 803.
Subsoil, *earth*, 342.
interior, 221.
Substance, *thing*, 3.
matter, 316.
interior, 221.
quantity, 25.
texture, 329.
compendium, 596.
meaning, 516.
important, 642.
wealth, 803.
Substantial, *dense*, 321.
existence, 1.
true, 494.
Substantiate, *demonstrate*, 478.
make good, 494.
Substantive, *substance*, 3.
Substitute, *means*, 634.
deputy, 759.
Substitution, *change*, 147.
Substratum, *substance*, 3.
interior, 221.
layer, 204.
base, 211.
support, 215.
materiality, 316.
Subsumption, *inclusion*, 76.
Subterfuge, *lie*, 546.
sophistry, 477.
Subterranean, *underground*, 208.
Subtile, *rare*, 322.
light, 320.
Subtilise, *sophistry*, 477.
Subtle, *cunning*, 702.
wise, 498.
texture, 329.
Subtract, *retrench*, 38.
arithmetical, 84.
to take, 789.
Suburban, *environs*, 227.
distance, 197.
Subvert, *invert*, 218
depress, 308.
change, 140.
destroy, 162.
Subway, *road*, 627.
Succedaneum, *substitute*, 147, 634.

Succeed, *answer*, 731.
follow, 63.
*Succès d'estime (Fr.), *approbation*, 931.
Success, *success*, 731.
Succession, *sequence*, 63.
continuity, 69.
of time, 109.
lateness, 117.
Successor, *sequel*, 65.
posterior, 117.
Succinct, *concise*, 572.
Succour, *help*, 707.
Succubus, *demon*, 980.
Succulent, *juicy*, 333.
edible, 298.
semiliquid, 352.
Succumb, *yield*, 725.
obey, 743.
fatigue, 688.
Such, *similarity*, 17.
Suck, *imbibe*, 296.
deprive, 789.
Suckle, *nourish*, 707.
Suckling, *youth*, 129.
Suction, *imbibition*, 296.
Sudatorium, *furnace*, 386.
Sudden, *early*, 132.
abrupt, 508.
transient, 111.
Suds, *froth*, 353.
Sue, *demand*, 765.
at law, 969.
Suet, *fat*, 356.
Suffer, *physical pain*, 378.
moral pain, 828.
to endure, 821.
to allow, 760.
disease, 655.
experience, 151.
Sufferance, *permission*, 760.
Sufficient, *enough*, 639.
Suffix, *sequel*, 65.
adjunct, 39.
Sufflation, *wind*, 349.
Suffocate, *choke*, 361.
Suffragan, *church*, 996.
Suffrage, *vote*, 609.
prayer, 990.
Suffragist, *dueness*, 924.
Suffuse, *mix*, 41.
feel, 821.
blush, 874.
Sugar, *sweet*, 396.
to flatter, 933.
Sugar-loaf, *convexity*, 250.
Suggest, *suppose*, 514.
advise, 695.
inform, 527.
Suggest, *recall*, 505.
occur, 451.
*Suggestio falsi (L.), *equivocalness*, 520.
falsehood, 544.
Suggestive, *impure*, 961.
Suicide, *kill*, 361.
*Sui generis (L.), *special*, 79.
unconformity, 83.
*Sui juris (L.), *freedom*, 748.
Suit, *accord*, 23.
class, 75.
expedient, 646.
clothes, 225.
courtship, 902.
at law, 969.
Suite, *series*, 69.
adjunct, 39.
sequel, 65.
retinue, 746.
Suiting, *accord*, 23.
Suitor, *love*, 897.
Sulcated, *furrow*, 259.
Sulky, *discourteous*, 895.
gloomy, 837.
Sullen, *discourteous*, 895.
gloomy, 837.
Sully, *deface*, 846.
dishonour, 874, 940.
Sulphur, *colour*, 436.
Sultan, *master*, 745.
Sultry, *heat*, 382.
Sum, *total*, 50.
number, 84.
to reckon, 85.
money, 800.
Sumless, *infinity*, 105.
Summary, *transient*, 111.
early, 132.
compendium, 201, 596.
Summation, *numeration*, 85.
Summer, *heat*, 382.
support, 215.
Summerset, *inversion*, 218.
Summit, *top*, 210.
climax, 33.
Summon, *command*, 741.
accuse, 938.
Summon up, *evoke*, 824.
Sumptuary, *expenditure*, 800, 809.
Sumptuous, *ostentation*, 882.
Sum up, *description*, 594.
Sun, *luminary*, 423.
Sunbeam, *light*, 420.
Sun-bonnet, *dress*, 225.
Sunder, *disjoin*, 44.
Sundries, *oddments*, 51.
Sundry, *multitude*, 102.
Sunk, *low*, 208.

Sunk, *vice*, 945.
Sunless, *dark*, 421.
Sunlight, *light*, 420.
cheerful, 836.
pleasing, 827.
prosperous, 734.
Sunny, *see* Sunlight.
Sunshine, *see* Sunlight.
Sup, *eat*, 296.
Superable, *facility*, 705.
Superabundant, *sufficient*, 641.
Superadd, *addition*, 37.
increase, 35.
Superannuated, *age*, 128.
Superannuation, *pension*, 803.
Superb, *proud*, 845.
Supercargo, *overload*, 694.
*Supercherie (Fr.), *deception*, 545.
Supercilious, *haughty*, 878.
insolent, 885.
contemptuous, 929.
Supereminence, *repute*, 873.
Supererogation, *uselessness*, 645.
activity, 682.
Superexalted, *repute*, 873.
Superexcellent, *goodness*, 648.
Superfetation, *addition*, 37.
Superficial, *shallow*, 209, 220.
ignorant, 491.
Superficies, *face*, 220.
Superfine, *best*, 648.
Superfluity, *redundance*, 641.
remainder, 40.
Superhuman, *divine*, 976.
perfect, 650.
great, 31.
Superimpose, *cover*, 220.
Superincumbent, *above*, 206.
weight, 319.
resting, 215.
Superinduce, *production*, 161.
change, 140.
addition, 37.
Superintend, *direction*, 693.
Superintendent, *director*, 694.
Superior, *greater*, 33.
important, 642.
good, 648.
Superlative, *perfect*, 650.
Superman, *hero*, 948.
Supernal, *lofty*, 206.
Supernatant, *overlying*, 206.
Supernatural, *deity*, 976.
Supernumerary, *redundant*, 641.
remaining, 40.
actor, 599.
Superpose, *addition*, 37.
cover, 222.
Superscription, *mark*, 550.
Superscription, *writing*, 590.
evidence, 467.
Supersede, *disuse*, 678.
substitute, 147.
Superstition, *credulity*, 486.
religious, 984.
Superstratum, *exteriority*, 220.
Superstructure, *completion*, 729.
Supertax, *tax*, 812.
Supervacaneous, *useless*, 645.
redundant, 641.
Supervene, *happen*, 151.
succeed, 117.
addition, 37.
Supervise, *direction*, 693.
Supervisor, *director*, 694.
Supine, *horizontal*, 213.
inverted, 218.
sluggish, 683.
torpid, 823.
Supper, *food*, 298.
Supplant, *substitution*, 147.
Supple, *soft*, 324.
servile, 886.
Supplement, *adjunct*, 39.
completion, 52.
addition, 37.
Suppletory, *addition*, 37.
Suppliant, *petitioner*, 767.
Supplicant, *petitioner*, 767.
Supplicate, *beg*, 765.
pity, 914.
worship, 990.
Supplies, *materials*, 635.
aid, 707.
Supply, *give*, 784.
provide, 637.
store, 636.
Support, *sustain*, 215.
operate, 170.
evidence, 467.
aid, 707.
preserve, 670.
endure, 821, 826.
Supporter, *prop*, 215.
Suppose, *supposition*, 514.
Supposing, *provided*, 469.
Supposition, *supposition*, 514.
Supposititious, *false*, 544, 925.
non-existing, 2.
Suppress, *conceal*, 528.
destroy, 162.
Supremacy, *superior*, 33.
authority, 737.
summit, 210.
Supremely, *great*, 31.
Surcease, *cessation*, 141.
Surcharge, *redundance*, 641.
dearness, 814.

Surcingle, *fastening*, 45.
Sure, *certain*, 474.
safe, 664.
Sure-footed, *careful*, 459.
skilful, 698.
Surely, *wonder*, 870.
Surety, *security*, 771.
evidence, 467.
Surf, *foam*, 353.
tide, 348.
Surface, *exterior*, 220.
Surfeit, *satiety*, 869.
redundance, 641.
Surge, *ocean*, 341.
rotation, 312.
swell, 305.
wave, 348.
Surgery, *remedy*, 662.
Surly, *gruff*, 895.
unkind, 907.
Surmise, *supposition*, 514.
Surmount, *rise*, 305.
tower, 206.
overcome, 731.
Surmountable, *facility*, 705.
Surname, *nomenclature*, 564.
Surpass, *superior*, 33.
grow, 194.
go beyond, 303.
Surpassing, *greatness*, 31.
Surplice, *gown*, 225.
canonical, 999.
Surplus, *remainder*, 40.
redundance, 641.
Surprise, *wonder*, 870.
non-expectation, 508.
disappoint, 509.
Surprisingly, *great*, 31.
Surrender, *submit*, 725.
obey, 743.
relinquish, 782.
Surreptitious, *false*, 544.
furtive, 528.
Surrogate, *consignee*, 758.
deputy, 759.
Surround, *circumjacence*, 227, 231.
Surtout, *dress*, 225.
Surveillance, *care*, 459.
direction, 693.
Survey, *view*, 441.
measure, 466.
Survive, *remain*, 40.
endure, 110.
Susceptible, *liable*, 177.
impressible, 822.
excitable, 901.
Suscitate, *cause*, 153.
produce, 161.
induce, 615.
Suscitate, *excite*, 825.
stir up, 173.
Suspect, *doubt*, 485.
suppose, 514.
Suspend, *hang*, 214.
discontinue, 141.
defer, 133.
stop, 265.
Suspense, *doubt*, 485.
uncertainty, 475.
hesitation, 603.
irresolution, 605.
Suspicion, *doubt*, 485.
incredulity, 487.
uncertainty, 475.
fear, 860.
Suspiration, *lamentation*, 839.
Susurration, *whisper*, 405.
Sustain, *support*, 215.
aid, 707.
operate, 170.
preserve, 670.
Sustenance, *food*, 298.
Sutler, *trader*, 797.
Suttee, *religion*, 991.
Suture, *joint*, 43.
Suzerainty, *authority*, 737.
*Svelte (Fr.), *lissom*, 324.
Swab, *cleanness*, 652.
Swaddle, *dress*, 225.
Swag, *hang*, 214.
lean, 217.
oscillation, 314.
drop, 306.
booty, 793.
Swagger, *boast*, 884.
bluster, 885.
smart, 845.
Swaggerer, *blusterer*, 887.
Swain, *rustic*, 876.
Swallow, *gulp*, 296.
believe, 484.
destroy, 162.
Swamp, *marsh*, 345.
destroy, 162.
Swamped, *failure*, 732.
Swank, *ostentation*, 882.
boasting, 884.
Swan-song, *end*, 67.
death, 360.
Swap, *interchange*, 148.
Sward, *plain*, 344.
Swarm, *crowd*, 72.
sufficiency, 639.
multitude, 102.
to climb, 305.
Swarthy, *black*, 431.
Swash, *spurt*, 348.
affuse, 337.

Swastika, *cross*, 219.
Swathe, *clothe*, 225.
fasten, 43.
Sway, *power*, 157.
influence, 175.
authority, 737.
induce, 615.
oscillate, 314.
Sweal, *calefaction*, 384.
Swear, *promise*, 768.
affirm, 535.
Swear-word, *expletive*, 641.
Sweat, *transude*, 348.
heat, 382.
labour, 686.
to fatigue, 688.
Sweater, *dress*, 225.
Sweep, *space*, 180.
curve, 245.
rapidity, 274.
clean, 652.
displace, 185.
destroy, 162.
devastation, 619, 649.
blackguard, 949.
Sweeping, *wholesale*, 50.
Sweepings, *refuse*, 653.
trifle, 643.
Sweet, *saccharine*, 396.
agreeable, 829.
lovely, 897.
melodious, 413.
Sweetheart, *love*, 897.
Sweetmeat, *sweet*, 396.
Swell, *increase*, 35.
expand, 194, 202.
bulge, 250.
tide, 348.
fop, 854.
emotion, 821, 824.
extol, 931.
swagger, 885.
Swelling, *bombastic*, 577.
Swell mob, *thief*, 792.
Swelter, *heat*, 382.
Swerve, *deviate*, 279.
diverge, 291.
irresolution, 605.
tergiversation, 607.
Swift, *velocity*, 274.
Swig, *drink*, 296.
tope, 959.
Swill, *drink*, 296.
tope, 959.
Swim, *float*, 305.
navigate, 267.
vertigo, 503.
Swimming, *successful*, 731.
buoyant, 320.
Swindle, *peculate*, 791.
cheat, 545.
Swindler, *defrauder*, 792.
sharper, 548.
Swine, *intemperance*, 954.
Swing, *space*, 180.
hang, 214.
play, 170.
oscillate, 314.
freedom, 748.
Swinge, *punish*, 972.
Swingeing, *great*, 31.
Swinish, *intemperance*, 954.
gluttony, 957.
Swipe, *blow*, 276.
Switch, *scourge*, 975.
shift, 279.
whisk, 311, 315.
Switchback, *obliquity*, 217.
Swivel, *hinge*, 312.
cannon, 727.
Swollen, *proud*, 878.
big, 192.
Swoon, *fainting*, 160.
fatigue, 688.
Swoop, *seizure*, 789.
descent, 306.
Swop, *see* Swap.
Sword, *arms*, 727.
Swordsman, *combatant*, 726.
Swot, *to study*, 539.
diligent, 682.
Sybarite, *intemperance*, 954.
Sycophant, *servility*, 886.
adulation, 933.
flatterer, 935.
Syllable, *word*, 561.
Syllabus, *list*, 86.
compendium, 596.
Syllogism, *logic*, 476.
Sylph, *sprite*, 979.
Sylvan, *woody*, 367.
Symbol, *sign*, 550.
metaphor, 521.
mathematical, 84.
Symmetry, *form*, 252.
order, 58.
beauty, 845.
equality, 27.
Sympathy, *kindness*, 906.
love, 897.
pity, 914.
Symphonic, *harmony*, 413.
Symphony, *music*, 415.
Symposium, *feast*, 299.
festivity, 840.
discussion, 461.
Symptom, *sign*, 550.
Synagogue, *temple*, 1000.

Synchronism, *time*, 120.
Syncopate, *shorten*, 201.
Syncopation, *rhythm*, 413.
Syncope, *cut*, 160.
Syndic, *master*, 745.
Syndicalism, *participation*, 778.
Syndicate, *partnership*, 712, 797.
Synecdoche, *metaphor*, 521.
substitution, 147.
Synod, *council*, 696.
church, 995.
assemblage, 72.
Synonym, *nomenclature*, 564.
Synopsis, *arrangement*, 60.
compendium, 596.
*Syntagma (Gr.), *arrangement*, 60.
Syntax, *grammar*, 567.
Synthesis, *combination*, 48.
Syrup, *sweet*, 396.
Systaltic, *pulse*, 314.
Systole, *pulse*, 314.
contraction, 195.
System, *order*, 58.
plan, 626.
Syzygy, *contiguity*, 199.

T

Tab, *adjunct*, 39.
Tabby, *variegated*, 440.
Tabernacle, *temple*, 1000.
Tabid, *morbid*, 655.
shrivelled, 195.
noxious, 649.
Table, *stand*, 215.
layer, 204.
list, 86.
record, 551.
repast, 298.
*Table d'hôte (Fr.), *food*, 298.
Table-land, *plain*, 344.
flat, 213.
Table-talk, *talk*, 588.
*Tableau (Fr,), *painting*, 556.
scene, 824.
Tablet, *record*, 551.
layer, 204.
Taboo, *spell*, 992, 993.
prohibition, 761.
Tabor, *music*, 417.
*Tabouret (Fr.), *support*, 215.
*Tabula rasa (L.), *ignorance*, 491.
oblivion, 506.
Tabulate, *arrange*, 60, 69.
register, 86.
Tachygraphy, *writing*, 590.
Tacit, *hidden*, 526.
Taciturn, *silent*, 585.
Tack, *direction*, 278.
nail, 45.
to turn, 279.
change course, 140.
Tack to, *add*, 37.
join, 43.
Tackle, *gear*, 633.
fastening, 45.
to undertake, 676.
encounter, 720.
Tact, *skill*, 698.
wisdom, 498.
taste, 850.
discrimination, 465.
Tactician, *proficient*, 700.
Tactics, *conduct*, 692.
plan, 626.
skill, 698.
warfare, 722.
Tactile, *touch*, 379.
Taction, *touch*, 379.
Tactless, *foolish*, 499.
Tactual, *touch*, 379.
Tadpole, *young*, 129.
Tag, *add*, 37, 39.
fastening, 45.
part, 51.
end, 67.
point, 253.
maxim, 496.
Tail, *end*, 67.
back, 235.
adjunct, 37, 214.
sequel, 65.
Taint, *disease*, 655.
decay, 659.
dirt, 653.
fault, 651.
disgrace, 874.
Taintless, *pure*, 652.
Take, *to appropriate*, 789.
receive, 785.
eat, 296.
believe, 484.
understand, 518.
please, 829.
Take aback, *surprise*, 870.
Take after, *similarity*, 17.
Take away, *remove*, 38, 789.
Take back, *retract*, 607.
Take care, *caution*, 864.
Take down, *swallow*, 296.
note, 551.
lower, 308.
humiliate, 879.
Take effect, *agency*, 170.
Take heed, *attention*, 457.
Take hold, *taking*, 789.
Take in, *include*, 54.

Take in, *admit*, 296.
understand, 518.
cheat, 545.
Take it, *believe*, 484.
suppose, 514.
Take off, *remove*, 185.
divest, 226.
imitate, 19.
personate, 554.
ridicule, 856.
jump, 305.
Take on, *anger*, 837.
undertake, 676.
Take out, *extract*, 301.
obliterate, 552.
Take part with, *aid*, 707.
Take place, *happen*, 151.
Take root, *dwell*, 186.
Take ship, *navigation*, 267.
Take the shine out of, *superiority*, 33.
Take up, *inquire*, 461.
Take up with, *sociality*, 892.
Take wing, *departure*, 293.
Taking, *vexation*, 828.
anger, 900.
pleasing, 829, 897.
Tale, *narrative*, 582, 594.
counting, 85.
Tale-bearer, *tell*, 534.
Talent, *skill*, 698.
intelligence, 498.
Tale-teller, *liar*, 548.
Talisman, *spell*, 993.
Talk, *speak*, 582.
rumour, 532.
conversation, 588.
Talkative, *talk*, 584.
Tall, *height*, 206.
Tallow, *fat*, 356.
Tally, *agreement*, 23.
numeration, 85.
Talmud, *revelation*, 985.
Talons, *claw*, 633.
authority, 737.
Talus, *slope*, 217.
Tambourine, *music*, 417.
Tame, *inert*, 172.
moderate, 174.
feeble, 575.
calm, 826.
teach, 537.
Tamis, *strainer*, 260.
Tamper with, *change*, 140.
meddle, 682.
Tan, *yellow*, 433.
to thrash, 972.
Tandem, *vehicle*, 272.
sequence, 69.
Tang, *taste*, 390.
Tangent, *contiguity*, 199.
Tangible, *touch*, 1, 379.
material, 316.
Tangle, *derange*, 61.
Tangled, *disordered*, 59.
matted, 219.
Tango, *dance*, 840.
Tank, *recipient*, 191.
reservoir, 636.
arms, 727.
Tankard, *receptacle*, 191.
Tantalise, *entice*, 615.
tease, 830.
tempt, 865.
Tantalus, *receptacle*, 191.
Tantamount, *equal*, 27.
synonymous, 516.
Tantara, *loudness*, 404.
Tantrum, *passion*, 900.
Tap, *hit*, 276.
plug, 263.
to let out, 297.
to intercept, 789.
Tape, *joint*, 45.
Taper, *narrow*, 203.
sharp, 253.
candle, 423.
Tapestry, *art*, 556.
Tar, *mariner*, 269.
Taradiddle, *untruth*, 546.
Tarantella, *dance*, 840.
Tardy, *dilatory*, 133.
slow, 275.
Target, *object*, 620.
laughing-stock, 857.
Tariff, *price*, 812.
Tarn, *lake*, 343.
Tarnish, *decoloration*, 429.
deface, 846.
spoil, 659.
disgrace, 874.
dishonour, 940.
Tarry, *remain*, 110.
continue, 142.
late, 133.
expect, 507.
rest, 265.
Tart, *acid*, 397.
rude, 895.
irascible, 901.
Tartan, *dress*, 225.
Tartar, *irascible*, 901.
Tartarus, *hell*, 982.
Tartness, *see* Tart.
Tartuffe, *hypocrisy*, 544, 548.
impiety, 989.
Task, *business*, 625.
to put to use, 677.
function, 644.

Task, *lesson*, 537.
Taskmaster, *director*, 694.
Tassel, *ornament*, 847.
Taste, *sapidity*, 390.
to experience, 821.
discrimination, 821.
small quantity, 32.
Tasteless, *vapid*, 391.
unattractive, 866.
Tasty, *savoury*, 394.
Tat, *knit*, 43.
*Tâtonnement (Fr.), *trial*, 463.
essay, 675.
Tatter, *part*, 51.
Tatterdemalion, *commonalty*, 876.
Tattle, *talk*, 588.
Tattoo, *roll*, 407.
Taunt, *reproach*, 938.
ridicule, 856.
hoot, 929.
Tautology, *repetition*, 104.
diffuseness, 573.
Tavern, *inn*, 189.
Tawdry, *vulgar*, 851.
Tawny, *grey*, 432.
brown, 433.
Tax, *impost*, 812.
to accuse, 938.
require, 765.
impose, 741.
employ, 677.
Taxi-cab, *vehicle*, 272.
Teach, *teaching*, 537.
Teachable, *learning*, 539.
Teacher, *instructor*, 540.
Tea-gown, *dress*, 225.
Team, *group*, 69.
Tear, *separate*, 44.
destroy, 162.
violence, 173.
move rapidly, 274.
weeping, 839.
Tear out, *extract*, 301.
Tearful, *lamenting*, 839.
Tease, *annoy*, 830.
Teaser, *secret*, 533.
Teat, *convexity*, 250.
Technical, *skill*, 698.
Technique, *skill*, 698.
musical, 415.
Technology, *skill*, 698.
Tedium, *fatigue*, 841.
Teem, *abound*, 639.
numerous, 102.
productiveness, 168
Teeming, *assemblage*, 72.
Teepee, *abode*, 189.
Teetotalism, *sobriety*, 958.
Teetotum, *rotation*, 840.
Tegument, *covering*, 222.
Telegraph, *signal*, 550.
Telegraphic, *concise*, 572.
velocity, 274.
Teleology, *thought*, 451.
Teleology, *intention*, 620.
Telephone, *hearing*, 418.
Telescope, *optical instrument*, 445.
Tell, *inform*, 527.
count, 85.
speak, 582.
describe, 594.
Tell off, *count*, 85.
Tell-tale, *evidence*, 467.
divulge, 529.
Temerity, *rashness*, 863.
Temper ,*nature*, 5.
state, 7.
elasticity, 323.
softness, 324.
affections, 820.
to moderate, 174.
soften, 826.
prepare, 673.
irascibility, 901.
Temperament, *nature*, 5.
disposition, 820.
music, 413.
Temperance, *moderation*, 953.
Temperate, *moderate*, 174.
mild, 826.
Temperature, *heat*, 382.
Tempest, *violence*, 173.
wind, 349.
excitement, 825.
Tempestivity, *occasion*, 134.
Temple, *church*, 1000.
side, 236.
Temporal, *transient*, 111.
laical, 997.
*Tempo (It.), *melody*, 413.
Temporary, *transient*, 111.
Temporise, *cunning*, 702.
policy, 698.
opportunity, 134.
Tempt, *entice*, 615.
desire, 865.
attempt, 676.
Ten, *number*, 98.
Tenable, *probable*, 472.
Tenacious, *retentive*, 781.
avaricious, 819.
resolved, 604.
obstinate, 606.
prejudiced, 481.
Tenacity, *toughness*, 327.
Tenant, *occupier*, 188.
possessor, 779.
present, 186.

Tenantless, *empty*, 187.
Tend, *aid*, 107.
contribute, 153.
conduce, 176.
direct to, 278.
Tendentious, *misjudgment*, 481.
Tender, *soft*, 324.
susceptible, 822.
loving, 897.
compassionate, 914.
to offer, 763.
smallness, 32.
Tenderfoot, *stranger*, 57.
Tendril, *infant*, 129.
Tenebrific, *darkness*, 421.
Tenement, *house*, 189.
property, 780.
Tenet, *belief*, 484.
creed, 983.
Tenor, *course*, 7.
degree, 26.
direction, 278.
meaning, 516.
musical, 413.
Tense, *hard*, 323.
Tensile, *elasticity*, 325.
Tension, *strength*, 159.
length, 200.
hardness, 323.
strain, 686.
Tent, *receptacle*, 189.
covering, 222.
Tentacle, *instrument*, 633.
Tentative, *experimental*, 463.
essaying, 675.
Tenter-hook, *expectation*, 507.
Tenuity, *rarity*, 322.
thinness, 203.
smallness, 32.
Tenure, *dueness*, 924.
Tephramancy, *prediction*, 511.
Tepid, *warm*, 382.
passionless, 823.
Teratology, *affectation*, 855.
Tercentenary, *period*, 138.
Terebration, *opening*, 260.
piercing, 302.
Tergiversation, *change*, 607.
equivocation, 520.
Term, *place in series*, 71.
end, 67.
limit, 233.
period of time, 106.
word, 562.
name, 564.
Termagant, *irascibility*, 901.
Terminal, *end*, 67.
Terminate, *completion*, 729.
Terminology, *word*, 562.
Terminus, *end*, 67.
Termless, *infinity*, 105.
Terms, *conditions*, 770.
circumstances, 8.
reasoning, 476.
Ternary, *number*, 93.
Terpsichore, *music*, 415.
Terrace, *plain*, 344.
level, 213.
buildings, 189.
*Terra firma (L.), *support*, 215.
*Terra incognita (L.), *ignorance*, 491.
Terraqueous, *land*, 342.
world, 318.
Terrene, *land*, 342.
world, 318.
Terrestrial, *land*, 342.
world, 318.
Terrible, *fearful*, 860.
great, 31.
Terrier, *list*, 86.
Terrific, *frightful*, 830.
Terrify, *affright*, 860.
Territory, *region*, 181.
Terror, *fear*, 860.
Terse, *concise*, 572.
Tertiary, *triality*, 92.
*Tertium quid (L.), *difference*, 15.
mixture, 41.
*Terza rima (It.), *poetry*, 597.
Tessellated, *variegation*, 440.
Test, *experiment*, 463.
Testament, *revelation*, 985.
Tester, *support*, 215.
Testify, *evidence*, 467, 560.
Testimonial, *record*, 551.
gift, 784.
Testimony, *evidence*, 467.
Test-tube, *receptacle*, 191.
Testy, *irascible*, 901.
rude, 895.
Tetchy, *irascible*, 901.
*Tête-à-tête (Fr.), *duality*, 89.
Tether, *fasten*, 43.
moor, 265.
restrain, 751.
Tetrad, *number*, 95.
Tetrarch, *master*, 745.
Text, *meaning*, 516.
prototype, 22.
theme, 454.
printing, 591.
Text-book, *lesson*, 537.
synopsis, 596.
Texture, *condition*, 7.
fabric, 329.
Thalassic, *ocean*, 341.
Thalia, *the drama*, 599

Thane, *master*, 745.
Thankful, *gratitude*, 916.
Thankless, *ingratitude*, 917.
painful, 830.
Thanks, *gratitude*, 916.
worship, 990.
Thatch, *cover*, 210.
Thaumatrope, *optical*, 445.
Thaumaturgy, *occult arts*, 992.
Thaw, *melt*, 335.
heat, 384.
mollify, 826.
relent, 914.
Theatre, *drama*, 599.
arena, 728.
school, 542.
spectacle, 441.
Theatrical, *ostentatious*, 882.
Theft, *steal*, 791.
Theism, *piety*, 98.
Theme, *topic*, 454.
music, 415.
Then, *time*, 121.
Thence, *cause*, 155.
departure, 293.
Thenceforth, *time*, 121.
Thenceforward, *time*, 121.
Theocratic, *deity*, 976.
Theology, *theology*, 983.
Theopathy, *piety*, 987.
Theorbo, *musical instrument*, 417.
Theorem, *proposition*, 535.
Theorise, *suppose*, 514.
Theory, *knowledge*, 490.
attribution, 155.
Theosophy, *theology*, 983.
heterodoxy, 984.
Therapeutics, *remedy*, 662.
There, *place*, 186.
Thereabouts, *nearly*, 32.
near, 107.
Thereafter, *time*, 117.
Thereby, *instrumentality*, 631.
Therefore, *reasoning*, 476.
attribution, 155.
motive, 615.
Therein, *interiority*, 221.
Thereof, *relation*, 9.
Thereupon, *posteriority*, 117.
Therewith, *accompany*, 88.
Theriac, *remedy*, 662.
Thermal, *heat*, 382.
Thermometer, *heat*, 389.
Thesaurus, *store*, 636.
words, 562.
Thesis, *theme*, 454.
dissertation, 595.
affirmation, 535.
Thetis, *ocean*, 341.
Theurgy, *occult arts*, 992.
Thew, *strength*, 159.
Thick, *broad*, 202.
dense, 321.
semiliquid, 352.
turbid, 426.
dirty, 653.
numerous, 102.
Thick-coming, *frequent*, 136.
Thicket, *plant*, 367.
Thick-skinned, *insensitive*, 376, 823.
Thief, *robber*, 792.
Thievery, *stealing*, 791.
Thimble, *instrument*, 633.
Thimbleful, *littleness*, 193.
smallness, 32.
Thimblerig, *deception*, 545.
Thin, *small*, 193.
narrow, 203.
rare, 322.
scanty, 640.
few, 103.
to subduct, 38.
Thing, *substance*, 3.
Things, *events*, 151.
Things, of all, *greatness*, 31.
Thingumbob, *trifle*, 643.
Think, *cogitate*, 451.
believe, 484.
Think of, *intend*, 620.
Think out, *plan*, 626.
Think upon, *remember*, 505.
Thin-skinned, *sensitive*, 375, 872.
Third part, *number*, 94.
Thirdly, *number*, 93.
Thirst, *desire*, 865.
Thistle, *sharpness*, 253.
Thistledown, *light*, 320.
Thither, *direction*, 278.
Thong, *join*, 45.
Thorn, *sharp*, 253.
painful, 830.
pain, 378.
Thorny, *difficult*, 704.
Thorough, *completeness*, 52.
Thorough-bass, *music*, 413.
Thoroughbred, *manners*, 852.
Thorough-going, *greatness*, 31.
Thoroughly, *great*, 31.
Thorough-paced, *great*, 31.
Thorp, *abode*, 189.
Though, *counteraction*, 179.
opposition, 708.
evidence, 468.
Thought, *reflection*, 451.
maxim, 496.
small quantity, 32, 193.
idea, 453.
Thoughtful, *reflecting*, 451.

Thoughtful, *wise*, 498.
Thoughtless, *incogitant*, 452.
careless, 460.
foolish, 499.
improvident, 674.
unskilful, 699.
Thousand, *number*, 98.
Thrall, *slave*, 746.
Thraldom, *slavery*, 749.
Thrash, *beat*, 972.
Thrash out, *inquire*, 461.
Thread, *tie*, 45.
filament, 205.
continuity, 69.
to pass through, 302.
Thread one's way, *journey*, 266.
experiment, 463.
Threadbare, *bare*, 226.
imperfect, 651.
Threat, *threaten*, 909.
Threaten, *future*, 121.
alarm, 669.
danger, 665.
Three, *number*, 90.
Threefold, *number*, 93.
Threnody, *lament*, 839.
Thresh, *see* Thrash.
Threshold, *beginning*, 66.
Thrice, *number*, 93.
Thrift, *success*, 731.
prosperity, 734.
economy, 817.
Thriftless, *prodigal*, 818.
Thrill, *touch*, 379.
affect, 821, 824.
Thrilling, *tingling*, 380.
charming, 829.
Thrive, *succeed*, 731.
prosper, 734.
Throat, *opening*, 260.
air-pipe, 351.
Throb, *agitate*, 315.
emotion, 821.
Throe, *violence*, 173.
agitation, 146, 315.
pain, 378, 828.
Throne, *seat*, 215.
abode, 189.
authority, 747.
Throng, *assembly*, 72.
Throttle, *seize*, 789.
occlude, 261.
suffocate, 361.
Through, *passage*, 302.
instrument, 631.
owing to, 154.
(go), *effect*, 729.
Throughout, *totality*, 50.
time, 106.
Throw, *propel*, 284.
exertion, 686.
Throw away, *lose*, 776.
relinquish, 782.
Throw down, *destroy*, 162.
overthrow, 308.
Throw in, *add*, 300.
Throw into the shade, *superiority*, 33.
Throw off, *eject*, 297.
do with ease, 705.
Throw over, *desert*, 624.
Throw up, *resign*, 757.
desert, 624.
Thrum, *music*, 415.
Thrush, *music*, 416.
Thrust, *push*, 276.
attack, 716.
Thrust in, *insert*, 300.
interpose, 228.
Thug, *thief*, 792.
Thuggism, *killing*, 361.
Thumb, *finger*, 379.
Thumbscrew, *scourge*, 975.
Thump, *beat*, 276.
punish, 972.
Thunder, *noise*, 404.
violence, 173.
Thunderbolt, *prodigy*, 872.
Thunder-clap, *prodigy*, 872.
Thunder-storm, *violence*, 173.
Thunder-struck, *wonder*, 870.
Thus, *reasoning*, 476.
Thus far, *smallness*, 32.
Thwack, *beat*, 276.
punish, 972.
Thwart, *obstruct*, 706.
intersect, 219.
Tiara, *diadem*, 747.
canonicals, 999.
Tick, *sound*, 407.
oscillation, 314.
indicate, 550.
credit, 805.
Ticket, *indication*, 550.
permission, 760.
Tickle, *touch*, 380.
please, 377, 829.
laugh, 838.
Tickled, *amused*, 827.
Ticklish, *difficult*, 704.
uncertain, 475.
dangerous, 665.
Tide, *ocean*, 341.
flood, 348.
abundance, 639.
Tidings, *news*, 532.
Tidy, *clean*, 652.
trim, 673.

Tie, *relation*, 9.
fasten, 43.
fastening, 45.
security, 771.
equality, 27.
obligation, 926.
Tie-beam, *support*, 215.
Tier, *continuity*, 69.
layer, 204.
Tiff, *discord*, 713.
anger, 900.
Tiffin, *food*, 298.
Tiger, *violence*, 173.
courage, 861.
servant, 746.
wretch, 913.
miscreant, 949.
Tight, *fast*, 43.
smart, 845.
drunk, 959.
Tike, *commonalty*, 876.
Till, *to cultivate*, 371.
coffer, 191, 802.
up to the time, 108.
Tilt, *slope*, 217.
tumble, 306.
cover, 222.
Tilt at, *attack*, 716.
Tilt over, *obliquity*, 218.
*Timbre (Fr.), *music*, 413.
Timbrel, *musical instrument*, 417.
Time, *period*, 106.
Time-ball, *indication*, 550.
Timeless, *untimely*, 135.
Timely, *early*, 132.
opportune, 134.
Timepiece, *chronometer*, 114.
Time-server, *servility*, 886.
apostate, 941.
cunning, 702.
versatile, 607.
selfish, 943.
Time-worn, *old*, 124.
exhausted, 659.
Timid, *fearful*, 860.
cowardly, 862.
humble, 881.
Timorous, *see* Timid.
Timpanist, *musician*, 416.
Tin, *money*, 800.
to preserve, 670.
Tinct, *colour*, 428.
Tincture, *mixture*, 41.
to colour, 428.
Tinder, *burn*, 388.
Tinge, *colour*, 428.
mix, 41.
Tingle, *pain*, 378, 828.
feeling, 821.
Tingling, *titillation*, 380.
Tink, *resonance*, 408.
Tinker, *improve*, 658.
Tinkle, *resonance*, 408.
Tinsel, *ornament*, 847.
glitter, 420.
tawdry, 851.
Tint, *colour*, 428.
*Tintamarre (Fr.), *loudness*, 404.
Tintinnabulation, *resonance*, 408.
Tiny, *little*, 32.
small, 193.
Tip, *summit*, 210.
to give, 784, 809.
hint, 527.
Tippet, *dress*, 225.
Tipple, *drink*, 296, 298.
drunkenness, 959.
Tipstaff, *police*, 965.
Tipsy, *drunk*, 959.
Tiptoe, *high*, 206.
curiosity, 455.
Tip-top, *summit*, 210.
first-rate, 648.
Tirade, *disapproval*, 932.
declamation, 582.
Tire, *weary*, 841.
worry, 830.
fatigue, 688.
band, 45.
Tiresome, *wearisome*, 841.
Tissue, *texture*, 329.
Tit, *small*, 193.
pony, 271.
Titanic, *greatness*, 31.
Tit-bit, *dainty*, 829.
Tit for tat, *retaliation*, 718.
Tithe, *tenth*, 99.
Titillate, *touch*, 380.
please, 838.
Title, *distinction*, 877.
name, 564.
mark, 550.
right, 924.
Title-page, *beginning*, 66, 593
Titter, *laugh*, 838.
Tittle, *small quantity*, 32.
little, 192.
Tittle-tattle, *interlocution*, 588.
Tittup, *frisk*, 266, 274.
Titubation, *fall*, 306.
failure, 732.
Titular, *title*, 564.
Toad, *ugliness*, 846.
Toad-eater, *servile*, 886.
flatterer, 935.
Toady, *to flatter*, 933.
Toast, *roast*, 384.
celebrate, 883.

Tobacco, *tobacco*, 298A.
Tobacco-pipe, *pipe*, 351.
Toccata, *music*, 415.
Tocsin, *alarm*, 669.
indication, 550.
Toddle, *walk*, 266.
limp, 275.
Toe, *base*, 211.
Toff, *notability*, 642.
fop, 854.
Toffee, *sweet*, 396.
*Toga (L.), *dress*, 225.
Together, *added*, 37.
simultaneous, 120.
accompanying, 88.
Toil, *exertion*, 686.
activity, 682.
trap, 667.
Toilet, *dress*, 225.
Token, *sign*, 550.
Toledo, *arms*, 727.
Tolerable, *endurable*, 651.
Tolerant, *patient*, 826.
Tolerate, *endure*, 821.
permit, 760.
licence, 750.
lenity, 740.
laxity, 738.
Toll, *sound*, 407.
tax, 812.
Tollbooth, *mart*, 799.
prison, 752.
Tolling, *interment*, 363.
Tomahawk, *arms*, 727.
Tomb, *interment*, 363.
Tomboy, *vulgar*, 851.
Tome, *volume*, 593.
Tomfoolery, *absurdity*, 497.
ridiculous, 856.
amusement, 840.
Tommy, *soldier*, 726.
Tompion, *stopper*, 263.
Tom-tom, *drum*, 416.
*Ton (Fr.), *taste*, 852.
Tonality, *melody*, 413.
Tone, *state*, 7.
strength, 159.
melody, 413.
minstrelsy, 415.
colour, 428.
Tone-colour, *music*, 415.
Tone down, *modify*, 174, 469.
Tone-poem, *music*, 415.
Tongue, *language*, 560.
Tongueless, *dumb*, 581.
Tongue-tied, *dumb*, 581.
Tonic, *remedy*, 662, 656.
music, 413.
Tonnage, *size*, 192.
Tonsure, *canonicals*, 999.
Too, *addition*, 37.
Too much, *redundance*, 641.
Tool, *instrument*, 631, 633.
Toot, *sound*, 408.
Tooth, *projection*, 250.
notch, 257.
sharp, 253.
link, 45.
taste, 390.
Toothsome, *savoury*, 394.
agreeable, 829.
Top, *summit*, 210.
good, 648.
to surpass, 33.
Topaz, *yellow*, 436.
Toper, *drunkard*, 959.
Top-full, *full*, 639.
Top-hamper, *hindrance*, 706.
Top-heavy, *inverted*, 218.
dangerous, 665.
tipsy, 959.
unbalanced, 28.
Tophet, *hell*, 982.
Top-hole, *excellent*, 648.
Topic, *topic*, 454.
Topical, *situation*, 183.
apt, 23.
Topmast, *height*, 206.
Topmost, *great*, 33.
high, 210.
Topography, *situation*, 183.
Topping, *excellent*, 648.
Topple, *fall*, 306.
ruin, 659.
Topple over, *inversion*, 218.
Top-sawyer, *profficient*, 700.
Topsy-turvy, *upside down*, 218.
nonsensical, 497.
Toque, *hat*, 225.
Torah, *revelation*, 985.
Torch, *light*, 423.
Torchlight, *light*, 420.
Toreador, *combatant*, 726.
Torment, *physical*, 378.
moral, 828, 830.
Tornado, *violence*, 173.
wind, 349.
Torpedo, *weapon*, 727.
car, 272.
Torpedo-boat, *ship*, 273.
Torpid, *inert*, 172.
insensible, 823.
inactive, 683.
Torrefy, *burn*, 384.
Torrent, *flow*, 348.
violence, 173.
Torrid, *heat*, 382.
Torsion, *twist*, 311.

Torso, *part*, 51.
Tortoise, *slow*, 275.
Tortoiseshell, *variegation*, 440.
Tortuous, *twist*, 248.
dishonest, 939.
style, 571.
Torture, *physical*, 378.
moral, 828, 830.
Toss, *throw*, 284.
oscillate, 314.
agitate, 315.
derange, 61.
Toss-up, *chance*, 156, 621.
Toss-pot, *drunk*, 959.
Tot, *dram*, 298.
Tot up, *numeration*, 85.
Total, *whole*, 50.
Totem, *indication*, 550.
*Toto cœlo (L.), *contrariety*, 14.
difference, 15.
greatness, 31.
completeness, 52.
Totter, *limp*, 275.
oscillate, 314.
agitate, 315.
decay, 659.
Tottering, *dangerous*, 665.
imperfect, 651.
Touch, *tact*, 379.
contiguity, 199.
to relate to, 9.
music, 415.
mix, 41.
small quantity, 32, 39.
act, 680.
treat on, 595.
excite, 824.
pity, 914.
test, 463.
Touch-and-go, *uncertainty*, 485.
danger, 665.
Touch up, *improve*, 658.
Touched, *feeling*, 821.
Touching, *relation*, 9.
Touchstone, *evidence*, 467.
Touchwood, *fuel*, 388.
Touchy, *irascibility*, 901.
Tough, *strong*, 327.
difficult, 704.
Tour, *journey*, 266.
Tourist, *traveller*, 268.
Toupee, *wig*, 225.
Tournament, *combat*, 720.
Tourney, *combat*, 720.
Tourniquet, *stopper*, 263.
hindrance, 706.
Tournure, *outline*, 229.
appearance, 448.
beauty, 845.
Tousle, *derange*, 61.
Tousled, *disorder*, 59.
Tout, *solicit*, 765, 767.
*Tout ensemble (Fr.), *whole*, 50.
Touter, *eulogist*, 935.
solicitor, 767.
Tow, *pull*, 285.
Towards, *direction*, 278.
Tower, *height*, 206.
building, 189.
defence, 717.
to soar, 305.
Towering, *great*, 31.
passion, 900.
Town, *city*, 189.
fashion, 852.
Town-talk, *news*, 532.
Townsman, *inhabitant*, 188.
Toxic, *poisonous*, 657.
Toxicology, *poison*, 663.
Toxin, *poison*, 663.
Toy, *amusement*, 840.
trifle, 643.
*Tracasserie (Fr.), *discord*, 713.
Trace, *inquire*, 461.
discover, 480.
vestige, 551.
Trace to, *discover*, 155.
Tracery, *lattice*, 219.
ornament, 847.
Traces, *harness*, 45.
Trachea, *air-pipe*, 351.
Track, *way*, 627.
to trace, 461.
Trackless, *difficult*, 704.
space, 180.
Tract, *region*, 181.
dissertation, 595.
Tract of time, *time*, 109.
Tractable, *easy*, 705.
malleable, 324.
Tractile, *easy*, 705.
malleable, 324.
Traction, *drawing*, 285.
transmission, 270.
Trade, *business*, 625.
traffic, 794.
Trade-mark, *indication*, 550.
Trade-wind, *wind*, 349.
Trader, *merchant*, 797.
Tradition, *record*, 551.
description, 594.
Traduce, *detract*, 934.
Traffic, *barter*, 794.
Tragedy, *drama*, 599.
disaster, 830.
Tragelaph, *unconformity*, 83.
Tragic, *distressing*, 830.
Tragi-comic, *the drama*, 599.

Tragi-comedy, *ridicule*, 856.
Trail, *sequel*, 65.
pendent, 214.
slow, 275.
drag, 285.
odour, 398.
indication, 551.
to track, 461.
Train, *series*, 69.
sequel, 65.
appendix, 39.
traction, 285.
teach, 537.
accustom, 613.
drill, 673.
Train-bearer, *servant*, 746.
Trained, *skill*, 698.
Trait, *appearance*, 448.
lineament, 550.
Traitor, *knave*, 941.
disobedient, 742.
Trajectory, *path*, 627.
Tram, *vehicle*, 272.
Trammel, *fetter*, 752.
restrain, 751.
hinder, 706.
*Tramontana (It.), *wind*, 349.
Tramontane, *distant*, 196.
Tramp, *to stroll*, 266.
stroller, 268.
Trample, *violate*, 927.
bully, 885.
spurn, 930.
Tramway, *way*, 627.
Trance, *lethargy*, 823.
inactivity, 683.
Tranquil, *calm*, 174, 826.
peaceful, 721.
quiet, 265.
to pacify, 723.
Transact, *conduct*, 692.
traffic, 794.
Transaction, *event*, 151.
Transalpine, *distance*, 196.
Transcend, *go beyond*, 303.
Transcendent, *great*, 31, 33.
perfect, 650.
good, 648.
glorious, 873.
Transcendental, *recondite*, 519.
Transcribe, *write*, 590.
copy, 21.
Transcript, *write*, 590.
copy, 21.
Transcursion, *transcursion*, 303.
Transept, *of church*, 1000.
crossing, 219.
Transfer, *things*, 270.
property, 783.
Transfer, *remove*, 185.
Transfiguration, *change*, 140.
divine, 998.
Transfix, *perforate*, 260.
Transform, *change*, 140.
Transformation, *wig*, 225.
Transfuse, *transfer*, 270.
mix, 41.
translate, 522.
Transgress, *go beyond*, 303.
infringe, 773.
violate, 927.
sin, 947.
Tranship, *transfer*, 270.
Transient, *passing*, 111.
Transilient, *transcursion*, 303.
Transit, *passage*, 144.
motion, 264.
transference, 270.
Transition, *motion*, 264.
Transitive, *passing*, 111.
Transitory, *passing*, 111.
Translate, *interpret*, 522.
transfer, 270.
promote, 995.
Translucent, *transparent*, 425.
Transmigration, *change*, 140.
conversion, 144.
Transmission, *moving*, 270.
of property, 783.
passage, 302.
Transmogrify, *change*, 140.
Transmute, *change*, 140.
conversion, 144.
Transparent, *pellucid*, 425.
obvious, 518.
perspicuous, 570.
Transpicuous, *transparent*, 425.
Transpierce, *pierce*, 260.
Transpire, *appear*, 525.
disclose, 529.
Transplant, *displace*, 185.
Transpontine, *drama*, 599.
Transport, *transfer*, 185, 270.
ship, 273.
feeling, 821.
excitation, 824.
pleasure, 827, 829.
Transpose, *displace*, 185.
invert, 218.
transfer, 270.
exchange, 148.
Transubstantiation, *rite*, 998.
Transude, *ooze*, 295.
exude, 348.
Transverse, *oblique*, 217.
Trap, *snare*, 667.
Trap-door, *escape*, 671.
pitfall, 667.

Trappings, *clothes*, 39, 225.
ornament, 847.
property, 780.
Trash, *absurdity*, 497.
trifle, 643.
Travail, *work*, 686.
Travel, *journey*, 266.
Traveller, *traveller*, 268.
Traverse, *move*, 266.
pass, 302.
investigate, 461.
obstruct, 706.
Travesty, *copy*, 21.
to imitate, 19.
misinterpret, 523.
burlesque, 856.
Tray, *receptacle*, 191.
Treachery, *deceit*, 940.
Treacle, *sweet*, 396.
Tread, *journey*, 266.
Treadle, *instrument*, 633.
Treadmill, *punishment*, 975.
wearisome, 841.
Treason, *revolt*, 742.
treachery, 940.
Treasure, *money*, 800.
perfection, 650.
Treasurer, *treasurer*, 801.
Treasury, *treasury*, 802.
store, 636.
Treat, *manage*, 692.
bargain, 769.
amuse, 840.
please, 827.
Treatise, *book*, 595.
Treatment, *action*, 692.
remedy, 662.
Treaty, *agreement*, 769.
Treble, *number*, 93.
music, 413.
Tree, *plant*, 367.
execution, 975.
Trefoil, *three*, 92.
Trek, *journey*, 266.
Trellis, *cross*, 219.
Tremble, *agitate*, 315.
waver, 149.
with cold, 385.
with fear, 860.
with emotion, 821.
Tremendous, *great*, 31.
fearful, 860.
Tremolo, *quaver*, 407.
Tremor, *agitation*, 315.
feeling, 827.
fear, 860.
Tremulous, *see* Tremor.
Trench, *furrow*, 259.
defence, 717.
Trenchant, *keen*, 171.
sharp, 253.
style, 574.
Trench on, *nearness*, 197.
encroach, 303.
Trencher, *plate*, 191.
layer, 204.
Trend, *direction*, 278.
curve, 245.
tendency, 176.
Trepan, *deceive*, 545.
perforator, 262.
Trepidation, *agitation*, 315.
emotion, 821.
fear, 860.
Trespass, *go beyond*, 303.
sin, 947.
Tress, *hair*, 256.
Trestle, *support*, 215.
Trey, *number*, 92.
Triad, *number*, 92.
Trial, *experiment*, 463.
essay, 675.
difficulty, 704.
suffering, 828.
lawsuit, 969.
Triality, *number*, 92.
Triangle, *angularity*, 244.
musical instrument, 417.
Tribe, *class*, 75.
assemblage, 72.
Tribulation, *pain*, 828.
Tribunal, *tribunal*, 966.
Tribune, *officer*, 745.
Tributary, *giving*, 784.
Tribute, *donation*, 784.
reward, 973.
approbation, 931.
Trice, *instantaneous*, 113.
Trichotomy, *trisection*, 94.
Trick, *deception*, 545.
contrivance, 626.
speciality, 79.
to dress, 225.
adorn, 845.
Trickery, *artifice*, 702.
tinsel, 851.
Trickle, *ooze*, 295.
drip, 348.
Trickster, *deceiver*, 548.
thief, 792.
Tricksy, *sportive*, 840.
Tricolour, *variegation*, 440.
Trident, *ocean*, 341.
Tried, *employed*, 677.
trusty, 939.
Trifid, *number*, 94.
Trifle, *unimportant*, 642.
small, 32.

Trifle away, *idle*, 683.
Trifle with, *neglect*, 460.
disparage, 483.
Triform, *number*, 92.
Trigeminal, *triple*, 93.
Trigger, *instrument*, 633.
Trill, *sound*, 407.
resonance, 408.
music, 415.
Trim, *state*, 7.
form, 240.
dress, 225.
ornament, 845, 847.
to adjust, 27.
prepare, 673.
scold, 932.
change sides, 607.
Trimmer, *fickle*, 607.
apostate, 941.
Trimmings, *ornament*, 847.
Trinal, *number*, 92.
Trine, *triplication*, 93.
Trinity, *Deity*, 976.
Trinket, *ornament*, 847.
Trinomial, *triality*, 92.
triplication, 93.
Trio, *number*, 92.
Triolet, *poetry*, 597.
Trip, *jaunt*, 266.
to fall, 306.
hasten, 274.
mistake, 495.
fail, 945.
guilt, 947.
Trip up, *overthrow*, 731.
deceive, 545.
Tripartition, *trisection*, 94.
Triple, *triplication*, 93.
Triplet, *triality*, 92.
Triplicate, *triplication*, 93.
Tripod, *support*, 215.
Tripper, *traveller*, 268.
Tripping, *nimble*, 682.
failing, 495.
Triquetra, *triality*, 93.
Trireme, *ship*, 273.
Trisect, *tripartition*, 94.
Tristful, *dejected*, 837.
Trisulcate, *tripartition*, 94.
furrow, 259.
Trite, *old*, 82.
hackneyed, 496.
unimportant, 643.
Tritheism, *heterodoxy*, 984.
Triturate, *pulverulence*, 330.
Triumph, *success*, 731.
trophy, 733.
exult, 838.
boast, 884.
Triumph, *celebrate*, 883.
Triumphant, *elated*, 836.
Trivet, *support*, 215.
Trivial, *trifling*, 643.
useless, 645.
flimsy, 477.
smallness, 32.
Troglodyte, *seclusion*, 893.
Troll, *roll*, 312.
sing, 415.
fairy, 980.
Trolley, *vehicle*, 272.
Trollop, *libertine*, 962.
Trombone, *musical instrument*, 417.
Troop, *army*, 726.
assemblage, 72.
Trooper, *combatant*, 726.
Trope, *metaphor*, 521.
Trophy, *triumph*, 733.
record, 551.
Tropical, *heat*, 382.
metaphor, 520.
Tropology, *metaphor*, 520.
Trot, *run*, 266.
velocity, 274.
journey, 266.
Trot out, *manifestation*, 525.
Troth, *truth*, 494.
promise, 768.
belief, 484.
Trothless, *faithless*, 940.
false, 544.
Troubadour, *musician*, 416.
Trouble, *derange*, 61.
evil, 619, 649.
pain, 828.
painful, 830.
exertion, 686.
Troublesome, *difficulty*, 704.
Troublous, *disorder*, 59.
Trough, *conduit*, 250.
trench, 259.
hollow, 252.
Trounce, *censure*, 932.
punish, 972.
Trousers, *dress*, 225.
*Trousseau (Fr.), *dress*, 225.
Trow, *think*, 451.
believe, 484.
know, 490.
Trowel, *instrument*, 191.
Truant, *idle*, 683.
Truce, *pacification*, 723.
*Trucheman (Fr.), *interpreter*, 524.
Truck, *vehicle*, 272.
barter, 794.
Truckle to, *submission*, 725.
Truculent, *malevolence*, 907.
Trudge, *slowness*, 275.

True, *real*, 1.
veracious, 543.
good, 648.
positive, 516.
faithful, 772.
True love, *love*, 897.
Truepenny, *probity*, 939.
Truism, *absurdity*, 497.
Trull, *impurity*, 962.
Truly, *really*, 31.
assent, 488.
verily, 494, 543.
Trump, *good man*, 948.
Trump card, *device*, 626.
success, 731.
Trump up, *falsehood*, 544.
Trumpery, *unimportance*, 643.
Trumpet, *musical instrument*, 417.
to publish, 531.
war-cry, 722.
Trumpeter, *messenger*, 534.
Trumpet-tongued, *publication*, 531.
Truncate, *shorten*, 201.
subduct, 38.
Truncheon, *club*, 727.
staff of office, 747.
mace, 633.
Trundle, *roll*, 312.
propel, 284.
Trunk, *whole*, 50.
origin, 153.
paternity, 166.
box, 191.
Truss, *join*, 43.
support, 215.
packet, 72.
Trust, *credit*, 805.
belief, 484.
hope, 858.
Trustee, *consignee*, 758.
Trustless, *improbity*, 940.
Trustworthy, *probity*, 939.
certainty, 474.
Trusty, *probity*, 939.
Truth, *truth*, 494.
Truthful, *veracity*, 543.
Truthless, *falsehood*, 544.
Try, *experiment*, 463.
endeavour, 675.
use, 677.
annoy, 830.
T-square, *angularity*, 244.
Tub, *vessel*, 191.
to bathe, 337.
Tuba, *musical instrument*, 417.
Tubby, *corpulent*, 192.
Tub-thumper, *ranter*, 584.
Tube, *opening*, 260.
Tubercle, *convexity*, 250.
Tuberosity, *convexity*, 250.
Tubular, *opening*, 160.
Tuck, *fold*, 258.
dagger, 727.
Tuck in, *eat*, 296.
locate, 184.
Tuft, *rough*, 256.
collection, 72.
Tuft-hunter, *sycophant*, 886.
time-server, 943.
Tug, *pull*, 285.
effort, 686.
ship, 273.
Tuition, *teaching*, 537.
Tulip, *variegation*, 440.
Tumble, *fall*, 306.
derange, 61.
spoil, 659.
fail, 732.
agitate, 315.
Tumble-down, *deterioration*, 259.
Tumbler, *glass*, 191.
buffoon, 844.
Tumbrel, *vehicle*, 272.
Tumefaction, *expansion*, 194.
Tumid, *size*, 192.
bombastic, 549, 577.
Tumour, *convexity*, 250.
Tumult, *disorder*, 59.
violence, 173.
agitation, 315, 825.
resistance, 719.
revolt, 742.
emotion, 825.
Tumultuous, *disorder*, 59.
Tumulus, *interment*, 363.
Tun, *large*, 192.
drunkard, 959.
Tunable, *harmony*, 413.
Tundra, *space*, 180.
Tune, *music*, 415.
to prepare, 673.
Tune, out of, *irrelation*, 10.
disagreement, 24.
Tune, to the — of, *amount*, 25.
Tuneful, *harmony*, 413.
Tuneless, *discord*, 414.
Tunic, *cover*, 222.
dress, 225.
Tuning-fork, *musical*, 417.
Tunnage, *size*, 192.
Tunnel, *opening*, 260.
way, 627.
*Tu quoque (L.), *retaliation*, 718.
Turban, *dress*, 225.
Turbid, *opaque*, 416.
foul, 653.
Turbinate, *convolution*, 248.
Turbine, *navigation*, 267.

Turbine, *instrument*, 633.
Turbulence, *disorder*, 59.
violence, 173.
agitation, 315.
excitation, 825.
Tureen, *receptacle*, 191.
Turf, *plain*, 344.
Turgescent, *expanded*, 194.
exaggerated, 549.
redundant, 641.
Turgid, *size*, 192.
exaggerated, 549, 577.
redundant, 641.
Turmoil, *confusion*, 59.
agitation, 315.
violence, 173.
Turn, *state*, 7.
juncture, 134.
form, 240.
period of time, 138.
curvature, 245.
deviation, 279.
circuition, 311.
rotation, 312.
change, 140.
translate, 522.
purpose, 630.
bout, 680.
aptitude, 698.
emotion, 820.
nausea, 867.
Turn away, *diverge*, 291.
dismiss, 756.
Turncoat, *tergiversation*, 607.
knave, 941.
Turn down, *reject*, 610.
Turn off, *dismiss*, 756.
execute, 361.
Turn out, *happen*, 151.
eject, 297.
strike, 742.
equipage, 852.
Turn over, *invert*, 218.
reflect, 451.
Turn round, *rotation*, 312.
Turn tail, *regression*, 283, 287.
Turn the scale, *superiority*, 33.
Turn the tables, *contrariety*, 14.
Turn turtle, *inversion*, 218.
Turn up, *happen*, 151.
arrive, 292.
chance, 621.
Turnpike, *hindrance*, 706.
Turnpike road, *way*, 627.
Turns, *periodicity*, 138.
Turnstile, *hindrance*, 706.
Turpitude, *dishonour*, 940.
disgrace, 874.
Turret, *height*, 206.
Turtle-dove, *love*, 897.
Tush, *contempt*, 930.
Tusk, *sharpness*, 253.
Tussle, *contention*, 720.
Tutelage, *safety*, 664.
Tutelary, *safety*, 664.
Tutor, *teacher*, 540.
to teach, 537.
*Tutoyer (Fr.), *friendship*, 888.
Twaddle, *absurdity*, 497.
loquacity, 584.
Twain, *duplication*, 90.
Twang, *taste*, 390.
sound, 402, 410.
voice, 583.
Tweak, *squeeze*, 195, 203.
punish, 972.
Twelfth, *number*, 99.
Twelve, *number*, 98.
Twenty, *number*, 98.
Twice, *duplication*, 90.
Twiddle, *rotation*, 312.
Twig, *part*, 51.
to notice, 457.
comprehend, 518.
Twilight, *morning*, 125.
evening, 126.
grey, 432.
Twill, *fold*, 258.
Twilled, *crossing*, 219.
Twin, *duplicate*, 90.
accompaniment, 88.
similar, 17.
Twine, *thread*, 45.
intersect, 219.
convolution, 248.
cling, 46.
Twinge, *bodily pain*, 378.
mental, 828, 830.
Twinkle, *light*, 420.
Twinkling, *moment*, 113.
Twirl, *agitation*, 315.
convolution, 248.
turn, 311, 312.
Twist, *cord*, 45.
distort, 243.
obliquity, 217.
convolution, 248.
bend, 311.
imperfection, 651.
prejudice, 481.
Twit, *disapprove*, 932.
Twitch, *pull*, 285.
convulsion, 315.
pain, 378.
mental, 828.
Twitter, *agitation*, 315.
cry, 412.
music, 415.

Twitter, *emotion*, 821.
Two, *number*, 89.
Twofold, *number*, 91.
Twopenny, *paltry*, 643.
Tyke, *commonalty*, 876.
Tympanum, *hearing*, 418.
Tympany, *expansion*, 194.
Tynewald, *council*, 696.
Type, *pattern*, 22.
rule, 80.
indication, 550.
printing, 591.
Typewriting, *writing*, 590.
Typhoon, *violence*, 173.
Typical, *ordinary*, 82.
special, 79.
Typify, *indication*, 550.
Typography, *printing*, 591.
Tyranny, *severity*, 739.
authority, 737.
Tyrant, *master*, 745.
Tyro, *learner*, 541.

U

Uberty, *sufficiency*, 639.
Ubiety, *presence*, 186.
Ubiquitous, *space*, 80.
presence, 186.
Udder, *teat*, 250.
*Uebermensch (Ger.), *hero*, 948.
Ugly, *ugliness*, 846.
cantankerous, 895.
formidable, 860.
Ukase, *order*, 741.
law, 963.
Ulcer, *disease*, 655.
care, 830.
Ulema, *judge*, 967.
priest, 996.
Ullage, *deficiency*, 53.
Ulster, *coat*, 225.
Ulterior, *in space*, 196.
in time, 121.
Ultimate, *end*, 67.
Ultimogeniture, *descent*, 167.
Ultimatum, *conditions*, 770.
Ultra, *superiority*, 33.
greatness, 31.
extremist, 604.
Ultramarine, *blueness*, 438.
Ultramontane, *authority*, 737.
Ululation, *cry*, 412.
Ulysses, *cunning*, 702.
Umber, *brown*, 433.
Umbilical, *centrality*, 223.
Umbrage, *shade*, 424.
darkness, 421.
Umbrage, *offence*, 900.
grudge, 898.
Umbrella, *shelter*, 666.
Umpire, *judge*, 480, 967.
Unabashed, *bold*, 861.
haughty, 873, 878.
insolent, 885.
conceited, 880.
Unabated, *great*, 31.
Unable, *impotence*, 158.
Unacceptable, *painfulness*, 830.
Unaccommodating, *disagreeing*, 24.
uncivil, 895.
disobliging, 907.
Unaccompanied, *alone*, 87.
Unaccomplished, *incomplete*, 730.
Unaccountable, *obscure*, 519.
wonderful, 870.
arbitrary, 964.
irresponsible, 927.
Unaccustomed, *unused*, 614.
unskilled, 699.
unusual, 83.
Unachievable, *difficult*, 704.
impossible, 471.
Unacknowledged, *ignored*, 489.
unrequited, 917.
Unacquainted, *ignorant*, 491.
Unactuated, *unmoved*, 616.
Unadmonished, *unwarned*, 665.
Unadorned, *simple*, 849.
style, 575.
Unadulterated, *simple*, 42.
genuine, 494, 648.
Unadventurous, *quiet*, 864.
Unadvisable, *inexpedient*, 647.
Unadvised, *unwarned*, 665.
foolish, 699.
Unaffected, *callous*, 376.
genuine, 494.
sincere, 543.
simple, 849.
in good taste, 850.
Unafflicted, *serene*, 831.
Unaided, *weak*, 160.
unsupported, 708.
Unalarmed, *courage*, 861.
Unalienable, *dueness*, 924.
Unallayed, *strength*, 159.
Unallied, *irrelative*, 10.
Unallowable, *wrong*, 923.
Unalluring, *indifference*, 866.
Unalterable, *identical*, 13.
unchanged, 142.
unchangeable, 150.
Unamazed, *expectance*, 871.
Unambiguous, *intelligibility*, 518.
Unambitious, *indifference*, 866.
Unamiable, *ill-natured*, 907.

Unanimity, *accord*, 714.
assent, 488.
Unannexed, *disjoined*, 44.
Unannounced, *inexpectation*, 508.
Unanswerable, *demonstrative*, 478.
certain, 474.
irresponsible, 927.
arbitrary, 964.
Unappalled, *courage*, 861.
Unapparent, *invisible*, 447.
latent, 526.
Unappeasable, *violence*, 173.
Unapplied, *disuse*, 678.
Unapprehended, *unknown*, 491.
Unapprehensive, *courage*, 861.
Unapprised, *ignorance*, 491.
Unapproachable, *distant*, 196.
great, 31.
Unapproved, *disapprobation*, 932.
Unapt, *incongruous*, 24.
inexpedient, 647.
unskilful, 699.
Unarmed, *weak*, 158, 160.
Unarranged, *in disorder*, 59.
unprepared, 674.
Unarrayed, *simplicity*, 849.
Unascertained, *ignorance*, 491.
Unasked, *voluntary*, 602.
Unaspiring, *indifferent*, 866.
modest, 881.
Unassailable, *safety*, 664.
Unassailed, *freedom*, 748.
Unassembled, *non-assemblage*, 73.
Unassisted, *unaided*, 708.
Unassociated, *disjunction*, 44.
Unassuming, *modesty*, 881.
Unatoned, *impenitence*, 951.
Unattached, *disjunction*, 44.
Unattackable, *safety*, 664.
Unattainable, *difficult*, 704.
impossible, 471.
Unattained, *failure*, 732.
Unattempted, *avoidance*, 623.
Unattended, *alone*, 87.
Unattended to, *neglect*, 460.
Unattested, *counter-evidence*, 468.
unrecorded, 552.
Unattracted, *dissuasion*, 616.
Unattractive, *indifference*, 866.
Unauthentic, *uncertainty*, 475.
Unauthorised, *undue*, 738, 925.
wrong, 923.
lawless, 964.
unwarranted, 514.
Unavailing, *useless*, 645.
failure, 732.
Unavoidable, *necessary*, 601.
certain, 474.
Unavowed, *dissent*, 489.
Unawakened, *inactivity*, 683.
Unaware, *ignorant*, 491.
unexpecting, 508.
impulsive, 601.
Unawed, *courage*, 861.
Unbalanced, *inequality*, 28.
Unballasted, *mutable*, 149.
foolish, 499.
Unbar, *liberate*, 750.
Unbearable, *pain*, 830.
Unbeaten, *success*, 731.
Unbecoming, *undue*, 925.
disgraceful, 874, 940.
incongruous, 24.
Unbefitting, *undue*, 925.
disgraceful, 940.
incongruous, 24.
Unbefriended, *alone*, 708.
Unbegotten, *inexistence*, 2.
Unbeguile, *disclosure*, 529.
Unbegun, *unprepared*, 674.
Unbeheld, *invisibility*, 447.
Unbelief, *doubt*, 485.
infidelity, 988.
incredulity, 487.
Unbeloved, *hate*, 898.
Unbend, *straighten*, 246.
repose, 687.
the mind, 452.
Unbending, *hard*, 323.
resolute, 604.
Unbenighted, *instructed*, 490.
Unbeseeming, *base*, 940.
Unbesought, *willingness*, 602.
deprecation, 766.
Unbestowed, *receiving*, 785.
Unbewailed, *disapprobation*, 932.
Unbiased, *wise*, 498.
impartial, 480.
spontaneous, 602.
uninfluenced, 616.
Unbidden, *spontaneous*, 600.
disobedient, 742.
Unbigoted, *knowledge*, 490.
Unbind, *detach*, 44.
release, 750.
Unblameable, *innocence*, 946.
Unblemished, *innocence*, 946.
Unblenching, *courage*, 861.
Unblended, *unmixed*, 42.
Unblest, *unhappy*, 838.
unapproved, 932.
Unblown, *non-preparation*, 674.
Unblushing, *impudent*, 885.
proud, 878.
vain, 880.
Unboastful, *modest*, 881.
Unbodied, *immateriality*, 317.
Unbolt, *liberate*, 750.

Unbonnet, *divestment*, 226.
Unborn, *future*, 121.
not existing, 2.
Unborrowed, *lending*, 787.
Unbosom, *disclosure*, 529.
Unbound, *free*, 748.
exempt, 927.
Unbounded, *great*, 31.
large, 192.
infinite, 105.
space, 180.
Unbrace, *relax*, 655.
weaken, 160.
Unbreathed, *latent*, 526.
Unbribed, *disinterested*, 942.
Unbridled, *lax*, 738.
free, 748.
Unbroken, *entire*, 50.
continuous, 69.
unviolated, 939.
Unbruised, *whole*, 50.
Unbuckle, *disjunction*, 44.
Unbusinesslike, *inactivity*, 683.
Unbuttoned, *freedom*, 748.
Uncage, *liberation*, 750.
Uncalled for, *useless*, 645.
not used, 678.
Uncandid, *morose*, 907.
insincere, 544.
Uncanny, *strange*, 83.
wonderful, 870.
Uncared for, *indifferent*, 866.
disliked, 867.
hated, 898.
Uncase, *divestment*, 226.
Uncaught, *freedom*, 748.
Uncaused, *chance*, 156.
Unceasing, *perpetuity*, 112.
Uncensured, *approbation*, 931.
Unceremonious, *rude*, 895.
Uncertain, *uncertainty*, 475.
irregular, 139.
Unchain, *unfasten*, 44.
liberate, 750.
free, 748.
Unchangeable, *immutable*, 150.
firm, 604.
Unchanged, *permanent*, 142.
Uncharitable, *malevolent*, 907.
Uncharted, *unknown*, 491.
Unchartered, *unauthorised*, 925.
illegal, 964.
Unchaste, *impure*, 961.
Unchastised, *acquittal*, 970.
Unchecked, *freedom*, 748.
Unchristian, *irreligion*, 988.
Uncial, *writing*, 590.
Uncivil, *rude*, 895.
vulgar, 851.

Unclad, *naked*, 226.
Unclaimed, *freedom*, 748.
Unclasp, *loosen*, 44.
Unclassed, *disorder*, 59.
Unclassical, *vulgarity*, 851.
Unclassified, *disorder*, 59.
Uncle, *relative*, 11.
pawnbroker, 787.
Unclean, *uncleanness*, 653.
impurity, 961.
Unclinch, *disjunction*, 44.
Unclipped, *whole*, 50.
Unclog, *liberate*, 705, 750.
Unclose, *opening*, 260.
Unclothe, *divestment*, 226.
Unclouded, *light*, 420.
joyful, 827.
Uncoif, *divestment*, 226.
Uncoil, *straighten*, 246.
evolve, 313.
Uncollected, *non-assemblage*, 73.
Uncoloured, *achromatism*, 429.
Uncombed, *vulgarity*, 851.
Uncombined, *single*, 47.
Uncomeatable, *difficult*, 704.
Uncomely, *ugliness*, 846.
Uncomfortable, *annoyed*, 828.
annoying, 830.
Uncommendable, *bad*, 945.
blamable, 932.
Uncommon, *unconformity*, 83.
greatness, 31.
infrequency, 137.
Uncommunicative, *close*, 585.
concealing, 528.
Uncompact, *rarity*, 322.
Uncompelled, *voluntary*, 600.
free, 748.
Uncomplaisant, *discourtesy*, 895.
Uncomplying, *refusing*, 764.
disobedient, 742.
Uncompounded, *simpleness*, 42.
Uncompressed, *light*, 320.
rare, 322.
Uncompromising, *strict*, 82.
severe, 739.
resolved, 604.
Unconceived, *unmeaning*, 517.
unintelligible, 519.
Unconcern, *indifference*, 866.
Unconcocted, *non-preparation*, 674
Uncondemned, *acquittal*, 970.
Unconditional, *absolute*, 768A.
Unconfined, *freedom*, 748.
Unconfirmed, *uncertainty*, 475.
Unconformable, *irrelation*, 10.
disagreeing, 24.
Unconformity, *irrelation*, 10.
irregular, 83.

Unconfused, *clear*, 518.
methodical, 58.
Unconfuted, *true*, 494.
demonstrated, 478.
Uncongealed, *fluidity*, 333.
Uncongenial, *disagreeing*, 24.
insalubrious, 657.
Unconnected, *irrelative*, 10.
discontinuous, 70.
Unconquerable, *power*, 157.
Unconquered, *resistance*, 719.
Unconsenting, *refusing*, 764.
unwilling, 603.
Unconsidered, *incogitancy*, 452.
Unconscionable, *excessive*, 31.
unprincipled, 945.
Unconscious, *insensible*, 823.
ignorant, 491.
Unconsolidated, *single*, 47.
Unconsonant, *disagreement*, 24.
Unconstitutional, *lawful*, 925.
Unconstrained, *free*, 748.
willing, 600.
unceremonious, 880.
Unconsumed, *remaining*, 40.
Uncontested, *certainty*, 474.
Uncontradicted, *true*, 488.
Uncontrollable, *violent*, 173.
emotion, 825.
Uncontrolled, *unrestrained*, 748.
Uncontroverted, *agreed*, 488.
Unconventional, *unconformity*, 83.
unhackneyed, 614.
Unconversant, *ignorant*, 491.
unskilled, 699.
Unconverted, *dissent*, 489.
Unconvinced, *dissent*, 489.
Uncopied, *non-imitation*, 20.
Uncork, *liberation*, 750.
Uncorrected, *imperfection*, 651.
Uncorrupted, *disinterested*, 942.
innocent, 946.
Uncorruptible, *probity*, 939.
Uncouple, *disjunction*, 44.
Uncourteous, *rude*, 895.
Uncourtly, *rude*, 895.
Uncouth, *ugly*, 846.
ridiculous, 853.
style, 579.
rude, 851.
Uncovenanted, *unsecured*, 768A.
Uncover, *open*, 260.
denude, 226.
disclose, 529.
bow, 894.
Uncreated, *inexistence*, 2.
Uncropped, *whole*, 50.
Uncrown, *abrogation*, 756.
Unction, *emotion*, 824.
Unction, *piety*, 987.
extreme, *rite*, 998.
Unctuous, *oily*, 355.
flattering, 933.
Unculled, *untouched*, 678.
relinquished, 782.
Uncultivated, *ignorant*, 491.
unprepared, 674.
Uncultured, *ignorant*, 491.
Uncurbed, *freedom*, 748.
Uncurl, *straightness*, 246.
Uncut, *whole*, 50.
Undamaged, *goodness*, 648.
Undamped, *dryness*, 340.
Undated, *waving*, 248.
time, 115.
Undaunted, *courage*, 861.
Undazzled, *wisdom*, 498.
Undebauched, *innocence*, 946.
Undecayed, *goodness*, 648.
Undeceive, *inform*, 527, 529.
Undeceived, *knowledge*, 490.
Undecided, *in question*, 461.
uncertain, 475.
irresolute, 605.
Undecipherable, *unintelligible*, 519.
Undecked, *simplicity*, 849.
Undecomposed, *simpleness*, 42.
Undefaced, *beauty*, 845.
Undefended, *submission*, 725.
Undefiled, *innocence*, 946.
Undefinable, *unmeaning*, 517.
obscure, 519.
uncertain, 475.
Undefined, *see* Undefinable.
Undemolished, *entire*, 50.
good, 648.
Undemonstrative, *modesty*, 881.
Undeniable, *certainty*, 474.
Undeplored, *hate*, 898.
Undepraved, *innocence*, 946.
Undeprived, *retention*, 781.
Under, *below*, 207.
less, 34.
Under-breath, *faintness*, 405.
Underbred, *rude*, 851.
Undercurrent, *stream*, 347.
latency, 526.
Underestimate, *depreciation*, 483.
Undergo, *feeling*, 821.
Undergraduate, *learner*, 541.
Underground, *low*, 207.
deep, 208.
Underhand, *concealment*, 528.
false, 544.
base, 940.
Underline, *mark*, 550.
emphatic, 642.
Underling, *servant*, 746.

Underlying, *lowness*, 207.
Undermanned, *insufficiency*, 640.
Undermine, *burrow*, 252.
counteract, 706.
damage, 659.
Undermost, *base*, 211.
Underneath, *lowness*, 207.
Underpin, *support*, 215.
Underplot, *plan*, 626.
Underprize, *underestimate*, 483.
Underprop, *support*, 215.
Underquote, *bargain*, 794.
Underrate, *depreciation*, 483.
Under-reckon, *depreciation*, 483.
Undersell, *sale*, 796.
Undersized, *littleness*, 193.
Understaffed, *insufficiency*, 640.
Understand, *know*, 490.
meaning, 516.
intelligible, 518.
Understanding, *intellect*, 450.
agreement, 714.
Understatement, *falsehood*, 544.
Understood, *implied*, 516.
metaphorical, 521.
Understrapper, *servant*, 746.
Understudy, *deputy*, 159.
Undertake, *promise*, 768.
pursue, 622.
endeavour, 676.
Undertaking, *enterprise*, 676.
business, 625.
Undertone, *faintness*, 405.
Undervalue, *depreciation*, 483.
Underwear, *dress*, 225.
Underworld, *commonalty*, 876.
Underwood, *plant*, 367.
Underwrite, *insure*, 769.
Undescribed, *unconformity*, 83.
Undescried, *invisible*, 447.
Undeserved, *undueness*, 925.
Undesigned, *necessity*, 601.
chance, 621.
Undesigning, *artlessness*, 703.
Undesirable, *unpleasant*, 830.
unattractive, 866.
Undesirous, *indifference*, 866.
Undespairing, *hope*, 858.
Undestroyed, *whole*, 50.
persisting, 142.
existing, 1.
Undetermined, *irresolute*, 605.
untried, 461.
obscure, 519.
chance, 156.
Undeterred, *resolute*, 604.
Undeveloped, *latent*, 526.
Undeviating, *progressing*, 282.
straight, 246.
Undeviating, *mid-course*, 628.
unchanged, 150.
Undevout, *irreligion*, 988.
Undigested, *unarranged*, 59.
crude, 674.
Undiluted, *strength*, 159.
Undiminished, *whole*, 50.
great, 31.
increase, 35.
Undine, *sprite*, 980.
Undirected, *deviating*, 279.
casual, 621.
Undiscerned, *invisibility*, 447.
Undiscerning, *blind*, 442.
stupid, 499.
Undisciplined, *unskilfulness*, 699.
Undisclosed, *concealment*, 528.
Undiscoverable, *concealment*, 528.
Undisguised, *explicit*, 516.
sincere, 543.
true, 494.
Undismayed, *courage*, 861.
Undispersed, *assemblage*, 72.
Undisposed of, *disuse*, 678.
retention, 781.
Undisputed, *certainty*, 474.
Undissolved, *entire*, 50.
dense, 321.
Undistinguished, *indiscrimination*, 465A.
Undistorted, *straight*, 246.
true, 494.
Undistracted, *attention*, 457.
Undisturbed, *quiet*, 265, 685.
calm, 826.
orderly, 58.
Undiverted, *resolution*, 604.
Undivided, *whole*, 50.
Undivulged, *concealment*, 528.
Undo, *untie*, 44.
do away with, 681.
counteract, 706.
reverse, 145.
Undoing, *ruin*, 735, 830.
Undone, *non-assemblage*, 73.
incomplete, 730.
foiled, 732.
hapless, 828.
Undoubted, *certainty*, 474.
Undraped, *nudity*, 226.
Undreaded, *courage*, 861.
Undreamed, *incogitancy*, 452.
Undress, *nudity*, 226.
morning dress, 225.
Undressed, *unprepared*, 674.
unadorned, 849.
Undrilled, *unprepared*, 674.
unaccustomed, 699.
Undriven, *willing*, 602.

Undrooping, *activity*, 682.
Undue, *wrong*, 923, 925.
Undulate, *oscillate*, 314.
wave, 248.
Undutiful, *vice*, 945.
Undyed, *achromatism*, 429.
Undying, *perpetual*, 112.
immutable, 150.
Unearth, *manifestation*, 525.
Unearthly, *immaterial*, 317.
heavenly, 981.
pious, 987.
Uneasy, *pain*, 828.
Uneatable, *unsavoury*, 395.
Unedifying, *misteaching*, 538.
Uneducated, *ignorant*, 491.
unprepared, 674.
unskilful, 699.
Unembarrassed, *manners*, 852.
Unemployed, *inactive*, 683.
not used, 678.
Unencumbered, *easy*, 705.
exempt, 927.
Unending, *infinite*, 105.
long, 200.
Unendowed, *impotence*, 158.
Unendurable, *painfulness*, 830.
Unenjoyed, *weary*, 841.
Unenlightened, *dark*, 421.
ignorant, 491.
foolish, 499.
Unenslaved, *free*, 748.
Unenterprising, *caution*, 864.
Unentertaining, *dullness*, 843.
Unentitled, *undueness*, 925.
Unequal, *inequality*, 28.
unable, 158.
unjust, 923.
Unequalled, *superior*, 33.
Unequipped, *non-preparation*, 674.
Unequivocal, *sure*, 474.
clear, 518.
Unequivocally, *sure*, 31.
Unerring, *certain*, 474.
true, 494.
innocent, 946.
Unespied, *invisible*, 447.
hidden, 526.
Unessayed, *disuse*, 678.
Unessential, *unimportance*, 643.
Uneven, *rough*, 256.
unequal, 28.
irregular, 83.
Unexaggerated, *truth*, 494.
Unexamined, *neglect*, 460.
Unexampled, *unconformity*, 83.
Unexceptionable, *good*, 648.
legitimate, 924.
innocent, 946.
Unexcited, *inexcitability*, 826.
Unexecuted, *non-completion*, 730.
Unexempt, *liability*, 177.
Unexercised, *unused*, 678.
unprepared, 674.
unskilled, 699.
Unexerted, *inertness*, 172.
Unexhausted, *vigorous*, 159.
abundant, 639.
Unexpanded, *contraction*, 195.
Unexpected, *unlooked for*, 508.
sudden, 132.
wonderful, 870.
Unexpensive, *cheapness*, 815.
Unexplained, *latent*, 526.
unknown, 491.
Unexplored, *latent*, 526.
unknown, 491.
Unexposed, *latent*, 526.
Unexpressed, *latent*, 526.
Unextended, *immateriality*, 317.
Unextinguished, *violent*, 172.
burning, 382.
Unfaded, *colour*, 428.
fresh, 648.
Unfading, *perpetuity*, 112.
Unfailing, *constant*, 142.
Unfair, *unjust*, 923.
dishonourable, 940.
false, 544.
Unfaithful, *faithless*, 940.
Unfaltering, *resolution*, 604.
Unfamiliar, *unconformity*, 83.
Unfashionable, *vulgarity*, 851.
Unfashioned, *formless*, 241.
unwrought, 674.
Unfasten, *disjunction*, 44.
Unfathomable, *deep*, 208.
infinite, 105.
Unfavourable, *obstructive*, 708.
out of season, 135.
Unfearing, *courage*, 861.
Unfeasible, *impracticable*, 471.
Unfed, *fasting*, 956.
deficient, 640.
Unfeeling, *insensibility*, 823.
Unfeigned, *veracity*, 543.
Unfelt, *insensibility*, 823.
Unfeminine, *vulgarity*, 851.
Unfertile, *unproductive*, 169.
Unfetter, *unfasten*, 44.
release, 750.
Unfettered, *spontaneous*, 600.
Unfinished, *non-completion*, 730.
Unfit, *inappropriate*, 24.
inexpedient, 647.
Unfix, *disjoin*, 44.
Unfixed, *irresolute*, 605.
mutable, 149.

Unflagging, *activity*, 682.
Unflattering, *sincere*, 543.
Unfledged, *unprepared*, 674.
young, 129.
Unflinching, *resolute*, 604.
bravery, 861.
persevering, 682.
Unfoiled, *success*, 731.
Unfold, *evolve*, 313.
straighten, 246.
disclose, 529.
interpret, 522.
Unforbidden, *permission*, 760.
Unforced, *free*, 748.
willing, 602.
Unforeseen, *unexpected*, 508.
surprising, 870.
Unforfeited, *retention*, 781.
Unforgettable, *importance*, 642.
Unforgivable, *vice*, 945.
Unforgiving, *revenge*, 919.
Unforgotten, *memory*, 505.
Unformed, *non-preparation*, 674.
Unfortified, *weakness*, 160.
Unfortunate, *failure*, 732.
adversity, 735.
unhappy, 828.
untimely, 135.
Unfounded, *falsehood*, 544.
Unfrequent, *seldom*, 137.
Unfrequented, *seclusion*, 893.
Unfriended, *weak*, 160.
enmity, 889.
Unfriendly, *enmity*, 889.
malevolent, 907.
Unfrock, *disqualify*, 925.
Unfruitful, *unproductiveness*, 169.
Unfulfilled, *non-observance*, 773, 925.
Unfurl, *evolution*, 213.
Unfurnished, *unprepared*, 674.
insufficient, 640.
Ungainly, *ugly*, 846.
rude, 895.
Ungarnished, *unadorned*, 849.
Ungathered, *disuse*, 678.
Ungenerous, *stingy*, 819.
selfish, 943.
Ungenial, *insalubrious*, 657.
uncivil, 895.
Ungenteel, *vulgar*, 851.
rude, 895.
Ungentle, *rude*, 895.
violent, 173.
Ungentlemanly, *vulgar*, 851.
rude, 895.
dishonourable, 940.
Ungird, *disjunction*, 44.
Unglue, *disjunction*, 44.
incoherence, 47.
Ungodly, *irreligion*, 988.
Ungovernable, *violent*, 173.
passion, 825.
Ungoverned, *freedom*, 748.
Ungraceful, *ugly*, 846.
vulgar, 851.
Ungracious, *uncivil*, 895.
unfriendly, 907.
Ungrammatical, *solecism*, 568.
Ungrateful, *ingratitude*, 917.
Ungratified, *pain*, 828.
Ungrounded, *error*, 495.
Ungrudging, *liberality*, 816.
Unguarded, *neglected*, 460.
dangerous, 665.
spontaneous, 612.
Unguent, *oil*, 356.
Unguided, *ignorant*, 491.
unskilful, 699.
Unhackneyed, *desuetude*, 614.
Unhallowed, *irreligion*, 988.
profane, 989.
Unhand, *liberation*, 750.
Unhandsome, *ugly*, 940.
Unhandy, *unskilfulness*, 699.
Unhappy, *pain*, 828.
Unhardened, *tender*, 914.
penitent, 950.
innocent, 946.
Unharmed, *safety*, 664.
Unharness, *disjoin*, 44.
liberate, 750.
Unhatched, *non-preparation*, 674.
Unhazarded, *safety*, 664.
Unhealthy, *ill*, 655.
unwholesome, 657.
Unheard of, *ignorant*, 491.
exceptional, 83.
impossible, 471.
wonderful, 870.
Unheeded, *neglected*, 460.
Unhelped, *unaided*, 708.
Unheralded, *inexpectation*, 507.
Unheroic, *cowardly*, 862.
Unhesitating, *resolution*, 604.
Unhewn, *formless*, 241.
unprepared, 674.
Unhindered, *free*, 748.
Unhinge, *weaken*, 169.
derange, 61.
Unhinged, *unsettled*, 605.
insane, 503.
Unholy, *evil*, 988.
Unhonoured, *disrespect*, 874.
Unhook, *disjoin*, 44.
Unhoped, *unexpected*, 508.
Unhouse, *displace*, 185.
Unhurt, *uninjured*, 670.
Unicorn, *monster*, 83.

Unicorn, *prodigy*, 872.
Unideal, *true*, 494.
existing, 1.
Uniform, *homogeneous*, 16.
simple, 42.
orderly, 58.
regular, 82.
symmetrical, 242.
livery, 225.
uniformity, 23.
Unify, *combine*, 48.
make one, 87.
Unilluminated, *dark*, 421.
ignorant, 491.
Unimaginable, *inconceivable*, 519.
Unimaginative, *dull*, 843.
Unimagined, *truth*, 494.
Unimitated, *original*, 20.
Unimpaired, *preserved*, 670.
sound, 648.
Unimpassioned, *inexcitable*, 826.
Unimpeachable, *innocent*, 946.
irrefutable, 478.
perfect, 650.
Unimpeded, *facility*, 705.
Unimpelled, *uninduced*, 616.
Unimportant, *insignificant*, 643.
Unimpressionable, *insensible*, 823.
Unimproved, *deterioration*, 659.
Uninfluenced, *unbiased*, 616.
obstinate, 606.
Uninfluential, *inert*, 172.
Uninformed, *ignorance*, 491.
Uninhabited, *empty*, 187.
Uninitiated, *unschooled*, 699.
Uninjured, *good*, 648.
preserved, 670.
healthy, 644.
Uninspired, *unexcited*, 823.
unactuated, 616.
Uninstructed, *ignorant*, 491.
Unintellectual, *ignorant*, 452.
imbecile, 499.
Unintelligent, *foolish*, 499.
Unintelligible, *difficult*, 519.
style, 571.
Unintentional, *change*, 621.
Uninterested, *incurious*, 456.
inattentive, 458.
indifferent, 823.
weary, 841.
Uninteresting, *wearisome*, 841.
Unintermitting, *unbroken*, 69.
durable, 110.
continuing, 143.
active, 682.
Uninterrupted, *continuous*, 69.
unremitting, 143.
Uninventive, *dull*, 843.
Uninvestigated, *unknown*, 491.
Uninvited, *exclusion*, 893.
Uninviting, *unattractive*, 866.
unpleasant, 830.
Union, *junction*, 43.
combination, 48.
concord, 23, 714.
concurrence, 178.
marriage, 903.
Unique, *special*, 79.
alone, 87.
exceptional, 83.
dissimilarity, 18.
non-imitation, 20.
Unison, *agreement*, 23.
concord, 714.
uniformity, 16.
melody, 413.
Unisonant, *harmony*, 413.
Unit, *number*, 87.
Unitarian, *heterodoxy*, 984.
Unite, *join*, 43.
agree, 23.
concur, 178.
assemble, 72.
converge, 290.
league, 712.
Unity, *singleness*, 87.
integrity, 50.
concord, 714.
Universal, *general*, 78.
Universe, *world*, 318.
University, *school*, 542.
Unjust, *wrong*, 923.
Unjustified, *undue*, 925.
Unkempt, *careless*, 653.
slovenly, 851.
Unkennel, *turn out*, 185.
disclose, 529.
Unkind, *malevolent*, 907.
Unknit, *disjoin*, 44.
Unknowable, *concealment*, 528.
Unknown, *ignorant*, 491.
latent, 526.
to fame, 874.
Unlaboured, *unprepared*, 674.
style, 578.
Unlace, *disjoin*, 44.
Unlade, *ejection*, 297.
Unladylike, *vulgar*, 851.
rude, 895.
Unlamented, *disliked*, 898.
unapproved, 932.
Unlatch, *disjoin*, 44.
Unlawful, *undue*, 925.
illegal, 964.
Unlearn, *forget*, 506.
Unlearned, *ignorant*, 491.
Unleavened, *non-preparation*, 674.

Unless, *circumstances*, 8.
qualification, 469.
condition, 770.
Unlettered, *ignorant*, 491.
Unlicensed, *unpermitted*, 761.
Unlicked, *clownish*, 876.
vulgar, 851.
unprepared, 674.
Unlike, *dissimilar*, 18.
Unlikely, *improbable*, 473.
Unlimited, *infinite*, 105.
space, 180.
great, 31.
Unlink, *disjoin*, 44.
Unliquefied, *solid*, 321.
Unlit, *darkness*, 421.
Unload, *unpack*, 297.
disencumber, 705.
transfer, 270.
Unlock, *unfasten*, 44.
explain, 462.
Unlooked for, *unexpected*, 508.
Unloose, *unfasten*, 44.
liberate, 750.
Unloved, *hate*, 898.
Unlucky, *inopportune*, 135.
failing, 732.
unfortunate, 735.
luckless, 828.
painful, 830.
bad, 649.
Unmaidenly, *ill-mannered*, 851.
Unmaimed, *uninjured*, 654.
Unmake, *reversion*, 145.
Unmanageable, *perverse*, 704.
unwieldy, 647.
Unmanly, *improbity*, 940.
Unmanned, *weak*, 160.
sad, 837.
Unmannerly, *rude*, 895.
Unmarked, *neglect*, 460.
Unmarred, *sound*, 654.
preserved, 670.
Unmarried, *celibacy*, 904.
Unmask, *show*, 525.
disclose, 529.
Unmatched, *different*, 15.
unparalleled, 20.
dissimilar, 18.
Unmeaning, *nonsense*, 517.
Unmeasured, *abundant*, 639.
infinite, 105.
undistinguished, 465A.
casual, 621.
Unmeet, *undue*, 925.
Unmelodious, *discord*, 414.
Unmelted, *density*, 321.
Unmentionable, *unseemly*, 961.
Unmentioned, *latency*, 526.
Unmerciful, *malevolence*, 907.
Unmerited, *undueness*, 925.
Unmethodical, *disorder*, 59.
Unmindful, *inattention*, 458.
neglect, 460.
ungrateful, 917.
Unmingled, *simpleness*, 42.
Unmirthful, *dejection*, 837.
Unmissed, *neglect*, 460.
Unmistakable, *clear*, 518.
visible, 446.
Unmitigated, *greatness*, 31.
Unmixed, *simpleness*, 42.
Unmodified, *permanence*, 142.
Unmolested, *content*, 831.
safe, 664.
Unmoral, *vice*, 945.
Unmourned, *hate*, 898.
Unmoved, *quiescent*, 265.
resolute, 604.
obstinate, 606.
torpid, 823.
uninduced, 616.
Unmusical, *discord*, 414.
Unmuzzled, *freedom*, 748.
Unnamed, *misnomer*, 565.
Unnatural, *unconformity*, 83.
Unnecessary, *inutility*, 645.
Unneeded, *inutility*, 645.
Unneighbourly, *unsociable*, 893.
Unnerved, *impotence*, 158.
weakness, 160.
Unnoted, *neglected*, 460.
ignoble, 874.
Unnoticed, *neglected*, 460.
ignoble, 874.
Unnumbered, *infinity*, 105.
Unobjectionable, *goodness*, 648.
Unobscured, *vision*, 420.
Unobservant, *inattention*, 458.
Unobserved, *unseen*, 460.
Unobstructed, *unopposed*, 709.
free, 748.
clear, 705.
Unobtainable, *impossibility*, 471.
Unobtained, *loss*, 776.
Unobtrusive, *modesty*, 881.
Unoccupied, *vacant*, 187.
unthinking, 452.
inactive, 683.
Unoffending, *innocuous*, 648.
innocent, 946.
Unofficial, *unauthorised*, 925.
Unopened, *closure*, 261.
Unopposed, *co-operation*, 709.
Unorganised, *mineral*, 358.
unprepared, 674.
Unornamental, *ugly*, 846.
Unornamented, *simple*, 849.

Unornamented, *style*, 576.
Unorthodox, *heterodox*, 984.
Unostentatious, *modesty*, 881.
Unpacified, *discord*, 713.
Unpack, *ejection*, 297.
Unpaid, *debt*, 806.
Unpaid for, *credit*, 805.
Unpalatable, *unsavoury*, 395.
disagreeable, 830, 867.
Unparagoned, *perfection*, 650.
Unparalleled, *great*, 31.
superiority, 33.
exceptional, 83.
unmatched, 20.
Unpardonable, *vice*, 945.
Unpatriotic, *selfish*, 911.
Unpeaceful, *warfare*, 722.
Unpeople, *displacement*, 185.
Unperceived, *latent*, 526.
neglected, 460.
unknown, 491.
Unperformed, *non-completion*, 730.
Unperjured, *probity*, 939.
Unperplexed, *wisdom*, 498.
Unpersuadable, *obstinacy*, 606.
dissuasion, 616.
Unperturbed, *impassive*, 823.
Unphilosophical, *folly*, 499.
Unpick, *disjunction*, 44.
Unpierced, *closure*, 261.
Unpin, *disjunction*, 44.
Unpitying, *ruthless*, 907.
angry, 900.
Unplagued, *content*, 831.
Unplayable, *difficult*, 704.
Unpleasant, *pain*, 830.
Unplumbed, *deep*, 208.
Unpoetical, *prose*, 598.
Unpolished, *rude*, 895.
vulgar, 851.
Unpolluted, *goodness*, 648.
Unpopular, *disliked*, 830.
Unpossessed, *loss*, 776.
Unpractical, *inactivity*, 683.
Unpractised, *unskilfulness*, 699.
disuse, 614.
Unprecedented, *unconformity*, 83.
Unprejudiced, *judicious*, 480.
wise, 498.
Unpremeditated, *impulsive*, 612.
unprepared, 674.
Unprepared, *non-preparation*, 674.
Unprepossessed, *wisdom*, 498.
Unprepossessing, *unpleasing*, 829.
Unpresentable, *vulgarity*, 851.
Unpretending, *modesty*, 881.
Unprincipled, *vice*, 945.
Unprivileged, *undueness*, 925.
Unproclaimed, *latency*, 526.
Unprocurable, *impossibility*, 471.
Unproductive, *barren*, 169.
useless, 645.
Unprofessional, *non-observance*, 614.
Unprofitable, *useless*, 645.
inexpedient, 647.
bad, 649.
unproductive, 169.
Unprolific, *barren*, 169.
Unpromising, *hopeless*, 859.
Unprompted, *impulse*, 612.
Unpromulgated, *latent*, 526.
Unpronounced, *latent*, 526.
Unpropitious, *hopeless*, 859.
inauspicious, 135.
Unproportioned, *disagreement*, 24.
Unprosperous, *adversity*, 735.
Unprotected, *danger*, 665.
Unproved, *sophistry*, 477.
Unprovided, *scanty*, 640.
unprepared, 674.
Unprovoked, *uninduced*, 616.
Unpublished, *latency*, 526.
Unpunctual, *tardy*, 133.
untimely, 135.
irregular, 139.
Unpunished, *exempt*, 960.
Unpurified, *uncleanness*, 653.
Unpurposed, *chance*, 621.
Uupursued, *relinquishment*, 624.
Unqualified, *inexpert*, 699.
unentitled, 925.
unprepared, 674.
Unquelled, *violence*, 173.
Unquenched, *violence*, 173.
burning, 382.
Unquestionable, *certainty*, 474.
Unquestioned, *certainty*, 474.
assent, 488.
Unquiet, *excitement*, 825.
Unravaged, *undamaged*, 648.
Unravel, *untie*, 44.
straighten, 246.
decompose, 49.
solve, 462.
interpret, 522.
disembarrass, 705.
arrange, 60.
Unravelled, *arranged*, 58.
Unreachable, *distance*, 196.
Unreached, *shortcoming*, 304.
Unread, *ignorance*, 491.
Unready, *non-preparation*, 674.
incompleteness, 53.
Unreal, *non-existing*, 2.
erroneous, 495.
imaginary, 515.
Unreasonable, *foolish*, 499.
exorbitant, 814.

Unreasonable, *unjust*, 923.
impossible, 471.
erroneous, 495.
Unreclaimed, *impenitence*, 951.
Unreconciled, *discord*, 713.
Unrecorded, *obliteration*, 552.
Unrecounted, *exclusion*, 55.
Unrecovered, *deterioration*, 659.
Unrectified, *imperfection*, 651.
Unredeemed, *greatness*, 31.
Unreduced, *greatness*, 31.
Unrefined, *vulgarity*, 851.
Unreflecting, *impulse*, 612.
Unreformed, *impenitence*, 951.
Unrefreshed, *fatigue*, 688.
Unrefuted, *demonstrated*, 478.
true, 494.
Unregarded, *neglected*, 460.
unrespected, 929.
Unregistered, *unrecorded*, 552.
Unrehearsed, *impulse*, 612.
Unrelated, *irrelation*, 10.
Unrelaxed, *unweakened*, 159.
Unrelenting, *malevolent*, 907.
revengeful, 919.
Unreliable, *dubious*, 485.
untrustworthy, 940.
Unrelieved, *aggravation*, 835.
Unremarked, *neglected*, 460.
Unremembered, *forgotten*, 506.
Unremitting, *continuing*, 110.
industrious, 682.
Unremoved, *location*, 184.
Unremunerative, *inutility*, 645.
Unrenewed, *unchanged*, 142.
Unrepealed, *unchanged*, 142.
Unrepeated, *fewness*, 103.
unity, 87.
Unrepentant, *impenitent*, 951.
Unrepining, *patient*, 831.
Unreplenished, *insufficient*, 640.
Unreported, *untold*, 526.
Unrepressed, *violent*, 173.
Unreproached, *innocence*, 946.
Unreproachful, *forgiveness*, 918.
Unreproved, *innocence*, 946.
Unrequited, *owing*, 806.
ingratitude, 917.
Unresented, *forgiven*, 918.
Unresenting, *enduring*, 826.
Unreserved, *frank*, 543.
Unresisting, *obedience*, 743.
Unresolved, *irresolute*, 605.
Unrespected, *disrespect*, 929.
Unresponsive, *insensibility*, 823.
Unrest, *moving*, 264.
change, 140.
changeable, 149.
Unrestored, *deterioration*, 659.
Unrestrained, *free*, 748.
unencumbered, 705.
Unrestricted, *undiminished*, 31.
free, 748.
Unretracted, *affirmation*, 535.
Unrevealed, *concealed*, 528.
Unrevenged, *jealousy*, 920.
Unreserved, *permanence*, 142.
continuance, 143.
Unrevoked, *continuance*, 143.
Unrewarded, *debt*, 806.
ingratitude, 917.
Unriddle, *solve*, 462.
interpret, 522.
disclose, 529.
Unrighteous, *evil*, 945.
Unrip, *uncover*, 260.
Unripe, *unprepared*, 674.
Unrivalled, *goodness*, 648.
Unrivet, *disjoin*, 44.
Unrobe, *divest*, 226.
Unroll, *straighten*, 246.
evolve, 313.
display, 525.
unravel, 47.
Unromantic, *true*, 494.
Unroof, *divest*, 226.
Unroot, *pull up*, 162.
Unruffled, *calm*, 174.
placid, 826.
unaffected, 823.
quiet, 265.
orderly, 58.
Unruly, *disobedient*, 742.
obstinate, 606.
Unsafe, *dangerous*, 665.
Unsaid, *unspoken*, 581.
Unsanctified, *unholy*, 988, 989.
Unsanitary, *insalubrious*, 657.
Unsanctioned, *undue*, 925.
Unsated, *desire*, 865.
Unsatisfactory, *discontent*, 832.
displeasing, 830.
Unsatisfied, *discontent*, 832.
Unsavoury, *unsavouriness*, 395.
Unsay, *retract*, 607.
Unscanned, *neglected*, 460.
Unscathed, *health*, 654.
Unschooled, *illiterate*, 491.
uneducated, 699.
Unscientific, *ignorant*, 495.
unskilled, 699.
Unscoured, *unclean*, 653.
Unscreened, *danger*, 665.
Unscrew, *disjoin*, 44.
Unscriptural, *heterodoxy*, 984.
Unscrupulous, *evil*, 940.
Unseal, *disclosure*, 529.
Unseam, *disjoin*, 44.

Unsearched, *neglect*, 460.
Unseasonable, *intempestivity*, 135.
inexpedient, 647.
inappropriate, 24.
Unseasoned, *unprepared*, 674.
unaccustomed, 614.
Unseat, *dismiss*, 756.
Unseconded, *unsupported*, 708.
Unsecured, *uncovenanted*, 768A.
Unseductive, *ugly*, 846.
Unseemly, *undue*, 925.
vicious, 945, 961.
vulgar, 851.
ugly, 846.
inexpedient, 647.
Unseen, *invisible*, 447.
neglected, 460.
Unselfish, *generous*, 942.
Unserviceable, *useless*, 645.
Unset, *disjoin*, 44.
Unsettle, *derange*, 61.
irresolute, 605.
mutable, 149.
insane, 503.
Unsevered, *whole*, 50.
Unshackle, *free*, 748.
liberate, 750.
untie, 44.
Unshaken, *strong*, 159.
resolute, 604.
belief, 484.
Unshapen, *amorphous*, 241.
ugly, 846.
Unshared, *possession*, 777.
Unsheathe, *uncover*, 226.
Unsheltered, *danger*, 665.
Unshifting, *continuance*, 143.
Unshocked, *unmoved*, 823.
Unshod, *divestment*, 226.
Unshorn, *whole*, 50.
Unshrinking, *resolution*, 604.
courage, 861.
Unsifted, *neglected*, 460.
Unsightly, *ugly*, 846.
Unsinged, *uninjured*, 670.
Unskilful, *unskilled*, 699.
Unslaked, *desire*, 865.
Unsleeping, *activity*, 682.
Unsociable, *exclusive*, 893.
Unsocial, *exclusive*, 893.
Unsoiled, *clean*, 652.
Unsold, *possessed*, 777.
Unsolder, *disjoin*, 47.
Unsolicited, *willing*, 602.
Unsolicitous, *indifferent*, 866.
Unsolved, *secret*, 526.
Unsophisticated, *genuine*, 494.
simple, 42.
good, 648.
Unsophisticated, *innocent*, 946.
Unsorted, *unarranged*, 59.
Unsought, *avoided*, 623.
unrequested, 766.
Unsound, *imperfect*, 651.
unhealthy, 655.
sophistical, 477.
Unsounded, *deep*, 208.
Unsown, *unprepared*, 674.
Unsparing, *ample*, 639.
Unspeakable, *great*, 31.
stammering, 583.
Unspecified, *general*, 78.
Unspent, *unused*, 678.
Unspoiled, *goodness*, 648.
Unspoken, *unsaid*, 581.
Unsportsmanlike, *improbity*, 940.
Unspotted, *clean*, 652.
innocent, 946.
beautiful, 845.
Unstable, *mutable*, 149.
irresolute, 605.
Unstained, *untouched*, 652.
honourable, 939.
Unstatesmanlike, *unskilful*, 699.
Unsteadfast, *irresolute*, 605.
Unsteady, *mutable*, 149.
irresolute, 605, 607.
dangerous, 665.
Unstinted, *plenteous*, 639.
Unstirred, *unmoved*, 826.
calm, 265.
Unstitch, *disjoin*, 44.
Unstopped, *open*, 260.
continuing, 143.
Unstored, *unprovided*, 640.
Unstrained, *unexerted*, 172.
relaxed, 687.
turbid, 653.
simple, 516.
Unstrengthened, *weak*, 160.
Unstrung, *weak*, 160.
Unsubdued, *free*, 748.
Unsubjugated, *free*, 748.
Unsubmissive, *disobedient*, 742.
Unsubstantial, *unsubstantiality*, 4.
rare, 322.
texture, 329.
imaginary, 515.
erroneous, 495.
Unsubstantiated, *erroneous*, 495.
Unsuccessful, *failure*, 732.
Unsuitable, *incongruous*, 24.
inexpedient, 647.
time, 135.
Unsuitability, *see* Unsuitable.
Unsuited, *see* Unsuitable.
Unsullied, *clean*, 652.
honourable, 939.

Unsullied, *guiltless*, 946.
Unsummed, *infinity*, 105.
Unsummoned, *voluntary*, 600.
Unsung, *untold*, 526.
Unsunned, *dark*, 421.
Unsupplied, *insufficiency*, 640.
Unsupported, *weak*, 160.
opposed, 708.
Unsuppressed, *persisting*, 142.
Unsurpassed, *great*, 31.
Unsusceptible, *unfeeling*, 823.
Unsuspected, *latent*, 526.
Unsuspicious, *credulous*, 484, 486.
hopeful, 858.
Unsustained, *weak*, 160.
opposed, 708.
Unswayed, *uninfluenced*, 616.
Unsweetened, *unsavoury*, 395.
Unswept, *dirty*, 653.
Unswerving, *straight*, 246.
determined, 604.
Unsymmetrical, *disorder*, 59.
distortion, 243.
Unsympathetic, *unfriendly*, 907.
Unsystematic, *disorder*, 59.
Untack, *disjoin*, 44.
Untainted, *healthy*, 654.
pure, 652.
honourable, 939.
Untalented, *unskilled*, 699.
Untalked of, *latency*, 526.
Untamed, *rude*, 851.
ferocious, 907.
Untangled, *order*, 58.
Untarnished, *probity*, 939.
innocence, 946.
Untasted, *taste*, 391.
Untaught, *ignorant*, 491.
Untaxed, *cheap*, 815.
Unteach, *misteach*, 538.
Unteachable, *unskilled*, 699.
Untempered, *greatness*, 31.
Untempted, *uninfluenced*, 616.
Untenable, *weak*, 160.
undefended, 725.
sophistical, 477.
Untenanted, *empty*, 187.
Untended, *neglected*, 460.
Untested, *neglected*, 460.
Unthanked, *ingratitude*, 917.
Unthankful, *ungrateful*, 917.
Unthawed, *solid*, 321.
cold, 383.
Unthinkable, *impossible*, 471.
Unthinking, *thoughtless*, 452.
Unthoughtful, *neglectful*, 460.
Unthought of, *neglected*, 460.
unconsidered, 452.
Unthreatened, *safe*, 664.
Unthrifty, *prodigal*, 818.
unprepared, 674.
Unthrone, *dismiss*, 756.
Unthwarted, *unhindered*, 748.
Untidy, *in disorder*, 59.
slovenly, 653.
Untie, *loose*, 44.
liberate, 750.
Until, *time*, 106, 108.
Untilled, *unprepared*, 674.
Untimely, *ill-timed*, 135.
Untinged, *simple*, 42.
uncoloured, 429.
Untired, *refreshed*, 689.
Untiring, *active*, 682.
Untitled, *commonalty*, 876.
Untold, *secret*, 526, 528.
countless, 105.
Untouched, *disused*, 678.
insensible, 376, 823.
Untoward, *bad*, 649.
unprosperous, 735.
unpleasant, 830.
Untraced, *latency*, 526.
Untracked, *latency*, 526.
Untrained, *unskilled*, 699.
unprepared, 674.
unaccustomed, 614.
Untrammelled, *free*, 705.
Untranslated, *misinterpretation*, 523.
Untravelled, *quiescent*, 265.
unknown, 491.
Untreasured, *unstored*, 640.
Untried, *undetermined*, 461.
Untrimmed, *simple*, 849.
unprepared, 674.
Untrodden, *new*, 123.
not used, 678.
impervious, 261.
Untroubled, *calm*, 174, 721.
Untrue, *false*, 544.
Untrustworthy, *dishonest*, 940.
Untruth, *falsehood*, 546.
Untunable, *discord*, 414.
Unturned, *straight*, 246.
Untutored, *ignorant*, 246.
Untwist, *straighten*, 246.
evolve, 313.
separate, 44, 47.
Unurged, *spontaneous*, 600.
Unused, *unaccustomed*, 614, 699.
untouched, 678.
Unusual, *unconformity*, 83.
greatness, 31.
Unutilised, *disuse*, 678.
Unutterable, *wonderful*, 870.
great, 31.
Unvalued, *depreciated*, 483.
undesired, 866.

Unvalued, *disliked*, 898.
Unvanquished, *free*, 748.
Unvaried, *permanent*, 142.
continued, 143.
monotonous, 576.
Unvarnished, *truth*, 494.
Unveil, *manifest*, 525.
disclose, 529.
Unventilated, *close*, 261.
Unverified, *indiscrimination*, 465A.
Unversed, *unconversant*, 491.
unskilled, 699.
Unvexed, *content*, 831.
Unviolated, *probity*, 939.
Unvisited, *exclusion*, 893.
Unvitiated, *unspoiled*, 648.
Unvouched for, *unattested*, 468.
Unwakened, *dormant*, 683.
Unwanted, *unnecessary*, 645.
Unwarlike, *cowardly*, 862.
Unwarmed, *cold*, 383.
Unwarned, *danger*, 665.
Unwarped, *unprejudiced*, 480.
Unwarranted, *unjustifiable*, 923, 925.
inconclusive, 477.
Unwary, *heedless*, 460.
Unwashed, *unclean*, 653.
vulgar, 851.
Unwasted, *unexhausted*, 639.
Unwatched, *neglected*, 460.
Unwatchful, *inattentive*, 458.
Unwatered, *dry*, 340.
undiluted, 159.
Unwavering, *resolute*, 604.
Unweakened, *strong*, 159.
Unwearied, *indefatigable*, 682.
refreshed, 689.
Unwedded, *celibacy*, 904.
Unweeded, *neglected*, 460.
Unweighed, *neglected*, 460.
Unwelcome, *disagreeable*, 830.
Unwell, *ill*, 655.
Unwept, *hate*, 898.
Unwholesome, *insalubrious*, 657.
Unwieldy, *large*, 192.
heavy, 319.
difficult, 704.
cumbersome, 647.
Unwilling, *unwillingness*, 603.
dissent, 489.
Unwind, *evolve*, 313.
straighten, 246.
Unwinking, *vigilant*, 457.
Unwiped, *unclean*, 653.
Unwise, *fool*, 499.
Unwished, *undesirable*, 866.
Unwithered, *strong*, 159.
Unwitnessed, *unseen*, 526.
Unwitting, *ignorant*, 491.
involuntary, 601.
Unwomanly, *unbecoming*, 940.
Unwonted, *unaccustomed*, 614.
unusual, 83.
Unworkmanlike, *unskilful*, 699.
Unworldly, *disinterested*, 943.
pious, 987.
Unworn, *unused*, 159.
Unworthy, *vicious*, 945.
base, 940.
shameful, 874.
Unwrap, *straighten*, 246.
Unwreathe, *straighten*, 246.
Unwrinkled, *smooth*, 255.
Unwrought, *unprepared*, 674.
Unyielding, *tough*, 323.
resolute, 604.
obstinate, 606.
resisting, 719.
Unyoke, *disjoin*, 44.
Upbear, *support*, 215.
raise, 807.
Upbraid, *disapprove*, 932.
Upbringing, *teaching*, 537.
Upcast, *elevation*, 307.
Upcountry, *interiority*, 221.
Upgrow, *height*, 206.
Upgrowth, *ascent*, 305.
Upheave, *elevation*, 307.
Uphill, *activity*, 217.
ascent, 305.
difficult, 704.
Uphold, *support*, 215.
aid, 707.
continue, 143.
Upholster, *cover*, 222.
furnish, 637.
Upkeep, *preservation*, 670.
Uplands, *height*, 206.
Uplift, *elevation*, 307.
Upper, *height*, 206.
Upper hand, *authority*, 737.
success, 731.
Uppermost, *height*, 206, 210.
Uppish, *self-assertive*, 885.
Upraise, *elevation*, 307.
Uprear, *elevation*, 307.
Upright, *vertical*, 212.
honest, 939.
virtuous, 944.
Uprise, *ascent*, 305.
Uproar, *noise*, 404.
turmoil, 173.
Uproot, *destruction*, 162.
Upset, *throw down*, 308.
disorder, 59.
derange, 61.
change, 140.

Upset, *invert*, 218.
destroy, 162.
Upside-down, *inversion*, 218.
Upshot, *end*, 66.
total, 50.
Upstart, *plebeian*, 876.
prosperous, 734.
Upturn, *inversion*, 218.
Upwards, *height*, 206.
Uranology, *world*, 318.
Urban, *abode*, 189.
Urbane, *courtesy*, 894.
Urchin, *small*, 193.
child, 129.
wretch, 949.
Urge, *impel*, 276.
incite, 615.
solicit, 765.
hasten, 684.
accelerate, 274.
violence, 173.
Urgent, *important*, 642.
required, 630.
Urn, *vase*, 191.
funereal, 363.
Usage, *custom*, 613.
rule, 80.
Usance, *debt*, 806.
Use, *employment*, 677.
waste, 638.
utility, 644.
habit, 613.
rule, 80.
Used up, *worn*, 651.
surfeited, 869.
Useful, *use*, 644.
Useless, *misuse*, 645.
Usher, *teacher*, 540.
servant, 746.
announce, 511.
precede, 62, 66.
prior, 116.
Usual, *ordinary*, 82.
customary, 613.
Usurp, *assume*, 739.
seize, 789.
illegality, 925.
Usury, *debt*, 806.
Utensil, *recipient*, 191.
instrument, 633.
Utilise, *use*, 644, 677.
Utilitarian, *philanthropy*, 910
Utility, *use*, 644.
Utmost, *superior*, 33.
Utopia, *visionary*, 515.
hopeful, 858.
Utter, *extreme*, 31.
to speak, 580.
disclose, 529.
Utter, *publish*, 531.
distribute, 73.
Uttermost, *greatness*, 31.
Uxorious, *love*, 897.

V

Vacant, *void*, 4.
absent, 187.
thoughtless, 452.
foolish, 499.
scanty, 640.
Vacate, *absence*, 187.
Vacation, *leisure*, 685.
Vaccination, *injection*, 300.
Vacillation, *changeableness*, 149.
undulation, 314.
wavering, 605.
Vacuity, *void*, 4, 180.
absence, 187.
inexistence, 2.
imbecility, 499.
*Vade-mecum (L.), *teaching*, 537.
school, 542.
Vagabond, *rogue*, 949.
wanderer, 268.
Vagary, *whim*, 608.
absurdity, 497.
imagination, 515.
antic, 856.
Vagrant, *moving*, 264.
roving, 266.
fickle, 149.
devious, 279.
traveller, 268.
Vague, *uncertain*, 475.
obscure, 519.
style, 571.
Vails, *expenditure*, 809.
Vain, *unreal*, 2.
unprofitable, 645.
conceited, 880.
unvalued, 866.
Vainglorious, *haughty*, 878.
boasting, 884.
vain, 880.
Valance, *edge*, 230.
Vale, *concavity*, 252.
Valediction, *departure*, 293.
courtesy, 894.
Valentine, *courtship*, 902.
Valet, *servant*, 746.
Valetudinarian, *disease*, 655.
Valhalla, *interment*, 363.
Valiant, *courage*, 861.
Valid, *strong*, 159.
powerful, 157.
influential, 175.

Valid, *cogent*, 467.
logical, 476.
Valise, *receptacle*, 191.
Valley, *concavity*, 252.
*Vallum (L.), *defence*, 717.
Valour, *courage*, 861.
Valuable, *goodness*, 648.
Value, *price*, 812.
goodness, 648.
importance, 642.
to measure, 466.
estimate, 480.
Valueless, *inutility*, 645.
Valve, *stop*, 263.
conduit, 350.
Vamp, *repair*, 658.
improvise, 612.
music, 415.
Vamp up, *furbish*, 673.
Vampire, *bane*, 663.
demon, 980.
Van, *front*, 234.
beginning, 66.
waggon, 272.
Vandal, *commonalty*, 876.
Vandalism, *vulgarity*, 851.
Vandyke, *point*, 253.
Vane, *indication*, 550.
Vanguard, *front*, 234.
beginning, 66.
Vanish, *disappear*, 449.
perish, 2.
transient, 111.
Vanity, *conceit*, 880.
worthlessness, 645.
Vanquish, *success*, 731.
Vanquished, *failure*, 732
Vantage-ground, *influence*, 175.
Vapid, *insipid*, 391.
unattractive, 866.
style, 575.
Vaporise, *vaporisation*, 336.
Vapour, *gas*, 334.
bubble, 353.
insolence, 885.
boasting, 884.
chimera, 515.
rare, 322.
Vapours, *dejection*, 837.
Variable, *changeable*, 149.
irresolute, 605.
Variance, *difference*, 15.
disagreement, 24.
discord, 713.
Variation, *non-imitation*, 20.
irrelation, 10.
music, 415.
Varied, *different*, 15.
Variegation, *colour*, 440.
Variety, *difference*, 15.
exception, 83.
Various, *different*, 15.
many, 102.
variation, 20.
Varlet, *sinner*, 949.
Varnish, *coat*, 222.
decorate, 845, 847.
sophistry, 477.
falsehood, 544.
excuse, 937.
Vary, *differ*, 15.
diversify, 18.
modify, 20.
change, 140.
fluctuate, 149.
Vase, *receptacle*, 191.
Vaseline, *unguent*, 356.
Vassal, *servant*, 746.
Vassalage, *subjection*, 749.
Vast, *in quantity*, 31.
in size, 192.
Vat, *receptacle*, 191.
Vaticination, *prediction*, 511.
Vaudeville, *the drama*, 599.
Vault, *cellar*, 191.
sepulchre, 363.
to leap, 305, 309
Vaulting, *superiority*, 33.
aspiring, 865.
Vaunt, *boasting*, 884.
*Vaurien (Fr.), *sinner*, 949.
Veda, *pseudo-revelation*, 986.
Vedette, *safety*, 664.
warning, 668.
Veer, *regression*, 283.
change, 140.
deviate, 279.
change intention, 607.
Vegetable, *vegetable*, 365.
plant, 367.
Vegetarian, *temperance*, 953.
Vegetate, *grow*, 194.
insensibility, 823.
Vehemence, *violence*, 173.
emotion, 825.
Vehicle, *vehicle*, 272.
*Vehmgericht (Ger.), *illegality*, 964.
Veil, *mask*, 530.
to conceal, 528.
shade, 424.
covering, 225.
Veiled, *invisible*, 447.
latent, 526.
Vein, *humour*, 602.
cast of mind, 820.
mine, 636.
Veined, *variegation*, 440.
Velleity, *will*, 600.

Vellum, *writing*, 590.
Velocipede, *locomotion*, 266.
Velocity, *swiftness*, 274.
Velvet, *soft*, 255.
plush, 256.
ease, 705.
physical pleasure, 277.
moral pleasure, 827.
Venal, *parsimony*, 819.
Vend, *sell*, 796.
*Vendetta (It.), *feud*, 713.
revenge, 919.
Vendible, *sale*, 796.
Vendor, *merchant*, 797.
Veneer, *covering*, 222.
Venerable, *old*, 128.
Veneration, *respect*, 928.
piety, 987.
Vengeance, *revenge*, 919.
(with a), *greatness*, 31.
Vengeful, *revenge*, 919.
Venial, *excusable*, 937.
Venom, *bane*, 663.
malignity, 907.
Venomous, *evil*, 649.
malignant, 907.
Vent, *air-pipe*, 351.
emit, 295.
disclose, 529.
sale, 796.
Ventilate, *perflate*, 349.
clean, 652.
discuss, 595.
examine, 461.
Ventilator, *wind*, 349.
Ventricle, *receptacle*, 191.
Ventriloquism, *voice*, 580.
Venture, *chance*, 156.
to try, 621, 675.
danger, 665.
courage, 861.
Venturous, *courage*, 861.
Venue, *place*, 182.
Venus, *beauty*, 845.
love, 897.
Veracity, *truth*, 543.
Veranda, *portico*, 191.
Verbal, *word*, 562.
Verbatim, *imitation*, 19.
interpretation, 522.
word, 562.
Verbiage, *diffuse*, 573.
nonsense, 497.
Verbose, *diffuse*, 573.
loquacious, 584.
Verdant, *green*, 435.
vegetation, 367.
credulous, 486.
ignorant, 491.
Verd-antique, *green*, 435.
Verdict, *opinion*, 480.
sentence, 969.
Verdigris, *green*, 435
Verdure, *green*, 435.
Verecundity, *modesty*, 881.
humility, 879.
Verge, *brink*, 230.
to tend, 278.
contribute, 176.
Verger, *churchman*, 996.
Verify, *test*, 463.
demonstrate, 478.
judge, 480.
warrant, 771.
Verily, *positively*, 32.
truly, 494.
Verisimilitude, *probable*, 472.
Veritable, *truth*, 494
Verity, *truth*, 494.
Verjuice, *sourness*, 397.
Vermicular, *convolution*, 248.
Vermiform, *convolution*, 248.
Vermilion, *redness*, 434.
Vermin, *base*, 876.
unclean, 653.
Vernacular, *language*, 560.
familiar, 82.
Vernal, *early*, 123.
spring, 125.
Versatile, *changeable*, 605.
skilful, 698.
*Vers de société (Fr.), *poetry*, 597.
*Vers libre (Fr.), *poetry*, 597.
Verse, *poetry*, 597.
Versed, *skill*, 698.
Versicolour, *variegation*, 440.
Versifier, *poetry*, 597.
Version, *interpretation*, 522.
Verso, *left hand*, 239.
Vert, *change belief*, 484.
Vertex, *summit*, 210.
Vertical, *verticality*, 212.
Vertigo, *insanity*, 503.
Verve, *imagination*, 515.
feeling, 821.
Very, *great*, 31.
Vesicle, *cell*, 191.
globe, 249.
Vespers, *rite*, 998.
Vespertine, *evening*, 126.
Vessel, *recipient*, 191.
ship, 273.
tube, 260.
Vest, *dress*, 225.
give, 784.
Vestal, *purity*, 960.
Vested, *legal*, 963.
Vestibule, *entrance*, 66.

Vestibule, *room*, 191.
Vestige, *record*, 551.
Vestments, *canonicals*, 999.
Vestry, *conclave*, 995.
church, 1000.
Vesture, *dress*, 225.
Veteran, *old*, 130.
adept, 700.
Veterinary, *remedy*, 662.
Veto, *prohibit*, 761.
*Vetturino (It.), *director*, 694.
Vex, *painful*, 830.
Vexation, *pain*, 828.
Vexatious, *painful*, 830.
Via, *way*, 627.
*Via media (L.), *mean*, 29.
middle, 68.
Viability, *life*, 359.
Viaduct, *way*, 627.
Vial, *bottle*, 191.
wrath, 900.
Viands, *food*, 298.
Viaticum, *rite*, 998.
Vibrate, *fluctuate*, 149.
oscillate, 314.
Vicar, *clergy*, 996.
Vicarage, *office*, 995.
house, 1000.
Vicarious, *substituted*, 149, 755.
Vice, *guiltiness*, 945.
imperfection, 651.
deputy, 759.
vinculum, 45.
Vicegerency, *commission*, 755.
Vicegerent, *consignee*, 758.
deputy, 759.
Vice-president, *master*, 745.
Viceroy, *deputy*, 759.
Vice versa (L.), *correlation*, 12.
contrariety, 14.
interchange, 148.
Vicinity, *nearness*, 197.
Vicious, *fallacious*, 477.
faulty, 651.
immoral, 945.
Vicissitude, *change*, 140.
mutable, 149.
Victim, *injured*, 732.
dupe, 547.
sufferer, 828.
Victimise, *deceive*, 545.
baffle, 731.
Victoria, *vehicle*, 272.
Victory, *success*, 731.
Victualling, *provision*, 637.
Victuals, *food*, 298.
*Videlicet (L.), *example*, 82.
namely, 522.
specification, 79.
Vie, *emulate*, 648.
contend, 720.
View, *sight*, 441.
appearance, 448.
to attend to, 457.
landscape, 556.
opinion, 484.
intention, 620.
View-finder, *optical*, 445.
Viewless, *invisible*, 447.
Viewy, *caprice*, 608.
Vigil, *watch*, 459.
eve, 116.
Vigilance, *attention*, 457.
care, 459.
Vignette, *engraving*, 558.
Vigour, *strong*, 159.
healthy, 654.
activity, 683.
energy, 171.
style, 574.
Viking, *pirate*, 792.
Vile, *bad*, 649.
odious, 830.
valueless, 643.
disgraceful, 874.
dishonourable, 940.
plebeian, 876.
Vilify, *censure*, 932.
shame, 874.
Vilipend, *censure*, 932.
shame, 874.
disrespect, 929.
Villa, *abode*, 189
Village, *abode*, 189.
Villager, *inhabitant*, 188.
Villain, *vice*, 945.
Villainage, *subjection*, 749.
Villainy, *vice*, 945.
Villanelle, *poetry*, 597.
Villous, *roughness*, 256.
Vim, *energy*, 171.
style, 574.
Vincible, *weakness*, 160.
Vinculum, *junction*, 45.
Vindicate, *justify*, 937.
a claim, 924.
Vindictive, *revengeful*, 919.
irascible, 901.
Vinegar, *sourness*, 397.
Vineyard, *agriculture*, 371.
Vintage, *agriculture*, 371.
Viola, *musical instrument*, 417.
Violate, *disobey*, 742.
engagement, 773.
right, 925.
duty, 927.
a usage, 614.
Violence, *physical*, 173.

Violence, *arbitrariness*, 964.
Violently, *great*, 31.
Violet, *purple*, 437.
Violin, *musical instrument*, 417.
Violinist, *musician*, 416.
Violoncello, *musical instrument*, 417.
Viper, *bane*, 663.
miscreant, 949.
Virago, *irascibility*, 901.
Virescent, *green*, 435.
Virgin, *girl*, 129.
celibacy, 904.
Virginal, *musical instrument*, 417.
Virginia, *tobacco*, 298A.
Viridescent, *green*, 435.
Virile, *manly*, 373.
adolescent, 131.
strong, 159.
style, 574.
Virtu, *taste*, 850.
Virtual, *real*, 1.
potential, 2.
Virtually, *truth*, 494.
Virtue, *goodness*, 944.
power, 157.
courage, 861.
Virtueless, *vice*, 945.
Virtuosity, *taste*, 850.
skill, 698.
Virtuoso, *taste*, 850.
performer, 416.
proficient, 700.
Virulence, *energy*, 171.
insalubrity, 657.
malignity, 649.
malevolence, 907.
Virus, *poison*, 663.
disease, 655.
Visage, *front*, 234.
appearance, 448.
*Vis-à-vis (Fr.), *front*, 234.
Viscera, *interior*, 221.
Viscid, *semiliquid*, 352.
Viscount, *master*, 875.
Viscous, *semiliquid*, 352.
*Visé (Fr.), *indication*, 550.
Vishnu, *deity*, 979.
Visible, *visibility*, 446.
Vision, *sight*, 441.
imagination, 515.
apparition, 980.
Visionary, *erroneous*, 495.
imaginary, 515.
heterodox, 984.
madman, 504.
Visit, *sociality*, 892.
arrival, 292.
Visitation, *pain*, 828.
calamity, 830.
Visiting-card, *indication*, 560.
Visitor, *director*, 694.
Visor, *concealment*, 528.
Vista, *point of view*, 441.
prospect, 448.
Visual, *vision*, 441.
Vital, *importance*, 642.
Vitality, *life*, 359.
strength, 159.
Vitals, *interior*, 221.
Vitiate, *deteriorate*, 659.
Vitreous, *density*, 321.
Vitrify, *density*, 321.
Vitriolic, *acrimonious*, 171.
malevolent, 907.
Vituperate, *disapprove*, 932.
*Viva voce (L.), *speech*, 582.
Vivacious, *active*, 682.
sensitive, 822.
cheerful, 836.
Vivid, *light*, 420.
colour, 428.
lively, 375.
energetic, 171.
style, 574.
Vivify, *life*, 359.
Vivisect, *anatomise*, 44.
Vixen, *scold*, 901, 932.
Vizier, *deputy*, 759.
Vocable, *word*, 562.
Vocabulary, *word*, 562.
Vocal, *voice*, 580.
loudness, 404.
music, 415.
Vocalise, *speech*, 580.
Vocalist, *musician*, 416.
Vocation, *business*, 625.
Vociferate, *cry*, 411.
loudness, 404.
voice, 580.
Vogue, *fashion*, 852.
custom, 613.
Voice, *speech*, 580.
sound, 402.
cry, 411.
choice, 609.
opinion, 484.
Void, *vacuum*, 2, 4.
absence, 187.
to emit, 297.
Voivode, *master*, 745.
Volant, *flight*, 267.
Volapük, *language*, 560.
Volatile, *vaporisable*, 336.
irresolute, 605.
Volatility, *caprice*, 608.
Volcanic, *violence*, 173.
Volitation, *flight*, 267.
Volition, *will*, 600.

W

Wander, *deviate*, 279, 291.
circuit, 629.
delirium, 503.
Wanderer, *traveller*, 268.
*Wanderlust (Ger.), *travel*, 266.
Wane, *decay*, 659.
decrease, 36.
contract, 195.
Wangle, *falsify*, 544.
plan, 626.
cunning, 702.
Want, *desire*, 865.
require, 630.
scant, 640.
poverty, 804.
incomplete, 53.
Wantless, *sufficiency*, 639.
Wanton, *unrestrained*, 748.
impure, 961.
War, *warfare*, 722.
War-cry, *indication*, 550.
War-whoop, *indication*, 450.
Warble, *music*, 415.
Ward, *restraint*, 751.
safety, 664.
asylum, 666.
Ward off, *defend*, 717.
avert, 706.
Warden, *guardian*, 664.
Warden, *deputy*, 759.
master, 745.
Warder, *keeper*, 263, 664, 753.
Wardmote, *tribunal*, 966.
Wardrobe, *dress*, 225.
receptacle, 191.
Wardship, *safety*, 664.
Ware, *merchandise*, 798.
Warehouse, *store*, 636.
mart, 799.
Warfare, *war*, 722.
Warlike, *contention*, 720.
Warlock, *spirit*, 980.
sorcerer, 994.
Warm, *hot*, 382.
to heat, 384.
ardent, 515, 821, 824, 888.
angry, 900.
irascible, 901.
violent, 173.
Warming-pan, *heater*, 386.
preparation, 673.
Warmth, *heat*, 382.
emotion, 821.
passion, 900.
Warn, *admonish*, 695.
forebode, 511.
Warning, *warning*, 668.
omen, 512.
alarm, 669.
Warp, *narrow*, 203.
deviate, 279.
prejudice, 481.
imperfect, 651.
texture, 329.
Warrant, *evidence*, 467.
order, 741.
permit, 760.
protest, 535.
money-order, 800.
security, 771.
to authorise, 737.
Warrantable, *defensible*, 937.
Warranty, *surety*, 771.
sanction, 924.
Warren, *productive*, 168.
Warrior, *combatant*, 726.
Wart, *convexity*, 250.
Wary, *cautious*, 864.
careful, 459.
Wash, *cleanse*, 652.
colour, 428.
water, 337.
marsh, 345.
Wash out, *obliterate*, 552.
Washy, *watery*, 337.
weak, 160.
valueless, 645.
style, 573.
Waspish, *discourteous*, 895.
irascible, 901.
Wassail, *feast*, 840.
Waste, *decrease*, 36.
contract, 195.
expend, 638.
destroy, 162.
vacant space, 180.
plain, 344.
misuse, 679.
useless, 645.
prodigality, 818.
refuse, 643.
loss, 776.
Wasted, *weakness*, 160.
Wasteful, *useless*, 645.
prodigal, 818.
Waste-pipe, *conduit*, 350.
Wastrel, *outcast*, 893.
Watch, *observe*, 441.
attend to, 457.
expect, 507.
sentinel, 753.
clock, 114.
Watchet, *blue*, 438.
Watch-fire, *indication*, 550.
Watchful, *care*, 459.
Watchman, *safety*, 664.
Watch-tower, *warning*, 668.
Watchword, *indication*, 550.

Water, *fluid*, 337.
to weaken, 160.
Watercourse, *conduit*, 350.
Waterfall, *river*, 348.
Water-gate, *conduit*, 350.
Waterlogged, *danger*, 665.
difficulty, 704.
Waterplane, *ship*, 273.
Waterproof, *dryness*, 340.
dress, 225.
Watershed, *summit*, 210.
Waterspout, *river*, 349.
Wave, *of water*, 348.
the sea, 341.
sinuous, 248.
oscillate, 314.
hint, 527.
curl, 245.
Waver, *unwilling*, 603.
hesitate, 605.
fluctuate, 149.
Wavy, *convolution*, 248.
Wax, *become*, 144.
increase, 35.
soft, 324.
unctuous, 355.
substance, 356.
Way, *road*, 627.
space, 180.
passage, 302.
conduct, 692.
habit, 613.
(under), *progression*, 282.
Wayfarer, *traveller*, 268.
Waylay, *deception*, 545.
Ways and means, *means*, 632.
Wayward, *obstinate*, 606.
capricious, 608.
discourteous, 895.
changeable, 149.
Wayworn, *fatigue*, 688.
Wayzgoose, *picnic*, 298.
Weak, *feeble*, 160.
small in degree, 32.
foolish, 499.
irrational, 477.
irresolute, 605.
compassionate, 914.
vicious, 945.
Weaken, *enfeeble*, 160.
decrease, 36.
invalidate, 468.
Weak-headed, *fool*, 499.
Weak-hearted, *coward*, 862.
Weak side, *vice*, 945.
Weal, *good*, 618.
ridge, 250.
Weald, *plant*, 367.
plain, 344.
Wealth, *rich*, 803.
Wean, *change habit*, 614.
change opinion, 484.
Weapon, *instrument*, 633.
arms, 727.
Weaponless, *impotent*, 158.
Wear, *decrease*, 36.
decay, 659.
use, 677.
clothe, 225.
Wear and tear, *waste*, 638.
injury, 619.
Wear off, *diminish*, 36.
cease, 141.
habit, 614.
Wear out, *damage*, 659.
fatigue, 688.
Wearisome, *fatigue*, 688.
ennui, 841.
Weary, *fatigue*, 688.
ennui, 841.
uneasy, 828.
Weasand, *air-pipe*, 260, 351.
Weather, *air*, 338.
succeed, 731.
disintegrate, 330.
Weatherbeaten, *weak*, 160.
Weathercock, *irresolute*, 605.
mutable, 149.
Weather-glass, *measure*, 466.
Weather-wise, *prediction*, 511.
Weave, *interlace*, 219.
produce, 161.
Web, *texture*, 329.
intersection, 219.
Wed, *marriage*, 903.
Wedded to, *habit*, 613.
opinion, 484.
obstinate, 606.
Wedge, *sharp*, 253.
angular, 244.
intervention, 228.
instrument, 633.
to insert, 300.
locate, 184.
join, 43.
ingress, 294.
Wedlock, *marriage*, 903.
Weed, *rubbish*, 643, 645.
reduce, 103.
mourning, 225, 839.
reject, 55.
tobacco, 298A.
Weekly, *period*, 108.
Weep, *lament*, 839.
Weigh, *heavy*, 319.
ponder, 451.
measure, 466.
lift, 307.

Weigh anchor, *depart*, 293.
Weigh down, *aggrieve*, 649.
Weigh with, *motive*, 615.
Weight, *influence*, 175.
gravity, 319.
importance, 642.
Weightless, *levity*, 320.
Weir, *hindrance*, 706.
Weird, *strange*, 83.
wonderful, 870.
supernatural, 980.
Welcome, *grateful*, 829.
sociality, 892.
reception, 894.
friendly, 888.
Weld, *coherence*, 46.
Welfare, *prosperity*, 734.
Welkin, *world*, 318.
Well, *water*, 343.
to flow, 348.
much, 31.
healthy, 654.
deep, 208.
assent, 488.
origin, 153.
Welladay, *lamentation*, 839.
Well-being, *prosperity*, 734.
gratification, 827.
Well-behaved, *good*, 944.
Well-born, *patrician*, 875.
Well-bred, *courteous*, 894.
genteel, 852.
Well-conducted, *good*, 944.
Well-disposed, *friendly*, 888.
Well-doing, *virtue*, 944.
Well done, *approbation*, 931.
Well enough, *imperfection*, 651.
Well-favoured, *beauty*, 845.
Well-founded, *probable*, 472.
Well-grounded, *knowledge*, 490.
Well-informed, *knowledge*, 490.
Well-intended, *virtue*, 944.
Well-judged, *intelligence*, 498.
Well-knit, *strength*, 159.
Well-mannered, *courtesy*, 894.
Well-meant, *benevolent*, 906.
Well met, *social*, 892.
Well-nigh, *great*, 32.
Well off, *prosperity*, 734.
Well-set, *strength*, 159.
Well-spent, *success*, 731.
Well-tasted, *savoury*, 394.
Well-timed, *opportune*, 134, 646.
Well-to-do, *prosperity*, 734.
Well-wisher, *friend*, 890.
Welsh, *to cheat*, 545.
Welsher, *deceiver*, 548.
Welt, *edge*, 230.
Welter, *rotation*, 312.
Welter, *agitation*, 315.
*Weltschmerz (Ger.), *weariness*, 841.
Wen, *convexity*, 250.
Wench, *young girl*, 129.
woman, 374.
Wend, *journey*, 266.
Werewolf, *demon*, 980.
Wet, *water*, 337.
moisture, 339.
Wet-nurse, *to pamper*, 954.
Whack, *blow*, 276, 972.
Whacker, *size*, 192.
Whale, *monster*, 192.
Whaler, *ship*, 273.
Wharf, *anchorage*, 189.
Whatnot, *receptacle*, 191.
Wheal, *convexity*, 250.
Wheedle, *flatter*, 933.
coax, 615.
endearment, 902.
Wheel, *circle*, 247.
circuition, 311.
deviation, 279.
rotation, 212.
instrument, 633.
means, 632.
Wheel (break on the), *torture*, 378.
pain, 830.
execution, 972.
rack, 975.
Wheelbarrow, *vehicle*, 272.
Wheeze, *blow*, 349.
hiss, 409.
joke, 842.
Whelm, *redundance*, 641.
Whelp, *young*, 129.
When, *time*, 119.
Whence, *attribution*, 155.
inquiry, 461.
departure, 293.
Whenever, *time*, 119.
Whensoever, *time*, 119.
Where, *presence*, 186.
Whereabouts, *situation*, 183.
nearness, 197.
Whereas, *reason*, 476.
Wherefore, *reason*, 476.
attribution, 155.
inquiry, 461.
motive, 615.
Wherever, *space*, 180.
Whereupon, *futurity*, 121.
Wherewith, *instrument*, 631.
Wherry, *boat*, 273.
Whet, *excite*, 824.
incite, 615.
sharpen, 253.
desire, 865.
meal, 298.

Whey, *fluid*, 337.
Whiff, *wind*, 349.
While, *duration*, 106, 120.
Whilom, *preterition*, 122.
Whim, *caprice*, 608.
desire, 865.
imagination, 515.
wit, 842.
Whimper, *lamentation*, 839.
Whimsical, *fanciful*, 515, 608.
ridiculous, 853.
Whimsy, *desire*, 865.
Whine, *cry*, 411.
complain, 839.
Whinny, *animal cry*, 412.
Whip, *to beat*, 276, 972.
scourge, 975.
rapidity, 274.
driver, 694.
trouble, 830.
Whip-hand, *success*, 731.
Whip off, *escape*, 671.
Whip-round, *giving*, 784.
Whip-up, *snatch*, 789.
Whipper-in, *director*, 694.
servant, 746.
Whippersnapper, *youth*, 129.
Whipping-post, *scourge*, 975.
Whirl, *rotation*, 312.
Whirligig, *rotation*, 312.
Whirlpool, *vortex*, 312.
eddy, 348.
confusion, 59.
Whirlwind, *wind*, 349.
Whisk, *rapidity*, 274.
circuition, 311.
agitation, 315.
Whisker, *hair*, 256.
Whisky, *vehicle*, 272.
Whisper, *faint sound*, 405.
stammer, 583.
tell, 527.
prompt, 615.
remind, 505.
Whist! *silence*, 403.
Whistle, *hiss*, 409.
music, 415.
instrument, 417.
Whistle at, *depreciate*, 483.
Whit, *point*, 32.
part, 51.
small, 193.
White, *whiteness*, 430.
White feather, *coward*, 862.
White-livered, *cowardice*, 862.
Whitewash, *whiten*, 430.
vindicate, 937.
acquit, 970.
Whither, *tendency*, 176.
Whither, *direction*, 278.
Whittle, *disjoin*, 44.
abbreviate, 201.
Whiz, *sibilation*, 409.
Whole, *entire*, 50.
healthy, 654.
Whole-hearted, *cordial*, 600.
Wholesale, *greatness*, 31.
whole, 50.
plenty, 639.
barter, 794.
Wholesome, *salubrity*, 656.
Wholly, *great*, 31.
whole, 50.
Whoop, *cry*, 411.
loud, 404.
weep, 839.
(war), 715, 722.
Whopper, *untruth*, 546.
Whopping, *size*, 192.
Whore, *libertine*, 962.
Why, *reason*, 615.
inquiry, 461.
cause, 155.
Wicked, *vice*, 945.
Wicker, *crossing*, 219.
Wicket, *entrance*, 66.
Wide, *broad*, 202.
Wide-awake, *hat*, 225.
Wide of, *distance*, 196.
Widespread, *dispersed*, 73.
Widowhood, *divorce*, 905.
Width, *breadth*, 202.
Wield, *use*, 677.
brandish, 315.
Wife, *marriage*, 903.
Wifeless, *celibacy*, 904.
Wig, *dress*, 225.
to scold, 932.
Wight, *man*, 373.
Wigwam, *abode*, 189.
Wild, *violent*, 173.
mad, 503.
excited, 825.
licentious, 954.
foolish, 499, 699.
useless, 645.
desert, 344.
Wilderness, *space*, 180.
useless, 645.
seclusion, 893.
Wild-fire, *heat*, 382.
Wile, *cunning*, 702.
stratagem, 545.
Wilful, *obstinacy*, 606.
Will, *volition*, 600.
Will-o'-the-wisp, *light*, 420.
phantom, 515.
Willing, *acquiescent*, 488.

Willing, *voluntary*, 600, 602.
Willow, *lamentation*, 839.
Willowy, *pliant*, 324.
Willy-nilly, *compulsion*, 744.
Wily, *sly*, 702.
Wimble, *perforator*, 262.
Wimple, *dress*, 225.
Win, *get*, 775.
succeed, 731.
engage, 897.
Wince, *flinch*, 860.
feel, 821, 825.
pain, 378, 828.
Winch, *instrument*, 633.
Wind, *blast*, 349.
circuition, 311.
convolution, 248.
rapidity, 274.
Wind up, *screw up*, 159.
end, 67.
complete, 729.
Wind-bound, *hindrance*, 706.
Windfall, *good*, 618.
luck, 621.
Winding, *curved*, 245.
undulating, 248.
Winding-sheet, *interment*, 363.
Windlass, *instrument*, 633.
Windmill, *rotation*, 312.
Window, *opening*, 260.
Windpipe, *air-pipe*, 351.
Windy, *air*, 338.
verbose, 573.
Winebag, *drunken*, 959.
Winebibber, *drunken*, 959.
Wing, *side*, 236.
limb, 633.
(under the) *asylum*, 666.
(take), *move*, 267.
Winged, *rapid*, 274.
Wink, *blind*, 442.
nictitate, 443.
hint, 527.
indicate, 550.
Wink at, *permit*, 760.
overlook, 460.
Winning, *pleasing*, 829.
lovely, 897.
Winnow, *sift*, 42.
exclude, 55.
clean, 652.
inquire, 461.
pick, 609.
Winter, *cold*, 383.
Wintry, *cold*, 383.
Wipe, *clean*, 652.
strike, 276.
Wipe off, *non-observance*, 773.
Wipe out, *obliterate*, 552.
Wipe out, *demolish*, 162.
Wire, *filament*, 205.
ligature, 45.
message, 532.
Wire-drawn, *lengthy*, 200.
thin, 203.
style, 571.
Wireless, *message*, 532.
Wireworm, *bane*, 663.
Wisdom, *wisdom*, 498.
Wise, *wisdom*, 498.
way, 627.
Wiseacre, *fool*, 501.
Wish, *desire*, 865.
Wish joy, *congratulation*, 896.
Wishy-washy, *insipid*, 391.
absurd, 497.
feeble, 575.
Wisp, *assemblage*, 72.
Wistful, *thoughtful*, 451.
Wit, *intellect*, 450.
humour, 842.
wisdom, 498.
humorist, 844.
Witch, *oracle*, 513.
proficient, 700.
sorceress, 994.
Witchcraft, *sorcery*, 992.
Witchery, *attraction*, 615.
sorcery, 992.
With, *addition*, 37.
accompanying, 88.
instrumental, 631.
Withal, *addition*, 37.
accompanying, 88.
Withdraw, *subduct*, 38.
recede, 287.
diverge, 291.
deny, 536.
depart, 293.
Wither, *shrink*, 195.
decay, 659.
Withershins, *rotation*, 312.
Withhold, *retain*, 781.
stint, 640.
prohibit, 761.
dissuade, 616.
Within, *interior*, 221.
Within an ace of, *smallness*, 32.
Without, *unless*, 8.
absence, 187.
exterior, 220.
subduction, 38.
exception, 83.
circumjacent, 227.
Withstand, *resist*, 719.
oppose, 179, 708.
Witless, *ignorant*, 491.
neglectful, 460.

Witless, *imbecile*, 499.
Witling, *fool*, 501.
Witness, *evidence*, 467.
voucher, 550.
Witness, with a, *greatness*, 31.
Wits, *intellect*, 450.
Witticism, *wit*, 842.
Witty, *wit*, 842.
Wive, *marriage*, 903.
Wizard, *sorcerer*, 994.
Wizened, *withered*, 193, 195.
Woe, *pain*, 828.
evil, 619.
Woebegone, *pain*, 828.
dejection, 837.
Woeful, *painfulness*, 830.
Wold, *plain*, 344.
Wolf, *to devour*, 296.
alarm, 669.
Woman, *woman*, 131, 374.
Womanly, *weakness*, 160.
Womb, *interior*, 221.
cause, 153.
Wonder, *astonishment*, 870.
prodigy, 872.
Wonderfully, *great*, 31.
Wonderment, *prodigy*, 872.
Wondrous, *wonder*, 870.
Wont, *habitual*, 613.
usual, 82.
Woo, *desire*, 865.
courtship, 902.
Wood, *plant*, 367.
Woodcut, *engraving*, 558.
Wood-note, *animal cry*, 412.
Wooer, *love*, 897.
Woof, *texture*, 329.
Wool, *hair*, 256.
Wool-gathering, *folly*, 499.
inattention, 458.
madness, 503.
Woolsack, *pillow*, 215.
authority, 747.
tribunal, 966.
Word, *vocable*, 562.
intelligence, 532.
promise, 768.
revelation, 985.
Deity, 976.
maxim, 496.
Wording, *expression*, 566.
Wordless, *aphony*, 581.
Words, *quarrel*, 713.
Wordy, *diffuseness*, 573.
Work, *product*, 154.
agency, 170.
to use, 677.
action, 680.
book, 593.
Work in, *introduce*, 37.
Work off, *get rid of*, 545, 672.
Work one's way, *progression*, 282.
Work out, *conduct*, 692.
achieve, 729.
Work up, *incite*, 615.
inflame, 824.
Work upon, *influence*, 175.
Workhouse, *poverty*, 804.
Working, *activity*, 682.
Workman, *agent*, 690.
originator, 164.
Workmanlike, *skill*, 698.
Workmanship, *production*, 161.
handiwork, 680.
Workshop, *workshop*, 691.
World, *universe*, 318.
mankind, 373.
fashion, 852.
events, 151.
great, 31.
Worldling, *selfish*, 943.
Worldly, *selfish*, 943.
irreligious, 988.
Worm, *small*, 193.
animal, 366.
spiral, 248.
Worm-eaten, *imperfect*, 651.
decayed, 659.
Worm in, *insert*, 300.
interpose, 228.
Worm out, *ascertain*, 480.
Wormwood, *unsavoury*, 395.
Worn, *imperfect*, 651.
decayed, 659.
Worry, *vexation*, 828.
to tease, 830.
harass, 907.
Worse, *badness*, 649.
Worship, *religious*, 990.
title, 877.
servility, 886.
Worshipful, *repute*, 873.
Worst, *defeat*, 731.
Worsted, *defeated*, 732.
Worth, *goodness*, 648.
value, 644.
virtue, 944.
price, 812.
Worthless, *useless*, 645.
profligate, 945.
Worth while, *utility*, 644.
Worthy, *virtuous*, 944.
saint, 948.
Wot, *knowledge*, 490.
Wound, *evil*, 619.
badness, 649.
hurt, 900.
Wrack, *evil*, 619.

Wraith, *spirit*, 980.
Wrangle, *dispute*, 713.
reason, 476.
Wrap, *cover*, 222.
circumscribe, 231.
Wrapped in, *attention*, 457.
Wrapper, *cover*, 222.
dress, 225.
Wrapt, *thought*, 451.
Wrath, *anger*, 900.
Wreak, *inflict*, 739, 918.
Wreath, *trophy*, 733.
ornament, 847.
honour, 877.
Wreck, *remainder*, 40.
destruction, 162.
failure, 732.
Wrench, *extract*, 301.
seize, 789.
twist, 243.
draw, 285.
Wrest, *seize*, 789.
twist, 243.
distort, 523.
Wrestle, *contention*, 720.
Wrestler, *combatant*, 726.
Wretch, *sinner*, 949.
apostate, 941.
Wretched, *unhappy*, 828.
bad, 649.
contemptible, 643.
petty, 32.
Wriggle, *agitation*, 315.
cunning, 702.
Wright, *workman*, 690.
Wring, *pain*, 378.
to torment, 830.
distort, 243.
Wring from, *taking*, 789.
Wrinkle, *fold*, 258.
hint, 527.
Writ, *order*, 741.
in law, 969.
Write, *writing*, 590.
Write off, *cancel*, 552.
Write up, *praise*, 931.
detail, 594.
Writhe, *agitate*, 315.
pain, 378, 828.
Writing, *book*, 593.
Wrong, *evil*, 619.
badness, 649.
vice, 945.
immoral, 923.
to injure, 907.
Wrong-doer, *sinner*, 949.
Wrong-headed, *foolish*, 499.
obstinate, 606.
Wrought up, *excitation*, 824.
Wry, *oblique*, 217.
distorted, 243.
Wynd, *abode*, 189.

X

Xanthippe, *shrew*, 901, 932.
Xebec, *ship*, 273.
Xylography, *engraving*, 558.
Xylophone, *musical instrument*, 417.

Y

Yacht, *ship*, 273.
Yahoo, *commonalty*, 876.
Yammer, *cry*, 411.
complain, 839.
Yank, *jerk*, 285.
Yap, *animal cry*, 412.
Yard, *workshop*, 691.
abode, 189.
Yarn, *filament*, 205.
prate, 584.
story, 594.
exaggeration, 549.
Yashmak, *dress*, 225.
Yataghan, *arms*, 727.
Yawl, *ship*, 273.
Yawn, *open*, 260.
fatigue, 688.
sluggish, 683.
insensible, 823.
Yea, *assent*, 488.
Yean, *produce*, 161.
Year, *period*, 108.
Yearn, *desire*, 865.
pine, 828.
pity, 914.
love, 897.
sad, 837.
Yeast, *bubble*, 353.
Yell, *cry*, 411.
complain, 839.
Yellow, *yellow*, 436.
Yelp, *animal cry*, 412.
Yeoman, *man*, 373.
Yeomanry, *army*, 726.
Yes, *affirmation*, 488.
consent, 762.
Yesterday, *preterition*, 122.
Yet, *exception*, 83.
time, 106, 122.
counteraction, 179.
compensation, 30.
Yield, *submit*, 725, 826.
regress, 283.
obey, 743.
consent, 762.

Yield, *furnish*, 784.
gain, 810.
price, 812.
facility, 705.
Yodel, *music*, 415.
Yoga, *asceticism*, 955.
Yoke, *join*, 43.
vinculum, 45.
couple, 89.
subjection, 749.
Yokel, *clown*, 876.
Yonder, *distance*, 196.
Yore, *preterition*, 122.
Young, *age*, 127.
Youngster, *youth*, 129.
Younker, *youth*, 129.
Youth, *age*, 127.
lad, 129.

Z

Zadkiel, *oracle*, 513.
Zany, *fool*, 501.
Zareba, *defence*, 717.
Zeal, *activity*, 682.
feeling, 821.
Zealot, *active*, 682.
resolute, 604.
obstinate, 606.
Zealotry, *obstinacy*, 606.
Zebra, *variegation*, 440.
Zenana, *apartment*, 191.
Zend-Avesta, *pseudo-revelation*, 986.
Zenith, *summit*, 210.
climax, 33.
Zephyr, *wind*, 349.
Zeppelin, *ship*, 127.
Zero, *nothing*, 4.
naught, 101.
Zest, *relish*, 394.
enjoyment, 827.
Zigzag, *angle*, 244.
obliquity, 217.
oscillation, 314.
circuit, 629.
Zither, *musical instrument*, 417.
Zodiac, *outline*, 229.
Zoilus, *envy*, 921.
*Zollverein (Ger.), *compact*, 769.
Zone, *circle*, 247.
belt, 229.
region, 181.
layer, 204.
Zoography, *zoology*, 368.
Zoology, *zoology*, 368.
Zoom, *deviation*, 279.
Zoophyte, *animal*, 366.
Zootomy, *zoology*, 368.
Zouave, *combatant*, 726.
Zoroaster, *pseudo-revelation*, 986.
Zymotic, *insalubrity*, 657.

THE END

EVERYMAN'S LIBRARY

By ERNEST RHYS

VICTOR HUGO said a Library was 'an act of faith,' and another writer spoke of one so beautiful, so perfect, so harmonious in all its parts, that he who made it was smitten with a passion. In that faith Everyman's Library was planned out originally on a large scale; and the idea was to make it conform as far as possible to a perfect scheme. However, perfection is a thing to be aimed at and not to be achieved in this difficult world; and since the first volumes appeared there have been many interruptions, chief among them Wars, during which even the City of Books feels the great commotion. But the series always gets back into its old stride.

One of the practical expedients in the original plan was to divide the volumes into separate sections, as Biography, Fiction, History, Belles-lettres, Poetry, Philosophy, Romance, and so forth; with a shelf for Young People. The largest slice of this huge provision of nearly a thousand volumes is, as a matter of course, given to the tyrranous demands of fiction. But in carrying out the scheme, publishers and editors contrived to keep in mind that books, like men and women, have their elective affinities. The present volume, for instance, will be found to have its companion books, both in the same class and not less significantly in other sections. With that idea too, novels like Walter Scott's *Ivanhoe* and *Fortunes of Nigel*, Lytton's *Harold*, and Dickens's *Tale of Two Cities*, have been used as pioneers of history and treated as a sort of holiday history books. For in our day history is tending to grow more documentary and less literary; and 'the historian who is a stylist,' as one of our contributors, the late Thomas Seccombe, said, 'will soon be regarded as a kind of Phoenix.'

As for history, Everyman's Library has been eclectic enough to choose its historians from every school in turn, including Gibbon, Grote, Finlay, Macaulay, Motley, and Prescott, while among earlier books may be found the Venerable Bede and the Anglo-Saxon Chronicle. On the classic shelf too, there is a Livy in an admirable translation by Canon Roberts, and Caesar, Tacitus, Thucydides, and Herodotus are not forgotten.

'You only, O Books,' said Richard de Bury, 'are liberal and independent; you give to all who ask.' The variety of authors old and new, the wisdom and the wit at the disposal of Everyman in his own Library, may even, at times, seem all but embarrassing. In the Essays, for instance, he may turn to Dick Steele in *The Spectator* and learn how Cleomira dances, when the elegance of her motion is unimaginable and 'her eyes are chastised with the simplicity and innocence of her thoughts.' Or he may take *A Century of Essays*, as a key to a whole roomful of the English Essayists, from Bacon to Addison, Elia to Augustine Birrell. These are the golden gossips of literature, the writers who learnt the delightful art of talking on paper. Or again, the reader who has the right spirit and looks on all literature as a great adventure may dive back into the classics, and in Plato's *Phaedrus* read how every soul is divided into three parts (like Caesar's Gaul). The poets next, and he may turn to the finest critic of Victorian times, Matthew Arnold, as their showman, and find in his essay on Maurice de Guerin a clue to the 'magical power of poetry,' as in Shakespeare, with his

> daffodils
> That come before the swallow dares, and take
> The winds of March with beauty.

Hazlitt's *Table Talk* may help us again to discover the relationship of author to author, which is another form of the Friendship of Books. His incomparable essay, 'On Going a Journey,' is a capital prelude to Coleridge's *Biographia Literaria*; and so throughout the long labyrinth of the Library shelves one can follow the magic clue in prose or verse that leads to the hidden treasury. In that way a reader becomes his own critic and Doctor of Letters, and may turn to the Byron review in Macaulay's *Essays* as a prelude to the three volumes of Byron's own poems, remembering that the poet whom Europe loved more than England did was, as Macaulay said, 'the beginning, the middle and the end of all his own poetry.' This brings us to the provoking reflection that it is the obvious authors and the books most easy to reprint which have been the signal successes out of the many hundreds in the series, for Everyman is distinctly proverbial in his tastes. He likes best of all an old author who has worn well or a comparatively new author who has gained something like newspaper notoriety. In attempting to lead him on from the good books that are known to those that are less known, the publishers may have at times been even too adventurous. But the elect reader is or ought to be a party to this conspiracy of books and book-men. He can make it possible, by his help and his co-operative zest, to add still more authors, old and new. 'Infinite riches in a little room,' as the saying is, will be the reward of every citizen who helps year by year to build the City of Books. With such a belief in its possibilities the old Chief (J. M. Dent) threw himself into the enterprise. With the zeal of a true book-lover, he thought that books might be alive and productive as dragons' teeth, which, being 'sown up and down the land, might chance to spring up armed men.' That is a great idea, and it means a fighting campaign in which every new reader who buys a volume, counts as a recruit.

> To him all books which lay
> Their sure foundation in the heart of man . . .
> From Homer the great Thunderer, to the voice
> That roars along the bed of Jewish song . . .
> Shall speak as Powers for ever to be hallowed!